ECONOMIC FORECASTS AND POLICY

CONTRIBUTIONS TO ECONOMIC ANALYSIS

XV

Edited by

R. STROTZ

J. TINBERGEN

P. J. VERDOORN

H. J. WITTEVEEN

1961

NORTH-HOLLAND PUBLISHING COMPANY – AMSTERDAM

ECONOMIC FORECASTS AND POLICY

by

H. THEIL

Professor of Econometrics,
Netherlands School of Economics

Assisted by

J. S. CRAMER * H. MOERMAN * A. RUSSCHEN

SECOND REVISED EDITION

N·H P&C

1961

NORTH-HOLLAND PUBLISHING COMPANY – AMSTERDAM

PRINTED IN THE NETHERLANDS

INTRODUCTION TO THE SERIES

This series consists of a number of hitherto unpublished studies, which are introduced by the editors in the belief that they represent fresh contributions to economic science.

The term *economic analysis* as used in the title of the series has been adopted because it covers both the activities of the theoretical economist and the research worker.

Although the analytical methods used by the various contributors are not the same, they are nevertheless conditioned by the common origin of their studies, namely theoretical problems encountered in practical research. Since, for this reason, business cycle research and national accounting, research work on behalf of economic policy, and problems of planning are the main sources of the subjects dealt with, they necessarily determine the manner of approach adopted by the authors. Their methods tend to be "practical" in the sense of not being too far remote from application to actual economic conditions. In addition they are quantitative rather than qualitative.

It is the hope of the editors that the publication of these studies will help to stimulate the exchange of scientific information and to reinforce international co-operation in the field of economics.

THE EDITORS

TO

J. TINBERGEN

FORECASTER AND POLICY-MAKER

The human race, to which so many of my readers belong, has been playing at children's games from the beginning... And one of the games to which it is most attached is called, "Keep to-morrow dark," and which is also named (by the rustics in Shropshire, I have no doubt) "Cheat the Prophet." The players listen very carefully and respectfully to all that the clever men have to say about what is to happen in the next generation. The players then wait until all the clever men are dead, and bury them nicely. They then go and do something else. That is all. For a race of simple tastes, however, it is great fun.

G. K. Chesterton, *The Napoleon of Notting Hill*

PREFACE

In 1953 the Director-General of Statistics and the Director of the Central Planning Bureau of the Netherlands agreed that it would be important to investigate in a systematic manner the possibilities of a new econometric model of the Netherlands. Such a model existed already and had been used for the formulation of the annual Central Economic Plans; it was felt, however, that major improvements were possible. It was planned that the greater part of the work would be carried out by staff members of the Central Planning Bureau; the contribution of the Central Bureau of Statistics would mainly involve the preparation of new and revised statistical data. Moreover, the collaboration of the Mathematical Centre, Amsterdam, and of the Netherlands Economic Institute, Rotterdam, was obtained, as well as a grant from the Netherlands Organization for the Advancement of Pure Research (Z.W.O.).

This volume is a first report on the research that has been carried out since then. It deals primarily with three basic issues in econometric model building. The first is that of the predictive quality of such models – a subject which is all the more important since it is not yet known with certainty whether model forecasts are superior to more naive forecasts. Chapter III and part of Chapter V deal in particular with this subject. As it is desirable to see these predictions in proper perspective, much time and effort was also spent on an entirely different kind of forecast, viz., that obtained by means of surveys. They form the subject of the Chapters IV and VI, the intermediate Chapter V being devoted to the phenomenon of underestimation of changes.

The second aspect considered in this volume is that of the relationship between decision-making and the econometric model which is used in order to formulate predictive statements. This is considered in the Chapters VII and VIII. The third aspect, finally, is of a statistical nature; it is largely concerned with the estimation of systems of simultaneous equations. This subject is considered in the second section of Chapter VI and in the Appendix to that chapter, after which it is taken up again in Chapter VIII, where it is considered from the standpoint of statistical decision theory.

There are numerous persons and organisations whose names deserve a place because of the contributions which they rendered to whatever positive value this book may prove to have. First, of course, are those whose names appear on the title page. Mr. A. Russchen of the Central Planning Bureau contributed to Chapter III by collecting the data and guiding the computations. Mr. J. S. Cramer contributed to the analysis of the survey data of the Chapters IV and VI; he was co-author of a paper that I read on this subject at the Uppsala Meeting of the Econometric Society in 1954. After he left the Bureau, Mr. H. Moerman guided the later part of the computations.

Thanks are also due to the Board of the *IFO-Institut für Wirtschaftsforschung*, Munich, and especially to Dr. W. Marquardt and Dr. O. Anderson Jun., who generously put the survey data at our disposal and supplied us with whatever additional information we needed; to the Boards of the four cooperating institutions and of the Netherlands Organization for the Advancement of Pure Research (Z.W.O.), for their constant support; and to those who read and criticised parts of the manuscript, in particular Professor D. van Dantzig of the University of Amsterdam (who read Chapter II), Professor T. C. Koopmans of Yale University (who read the statistical sections of Chapter VI), and Professor H. A. Simon of the Carnegie Institute of Technology (who read the Chapters VII and VIII). I am also much indebted to the University of Chicago, where I held a visiting professorship during the academic year 1955–56, and to Stanford University, where I spent the summer of 1956. This period was a stimulating one and highly productive with respect to the material covered by this book. Finally, thanks are due to the following staff members of the Econometric Institute of the Netherlands School of Economics: Messrs. T. Kloek and H. Neudecker, who assisted in the last phase of the computations; Mr. John W. Hooper, who improved my English; Miss P. van Baarle for her efficient typing; and Miss E. van der Hoeven and Messrs. D. B. Jochems, E. Kaptein and P. J. M. van den Bogaard, who assisted me in reading the proofs. Needless to say, none of those mentioned here should be held responsible for any remaining errors.

Rotterdam, July 1958 H. THEIL

PREFACE TO THE SECOND EDITION

The main change in the second edition compared with the first involves the statistical part of the book. The discussion in the text of Chapter VI has been simplified in order to make it more suitable for teaching purposes. Several new results have been added: the procedure of mixed estimation, small-sample properties of simultaneous-equation estimators, the trace correlation of a simultaneous system, as well as extensions of the Gauss-Markov theorem to the residual variance and to least-squares under linear constraints.

I am indebted to Messrs. J. C. G. Boot and S. P. van der Zee for their help in reading the proofs and correcting the Index.

Rotterdam, November 1960 H. THEIL

ABBREVIATED CONTENTS

TABLE OF CONTENTS

PREFACE XI

PREFACE TO THE SECOND EDITION XIII

ABBREVIATED CONTENTS XIV

TABLE OF CONTENTS XV

LIST OF TABLES XXIV

LIST OF FIGURES XXIX

I. INTRODUCTION

1.1. Forecasts 1

1. Definition of forecasts (predictions); economic predictions and quantitative economic predictions – 2, 3. Plans and expectations; the relative abundance of expectations

1.2. Forecasts and Policy 2

1. *Gouverner c'est prévoir* – 2. Necessity of a preliminary empirical analysis of forecasts

1.3. Survey of Contents 3

II. ELEMENTARY ASPECTS OF THE METHODOLOGY OF FORECASTING

2.1. Some Concepts and Definitions 6

1. Conditional and unconditional predictions – 2. Point and interval predictions; an example in regression analysis – 3. Single and multiple predictions – 4. Combinations of these distinctions; conditional point predictions and unconditional interval predictions

2.2. Requirements Which Scientific Predictions Should Meet. . . 11

1. Verifiability – 2, 3, 4. Implications of verifiability: unambiguity; probability statements; verifiability of the prediction procedure – 5. Internal consistency

2.3. Three Types of Problems in Forecasting 15

1. The problems: verification and accuracy analysis; generation of predictions; influence on behaviour – 2. Justification of straightforward accuracy analyses – 3. "Higher-order" predictions; constancy assumptions as the theory used in forecasting – 4. Causal hierarchy among plans, judgments, and expectations – 5. Plans having a separate and distinct influence on behaviour

2.4. On the Methodology of Verification and Accuracy Analysis . . 22

1. Statistical methods of verification – 2. Incorrect forecasting procedures and imperfect forecasts; accuracy analysis of interval predictions; "net forecasting value" – 3. Errors of observation and errors of forecasting – 4.

LIST OF TABLES

Chapter II

Chapter III

CHAPTER IV*

CHAPTER V

* Unless otherwise stated (or when the opposite is self-evident), all tables of this chapter refer to the German leather and shoe industry in the period 1951–1953.

Chapter VI*

* Unless otherwise stated, all tables of this chapter refer to the German leather and shoe industry.

Chapter VII

LIST OF FIGURES

Chapter II

Chapter III

CHAPTER IV*

CHAPTER V

* Unless otherwise stated, all figures of this chapter refer to the German leather and shoe industry in the period 1951–1953.

CHAPTER VI*

* Unless otherwise stated, all figures of this chapter refer to the German leather and shoe industry.

CHAPTER VII

CHAPTER VIII

I. Introduction

1.1. Forecasts

1.1.1. A *forecast* or a *prediction* is generally defined as a statement concerning unknown, in particular future, events. The terms "statement" and "events" will be interpreted here in a liberal way: it is not necessary that the statement is written down, published, or communicated in any other sense, and the event described may be the mere absence of certain other events. For instance, "There will be no war between the United States and Russia before 1970" is a prediction although the event predicted is the absence of a war; and it remains a "prediction" even if its author, the *forecaster*, does not communicate it to others.

We shall confine ourselves mainly to *economic predictions*; i.e., statements which are limited to one or more economic aspects of the events predicted. *Quantitative economic predictions*, furthermore, are those economic predictions for which these aspects can be described by one or more numbers; e.g., the national income of some country in some year, the international raw material price level, etc. The greater part of this book is devoted to this type of predictions, which will hence often be called simply "predictions" or "forecasts," and it is then implicitly assumed that they belong to this type.

1.1.2. Although a further typology of predictions can be postponed until Section 2.1, it is useful to make here a distinction according to their authorship. *Plans* or *intentions* are statements concerning the forecaster's own actions in the future; they have hence reference to his "instruments," i.e., to variables which he controls. *Expectations* are statements concerning events which are not controlled by the forecaster's actions.[1] Examples of the first category are an entrepreneur's

[1] In order to avoid misunderstandings, the statistical term "expectation" or "mathematical expectation" will be replaced throughout by "mean value."

production plan, and plans concerning future selling prices of price adjusting firms. Of the second: a consumer's price expectations, a retailer's sales expectations, etc. Another example of the second category is the change over time of a firm's stocks of finished products. This change is partly determined by the firm's production, partly by its sales. Although the production is an instrument variable from the standpoint of this firm, the sales are not, so that the change in stocks is not a variable controlled by it and, hence, statements concerning future changes are expectations, not plans.

1.1.3. The number of expectations concerning one event ma y b large; indeed, it is as large as the number of people or institutions who consider the event so interesting that they are prepared to make a prediction—provided, of course, these forecasters do not control the event, for otherwise the prediction is a plan rather than an expectation. The number of plans concerning one event is, however, zero or one. It is one if a plan is made by the individual or institution controlling the event, it is zero if this individual refrains from doing so; but it may also be necessarily zero, viz., if the event is not controlled by a single authority. An example is the above-mentioned change in stocks: neither the producing firm, nor the buying firms or consumers can be said to control this change, so that there is simply no single individual for whom the change is an instrument variable. The same holds, at least in Western economic systems, for most of the strategic macroeconomic variables, like employment, national product, aggregate exports and so on. Consequently, as far as the mere possibilities of making forecasts are concerned, the number of expectations must be expected to exceed the number of plans considerably.

1.2. Forecasts and Policy

1.2.1. *Gouverner c'est prévoir* is perhaps an exaggeration—it means that policy-making does not only require prediction, or literally prevision, but that there is an identity relationship between both concepts—; on the other hand, however, prediction plays such an essential rôle in the policy-making process that this French dictum may be accepted as a vivid expression of an important requirement for rational policy.

Rational policy-making is the adaptation of the policy-maker's instruments to his changing environment in such a way that the result is "good" or even "optimal." Consequently, there are several ways in which forecasting affects rational behaviour. The following (preliminary) sketch may illustrate this. First, the changing environment has to be predicted; second, a forecast of the effects of the policy-maker's measures, i.e., of changes of instrument values, is required; third, a plan of action must be made. For instance, in the case of employment policy, it is necessary to obtain some idea as to the factors controlling next year's or next quarter's employment level. If this leads to a predicted employment which is considered too low, the policy-maker will try to find measures in order to increase the level; and then it is necessary to predict the effectiveness of alternative measures, i.e., of the reaction of variables which are not controlled to changes in controlled variables. This leads to a plan of actions, which may be followed or abandoned in the light of subsequent events.

1.2.2. A realistic analysis of the relationship between forecasts and policy must be based on the assumption of several variables controlled and not controlled by the policy-maker, of their interrelationships, of the policy-maker's preferences which serve to formalise the optimality criterion of 1.2.1, etc. Later chapters are devoted to this purpose. But this will be clear even here: if there are any errors in the forecasting process on which the measures taken are based, the measures themselves will in general be suboptimal. Hence a preliminary analysis of forecasts and especially of forecasting errors must be considered useful. Of course, forecasting in the field of economics is a hazardous enterprise, so that errors as such need not amaze us; but if it were possible to detect forecasting errors which we might call "systematic," this could be helpful to find systematic failures in the adaptation of instruments, and it might be possible to indicate ways in which such failures can be avoided, at least approximately.

1.3. Survey of Contents

1.3.1. Out of the next Chapters II–VIII, the last two are mainly theoretical, the four from III onwards mainly empirical, and Chapter II is preliminary to these four. This order is not conventional (it is more usual to begin with theory), but it has at least the virtue that it is the order according to an increasing degree of sophistication. Moreover, since the empirical work on forecasting data was until recently not very impressive, it is virtually necessary to work on facts before proceeding to theory, for otherwise the probability of postulating irrelevant truth is too large.

In Chapter II a distinction is made between three main types of problems in the analysis of forecasts, viz., verification and accuracy analysis; the analysis of the generation of predictions; and the use of forecasts for policy purposes. Some new measures for judging the accuracy of forecasts are proposed and discussed. Otherwise, however, the discussion is confined to the minimum which is necessary for the empirical chapters.

1.3.2. The Chapters III and IV are devoted to problems of accuracy analysis. Chapter III deals with the macroeconomic forecasts that have been prepared for the Dutch and the Scandinavian economies in recent years, IV with monthly survey data of plans, expectations, and behaviour of a large number of firms of the German leather and shoe industry. The treatment of the macroeconomic predictions is mainly descriptive. The availability of a larger number of data in the case of the microeconomic surveys makes it possible to obtain more elaborate results, *i.a.* on differences in forecasting quality of separate types of firms and of separate economic variables.

The most conspicuous result of both of these chapters is that of the general underestimation of changes. This phenomenon is analysed in more detail in Chapter V. It is shown why we should expect a bias of this kind; and several further illustrations, derived from American, German and Dutch studies, are presented there and discussed.

1.3.3. The generation of plans and expectations is the subject of Chapter VI. The object analysed is the set of price data of the German firms discussed earlier in Chapter IV.

The first two sections of Chapter VI are devoted to problems of methodology, viz., that of the particular type of data analysed (including problems of aggregation) and that of statistical inference. The latter section starts with some general remarks on desirable properties of econometric and statistical approaches, after which the classical method of least-squares is generalised successively for the complications of autocorrelated disturbances, simultaneous equations, etc., and mixtures of these. A choice is made out of the available methods, which is based *i.a.* on the problems of specification errors.

After these methodological sections an attempt is made to test and estimate relations between expected, planned, and actual price data. A large number of such relations is the result; they are subsequently used for predictions outside the sample analysed.

1.3.4. The Chapters VII and VIII are devoted to the relationship between forecasting and policy. In Chapter VII the problems are posed, in VIII an attempt is made to solve them. Special attention is paid to the uncertainty which characterises most decision processes —and which is at the same time the rationale of making predictions. It is shown under which circumstances the neglect of uncertainty leads to appropriate behaviour, and under which conditions a suboptimal behaviour is the consequence; and, in the latter case, what are the characteristics of this suboptimality. Furthermore, it is analysed how changes in the policy-maker's environment affect his optimal behaviour; how incorrect predictions of such changes, especially those which have been found to be rather frequent in the preceding empirical chapters, lead to deviations below the optimum; how these deviations can be measured; and what should be done in order to minimise them.

Chapter IX gives a conclusion. The reader who is mainly interested in results is advised to proceed to that chapter immediately after the present one.

II. *Elementary Aspects of the Methodology of Forecasting*

2.1. Some Concepts and Definitions

2.1.1. In addition to the concepts of Section 1.1, the following distinctions will prove to be useful.

First, we may have *conditional* and *unconditional predictions*. The former adjective applies when the statement concerning the unknown events is supposed to hold only if some other, more basic, event occurs. Some examples: "I will increase my selling prices next month by 10 per cent if the raw material prices go up by 15 per cent;" "I expect the national product of this country to decrease in the next year by 5 per cent if the Government outlays will be reduced as drastically as is planned now." Another example is the prediction of the effectiveness of alternative measures of policy, mentioned at the end of 1.2.1; e.g., "If all tax rates are reduced by 10 per cent, employment will increase by 5 per cent."

Forecasts are called unconditional if no such provisos are made.

2.1.2. Next, we have the important distinction between *point* and *interval predictions*. Interval predictions give a set of situations, not a single situation, such that one of these will be realised—at least according to the forecaster. An example: "I expect the international raw material price level to increase by something between 5 and 15 per cent next year." Another: "I expect the national income of the United States in 1970 to be somewhere between \$350 and \$450 billions." Point predictions give a single situation: "I expect the national income of the United States in 1970 to be \$403,768,599,423.17." Writing down so many figures seems rather ridiculous; indeed, it is customary to round this off to e.g. \$404 billions. Strictly speaking, this means that the actual value is expected to lie between \$403.5 and \$404.5 billions—which is an interval prediction, not a point prediction! It is useful to modify these definitions slightly such that the above prediction can be considered as a point prediction; it will be shown in the next section, 2.2, that this can be done in a satisfactory way.

A classical example of point and interval predictions in the field of statistics (which will prove instructive for the analysis of Chapter III) is the following. Suppose it is known that one variable, y, depends linearly on another, x, except for random disturbances:

$$y_t = \alpha + \beta x_t + u_t, \tag{2.1}$$

where α and β are the parameters of this relation, u the disturbance (with zero mean), and t refers to separate numerical observations, e.g., to values observed in successive years. An example: x is real per capita income per year in some country, y real per capita consumption.

Suppose furthermore that time series of length T for x and y are available:

$$x_1, x_2, \ldots, x_T$$

$$y_1, y_2, \ldots, y_T,$$

and that a prediction of the y-value in the future year $T + 1$ is required, given the fact that x in that year equals a fixed value x_{T+1}. A point prediction of y_{T+1} is then obtained as follows. First, β and α of (2.1) are estimated according to least-squares:

$$b = \frac{\Sigma(x_t - \bar{x})(y_t - \bar{y})}{\Sigma(x_t - \bar{x})^2}; \qquad a = \bar{y} - b\bar{x},$$

$\bar{x}$ and $\bar{y}$ being the means of the series $x_1, \ldots, x_T$ and $y_1, \ldots, y_T$, respectively. A point prediction y^*_{T+1} of y_{T+1} can then be given by (2.1) after replacing t by $T + 1$, α and β by their estimates, and dropping the disturbance u:

$$y^*_{T+1} = a + bx_{T+1}, \tag{2.2}$$

whereas, of course, the true value y_{T+1} is

$$y_{T+1} = \alpha + \beta x_{T+1} + u_{T+1}.$$

The difference, $y^*_{T+1} - y_{T+1}$, is the error of the point prediction. Under certain conditions this forecasting error can be shown to have a probability distribution with zero mean and variance

$$(2.3) \qquad \text{var}\,(y^*_{T+1} - y_{T+1}) = \sigma^2\left(1 + \frac{1}{T}\right) + \frac{\sigma^2}{\Sigma(x_t - \bar{x})^2} \cdot (x_{T+1} - \bar{x})^2,$$

σ^2 being the variance of the disturbances u. When replacing σ^2 by its

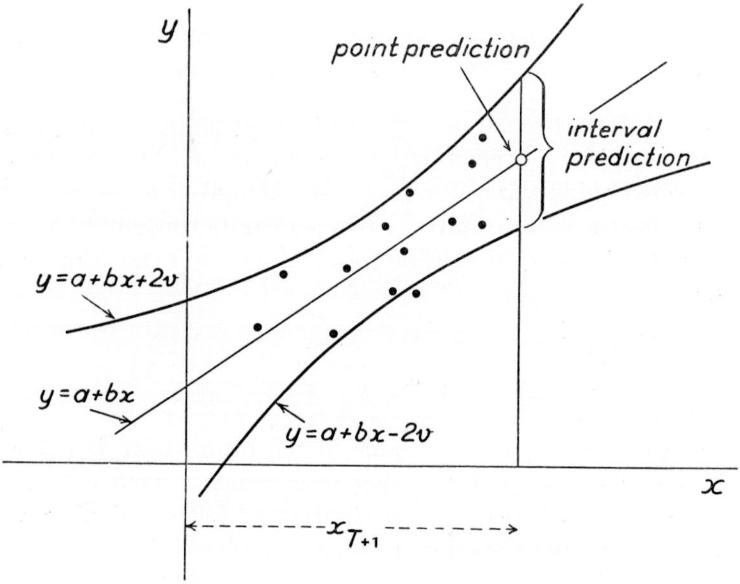

Fig. 2.1. Point and interval predictions in regression analysis

unbiased estimator $s^2T/(T-2)$, s^2 being the observed variance of the residuals u'_t in the regression equation

$$y_t = a + bx_t + u'_t \qquad (t = 1, \ldots, T),$$

an unbiased estimator, v^2 say, of the variance (2.3) is obtained. Its square root, v, estimates the standard deviation of the forecasting error and can hence be used for an interval prediction: when taking, say, twice this standard deviation, and adding it to and subtracting it from the regression $y = a + bx$, we obtain two curves (cf. Fig. 2.1), viz.,

$$y = a + bx + 2v \quad \text{and} \quad y = a + bx - 2v;$$

these curves give, for any value of x, an interval prediction of the y belonging to this x, such that the probability that this interval contains the true y is of the order of 0.9. The numerical value of this probability depends, of course, on the factor by which v is multiplied—a smaller factor leads to smaller intervals and hence to more precise interval predictions, but also to a smaller probability and hence to less reliability; it depends also on the distribution of the disturbances u. The shape of the two curves of Fig. 2.1 is that of a hyperbola; the smallest interval is obtained when x_{T+1} equals $\bar{x}$, the average of the x-values observed during the period analysed, and the length of the interval grows indefinitely when x_{T+1} moves away from $\bar{x}$, in either direction. If the sample size T is enlarged such that $\Sigma(x_t - \bar{x})^2$ increases indefinitely, the two curves become asymptotically straight lines parallel to the regression line—but they will never coincide with this line because $\sigma > 0$.[1]

This example shows further that it is in principle possible to make a set of alternative interval predictions, all with different probabilities, rather than a single interval prediction. In the extreme case a whole probability distribution results. It shows also that we may have two distinct kinds of uncertainty, one of which deals with the inherent randomness of the quantity to be predicted (due to the disturbance u_{T+1}), and the other with the randomness of the estimators of parameters of its distribution (a and b).

2.1.3. The third distinction is that between *single* and *multiple predictions*. Single predictions are confined to one event or even to one aspect of an event; and if the prediction is of the quantitative type, it is given by one number only in the case of point predictions and by one pair of numbers in the case of interval predictions. Conversely, multiple predictions refer to several events or at least to several aspects of one event; and hence, if they belong to the quantitative type, they are expressed by several numbers. An example of the latter type is the

[1] The following assumptions are used in this analysis: (*i*) the x's are fixed in repeated samples, and hence contain no errors of measurement; (*ii*) the u's are independently distributed (and hence not serially correlated), and they have all the same variance σ^2. For an exposition of the more general multiple-regression case, see e.g. J. R. N. STONE, *The Measurement of Consumers' Expenditure and Behaviour in the United Kingdom, 1920–1938*, Vol. I (Cambridge, 1954), p. 283.

simultaneous prediction of the percentage change of the population of some country during, say, half a century, and of the available labour force during the same period. If the prediction is of the interval type, it has often an ellipsoidal shape like that of Fig. 2.2. The fact that the axes of the ellipse are not parallel to the axes of the system of coordinates indicates that the quantities to be predicted are not independent—which is in many cases true for multiple predictions.

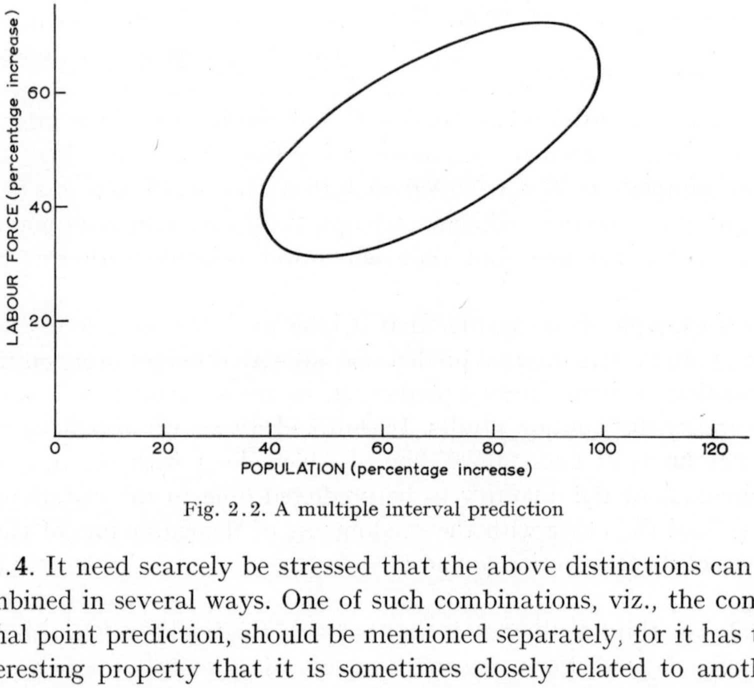

Fig. 2.2. A multiple interval prediction

2.1.4. It need scarcely be stressed that the above distinctions can be combined in several ways. One of such combinations, viz., the conditional point prediction, should be mentioned separately, for it has the interesting property that it is sometimes closely related to another combination, viz., the unconditional interval prediction. For suppose that several alternative point predictions are made, all based on different conditions; for example, that alternative estimates are made of the population of France on January 1st, 1970, all under different assumptions concerning the development of the birth rate. In general, the function of such alternative conditions is to set limits to the possible variation of those factors determining the phenomenon to be predicted about which the forecaster feels least sure. Consequently, the extrema of the point predictions obtained form in many cases an unconditional interval prediction, and the main advantage of the alternative point predictions over this interval prediction is that some specification is given of the relationships governing the predicted phenomenon—at least, of those relationships that have been used by the forecaster.

2.2. Requirements which Scientific Predictions should Meet

2.2.1. Sometimes predictions are simply the result of "feeling" or even of the forecaster's imagination—the latter of which applies to all examples given above. Such a simple forecasting procedure does not, however, necessarily imply that the prediction is unimportant; first, the prediction may nevertheless turn out to be right—which does certainly not apply to most of the examples—and second, even if the prediction is quite wrong, it may affect the forecaster's behaviour so that it remains interesting. But this section is not devoted to forecasts of this kind; it deals, instead, with predictions to which we shall attach the weighty adjective "scientific." The exposition will be confined to the expectation category;[1] "scientific plans" are the subject of the much more elaborate analysis of the Chapters VII and VIII.

The requirements which we shall impose can be indicated by the term *verifiability*: it must be possible to conclude, after a certain time, in an unambiguous way whether the prediction has turned out to be correct or not, and both possibilities must exist; and it must be possible to verify the procedure by which the prediction itself was derived. This will be worked out in the remainder of this section. It is to be noted that this condition excludes trivial predictions, e.g., "The national income of Canada in 1970 will be positive but finite," for it is never possible to conclude that such a forecast is not correct. Similarly, meaningless forecasts are excluded, e.g., "If the industrial production of the Netherlands in 1965 will exceed the 1960-level by 100 percent, the imports of this country will exceed its exports by 5.5 billions of guilders." This conditional prediction is meaningless, for there is not the remotest chance that the production increase will be as high as that; and hence there is no possibility of verification.

[1] Part of the ideas to be expounded below are derived from Professor D. VAN DANTZIG's address "Voorspelling en Profetie" (Prediction and Prophecy) read at the Sixth Dutch Statistical Day; see *Statistica*, Vol. 6 (1952), pp. 195–203.

2.2.2. Verifiability has the following further implications.

First, there should be no ambiguity as to the concepts used in the prediction. Hence, if the national income of some country in some year is predicted, it is necessary to state explicitly whether it is computed at factor prices or at market prices, whether it is deflated or not, etc. Sometimes, of course, it is clear from the context which of these concepts is used by the forecaster.

Secondly, there should be no ambiguity as to the time or the time interval to which the prediction refers, and the distance between this time or time interval and the time of prediction should be finite. It is hence not permissible to say that some event will occur somewhere in the future, but it remains permissible to say that it will occur somewhere between January 1st, 1970, and January 1st, 1980. Obviously, if this requirement is not fulfilled, verification is impossible, for the forecaster can always maintain that "his time" has not yet arrived.

2.2.3. The next implication of verifiability deals with the relationship between the forecast and the actual outcome with which this forecast is concerned. It is clear that in the case of point predictions this relationship is usually very simple: forecast and actual result will generally not be exactly equal, so that verification is then equivalent with rejection. However, this rather trivial result is not what is meant by the forecaster. It is not the function of point predictions to "hit" reality exactly, but their function is to be statements such that the resulting forecasting errors have certain desirable properties. We shall therefore require that, in the case of quantitative point predictions—we disregard here the nonquantitative type—, a probability statement about their relationship to the corresponding actual values is given. For instance, it may be stated that the probability that the prediction exceeds the actual value equals the probability that it is smaller; then we have a point prediction of the median type. Or it may be given that the prediction has been derived in such a way that the resulting forecasting error has zero mean; then we have an "unbiased prediction." To put it in another way: scientific point predictions are parameters or at least point estimates of parameters of the distribution of the quantity to be predicted.[1] It is not necessary that the errors of forecasting

[1] The regression prediction $y^*_{T+1} = a + bx_{T+1}$ is an example: it is an unbiased estimate of $\alpha + \beta x_{T+1}$, which is itself the mean value of y_{T+1} (the quantity to be predicted). Hence y^*_{T+1} is an unbiased point prediction of y_{T+1}: $\mathscr{E}(y^*_{T+1} - y_{T+1}) = 0$.

have zero as a parameter of central tendency; sometimes it is useful to give "conservative" point predictions, and then quartiles, etc., may play a rôle.

Similarly, for interval predictions—here we need not confine ourselves to the quantitative type—a probability statement is required, viz., in this slightly different form: the probability p that it will be fulfilled (viz., that one of the situations covered by the forecast will coincide with the actual outcome) should be given. In general, this probability will be chosen in the neighbourhood of 1 (e.g., 0.9 or 0.95), because most interval forecasters give the (implicit) advice to disregard the possibility that the forecast will not be realised. This, at the same time, makes it possible to give a more satisfactory definition of point predictions when rounding off would give them the appearance of interval predictions (cf. 2.1.2). Such an interval, e.g., that between $403.5 and $404.5 billions for the American national income in 1970, has obviously a very small chance to contain the true national income. Therefore, we shall define point predictions as those predictions which have, according to the forecaster, a chance p of being fulfilled that is smaller than the chance $1 - p$ of being not fulfilled (i.e., $p < 0.5$); for interval predictions we then have $p \geq 0.5$. Under this definition rounding off will shift a prediction from the point into the interval class only if this rounding has a sufficiently appreciable effect on the nature of the forecast. Finally, as to the "point" probability statements of the preceding paragraph in the case of rounding, if the forecast remains a point prediction according to the above definition, then this forecast will be said to be a median (mean, etc.)–type prediction if the interval of rounding contains a value which has this median (mean, etc.) character.

2.2.4. Even if it is stated that the $404 billions forecast of the American national income (at factor prices, in prices of 1955, etc.) in the calendar year 1970 is a median prediction, even then it is not necessarily a scientific prediction. For it may be that it is merely the result of the forecaster's imagination. It is therefore not sufficient that the predictions themselves can be verified afterwards; it is, in addition to this, necessary that the line of thought which underlies the prediction can be verified. This does not imply that everyone should be in a position to scrutinise the procedure that has been followed; not everyone e.g., is a good mathematician. But it implies that such a line of thought exists and that it can be followed by others than the forecaster himself.

It is not easy and even not fruitful to generalise about this point, but this at least can be said: the forecasting procedure must be based on theoretical considerations—however simple—and on empirical observations obtained beforehand—however scanty and crude.

2.2.5. There is another requirement, which is sometimes imposed on multiple predictions; one might call it "internal consistency." It is concerned with the question whether forecasts should obey the same equations and inequalities among themselves as the corresponding actual outcomes do. An example: Suppose one wants to predict for a certain commodity next year's price (p), the quantity sold (q) and the amount spent on it (v). Obviously

$$pq = v. \tag{2.4}$$

Suppose also that point predictions of these three variables are made: $\bar{p}$, $\bar{q}$, $\bar{v}$. The question arises: Must these predictions satisfy the same relation as (2.4) for the quantities to be predicted? In other words, must prediction take place subject to the restriction

$$\bar{p}\bar{q} = \bar{v}\,? \tag{2.5}$$

An affirmative answer seems rather obvious and, indeed, sometimes restrictions of the type (2.5) are legally imposed: The Law on the Central Economic Plan of the Netherlands requires that annually "a well-balanced system of predictions... concerning the Dutch economy" should be presented and, no doubt, the adjective "well-balanced" should be interpreted in such a way that restrictions of the type (2.5) cannot be avoided. Nevertheless, if the definition of point predictions given in 2.2.3 is accepted, there is no reason why we should feel obliged to impose (2.5); for according to this definition the forecaster does not pretend that prediction and actual outcome will turn out to be identical, and hence there is no reason to expect the identity (2.4) which is satisfied by the outcomes to be satisfied by the forecasts as well. Actually, it is not difficult to see that (2.5) is easily contradicted by other prediction requirements which are sometimes rather plausible. Suppose, e.g., that $\bar{p}$, $\bar{q}$, $\bar{v}$ are all unbiased point predictions:

$$\mathscr{E} e_p = 0; \qquad \mathscr{E} e_q = 0; \qquad \mathscr{E} e_v = 0,$$

$e_p\,(= \bar{p} - p)$, e_q, e_v being the forecasting errors of price, quantity and value, respectively, and $\mathscr{E}$ the mean-value operator. Then, assuming the realisations to be stochastic and the forecasts nonstochastic,

$$\mathscr{E}(\bar{p}\bar{q} - pq) = - \operatorname{cov}(e_p, e_q).$$

But also

$$\mathscr{E}(\bar{p}\bar{q} - pq) = \mathscr{E}(\bar{v} - v) = 0.$$

It follows that (2.5) cannot be satisfied by unbiased point predictions $\bar{p}$, $\bar{q}$, $\bar{v}$, unless the forecasting errors in $\bar{p}$ and $\bar{q}$ are uncorrelated. If they are correlated, either (2.5) should be dropped, or at least one of the three forecasts should not be unbiased.

For multiple interval predictions these requirements are more natural, as in such cases the forecaster has indeed the pretention of being right as far as his intervals are concerned—except, of course, for a small probability. But at the same time the condition is much weaker here, for it is sufficient that each interval contains one value for which restrictions of the type (2.5) are satisfied.

2.3. Three Types of Problems in Forecasting

2.3.1. It is useful to divide the analysis of forecasts into three main categories.

First, we have the problem of *verification*: does the prediction come true? For the interval predictions considered in the preceding section this means: do the intervals cover the actual outcomes with the frequency postulated by the forecaster? For point predictions: is the mean forecasting error indeed zero, or is it true that the outcomes are equally often above and below their predictions? Closely related to this problem is the *accuracy analysis* of predictions, which is concerned with their empirical variation around the realisations. These topics will be considered in more detail in the next section, 2.4; but it is of some interest to note even here that accuracy analysis is not necessarily confined to scientific predictions.

Second, there is the problem of the *generation* of predictions: what is the basis used by the forecaster when he formulates his plans and expectations? What kind of observations are used, which are the theoretical relationships assumed?

Third, what is the *purpose* of the predictions? More specifically: what is their influence on the actual behaviour of individuals?

One may object that there is still another problem with respect to forecasts, viz., how to make good or even "best" predictions? Contrary to the three problems mentioned above, this one is of the normative type. Its solution depends on the purpose for which the prediction is made, so that the third problem can be said to be preliminary to this. We must therefore postpone its treatment to the Chapters VII and VIII, where the relation between prediction and behaviour—the third problem—is considered in more detail.

2.3.2. One might think that it can be maintained, strictly speaking, that the first problem—verification and accuracy analysis—is super-

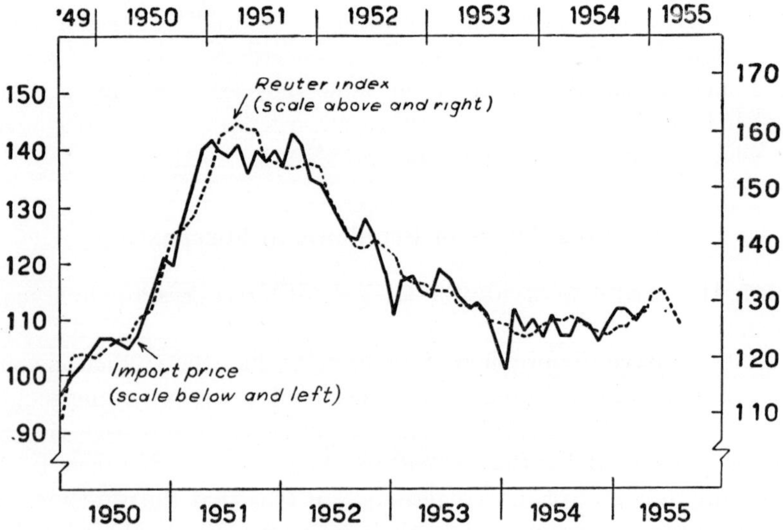

Fig. 2.3. The lagged association between the Reuter index of raw material prices (time scale above) and the Dutch import price level (time scale below)

fluous. For suppose that it is known how the prediction is based on observable data (i.e., that the second problem has been solved) and also by what mechanism the actual phenomenon is generated. Then we would also know how the forecasting errors are generated, so that we would know their characteristics even under circumstances that have not revealed themselves so far; and this is much more than we can ever hope to derive from a direct verification analysis. An example: the Dutch import price level has to be predicted for the next year. It is known that this price level is determined, except for minor deviations which we shall neglect for the sake of the argument, by the international raw material price level with a lag of four months; this is illustrated in Fig. 2.3. The actual import price level to be predicted is hence determined by the international level in the last four months of the preceding year (which is known) and that in the first eight months of the year of prediction (which is unknown). For the latter determining quantity a substitute has to be found; suppose that recent speeches of leading American officials are taken for this purpose, which sometimes contain communications about future strategic purchases and which may hence shed some light on the probable future movement of the international raw material price level. It follows that, if this is the way in which the prediction is made, any forecasting error in the Dutch import price level must be ascribed to an incorrect or incomplete relationship assumed between these speeches and the raw material price level. Hence it is hardly necessary to investigate the accuracy of the import price level predictions themselves; it is sufficient and even more satisfactory to analyse the accuracy of a "preliminary" prediction (or a prediction "of a higher order"), viz., that of the international raw material price level in the first eight months of the year of prediction; the reason being that the latter forecasts determine everything and are more basic. Similarly, as to the verification in contrast to the accuracy analysis, if this leads to a favourable (or unfavourable) conclusion about the "higher-order" prediction, the same must hold for the prediction of the import price level.

However, it cannot be really maintained that a direct verification and accuracy analysis is meaningless simply because of the superiority of a twofold analysis of the generation of predictions and of actual phenomena, supplemented by an investigation of higher-order predictions. For practically always such analyses are based on observations of limited size and quality, so that the results are subject to uncertainties which are sometimes sizable. Accuracy analysis is concerned with forecasting errors, i.e., with the differences between predictions and outcomes; hence, if the generation processes of the latter quantities can only be known imperfectly, the same applies with even greater force in general to the generation process of the errors of prediction. To take the above example: if it is known that the forecaster derives his predictions in the way described and if it is also known how the actual import price level is determined, then one is perhaps justified in rejecting the idea of a direct verification and accuracy analysis. But the generation of actual phenomena is hardly ever known exactly; and that of the predictions is in many cases not known either, e.g., if these predictions are entrepreneurial plans. In such cases it is certainly reasonable to attack the problem in a direct way, as will be done in Section 2.4.[1]

2.3.3. The remainder of this section is devoted to the last two types of problems mentioned in 2.3.1, as far as this is necessary for the next four empirical chapters. Two remarks of a general nature can then be made.

First, as stated above, predictions are often determined by predictions of other quantities, which are therefore called "of a higher order" with respect to the former forecasts. For instance, an entrepreneur may intend to raise his selling prices in the next month because he expects his buying prices to increase in that month; then the expectation is a higher-order prediction with respect to the plan. This will be considered in more detail in 2.3.4.

Second, it can be maintained that predictions—at least expectations which fall under the scientific category—are generated by means of the assumption that something remains constant; the constancy of this "something" is the theory used in the formulation of the prediction. An example: suppose one wants to predict the American national income of the next year. If the procedure is simply that the value of this year is taken, "something" is national income itself; if the procedure is adjusted for the growth of the population, then "something" is per capita income; if the prediction is derived by linear extrapolation, "something" is the average annual rate of change of national income during some previous period; if it is derived by means of an econometric equation system fitted to earlier periods, then "something" is the array of all coefficients of this system; etc. Needless to say, in many cases such a constancy assumption is not rigidly adhered to and allowance is made for specific disturbances; but the way in which this is done is such that a link is made with the effects of similar disturbances in the past, and then in principle the same situation arises.

2.3.4. As to the generation of predictions, it has become a tradition in econometrics to distinguish between four types of economic relations, viz., behavioural, technical, institutional and definitional relations,

[1] It should also be noted that the accuracy analysis may lead to results which are useful for the formulation of statistical hypotheses about the generation of predictions if this generation is unknown.

which serve to describe the behaviour patterns of individuals or of groups of individuals, relationships that are imposed by technical or physical conditions, relations between variables which hold because of the social and institutional framework of the economy, and interrelationships between variables that follow simply from their definitions, respectively.[1] Examples of these successive types are: consumers' demand equations, production functions, income tax rates as a function of income, and the identity: price times quantity equals value.

The introduction of expectations and plans makes it possible to use a finer distinction, especially in the field of behaviour relations. It will prove useful, in view of the availability of certain empirical data in the next chapters, to add a third concept, viz., "judgments." A judgment variable does not give a description of an actual situation or a prediction, but it gives an appraisal of a situation. For example, a Minister of Finance may formulate at the beginning of each month the excess of the money circulation over the level which he considers desirable in the light of prevailing circumstances; such a series of monthly values may be regarded as observations on a judgment variable. Let us then consider what kind of relationships among these three types of variables (plans, expectations, judgments) must be supposed to exist. We shall follow the traditional line of the economist's approach when he formulates the general form of his equations; later, in the Chapters VII and VIII, we shall go deeper into this matter. For simplicity's sake, we shall suppose that all predictions are of the point, not of the interval, type; this is in accordance with the majority of the empirical data to be analysed in the next chapters.

Expectations are determined by the existing situation and its recent history (i.e., by "predetermined" variables) and by expectations of higher order.[2] Determination by the former type of variables alone is a well-known feature of many econometric analyses; it is e.g. often assumed that expected profits can be regarded as determined by recent profits, at least approximately. It is clear, however, that this is a one-sided procedure which is only justified by lack of data; and, taking

[1] See e.g. J. TINBERGEN, *Econometrics* (New York, 1951), p. 16.

[2] The higher-order formulation implies that the relationships governing the expectations are supposed to be of the recursive type. In most cases this will be correct, but it is certainly imaginable that a non-recursive system of relations is adjusted to some previous period, after which it is applied to the present and the immediate future in order to obtain predictions. Such expectations cannot be ordered according to "higher" and "lower," and we should then say that they are all simultaneously determined by predetermined variables; an example will be given in Section 3.1.

again the above example, when expectation figures concerning the volume of sales would be available, these would almost certainly contribute to the "explanation" of expected profits.

Judgments are determined by predetermined variables and by ex-

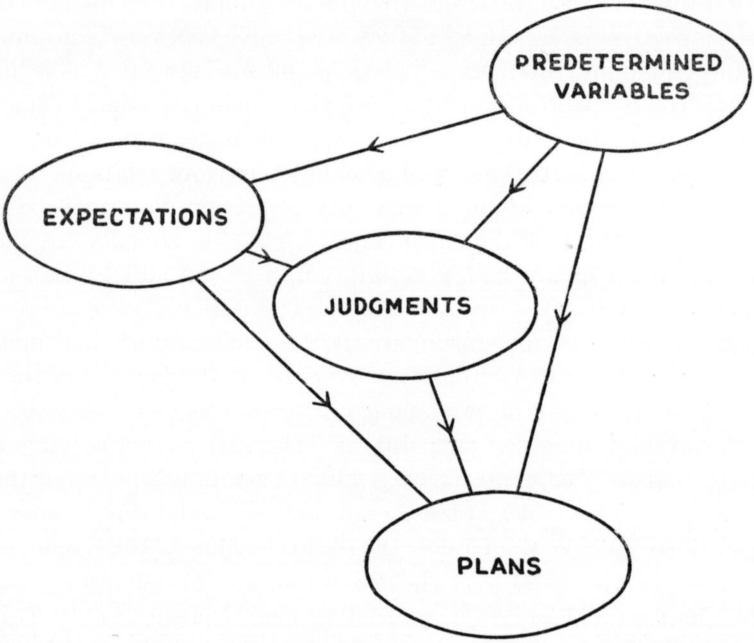

Fig. 2.4. Causal hierarchy among plans, judgments and expectations

pectations. An example: an entrepreneur will consider his stock of finished products too large or too small when his present stock does not stand in the normal relation to his sales in the present and in the near future. Present stocks and sales are predetermined, future sales represent an expectation.

Plans, finally, are determined by predetermined variables, expectations and judgments. An example: the above-mentioned entrepreneur will plan the rate of his production with the following factors in mind: the present conditions of the labour market (predetermined variables), the possibility of obtaining raw materials in the near future (expectations), and his appraisal of the size of the present stocks. Needless to

[1] This concept is used in the sense introduced first by H. A. SIMON; cf. his "On the Definition of the Causal Relation," *Journal of Philosophy*, Vol. 49 (1952), pp. 517–528, and "Causal Ordering and Identifiability," Chapter III of *Studies in Econometric Method*, edited by W. C. HOOD and T. C. KOOPMANS (New York–London, 1953).

say, not always all types of determining factors are relevant and the "real world" may sometimes allow a simpler representation; but the above is sufficient to show that the causal hierarchy[1] (footnote p. 20) among these concepts is in the general case as drawn in Fig. 2.4.[1]

2.3.5. In this connection we have to consider a particular aspect of the influence of plans and expectations on actual behaviour—the third problem mentioned in 2.3.1. There are well-known textbook cases of expectations affecting behaviour, e.g., an expected rise of prices leading to additional purchases; but plans having a separate and distinct influence on actual behaviour are mentioned less frequently. In a trivial sense, of course, plans and behaviour are related to each other, for plans are announcements of a planner that he will do something in the future; and we must expect that he will act accordingly at least sometimes. But this does not imply that the plan as such has a distinct influence on behaviour, since behaviour may be determined by other factors. An example: I intend to go to Paris next spring because an Econometric Society Meeting will be held there. Suppose then that the Meeting is canceled. If I remain at home, the plan evidently does not affect my behaviour. But I may have enjoyed the idea of going to Paris so much that I decide to go in spite of the fact that there is no Meeting; and in such a case the plan can be said to have a separate and distinct influence on behaviour.[2] Or in more "economic" terms, an individual may commit himself to the fulfilment of his intentions (e.g., because they leak out), at least partly, even if circumstances do not correspond to his original ideas about them at the time when he first decided on his plans. In such cases it is conceivable that actual behaviour should be described as a "correction" on the original plan; i.e., not the behaviour variable itself should be the object of scientific description, but its difference with the corresponding plan. The determining factors are then: (*i*) the differences between the actual and expected values

[1] Sometimes plans lead to ("cause") certain expectations, which seems in contradiction with Fig. 2.4. This is not the case, however, since this determination of expectations is always subject to the condition that the determining plan is carried out. An example: "I plan to raise my selling prices; so (if I carry out the plan) I must expect my competitors to follow suit." Such effects can be easily explained by means of Fig. 2.4: if plans are carried out, the resulting action is a fact which falls under the category of predetermined values, and this in turn leads to certain expectations, etc.

[2] Compare this with F. Modigliani's and O. H. Sauerlender's analysis in "Economic Expectations and Plans of Firms in Relation to Short-Term Forecasting," in: *Short-Term Economic Forecasting*, Studies in Income and Wealth, Vol. 17, edited by the National Bureau of Economic Research (Princeton, 1955), esp. pp. 317 ff.

assumed by those predetermined variables which are relevant for the decision; (*ii*) expectations of future values of these variables; (*iii*) relevant judgments, as a correction on earlier judgments upon which the intentions were based.

It is easy to see that this type of behaviour equation (that of the "correction approach") is more general than the familiar one. Suppose for example that the factor under (*i*) alone is relevant, and call y the behaviour variable, $\bar{y}$ the corresponding plan, x the actual predetermined variable and $\bar{x}$ its expectation; both $\bar{x}$ and $\bar{y}$ are considered as point predictions. Under linearity assumptions we have for the intention equation

$$\bar{y} = \alpha_1 + \beta_1 \bar{x} \tag{2.6}$$

and for the behaviour equation under the correction approach

$$y - \bar{y} = \beta_2(x - \bar{x}), \quad \text{say.} \tag{2.7}$$

It follows immediately that, unless $\beta_1 = \beta_2$, the plan $\bar{y}$ has a distinct influence on actual behaviour. A rather plausible case is $0 < \beta_2 < \beta_1$ (or $\beta_1 < \beta_2 < 0$), which implies a reluctance to revise the original plans. If $\beta_1 = \beta_2$, addition of both equations gives a relation between actual variables only, so that in this special case the traditional approach is rehabilitated.

2.4. On the Methodology of Verification and Accuracy Analysis

2.4.1. Verification of a single interval or point prediction is usually not very meaningful; instead, prediction series of sufficient length are more adequate instruments in judging forecasting quality. Suppose then that successive values assumed by some variable have been predicted in terms of interval forecasts, all of which have—at least according to the forecaster—a chance p of "success." The hypothesis to be tested is that the forecaster is right, i.e., that the intervals cover the actual values indeed with probability p. The binomial distribution can then, under certain conditions, be conveniently applied: call the observed fraction of "successes" f and consider the differences $(f - p)$; if this difference is so small that this or still larger differences are sufficiently probable under the assumption that the probability of success is really p, then our forecaster should not be recorded as a "liar." If, on the other hand, the difference is too unprobable, this is a significant result which leads us to reject the correctness of the assertion; but it does not necessarily imply that the forecaster is less reliable than he pretends to be, for we may have a significant positive difference $(f - p)$! Similarly, in the case of point predictions, we may use the symmetrical binomial distribution for testing median predictions, Student's distribution (under normality assumptions) for unbiased predictions, etc.

An essential condition in the application of the above-mentioned distributions is that the predictions be independent. This condition is not unsurmountable when the forecasts are made at the beginning of their period of prediction; but it will not be fulfilled in general when on one point of time a series of simultaneous predictions is made of successive values to be assumed by some variable. Suppose for example that the real national income of the United States has to be predicted on January 1, 1959, for the years 1959, 1960, 1961. If interval predictions are made (with probability p of success) and if the 1959-value happens to fall in the middle of its interval, then the chance that the 1960-value will lie in its prediction interval, given the 1959-value, will in general exceed p; conversely, if the 1959-value falls outside its interval, the latter chance will be smaller than p. This effect is caused by the considerable positive serial correlation which characterises real income and also most other economic variables. In such cases, clearly, some caution is necessary when applying the ideas of the preceding paragraph.

2.4.2. Whereas verification amounts to testing the hypothesis that the *forecasting procedure* is *correct*, accuracy analysis deals with the degree to which the *forecasts* are *imperfect*. A forecast is to be considered perfect if it turns out to be identical with the quantity to be predicted. In all other cases it is imperfect—which is usually the case. In particular, an interval prediction is never perfect except when it degenerates to a point prediction and coincides with the phenomenon to be predicted. A short sketch of the accuracy analysis of interval predictions can be given as follows.

In general, one might expect that a greater precision (i.e., a smaller interval in the case of quantitative predictions) can only be obtained at the cost of less reliability (i.e., of smaller p). But it is conceivable that a smaller interval can be given without affecting the reliability of the prediction. Consider Fig. 2.5; the bell-shaped curve represents the frequency distribution of actual outcomes. Suppose that the forecaster's prediction interval is PQ; then its length can be reduced to that of AB without affecting p, for p equals both areas below the curve, $PQQ'P'$ and $ABB'A'$, whereas $AP < BQ$. It follows that the prediction PQ should be replaced by AB, at least when the precision criterion is adopted. In principle, it is possible to investigate such cases empiri-

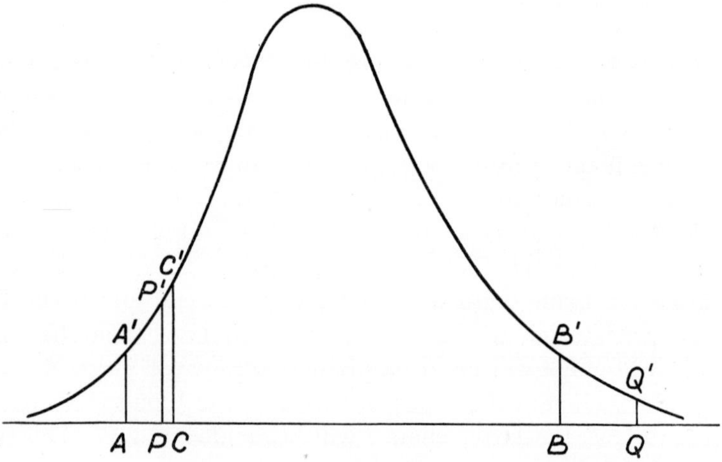

Fig. 2.5. Accuracy analysis of interval predictions

cally. For suppose that we have a series of interval predictions at our disposal, together with the actual outcomes; then we can try to shift these intervals according to a fixed pattern in such a way that the frequency of success is increased, and thereupon see whether their length can be reduced without reducing the success frequency below the original level. If, on the other hand, the forecaster is only interested in a lower limit of the quantity to be predicted, this limit should be C, the area below the frequency curve to the right of the line CC' being equal to p. In such a case the precision criterion loses its relevance; actually, the interval of prediction is then of infinite length.

Since interval predictions play a relatively minor rôle in the further analysis, we shall not continue this discussion. Instead, we proceed with another subject which may be regarded as falling under the general topic of accuracy analysis, viz., that of the "net forecasting value." It occurs rather frequently that predictions show large errors but that, when handled appropriately, they nevertheless have a certain value for forecasting purposes. This can be illustrated conveniently with the following example, which is due to M. HASTAY.[1] Hastay's analysis is concerned with the Dun and Bradstreet surveys, which cover four groups of firms (durable and nondurable goods manufacturers, wholesalers and retailers) and five variables in the case of traders (sales, employees, prices, inventories, profits) and six in the case of manufacturers (new orders in addition to these five). So, as a whole, there are

TABLE 2.1

BIVARIATE FREQUENCY TABLE OF CORRELATIONS BETWEEN PREDICTED AND ACTUAL CHANGES (P_{t+2} AND A_{t+2}) AND BETWEEN PREDICTED AND LAGGED ACTUAL CHANGES (P_{t+2} AND A_{t+1}) FOR DUN & BRADSTREET DATA, 1949–1953 (Hastay, 1954)

		P_{t+2} *and* A_{t+2}				
		0.21–0.40	0.41–0.60	0.61–0.80	0.81–0.90	0.91–1
P_{t+2} *and* A_{t+1}	0.21–0.40	*0*	.	.	.	.
	0.41–0.60	1	*0*	.	.	.
	0.61–0.80	.	4	*0*	.	.
	0.81–0.90	.	.	5	*2*	.
	0.91–1	.	.	8	2	*0*

twenty-two variables. The precise form of the surveys will be considered later, in Chapter IV; for our present purposes it is sufficient to know that, at the end of quarter t, they give predicted changes for quarter $t+2$ relative to the same quarter of the preceding year, $t-2$. We shall indicate such a prediction by P_{t+2}. Table 2.1 above gives a bivariate frequency distribution of the following correlation coefficients: for each of the twenty-two variables, the correlation over time between P_{t+2} and the corresponding actual change to be predicted (A_{t+2}) is computed, and also the correlation between P_{t+2} and the earlier actual change A_{t+1}. *A priori* it seems reasonable to expect the former correlations to be larger, since there is little reason for a considerable correlation between forecasts and actual changes to which these forecasts are not supposed to refer. So we should expect to find the highest density of the bivariate frequency table above and to the right of the main diagonal (the entries of which are printed in italics). However, the opposite is true: there are only two cases in the diagonal and all others are to the left and below, thus implying that the correlation between P_{t+2} and A_{t+2} tends to be smaller than that between

[1] "The Dun and Bradstreet Surveys of Businessmen's Expectations," *Proceedings of the Business and Economic Statistics Section of the American Statistical Association*, September 1954, pp. 93–123.

P_{t+2} and A_{t+1}. Indeed, the median of the latter correlations is 0.9 and exceeds the median of the former by almost 0.2. This suggests that, although P_{t+2} as a forecast of A_{t+2} may have limited value, it is still valuable as a forecast of A_{t+1}. The conclusion seems therefore justified that the participants of the survey, although asked for their ideas about the quarter $t + 2$, answer as if they were asked about the next quarter $t + 1$.

Two qualifications should be made. First, a high correlation does not necessarily imply a successful set of forecasts, and it may be necessary to apply a linear transformation to them in order to obtain a reasonable fit even if the correlation is high; we shall come back to this point in Section 2.5. Second, it is conceivable that a correction of the forecasts by means of further additional information improves their quality. For instance, a multiple regression of A_{t+1} on P_{t+2} and still earlier (and known) A's may give significantly better results; this was analysed by Hastay in his above-mentioned article, to which we may therefore refer.

2.4.3. Since interval predictions give at least some idea of the uncertainty of the phenomenon to be predicted but point predictions not at all, a straightforward analysis of the accuracy of the latter category deserves our attention. A great many statistical measures are available for this purpose: the standard deviation of the forecasting errors, the mean of their absolute values, etc. Further, it is often interesting to analyse the development of these measures over time, because the forecasts may gradually improve or their errors may be correlated with general trade cycle fluctuations, etc. But we shall not deal with these possibilities extensively here, since several of the subsequent chapters are devoted to empirical analyses in this field. Only turning point errors and inequality measures need a preliminary discussion, which will take place in 2.4.4 and in Section 2.5, respectively.

There is, however, one problem which is preliminary to all analyses of this kind, viz., that of the *errors of observation* in observed values. Although these errors are relevant for interval predictions and for verification as well, their practical importance is predominant for the accuracy analysis of point predictions. Let us therefore call

$$A; \qquad A + e_m; \qquad A + e_f$$

the "true" actual value, the observed actual value, and the predicted value, respectively; hence e_m is the error of measurement, e_f the error of forecasting. The observed forecasting error is

$$A + e_f - (A + e_m) = e_f - e_m,$$

so that the accuracy analysis is disturbed by the errors of measurement. Suppose that this analysis is based on the variance of a series of observed forecasting errors, i.e., on

$$\begin{aligned} \text{var}\,(e_f - e_m) &= \text{var}\,e_f + \text{var}\,e_m - 2\,\text{cov}\,(e_f, e_m) = \\ &= s_f^2 + s_m^2 - 2rs_f s_m, \end{aligned} \tag{2.8}$$

s_f and s_m being the standard deviations of forecasting and of observational errors, respectively, and r their correlation coefficient. It follows that, if the errors are uncorrelated, the variance of the observed forecasting errors exceeds the variance of the true forecasting errors, so that the actual prediction process is better than its accuracy analysis suggests—at least, when the variance criterion is adopted.[1] Absence of correlation between forecasting and observational errors is often very plausible, but two exceptions should be mentioned. First, the forecasts may be largely based on recent values of the variable to be predicted, and there may be a considerable positive serial correlation between the errors of measurement. Second, it sometimes happens that the actual phenomenon to be predicted cannot be estimated accurately because of poor data, and the estimate is therefore partly based on the prediction or on the same method on which the prediction is based. For instance, if an economic statistician estimates aggregate consumption while strongly believing that its change should be approximately equal to 0.7 times the change in the total disposable income, then it is easy to see that the use of the same relation for prediction purposes gives rise to a positive correlation between the two types of errors. These examples suggest that, if correlation is not absent, it is more likely to be positive than negative; and if it is positive, the variance of the observed forecasting errors may underestimate the true variance. However, this effect will in general be small, for the relative difference of these variances is $x^2 - 2rx$, where x stands for the ratio s_m/s_f; this ratio will be below unity—otherwise the accuracy analysis cannot be said to be very meaningful—, the two terms of this difference have

[1] If the variance criterion is rejected because it does not take account of possible nonzero mean values of the errors, second moments around zero might be taken instead; s_f and s_m should then be interpreted as square roots of these moments, and r should be interpreted accordingly.

opposite signs if $r > 0$, and r itself will usually not be very large either (and it should exceed $\frac{1}{2}s_m/s_f$ before the difference becomes negative). We should therefore conclude that observational errors often lead to

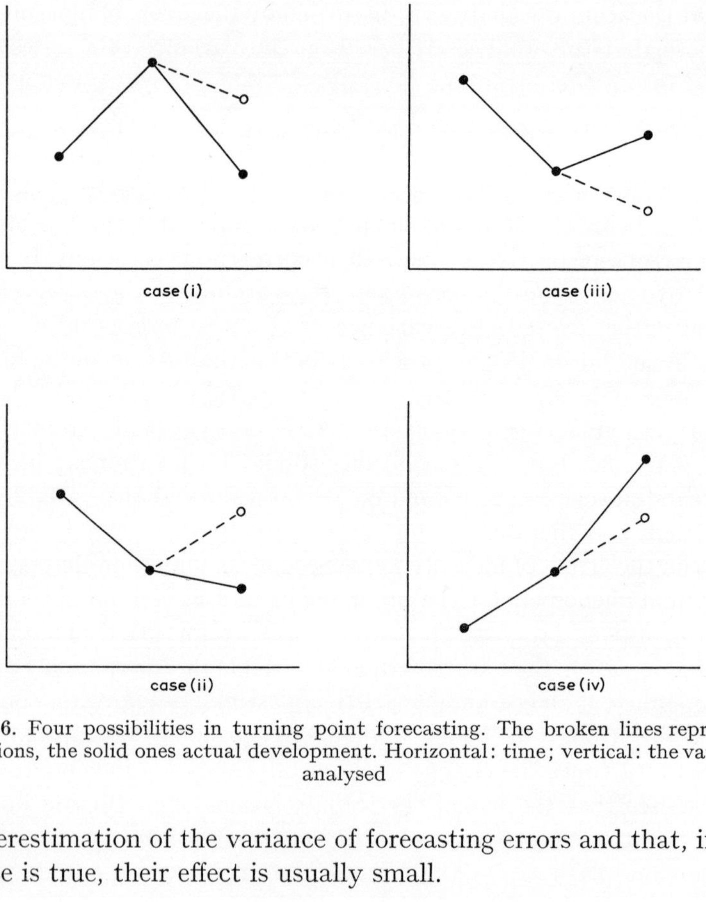

Fig. 2.6. Four possibilities in turning point forecasting. The broken lines represent predictions, the solid ones actual development. Horizontal: time; vertical: the variable analysed

an overestimation of the variance of forecasting errors and that, if the reverse is true, their effect is usually small.

2.4.4. We proceed to a well-known criterion for judging the quality of time series of predictions, viz., that of the *turning points*. The idea is that, given the considerable positive serial correlation of most economic time series, it is rather easy to predict a continuation of expansions or of contractions; and that, therefore, a real success is only obtained if the end of such a one-sided movement is correctly predicted.

There are four possibilities with respect to the prediction of turning points, viz.:

(*i*) A turning point is correctly predicted; i.e., a turning point is predicted, and an actual turning point in the same period is recorded afterwards. Examples of this and the three other cases are drawn in Fig. 2.6.

(*ii*) A turning point is incorrectly predicted; i.e., a turning point is predicted, but there is no actual turning point.

(*iii*) A turning point is incorrectly not predicted; i.e., a turning point is recorded, but it was not predicted before.

(*iv*) A turning point is correctly not predicted; i.e., a turning point is neither predicted nor recorded.

The cases (*ii*) and (*iii*) represent failures; we shall call them *turning point errors of the first kind* and of the *second kind*, respectively. This is

TABLE 2.2

DICHOTOMY OF TURNING POINT FORECASTING

		predicted	
		turning point	no turning point
actual	turning point	(*i*)	(*iii*)
	no turning point	(*ii*)	(*iv*)

formally comparable with the familiar statistical distinction of first-kind (incorrect rejection of a hypothesis) and second-kind (incorrect not-rejection) errors; hence the names. Now suppose that time series of predictions and of corresponding actual values are given. Then the observations can be split up according to these four categories. When using the above small Roman numerals for frequencies of observations, the result is Table 2.2. Clearly, perfect turning point forecasting requires the off-diagonal cells to be empty, i.e., $(ii) = (iii) = 0$. We have failures if the set of predicted turning points [their total number being $(i) + (ii)$] contains cases of no actual turning point; similarly, we have failures if the set of actual turning points [with total frequency $(i) + (iii)$] contains cases of no predicted turning point. Adequate quantitative measures for the description of both types of failure are then

$$(2.9) \qquad \varphi_1 = \frac{(ii)}{(i) + (ii)}; \qquad \varphi_2 = \frac{(iii)}{(i) + (iii)},$$

where, of course, whenever determinate, $0 \leq \varphi_1,\ \varphi_2 \leq 1$, small φ's being indications of successful turning point forecasting. If none of the predicted turning points coincides with any of the actual turning points, i.e., if $(i) = 0$, then $\varphi_1 = \varphi_2 = 1$. A further analysis of these ratios will be given in a later part where empirical results are discussed (cf. Section 4.3).

Another graphical picture of turning point errors is presented in

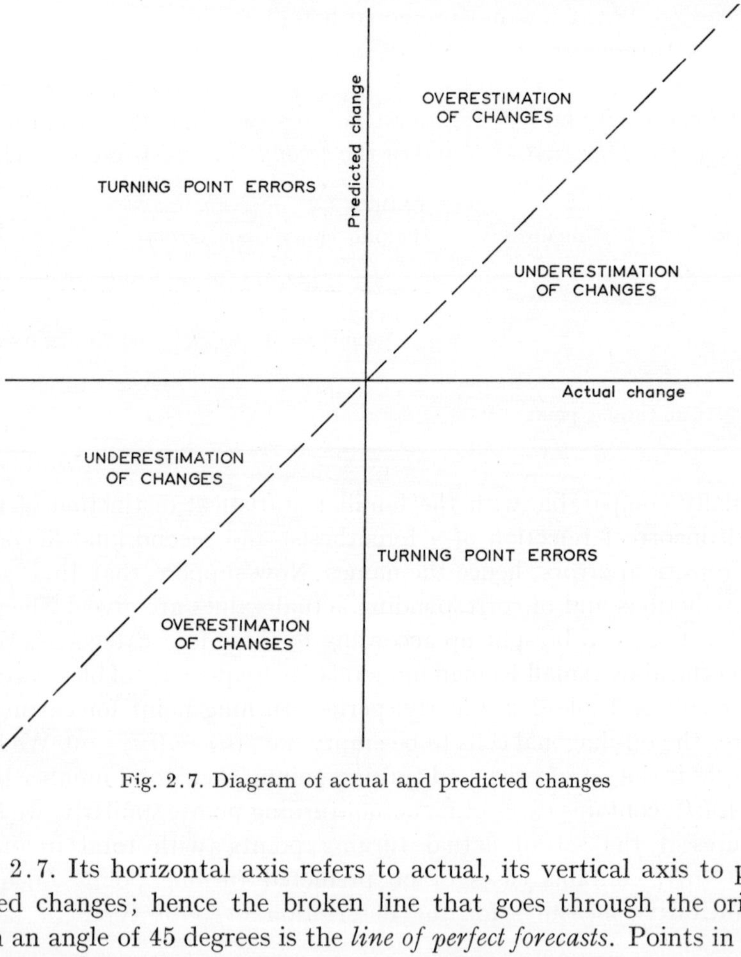

Fig. 2.7. Diagram of actual and predicted changes

Fig. 2.7. Its horizontal axis refers to actual, its vertical axis to predicted changes; hence the broken line that goes through the origin with an angle of 45 degrees is the *line of perfect forecasts*. Points in the second and fourth quadrants always represent turning point errors, simply because the signs of the predicted changes are then different from those of the actual changes. The question of first-or second-kind turning point errors depends on the sign of the preceding actual change in the same variable, which is not indicated in the figure. As to the other two quadrants (the first and the third), the line of perfect forecasts divides these into equal areas of *overestimation of changes* and of *underestimation of changes*.

Although a turning point analysis may often yield a valuable insight, its importance should not be exaggerated. First, the analysis is not invariant against a replacement of the variables used by related variables. Suppose for example that aggregate consumption is replaced by per capita consumption and that the population increases annually by 1 per cent. If total consumption decreased last year by 1 per cent and increases by $\frac{1}{2}$ per cent in the present year, the prediction being an increase of $1\frac{1}{2}$ per cent, then this is a correctly predicted turning point; but for per capita consumption these three percentage increases are -2, $-\frac{1}{2}$, $\frac{1}{2}$, which implies a turning point error of the first kind. Secondly, actual and predicted turning points will sometimes represent sharp peaks and troughs, but they may also be so flat as to have very little meaning as such, and sometimes actual turning points are even dubious because of errors of measurement.

2.4.5. It should be stressed that a final appraisal of the quality of forecasts cannot in general be obtained by means of such purely statistical criteria. This is due to the fact that this quality has to be judged in relation to the use that is made of the forecasts; and it is necessary, therefore, that these criteria have an economic significance. We shall return to this topic in the Chapters VII and VIII.

Still, a careful accuracy analysis may have a considerable value; the next two chapters are an attempt to show just this. And it will also appear that several of the statistical criteria (like those to be considered in the next section) are indeed conceptually related to economic criteria which are highly relevant.

2.5. Measures of Inequality

2.5.1. One of the measures that has sometimes been used for analysing the accuracy of forecasts is the classical (product-moment) correlation coefficient of the series of predictions and actual outcomes. Its disadvantage is that perfect (positive) correlation does not imply perfect forecasting, but only the existence of an exact linear relation with positive slope between the individual predictions (P_i) and the actual values (A_i),

$$P_i = \alpha + \beta A_i, \qquad \beta > 0,$$

whereas perfect forecasting requires, in addition to this, $\alpha = 0$ and $\beta = 1$.[1] An alternative coefficient, viz.

$$U = \frac{\sqrt{\frac{1}{n}\Sigma (P_i - A_i)^2}}{\sqrt{\frac{1}{n}\Sigma P_i^2} + \sqrt{\frac{1}{n}\Sigma A_i^2}}, \tag{2.10}$$

$P_1, \ldots, P_n$ being the predictions and $A_1, \ldots, A_n$ the corresponding actual outcomes, is preferable in this respect. We shall call it the *inequality coefficient* of the series P_i, A_i. It is to be considered as an estimator of the parent coefficient

$$Y = \frac{\sqrt{(\mu_{20} + \mu_{02} - 2\mu_{11})}}{\sqrt{\mu_{20}} + \sqrt{\mu_{02}}}, \tag{2.11}$$

where the moment μ_{hk} stands for the mean value of $P^h A^k$. It is shown in the Appendix of this chapter (Section 2.A) that the following inequality holds for the variance of U under the assumptions of independence and bivariate normality:

$$\operatorname{var} U \leq \frac{1}{n} Y^2 (1 - Y^2)^2. \tag{2.12}$$

In most cases the inequality sign can be replaced by the equality sign without serious error, but it should be added that (2.12) is only valid for large samples. With this qualification we may say that, if the inequality coefficient is not too large (below 0.3 or 0.4, say), its standard error is roughly proportional to itself, the proportionality factor being $1/\sqrt{n}$.

The coefficient U is—except for the trivial case where all P's and A's are zero, when it is indeterminate—confined to the closed interval between zero and unity; the proof can be given most easily in geometric terms, as will be done in 2.5.5. We have $U = 0$ in the case

[1] The correlation criterion can be improved in this respect by taking correlations based on moments around zero instead of moments about the means. However, $\beta = 1$ is then still a requirement which has to be additionally imposed for perfect forecasting.

of equality: $P_i = A_i$ for all i. This is clearly the case of perfect forecasts. We have $U = 1$ (the "maximum of inequality") if there is either a negative proportionality, or if one of the variables is identically zero: $rP_i + sA_i = 0$ for all i and for some nonnegative r and s (not both zero). In other words, $U = 1$ if there is a non-positive proportionality be-

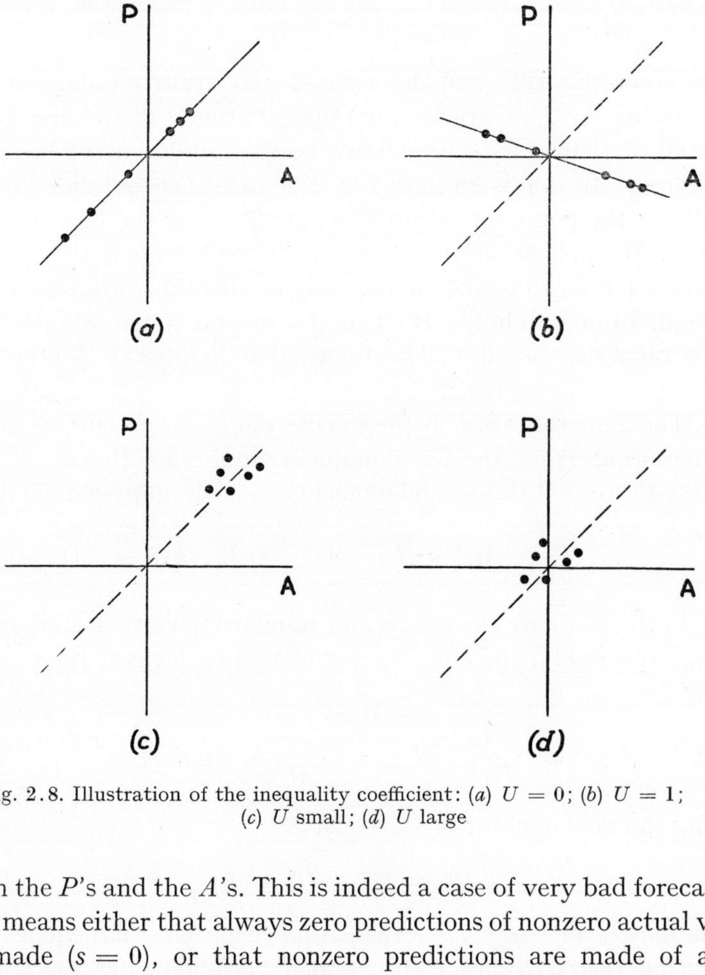

Fig. 2.8. Illustration of the inequality coefficient: (*a*) $U = 0$; (*b*) $U = 1$; (*c*) U small; (*d*) U large

tween the P's and the A's. This is indeed a case of very bad forecasting, for it means either that always zero predictions of nonzero actual values are made ($s = 0$), or that nonzero predictions are made of actual values which are always zero and hence easy to predict ($r = 0$), or that predictions are positive (negative) if actual outcomes are negative (positive) in a remarkably regular manner (r and $s \neq 0$). It is clear, furthermore, that the inequality coefficient—contrary to the correlation coefficient—is not invariant against additive variations. For instance, the correspondence between the two series

-3	5	10	-4
-1	7	7	-1

s less than that between the same series but increased by 100:

97	105	110	96
99	107	107	99,

at least according to U (and also according to intuitive judgment!) but not according to the correlation coefficient; the U of the first pair of series is 0.23, that of the second 0.01, and the correlation is 0.95 in both cases. An illustration is given in Fig. 2.8; case (*d*) is obtained from (*c*) by shifting the point set towards the origin along the line of perfect forecasts. All applications of the inequality coefficients in the following chapters will refer to predicted and actual changes in variables, so that the origin from which the P's and A's are measured is then fixed. Further numerical details will be discussed in Chapter IV (Section 4.4).

2.5.2. The numerator of U is the square root of the second moment of the forecasting errors; the denominator is simply such that $0 \leq U \leq 1$. It is easy to see that this second moment can be decomposed as follows:

$$\frac{1}{n}\Sigma(P_i - A_i)^2 = (\bar{P} - \bar{A})^2 + (s_P - s_A)^2 + 2(1 - r)s_P s_A, \tag{2.13}$$

where $\bar{P}$, $\bar{A}$, s_P, s_A are the means and standard deviations of the series P_i, A_i, respectively, and r is their correlation coefficient. Hence, when writing

$$U_M = \frac{\bar{P} - \bar{A}}{D}; \quad U_S = \frac{s_P - s_A}{D}; \quad U_C = \frac{\sqrt{2(1-r)s_P s_A}}{D}, \tag{2.14}$$

D being the denominator of U, we have

$$U_M^2 + U_S^2 + U_C^2 = U^2, \tag{2.15}$$

and we may term U_M, U_S, U_C the *partial* coefficients of inequality due to *unequal central tendency*, to *unequal variation*, and to *imperfect covariation*, respectively. Furthermore, when writing

$$U^M = \frac{U_M^2}{U^2}; \quad U^S = \frac{U_S^2}{U^2}; \quad U^C = \frac{U_C^2}{U^2}, \tag{2.16}$$

we have

$$U^M + U^S + U^C = 1, \tag{2.17}$$

and we may term U^M, U^S, U^C the *proportions of inequality* due to these three different sources. We shall indicate them briefly as the *bias*, the *variance* and the *covariance proportions*, respectively.

So it appears to be possible to describe the "inequality" of two series P_i, A_i and its "composition" in a very simple way. It is of some interest to give a number of special cases; this is done in Fig. 2.9. The three scatters in the first row illustrate the cases $U^M = 0$ (which implies a centre of gravity on the line of perfect forecasts), $U^S = 0$ (then the orthogonal regression line through the n points is parallel to this line), and $U^C = 0$ (which implies either a perfect positive correlation, or zero variation in one of the variables). The second row refers to the cases U^M, U^S, $U^C = 1$. We have $U^M = 1$ if there is either a perfect correlation with slope 1, or no variation at all in P and A; $U^S = 1$ if the centre of gravity lies on the line of perfect forecasts and, moreover, either the correlation is positive and perfect or one of the variables has zero variation; and $U^C = 1$ if the line of perfect forecasts is the orthogonal regression line. The third row illustrates the cases of partial inequality coefficients equal to unity in absolute value (each of which implies $U = 1$): $U_M = \pm 1$ implies zero variation in both variables, the single point lying in one of the "wrong" quadrants; $U_S = \pm 1$ implies a zero mean for one of the variables, and for the other zero values only; $U_C = 1$ if there is a negative perfect correlation (slope -1) through the origin, which is at the same time the centre of gravity. The fourth row, finally, is concerned with maximum inequality arising from two of the three sources. In each of the cases the points must lie on a straight line through the origin with non-positive inclination, but $U^M = 0$ requires, in addition to this, that the origin is the centre of gravity, $U^S = 0$ that the line is perpendicular to the line of perfect forecasts, $U^C = 0$ that it coincides with one of the axes.

2.5.3. It is of some interest to consider the three proportions more closely. We shall do so in a rather heuristic manner.

Inequality of central tendency is a type of forecasting error which, if significant, is certainly not of a desirable type; we might call it a "systematic error." We may therefore say that, from the forecaster's standpoint, if the (total) inequality coefficient U cannot attain the

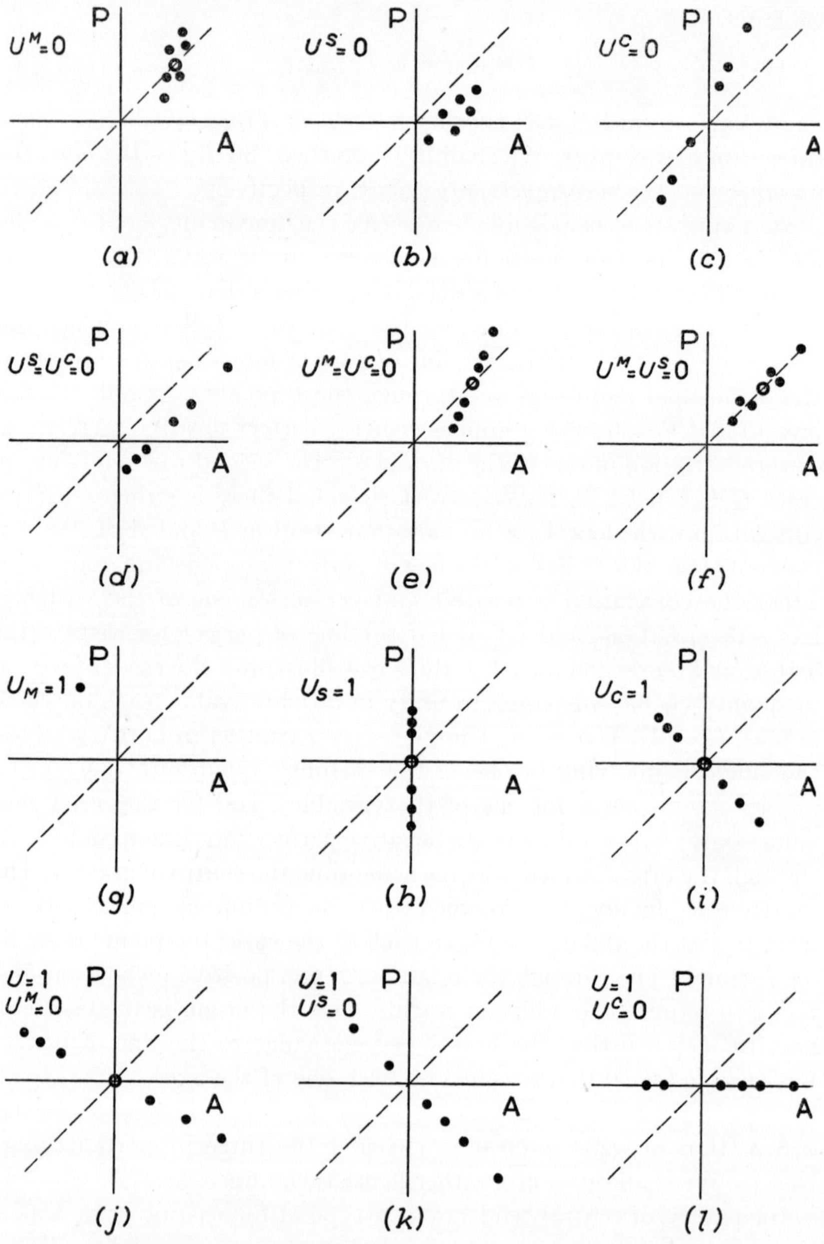

Fig. 2.9. Illustration of the inequality proportions and partial inequality coefficients. The centres of gravity, when relevant, are denoted by small circles

desirable level 0, the most desirable level of U^M is 0. The same is not true for the inequality due to imperfect covariation. There is no reason to expect an imperfect forecaster to make predictions which are perfectly correlated with the actual outcomes; indeed, we might call errors of this kind "unsystematic." As to unequal variation, consider the following example. Suppose that a time series analysis of the labour productivity in some country reveals that this variable has been characterised by a trend increase of 2 per cent per year. Suppose also that this "law" is used for prediction purposes, i.e., that for each year a 2 per cent increase is predicted, whereas the actual development continues to fluctuate around this trend line. Then, if a sufficient number of predictions is available, and if the U's are calculated for annual percentage changes, we should expect $U_M = 0$ because the forecasts are on the average correct, $U_C = 0$ because there is no variation in the predictions, but $U_S \neq 0$. This might again be called "systematic," because the error is due to the forecaster's neglect of fluctuations in labour productivity caused by trade cycle fluctuations, etc.

It seems that we must draw the conclusion that, if the forecaster's ability does not allow him to attain perfection, the desirable distribution of inequality over the three sources is $U^M = U^S = 0$, $U^C = 1$. It seems plausible, furthermore, that this particular distribution can be more easily attained or approximated by a good forecaster than by a less able man, for small proportions U^M, U^S indicate that systematic errors play a minor rôle. Since the inequality coefficient U itself is a measure of forecasting ability, the following empirical hypothesis for a set of prediction series of the same series of actual phenomena is wellworth trying: U^M and U^S are, *ceteris paribus*, increasing functions of U, and U^C is a decreasing function of U.

It is interesting in this connection that the (asymptotic) sampling variances of the three proportions are given by (cf. the Appendix, Section 2.A):

$$\text{(2.18)} \qquad \operatorname{var} U^M = \frac{2}{n} Y^M (1 - Y^M)^2 (2 - Y^M);$$

$$\text{(2.19)} \qquad \operatorname{var} U^S \leqq \frac{4}{n} Y^S [(Y^C)^2 + Y^M (1 - Y^M)];$$

$$\text{(2.20)} \qquad \operatorname{var} U^C \leqq \frac{4}{n} (Y^C)^2 (1 - Y^C),$$

the right-hand Y's being the same functions of the parent moments as the sample proportions are of the sample moments. As in the case of the variance of U, no serious errors are involved in general if we replace $\leq$ by $=$. It follows from (2.18) – (2.20) that, as long as the parent proportions are not far from their desirable levels (0, 0, 1), the sampling variance of each sample proportion is about equal to (slightly less than) $4/n$ times the difference between the corresponding parent proportion and its desirable level. It will be noted that, unless these differences are very small and Y is very large, these variances tend to be larger than the variance of U.

2.5.4. Several modifications and generalisations of the inequality measures can be formulated; a short survey is presented in the Appendix to this chapter, Section 2.B. Here, we shall confine ourselves to those variants which will prove to be useful in the subsequent analysis.

First, the decomposition (2.13) is not the only one; we may also use

$$(2.21) \qquad \frac{1}{n}\Sigma(P_i - A_i)^2 = (\bar{P} - \bar{A})^2 + (s_P - rs_A)^2 + (1 - r^2)s_A^2.$$

This decomposition makes sense in the following situation. Suppose that the actual outcomes $A_1, \ldots, A_n$ consist each of a stochastic and a nonstochastic part, and that the forecaster always predicts the nonstochastic part perfectly but disregards the stochastic part.[1] Then, when assuming that the latter part has zero mean, we may conclude that the parent regression of the A's on the P's has zero intercept and unit slope:

$$A_i = P_i + u_i,$$

u_i being the disturbance of the regression. In this situation the first term in the right-hand side of (2.21) has obviously a zero parent value; i.e., $\mathscr{E}\bar{P} = \mathscr{E}\bar{A}$. The same is true for the second, since the sample regression of A on P has slope rs_A/s_P, which is 1 if and only if the second term vanishes; and it is indeed 1 in the population, so that the second term must vanish there. So, under the above specifications, the only term which does not vanish in the population is the third, which equals the variance of the disturbances u_i. These considerations suggest that

[1] Note that this assumption has also been used in the price-quantity-value example of 2.2.5.

an alternative decomposition of U in terms of U_M and the following two partial inequality coefficients has some merits:

(2.22) $$U_R = \frac{s_P - r s_A}{D}; \qquad U_D = \frac{\sqrt{(1 - r^2)}\, s_A}{D},$$

D being the denominator of U; and we may say that U_R and U_D refer to the inequality due to an incorrect regression slope and to nonzero regression disturbances, respectively. As in (2.15), we have

(2.23) $$U_M^2 + U_R^2 + U_D^2 = U^2,$$

and we can introduce two new inequality proportions, viz.

(2.24) $$U^R = \frac{U_R^2}{U^2}; \qquad U^D = \frac{U_D^2}{U^2},$$

to be called the *regression* and the *disturbance* proportions, respectively. Obviously

(2.25) $$U^M + U^R + U^D = 1.$$

For the variances of these proportions we have (cf. the Appendix to this chapter, Section 2.B):

(2.26) $$\text{var } U^R = \frac{4}{n} Y^R [Y^D(1 - Y^R) + Y^M Y^R (1 - \tfrac{1}{2} Y^M)]$$

(2.27) $$\text{var } U^D = \frac{4}{n} (Y^D)^2 [1 - Y^D - \tfrac{1}{2} (Y^M)^2],$$

the right-hand Y's being the same functions of the parent moments as the U's are of the sample moments. These results imply, as in the case of the first decomposition (2.13), that the variances are approximately equal to $4/n$ times the difference between the parent proportions (Y^R, Y^D) and the numerical values (0, 1, respectively) discussed above.[1]

The decomposition (2.21) has evidently its merits, but it has not been applied in the next two empirical chapters, first because it was deemed unsatisfactory to impose the probabilistic ideas underlying

[1] It will be noted that these numerical values are not identical with the desirable levels of 2.5.3; i.e., $(U^M, U^S, U^C) = (0, 0, 1)$ is not equivalent to $(U^M, U^R, U^D) = (0, 0, 1)$. But the difference is in general small. For suppose that $(U^M, U^S, U^C) = (0, 0, 1)$; then $U^R = 1 - U^D = \frac{1}{2}(1 - r)$, which is usually close to zero because the correlation between P and A is, though not perfect, generally substantial. Similarly, if $(U^M, U^R, U^D) = (0, 0, 1)$, then $U^S = 1 - U^C = (1 - r)/(1 + r)$, which tends to be small, too.

(2.21) *a priori*, second because some experimentation with the data of these chapters suggested that there was no reason to suppose that s_P equals rs_A, even approximately. However, we shall come back to this decomposition in Chapter V (Section 5.2) and Chapter VI (Section 6.8).

Finally, we should mention that a generalisation of U can be obtained by introducing the following "generalised inequality coefficient:"

$$(2.28) \qquad U^* = \frac{\sqrt{\Sigma\Sigma q_{ij}(P_i - A_i)(P_j - A_j)}}{\sqrt{\Sigma\Sigma q_{ij}P_iP_j} + \sqrt{\Sigma\Sigma q_{ij}A_iA_j}},$$

where $[q_{ij}] = \mathbf{Q}$ is a positive-definitive matrix. In matrix notation:

$$(2.29) \qquad U^* = \frac{\sqrt{(\mathbf{p} - \mathbf{a})' \mathbf{Q}(\mathbf{p} - \mathbf{a})}}{\sqrt{\mathbf{p}'\mathbf{Q}\mathbf{p}} + \sqrt{\mathbf{a}'\mathbf{Q}\mathbf{a}}},$$

$\mathbf{p}$ and $\mathbf{a}$ being column vectors of predictions and actual outcomes, respectively. If $\mathbf{Q} = \lambda\mathbf{I}$, λ being any positive scalar and $\mathbf{I}$ the unit matrix of order n, then $U^* = U$. It can be proved that $0 \leq U^* \leq 1$, and that U^* can be decomposed in a way similar to U.

2.5.5. The remainder of this section is devoted to a geometric picture of the U's in the n-dimensional Cartesian space. Along the first axis (a_1) we measure the first value of the series of predictions (P_1) and of the series of actual outcomes (A_1); similarly along the second axis (a_2, P_2, A_2), etc. Hence the series of n observations P_i, A_i are represented by two points in the n-dimensional space, to be called P^0 and A^0 respectively. The inequality coefficient U is then equal to the distance P^0A^0 divided by the sum of the distances OP^0 and OA^0, O being the origin. It follows immediately that $0 \leq U \leq 1$, unless O, P^0 and A^0 coincide (the indeterminate case).

Consider furthermore the $(n - 1)$-dimensional plane

$$\sum_{i=1}^{n} a_i = 0,$$

and the projections P^1 and A^1 of P^0 and A^0, respectively, in this plane. The five points O, A^0, P^0, A^1 and P^1 all lie in a three-dimensional subspace R_3, since A^0A^1 and P^0P^1 are parallel, both being perpendicular to the hyperplane. This subspace is given in Fig. 2.10; the figure contains also a point Q on the line P^0P^1 such that $P^0Q = A^0A^1$. Then we have

$$OP^0 = \sqrt{\Sigma P_i^2}; \quad OA^0 = \sqrt{\Sigma A_i^2}; \quad P^0A^0 = \sqrt{\Sigma(P_i - A_i)^2};$$

$$P^0P^1 = \bar{P}\sqrt{n}; \quad A^0A^1 = \bar{A}\sqrt{n}; \quad P^1Q = (\bar{P} - \bar{A})\sqrt{n};$$

$$OP^1 = s_P\sqrt{n}; \quad OA^1 = s_A\sqrt{n}; \quad P^1A^1 = \sqrt{\{(s_P^2 + s_A^2 - 2rs_Ps_A)n\}}.$$

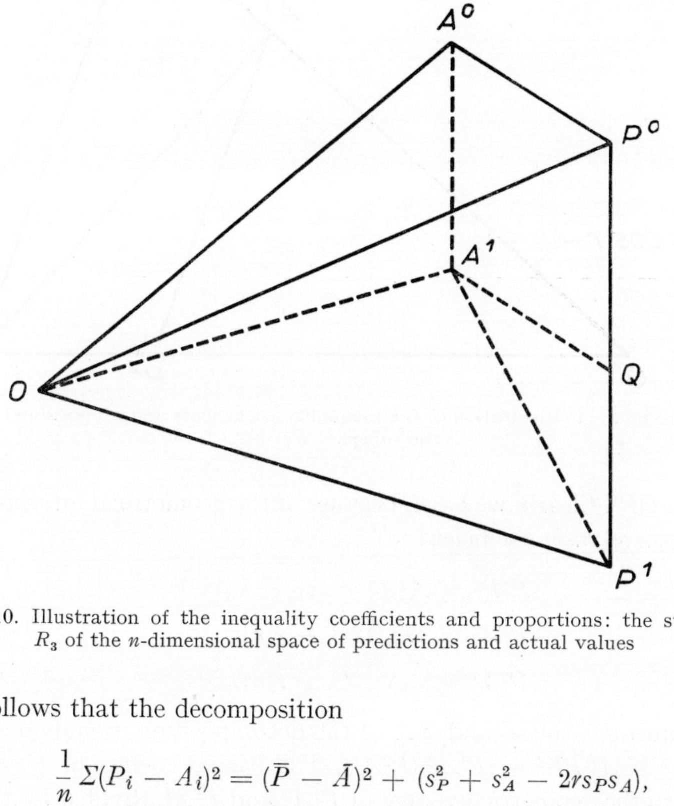

Fig. 2.10. Illustration of the inequality coefficients and proportions: the subspace R_3 of the n-dimensional space of predictions and actual values

It follows that the decomposition

$$\text{(2.30)} \qquad \frac{1}{n}\Sigma(P_i - A_i)^2 = (\bar{P} - \bar{A})^2 + (s_P^2 + s_A^2 - 2rs_Ps_A),$$

which may be regarded as a first step towards the decomposition (2.13) [and also as a first step with respect to (2.21)], is geometrically equivalent with the relation $(P^0A^0)^2 = (P^1A^1)^2 + (P^1Q)^2$; hence the partial coefficient U_M equals P^1Q divided by $OP^0 + OA^0$. As to the further decomposition

$$\text{(2.31)} \qquad s_P^2 + s_A^2 - 2rs_Ps_A = (s_P - s_A)^2 + 2(1 - r)s_Ps_A,$$

consider Fig. 2.11, which illustrates the subspace R_2 of R_3 containing the triangle OP^1A^1; in this figure two points P^2 and A^2 on the lines OP^1 and OA^1, respectively, are drawn such that $OP^2 = OA^1$ and

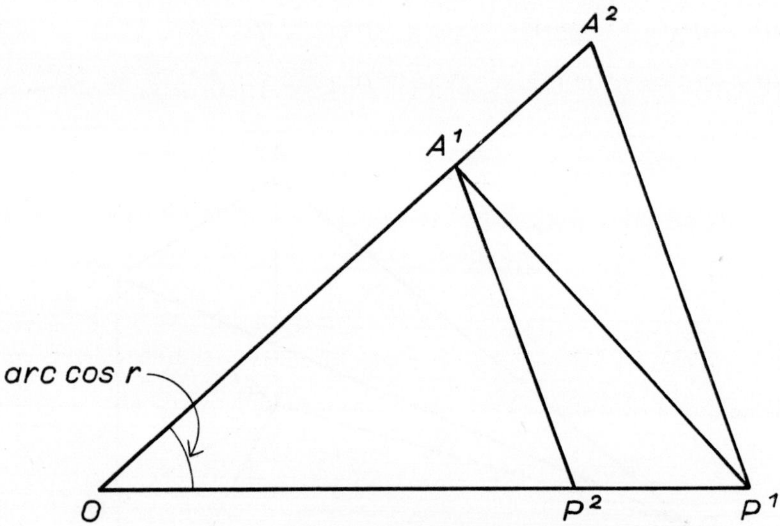

Fig. 2.11. Illustration of the inequality coefficients and proportions: the subspace R_2 of R_3

$OA^2 = OP^1$. Clearly we have, because of the geometrical interpretation of the correlation coefficient:

$$P^1P^2 = A^2A^1 = (s_P - s_A)\sqrt{n};$$
$$P^1A^2 = s_P\sqrt{\{2(1-r)n\}};$$
$$P^2A^1 = s_A\sqrt{\{2(1-r)n\}}.$$

Consequently, the second step of the decomposition is equivalent with $(P^1A^1)^2 = (P^1P^2)^2 + (P^1A^2)(P^2A^1)$. The partial coefficient U_C is then equal to the geometric average of P^1A^2 and P^2A^1, divided by the sum of OP^0 and OA^0; and U_S equals P^1P^2 (or A^2A^1) divided by this sum. The geometrical equivalents of the inequality proportions can then be easily derived. The second step corresponding to (2.21), finally, is derived in a similar way by drawing a vertical line through A^1; cf. Section 2.B of the Appendix.

Appendix to Chapter II

2.A. The Sampling Variance of the Inequality Measures

2.A.1. The asymptotic sampling variances of the inequality coefficient U and the proportions U^M, U^S, U^C, all being functions of sample moments, can be evaluated as follows.[1] Take U; the differential of its logarithm is given by

$$(2.32)\qquad \frac{dU}{U} = \tfrac{1}{2}\,\frac{d(m_{20}+m_{02}-2m_{11})}{m_{20}+m_{02}-2m_{11}} - \frac{d(\sqrt{m_{20}}+\sqrt{m_{02}})}{\sqrt{m_{20}}+\sqrt{m_{02}}},$$

where m_{hk} is the sample moment corresponding to the parent moment μ_{hk}. If we square both sides of this equation and take mean values, the following result holds asymptotically:

$$(2.33)\qquad \frac{\operatorname{var} U}{Y^2} = \tfrac{1}{4}\,\frac{\operatorname{var}(m_{20}+m_{02}-2m_{11})}{(\mu_{20}+\mu_{02}-2\mu_{11})^2} + \frac{\operatorname{var}(\sqrt{m_{20}}+\sqrt{m_{02}})}{(\sqrt{\mu_{20}}+\sqrt{\mu_{02}})^2}$$
$$- \frac{\operatorname{cov}(m_{20}+m_{02}-2m_{11},\ \sqrt{m_{20}}+\sqrt{m_{02}})}{(\mu_{20}+\mu_{02}-2\mu_{11})(\sqrt{\mu_{20}}+\sqrt{\mu_{02}})}.$$

The right-hand side can be reduced to combinations of variances and covariances of sample moments, either directly or—as in the case of the square roots—by applying the same procedure once more. It should be noted that the classical formulae in this field (which are applied here throughout) are based on the assumption that the n pairs (P_i, A_i) are independent random drawings from the same universe.

2.A.2. The result for (2.33) is a complicated expression involving

[1] See e.g. M. G. Kendall, *The Advanced Theory of Statistics*, Vol. I (London, 3rd edition, 1947), Chapter 9.

parent moments of the fourth order, which can however be simplified considerably if the assumption is made that the parent distribution is normal.[1] The first fraction of the right-hand side of (2.33) becomes then $\frac{1}{4}(2/n)[1-(Y^M)^2]$, and the result as a whole is

$$\frac{n \operatorname{var} U}{Y^2} = \tfrac{1}{2}[1 + A - 2B - (Y^M - C)^2], \tag{2.34}$$

in which

$$A = \frac{\mu_{20} + \mu_{02} + 2\mu_{11}^2/\sqrt{\mu_{20}\mu_{02}}}{(\sqrt{\mu_{20}} + \sqrt{\mu_{02}})^2}; \tag{2.35}$$

$$B = \frac{\dfrac{(\mu_{20} - \mu_{11})^2}{\sqrt{\mu_{20}}} + \dfrac{(\mu_{02} - \mu_{11})^2}{\sqrt{\mu_{02}}}}{(\mu_{20} + \mu_{02} - 2\mu_{11})(\sqrt{\mu_{20}} + \sqrt{\mu_{02}})}; \tag{2.36}$$

$$C = \frac{\dfrac{\mu_{10}^2}{\sqrt{\mu_{20}}} + \dfrac{\mu_{01}^2}{\sqrt{\mu_{02}}}}{\sqrt{\mu_{20}} + \sqrt{\mu_{02}}}. \tag{2.37}$$

It will be observed that $-(Y^M - C)^2$ is the only term of (2.34) that contains parent moments of the first order. This term cannot be expressed as a function of the parent inequality coefficient.

The arithmetic can be simplified if we introduce

$$w = \frac{\mu_{11}}{\sqrt{\mu_{20}\mu_{02}}}, \qquad -1 \leq w \leq 1, \tag{2.38}$$

and the square of the ratio of the geometric average of $\sqrt{\mu_{20}}$ and $\sqrt{\mu_{02}}$ to their arithmetic average,

$$\theta = \frac{4\sqrt{\mu_{20}\mu_{02}}}{(\sqrt{\mu_{20}} + \sqrt{\mu_{02}})^2}, \qquad 0 \leq \theta \leq 1. \tag{2.39}$$

[1] Under this assumption, the "division of inequality" into the three components can be justified in a natural way: a bivariate normal distribution is determined by five parameters, viz., the two means, the two standard deviations and the correlation; and hence, the simplest division is that according to means, to standard deviations, and to the difference between the correlation and 1.

Combining (2.35), (2.36), (2.38) and (2.39), we find

$$(2.40) \qquad 1 + A - 2B = \frac{\frac{1}{4}(1-w)(1+w)^2\theta^2}{1-\frac{1}{2}(1+w)\theta}.$$

Also

$$(2.41) \qquad Y^2 = 1 - \tfrac{1}{2}(1+w)\theta;$$

$$(2.42) \qquad (1-Y^2)^2 = \tfrac{1}{4}(1+w)^2\theta^2.$$

Combining (2.40), (2.41) and (2.42) gives

$$(2.43) \qquad 1 + A - 2B = \frac{(1-w)(1-Y^2)^2}{Y^2}.$$

But it follows from (2.41) that

$$(2.44) \qquad 1 - w = 2\left[1 - \frac{1-Y^2}{\theta}\right] \leq 2Y^2,$$

so that

$$(2.45) \qquad 1 + A - 2B \leq 2(1-Y^2)^2.$$

From this and from (2.34) the result (2.12) follows. The overestimation of the variance which takes place if the expression $(1/n)Y^2(1-Y^2)^2$ is used is in most cases not very serious. First, the difference between the geometric and the arithmetic averages of $\sqrt{\mu_{20}}$ and $\sqrt{\mu_{02}}$ is of the second order, and so is the difference between $1-w$ and $2Y^2$ in (2.44). Second, the expression $-(Y^M - C)^2$, which involves the squaring of the difference of two positive numbers, both ≤ 1, is usually small compared with $2(1-Y^2)^2$. In our applications the U's will generally be of the order of 0.2–0.4, so that $2(1-Y^2)^2$ is then of the order of 1.4 or higher; and both the U^M's and the C's tend to be rather small.[1] Nevertheless, some "safety margin" is useful because of the restrictive underlying assumptions of normality and independence, and because of the fact that it is an asymptotic result.

2.A.3. The same procedure can be applied to the inequality proportions. The result (2.18) for the variance of U^M is then obtained in a straightforward way. For the variance of U^S we find

[1] The applications referred to in this Appendix are those of Chapter IV.

$$(2.46) \qquad n \operatorname{var} U^S = 4Y^S[Y^S Y^M(1 - \tfrac{1}{2} Y^M) + \tfrac{1}{2}(1+\varrho)(1-Y^S)Y^C],$$

where ϱ is the parent correlation of predictions and actual outcomes,

$$(2.47) \qquad \varrho = \frac{\bar{\mu}_{11}}{\sqrt{\bar{\mu}_{20}\bar{\mu}_{02}}},$$

the $\bar{\mu}$'s being moments about the means. Since $\frac{1}{2}U^M$ is usually close to zero and the correlations are not very far from 1, we may simplify accordingly. This leads to (2.19).

For the variance of U^C we find

$$(2.48) \qquad n \operatorname{var} U^C = 4(Y^C)^2[1 - Y^C - \tfrac{1}{2}\{(Y^M)^2 + (1-\varrho)Y^S\}].$$

The term between curled brackets, multiplied by $\frac{1}{2}$, is relatively small; it has been left out in the final result (2.20).

2.B. Generalisations and Modifications of the Inequality Measures

2.B.1. As stated in the text, U can be generalised to

$$(2.29) \qquad U^* = \frac{\sqrt{(\mathbf{p}-\mathbf{a})'\mathbf{Q}(\mathbf{p}-\mathbf{a})}}{\sqrt{\mathbf{p}'\mathbf{Q}\mathbf{p}} + \sqrt{\mathbf{a}'\mathbf{Q}\mathbf{a}}},$$

where $\mathbf{Q}$ is a positive-definite matrix of order n. Such a matrix can always be written as the product $\mathbf{R}'\mathbf{R}$, $\mathbf{R}$ being a square and nonsingular matrix of rank n.[1] Hence U^* can be interpreted as the original coefficient U corresponding to the linear prediction combinations $\mathbf{Rp}$ and those of the actual values $\mathbf{Ra}$. This means that all results obtained for U and its proportions can be immediately applied to U^*, provided $\mathbf{p}$ and $\mathbf{a}$ are replaced by $\mathbf{Rp}$ and $\mathbf{Ra}$, respectively.

A particular case occurs when $\mathbf{Q}$ is the inverse of the moment matrix of the forecasting errors:

$$(2.49) \qquad \mathscr{E}[(\mathbf{p}-\mathbf{a})(\mathbf{p}-\mathbf{a})'] = \mathbf{Q}^{-1}.$$

[1] See e.g. T. C. KOOPMANS and W. C. HOOD, "The Estimation of Simultaneous Linear Economic Relationships," p. 188 (Chapter VI of *Studies in Econometric Method*, edited by W. C. Hood and T. C. Koopmans, New York-London, 1953).

The parent value of U^* is then simplified to

$$(2.50)\qquad Y^* = \frac{1}{\sqrt{\mathscr{E}\left(\frac{1}{n}\,\mathbf{p}'\mathbf{Q}\mathbf{p}\right)} + \sqrt{\mathscr{E}\left(\frac{1}{n}\,\mathbf{a}'\mathbf{Q}\mathbf{a}\right)}}.$$

2.B.2. The inequality coefficient can also be generalised for the case in which several (say N) variables have to be compared. Suppose that n vectors of values have been observed, each component of each

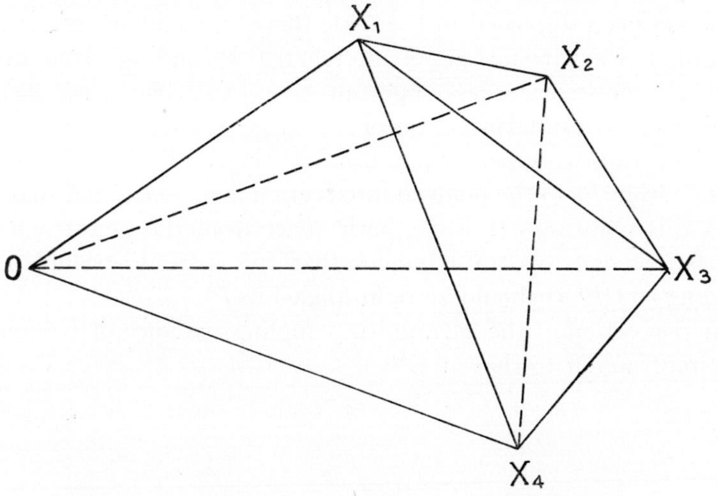

Fig. 2.12. Illustration of the multiple inequality coefficient

vector corresponding to one variable. This situation can be conveniently illustrated in the n-dimensional space which was used in the text for $N = 2$; cf. Fig. 2.12 for the case $N = 4$. The "multiple" inequality coefficient is then

$$(2.51)\qquad U_{12\,..\,N} = \frac{\sum\limits_{h}\sum\limits_{k>h}(X_hX_k)}{2\sum\limits_{h}(OX_h)},$$

where (X_hX_k) and (OX_h) stand for the distances from X_h to X_k and to O, respectively. It is easily verified that the bounds of this coefficient, too, are 0 and 1. The maximum 1 can be attained only if $N-2$ or $N-1$ of the X's coincide with O; this is in accordance with the situation of nonpositive proportionality described in 2.5.1. The multiple coefficient is a weighted average of the coefficients of lower order; for example,

$$U_{123} = \frac{[(OX_1)+(OX_2)]U_{12}+[(OX_2)+(OX_3)]U_{23}+[(OX_3)+(OX_1)]U_{31}}{2\Sigma(OX_h)}.$$

2.B.3. Apart from the alternative decomposition

$$(2.21) \qquad \frac{1}{n}\Sigma(P_i - A_i)^2 = (\bar{P} - \bar{A})^2 + (s_P - rs_A)^2 + (1 - r^2)s_A^2,$$

which has been discussed in the text, there is a similar one, viz., the expression which results if we interchange s_P and s_A. That decomposition is, however, of less importance.

The geometric interpretation of (2.21) is as follows. Consider Fig. 2.11 and drop a perpendicular from A^1 on the line OP^1. Then the distance from P^1 to the point of intersection is $s_p - rs_A$ and that from A^1 to this point $s_A\sqrt{(1 - r^2)}$, both apart from the factor $\sqrt{n}$. The stochastic theory of 2.5.4 implies that the "parent" triangle corresponding to OP^1A^1 should be right-angled in P^1.

The derivation of the asymptotic sampling variance of U^R and U^D is entirely similar to that of U^M.

III. *Postwar Macroeconomic Forecasts in The Netherlands and Scandinavia*

3.1. Macroeconomic Forecasting: Nature and Procedure

3.1.1. This chapter is devoted to an analysis of a number of macroeconomic forecasts which have in recent years been prepared by Government Agencies of several European countries. The function of this analysis, which is mainly concerned with Dutch forecasts, supplemented with certain Scandinavian data, is primarily that of an application of some of the ideas expounded in Chapter II. Although it will appear to be possible to draw certain interesting conclusions about the forecasts themselves, there are obvious difficulties which hamper a final appraisal of their adequacy. First, a satisfactory analysis would require a rather detailed and coherent picture of the development of the economies involved, which is beyond the scope of this book. Second, the character of the forecasts themselves is not always entirely clear. Sometimes they were "plans" in the sense of targets which "should" be realised—which does not imply that the Governments had full control over the variables involved—, sometimes they were expectations on probable development, and it has not always been stated unambiguously which of these alternatives applies; this holds e.g. for the earlier Central Economic Plans of the Netherlands. Third, the observed actual values to be presented below are not free from errors of measurement, especially since provisional data on actual development must be used for the more recent years. Finally, the series to be analysed are very short, they are presumably not independent in the statistical sense, and the predictions were sometimes published rather late; the last two points will be reconsidered in Section 3.2.

In spite of this list of objections it remains true that we are concerned here with predictions in the sense of statements concerning unknown (future) events; and it remains interesting to see to what extent they have been realised—even if the actual values are known imperfectly—, for the forecasts represent important attempts to deal with strategic economic variables in a scientific manner, although they are themselves not scientific in the sense of Section 2.2.

The forecasts are all of the point, not of the interval class; and they have a multiple character because several future events are predicted simultaneously. The variables analysed are listed in Table 3.1, and their numerical values (actual and predicted), are presented in the Appendix of this chapter, in Table 3.9. The period analysed is 1949–1951 and 1953 for the Netherlands, 1949–1952 for the three Scandinavian countries; 1952 has been omitted for the Netherlands because that year's forecasts were of the alternative conditional type, and it is not satis-

TABLE 3.1

LIST OF DUTCH AND SCANDINAVIAN VARIABLES ANALYSED

Netherlands	*Scandinavia*
(a) *Price indices of:*	
commodity exports commodity imports consumption	commodity exports commodity imports
(b) *Quantities and volumes:*	
commodity exports commodity imports consumption industrial production construction activity available labour force labour productivity employment in private sector employment in public sector	commodity exports commodity imports national product industrial production construction activity gross fixed investment*
(c) *Money values:*	
commodity exports commodity imports consumption net investment value added in private sector Government wage bill Government commodity purchases indirect taxes minus subsidies exports of services imports of services surplus on the balance of services	

* For Sweden and Denmark only.

factory to select a particular one out of the alternatives. As a whole, there are 92 Dutch and 82 Scandinavian forecasts.

3.1.2. The remainder of this section is devoted to a short sketch of some prediction procedures which are frequently used in this field. This is a subject which obviously belongs to the second category of problems in forecasting (that of the generation of predictions), mentioned in Section 2.3.

A simple method of macroeconomic forecasting, which is rather often adopted, is the following trial-and-error procedure.[1] We start from certain numerical assumptions (usually plausible guesses) concerning a number of basic variables, derive from these the values to be assumed by other variables by means of simple economic hypotheses (e.g. fixed imports-income ratios, etc.), and proceed in this way until results are obtained which are, when applied to the actual phenomena which they serve to predict, untenable; for example, the result may be an employment level considerably above the full-employment ceiling. Some alterations in the assumptions are then made which remove this feature but perhaps lead to other contradictions, after which new alterations are made, and so on until the results are free from such defects. We might hence describe this trial-and-error method as an iterative procedure, starting from *a priori* plausible assumptions and ending when all internal-consistency requirements[2] are met.

This procedure has several defects, even if we are prepared to disregard the predominant rôle of the internal-consistency criterion (cf. above, 2.2.5). First, although the method itself is very simple, its working is far from transparent; second, it is not at all easy to use the method for policy purposes—a feature the importance of which will become clear in later chapters. An econometric equation system is superior in both respects, though not necessarily in all respects (for instance, it may predict badly!). The next few pages are devoted to a brief exposition of the system used for the Dutch Central Economic Plan of 1955.[3] It should be admitted that prediction according to such a system requires in general a preliminary prediction of exogenous changes (i.e., a set of higher-order forecasts); and this aspect is not always very

[1] Cf. also R. L. MARRIS, "The Position of Economics and Economists in the Government Machine; a Comparative Critique of the United Kingdom and the Netherlands," *Economic Journal*, Vol. 64 (1954), pp. 759–783.

[2] This term is used here in a wide sense.

[3] Cf. *Centraal Economisch Plan 1955* (The Hague, 1955), pp. 110–119.

much different from the initial stages of the trial-and-error method. However, the mechanism of an economy is much more clearly pictured by an equation system than by iteration.

3.1.3. The 1955-system for the Dutch economy consists of 27 equations, 12 of which are definitions, 4 institutional, and the remainder behavioural equations.[1] Five sectors are distinguished: Government, enterprises, wage-earners, entrepreneurs, and the rest of the world. All relations are assumed to be linear, or are linearised; for example, the product of two variables can be written as

$$xy = (\bar{x} + \Delta x)\,(\bar{y} + \Delta y),$$

where x and y are the values in the year of prediction, $\bar{x}$ and $\bar{y}$ those of the preceding year, and Δx, Δy increments. In most cases these increments are small relative to the values $\bar{x}$, $\bar{y}$, so that the increment of the product is approximately given by

$$xy - \bar{x}\bar{y} = \bar{x}\Delta y + \bar{y}\Delta x,$$

which is linear in Δx and Δy. In what follows all variables are assumed to be differences between the value of the year of prediction and the corresponding value of the preceding year; when the latter (base) values occur, they are denoted by a bar above the symbol (e.g. $\bar{e}$, $\bar{n}$). Furthermore, quantities and prices are denoted by lower-case, money amounts by corresponding capital letters; and, unless otherwise stated, prices are measured as indices with base 1 in the preceding year, and the other variables in billions (10^9) of guilders.

The first equation defines the aggregate value of the sales of enterprises (V) as the sum of its components:

$$V = C + X_G + I + D + N + E, \tag{3.1}$$

where C refers to aggregate consumption bought by families from firms, X_G to Government commodity purchases, I to net investment, D to depreciation, N to addition to stocks, E to exports.[2] In terms of volumes and prices we have, after linearisation,

[1] Note that the actual values of the variables to be introduced are assumed to satisfy the behavioural equations *stochastically*, whereas the predictions are – after allowance is made for specific numerical values of disturbances – determined *exactly* by all equations. The fact that the predictions satisfy the definitional equations implies that the consistency criterion is accepted. The fact, furthermore, that the system is not of the recursive type implies that the predictions are simultaneously determined by predetermined values; cf. p. 19 n. 2.

[2] In 1954 this composition was the following (in billions of guilders): $C = 16$; $X_G = 2$; $I = 2$; $D = 2$; $N = 1$; $E = 13$. A list of variables of this equation system is given in the Appendix of this chapter, Table 3.11.

$$V = v + \bar{c}p_c + \bar{x}_G p_{x_G} + (\bar{\imath} + \bar{d})p_i + \bar{n}p_n + \bar{e}_c p_{e_c} + \bar{e}_s p_{e_s}, \tag{3.2}$$

where e_c and e_s represent exports of commodities and of services, respectively; the other symbols are volumes and prices corresponding to the above amounts denoted by capitals.

Consumption is split up according to the amounts spent by wage-earning and entrepreneurial families (X_W and X_Z), with different marginal propensities:

$$C = X_W + X_Z - C' \tag{3.3}$$

$$X_W = 0.85\,(W + U - T_W + W') \tag{3.4}$$

$$X_Z = 0.4\,(Z - T_Z + Z'), \tag{3.5}$$

where C' is the consumption bought from the rest of the world and the Government, W the private wage bill, U payments made by the Unemployment Fund, T_W income taxes paid by wage-earners, W' wages paid by the Government, foreign countries, etc., minus certain premiums, Z non-wage income, T_Z income taxes paid by this group, Z' income received by the same group from abroad minus certain premiums. Out of these variables, Z is determined by the profit-and-loss account

$$Z = V - W - T_I - D - M, \tag{3.6}$$

T_I being indirect taxes minus subsidies and M imports.

The tax variables of (3.4), (3.5), (3.6) are determined by the institutional equations

$$T_W = 0.09\,(W + U + W') + T_W^{\text{au}} \tag{3.7}$$

$$T_Z = 0.3\,(Z + Z') + T_Z^{\text{au}} \tag{3.8}$$

$$T_I = 0.03\,W + 0.04M + 0.09\,(V - E) + T_I^{\text{au}}. \tag{3.9}$$

The coefficients represent average marginal tax rates in the relevant area, and the last terms (with superscript au) serve to estimate the effect of the acceleration of the collection of taxes. Another institutional equation determines the variable U of (3.4):

$$U = 0.54\,\bar{B}\bar{R}(b - a), \tag{3.10}$$

where a represents the employment in the private sector, b the available labour force (both increments with base 1 in 1954), $\bar{B}$ the number of employees working in the private sector in 1954 (about 2.6 millions), and $\bar{R}$ is the annual amount paid by the Unemployment Fund per unemployed man in that year. Hence $\bar{B}\bar{R}(b - a)$ would represent the increase in the aggregate amount to be paid by the Unemployment Fund if all unemployed would receive the benefits; but actually, it applies to only 54 per cent of them.

The employment variable a enters, together with the wage rate w, into the equation defining the private wage bill,

$$W = \bar{W}(a + w), \tag{3.11}$$

and it is itself described as a function of home production, i.e., of the volume of sales minus imports $(v - m)$:

$$a = 0.4\,(v - m)/(\bar{v} - \bar{m}). \tag{3.12}$$

This implies an elasticity of 0.4 for employment with respect to home production, which leaves scope for an increase of labour productivity when production rises. The volume of imports [the correction on v in (3.12)] is described as a function of the components of the sales of enterprises, all with different marginal import ratios:

$$\begin{aligned} m = 0.38\,c + 0.39\,x_G + 0.71\,(i + d) + 0.79\,n\,+ \\ + 0.63\,e_c + 0.28\,e_s + m_s, \end{aligned} \tag{3.13}$$

where m_s represents the imports of services, which are estimated autonomously. The amount of imports (M) is defined as

$$M = m + \bar{m}_c p_{m_c} + \bar{m}_s p_{m_s}, \tag{3.14}$$

where $\bar{m}_c$ and p_{m_c} refer to the imports of commodities. Similar definitions connect the values, volumes, and prices of the constituents of V [cf. equation (3.1)]:

$$C = c + \bar{c}p_c \tag{3.15}$$

$$X_G = x_G + \bar{x}_G p_{x_G} \tag{3.16}$$

$$I = i + \bar{i}p_i \tag{3.17}$$

$$D = d + \bar{d}p_i \tag{3.18}$$

$$N = n + \bar{n}p_n \tag{3.19}$$

$$E = e_c + e_s + \bar{e}_c p_{e_c} + \bar{e}_s p_{e_s}. \tag{3.20}$$

Two of these constituents have still to be considered, viz., exports and investment. The volume of commodity exports is described as a function of the ratio of its price level to the competitive world price level (p_w)—with elasticity -2—, except for an autonomous increase:

$$e_c = -2\,(p_{e_c} - p_w)\,\bar{e}_c + e_c^{\mathrm{au}}. \tag{3.21}$$

As to the description of net investment, we may split up aggregate investment either into net investment and depreciation or into expansion and replacement. Consequently, when net investment is the variable in the system, and expansion the variable described by the equation, we should add in this equation replacement (r) and subtract depreciation (d) in order to get the variable which we really need. The equation is then

$$i = 0.25\,(v - n) - 0.1\,\bar{i} + r - d, \tag{3.22}$$

which implies that the expansion of enterprises is written as a function of the volume of sales (except for changes in inventories) and of the stock of capital goods at the beginning of the year. In (3.22), being an equation in first differences, the latter variable is represented by $\bar{i}$.

Finally, there are five equations describing price indices as functions of the wage rate and of the price level of commodity imports—with different weights—, except for estimated effects of certain tax changes:

$$p_c = 0.35\,w + 0.2 p_{m_c} + T_{I;c}^{\mathrm{au}}/\bar{c} \tag{3.23}$$

$$p_{x_G} = 0.3\,w + 0.5\,p_{m_c} + T_{I;x_G}^{\mathrm{au}}/\bar{x}_G \tag{3.24}$$

$$p_i = 0.25\,w + 0.5\,p_{m_c} + T_{I;i}^{\mathrm{au}}/\bar{i} \tag{3.25}$$

$$p_n = 0.1\,w + 0.7\,p_{m_c} + T_{I;n}^{\mathrm{au}}/\bar{n} \tag{3.26}$$

$$p_{e_c} = 0.5\,\{0.35\,w + 0.3\,p_{m_c} + T_{I;e_c}^{\mathrm{au}}/\bar{e}_c\} + 0.5\,p_w. \tag{3.27}$$

The last equation expresses the dependence of the export price level on cost factors as well as on the competitive world price level.

3.1.4. Together, these 27 equations describe 27 endogenous variables as determined by exogenous variables. The former category consists of

(*i*) prices: p_c, p_{x_G}, p_i, p_n, p_{e_c};

(*ii*) quantities and volumes: v, c, i, a, m, e_c;

(*iii*) money variables: V, C, X_G, I, D, N, E, X_W, X_Z, Z, T_W, T_Z, T_I, U, W, M.

All other variables are considered exogenous. This does not necessarily imply that mutual relationships between these variables and the endogenous ones are wholly absent, but rather that these relations, if existent, are so uncertain that at the present stage not much is lost by neglecting them. Actually, the system was often revised, even as far as its variables are concerned. This is an obvious necessity when, say, the Government would decide to relax the control over wage rates—an additional wage rate equation would then have to be inserted—; but even apart from this, model building in econometrics is a young science which tries to advance by absorbing all new ideas and new observations that are presented when time proceeds. The system described in 3.1.3 has therefore no pretentions of being adequate in the sense that no rival method can be conceived of which would perform its job better; but it is at least useful as an illustration of the way in which the forecasts to be analysed have been prepared. Of course, it is not necessary to use a whole system for the prediction of all of the variables: some, like the size of the population, can be conveniently extrapolated, at least in the short run; others can be estimated by means of a single equation, e.g., the price level of commodity imports (cf. 2.3.2); still others can be determined from Government regulations, like wages; etc. Nevertheless, the equation system remains the kernel of the forecasting procedure, the numerical outcomes of which are, of course, decidedly influenced by exogenous predictions of the above-mentioned types.

3.2. On the Interdependence of Forecasts and of Actual Changes, and the Time of their Publication

3.2.1. One may wonder whether there is any sense in applying accuracy analysis to a set of forecasts of variables which are supposed to be connected so closely that twenty-seven equations are deemed necessary to describe this fact. Isn't it preferable to test the validity of the separate equations?

The answer to this question is the following. There are three levels at which one can analyse the accuracy of forecasts of this kind, viz.:

(*i*) One can take the predictions as they are and compare them with the corresponding observed actual data. This is the most straightforward procedure.

(*ii*) One can separate the endogenous variables from the exogenous ones, insert the observed values of the latter category in the equation system, and derive conditional predictions of the endogenous values by means of this system, the condition being that the exogenous values are as observed. Comparing these predictions with the observed endogenous values is then a method of measuring the accuracy of the model.

(*iii*) One can insert, for each equation of the model, the observed values of the right-hand (explanatory) variables, and compare the implied value of the left-hand variable with the observed value.

These three different approaches stand more or less in the order of increasing sophistication and also of increasing requirements as to quality and size of the sample in order to carry out the approach successfully. The latter aspect rules out approach (*iii*);[1] approach (*ii*) will be considered in Chapter V (Section 5.2). The approach of this chapter is, therefore, (*i*). The uniqueness of this choice should not, however, be regarded as implying that the approach has no drawbacks. On the contrary, we should expect—as indicated above—a certain degree of interdependence of the separate forecasts and of the separate actual changes, and also of the separate forecasting errors. This will almost surely make an appraisal of the forecasting quality more difficult. On the other hand, it should be realised that in the actual forecasting procedure the equation system was not (and will in general not be) accepted without assumptions concerning disturbances. Such numerical disturbances are introduced in order to take account of plausible deviations from the "normal" behaviour pattern; an example is the autonomous term of the export equation (3.21), which was in several years considerably larger than the price term. Since the numerical outcomes of the forecasting procedure are in many respects highly dependent on these deviations, it must be considered interesting to analyse the results of such a "combined" approach, which was really adopted—in contrast with those of a mechanical application of the equation system. These disturbances are not introduced into definitional equations, like that connecting price, volume and value of consumption, so that the argument cannot be applied to these relations.

[1] For an application of this approach, see C. Christ's paper "A Test of an Econometric Model for the United States, 1921–1947" in: *Conference on Business Cycles*, edited by the National Bureau for Economic Research (New York, 1951), pp. 35–107; and "Aggregate Econometric Models," *American Economic Review*, Vol. 46 (1956), pp. 385–408. It should be noted that some of Christ's more refined tests cannot be applied here, because the constant terms and the covariance matrix of the disturbances of the Dutch system have not been specified.

But even in such cases it is interesting to analyse the accuracy of all variables involved, for the omission of one of them may lead to a loss of insight; for example, the average forecasting quality (measured by means of some standard chosen before) of the value of consumption is not necessarily uniquely determined by the quality of the corresponding price and volume predictions, since the forecasting errors of the last two series may or may not cancel out.

3.2.2. Granted the above arguments on deliberate deviations from a mechanical application of the equation system, it remains true that some of the forecasts represent mere duplications. There is, of course, no need to test the hypothesis that the values of the variables to be analysed are independently distributed, for we know that this cannot be true; but we may try to find out to what extent it is untrue.

In order to analyse the variables in a comparable way, all forecasts for year t will be expressed (as will be done throughout in this chapter) as percentage deviations from the corresponding actual values in $t - 1$, such as these were known at the moment when the forecast was made; and all actual outcomes will be expressed as percentage deviations from the corresponding "final" actual values in the preceding year. In formulae:

$$P_t = \frac{p_t - a'_{t-1}}{a'_{t-1}} 100; \qquad A_t = \frac{a_t - a_{t-1}}{a_{t-1}} 100,$$

p_t being the value predicted for year t, a_t the observed actual value, and $a_t{}'_{-1}$ the (provisional) observed actual value for $t - 1$ as it was known when the forecast for t was made. These definitions imply that the influence of incomplete knowledge of the previous year $t - 1$ (which is not to be predicted) is eliminated; this is clearly desirable for the accuracy analysis.

3.2.3. A simple method of analysing the degree of interconnection between the series of forecasts (P) and that between those of the actual values (A) is to compute all possible correlation coefficients and to see to what extent their empirical distribution deviates from the theoretical distribution that holds under the assumption of independence. This method is, however, somewhat restrictive because the classical product-moment correlation is an indicator of linearity, whereas in fact the relationships may be of a more complicated type. Two examples are given in Fig. 3.1, where the A-values of some price series are shown to satisfy approximately nonlinear, although monotonous relationships. This does not, of course, imply that such curves represent

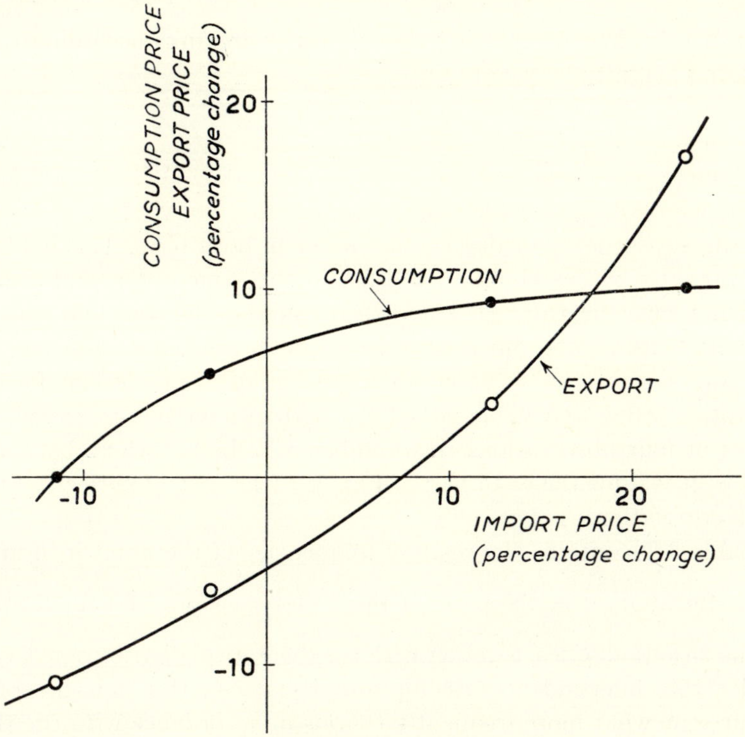

Fig. 3.1. Examples of curvilinear association. Horizontal: price level of commodity imports; vertical: price level of consumption and of commodity exports (all in percentage deviations from the previous year)

"true" economic interconnections; instead, we should interpret the cases of perfect monotony of Fig. 3.1 in the sense that they should not occur too often, for otherwise the separate series would indeed be largely repetitions of each other and we would gain very little by applying accuracy analysis to all of them.

The simplest way to investigate the degree of monotony is counting the number of inversions for pairs of series; this amounts to calculating rank correlation coefficients.[1] Consider therefore the forecast

[1] See e.g. M. G. KENDALL, *The Advanced Theory of Statistics*, Vol. I (London, 3rd edition, 1947), Chapter 16. Ties have been considered as half inversions, and distributed evenly over adjacent integral values in Table 3.2 below.

series of the value of consumption and of the value added in the private sector; these P's are, in the chronological order 1949, 1950, 1951, 1953:

1.3	6.5	7.7	2.3
3.1	6.7	8.5	2.1,

respectively. When replacing the P's by their ranks according to increasing magnitude, we obtain

1	3	4	2
2	3	4	1.

Next, we take all possible pairs of ranks, and see whether they show the same (ascending or descending) order in both rows. This holds for the first two places: 1–3 and 2–3 are in the same order, and also for the first and the third (1–4 and 2–4), but not for the first and the fourth: 1–2 and 2–1. Since all other pairs (3–4 and 3–4; 3–2 and 3–1; 4–2 and 4–1) are in the same order, the series of predictions for consumption value and value added are said to have one inversion. For series of four observations this number may be anywhere between 0 and 6; it is 0 for the examples of Fig. 3.1 (the case of perfect positive rank correlation).

Table 3.2 contains the relative frequencies of the number of inversions for all $\binom{23}{2} = 253$ pairs of the 23 forecasts and for all 253 pairs of the 23 actual series, together with the theoretical distribution derived under the independence assumption. It is seen that few inversions occur somewhat more frequently than is in accordance with the theoretical distribution, but that the effect is rather small: the average number of inversions is 2.8, both for the forecasts and for the actual outcomes, as against 3 in the theoretical case. It may be, however, that this result is rather artificial. For suppose that we replace employment by unemployment, and let us disregard for the sake of the argument any changes in the available labour force. Then all P's and A's of employment obtain different signs, which affects the distribution of the number of inversions. It seems, therefore, that Table 3.2 is the result of the arbitrary way in which the variables are defined. On the other hand, this objection is only partly valid, since most of the variables have the property that they are positively associated with general trade cycle movements—a property which they would lose if the above-mentioned transformation were applied to them. There are only six variables about which we should be less sure in this respect;[1] it is therefore interesting to see whether the remaining 17 variables show a different picture. Indeed, it follows from Table 3.2 that for this sub-

TABLE 3.2

RELATIVE FREQUENCIES OF THE NUMBER OF INVERSIONS, AND THEIR MEANS, FOR PAIRS OF DUTCH PREDICTION AND ACTUAL SERIES

Nature of series	*Number of inversions*							*Mean*
	0	*1*	*2*	*3*	*4*	*5*	*6*	
Forecasts:								
23 variables	0.09	0.13	0.22	0.19	0.20	0.13	0.03	2.8
17 variables	0.13	0.19	0.23	0.14	0.17	0.11	0.04	2.5
Actual values:								
23 variables	0.07	0.15	0.20	0.24	0.18	0.13	0.03	2.8
17 variables	0.10	0.18	0.21	0.22	0.16	0.12	0.01	2.6
Theoretical distribution under independence	0.04	0.12^5	0.21	0.25	0.21	0.12^5	0.04	3

group few inversions are still more frequent than for the larger group of all 23 variables; moreover, that they are more frequent for the forecasts than for the actual values. Although it is difficult to establish statistical significance here because inversions corresponding to the same series are not independent, the reliability of this result is supported by its plausibility: economic phenomena are characterised by some degree of interdependence, which raises the frequency of few inversions above the level of independence; and economic predictions are based on exactly this interdependence, so that—even if this is done imperfectly, and even if allowance is made for disturbances—we should expect them to be characterised by still more regularity. Too much regularity is presumably a normal error of forecasts which are derived by means of scientific methods. On the other hand, the results of Table 3.2 for all 23 variables together, on which the subsequent analysis for Dutch predictions is based, do not suggest that the interdependence is considerable; though it cannot be maintained, of course, that the 92 forecasts are as valuable for accuracy analysis as a similar number of independent predictions would be.[2]

[1] These variables are: available labour force; employment in the public sector; Government wage bill; Government commodity purchases; indirect taxes minus subsidies; surplus on the balance of services.

[2] There may be other types of interdependence than the one analysed here, e.g., lagged and multiple correlations. But the paucity of data and the findings reported here suggest that such an analysis will not be very fruitful.

3.2.4. There is another problem affecting the nature and quality of the forecasts which should be considered, viz., the time of their publication. Whereas the Scandinavian forecasts were generally published in the beginning of the year to which they refer, the publication data of the Dutch predictions were often much later. The reasons were mainly political, and not interesting for our present purposes. Instead, our first question should be: Are we justified in accepting the published figures as predictions, if the time interval to which they refer is only partly future? The answer should be: To a certain extent, yes, for whereas the calendar year may belong partly to the past, the "statistical year" lags considerably behind because of the delay in the supply of economic information, so that the predictions refer indeed largely to "unknown" events. However, this applies to Scandinavia as well, so that, if we want to compare the quality of the Dutch and the Scandinavian forecasts, we are faced with a second problem: What is the influence of the lapse of time on the quality of forecasting? This we shall now consider.

The simplest way of investigating the influence of time is to analyse the successive unpublished versions of the Dutch forecasts. To take an extreme example: there are four versions of the Central Economic Plan 1949, viz., three preliminary versions (of August 1948, May 1949 and September 1949) and the final version. Two successive versions imply, for each predicted variable, a revision—either a successful or an unsuccessful revision. An example: in August 1948 the Government wage bill was predicted to increase by 4.2 per cent in 1949; in May 1949 this was revised to a decrease of 0.7 per cent; the actual result was a decrease of 6.5 per cent, so that the revision, although far from perfect, was a successful one. More formally, write P' for the original and P'' for the revised forecast; and consider the "revision ratio"

$$R = \frac{P'' - P'}{A - P'}. \tag{3.28}$$

Clearly, a perfect revision requires $R = 1$. An R between 0 and 2 may be said to correspond to a successful revision; if $0 < R < 1$, then the revision is, though successful, too small; if $R > 1$, it is too large; if $R > 2$, the revised forecast is farther from A than the original forecast was, just as in the case $R < 0$. It appears that the majority of the revisions was indeed successful according to this criterion, which is true for all separate years; but there is an appreciable difference between small and large changes. Table 3.3 below shows that, for increases and decreases which turned out to be less than 5 per cent, about one half of the R's are outside the interval (0, 2).[1] The picture is somewhat more favourable for changes between 5 and 15 per cent; but a considerable majority of successful revisions exists only when actual changes exceeding 15 per cent are considered. It follows that revisions have been

TABLE 3.3

FREQUENCY DISTRIBUTIONS OF REVISION RATIOS OF THE DUTCH FORECASTS, 1949–1951 AND 1953

Percentage range of actual change	$\leqq 0.00$	*0.01–1.00*	*1.01–2.00*	$\geqq 2.01$	*Total*
$\lvert A \rvert < 5$	11	10	3	3	27
$5 \leqq \lvert A \rvert < 15$	14	16	9	2	41
$15 \leqq \lvert A \rvert$	4	23	1	2	30

clearly successful only when they concerned large movements—a feature which could perhaps have been predicted before. Another conclusion from Table 3.3 is that there is a considerable tendency to make revisions which are too small, the total number of R's between 0 and 1 being about four times as large as the number between 1 and 2. The large number of revisions in the wrong direction ($R < 0$) is also striking.

3.2.5. Our conclusion from this section cannot be that the interdependence of forecasts facilitates their accuracy analysis, nor that the delay in publishing the Dutch predictions is a point in their favour. Instead, we should conclude, first, that the interdependence exists and hampers the accuracy analysis, but that its importance is not such as to make further analysis fruitless; second, that the delay in publication represents a Dutch lead over Scandinavia in the international forecasting league. The comparison of Dutch and Scandinavian forecasts should show a better record for the former before we can consider them equally good or bad—provided, of course, such a comparison of different variables under different circumstances can be said to be meaningful.

[1] For a survey of the revisions, cf. the Appendix to this chapter, Table 3.12. The fact that not all of the 23 variables have been predicted in the preliminary versions is a reflection of the greater care paid to the final published versions. This is the reason why the analysis of this chapter is mainly based on the latter forecasts, the former being used primarily for purposes of qualification. It will appear, however, that these qualifications are of minor importance.

3.3. Accuracy Analysis of the Forecasts (1)

3.3.1. Our first and main approach will be to take all 92 Dutch and all 82 Scandinavian forecasts together, and to see what can be said about these two aggregates. There are obvious objections to such a procedure, particularly because of possible differences between separate variables and years, and the only apology that can be made is that of the small

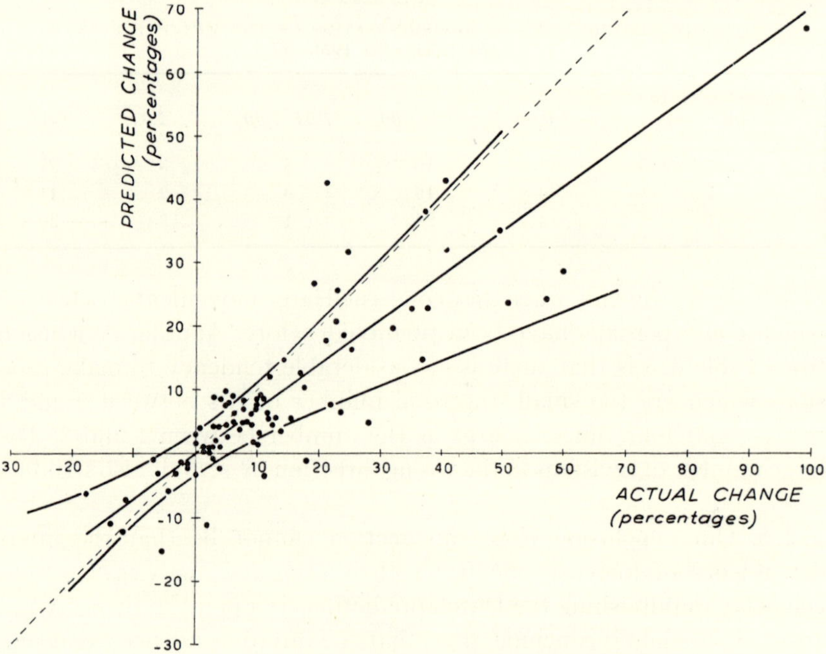

Fig. 3.2. Forecasts for the Netherlands, 1949–51, 1953

number of data resulting from finer classifications. Something will be done for separate years in this section; the next section is devoted to differences between variables, as far as this can be done.

The Figs. 3.2 and 3.3 give a picture of the forecasts for the Netherlands and Scandinavia, respectively. The broken lines are the lines of perfect forecasts; the solid lines and curves will be explained below, in 3.3.2. It appears that each of the point sets is more or less clustered around a straight line through the origin with positive slope. However, most of the points lying to the right of the vertical axis ($A > 0$) are below the line of perfect forecasts. This implies a tendency towards underestimation of changes, to which we shall return in 3.3.2.

The Figs. 3.4 and 3.5 show how the forecasts would have been if they had been based on the cheaper method of exponential extrapolation, i.e., on $P_t = A_{t-1}$. The result is evidently much worse, both for the Netherlands and Scandinavia; the percentage of turning point errors (sgn $P_t \neq$ sgn A_t) increases from 7 to 15 for the Netherlands and from 10 to 23 for Scandinavia. Of course, this extrapolation method is rather rough, and in particular there is no reason why a

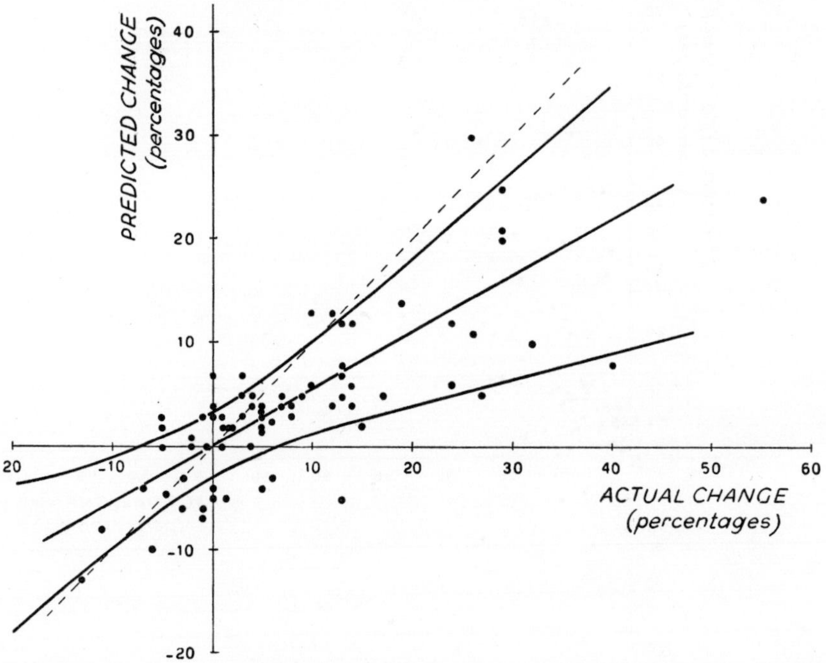

Fig. 3.3. Forecasts for Scandinavia, 1949–52

variable like net investment (including inventory changes) should be governed by a development pattern $A_t = A_{t-1}$, even approximately. It seems therefore preferable to extrapolate in a more refined way. Unfortunately, the possibilities in this field are in principle almost unlimited; and it is moreover practically impossible to take earlier changes ($A_{t-2}, \ldots$) into account, because this would require statistical data for the years preceding 1947, the weighting systems of which are too much based on prewar conditions. The best way is presumably to use an extrapolation method based on A_{t-1} which is bound to lead to a maximum of forecasting quality in a certain sense. Therefore, for each variable an "extrapolation factor" k has been determined such that the regression

$$A_t = kA_{t-1} \tag{3.29}$$

leads to a minimal second moment of residuals; these factors, which are of course positive for most of the variables, are summarised in the Appendix of this chapter, Table 3.9. The Figs. 3.6 and 3.7 show, how-

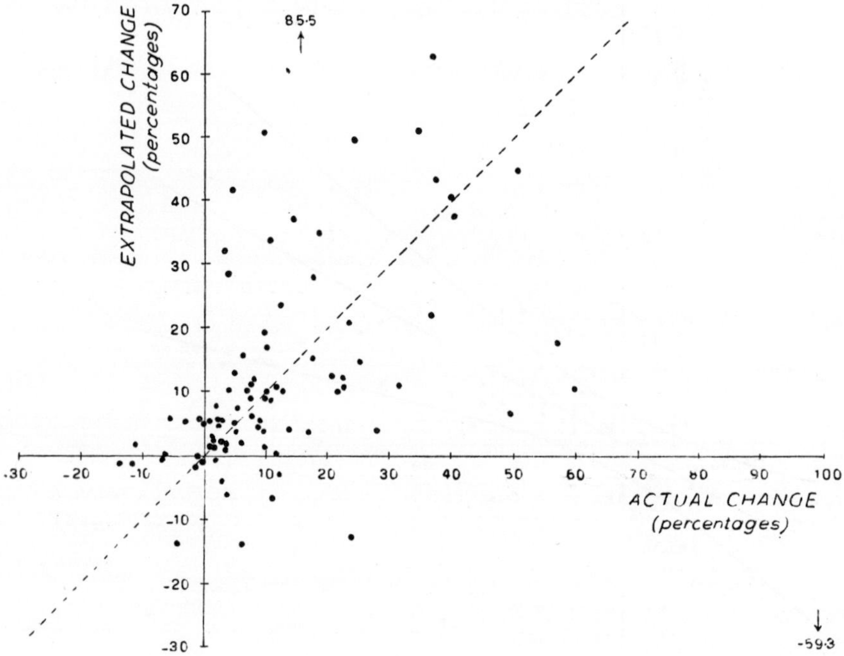

Fig. 3.4. Simple extrapolations ($P_t = A_{t-1}$) for the Netherlands, 1949–51, 1953

ever, that even if kA_{t-1} is taken as forecast of A_t, the results are still considerably below the level of the Figs. 3.2 and 3.3, respectively, although they are indeed somewhat better than those based on the simpler extrapolation $P_t = A_{t-1}$. Given the extreme character of the second extrapolation method—it is clear, parenthetically, that it could not have been applied in practice because the k's required knowledge of future A's—, the conclusion seems justified that no such method, based on the development of the variables considered since the preceding year, is able to compete with the actual forecasts made.

3.3.2. It will be observed that the point sets of the Figs. 3.2 and 3.3 have about the same shape as the hyperbolic area of Fig. 2.1: the individual points are scattered along a "regression line" which goes through the origin, and their variance around this line increases when we move away from the origin. Perhaps this is rather natural, at least qualitatively; for the prediction of large changes (say 20 or 30 per cent) will usually be characterised by larger errors than the prediction of

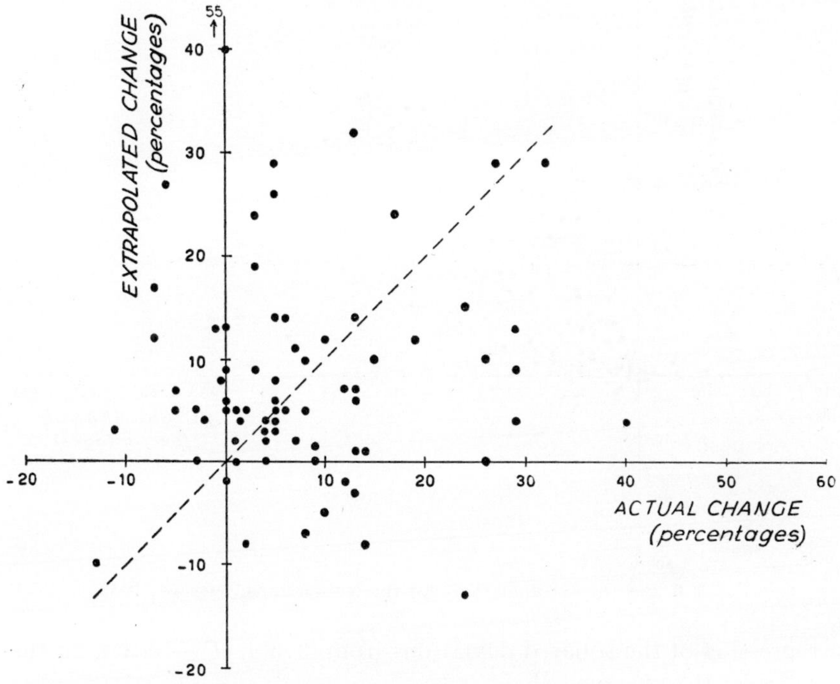

Fig. 3.5. Simple extrapolations ($P_t = A_{t-1}$) for Scandinavia, 1949–52

changes of, say, 5 per cent. We should not, of course, expect a proportionality between the error variance and the actual change, since this would imply perfect forecasting of zero changes. To assume that the variation of the forecasts consists of a part which is a constant with respect to the actual change and a part which increases with it is obviously better.

Let us accept this hyperbolic picture for descriptive purposes; it is then rather simple to give a mathematical summary of the forecasts as a whole. This summary consists of two parts: first, a regression of predictions on observed actual changes,

$$P = mA, \tag{3.30}$$

m being about 0.7 for the Netherlands and 0.55 for Scandinavia; second,

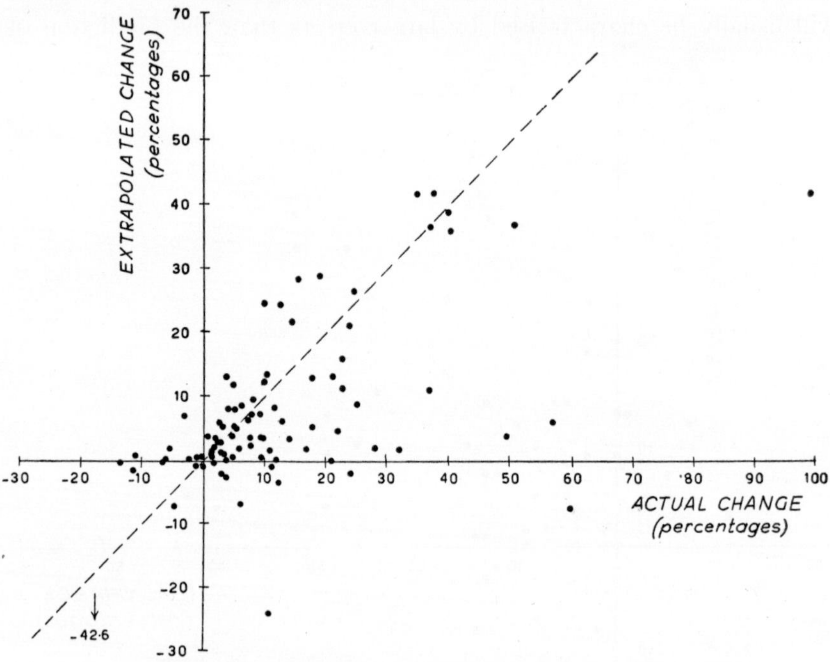

Fig. 3.6. Best-fit extrapolations for the Netherlands, 1949–51, 1953

a regression of the squared deviations from (3.30), $(P - mA)^2$, on the squares of the observed changes:[1]

[1] This regression is geometrically described as the "scedastic curve;" see e.g. M. G. KENDALL. *The Advanced Theory of Statistics*, Vol. II (London, 2nd edition, 1948), p. 142. The numerical outcomes in (3.31) and Table 3.4 below were derived by means of an iterative procedure. First, the median (m') of the individual ratios P/A was used as a preliminary estimate of m; next, the squares of the deviations $P - m'A$ were grouped according to increasing order of $|A|$ and plotted in a scatter against the square of A. This yields the estimates 10 and 0.1 of (3.31). The final estimates of m in Table 3.4 below are all obtained by taking a weighted average of the ratios P/A, the weights being equal to $A^2/(10 + 0.1\,A^2)$. This is in accordance with generalised least-squares; cf. A. C. AITKEN, "On Least Squares and Linear Combination of Observations," *Proceedings of the Royal Society of Edinburgh*, Vol. 55 (1934–35), pp. 42–48. No more rounds were made in iteration, first because the preliminary estimates m' are already close to the accepted estimates, second because the scatter diagram of (3.31) shows much more scatter than regression (which is to be expected), third because it is virtually

$$(P - mA)^2 = 10 + 0.1\,A^2. \tag{3.31}$$

Equation (3.30) tells us that the Dutch forecasts were on the average about 70 per cent of the corresponding observed changes, whereas for Scandinavia this figure is 55. Equation (3.31) implies that the variance of the forecasts around the regression (3.30)—or alternatively, the

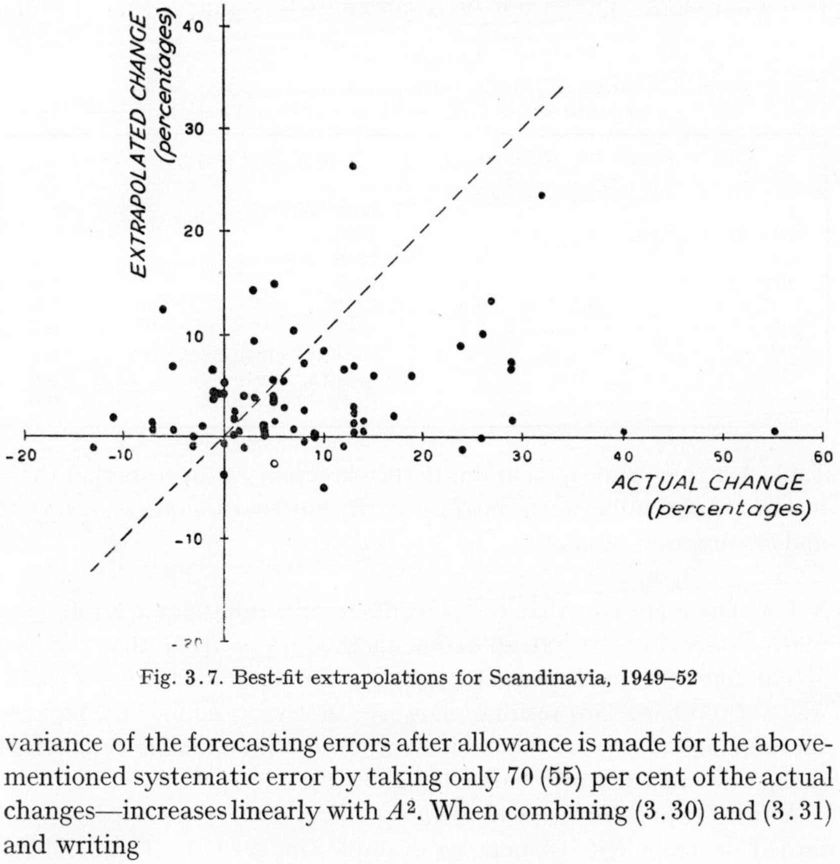

Fig. 3.7. Best-fit extrapolations for Scandinavia, 1949–52

variance of the forecasting errors after allowance is made for the above-mentioned systematic error by taking only 70 (55) per cent of the actual changes—increases linearly with A^2. When combining (3.30) and (3.31) and writing

$$P = mA \pm \sqrt{10 + 0.1\,A^2}, \tag{3.32}$$

we obtain the hyperbolic curves of the Figs. 3.2 and 3.3, which describe the forecasts according to the regression (mA) $\pm$ the standard deviation. Hence, under normality assumptions, about two thirds of

impossible to take account of nonzero correlations between the deviations $P - mA$ (which is, strictly speaking, necessary for the application of Aitken's method). Later, in the Sections 6.2 and 8.5, we shall come back to methods of this kind.

the points lie in the hyperbolic area. The minimum standard deviation is about 3 per cent (for $A = 0$), and it increases with $|A|$, slowly in the beginning, but later rapidly (3.5 per cent for $A = 5$; 4.5 for $A = 10$; 16 for $A = 50$).

The regressions (3.30) are represented in the Figs. 3.2 ($m = 0.7$) and 3.3 ($m = 0.55$) by the solid straight lines. There is no need to stress that their slopes should not be regarded as fundamental parameters.

TABLE 3.4

ESTIMATED MEAN VALUES OF DUTCH AND SCANDINAVIAN FORECASTS AS FRACTIONS OF CORRESPONDING ACTUAL CHANGES

Country and year	*Mean fraction*		*Country and year*	*Mean fraction*	
Netherlands:			Scandinavia:		
1949–51 and 1953	0.7		1949–52	0.55	
1949		0.6	1949		0.6
1950		0.6	1950		0.5
1951		0.9	1951		0.6
1953		0.7	1952		0.5
			Norway, 1949–52		0.4
			Sweden, 1949–52		0.6
			Denmark, 1949–52		0.6

Table 3.4 gives some indications in this direction; it suggests that there is some variation between separate years, but that the phenomenon of underestimation of changes itself is persistent.

3.3.3. The mere fact that the percentage of turning point errors is so much larger for the extrapolation method $P_t = A_{t-1}$ than for the actual forecasts made suggests that the prediction of turning points was not too bad. This result is, however, not very significant, because the absence of serious depressions reduced the available number of such cases considerably. Table 3.5 gives a numerical survey.[1]

A further problem is that of the prediction of accelerated and retarded development. To take an example: in 1949 the Dutch labour productivity increased by 7.4 per cent, in 1950 by 5.2 per cent; hence the development showed a retardation, which was correctly predicted,

[1] Actual turning points which refer to three successive years (because the second year shows an $A_t = 0$) are considered as one change, and the appraisal in Table 3.5 is not affected by the sign of the forecast made for this second year. In one case (the Danish national product of 1951) the turning point was "half-way" predicted, the forecast being zero; this case is not represented in the column "correctly predicted," since it would otherwise lead to a frequency of correct Danish predictions exceeding the total number of turning point predictions.

TABLE 3.5

FREQUENCIES OF TURNING POINTS OF DUTCH AND SCANDINAVIAN VARIABLES, PREDICTED AND ACTUAL

Country	*Turning Points*			*Errors*			
	Predicted	*Actual*	*Correctly Predicted*	*1st kind*	*2nd kind*	φ_1	φ_2
Netherlands	18	14	13	5	1	0.3	0.1
Scandinavia	18	21	15	3	6	0.2	0.3

the 1950 forecast being an increase of 4.7 per cent. A survey of the success in this field is given in Table 3.6, where the predictions P_t which satisfy

$$\text{sgn}\,(P_t - A_{t-1}) = \text{sgn}\,(A_t - A_{t-1}) \tag{3.33}$$

are accepted as correctly predicted, all others as incorrectly predicted.[1] The results show a substantial majority falling under the former category.

TABLE 3.6

PREDICTION OF ACCELERATED AND RETARDED DEVELOPMENT OF DUTCH AND SCANDINAVIAN VARIABLES

Country and year	*Correctly Predicted*	*Incorrectly Predicted*	*Total*	*Fraction of Incorrect Predictions*
Netherlands				
1949–51, 1953	71	20	91	0.22
1949	19	4	23	0.2
1950	15	7	22	0.3
1951	20	3	23	0.1
1953	17	6	23	0.3
Scandinavia				
1949–52	62	12	74	0.16
1949	15	3	18	0.2
1950	14	7	21	0.3
1951	20	1	21	0.0
1952	13	1	14	0.1
Norway, 1949–52	18	4	22	0.2
Sweden, 1949–52	25	4	29	0.1
Denmark, 1949–52	19	4	23	0.2

A third problem is the following. Just as the predicted changes have been found to be too small—which implies that the predicted future

[1] All cases $A_t = A_{t-1}$ are omitted; the case $P_t = A_{t-1}$ is considered as incorrectly predicted.

values show a bias towards present values—, in just the same way it is conceivable that the predicted changes themselves show a bias towards present (or better, recent) changes. This cannot, of course, be true in the extreme sense that the predicted changes P_t are all identical with the corresponding actual recent changes A_{t-1}, for this would amount to the extrapolation method $P_t = A_{t-1}$ which has been found to be inferior to the actual forecasts made. Nevertheless, some bias in this direction is possible, and it is interesting to test this. The following regression, applied to each of the variables, seems useful for this purpose:

$$P_t = h_1 A_t + h_2 A_{t-1}. \tag{3.34}$$

Perfect forecasting requires $h_1 = 1$, $h_2 = 0$, and zero residuals. Underestimation of changes without bias towards recent changes implies $0 < h_1 < 1$ and $h_2 = 0$; and the bias would imply $h_2 > 0$. A survey of the coefficients of (3.34) obtained according to least-squares—no other method applied to only four observations can claim superiority—is given in the Appendix to this chapter, Table 3.9; Table 3.7 gives their frequency distributions. It appears that almost all of the h_1's are concentrated in the interval (0, 1), as is to be expected. The h_2-test is, however, rather inconclusive: Scandinavia shows a majority of positive values (though the mean of the 23 coefficients is not more than 0.1), and the h_2's of the Netherlands are distributed almost symmetrically around zero. The bias, if existent, is therefore presumably not large.

TABLE 3.7

BIAS TOWARDS RECENT CHANGES OF DUTCH AND SCANDINAVIAN PREDICTIONS: FREQUENCY DISTRIBUTIONS OF h_1 AND h_2 OF (3.34)

Country	$h_1 \leq 0$	$0 < h_1 < 1$	$h_1 \geq 1$	$h_2 < -0.10$	$-0.10 \leq h_2 \leq 0.10$	$h_2 > 0.10$
Netherlands	1	20	2	9	5	9
Scandinavia	2	20	1	4	9	10

3.3.4. It is good to pause here for a moment, and to make some comments on the results that have been obtained so far.

First, the regressions introduced in 3.3.2 are all regressions with the actual changes as "fixed variables." In other words, the approach was: Given the fact that these actual changes are as observed, how are the predicted changes distributed around them? This approach is not the same as the one implied by the following question: Given the predicted changes such as they are, how are the actual changes distributed around their predictions? The difference between both is that of the classical distinction of the first and the second regression line. No doubt, the former approach is the more modest one from the forecaster's standpoint, for it takes the goal of prediction as given, whereas the latter takes the forecaster's achievement as given. Nevertheless, we should pay serious attention to the latter, because—as is well-known—the regression of forecasts on actual changes tends to reduce the regression coefficient below unity, even if the number of observations Northwest and Southeast of the line of perfect forecasts are equal. This situation seems especially serious, because the stochastic model of 2.5.4 suggests that the case of P fixed, A stochastic is not at all unreasonable. Also, a regression of A on P makes sense because P is known at an earlier date than A, and hence one may ask: What is the distribution of A, given the available P? The danger exists, therefore, that the underestimation of changes is a spurious effect produced by the regression technique, so that we should ask the question whether the effect still manifests itself if we accept the second approach. The answer is in the affirmative; if we apply the same approach to our data but with P and A interchanged, the result is a regression coefficient above unity, both for the Netherlands and Scandinavia.[1] Thus the phenomenon of underestimation as such seems well-established.

Second, it is of some importance to compare these results with those obtained by CHRIST for the United States.[2] They are indeed highly different. Christ finds that, when he uses KLEIN's well-known models for prediction purposes, the outcomes are on the average not much better than those supplied either by the assumption that no change at all occurs, or by the assumption that next year's change equals last year's change for each variable. To see how much different this result is, it is sufficient to go back to the Figs. 3.2, 3.3, 3.4 and 3.5, and to realise that so far nothing has been said about the forecasting quality of the no-change assumption in the Dutch and the Scandina-

[1] This alteration implies that the scedastic curve (3.31) has to be changed to the form $(A - m^*P)^2 = a + bP^2$. The coefficients a, b are approximately three times as large as the corresponding coefficients of (3.31).

[2] Cf. p. 57 n. For Klein's models, mentioned below, cf. L. R. Klein, *Economic Fluctuations in the United States, 1921–1941* (New York-London, 1950) and L. R. Klein and A. S. Goldberger, *An Econometric Model of the United States, 1929–1952* (Amsterdam, 1955).

vian case, simply because it is of such a low standard; this can easily be derived from the Figs. 3.2 and 3.3, viz., by shifting all points in vertical direction until they reach the horizontal axis. The question arises to what factors this difference must be ascribed. A satisfactory answer would no doubt be complicated, since it would require an analysis of the predictability of the economies involved; but the following factors are almost certainly of importance. First, Christ's forecasts are conditional predictions based on the models, and their derivation is entirely mechanical; and in the Dutch case the models were changed and disturbances were specified whenever the forecasters thought it was good to do so. When we make the benevolent assumption that these forecasters were of reasonable quality, we should conclude that this point contributes to the difference observed. Secondly, however, Christ's forecasts are conditional predictions based on the observed values of the exogenous variables; and in the Dutch and Scandinavian case all variables, including the exogenous category, were subject of prediction. This clearly widens the gap. We shall come back to this point later (in Section 5.2), when an approach closer to Christ's will be adopted.

3.3.5. The most important systematic error which we have been able to find in this section is the underestimation of changes. Table 3.4 suggests that this error is more serious for Scandinavia than for the Netherlands; however, this may be due to the unequal dates of publication. The simplest way to analyse this is to investigate the underestimation of changes for those preliminary versions of the Dutch Central Economic Plans which were made around the month of January of the year to which they refer.[1] This leads to 44 observations, for which the average ratio of forecasts to actual changes is slightly below 0.6. Although this figure is unfavourably affected by the less-than-proportionate representation of the "good" year 1951, it seems reasonable to conclude that there is not much difference between the Netherlands and Scandinavia as to the underestimation.

Fig. 3.8 gives a final picture of the errors of forecasting and extrapo-

[1] These versions are: of May 1949 for the Plan 1949, January 1950 for 1950, October 1950 for 1951, March 1953 for 1953. The ratio 0.6, mentioned below, is derived in the same way as the ratios of Table 3.4. It is of some interest to add that about 80 per cent of the preliminary forecasts are closer to the corresponding observed changes than no-change extrapolations, one half of the remainder consisting of ties. Similarly, the extrapolations $A_t = A_{t-1}$ are worse than these forecasts in about 70 per cent of the cases.

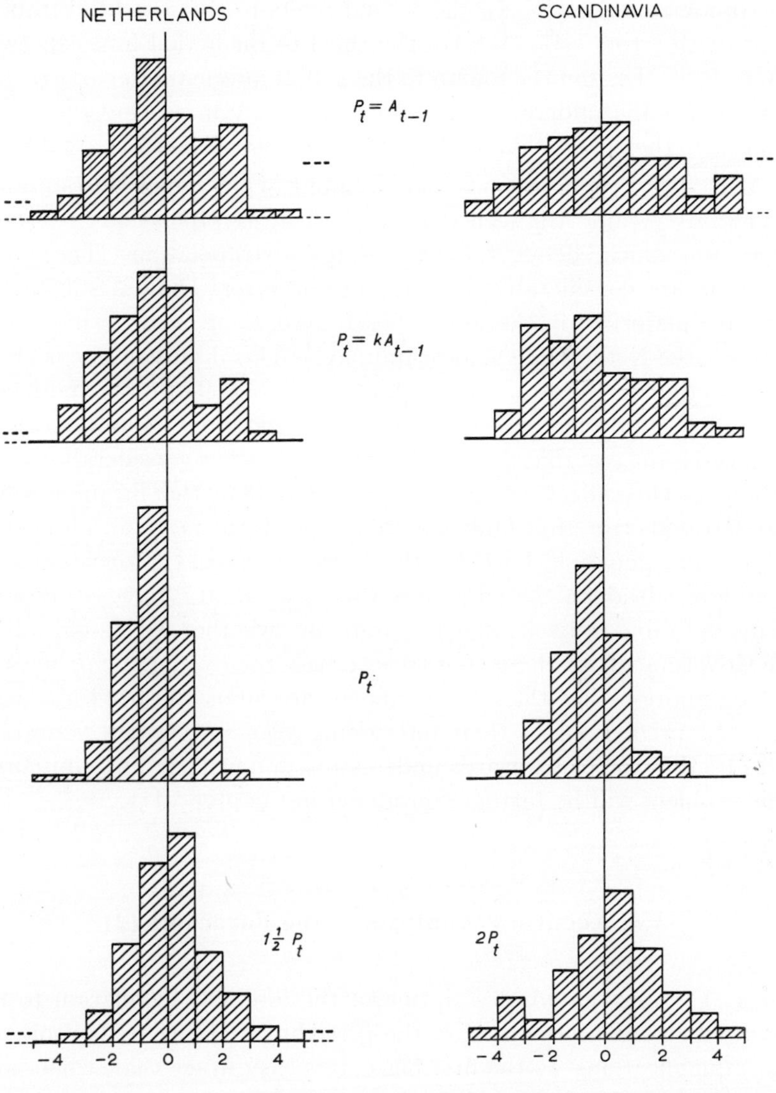

Fig. 3.8. Frequency distributions of standardised forecasting errors according to simple exponential extrapolations (first row), best-fit extrapolations (second row), actual predictions (third row), and actual predictions multiplied by $1\frac{1}{2}$ for the Netherlands and by 2 for Scandinavia (fourth row). Frequencies for the open intervals above 5 and below −5 are denoted by broken lines

lation. The first row contains the frequency distributions of the extrapolation errors $A_{t-1} - A_t$, the second refers to the best-fit extrapolations (with errors $kA_{t-1} - A_t$), the third to the actual forecasts (with errors $P_t - A_t$), and the fourth to the actual forecasts after a correction is made for the underestimation of changes by increasing the Dutch P's by 50, the Scandinavian P's by 100 per cent. All errors are divided by $\sqrt{10 + 0.1\, A_t^2}$ in order to take account of the hyperbolic standard deviations. Again, it is seen that the best-fit extrapolations are somewhat, not much, better than the simple extrapolations. The actual forecasts are considerably better, but the errors show a substantial negative majority; in the units chosen here, their mean is about $-\frac{1}{2}$, both for the Netherlands and Scandinavia. This disadvantage is eliminated in the fourth row, although the mark is overshot for Scandinavia, its multiplication factor 2 being somewhat too large. More important, however, is the fact that the multiplication leads to a considerably larger variance. This effect is indeed so sizable that the mean absolute standardised error after multiplication exceeds the mean absolute error before multiplication, both for the Netherlands and for Scandinavia. Therefore, although the elimination of a systematic forecasting error seems desirable in itself, it is far from sure whether we should advise the Governments of these countries to base their economic policies on the assumption that the actual changes are 50 or 100 per cent larger than the predictions of their forecasting agencies, even if we would feel sure that the bias towards underestimation will remain unimpaired. This problem will be further considered in Chapter VIII.

3.4. Accuracy Analysis of the Forecasts (2)

3.4.1. The aggregative description of the forecasts in relation to the observed changes, presented in the preceding section, needs some obvious qualifications. In the first place, it is easy to see that, when both the price change and the volume change of consumption (say) are underestimated by a certain percentage, this may have certain implications for the value change; and these implications may be in conflict with a description in terms of equal mean ratios of predictions to corresponding actual outcomes. Let us consider this briefly.

The predicted relative value change (P_v) can, under the assumption that the internal consistency criterion is applied, be expressed in terms of the predicted price (P_p) and quantity (P_q) changes:[1]

$$P_v = P_p + P_q + P_p P_q. \tag{3.35}$$

Similarly, for the actual changes:

$$A_v = A_p + A_q + A_p A_q. \tag{3.36}$$

Suppose then that there is a proportionate underestimation of both price and quantity changes with parameter m ($0 < m < 1$), except for certain deviations which are zero on the average:

$$P_p = mA_p + \epsilon_p; \qquad P_q = mA_q + \epsilon_q. \tag{3.37}$$

The ratio of P_v to A_v is then

$$\frac{P_v}{A_v} = m + \frac{-m(1-m)A_p A_q + (1 + mA_q)\,\epsilon_p + (1 + mA_p)\,\epsilon_q + \epsilon_p \epsilon_q}{A_p + A_q + A_p A_q}. \tag{3.38}$$

It follows that the underestimation of the value changes is in general not characterised by the same average m. The difference between the average of P_v/A_v and m is, under the assumption that the A's can be taken as fixed, determined by the first and the last term of the numerator of the right-hand fraction of (3.38) (given the denominator). It is easy to see that this difference tends to be small if the ϵ's have a moderate covariance, if A_p, A_q are of moderate size, and if the latter changes have the same sign (which they usually had). Neglecting the two terms amounts to linearising the value identity; and under linearity assumptions there are no conflicts resulting from the hypothesis of proportionate underestimation of changes.

3.4.2. Of more importance, perhaps, is the fact that our analysis relates the forecasting errors only to the size of the actual changes to be predicted. There are obviously other determining factors. First, we may think of the average variability of the variable considered. Since an increase of, say, 5 per cent of a normally highly fluctuating variable like net investment will usually be predicted less accurately than the same increase for a relatively rigid variable (e.g., the volume of consumption), we should expect the average variability of the variable

[1] Note that in the equations (3.35)–(3.38) the P's and A's are to be considered as fractions of unity, not as percentages.

to have a positive influence on the size of the forecasting errors. Table 3.8 gives some empirical indications in this direction. It contains, for variables with average absolute changes in the period 1949–52 (for the Netherlands: 1949–53) below 5 per cent, between 5 and 10 per cent, and above 10 per cent, the square root of the average value of

$$\frac{(sP - A)^2}{s^2(10 + 0.1\,A^2)} \qquad \begin{aligned}(s &= 1\tfrac{1}{2} \text{ for the Netherlands}\\ &= 2 \text{ for Scandinavia}),\end{aligned} \tag{3.39}$$

where averaging takes place over all variables of each of these groups, and over all of the four years. If the magnitude of the actual change were the only factor determining the distribution of the forecasts, then—as follows from Section 3.3—the square root would be about unity both for the Netherlands and for Scandinavia, for each of the three groups. If, however, the average variability of the variable—contrary to the variation A in the year to be predicted—has an independent positive influence on the size of the prediction errors, we should expect the root to increase from left to right in the table. It follows from Table 3.8 that the latter effect is indeed likely to exist, especially for the Netherlands.[1] The drop from 1.2 to 1.0 in the second row (for Scandinavia) is not significant.

TABLE 3.8

THE INFLUENCE OF THE AVERAGE VARIABILITY OF VARIABLES ON THEIR FORECASTING ERRORS: SQUARE ROOTS OF MEANS OF (3.39) FOR DUTCH AND SCANDINAVIAN VARIABLES

Country	*Variables with mean absolute annual change*		
	Below 5%	*Between 5 and 10%*	*Above 10%*
Netherlands	0.4	0.9	1.4
Scandinavia	0.7	1.2	1.0

3.4.3. Neither the size of the actual change to be predicted, nor the normal variability of the variable to be predicted determine the distribution of the forecasting errors completely. There are "natural" differences of forecasting power with respect to separate variables, which are independent of the above-mentioned factors. An impression of

[1] The results of Table 3.8 may be partly due to the possibility that the average underestimation of changes is somewhat overestimated by the numerical specification of s; cf. the end of 3.3.5. This is not, however, sufficient to explain the whole result.

these differences can be obtained by computing the inequality measures proposed in Section 2.5, although the value of these measures is obviously depressed by the small number of observations on which they must be based. The results are presented in the Appendix to this chapter, in Table 3.10, together with the means ($\bar{P}$, $\bar{A}$), standard deviations (s_P, s_A) and correlation (r) of forecasts and actual outcomes. Here, we shall confine ourselves to a brief summary.

About nine tenths of the variables show positive correlations between predictions and realisations, and the median correlation is as high as 0.9, both for the Netherlands and Scandinavia. Frequency distributions of the (total) inequality coefficients U are given in Fig 3.9.

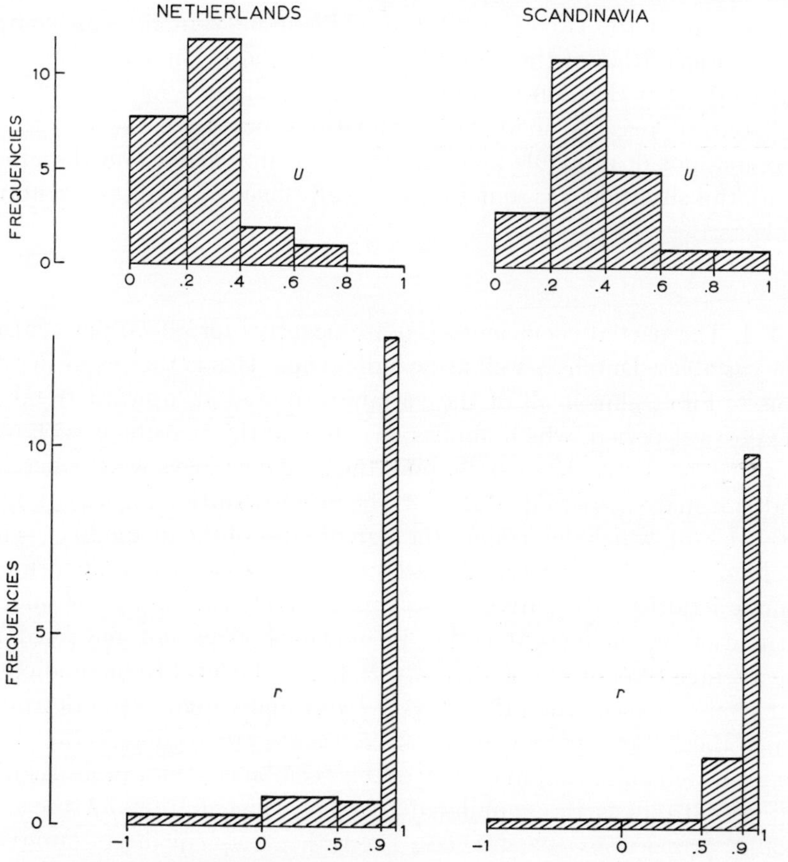

Fig. 3.9. Frequency distributions of the (total) inequality coefficients (U) for predictions and actual changes, and of the correlation coefficients (r)

Some 50 per cent of the coefficients are concentrated in the interval (0.2, 0.4), again both for the Netherlands and Scandinavia, but the results as a whole look somewhat more favourable for the Netherlands. The "best" variable for this country is the import price level, $U = 0.04$; the Scandinavian U's of the same variable are of the order of 0.15, and this difference may well reflect the unequal dates of publication. Examples of bad forecasting are the Dutch Government wage bill and the exports and imports of services. For the last two variables this result is not astonishing, since very little is known about the international service sector; satisfactory price indices, e.g., are not easily available in this field. More surprising is the bad result for the Government wage bill, since this variable might be regarded as an instrument from the standpoint of the Government whose Planning Bureau is in charge of the preparation of the Central Economic Plans. The effect is partly due to the fact that, on the one hand, the predictions had to be based for political reasons on budget estimates which have the nature of maxima, not of probable amounts to be spent, whereas, on the other hand, this situation was sometimes radically changed by supplementary budgets.

3.4.4. The partial coefficients U_M are negative for 80–90 per cent of the variables, Dutch as well as Scandinavian. This is the result of two causes. First, almost all of the variables showed an upward trend in the postwar period, which implies $\bar{A} > 0$; and this feature as such was correctly predicted: $\bar{P} > 0$. Second, the actual changes were generally underestimated, so that $\bar{P}/\bar{A} < 1$. These inequalities together imply $\bar{P} - \bar{A} < 0$, which determines the sign of most of the inequality coefficients of central tendency. Similarly, there is for each country a three-fourth majority of negative U_S's. This is largely caused by the underestimation of changes, for this phenomenon does not only reduce the average level of the predictions, $\bar{P}$, below the level to be predicted, but it also reduces the differences between individual predictions and hence their standard deviation, s_P. Actually, the median ratio s_P/s_A for all Dutch and Scandinavian variables combined is not more than $\frac{2}{3}$.

Fig. 3.10 gives the cumulated frequency distributions of the inequality proportions U^M, U^S, U^C. The rather frequent intersections of the three lines in the two figures suggest that the three proportions are on the average not much different from each other. Another picture

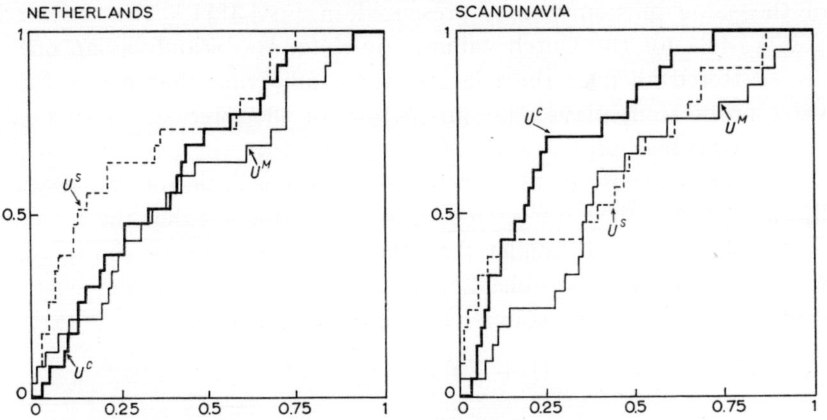

Fig. 3.10. Cumulated frequency distributions of inequality proportions

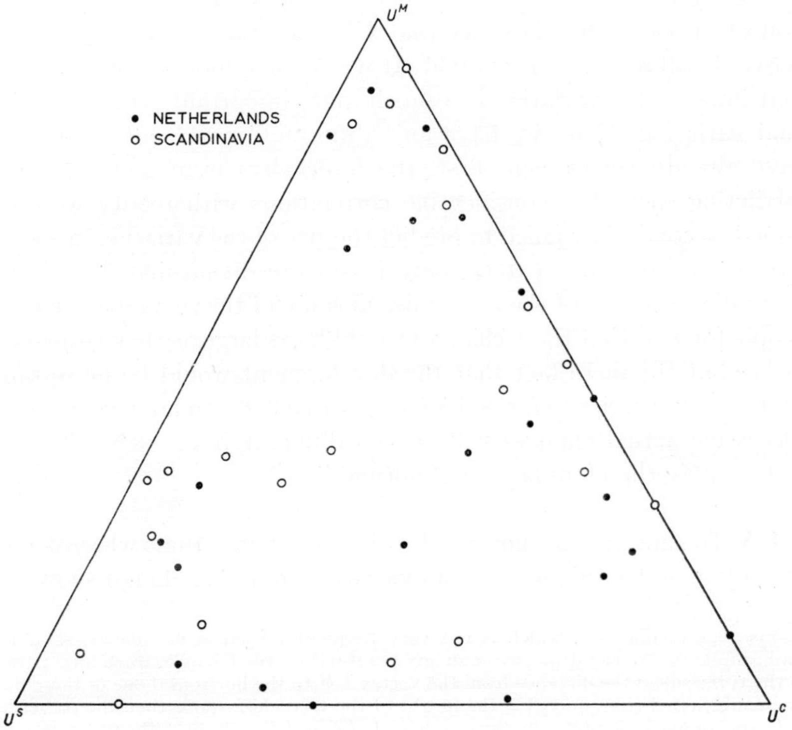

Fig. 3.11. Triangular illustration of the inequality proportions

of the same phenomenon is presented in Fig. 3.11.[1] The observed points (dots for the Dutch values, circles for the Scandinavian ones) are scattered all over the triangle, thus indicating that none of the three proportions plays a dominant rôle for the forecasts as a whole.

That the bias proportion U^M is not small on the average can be easily ascribed to the combined effect of underestimation of changes and upward trends. More interesting, however, is the fact that the U^S's do not tend to be much smaller than the U^C's, for it can be shown that $U^S < U^C$ is rather plausible. Let us therefore write δ for the relative difference between the standard deviations s_P and s_A:

$$s_P = s\,(1 + \tfrac{1}{2}\,\delta); \qquad s_A = s\,(1 - \tfrac{1}{2}\,\delta).$$

Then the ratio U^S/U^C is given by

$$\frac{U^S}{U^C} = \frac{\delta^2}{2\,(1 - r)\,(1 - \frac{1}{4}\,\delta^2)}.$$

Hence a relative difference of 10 per cent ($\delta = 0.1$) requires a correlation of at least 0.995 in order that $U^S \geq U^C$; and a difference of 25 per cent still requires an r of 0.97. It would therefore be normal to find that imperfect covariation is a much more important error than unequal variation. Here, we have an "abnormal" case, and the reasons have already been given: first, the forecasters were quite clever in predicting such that considerable correlations with reality were obtained; second, they failed to predict the size of the variation in successive years. To a large extent, both reasons result ultimately from the rapid development of the economies in some of the years analysed: few people foresaw that these changes would be as large as they turned out to be, but the mere fact that the development would be more rapid or slower was easier to foretell (cf. also Table 3.6). In later years, when successive actual changes will be less different from each other, the picture may therefore be more "normal."

3.4.5. To sum up our main results, we have found that, whereas both prediction and actual series of all variables combined do not show very

[1] This type of diagram, which is not very frequently used in economics, should be read as follows. We can draw, through any point within the triangle, three lines parallel to the three sides; the distance from the vertex U^M to the horizontal one of these lines, when subtracted from unity (= the height of the triangle), equals then the proportion U^M; and similarly for U^S, U^C. So, if $U^M = 1$, $U^S = U^C = 0$, then the point coincides with the vertex (U^M) of the triangle.

much more rank correlation than independent series do, the forecasts and corresponding actual values of the same variables are generally highly correlated.[1] However, even perfect correlation does not imply perfect forecasting. On the average, the actual changes were underestimated by almost 50 per cent—a defect which was to some extent, but far from perfectly, remedied when the forecasts were formulated later in the year of prediction.

It is not possible to verify the forecasts in the sense of Section 2.4, because their probability relation to actual outcomes was not stated before. If this had been done and if the stated relation had been that of unbiased point predictions—or, more generally, central-tendency predictions—, then the correctness of the assertion would probably have to be rejected because of the systematic underestimation of changes. But the superiority of the forecasts over extrapolations suggests that they should be taken seriously, especially when their scientific nature is established more firmly. We shall come back to this point in Chapter VIII, where we shall also pay attention to the question whether it is appropriate to "weight" the separate predicted variables according to their importance—a problem which was entirely disregarded in this descriptive analysis.

[1] They are also highly rank-correlated: not much less than one half of the pairs of prediction and corresponding actual series have no inversion at all, and the average number of inversions is about one half of the mean value under the independence assumption.

Appendix to Chapter III

3.A. Survey of Figures and List of Variables

Table 3.9 contains the actual (A) and predicted (P) percentage changes of the 23 Dutch, 7 Norwegian, 8 Swedish and 8 Danish variables, together with the extrapolation factors k [equ. (3.29)] and the coefficients h_1, h_2 [equ. (3.34)]. The years covered are 1948–1953, except for (*i*) predictions for 1948, (*ii*) Dutch predictions for 1952 (for that year alternative forecasts were prepared), (*iii*) Scandinavian predictions and actual values for 1953, (*iv*) some other forecasts and results for Scandinavia in 1948, 1951, 1952, which are not available. The Dutch actual data are derived from publications of the Central Bureau of Statistics of the Netherlands, supplemented by computations of the Central Planning Bureau. The Dutch forecasts are derived from the Central Economic Plans. The Plans 1951 and 1953 contain two alternative plans, one of which is based on certain Government measures, the other on the absence of these measures. Since the latter alternative was improbable even at the time when the Plan was published—because the measures had already been announced or taken—, the former alternative is represented in the table. The Scandinavian data are derived from the *Economic Bulletin for Europe* of July 1953, published by the Economic Commission for Europe (E.C.E.). All figures are given in one decimal place, whenever possible.

Table 3.10 contains the means ($\bar{P}$, $\bar{A}$), standard deviations (s_P, s_A), correlations (r) and inequality coefficients and proportions. The Swedish and Danish industrial production figures are omitted because of paucity of observations.

Table 3.11 gives a survey of variables and their symbols of the Dutch equation system 1955, with endogenous and exogenous variables separated.

Table 3.12 deals with the preliminary versions of the Central Economic Plans; they are derived from unpublished papers of the Central Planning Bureau. It should be noted that the September 1952 version represents the average of four alternative versions, and that the March 1953 version is the "central-case" alternative of that month.

TABLE 3.9

PREDICTED AND ACTUAL PERCENTAGE CHANGES IN DUTCH AND SCANDINAVIAN MACROECONOMIC VARIABLES, 1948–1953, AND THE COEFFICIENTS k OF (3.29) AND h_1, h_2 OF (3.34)

Countries and variables	*1948*	*1949*		*1950*		*1951*		*1952*		*1953*		k	h_1	h_2
	A	*P*	*A*	*P*	*A*	*P*	*A*	*P*	*A*	*P*	*A*			
NETHERLANDS														
(a) *Price indices of:*														
commodity exports	0	− 3	− 6	+ 9	+ 4	+13	+17	.	+ 1.7	− 7	−11	+0.46	+0.75	−0.04
commodity imports	+ 5.3	− 3	− 3	+12.4	+12.4	+21.0	+22.9	.	− 1.5	−12	−11.5	+1.28	+0.96	−0.14
consumption	+ 4.0	+ 3	+ 5.4	+ 5	+ 9.2	+ 9	+10	.	− 0.8	− 3.1	0	+1.31	+0.89	−0.23
(b) *Quantities and volumes:*														
commodity exports	+44.9	+24	+51	+23	+35	+27	+19	.	+ 4.0	+ 4	+14	+0.82	−0.12	+0.63
commodity imports	+ 8.7	+ 9	+11	+20	+32	+ 9	+ 3	.	−12.6	+19	+24	+0.17	+0.63	+0.21
consumption	+ 5.8	− 2	− 0.9	+ 2	0	− 1	− 2.3	.	+ 1.9	+ 4.5	+ 3.7	+0.05	+0.83	−0.31
industrial production	+19.4	+ 8	+10	+ 6	+13	+10	+ 5	.	0	+ 6	+12	+0.60	+0.21	+0.42
construction activity	+41.7	+ 8	+ 5	+ 8	+ 5	+ 3	0	.	− 2.4	+18	+21	+0.10	+0.88	+0.10
available labour force	+ 4.6	+ 1.1	+ 2.5	+ 0.6	+ 1.5	+ 1.0	+ 1.3	.	+ 1.1	+ 1.1	+ 1.4	+0.61	+1.05	−0.32
labour productivity	+10.1	+ 4	+ 7.4	+ 4.7	+ 5.2	+ 4.2	+ 1.0	.	+ 2.2	+ 5.2	+ 6.2	+0.70	+0.60	+0.14
employment in private sector	+ 5.8	+ 0.6	+ 2.4	+ 1.2	+ 2.9	+ 1.5	+ 1.5	.	− 0.6	+ 1.4	+ 1.8	+0.50	+0.63	−0.09
employment in public sector	− 2.0	− 1.8	− 1.1	−10.9	−13.5	− 5.8	− 4.3	.	+ 6.2	+ 5.3	+ 7.9	+0.55	+0.79	+0.19
(c) *Money values:*														
commodity exports	+43.5	+23.0	+37.6	+32.5	+40.5	+43.4	+40.2	.	+ 5.9	− 0.6	+ 2.8	+0.96	+0.95	−0.11
commodity imports	+15.7	+ 6.4	+ 6.3	+35.1	+49.6	+32.1	+24.6	.	−13.9	+ 9.3	+ 6.2	+0.53	+0.68	+0.28
consumption	+10.1	+ 1.3	+ 4.4	+ 6.5	+ 9.1	+ 7.7	+ 7.9	.	+ 1.1	+ 2.3	+ 3.6	+0.78	+0.88	−0.12
net investment (incl. inventories)	+33.8	+ 9.3	+10.7	+29.0	+60.0	− 6.1	−17.5	.	−59.3	+66.9	+99.1	−0.71	+0.62	+0.04
value added in private sector	+16.8	+ 3.1	+10.4	+ 6.7	+11.9	+ 8.5	+ 8.1	.	+ 4.0	+ 2.1	+ 9.8	+0.79	+0.31	+0.15
Government wage bill	− 0.8	− 0.7	− 6.5	− 3.2	+11.4	+ 5.4	+ 7.9	.	+ 1.3	+ 7.3	+ 9.8	+0.19	+0.08	+0.57
Governmentcommoditypurchases	+20.5	+ 6.7	+23.7	+ 5.0	+12.5	+42.9	+21.0	.	+10.8	+26.1	+22.8	+1.03	+2.02	−1.10
indirect taxes minus subsidies	+62.9	+38.5	+37.3	+14.9	+14.6	+16.9	+25.4	.	− 3.8	+ 4.6	+ 3.2	+0.58	+0.65	+0.19
exports of services	+50.9	+ 2	+10	+ 8	+22	+15	+37	.	+ 7.6	−11	+ 2	+0.48	+0.50	−0.16
imports of services	+28.7	− 2	+ 4	+ 5	+28	− 1	+18	.	+ 9.7	− 1	−10	+0.45	+0.18	−0.13
surplus on the balance of services	+85.5	+ 5.9	+15.5	+10.8	+17.7	+24.5	+57.2	.	+ 5.9	−15.1	− 5.1	+0.33	+0.51	−0.08

TABLE 3.9 (concluded)

Countries and variables	1948	1949		1950		1951		1952		1953		k	h_1	h_2
	A	*P*	*A*	*P*	*A*	*P*	*A*	*P*	*A*	*P*	*A*			
NORWAY														
(a) *Price indices of:*														
commodity exports	.	−5	0	0	+4	+8	+40	+3	0	.	.	+0.10	+0.19	+0.08
commodity imports	.	0	−2	+13	+12	+14	+19	+7	+3	.	.	+0.51	+0.79	+0.13
(b) *Quantities and volumes:*														
commodity exports	.	+7	0	+11	+26	+3	+5	+3	−5	.	.	+0.15	+0.38	+0.08
commodity imports	.	+6	+14	−3	+6	−5	+13	+7	0	.	.	+0.40	−0.65	+0.31
national product	+4	+3.5	+5	+2	+5	+2	+2	+3	+1	.	.	+0.81	+0.28	+0.34
industrial production	+12	+6	+10	+4	+8	+4	+5	+4	0	.	.	+0.72	−0.39	+0.77
construction activity	−8	+4	+14	−4	+5	−6	−3	.	.	.	.	−0.20	+0.14	−0.39
SWEDEN														
(a) *Price indices of:*														
commodity exports	+12	−7	−7	+3	+8	+24	+55	+3	−1	.	.	+0.07	+0.44	+0.04
commodity imports	+5	0	+1	+12	+13	+21	+29	+4	+5	.	.	+0.52	+0.76	−0.01
(b) *Quantities and volumes:*														
commodity exports	+10	+3	+15	+6	+24	+25	+3	−8	−11	.	.	+0.60	+0.27	+0.07
commodity imports	−10	−13	−13	+12	+24	+5	+17	−4	−7	.	.	+0.09	+0.53	−0.03
national product	+6	+1.5	+5	+2.5	+6	+3	0	+2	+1	.	.	+0.62	+0.01	+0.41
industrial production	.	.	.	+4	+4	+4	+4	+1	−2	.	.	+0.25	+0.50	+0.50
construction activity	−8	−5	+2	+5	+4	+2	+1.5	+5	+9	.	.	+0.14	+0.48	+0.70
gross fixed investment	−2	−4	0	+5	+9	+3	+3	+4	+4	.	.	+0.41	+0.56	+0.27
DENMARK														
(a) *Price indices of:*														
commodity exports	+9	0	0	−3	−3	+8	+13	.	.	.	.	−0.43	+0.64	+0.01
commodity imports	+7	+2	−5	+13	+10	+30	+26	.	.	.	.	+1.01	+1.04	+0.39
(b) *Quantities and volumes:*														
commodity exports	+9	+20	+29	+10	+32	+8	+13	.	.	.	.	+0.82	+0.57	−0.10
commodity imports	+4	+25	+29	+5	+27	−10	−6	.	.	.	.	+0.46	+0.74	−0.36
national product	+3	+4	+5	+3	+8	0	−0.5	.	.	.	.	+0.52	+0.48	+0.03
industrial production	+11	+5	+7	+4	+12	.	.	0	−5	.	.	+0.95	+0.11	+0.39
construction activity	+2	+4	+7	+7	+13	−7	−1	.	.	.	.	+0.41	+0.77	−0.47
gross fixed investment	+1	+12	+14	+5	+13	−6	−1	.	.	.	.	+0.50	+0.86	−0.42

TABLE 3.10

MEANS, STANDARD DEVIATIONS, AND CORRELATION AND INEQUALITY COEFFICIENTS AND PROPORTIONS FOR DUTCH AND SCANDINAVIAN PREDICTION AND ACTUAL SERIES

Countries and variables	$\bar{P}$	$\bar{A}$	s_P	s_A	r	U	U_M	U_S	U_C	U^M	U^S	U^C
NETHERLANDS												
(a) *Price indices of:*												
commodity exports	+ 3.0	+ 1.0	8.3	10.7	+0.96	0.21	+0.10	−0.13	0.13	0.24	0.36	0.40
commodity imports	+ 4.6	+ 5.2	12.9	13.3	+1.00	0.04	−0.02	−0.02	0.02	0.37	0.21	0.42
consumption	+ 3.5	+ 6.2	4.4	4.0	+0.97	0.23	−0.21	+0.03	0.08	0.84	0.02	0.14
(b) *Quantities and volumes:*												
commodity exports	+19.5	+29.8	9.1	14.5	+0.53	0.30	−0.19	−0.10	0.20	0.41	0.11	0.48
commodity imports	+14.3	+17.5	5.3	11.2	+0.95	0.20	−0.09	−0.16	0.07	0.21	0.67	0.12
consumption	+ 0.9	+ 0.1	2.6	2.2	+0.89	0.28	+0.15	+0.07	0.22	0.30	0.06	0.64
industrial production	+ 7.5	+10.0	1.7	3.1	−0.98	0.29	−0.14	−0.08	0.25	0.22	0.07	0.71
construction activity	+ 9.3	+ 7.8	5.5	7.9	+0.99	0.07	+0.03	−0.06	0.02	0.25	0.67	0.08
available labour force	+ 1.0	+ 1.7	0.2	0.5	+0.31	0.32	−0.27	−0.10	0.13	0.71	0.11	0.18
labour productivity	+ 4.5	+ 5.0	0.5	2.4	+0.19	0.24	−0.04	−0.19	0.13	0.03	0.65	0.32
employment in private sector	+ 1.2	+ 2.2	0.4	0.5	−0.56	0.36	−0.28	−0.06	0.22	0.60	0.02	0.38
employment in public sector	− 3.3	− 2.8	5.9	7.7	+0.99	0.14	−0.04	−0.12	0.06	0.07	0.74	0.19
(c) *Money values:*												
commodity exports	+24.6	+30.3	16.2	15.9	+0.92	0.14	−0.09	+0.01	0.10	0.45	0.00	0.55
commodity imports	+20.7	+21.7	13.0	17.8	+0.90	0.16	−0.02	−0.09	0.13	0.01	0.34	0.65
consumption	+ 4.5	+ 6.3	2.7	2.3	+0.91	0.18	−0.15	+0.03	0.09	0.71	0.04	0.25
net investment	+24.8	+38.1	27.3	44.8	+0.98	0.24	−0.14	−0.18	0.07	0.33	0.58	0.09
value added in private sector	+ 5.1	+10.1	2.6	1.4	−0.26	0.37	−0.31	+0.08	0.19	0.71	0.04	0.25
Government wage bill	+ 2.2	+ 5.7	4.3	7.1	+0.27	0.58	−0.25	−0.20	0.48	0.19	0.12	0.69
Government commodity purchases	+20.2	+20.0	15.5	4.4	+0.38	0.32	+0.00	+0.24	0.20	0.00	0.59	0.41
indirect taxes minus subsidies	+18.7	+20.1	12.3	12.7	+0.95	0.09	−0.03	−0.01	0.09	0.10	0.00	0.90
exports of services	+ 3.5	+17.8	9.6	13.1	+0.96	0.47	−0.44	−0.11	0.10	0.90	0.06	0.04
imports of services	+ 0.3	+15.0	2.8	9.0	+0.89	0.80	−0.73	−0.31	0.11	0.83	0.15	0.02
surplus on the balance of services	+ 6.5	+21.3	14.2	22.5	+0.94	0.39	−0.32	−0.18	0.13	0.67	0.21	0.12

TABLE 3.10 (*concluded*)

Countries and variables	$\bar{P}$	$\bar{A}$	s_P	s_A	r	U	U_M	U_S	U_C	U^M	U^S	U^C
NORWAY												
(a) *Price indices of:*												
commodity exports	+ 3.7	+14.7	3.3	18.0	+0.89	0.66	−0.39	−0.52	0.13	0.35	0.61	0.04
commodity imports	+11.3	+11.3	3.1	6.6	+0.95	0.15	+0.00	−0.14	0.06	0.00	0.85	0.15
(b) *Quantities and volumes:*												
commodity exports	+ 5.7	+ 8.7	3.8	12.9	+0.95	0.44	−0.13	−0.41	0.10	0.09	0.86	0.05
commodity imports	− 0.3	+ 6.3	5.3	5.3	−0.92	0.91	−0.49	0.00	0.76	0.29	0.00	0.71
national product	+ 2.6	+ 3.3	0.7	1.8	+0.08	0.30	−0.10	−0.18	0.23	0.10	0.34	0.56
industrial production	+ 4.5	+ 5.8	0.9	3.8	+0.64	0.31	−0.11	−0.25	0.13	0.13	0.68	0.19
construction activity	− 2.0	+ 5.3	4.3	6.9	+0.96	0.59	−0.54	−0.19	0.12	0.85	0.11	0.04
SWEDEN												
(a) *Price indices of:*												
commodity exports	+ 5.8	+13.8	11.3	24.4	+0.97	0.39	−0.20	−0.32	0.09	0.26	0.68	0.06
commodity imports	+ 9.3	+12.0	8.0	10.7	+0.99	0.14	−0.10	−0.09	0.05	0.46	0.43	0.11
(b) *Quantities and volumes:*												
commodity exports	+ 1.5	+ 7.8	5.6	13.1	+0.84	0.52	−0.30	−0.36	0.23	0.33	0.47	0.20
commodity imports	0.0	+ 5.3	9.4	15.6	+0.97	0.33	−0.20	−0.24	0.11	0.37	0.52	0.11
national product	+ 2.3	+ 3.0	0.6	2.6	−0.44	0.47	−0.12	−0.32	0.32	0.07	0.46	0.47
construction activity	+ 1.8	+ 4.1	4.1	3.0	+0.60	0.43	−0.25	+0.12	0.33	0.34	0.07	0.59
gross fixed investment	+ 2.0	+ 4.0	3.5	3.2	+0.83	0.31	−0.22	+0.03	0.22	0.50	0.01	0.49
DENMARK												
(a) *Price indices of:*												
commodity exports	+ 1.7	+ 3.3	4.6	6.9	+1.00	0.23	−0.13	−0.18	0.03	0.34	0.64	0.02
commodity imports	+15.0	+10.3	11.5	12.7	+0.99	0.14	+0.13	−0.03	0.04	0.88	0.05	0.07
(b) *Quantities and volumes:*												
commodity exports	+12.7	+24.7	5.3	8.3	+0.51	0.35	−0.30	−0.08	0.17	0.73	0.05	0.22
commodity imports	+ 6.7	+16.7	14.3	16.1	+0.85	0.34	−0.26	−0.04	0.21	0.58	0.02	0.40
national product	+ 2.3	+ 4.2	1.7	3.5	+0.83	0.35	−0.22	−0.22	0.17	0.38	0.38	0.24
construction activity	+ 1.3	+ 6.3	6.0	5.7	+0.97	0.35	−0.34	+0.02	0.09	0.93	0.00	0.07
gross fixed investment	+ 3.7	+ 8.7	7.4	6.9	+0.94	0.29	−0.26	+0.03	0.12	0.81	0.01	0.18

TABLE 3.11

LIST OF VARIABLES, AND OF THEIR SYMBOLS, OF THE DUTCH EQUATION SYSTEM 1955

Symbols	*Endogenous variables*	*Symbols*	*Exogenous variables*
	(a) *Price indices of:*		
p_c	consumption	w	wage level
p_{x_G}	Government commodity purchases	p_{m_c}	commodity imports
p_i	investment goods	p_{m_s}	imports of services
p_n	changes in stocks	p_{e_s}	exports of services
p_{e_c}	commodity exports	p_w	foreign goods competing with Dutch goods abroad
	(b) *Quantities and volumes:*		
v	aggregate sales of enterprises	x_G	Government commodity purchases
c	consumption	d	depreciation of enterprises
i	net investment	n	changes in stocks
e_c	commodity exports	e_c^{au}	autonomous increase of commodity exports
m	imports	e_s	exports of services
a	labour productivity	m_s	imports of services
		r	replacement investment of enterprises
		b	available labour force

TABLE 3.11 *(concluded)*

Symbols	*Endogenous variables*	*Symbols*	*Exogenous variables*
	(c) *Money values:*		
V	aggregate sales of enterprises	C'	consumption bought from the rest of the world and the Government
C	consumption	Z'	income received by non-wage-earners from abroad minus certain premiums
X_G	Government commodity purchases	W'	wages paid by the Government, foreign countries, etc., minus certain premiums
I	net investment	T_Z^{au}	autonomous increase in income taxes to be paid by entrepreneurs
D	depreciation	T_W^{au}	do., by wage-earners
N	changes in stocks	T_I^{au}	autonomous increase of indirect taxes
E	exports	$T_{I;c}^{au}$	autonomous increase of indirect taxes on consumption goods
M	imports	$T_{I;x_G}^{au}$	do., on Government commodity purchases
Z	non-wage income	$T_{I;i}^{au}$	do., on investment goods
W	private wage bill	$T_{I;n}^{au}$	do., on changes in stocks
U	payments made by the Unemployment Fund	$T_{I;e_c}^{au}$	do., on commodity exports
X_Z	consumption of entrepreneurs		
X_W	consumption of wage-earners		
T_Z	income taxes paid by entrepreneurs		
T_W	income taxes paid by wage-earners		
T_I	indirect taxes (minus subsidies)		

TABLE 3.12

PREDICTED PERCENTAGE CHANGES ACCORDING TO PRELIMINARY VERSIONS OF THE DUTCH CENTRAL ECONOMIC PLANS*

Plans and variables	*Versions of:*		
Plan 1949	*Aug. 1948*	*May 1949*	*Sept. 1949*
commodity exports	+15.7	+17.9	+19.2
commodity imports	+11.8	+ 0.8	+ 6.0
consumption	+ 8.4	+ 1.6	+ 3.1
net investment	+27.0	− 7.2	+14.7
value added in private sector	+ 6.0	+ 2.4	+ 3.2
Government wage bill	+ 4.2	− 0.7	− 5.1
Government commodity purchases	0	+19.5	+ 2.2
indirect taxes minus subsidies	+60.9	+38.5	+56.5
exports of services	+ 3.4	0	+ 3.4
imports of services	+ 2.6	0	+ 2.6
surplus on the balance of services	+ 4.2	0	+ 4.2
Plan 1950	*July 1949*	*Jan. 1950*	*July 1950*
consumption (price)	.	+ 5.1	+ 4.8
commodity exports (vol.)	+15.6	.	.
commodity imports (vol.)	+ 3.8	.	.
consumption (vol.)	+ 2.8	+ 1.8	− 0.4
industrial production (vol.)	+ 7.4	+ 5.5	+ 6.4
available labour force	+ 0.9	+ 1.0	+ 0.6
labour productivity	+ 4	+ 4.3	+ 5.7
employment in private sector	+ 1.0	+ 1.0	+ 1.2
employment in public sector	− 7.3	− 6.5	−10.9
commodity exports	.	+30.3	+32.5
commodity imports	.	+21.9	+32.3
consumption	.	+ 7.0	+ 4.4
net investment	.	+ 5.0	+21.2
value added in private sector	.	.	+ 7.1
Government wage bill	.	0	− 9.2
Government commodity purchases	.	+19.6	+37.3
indirect taxes minus subsidies	.	.	+ 5.8
surplus on the balance of services	.	.	+10.8
Plan 1951	*Oct. 1950*	*July 1951*	
commodity exports (price)	+ 9.2	+13	
commodity imports (price)	+16.8	+21	
consumption (price)	.	+ 9	
commodity exports (vol.)	+17.5	+27	
commodity imports (vol.)	+ 4.9	+ 9	
consumption (vol.)	.	− 1	
industrial production (vol.)	.	+ 9.8	
construction activity (vol.)	.	+ 3.3	
available labour force	.	+ 1.1	
labour productivity	+ 4.4	+ 4.0	
employment in private sector	.	+ 1.5	
employment in public sector	.	− 5.2	

* Except when otherwise stated (or when the alternative is clear anyhow), all variables are money variables.

TABLE 3.12 (*concluded*)

Plans and variables	*Versions of:*	
Plan 1951 (*concluded*)	*Oct. 1950*	*July 1951*
commodity exports	+29.8	+43.7
commodity imports	+22.1	+31.7
consumption	.	+ 7.7
net investment	.	— 6.1
value added in private sector	.	+ 8.5
Government wage bill	.	+ 5.3
Government commodity purchases	.	+42.9
indirect taxes minus subsidies	.	+16.9
exports of services	.	+12.6
imports of services	.	— 3
surplus on the balance of services	.	+22.2
Plan 1953	*Sept. 1952*	*March 1953*
commodity exports (price)	— 1.6	— 4.8
commodity imports (price)	— 0.5	— 7.0
consumption (price)	+ 2.9	— 2.6
commodity exports (vol.)	+ 3.3	+ 2.6
consumption (vol.)	+ 1.4	+ 3.6
construction activity (vol.)	.	+18
labour productivity	.	+ 6.3
commodity exports	+ 1.7	— 2.3
consumption	+ 4.3	+ 0.9
net investment	.	+66.2
Government wage bill	.	+ 7.3
Government commodity purchases	.	+26.1
indirect taxes minus subsidies	.	+ 3.5

3.B. Additional Dutch Data for the Years 1954 and 1955

After the analysis of this chapter was completed, new data for the years 1954 and 1955 became available. They are presented in Table 3.13 below. Two variables (industrial production and construction activity) are deleted because of lack of data. As a whole there are 42 pairs of predicted and actual changes, of which 27 are cases of underestimation, 7 of overestimation, 5 turning point errors, and 3 zero predictions of nonzero changes or nonzero predictions of zero changes. Four of the five turning point errors fall under the international service and the Government sector. A graphical picture is presented in Fig. 3.12. The general quality of the predictions seems to be somewhat below the level of 1949–1953, which may be due to the early publication of the present forecasts.[1] The underestimation of changes is considerable; it may be that there is also an underestimation of the level of the variables predicted.[2]

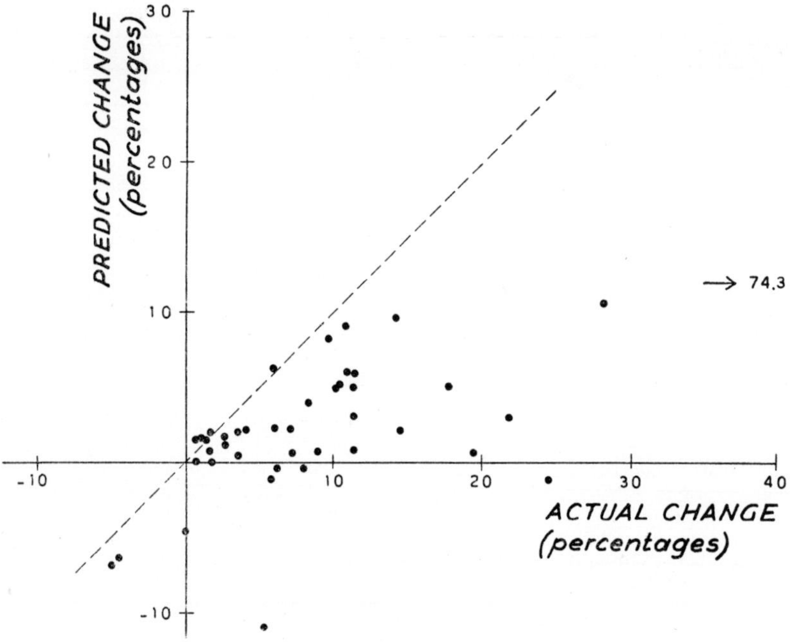

Fig. 3.12. Forecasts for the Netherlands, 1954–55

[1] Note that the observed actual changes of Table 3.13 are partly based on preliminary data. There are discrepancies between these figures and some of the figures used in Section 5.2 below, the present ones being computed later. Rather than removing these discrepancies, we prefer to leave them as they are, since they give a clear insight into the necessary qualifications of our conclusions.

[2] For a further analysis including the year 1956, see C. van de Panne, "De voorspellingskwaliteit van de Centrale Economische Plannen, 1949–1956," *De Economist*, Vol. 107 (1959), pp. 91–123.

TABLE 3.13

PREDICTED AND ACTUAL PERCENTAGE CHANGES IN DUTCH MACROECONOMIC VARIABLES, 1954–1955

Variables	*1954*		*1955*	
	P	*A*	*P*	*A*
(a) *Price indices of:*				
commodity exports	−4.5	0	0	1
commodity imports	−6.7	−5.0	0	1.8
consumption	2.0	3.6	1.7	1.0
(b) *Quantities and volumes:*				
commodity exports	6.0	11.4	5.0	10.3
commodity imports	10.6	28.2	0.8	7.2
consumption	6.2	5.9	2.3	7.3
available labour force	1.7	2.6	1.4	1.3
labour productivity	1.6	0.7	0.6	3.4
employment in private sector	2.3	4.2	1.3	2.7
employment in public sector	2.4	6.0	2.1	1.6
(c) *Money values:*				
commodity exports	1.2	11.4	5.0	11.4
commodity imports	3.2	21.9	0.8	9.1
consumption	8.3	9.7	4.0	8.3
net investment (incl. inventories)	12.1	74.3	−10.9	5.2
value added in private sector	6.1	11.0	3.1	11.4
Government wage bill	9.5	14.4	8.9	11.1
Government commodity purchases	−0.5	6.3	−0.4	8.0
indirect taxes minus subsidies	5.3	10.7	1.1	2.1
exports of services	−1.0	5.8	0.7	19.5
imports of services	5.1	17.9	2.2	14.7
surplus on the balance of services	−6.3	−4.5	−1.0	24.5

IV. Accuracy Analysis of Entrepreneurial Predictions by Means of Business Test Data

4.1. The Munich Business Test and the German Leather and Shoe Industry

4.1.1. This chapter deals with entrepreneurial plans and expectations. It is in one sense more pretentious than the preceding chapter, in another sense less pretentious, in still another sense quite different. It may be more pretentious as to the accuracy analysis proper, because the number of observations on which it is based is considerably larger. It has few or no pretentions with respect to the problem of the ways in which plans and expectations are determined. Indeed, whereas it was relatively easy to sketch the derivation of the figures of the Dutch Central Economic Plans because this was recorded, the same is not true for entrepreneurial predictions. The actual determination of these forecasts is, therefore, a problem which needs separate study; this will be postponed till Chapter VI.

The present chapter is, finally, different from the preceding one with respect to the form in which the basic data are presented. Until now, we dealt with "conventional" macrovariables like averages, indices and national totals; here, however, we shall work with percentages of firms reporting, planning, or expecting either an increase, or no change, or a decrease in certain variables. This will be considered in more detail in 4.1.2. The remainder of this section is devoted to a description of the set of firms analysed in this chapter, viz., the German leather and shoe industry.

4.1.2. Since the beginning of 1950, the *IFO-Institut für Wirtschaftsforschung* in Munich, Germany, has sent monthly questionnaires to a large number (at present more than 5,000) of firms all over Western Germany. These questions (which are supposed to be answered by leading personalities of the firms) have reference to actual, planned, and expected directions of change of certain microvariables. It is asked, for example, whether the sales of certain products have increased as compared with the previous month, or decreased, or remained the same; also, whether the entrepreneur expects these sales to increase, decrease, or remain constant in the next month. Similar questions refer to other variables including those which are exogenous from the entrepreneur's point of view as well as instrumental variables. For instance, it is asked whether the entrepreneur raised, lowered, or kept unchanged his selling prices in this month, and whether he intends to raise (lower, etc.) them in the next month. There is also a judgment variable, for entrepreneurs are asked: Do you consider your stocks too large, too small, or normal? In Table 4.1, where a list of the variables currently

TABLE 4.1

VARIABLES COVERED BY THE MUNICH BUSINESS TEST

Manufacturing industry	*Wholesale and retail trade**
Position with regard to orders	*sales value***
new orders received (total)	*purchases***
new orders received from abroad (if any)	*goods ordered***
production (daily)	*stocks***
acquirement of new capacity***	appraisal of stocks
daily work-time	*buying prices*
stocks of raw materials	*selling prices*
stocks of finished goods (if any)	
appraisal of stocks of raw materials	
appraisal of stocks of finished goods (if any)	
selling prices	

Note: Those variables for which actual as well as planned or expected directions of change are asked are printed in italics; all other refer to actual changes only.
* Questions for wholesalers are confined to their domestic operations.
** For this variable a question is also put with respect to actual changes as compared with the same month of last year.
*** This includes the question: Did you acquire additional capacity for the production of the commodity considered in this month, yes or no?

covered is given, this question is indicated by "appraisal of stocks." As a whole, these variables refer at present to more than 150 commodities in various manufacturing classifications, about 90 in the wholesale trade and about 50 in the retail trade.[1]

[1] For the description of the survey in German, cf. H. LANGELÜTKE and W. MARQUARDT, "Das Konjunkturtest-Verfahren," *Allgemeines Statistisches Archiv*, Vol. 35 (1951) pp. 189–208; this paper is, however, no longer fully up-to-date with respect to the

The primary object of this "Munich Business Test" (abbreviated as M.B.T.; German, *Konjunkturtest*) is to supply detailed information at short, regular, intervals, which is available soon after the period to which the information refers. Indeed, the results are published within two or three weeks after the questionnaires have been sent out. The outcomes are presented in the form of "weighted percentages:" each individual answer is weighted according to the size of the firm (the number of employees for manufacturers, the value of sales for traders), and they are aggregated in terms of percentages of participants in each separate industry or trade classification who report a rise, no change, or a fall in a particular variable. Hence, for each variable and each month, we can represent the M.B.T. outcomes by a column vector of *test variates*,

$$\mathbf{x} = \{x^1 \quad x^2 \quad x^3\},$$

where x^1 is the fraction of firms reporting (or planning or expecting) an increase, x^2 for no change, and x^3 for a fall; their sum is, of course, unity.

Our information concerning entrepreneurial predictions and actual variables consists of a number of time series of such test vectors. Nothing is asked about the exact magnitude of the quantities involved. The reason is that the organisers of the survey felt that such far-going questions would induce the leaders of enterprises either not to answer at all, or to have them answered by their subordinates, who are not so well-informed.

4.1.3. The leather and shoe industry, which will be the object of our analysis, consists of the following six stages:

I. Wholesale traders in raw hides
II. Tanneries (leather manufacturers)
III. Wholesale traders in leather

questions asked. The same or similar surveys have recently been set up in several other countries, viz., in the Netherlands, Belgium, South Africa, Japan, Sweden, and (with rather important modifications) in France, Luxemburg and Italy; for more details, cf. W. STRIGEL, "Über die Anwendung von Tendenzbefragungen als Mittel der Konjunkturbeobachtung im Ausland," *Allgemeines Statistisches Archiv*, Vol. 38 (1954), pp. 142–153.

Short descriptions in English have been given by H. THEIL in "Recent Experiences with the Munich Business Test," *Econometrica*, Vol. 23 (1955), pp. 184–195; and in an article "Short-Term Business Indicators in Western Europe," by the Economic Commission for Europe in *Economic Bulletin for Europe*, Vol. 7 (1955), pp. 34–78.

IV. Shoe manufacturers
V. Wholesale traders in shoes
VI. Retail traders in shoes.

Four of these stages consist of traders (I, III, V, VI), two of manufacturers (II, IV). A survey of their samples as covered by the Business Test, and of their fluctuations through time, is given in Table 4.2. In what follows, we shall often denote a stage by its roman numeral as indicated above; and we shall adopt the convention to call one stage "higher" ("lower") than another if it is farther from (nearer to) the ultimate consumer, i.e., if its roman numeral stands for a smaller (larger) number.

Whereas the postwar characteristics of the economies considered in the preceding chapter are sufficiently well-known, at least in outline, the same cannot be said with respect to the firms mentioned above. The remainder of this section is, therefore, devoted to a brief description of their situation in recent years, the period of our analysis being, for the greater part of the time series, February 1951 until November 1953—a period characterised by violent movements, due *i.a.* to the Korean boom and the subsequent contraction.[1]

4.1.4. In Western Germany there are about 1000 traders in raw hides, who employ some 3000 people. About one half of the hides is imported, the remainder is produced in Germany. The large proportion of imported hides has led to some price instability of the national market, owing to export restrictions of other European countries and to the economic policy of Argentine. The traders' sales volume has a normal seasonal peak in the autumn.

The leather industry (tanneries) consists of about 600 firms, of which 200 have less than 10 employees; the 39 largest firms (with more than 200 employees) are responsible for about one half of the aggregate volume of sales. There is some surplus capacity in the industry, which is due to the division of Germany into a Western and an Eastern part, and to the increasing importance of rubber soles and other substitutes. The war damage was not very important. Production increased from 1949 till 1952 by only 14 per cent, whereas this percentage for the other German industries was of the order of 60. The industry has a normal seasonal peak from the autumn until spring, which corresponds with the

[1] The factual information supplied in 4.1.4 has been derived from the *Branchenhandbücher* for leather and for shoes, published by the IFO-Institute in recent years.

TABLE 4.2

NUMBERS AND SIZE DISTRIBUTIONS OF FIRMS TAKING PART IN THE MUNICH BUSINESS TEST: GERMAN LEATHER AND SHOE INDUSTRY, 1951–1953

Stage	*1951*				*1952*				*1953*			
	Jan.	*April*	*June*	*Oct.*	*Jan.*	*April*	*June*	*Oct.*	*Jan.*	*April*	*June*	*Oct.*
Wholesale trade in hides: total only	—	9	14	16	16	14	12	12	11	13	13	11
Tanneries: number employed:												
1– 19	3	4	6	10	11	13	10	14	14	9	12	9
20– 49	9	10	7	10	9	8	12	11	15	11	9	13
50– 99	9	9	8	9	7	8	6	8	13	14	16	15
100–199	8	8	8	9	8	11	9	8	6	7	7	8
200–499	3	3	3	5	7	4	6	6	6	7	6	6
over 500	3	3	3	2	2	2	1	3	3	2	1	2
total	35	37	35	45	44	46	44	50	57	50	51	53
Wholesale leather trade: total only	—	17	23	21	19	21	19	21	19	20	22	23
Shoe manufacturers: number employed:												
10– 19	4	4	5	3	3	2	1	—	2	1	1	2
20– 49	8	7	7	9	6	6	8	9	8	10	10	7
50– 99	16	19	17	14	15	19	17	15	14	13	15	15
100– 199	12	12	10	13	11	12	9	13	15	13	15	17
200– 499	13	12	12	9	10	11	9	13	9	12	13	14
500– 999	7	6	6	6	4	5	7	6	5	1	3	5
over 1000	7	8	6	6	7	5	5	6	6	8	8	9
total	67	68	63	60	56	60	56	62	59	58	65	69
Wholesale shoe trade: total only	—	11	20	16	16	19	22	22	23	26	23	23
Shoe retail trade: annual sales in DM.1000												
0– 200	36	31	21	29	39	22	29	22	19	23	23	17
200– 500	28	24	16	22	19	24	20	22	23	16	23	24
500–1000	18	15	15	11	14	25	21	22	29	20	16	11
1000–2000	7	7	7	5	7	8	9	7	7	6	7	4
over 2000	4	7	3	4	4	3	3	1	4	3	3	4
total	93	84	62	71	83	82	82	74	82	68	72	60

seasonal pattern of the purchases of the manufacturers. Raw material expenses are the most important item in cost calculations.

The wholesale leather traders are about 1600 in number; they employ somewhat more than 6000 people. Before the monetary reform in 1948, leather could be obtained by shoemakers only *via* wholesalers; but this strong position was attacked by the tanners and by unions of shoemakers, who tried to eliminate these wholesalers. Some opposite tendencies could be observed in later months, when the tanners proved to be afraid of monopsonistic tendencies of the shoemakers' unions. As a whole, however, the wholesalers' situation was not very favourable, even apart from the above-mentioned evolution, because of the rubber soles competition; moreover, their war damage was considerable. As to the international leather trade, during the winter 1950–1951 leather imports were liberalised, but after a few months new restrictions were imposed; in the summer of 1952 the imports were partly reliberalised. Leather exports are relatively insignificant.

In the shoe industry there are about 900 firms with 10 or more employees; the 23 largest (with more than 500 employees) are responsible for about one third of the aggregate volume of sales. The industry buys 75–80 per cent of the leather produced by the tanneries, mainly directly (i.e., not *via* the wholesale leather traders). The raw material expenses are high, just as in the case of the tanneries. Changes in raw material prices seem to be sometimes reflected in quality variations. The reconstruction cost, incurred after the war, was considerable and had frequently to be financed from outside funds.

There are about 300 firms engaged in the wholesale trade of shoes, with some 2000 employees. Their situation was in general not very favourable in view of war damage, direct relations between manufacturers and retailers and even direct supply of manufacturers to consumers *via* their own shops. It is estimated that about 15 per cent of the aggregate retailers' sales is supplied by manufacturer-owned shops. A great many of the numerous other retailers established collective purchasing agencies.

4.1.5. The available test data for the leather and shoe industry are presented in the Appendix of this chapter (Table 4.19). Table 4.3 gives a summary of the availability of the data, together with the notation of variables that will be adopted from now on. A t in Table 4.3 means "available for all traders," an m "available for all manufacturers." Planned and expected variables are denoted by a bar above the symbol of the corresponding "actual" variables.

TABLE 4.3

AVAILABILITY AND NOTATION OF VARIABLES: GERMAN LEATHER AND SHOE INDUSTRY, 1951–53

Variables	*Actual*		*Predicted*	
	availability	*notation*	*availability*	*notation*
position with regard to orders	m	O		
production	m	P	m	$\bar{P}$
daily work-time	m	W		
sales value	t	T	t	$\bar{T}$
purchases	t	I	t	$\bar{I}$
stocks of finished goods	m, t	S	t	$\bar{S}$
appraisal of stocks	m	S_A		
buying prices	t	p_b	t	$\bar{p}_b$
selling prices	m, t	p_s	m, t	$\bar{p}_s$

4.2. Balances and Disconformity Indices

4.2.1. Business Test forecasts are obviously of the multiple type, since the participants are asked several questions in each month. It is not possible to give a conclusive answer to the question whether the predictions are of the point or of the interval type. First, the participants can reply in three alternative ways (increase, no change, decrease), so that the only thing we can reasonably conclude is that the answer given has, in the forecaster's eyes, a probability exceeding one third. Hence the probability in each particular case may or may not exceed one half. Second, the forecasters give neither probabilities nor even an explanation of what "no change" really means. So there is no possibility to verify the predictions; but this does not exclude an analysis of their accuracy. We shall do so by aggregating the forecasts in the form of test variates (so that the forecasts of individuals become, after aggregation, predictions of industries, which are obviously of the point type), and by comparing these with the test variates of the corresponding "actual" variables; where the term "actual" should be interpreted according to the forecasters' own reports on actual development in the Business Test. More precisely: if, in some month, the fractions of changes reported, x^1, x^2, x^3, are all equal to the corresponding fractions of changes expected or planned for that month, $\bar{x}^1$, $\bar{x}^2$, $\bar{x}^3$ (in vector form: $\mathbf{x} = \bar{\mathbf{x}}$), then the forecasts for that month will be called "perfect." Similarly, if for one variable the time series of test vectors of "actual" and of prediction fractions are closer to each other according to some criterion than for another variable, the former will be said to have been predicted better according to this criterion.

Naturally, this convention is not identical with the ordinary use of the terms. First, an entrepreneur may expect an increase and, indeed, may be confronted with an increase afterwards, but both changes need not be numerically the same. This aspect is not revealed by our test variates. More generally, test variates are the result of a particular aggregation procedure and may hence conceal certain prediction imperfections in the microsphere. To take another example, one entrepreneur may expect an increase and report a decrease afterwards, and another (whose firm is of equal size) may expect and report just the contrary; these forecasting errors cancel out in the test variates. Although effects of this kind are not at all absent in the case of other aggregation procedures, it is nevertheless appropriate to state explicitly that the vector equality $\mathbf{x} = \bar{\mathbf{x}}$ is a necessary, not a sufficient condition for perfect forecasting at the microlevel. But actually, even this is not fully true, for the sets of responding entrepreneurs in successive months are not always identical. This last aspect is however not very important in a quantitative sense, especially when samples of sufficient size are examined. It seems reasonable to examine the test variates as they are, and to postpone a judgment on their quality and suitability until results are obtained. But, of course, the necessary qualifications should be kept in mind.

Granted the above arguments, the question arises whether we should extend our accuracy analysis to all three fractions, or whether we should confine ourselves to only two of them, the three fractions together being always unity. For certain reasons to be given below—which are comparable with the arguments given in 3.2.1 on the analysis of interrelated macroeconomic series—, we shall consider all three fractions; and we shall even introduce two additional characteristics, to be called the *derived test variates* in contrast with our original three fractions, the *basic test variates*.

4.2.2. Since present-day economic thinking is so closely tied to conventional statistical aggregates like indices and national totals, it would be convenient if we could transform our test variates in such a way that the result of this transformation has a closer resemblance to these classical aggregates. The following intuitive argument, due to O. ANDERSON, Jr.,[1] seems valuable in this connection.

The M. B. T. questionnaires refer to changes in entrepreneurial variables. Hence we should compare the test variates with the first differences of a conventional aggregate—say, of the index of the same variable to which the test variates considered belong (e.g., a production index). Now suppose that the percentage of firms reporting a rise is large, whereas the percentage reporting a fall is small; then this over-all tendency of increases will generally be accompanied by a large positive value of the first difference of the index, and *vice versa*. It seems plausible, therefore, that the change in the index is positively associated with the fraction of increases and negatively with the fraction of decreases. We might even hope that there is a rather close association between the first difference of the index and the difference of these fractions, to be called the *balance* of the test variates:

$$b(\mathbf{x}) = x^1 - x^3.$$

Actually, Anderson computed a number of regressions of first differences on corresponding balances for several large groups of aggregated industrial and trade classifications, and he found correlations of the order of 0.9, which may be considered as a first indication that this new type of data has some positive value.[2]

4.2.3. Another approach is the following. Consider the frequency distribution of the first differences of the microvariables corresponding to the macroindex in some month. Six examples are given in Fig. 4.1, all referring to the Dutch shoe industry; along the horizontal axis production is measured as a percentage of the production in the preceding month, along the vertical axis the corresponding number of firms (weighted proportionally to their production in the previous month). The distributions in the first row (the transitions October-November 1950 and March-April 1951) show a relatively small variance

[1] "Konjunkturtest und Statistik," *Allgemeines Statistisches Archiv*, Vol. 35 (1951), pp. 209–220; "The Business Test of the IFO-Institute for Economic Research, Munich, and Its Theoretical Model," *Review of the International Statistical Institute*, Vol. 20 (1952), pp. 1–17.

[2] The aggregation procedure implied by taking balances has been developed independently at the National Bureau for Economic Research, and the aggregates are known there as "diffusion indices." The Dun and Bradstreet data mentioned in Section 2.4 have also the form of balances; the correlations of Table 2.1 are correlations between balances of predictions and balances of reported changes. The Dun and Bradstreet data are, contrary to those of the M.B.T., unweighted. See HASTAY, *loc. cit.*

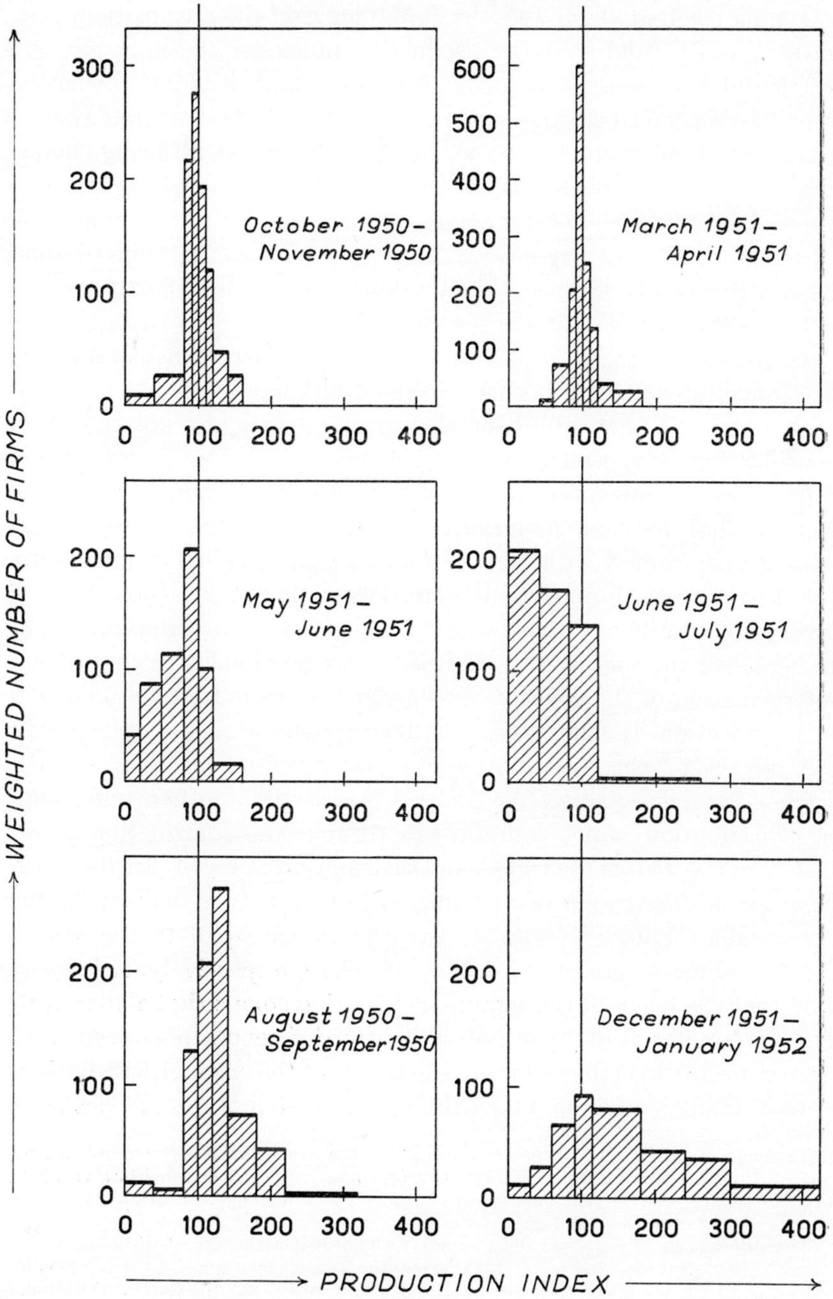

Fig. 4.1. Frequency distributions of first differences of microvariables: monthly production changes in the Dutch shoe industry

around a mean of about 100, thus implying that these transitions were rather "quiet" and that the production index for the industry as a whole did not change very much. The other four distributions have a much larger variance, those of the second row about means smaller than 100, those of the third about means above 100, all being characterised by appreciable skewness. The transition June-July 1951 shows even a larger frequency for the interval 0–40 than for any other interval of the same size—a natural result when production is reduced sufficiently drastically. Seasonal fluctuations are no doubt partly responsible for the large changes observed.[1]

In the same way, it is possible to derive frequency distributions of first microdifferences for other variables, although it should be added that, naturally, they will display a varying degree of regularity. Now consider Fig. 4.2, which contains a hypothetical distribution of first differences for entrepreneurs participating in the Business Test; and suppose that, for some nonnegative fractions a, b, those entrepreneurs who are confronted with relative increases $> b$ report an increase in the Test, those whose decreases are larger than a in absolute value report a decrease, and those whose changes are in the interval $(-a, b)$, to be called the *indifference interval,* report no change. Such a liberal interpretation of the concept "no change" seems indeed reasonable in this connection. It follows that the test variates x^1, x^2, x^3 are equal to the masses of this distribution for the intervals (b, ∞), $(-a, b)$, $(-\infty, -a)$, respectively. We proceed to consider another, much simpler distribution, which contains exactly the same information as our test variates. This is the right-hand distribution of Fig. 4.2, to be called the *signum distribution* of first microdifferences. It is defined for the three values 1, 0, -1, and its frequencies are equal to the abovementioned masses and test variates, x^1, x^2, x^3, respectively. It is easily seen that the mean of the signum distribution equals the balance, $b(\mathbf{x})$. This parameter is comparable with first differences of conventional aggregates, because the latter are the means of the original distributions of first differences, from which the signum distributions are derived.[2]

[1] The diagrams are derived from H. Theil, "On the Time Shape of Economic Microvariables and the Munich Business Test," *Review of the International Statistical Institute,* Vol. 20 (1952), pp. 105–120. This paper contains also some suggestions on the nature of the types of distributions found.

[2] First differences of weighted indices may be regarded as means of distributions of microchanges, provided due account is taken of the weights by adjusting the frequencies belonging to the elements that are weighted differently; first differences of national totals are obtained by multiplying the mean by the number of elements; etc.

Hence balances are analogous to more familiar aggregates in the sense that both describe the central tendency of microchanges.

Secondly, however, we may consider the variance of the signum distribution,

$$d(\mathbf{x}) = x^1 + x^3 - \{b(\mathbf{x})\}^2,$$

to be called the *disconformity index*. This statistic can be regarded as a measure of the dispersion of changes of individual microvariables around their central tendency. Together, the balance and the discon-

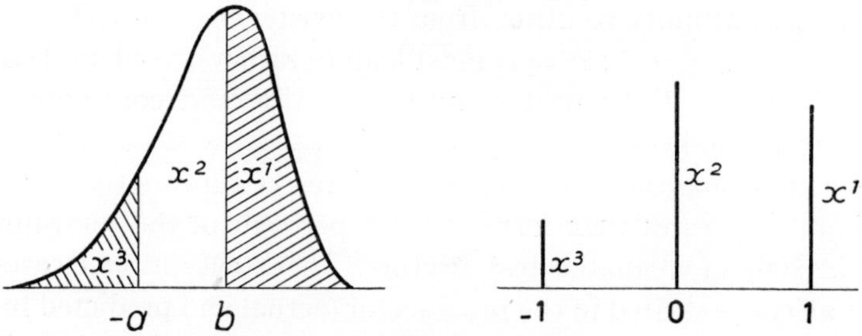

Fig. 4.2. Hypothetical frequency distribution of first differences of microvariables, and its signum distribution

formity index are derived test variates which determine the basic test variates completely. The remainder of this chapter is based on all five test variates, each of them being interesting in its own way; and the remainder of this section is devoted to an empirical analysis of disconformity, which may be expected to shed some light on properties of the microsphere and possibly also on some features of forecasting.

4.2.4. Whereas the balance is numerically restricted to the interval $(-1, 1)$, the disconformity index is confined to the smaller interval $(0, 1)$. We have $d = 0$ in the case of unanimity: either $x^1 = 1$, or $x^2 = 1$, or $x^3 = 1$. We have $d = 1$ if 50 per cent of the firms report increases and 50 per cent decreases: $x^1 = x^3 = \frac{1}{2}$. Still another critical value is $d = \frac{1}{4}$. This is the maximum attainable when all firms report either increases or no change, or either decreases or no change. Or in other words: if we have $d > \frac{1}{4}$, then we are sure that there are "contradictions" in the sense that some entrepreneurs report or expect increases and others decreases—each for his own variable, of course. An analysis of disconformity seems indeed interesting, because it may reveal something about the applicability of the concept of a homogeneous industry, so beloved in economic theory. Apart from this, such an analysis is useful for the M.B.T. itself, for it will be intuitively clear that the total absence of disconformity, $d \equiv 0$, is an impediment to a close association between balances (or any other measures of central tendency derived from test variates) and the first differences of the corresponding conventional aggregate. We have $d \equiv 0$ if the industry consists of only one firm. This is natural, since we should have no disconformity if there is only one unit making decisions and reporting plans, expectations, and observations on exogenous variables. But the extreme discontinuity resulting from the existence of only three possibilities ($x^1 = 1$; $x^2 = 1$; $x^3 = 1$) must lead to rather considerable deviations between the test variates and the usually more continuous time pattern of the indices.

When analysing the available test variates, it appears that the cases $d = 0$ are very rare: they form about 3 per cent of the total number (about 1,900) of available test vectors. These exceptional cases are almost all concentrated in the price sector (actual and predicted buying and selling prices), for which the percentage is about three times larger but still rather small. The last problem of the preceding paragraph presents, therefore, no real difficulties. As to other numerical values of the disconformity index, Table 4.4 gives the quartiles of these coefficients for each variable and each industry stage. It appears that a great many of them must exceed the critical value $\frac{1}{4}$: about three fourths of the upper quartiles are equal to 0.25 or larger, and the same holds for about one half of the medians and about one third of the lower quartiles. There are hence rather appreciable differences between the monthly directions of change for the same variables of separate firms of the same branch of industry or trade. It is also interesting to note that the disconformity is in general more considerable for quantity and value variables than for price variables. For instance, if we take the trading firms (the stages I, III, V, VI) and the four price variables belonging to each stage (buying and selling prices, actual and predicted), then the resulting sixteen medians of disconformity indices are distributed about a mean of 0.16 with a standard deviation of 0.05, whereas these statistics are 0.40 and 0.08, respectively, for the twenty-four quantity and value variables of the same stages. It follows from Table 4.5 that similar conclusions hold for the other quartiles and also for the manufacturing stages; both for the traders and for the manufac-

TABLE 4.4

QUARTILES OF DISCONFORMITY INDICES: GERMAN LEATHER AND SHOE INDUSTRY, 1951–1953

Stages	Quartiles	*Variables* O	P	$\bar{P}$	W	T	$\bar{T}$	I	$\bar{I}$	S	$\bar{S}$	S_A	p_b	$\bar{p}_b$	p_s	$\bar{p}_s$
I	lower					0.28	0.16	0.35	0.20	0.27	0.22		0.06	0.15	0.03	0.15
	median					0.38	0.25	0.43	0.30	0.38	0.29		0.19	0.24	0.20	0.24
	upper					0.54	0.43	0.52	0.40	0.50	0.42		0.38	0.28	0.37	0.28
II	lower	0.33	0.18	0.13	0.07					0.31		0.25			0.17	0.11
	median	0.45	0.21	0.16	0.13					0.35		0.31			0.22	0.19
	upper	0.58	0.26	0.21	0.20					0.43		0.40			0.27	0.25
III	lower					0.33	0.24	0.37	0.24	0.35	0.24		0.05	0.11	0.07	0.12
	median					0.44	0.39	0.43	0.32	0.43	0.33		0.15	0.19	0.12	0.18
	upper					0.55	0.51	0.51	0.48	0.54	0.40		0.24	0.25	0.22	0.25
IV	lower	0.33	0.20	0.14	0.11					0.30		0.20			0.07	0.04
	median	0.39	0.25	0.18	0.21					0.37		0.24			0.13	0.11
	upper	0.48	0.31	0.24	0.24					0.54		0.28			0.23	0.19
V	lower					0.36	0.25	0.44	0.31	0.32	0.25		0.05	0.05	0.03	0.00
	median					0.51	0.37	0.56	0.42	0.42	0.40		0.09	0.13	0.06	0.14
	upper					0.64	0.53	0.66	0.56	0.56	0.52		0.21	0.24	0.21	0.23
VI	lower					0.19	0.13	0.37	0.28	0.30	0.23		0.04	0.07	0.03	0.06
	median					0.43	0.32	0.59	0.48	0.43	0.41		0.14	0.19	0.13	0.18
	upper					0.63	0.51	0.77	0.58	0.61	0.51		0.23	0.25	0.20	0.23

turers the upper quartile of the price disconformity indices is on the average approximately equal to the lower quartile of the quantity indices. It seems, therefore, that behaviour, plans and expectations with respect to prices are—given the indifference intervals—much more similar for separate firms than those with respect to quantities and values. A possible explanation is that information about prices of other firms is much easier to obtain and at the same time more important to have, since the other (quantity) variables have no official or semi-official quotations and are not instruments of competition, like prices.

TABLE 4.5

DISTRIBUTION OF QUARTILES OF DISCONFORMITY INDICES BY STAGES AND VARIABLES: GERMAN LEATHER AND SHOE INDUSTRY, 1951–1953

Firms	*Quartiles*	*Prices**		*Quantities and values***	
		mean	*standard deviation*	*mean*	*standard deviation*
traders	lower	0.07	0.04	0.28	0.07
	median	0.16	0.05	0.40	0.08
	upper	0.25	0.05	0.54	0.08
manufactures	lower	0.10	0.05	0.24	0.07
	median	0.16	0.04	0.29	0.09
	upper	0.24	0.03	0.37	0.12

* Buying and selling prices, actual and predicted.
** Position with respect to orders, production, sales, purchases, and stocks; actual, predicted and appraisal. Daily work-time has been excluded, because this variable is, for obvious reasons, characterised by monthly changes that are much smaller than those of the other variables.

4.2.5. Another interesting question with respect to disconformity is whether there is any association between the degree of "bewilderment" for some variable in one month and the next. A convenient method for testing the absence of association consists of computing the first serial correlation coefficient for time series of disconformity indices,

$$r_1 = \frac{\Sigma (d_t - \bar{d})(d_{t-1} - \bar{d}')}{\sqrt{\Sigma (d_t - \bar{d})^2 \, \Sigma (d_{t-1} - \bar{d}')^2}},$$

$\bar{d}$ being the mean of the current d's and $\bar{d}'$ that of the lagged d's.

The results are gathered in Table 4.6 and illustrated in Fig. 4.3. Although a great many coefficients are close to zero, for the set of outcomes as a whole it seems better not to accept the hypothesis of zero autocorrelation. About 60 per cent of the fifty-six coefficients is

TABLE 4.6

FIRST SERIAL CORRELATION COEFFICIENTS OF DISCONFORMITY INDICES: GERMAN LEATHER AND SHOE INDUSTRY, 1951–1953

Variables	*Stages of the industry*					
	I	*II*	*III*	*IV*	*V*	*VI*
O	.	0.50	.	0.49	.	.
P	.	0.24	.	0.31	.	.
$\bar{P}$	.	0.37	.	0.12	.	.
W	.	0.54	.	0.18	.	.
T	−0.13	.	0.63	.	0.02	−0.09
$\bar{T}$	−0.05	.	0.47	.	−0.01	−0.15
I	0.17	.	−0.05	.	−0.25	0.12
$\bar{I}$	0.14	.	0.19	.	0.17	0.04
S	−0.28	0.32	0.02	0.58	−0.25	0.30
$\bar{S}$	0.30	.	0.29	.	0.06	−0.21
S_A	.	−0.06	.	0.37	.	.
p_b	−0.09	.	0.43	.	0.68	0.77
$\bar{p}_b$	0.00	.	0.33	.	0.46	0.66
p_s	−0.14	0.16	0.31	0.26	0.58	0.67
$\bar{p}_s$	0.05	0.47	0.36	0.39	0.71	0.70

concentrated in the interval (0, 0.5), and the remainder is approximately equally divided between negative and larger positive values. About one third exceeds the value 0.35 (which is approximately twice the standard error under the hypothesis of zero autocorrelation), and the average of all is about one quarter. Some caution is necessary when

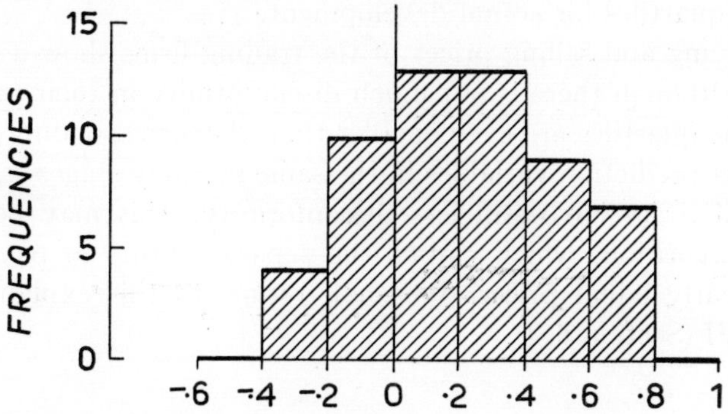

Fig. 4.3. Frequency distribution of first serial correlation coefficients of disconformity indices

judging these aggregate outcomes in view of the fact that the correlations may not be—and are presumably not—independent, but a moderate positive association between the disconformity in one month and that in the next seems nevertheless plausible.

4.2.6. Finally, we may ask whether there are any systematic differences between the disconformity indices of corresponding actual and predicted variables. A closer inspection of the quartiles of Table 4.4 suggests that the answer should be positive. Let us first disregard the traders' prices. Then sixteen variables of separate stages remain for which both actual data and predictions are available. Table 4.4 reveals that the resulting forty-eight quartiles of disconformity indices for predictions are all, without exception, smaller than the corresponding quartiles for actual development. This means that the entrepreneurs' opinions about future changes of variables are not so much divided as their reports on recent changes are. Various explanations are possible, but the following has at least the virtue of simplicity. It will appear later that "no change" is, for most of the variables, planned or expected more frequently than observed afterwards. This implies a concentration of predicted changes (relative to actual changes) around zero, which will usually—though not necessarily—lead to less disconformity. It is also conceivable that the entrepreneurs' outlook is more concerned with conditions of their branch of industry or trade than with those of their separate firms. It is not possible to be more conclusive at the present stage. Whatever the causes may be, however, Fig. 4.4 reveals that, for this group of variables, the disconformity quartiles of predictions are on the average equal to 70–80 per cent of the corresponding quartiles for actual development.

The buying and selling prices of the trading firms show a different picture. Although there is not much disconformity in their prediction series—the quartiles are even smaller than the corresponding quartiles of all other prediction variables in the same industry stages—, most of the actual series have still less disconformity. This may be due to sharp competition, which causes the separate firms to pay and to charge nearly equal prices. We shall return to this explanation in Chapter VI (Section 6.4).

4.3. Analysis of Turning Point Errors

4.3.1. In order to give a general preliminary impression of the entrepreneurs' success of forecasting, we shall now turn to the degree to which turning points for the various variables have been predicted correctly. This measure has some intuitive value which justifies its use for this limited purpose, even though it will appear necessary to supplement some of the findings of this section later on.

Clearly, turning points have to be re-defined here in order to be

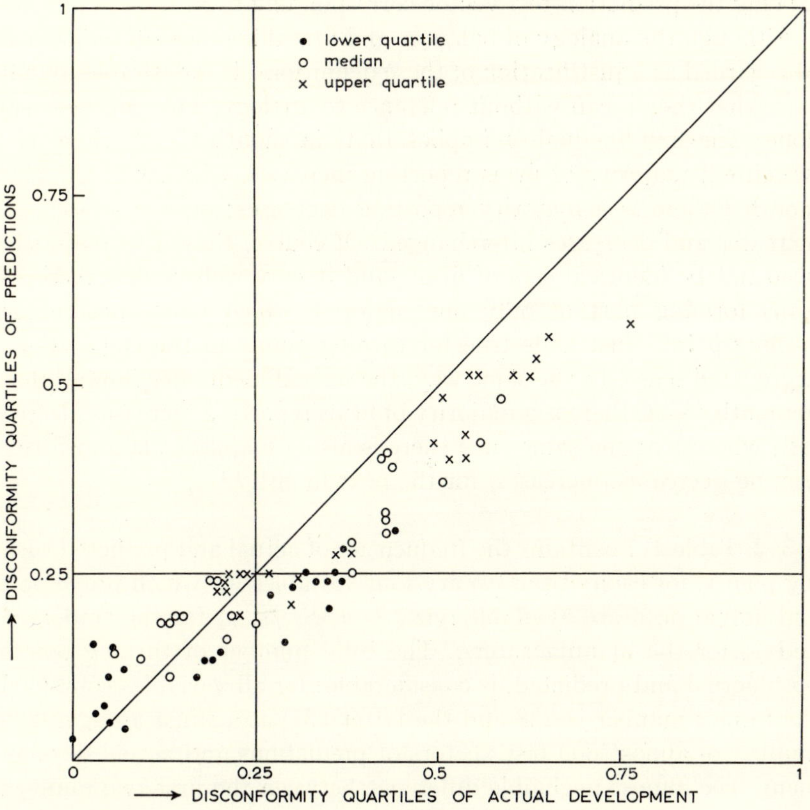

Fig. 4.4. Pairs of quartiles of disconformity indices for predicted and actual development; German leather and shoe industry, 1951–1953. *Note:* all circles, dots and crosses above the upward sloping line through the origin belong to the price variables of the traders

analysed by means of test variates. For this purpose, the other derived test variate, the balance, can be conveniently employed. This will be immediately clear when it is recalled that this coefficient is a measure of central tendency of changes. Consequently, we define an actual turning point as a pair of successive months $t-1$, t, for which

$$\operatorname{sgn} b(\mathbf{x})_t \neq \operatorname{sgn} b(\mathbf{x})_{t-1},$$

i.e., the case of balances of opposite signs in successive months. Similarly, we define a predicted turning point as a pair $t - 1, t$ for which

$$\operatorname{sgn} b(\bar{\mathbf{x}})_t \neq \operatorname{sgn} b(\mathbf{x})_{t-1},$$

$\bar{\mathbf{x}}$ being the prediction test vector corresponding to $\mathbf{x}$.

Although the analogy of balances and first differences of indices can be regarded as a justification of these definitions, it is desirable to indicate what they mean without reference to analogy. This can be easily done. The first inequality implies that, in month $t - 1$, there is a (weighted) majority of firms reporting increases, whereas in the next month t there is a majority reporting decreases; or *vice versa*, with increases and decreases interchanged. Of course, these two majorities need not be identical sets of firms, and it may well be that there are firms forming part of only one majority which hence observe no turning point—just as is true for turning points in the conventional aggregated sense. In the same way, the second inequality implies that, in month $t - 1$, there is a majority of firms reporting increases (decreases), whereas at the same time there is also a majority planning or expecting decreases (increases) for the next month t.[1]

4.3.2. Table 4.7 contains the frequencies of actual and predicted turning points, for each of the twenty-four variables for which predictions and actual data are available (viz., T, I, S, p_b, p_s for the traders, P and p_s for the manufacturers). The total number of turning points, both actual and predicted, is considerable: for all variables combined, the former number is 228 and the latter 237, as against an aggregate number of almost 800 test vectors of predictions and actual development. The almost negligible difference between the first two numbers does not mean, however, that the forecasting success was complete: both the turning point errors of the first kind as a fraction of the total number of predicted turning points (φ_1) and the second-kind errors as a fraction of all actual turning points (φ_2) amount to about 0.35–0.4.

[1] "Majorities" (or "pluralities") should of course be interpreted with respect to increases and decreases only, not in the sense that a majority of (say) increases implies $x^1 > \frac{1}{2}$.
Some arbitrary conventions are necessary for the cases $b(\mathbf{x}) = 0$ and $b(\bar{\mathbf{x}}) = 0$. The following are adopted in the tables below: (*i*) $b(\bar{\mathbf{x}}) = 0$ is not a predicted turning point; (*ii*) if $b(\mathbf{x})_t = 0$, then $b(\bar{\mathbf{x}})_{t+1} \neq 0$ is a predicted turning point only if $\operatorname{sgn} b(\bar{\mathbf{x}})_{t+1} \neq \operatorname{sgn} b(\mathbf{x})_{t-1}$; (*iii*) the cases $b(\mathbf{x})_{t-1} < b(\mathbf{x})_t = 0 > b(\mathbf{x})_{t+1}$ and $b(\mathbf{x})_{t-1} > b(\mathbf{x})_t = 0 < b(\mathbf{x})_{t+1}$ are no turning points; (*iv*) the cases $b(\mathbf{x})_{t-1} < b(\mathbf{x})_t = 0 < b(\mathbf{x})_{t+1}$ and $b(\mathbf{x})_{t-1} > b(\mathbf{x})_t = 0 > b(\mathbf{x})_{t+1}$ are turning points, which are temporally localised in the pair of months $t, t + 1$.

TABLE 4.7

FREQUENCIES OF TURNING POINTS, ACTUAL AND PREDICTED: GERMAN LEATHER AND SHOE INDUSTRY, 1951–1953

Variables	*Stages*	*Turning points*			*Errors*		*Significance*
		predicted	*actual*	*correctly predicted*	*first-kind*	*second-kind*	
			Traders				
T	I	14	11	8	6	3	*
	III	10	14	6	4	8	
	V	14	12	9	5	3	*
	VI	15	17	15	0	2	*****
I	I	8	8	5	3	3	*
	III	12	10	5	7	5	
	V	15	13	12	3	1	****
	VI	14	11	9	5	2	**
S	I	8	8	1	7	7	
	III	14	10	6	8	4	
	V	14	11	9	5	2	**
	VI	17	11	10	7	1	**
p_b	I	9	13	8	1	5	**
	III	6	6	3	3	3	*
	V	3	6	2	1	4	
	VI	6	5	2	4	3	
p_s	I	10	15	10	0	5	***
	III	5	8	4	1	4	**
	V	3	3	1	2	2	
	VI	8	6	4	4	2	*
			Manufacturers				
P	II	10	8	6	4	2	**
	IV	9	8	6	3	2	**
p_s	II	6	9	2	4	7	
	IV	7	5	4	3	1	**

On the other hand, we should not interpret this rather negative result as an indication that the predicted turning points are, although their total number is satisfactory, randomly distributed. Take e.g. the outcomes of the first row of Table 4.7; when writing them in the double-dichotomy form of Table 2.2, we obtain[1]

$$\begin{matrix} 8 & 3 \\ 6 & 16. \end{matrix}$$

[1] The frequency 16 in the lower right-hand cell is obtained by deducting the other frequencies from the total number (33). The χ^2's, mentioned below, have been derived by applying Yates' correction for continuity; see e.g. M. G. KENDALL, *The Advanced Theory of Statistics*, Vol. I (London, 3rd edition, 1947), p. 303.

This yields a χ^2 of 4.5, which is significant at the 5 per cent level. In the last column of Table 4.7,* denotes significance at the 10 per cent level,** (***) significance at the 1 (0.1) per cent level, etc. As a whole, there are so many asterisks that there can be no doubt that the predicted turning points are not randomly distributed.

4.3.3. Table 4.8 gives a survey by types of variables (all industry stages combined) and by the successive stages (all variables combined); perhaps we may hope that this aggregation results in increased stability of the figures obtained. It appears then that turning points occur more frequently, and are also more frequently predicted, for quantity and

TABLE 4.8

AGGREGATED FREQUENCIES OF TURNING POINTS: GERMAN LEATHER AND SHOE INDUSTRY, 1951–1953

Variables or stages	*Turning points*			*Errors*			
	predicted	*actual*	*correctly predicted*	*first-kind*	*second-kind*	φ_1	φ_2
			All traders combined				
T	53	54	38	15	16	0.28	0.30
I	49	42	31	18	11	0.37	0.26
S	53	40	26	27	14	0.51	0.35
p_b	24	30	15	9	15	0.37	0.50
p_s	26	32	19	7	13	0.27	0.41
			All manufacturers combined				
P	19	16	12	7	4	0.37	0.25
p_s	13	14	6	7	8	0.54	0.57
			All variables combined				
I	49	55	32	17	23	0.35	0.42
III	47	48	24	23	24	0.49	0.50
V	49	45	33	16	12	0.33	0.27
VI	60	50	40	20	10	0.33	0.20
II	16	17	8	8	9	0.50	0.53
IV	16	13	10	6	3	0.37	0.23

value variables than for prices; hence more significant conclusions can be drawn about the former variables. Among these, the stocks seem to be the "worst" variable. As to differences between the separate stages, the lower ones seem to have been somewhat more successful than those which are farther from the ultimate consumer, especially according to the φ_2-criterion.

It will be noted that every forecaster can "protect" himself mechanically against turning point errors of the first kind, viz., by never

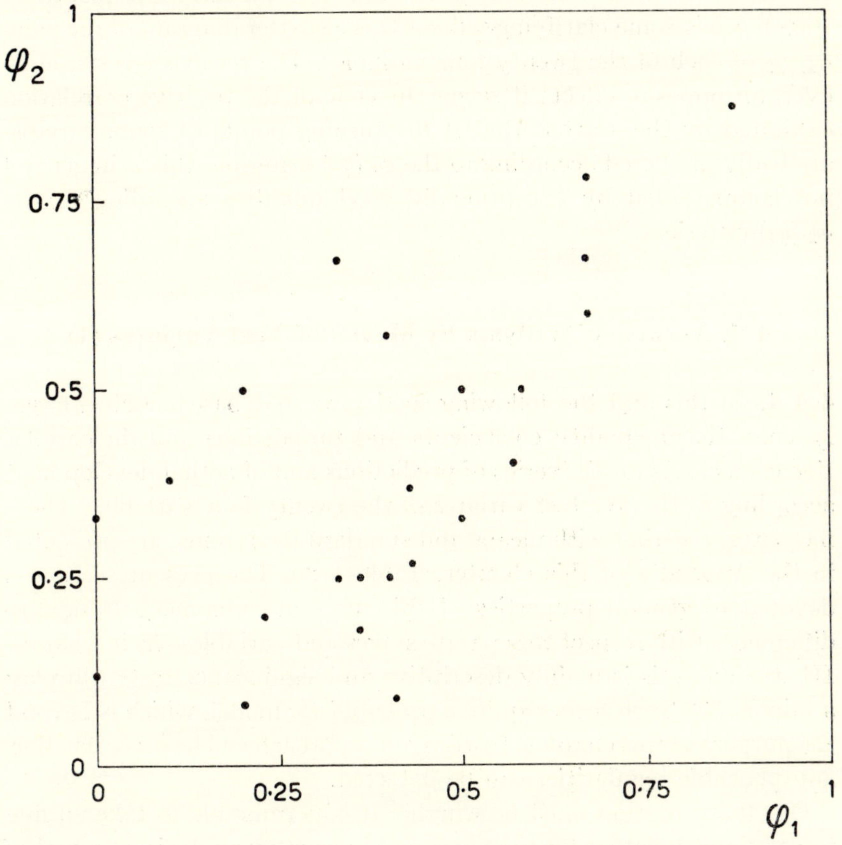

Fig. 4.5. Twenty-four pairs of φ_1, φ_2-ratios of the turning points of variables of the German leather and shoe industry, 1951–1953

predicting any turning point; for example, by extrapolating directions of change. Similarly, he can "protect" himself against second-kind errors, viz., by predicting a turning point at every occasion. The first procedure leads to a φ_1 with zero numerator (though of the indeterminate form 0/0), but to a φ_2 equal to 1; the second leads to a zero value of φ_2 (or 0/0 if there are no turning points), but to a φ_1 equal to the frequency of observations which represent no actual turning points.

When expressed in this way, it seems that there is some kind of substitution relationship between the two types of errors, and it is interesting to analyse this empirically. Naturally, this cannot be done with test variates for individual forecasters, but for the sets of firms representing entire stages in the leather and shoe industry the picture of Fig. 4.5 has some clarifying value.[1] It is a scatter diagram of the pairs φ_1, φ_2 of each of the twenty-four variables. The result suggests, however, an opposite effect: it seems, in view of the positive correlation exhibited by the scatter, that if the turning points of some variable are badly predicted according to the φ_1 (φ_2)-criterion, this is in general not compensated by exceptionally good qualities according to the φ_2 (φ_1)-criterion.

4.4. Accuracy Analysis by Means of Test Variates (1)

4.4.1. In this and the following section we shall base ourselves largely upon the inequality coefficients and proportions and the correlation coefficients for the series of predictions and of actual development according to the five test variates of the twenty-four variables. These measures, together with means and standard deviations, are presented in the Appendix of this chapter, Table 4.20. The present section is devoted to general properties of this mass of outcomes, the next to differences with respect to separate stages and variables. As in Chapter III, the analysis is mainly descriptive and significance tests will play a minor rôle. Such tests require a probabilistic model, which is beyond the purpose of this chapter. Instead, our approach will be to see whether any plausible regularities can be detected.

Our first question must be whether it is permissible to take all five test variates together for the purposes of accuracy analysis, or whether it is preferable to analyse them separately. Table 4.9 may be regarded as an answer. It contains five frequency distributions of U, corre-

[1] The following example shows that important differences may exist between micro and macrosphere. Suppose there are three firms, A, B and C, all of equal size; furthermore that all observe decreases in the present month, that A and B predict decreases for the next but C an increase, and that these forecasts come true. Hence there is no turning point error in the microsphere. But if A's and B's predicted decreases amount to 5 per cent each, C's predicted increase to 15 per cent, A's and B's actual decreases to 15 per cent each, and C's actual increase to 20 per cent, then there is a first-kind error in the macrosphere in terms of the conventional macrovariable, which is detected by means of test variates only if A's and B's predicted increases fall in the indifference interval.

TABLE 4.9

FREQUENCY DISTRIBUTIONS OF THE INEQUALITY AND CORRELATION COEFFICIENTS FOR PREDICTION AND ACTUAL DEVELOPMENT OF 24 VARIABLES, BY TEST VARIATES: GERMAN LEATHER AND SHOE INDUSTRY, 1951–1953

Intervals	*Test variates*				
	increases	*no change*	*decreases*	*balance*	*disconformity index*
	Distributions of U				
$\leqq 0.10$	0	5	0	0	0
0.11 – 0.20	6	8	6	2	3
0.21 – 0.30	8	6	8	7	16
0.31 – 0.40	10	4	9	6	3
0.41 – 0.50	0	0	1	4	2
0.51 – 0.60	0	1	0	5	0
	Distributions of r				
$\geqq 0.91$	3	2	3	3	0
$\geqq 0.81$	8	2	10	12	0
0.61 – 0.80	8	9	6	9	3
0.41 – 0.60	6	3	6	1	6
0.21 – 0.40	1	7	2	2	8
0.01 – 0.20	1	3	0	0	5
$\leqq 0.00$	0	0	0	0	2

sponding to each of the test variates, for all twenty-four variables combined, and the corresponding distributions of r. It appears that (0.2, 0.4) is, for almost all of the test variates, the interval containing the largest number of U's, just as is true for the macroeconomic forecasts of the preceding chapter (cf. Fig. 3.9); but otherwise there are important differences between the separate distributions. Whereas both the U- and the r-distributions of the fractions of increases and of decreases are very similar, the no-change fractions show a greater forecasting success than these according to U but a smaller success according to r. About one half of the variables have inequality coefficients of 0.20 or smaller for their series of fractions of no-change, actual and predicted, but this holds for only one fourth of the variables when no change is replaced by increase or decrease. On the other hand, almost 40 per cent of the variables show correlations as large as 0.80 or still larger when their x^1 or x^3-series is compared with the corresponding prediction series, but there are only two variables for which this is true if we take x^2 instead. These differences become even larger when we proceed to the balances. When these test variates are compared with the other four, it appears that their forecasting success ranks first according to r but last according to U![1] We must conclude, therefore, that it is preferable not to combine the separate test variates when their inequality coefficients are analysed.

The cause of this heterogeneous picture is rather simple. It was observed earlier (cf. 2.5.1) that the correlation coefficient is invariant against changes of the origin from which the variables are measured, whereas the inequality coefficient is not; more specifically, the inequality coefficient becomes smaller when the origin moves away from the means of both series. The balance is the only test variate which can assume both positive and negative values; and the fractions of no-change are, for about 80 per cent of the forty-eight time series of test vectors, larger on the average than the other two basic test variates. It is obvious, therefore, that the forecasting picture of the no-change fractions is deteriorated compared with that of the balances when this picture is based on a measure that is independent of the origin.

Granted this, the question arises whether something more can be said about the meaning of a particular numerical value of U for our test variates. An attempt to answer this question is made in Table 4.10, which contains, for the separate trade classifications of the leather and shoe industry and for all five test variates, inequality coefficients for the following pairs of variables: expected and actual buying prices; planned and actual selling prices; expected buying and planned selling prices; actual buying and actual selling prices. A comparison with the inequality coefficients of the last two pairs seems reasonable, because it is intuitively obvious that changes in selling prices must stand in some relationship to changes in buying prices, although this relation is not, of course, necessarily a unique one. It follows from Table 4.10 that the U's for the pairs $\bar{p}_b$, $\bar{p}_s$ and p_b, p_s are considerably smaller than the U's of the upper half of the table; the mean of the former U's is less than 0.1, that of the latter about three times larger, and there are only two cases in which a U in the upper half is smaller than the U in the corresponding place of the lower half. We should hence conclude that the entrepreneurs are much more inclined to react on observed and expected buying price changes than capable to make correct predictions of such changes and prepared to carry out their price plans. Inequality coefficients of the order of 0.3, such as these

[1] The results for the disconformity indices will be discussed in 4.5.4, since the best insight into their properties can be obtained after a sufficiently complete picture of the properties of the other test variates is presented.

have been found in Table 4.9 for series of forecasts and actual development, cannot be considered as indicators of a very close relationship for test variates.

TABLE 4.10

INEQUALITY COEFFICIENTS FOR FOUR PAIRS OF TRADERS' PRICE VARIABLES: GERMAN LEATHER AND SHOE INDUSTRY, 1951–1953

Test variates	*Industry stages*				*Industry stages*			
	I	*III*	*V*	*VI*	*I*	*III*	*V*	*VI*
	$\bar{p}_b$ *and* p_b				$\bar{p}_s$ *and* p_s			
x^1	0.36	0.35	0.14	0.18	0.38	0.27	0.19	0.20
x^2	0.39	0.21	0.11	0.08	0.40	0.17	0.11	0.08
x^3	0.36	0.33	0.30	0.12	0.36	0.31	0.27	0.14
b	0.44	0.38	0.23	0.17	0.45	0.34	0.24	0.18
d	0.43	0.33	0.33	0.18	0.43	0.33	0.29	0.20
	$\bar{p}_b$ *and* $\bar{p}_s$				p_b *and* p_s			
x^1	0.05	0.09	0.10	0.12	0.05	0.24	0.12	0.22
x^2	0.04	0.04	0.04	0.05	0.09	0.10	0.04	0.08
x^3	0.05	0.06	0.10	0.08	0.05	0.04	0.08	0.07
b	0.05	0.08	0.10	0.10	0.05	0.14	0.09	0.16
d	0.08	0.07	0.13	0.12	0.10	0.18	0.12	0.22

4.4.2. Next, we consider the inequality proportions U^M, U^S and U^C. Contrary to our findings for the macroeconomic forecasts of the preceding chapter, these three proportions are numerically so much different from each other that it seems permissible to combine them for all variables and all test variates. According to Table 4.11, by far the largest "source" of forecasting errors—at least according to the test variates employed—is imperfect covariation. A secondary rôle is played by unequal central tendency, the bias proportion U^M being less than

TABLE 4.11

FREQUENCY DISTRIBUTIONS OF 120 INEQUALITY PROPORTIONS: GERMAN LEATHER AND SHOE INDUSTRY, 1951–1953

Inequality proportions	*Proportion intervals*									
	0–0.10	*0.11–0.20*	*0.21–0.30*	*0.31–0.40*	*0.41–0.50*	*0.51–0.60*	*0.61–0.70*	*0.71–0.80*	*0.81–0.90*	*0.91–1*
U^M	53	27	18	14	6	2	0	0	0	0
U^S	97*	15	6	2	0	0	0	0	0	0
U^C	0	1	1	1	4	7	22	21	33	30

* Of which 82 in the interval $U^S \leqq 0.05$.

0.2 in two thirds of all cases. Unequal variation is a still smaller source: only one third of the variance proportions exceeds 0.05. A graphical picture—more "normal" than that of the proportions of Chapter III—is given in the Figs. 4.6 and 4.7.

We proceed to consider the hypothesis formulated in 2.5.3, viz., that U^M, U^S and $-U^C$ are, *ceteris paribus*, increasing functions of U. It is obviously rather difficult to enforce the *ceteris paribus* clause, but

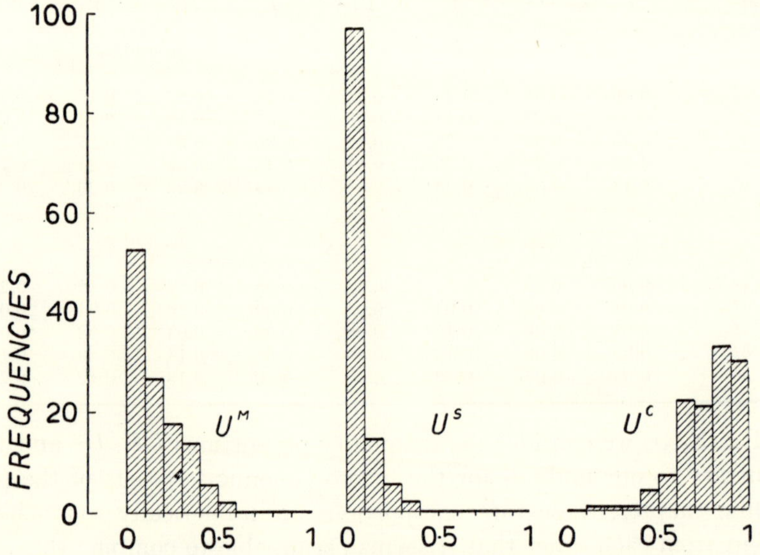

Fig. 4.6. Frequency distributions of the inequality proportions for 120 series of predictions and actual development (test variates): German leather and shoe industry, 1951–1953

the following procedure will perhaps approximate this condition.[1] First, it follows from Table 4.9 that it is preferable not to combine the heterogeneous test variates. Since the same is true for the different variables, the analysis should be carried out separately for each variable and for each test variate. The only remaining criterion is then the industry stage. However, the number of manufacturing stages and that of their available variables are both only two, so that it seems better to confine the attention to the traders. Hence we can compare, for each of the five variables T (sales), I (purchases), S (stocks), p_b and p_s (buying and

[1] The best way to test this hypothesis is, of course, to consider the forecasts of a series of phenomena made by a large number of competing forecasters.

selling prices) and for each of the five test variates, the coefficients U and the proportions U^M, U^S, U^C of the four stages I, III, V and VI. But it follows from Section 2.5 that the sampling fluctuations of the

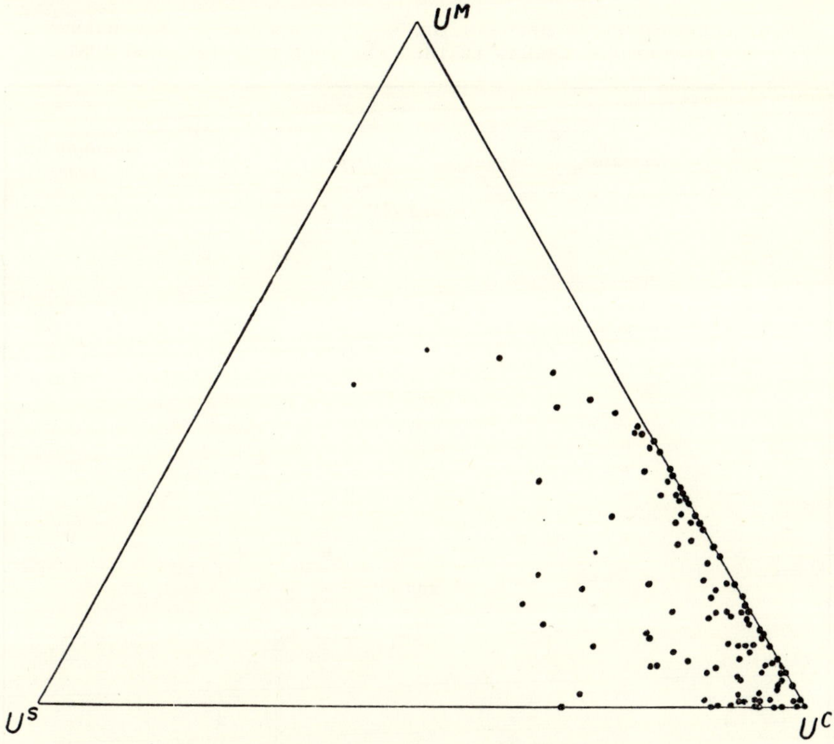

Fig. 4.7. Triangular illustration of the inequality proportions of Fig. 4.6

inequality proportions are rather large; therefore, the coefficients and proportions of the upper (I, III) and the lower (V, VI) stages have been averaged. If, for some variable and some test variate, the difference between the I–III-average of U and the V–VI-average has the same sign as the similar difference for U^M (U^S, U^C), this is denoted by + in Table 4.12; if the signs are different, then − is used; 0 indicates that one of the differences is zero in two decimal places.[1]

It appears that 10 of the 15 signs for the basic test variates are positive in the comparison between U and U^M, that the same holds for

[1] Another method, which might be valuable in some cases, is that of determining rank correlations between U and U^M (U^S, U^C). In the present case, however, its application is cumbersome in view of the large number of ties.

11 of the 15 signs in the comparison between U and U^S, whereas it is only 4 out of 15 in the comparison between U and U^C. As to the balan-

TABLE 4.12

SIGN CORRESPONDENCE BETWEEN THE TRADERS' INEQUALITY COEFFICIENTS AND PROPORTIONS: GERMAN LEATHER AND SHOE INDUSTRY, 1951–1953

Variables	*Test variates*				
	increases	*no change*	*decreases*	*balance*	*disconformity index*
			U and U^M		
T	+	+	−	+	+
I	−	+	+	+	−
S	−	−	+	−	+
p_b	+	+	+	−	−
p_s	−	+	+	−	−
			U and U^S		
T	0	+	+	0	+
I	+	+	+	+	−
S	−	+	0	−	−
p_b	+	−	+	+	−
p_s	+	+	+	+	0
			U and U^C		
T	−	−	+	−	−
I	+	−	−	−	+
S	+	+	−	+	−
p_b	−	−	−	−	+
p_s	−	−	−	−	+

ces, we find the same sign pattern (+ for U^M and U^S, − for U^C) in 9 cases out of 15. Combining balances and basic test variates and disregarding ties, we find 41 signs which are in accordance with the hypothesis and 16 which contradict it. When viewed as a whole, therefore, the outcomes of Table 4.12 may be regarded as a moderately strong corroboration of the hypothesis formulated in 2.5.3. That we cannot be more certain is due to the complicated interdependence of the signs of the table: there is not only the mathematical relation between the three proportions (+ signs in corresponding places of the comparisons between U and U^M and between U and U^S imply always a — sign for U and U^C), but there is also the economic relationship between different variables, like buying and selling prices.

4.4.3. We proceed to the partial inequality coefficients U_M, U_S, U_C. Since their numerical magnitude has already been considered implicitly in the analysis of the inequality proportions, we shall confine ourselves here to their signs. A survey of signs is given in Table 4.13.

TABLE 4.13

SIGNS OF THE PARTIAL INEQUALITY COEFFICIENTS U_M AND U_S: GERMAN LEATHER AND SHOE INDUSTRY, 1951–1953

Variables	*Stages*	*Test variates*					*Test variates*				
		x^1	x^2	x^3	b	d	x^1	x^2	x^3	b	d
		Traders									
		signs of U_M					*signs of U_S*				
T	I	−	+	−	+	−	+	+	−	−	−
	III	+	+	−	+	−	+	+	−	−	−
	V	+	+	−	+	−	+	+	−	−	−
	VI	−	+	−	+	−	−	+	−	−	+
I	I	−	+	−	+	−	−	−	−	−	+
	III	+	+	−	+	−	+	−	−	−	+
	V	−	+	−	−	−	+	+	+	+	−
	VI	−	+	−	−	−	+	+	+	−	−
S	I	−	+	−	+	−	−	−	−	−	−
	III	−	+	−	+	−	−	+	+	+	+
	V	−	+	+	−	−	−	−	+	−	+
	VI	−	+	+	−	−	−	+	−	−	+
p_b	I	−	+	−	+	+	−	−	−	−	−
	III	−	+	−	+	+	−	−	−	−	−
	V	+	+	−	+	+	−	−	−	−	+
	VI	−	+	+	−	+	−	−	−	−	+
p_s	I	−	+	−	+	+	−	−	−	−	−
	III	−	+	−	+	+	−	−	−	−	+
	V	+	−	−	+	+	−	−	−	−	+
	VI	+	−	−	+	+	−	−	−	−	+
		Manufacturers									
		signs of U_M					*signs of U_S*				
P	II	−	+	−	+	−	−	−	−	−	+
	IV	−	+	−	+	−	−	+	−	−	−
p_s	II	−	+	−	+	−	−	−	−	−	−
	IV	+	+	−	+	−	+	+	−	−	+

First, we consider U_M. It is seen that this coefficient has by far the simplest sign pattern for the fractions of no change: their U_M's are positive for 22 of the 24 variables, and the two exceptions are numerically almost negligible. The obvious conclusion is that the entrepreneurs consistently underestimated the actual changes in their variables. However, one objection can be made against this conclusion: it may be that the *minimum sensibile* which thc leaders of enterprises take into account before they call small changes really changes and not cases of (approximately) no change is different for predictions and for actual development. Or in other words: the indifference intervals for predicted and actual changes need not be identical. On the other hand, although it is not easy to verify such a hypothesis, it seems at least plausible that such differences cannot be very important, for the monthly questions on recent and future development are always asked in the same questionnaire, which will generally be answered within five minutes time.

TABLE 4.14

UNDERESTIMATION OF CHANGES COMPARED WITH CORRELATIONS BETWEEN THE BALANCES OF PREDICTIONS AND OF ACTUAL DEVELOPMENT: GERMAN LEATHER AND SHOE INDUSTRY, 1951–1953

Variables	*Traders*						
		Industry stages				*Inversions*	
		I	*III*	*V*	*VI*	*all*	*excl. VI*
T	underestimation ($\bar{P}$–$\bar{A}$)* correlation (r_b)*	0.11 0.62	0.13 0.67	0.06 0.77	0.15 0.86	2	2
I	underestimation correlation	0.13 0.46	0.10 0.62	0.10 0.85	0.12 0.86	$3\frac{1}{2}$	$2\frac{1}{2}$
S	underestimation correlation	0.11 0.29	0.12 0.21	0.02 0.78	0.08 0.86	4	2
p_b	underestimation correlation	0.19 0.65	0.15 0.78	–0.00 0.90	0.00 0.95	$5\frac{1}{2}$	3
p_s	underestimation correlation	0.20 0.64	0.10 0.82	–0.00 0.88	–0.01 0.94	6	3

	Manufacturers			
		Industry stages		*Inversions*
		II	*IV*	
P	underestimation correlation	0.07 0.72	0.07 0.82	$\frac{1}{2}$
p_s	underestimation correlation	0.17 0.82	0.04 0.91	1

* See text.

It is possible to specify these outcomes for the no-change fractions a little further. Table 4.14 contains, for each of the twenty-four variables, the average no-change fraction of predictions ($\bar{P}$, say) minus that of actual outcomes ($\bar{A}$), and the correlation (r_b) between the balance series of these two quantities. The no-change difference $\bar{P} - \bar{A}$ may be regarded as a quantitative indicator of the underestimation of changes; the balance correlation describes the degree to which the ups and downs in the central tendency of actual microchanges are reflected in the central tendency of predicted changes.[1] When taking the seven variables (i.e., the successive double rows of Table 4.14) separately, it seems that the two measures are negatively associated: as a whole, there are $22\frac{1}{2}$ inversions between the r_b- and the corresponding $\bar{P} - \bar{A}$-rankings as against an attainable maximum of 32, or about 70 per cent of the maximum. The greater part of the "exceptions" is concentrated in the last stage, VI; if it is excluded, the percentage rises above 80. We should conclude, therefore, that the underestimation of changes is often greater when the entrepreneurs show the least forecasting power as far as the central tendency of their opinions is considered; possibly, however, with the exception of the retailers in shoes. It may be that this deviation is due to the sociological structure of this group of firms, which consists of retailers only. Small firms are in general not well-equipped for forecasting purposes and must, hence, often report "no change" when "no idea" would be a more realistic alternative, even though the stage as a whole is in a position to predict at least the direction of the aggregate fluctuations relatively precisely.

4.4.4. Next, we consider the U_M's of the other basic test variates and of the balances.

The mere fact that U_M is generally positive for the no-change category implies that this coefficient must be negative in the majority of cases for the fractions of increases and of decreases. Indeed, U_M is negative for the fractions of increases for 17 of the 24 variables, and the same holds for the decreases for 21 variables. Negativity of U_M is a more pronounced trait of the latter fractions, which also follows

[1] Correlations are to be preferred here to inequality coefficients, because the latter —contrary to the former—are influenced by the inequality of the means of the balance series, so that the association analysed in this paragraph could be partly spurious when inequality coefficients had been used.

In Table 4.14 (as well as in the further tables of this chapter), ties in two decimal places are considered as half inversions.

from the fact that U_M of the balances is positive for 19 variables. Since all variables (except possibly stocks) are positively associated with general trade cycle conditions, we should conclude that the entrepreneurs had on the average more optimistic (or less pessimistic) expectations of these conditions than their own reports on actual outcomes justified—at least, during the period considered. The few exceptions to this rule are all concentrated in the stages V and VI, so that the conclusion may be given for the higher stages with greater confidence.

4.4.5. It may be considered rather remarkable that the inequality of central tendency is characterised, in spite of its rather small contribution to total inequality as measured by the bias proportions, by such regular features as those found above. Nevertheless, it seems rather obvious that, when proceeding to the coefficients U_S which are still smaller than U_M, we should not expect to find so much regularity here. But two interesting traits can be indicated.

First, U_S of the balance series is negative for 22 of the 24 variables. This, together with the fact that the U_M's of the balances are generally positive (cf. 4.4.4), implies that the balances of the forecast test series are frequently distributed with smaller variation around algebraically larger averages than the corresponding actual outcomes. We could say, therefore, that the waves of optimism and pessimism show smaller amplitudes and more optimism on the average than the actual outcomes, as reported afterwards by the forecasters themselves, justify. This effect is closely related to the underestimation of changes, first because the larger no-change fractions of predictions reduce the range of their balances, second because a reduction of the fractions of increases and decreases resulting from these larger no-change fractions compels the balances to move in the direction of zero; and, indeed, the above-mentioned algebraically larger averages are frequently means closer to zero, most of the balance series having negative averages.

Secondly, the U_S's of the basic test variates of the traders' prices are all negative. Similarly, there is a slight negative majority for the basic test variates of all other variables combined, which becomes somewhat more substantial (about two thirds) when the no-change category is disregarded. Part of this effect is no doubt due to the reduction of the individual fractions of increases and decreases for predictions as compared with actual development; but, obviously, this does not apply to the traders' prices, where $U_S < 0$ for all basic test variates, including the no-change category. The appropriate explanation is perhaps that, if a particular type of change (increase, no change or decrease) is predicted for next month, and if this change does not take place, the forecaster will often predict the same type again. The existence of such a "tenacity effect," which may be quite rational when the forecaster feels sure about the phenomenon itself but not about the time of its appearance, is corroborated to some extent by the fact that turning points as measured by balances (cf. Section 4.3) were rather frequently predicted too early: not much less than one half of the first-kind errors can be "explained" in this way that turning points were predicted for the months t and $t+1$ but occurred only in $t+1$, or even for t, $t+1$, $t+2$ with an actual turning point not before $t+2$. If we accept this explanation, the turning point prediction of the firms under consideration can no longer be considered as satisfactory as the first sentences of 4.3.2 suggested: the total number of turning points, though about equal to the total number of actual turning points, is then "inflated" by "double-counting."

4.5. Accuracy Analysis by Means of Test Variates (2)

4.5.1. We proceed to consider whether any accuracy differences exist with respect to the separate stages of the industry and with respect to other criteria. Table 4.15 gives some indications for our traders. It contains, for each variable and for each test variate, the number of inversions between the ranking of their stages in the order I, III, V, VI (i.e., according to decreasing distance from the ultimate consumer) and two alternative rankings describing the success of forecasting, viz., according to decreasing values of U and according to increasing values of r. It appears that the total number of inversions in the U-comparisons for all basic test variates combined is 20, as against an attainable maximum of 90; and for r it is only $9\frac{1}{2}$. This suggests that the quality of the forecasts increases when we approach the stages near to the consumer.[1] Although the individual outcomes of the table are significant at the 5 per cent level only if the number of inversions is zero, there can

[1] It is interesting in this connection that the fraction of first-kind turning point errors that can be ascribed to the tenacity effect (cf. 4.4.5) increases in the neighbourhood of the consumer: for stage I it is 0.1; for III, 0.3; for V, 0.6; for VI, 0.7. An adequate explanation is perhaps that lower stages feel surer about their predictions.

be no doubt that the results for all basic test variates together are highly significant. The same holds for the balances, where the total number of inversions is 2 according to U and 1 according to r; and the same probably holds for the manufacturers as well, although the number of supporting data is small. The difference between the results of the U- and those of the r-rankings for the basic test variates is wholly due to the no-change category, which shows thirteen inversions for the U-ranking. This, in turn, is largely due to the relatively substantial underestimation of changes by the shoe retailers (cf. 4.4.3); if their stage is disregarded, only four inversions for the no-change fractions remain.

Confining ourselves to the inversions according to U in Table 4.15,

TABLE 4.15

INVERSIONS BETWEEN THE RANKING OF THE TRADERS ACCORDING TO DECREASING DISTANCE FROM THE CONSUMER AND THOSE ACCORDING TO INEQUALITY AND CORRELATION COEFFICIENTS OF THEIR PREDICTIONS AND ACTUAL SERIES: GERMAN LEATHER AND SHOE INDUSTRY, 1951–1953

Variables	*Test variates*					*Test variates*				
	x^1	x^2	x^3	b	d	x^1	x^2	x^3	b	d
	according to decreasing U					*according to increasing r*				
sales	0	3	2	1	3	1	0	1	0	4
purchases	1	5	1	1	$1\frac{1}{2}$	0	$\frac{1}{2}$	0	0	1
stocks	$\frac{1}{2}$	5	$\frac{1}{2}$	0	$3\frac{1}{2}$	0	2	1	1	3
buying prices	1	0	0	0	$\frac{1}{2}$	1	0	$\frac{1}{2}$	0	0
selling prices	1	0	0	0	0	1	$\frac{1}{2}$	1	0	0

we see that the prices show the clearest association between the distance from the consumer and forecasting quality. Perhaps this is natural, because the lower stages (those engaged in shoe manufacturing and selling) are in a position to observe the price movements of their raw materials occurring in higher stages, whereas the latter do not have such a source of information at their disposal. On the other hand, just these stages should be in a somewhat better position to observe fluctuations in quantities, since these are generally generated by the ultimate consumer and propagated by the lower stages to the higher ones. Some corroboration of these different propagation directions is given in Table 4.16, which contains the number of inversions between the ranking of the traders according to decreasing distance from the consumer and the ranking according to decreasing quartiles of disconformity indices (cf. Table 4.4 above). It appears that the price

TABLE 4.16

INVERSIONS BETWEEN THE RANKING OF THE TRADERS ACCORDING TO DECREASING DISTANCE FROM THE CONSUMER AND THAT ACCORDING TO DECREASING QUARTILES OF DISCONFORMITY INDICES: GERMAN LEATHER AND SHOE INDUSTRY, 1951–1953

Quartiles	*Variables*				
	T	I	S	p_b	p_s
lower	3	$4\frac{1}{2}$	3	$\frac{1}{2}$	$2\frac{1}{2}$
median	4	$5\frac{1}{2}$	$4\frac{1}{2}$	1	2
upper	5	5	6	1	0
	$\bar{T}$	$\bar{I}$	$\bar{S}$	$\bar{p}_b$	$\bar{p}_s$
lower	3	5	4	1	1
median	3	6	6	$1\frac{1}{2}$	$1\frac{1}{2}$
upper	$4\frac{1}{2}$	6	4	$1\frac{1}{2}$	$\frac{1}{2}$

variables show a small number of inversions, their average for all quartiles combined being about 1 for predictions as well as actual development (the attainable maximum being 6), whereas for the other variables (T, I, S) this figure is about $4\frac{1}{2}$. Similar results can be obtained for the manufacturers, although they are small in number. These outcomes suggest that the disconformity among entrepreneurs decreases in the neighbourhood of the consumer when prices are considered, whereas the opposite takes place for the other variables. Or, to put it more picturesquely, the variance of reality and ideas diminishes when we leave the place of their generation. Therefore, one might think that, in view of the propagation "from below," higher stages should be superior forecasters of non-price variables—which is, except for the no-change category, opposite to the findings of Table 4.15. The reason for this different outcome is probably twofold. First, although it is true that the propagation direction for these variables is as stated above, this is of limited help for the higher stages when they do not know very much about what is happening below them. In the extreme case of total absence of information of this kind this would imply that, *ceteris paribus*, all stages are equally successful in forecasting these variables. Second, there may be seasonal fluctuations which facilitate forecasting. If the seasonal patterns are more pronounced for the lower stages, the *ceteris paribus* clause is not fulfilled, and we should expect a better forecasting record for these firms. Table 4.17 gives some indications in this direction. It contains the correlations between the balances of all non-price variables of the traders, both actual and predicted, and the same balance series lagged twelve months. If there is some pronounced seasonality, we should expect positive correlations; if there is none, we should expect them to be distributed around zero, trends

TABLE 4.17

TWELVE-MONTH LAG CORRELATIONS OF THE BALANCES OF THE TRADERS' NON-PRICE VARIABLES: GERMAN LEATHER AND SHOE INDUSTRY, 1951–1953

Stages	*Variables*					
	T	I	S	$\bar{T}$	$\bar{I}$	$\bar{S}$
I	0.41	0.42	0.39	0.19	0.60	0.27
III	0.79	0.58	0.30	0.80	0.79	0.23
V	0.45	0.47	0.32	0.87	0.75	0.73
VI	0.75	0.86	0.83	0.90	0.84	0.79

being of minor importance. Table 4.17 reveals that all twenty-four correlations are positive, and that twelve of them exceed 0.7; it is therefore reasonable to conclude that some seasonality does exist, which is in accordance with the information supplied in 4.1.4. This is certainly a factor which should be taken into account when appraising forecasting success.[1] The correlations show some tendency to increase in the consumer's neighbourhood; the total number of inversions of the rankings according to increasing correlation and to decreasing distance from the consumer is only 2 in the case of the prediction series, and 5 in that of actual development (18 being the attainable maximum in both cases). These results lead us to the tentative conclusion that the better forecasting records of the lower stages with respect to non-price variables are at least partly due to the fact that they made a larger use of seasonality than the higher stages; and perhaps that they made even more use of it than the actual outcomes justified—cf. the somewhat higher correlations for the predictions of V and VI compared with those of their actual development.

4.5.2. Table 4.18 is devoted to a comparison of variables. It contains, for each of the four industry stages I, III, V, VI and for each of the five test variates, the ranking of the five variables (T, I, S, p_b, p_s) according to increasing inequality and decreasing correlation coeffi-

[1] This point, and the "tenacity effect," are the two main qualifications of the turning point analysis; cf. the beginning of 4.3.1 and the end of 4.4.5.

TABLE 4.18

RANKING OF VARIABLES ACCORDING TO INCREASING INEQUALITY AND DECREASING CORRELATION COEFFICIENTS, BY STAGES AND TEST VARIATES: GERMAN LEATHER AND SHOE INDUSTRY, 1951–1953

Test variates	*Variables*	*Stages* according to increasing *U*				*Sum*	*Stages* according to decreasing *r*				*Sum*
		I	*III*	*V*	*VI*		*I*	*III*	*V*	*VI*	
x^1	*T*	2	1	4	1	8	3	3	4	3	13
	I	1	2	3	4	10	4	4	3	4	15
	S	5	4–5	5	5	19½	5	5	5	5	20
	p_b	3	4–5	1	2	10½	1	2	1	1	5
	p_s	4	3	2	3	12	2	1	2	2	7
x^2	*T*	3	5	3–4	5	16½	3	4	4	4	15
	I	2	3	3–4	3–4	12	1	3	3	3	10
	S	1	1	5	3–4	10½	2	5	5	5	17
	p_b	4	4	1–2	1–2	11	5	2	1	1	9
	p_s	5	2	1–2	1–2	10	4	1	2	2	9
x^3	*T*	3–5	5	3	5	17	3	3	2	5	13
	I	2	4	1	2–3	9½	4	4	1	3	12
	S	1	1	2	4	8	5	5	3–4	4	17½
	p_b	3–5	3	5	1	13	2	2	5	1	10
	p_s	3–5	2	4	2–3	12½	1	1	3–4	2	7½
b	*T*	1–3	3–4	5	3	13½	3	3	5	3–5	15
	I	4	3–4	3	4	14½	4	4	3	3–5	15
	S	5	5	4	5	19	5	5	4	3–5	18
	p_b	1–3	2	1	1	6	1	2	1	1	5
	p_s	1–3	1	2	2	7	2	1	2	2	7
d	*T*	3	2	3	5	13	3	1	5	5	14
	I	2	1	2	3	8	2	2	4	3	11
	S	1	3	1	4	9	1	5	3	4	13
	p_b	4–5	4–5	5	1	15	5	4	2	1	12
	p_s	4–5	4–5	4	2	15	4	3	1	2	10

cients. Low rank numbers are hence indicators of relatively good forecasting. The table contains also the sum of the rank numbers over all four stages, for each variable and test variate separately. Ties in two decimal places are indicated by double or triple ranks (1–2, 3–5, etc.), but in the sum columns these are replaced by averages (viz., 1½, 4, etc.).

Confining ourselves first to the basic test variates, we find a fairly regular pattern for the rankings according to decreasing correlation coefficients. The lowest ranks are those of buying and selling prices (with total rank numbers of 24 and $23\frac{1}{2}$, respectively), next are purchases and sales (with total ranks of 37 and 41, respectively), and the last is stocks, with a total number of $54\frac{1}{2}$. In view of these large differences it seems rather safe to conclude that, as far as the basic test variates are considered, the best predictions according to the correlation criterion have been made for buying and selling prices, and that stocks are worst among the non-price variables. It will be noted that the latter conclusion corroborates the turning point analysis of 4.3.3. It is also interesting to note that there are no appreciable differences between related expectations and plans, i.e., between buying and selling prices, and between sales and purchases.

The inequality criterion shows much less regularity for the basic test variates, with the result that the difference between the largest and the smallest total number of ranks, which is 31 when the correlation criterion is adopted ($54\frac{1}{2}$ for stocks minus $23\frac{1}{2}$ for buying prices), is here only 10. We must conclude that the regularity found in the preceding paragraph is a matter of general linearity, not of equality. On the other hand, when leaving the realm of basic test variates and proceeding to the balances, the regularity is fully restored: the price variables occupy —either individually or jointly—the first two places, and stocks the last, according to both criteria (U and r) and for practically all traders. For the manufacturers we have exactly the same situation: selling prices have been predicted better than production (a non-price variable) if we take the basic test variates and accept the correlation criterion, not if we take the inequality criterion; but both criteria show the same picture when we consider balances instead of basic test variates. Our conclusion must be, therefore, that there exists a clear pattern of forecasting quality differences with respect to separate variables if we accept the central-tendency aggregation procedure implied by the use of balances; but that the components of this aggregation—more generally, the basic test variates—show such a pattern only if the criterion of forecasting quality is that of a linear relationship with positive slope between forecasts and actual values.

4.5.3. Balances were introduced in Section 4.2 in order to serve as a measure of central tendency of microchanges. There is a wide-spread belief among economists that such measures are subject to more stability and regularity than their components. If we accept this, we should expect balance series of predictions and of actual development to be characterised by more, certainly not less, regularity than that found for basic test variates.

When reconsidering our empirical results, it is seen that this at least is an expectation which is rather well fulfilled. The correlations between balances of predictions and those of actual development are on the average larger than those of the basic test variates (cf. Table 4.9). It is true, the inequality coefficients show a different picture, but this could be easily explained. The signs of the partial inequality coefficients U_M of the balances show a high degree of regularity—just as those belonging to the basic test variates—, and the regularity of the signs of their U_S's exceeds that of the signs for the basic test variates (cf. Table 4.13). Both according to U and according to r there is an almost perfect rank correlation between the traders' distance from the ultimate consumer and the quality of their forecasts when balances are considered, but a lower correlation when any of the basic test variates is taken instead (cf. Table 4.15).

Finally, only when balances are considered there is a clear pattern of differences of forecasting power with respect to separate variables, according to both U and r – cf. 4.5.2. An attempt to exhibit this effect geometrically is made in Fig. 4.8. It is a three-dimensional scatter, with the inequality coefficients of the balance series of predictions and actual development along the vertical axis, and the successive industry stages and the variables along the horizontal axes. For this purpose, stages and variables have to be "quantified," i.e., they have to be represented by two numerical variables. In the diagram this is performed in such a way that a satisfactory fit is obtained. It is seen that the fit is indeed satisfactory; but it must be admitted, of course, that the "quantification" implies the adjustment of a rather large number of parameters.

4.5.4. When proceeding to the other derived test variates, the disconformity indices, we find an entirely different picture. Table 4.9 shows that the correlations between predictions and actual outcomes are lowest for this category, and the only two negative correlations belong to these test variates. Whereas Table 4.12 shows a plausible and fairly regular sign pattern for the basic test variates and the balances, the signs for the disconformity indices seem for the greater part opposite to what could be expected *a priori*. It is preferable, however, not to attach too much value to this result, because Table 4.12 is

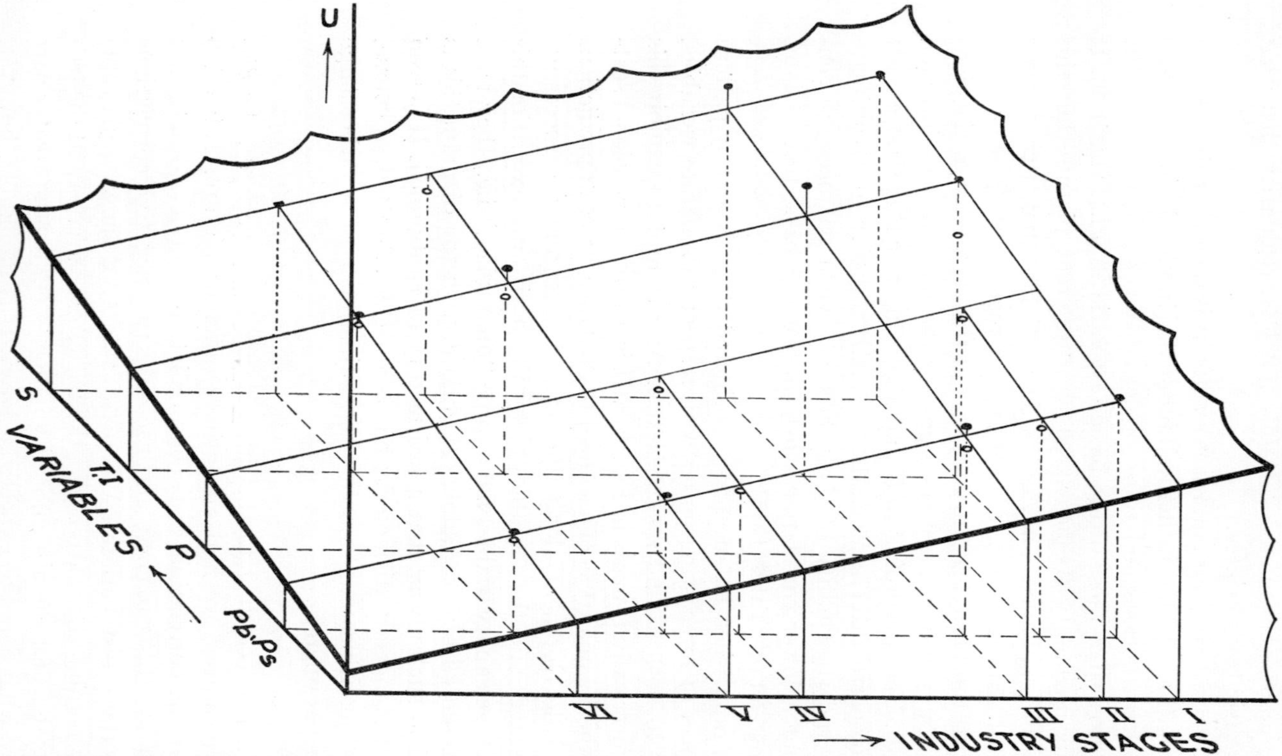

Fig. 4.8. Three-dimensional scatter and regression connecting the inequality coefficients (U) of the balance series of predictions and actual development with the successive predicting stages of the German leather and shoe industry (I, traders in hides; II, tanneries; III, leather traders; IV, shoe manufacturers; V, shoe wholesalers; VI, shoe retailers), and with the variables predicted (p_b, buying prices; p_s, selling prices; P, production; T, sales; I, purchases; S, stocks). Dots are points above the regression plane, small circles points below the plane

based on differences between inequality coefficients, which are quite small for the disconformity indices, two thirds of these U's being concentrated in the interval (0.2, 0.3). Furthermore, as to the signs of the partial inequality coefficients U_S, it seems impossible to detect any regularity for the U_S's of these test variates in Table 4.13. Table 4.15 shows a negligible rank correlation between the rankings according to distance from the consumer and forecasting quality when disconformity indices and non-price variables are considered. Table 4.18 shows that the rankings of variables are, in the case of these test variates, rather irregular. It is remarkable indeed to find that, whereas the basic test variates show regularity according to r only and the balances according to both U and r, the disconformity indices do not show much regularity at all, either according to U or according to r.

Only two regular traits can be detected for these test variates from the tables of this and the preceding section. First, their U_M's are positive for the traders' prices and negative for all other variables. Second, there is an almost perfect rank correlation between the forecasting quality of these prices and the distance from the consumer. The first phenomenon is nothing else than a restatement of the remarks made in 4.2.6, to which we may therefore refer; it is clear that the underestimation of changes is at least partly responsible for the negative U_M's of the disconformity indices. The second is due to the extremely low (and sometimes negative) correlations for the disconformity indices in the higher stages, and to the fact that the correlations for the basic test variates in the lower stages are so close to unity (in stage VI, e.g., they are all above 0.9) that the disconformity indices, being single-valued functions of the basic test variates, cannot have very low correlations.

As a whole, therefore, the disconformity indices of prediction series as compared with those of corresponding actual series show very little regularity, and the results obtained here suggest an "irregular Kollektiv"[1] rather than anything else. Perhaps this is a good thing for the classical type of economic research, which is primarily concerned with the analysis of central tendencies of microchanges, not with the variance around these tendencies. For, if such variances would show

[1] Cf. R. VON MISES, *Probability, Statistics and Truth* (London, 1939). The only exception is (cf. above) that the disconformity indices of prediction series are in general smaller than those of the corresponding series of actual development.

clear and well-defined patterns, their neglect might lead to new types of bias beyond those with which we are already familiar.

4.5.5. When reconsidering the analysis of this chapter, it seems that two main types of conclusions can be drawn.

The first deals with the adequacy of the data. All figures underlying the analysis have been collected from the participating firms on a voluntary basis, and nothing prevents entrepreneurs to falsify their reports and plans—nothing, except for the common sense of the collectors of the data. The best method for judging their adequacy is, therefore, to see whether the conclusions derived from them are plausible. This appraisal can be rather positive. Underestimation of changes is a prediction error which we already observed in the preceding chapter. Better forecasting results for prices in lower stages is another plausible result. A third example is the greater regularity found for balances when compared with disconformity indices. A fourth is the rather poor forecasting record for stocks.

Given a favourable appraisal of the underlying data as a whole, we may have some confidence in results that are not so immediately plausible. One example is that of the nearly identical forecasting qualities of comparable instruments and exogenous variables: selling and buying prices, and purchases and sales. Another is the quantitative result of the turning point analysis, both φ's being about 0.35–0.4 for all variables combined—though we must add that seasonality and tenacity effects have contributed to this result. Still another is the remarkably simple picture of Fig. 4.8, which shows that the forecasting record of all twenty-four variables can be approximately described by a two-dimensional plane, provided that stages and variables are suitably arranged. This arrangement suggests that the leather and shoe industry consists of two "clusters" as regards forecasting success, viz., the firms engaged in the selling and manufacturing of leather and hides, and those engaged in the selling and manufacturing of shoes; furthermore, that the "forecasting quality distance" (measured by the inequality coefficient) between stocks on the one hand and sales and purchases on the other is smaller than that between the latter variables and prices.

Appendix to Chapter IV

4.A. Tables and Comments

Table 4.19 contains the monthly fractions of increases and decreases (multiplied by 100) for the variables analysed in this chapter. Two things should be noted. First, as to the manufacturer's stocks, the questionnaire contains a question whether the firm has any stocks at its disposal. The percentage of entrepreneurs who answer negatively (which is usually small) are to be found in the columns under 0. The computations reported in this chapter are based on the conditional distribution over the three possibilities (increase, no change, decrease), the condition being that stocks are not absent. Second, the questionnaire asks the manufacturers for predicted changes over two-month periods instead of one-month periods. The analysis of this chapter is based on the assumption that, in fact, the manufacturers predict, just as the traders, over one-month periods; the reason being, first, that O. ANDERSON, R. K. BAUER and E. FELS suggested that this was presumably true,[1] second that the "weight" of the manufacturers in the present analysis is relatively small, viz., only four of the twenty-four variables. Hence the analysis as a whole cannot be seriously affected even if the assumption is incorrect.

Table 4.20 contains the means, standard deviations, correlations, etc., of the test vector series. They are also multiplied by 100.

[1] "On the Accuracy of Short-Term Expectations," *Proceedings of the Business and Economic Statistics Section of the American Statistical Association* (September 1954), pp. 124–147. We shall come back to this point in Chapter V (Section 5.4).

TABLE 4.19

TEST VARIATES (MULTIPLIED BY 100) OF THE GERMAN LEATHER AND SHOE INDUSTRY, 1951–1953

	Variables (and industry stages)											
	sales (*I*)		*sales expected* (*I*)		*purchases* (*I*)		*purchases planned* (*I*)		*stocks* (*I*)		*stocks expected* (*I*)	
	x^1	x^3	x^1	x^3	x^1	x^3	x^1	x^3	x^1	x^3	x^1	x^3
1951, J	67	16	.	.	50	33	.	.	16	67	.	.
F	15	54	50	17	8	46	33	0	0	42	17	0
M	14	29	23	23	8	8	23	0	21	21	0	8
A	0	100	0	43	13	62	14	0	56	0	7	7
M	6	65	11	78	19	31	22	34	30	35	45	11
J	17	50	38	6	23	39	20	20	15	31	19	25
J	20	73	29	7	33	33	15	39	27	27	21	29
A	8	46	27	46	15	39	0	27	31	23	33	20
S	56	5	61	0	39	11	46	0	28	16	23	38
O	63	0	61	0	63	6	33	6	25	25	11	11
N	27	20	0	19	43	7	31	6	14	14	37	6
D	0	25	0	50	25	17	0	7	25	8	29	7
1952, J	31	38	8	38	25	25	15	8	6	38	15	15
F	0	82	0	25	0	75	25	31	8	75	6	25
M	23	46	17	66	15	54	25	42	8	46	16	42
A	7	64	8	23	14	36	0	15	43	21	0	31
M	15	54	7	79	15	46	14	29	8	23	29	7
J	42	16	23	15	17	33	8	15	17	67	15	31
J	40	13	58	17	20	53	25	42	0	50	0	58
A	47	20	29	0	60	20	36	21	33	34	14	36
S	15	0	15	23	31	15	38	8	8	17	23	15
O	17	8	0	17	17	17	25	0	17	33	20	10
N	47	6	17	0	53	14	25	0	21	29	25	8
D	38	8	20	0	38	8	14	14	22	8	0	20
1953, J	9	18	17	8	0	20	17	17	27	18	17	8
F	7	29	0	33	7	21	0	27	7	14	18	18
M	23	15	8	7	0	15	0	28	0	38	0	21
A	27	27	0	9	9	36	15	15	9	36	15	8
M	15	23	16	42	8	30	17	50	8	38	17	25
J	35	9	9	0	35	26	8	46	9	26	0	38
J	9	36	0	19	9	36	9	26	0	32	0	18
A	23	9	53	12	23	32	15	20	18	18	10	15
S	16	4	50	0	17	9	36	9	0	32	14	14
O	24	28	12	0	24	19	24	0	24	24	24	8
N	.	.	24	19	.	.	52	0	.	.	48	0

TABLE 4.19 (*continued*)

	Variables (and industry stages)									
	buying prices (*I*)		*buying prices expected* (*I*)		*selling prices* (*I*)		*selling prices planned* (*I*)		*position with regard to orders* (*II*)	
	x^1	x^3	x^1	x^3	x^1	x^3	x^1	x^3	x^1	x^3
1951, J	100	0	.	.	100	0	.	.	29	4
F	85	0	67	0	85	0	67	0	0	19
M	0	21	38	24	0	43	38	24	2	67
A	0	100	0	79	0	100	0	79	3	74
M	18	76	0	89	12	82	0	89	3	49
J	77	8	47	0	72	14	47	0	18	36
J	0	93	50	14	0	100	57	14	7	46
A	0	85	13	54	0	85	13	54	28	15
S	100	0	61	0	100	0	50	0	56	3
O	69	12	83	0	57	6	83	0	75	6
N	14	40	6	50	14	33	6	50	20	23
D	0	100	0	57	0	100	0	57	5	37
1952, J	0	100	0	62	0	100	0	62	9	55
F	0	100	0	50	0	100	0	56	5	63
M	8	46	0	92	8	54	0	92	5	44
A	0	93	8	15	0	100	8	15	22	34
M	8	53	0	86	8	69	0	86	16	38
J	83	0	46	0	83	0	38	0	58	13
J	100	0	42	0	93	0	42	8	33	30
A	29	57	64	0	29	57	64	0	47	11
S	0	54	16	42	0	54	16	42	42	25
O	0	25	0	50	0	27	0	58	48	18
N	86	0	17	0	86	0	9	0	59	9
D	38	0	27	7	41	0	27	7	34	35
1953, J	0	82	0	17	0	82	0	17	22	49
F	7	7	0	64	0	7	0	64	15	61
M	31	0	7	7	38	0	7	7	18	52
A	0	73	8	15	0	73	8	15	4	67
M	69	0	8	25	69	0	8	25	25	40
J	43	0	23	0	43	0	23	0	30	35
J	26	26	0	17	14	24	0	17	19	26
A	64	0	35	15	77	0	40	0	33	30
S	24	16	50	0	24	16	50	0	31	24
O	0	53	0	32	0	52	0	24	35	18
N	.	.	0	43	.	.	0	43	.	.

TABLE 4.19 (*continued*)

	Variables (and industry stages)										
	production (II)		production planned (II)		daily work-time (II)		stocks (II)			appraisal of stocks (II)	
	x^1	x^3	x^1	x^3	x^1	x^3	x^1	x^3	0	x^1	x^3
1951, J	20	4	.	.	1	5	1	54	11	0	62
F	11	10	6	4	0	5	3	53	10	0	54
M	2	15	1	17	0	6	15	13	7	1	37
A	0	36	0	15	0	31	67	4	6	18	6
M	0	50	0	30	0	39	72	6	2	42	0
J	2	51	3	41	0	44	59	4	2	38	0
J	0	43	4	19	0	43	79	5	3	45	5
A	3	18	1	11	3	20	53	11	2	44	1
S	3	6	11	7	18	0	12	37	4	14	6
O	36	2	19	17	23	2	5	55	1	11	7
N	27	12	14	6	25	11	2	47	5	22	10
D	5	14	9	16	3	12	15	33	3	11	9
1952, J	8	12	6	24	5	9	30	12	2	33	8
F	2	20	7	2	0	10	43	6	1	51	0
M	0	23	2	25	0	16	55	3	2	45	0
A	7	22	5	17	4	14	39	5	0	37	0
M	3	36	7	12	3	33	47	16	1	49	3
J	16	13	0	16	18	5	20	32	1	22	5
J	27	3	14	1	6	3	21	22	2	29	7
A	24	2	20	0	6	1	4	25	1	15	3
S	31	0	1	1	13	0	8	35	3	17	5
O	24	0	8	1	15	0	7	49	4	19	10
N	26	5	11	0	14	1	3	34	5	13	13
D	18	7	15	3	8	0	5	51	5	6	13
1953, J	6	16	14	2	6	7	15	23	8	10	8
F	11	4	9	2	3	2	29	9	13	15	8
M	10	8	10	3	1	7	45	3	15	25	10
A	0	13	5	9	0	10	42	5	11	28	7
M	1	18	2	17	0	8	40	14	6	32	1
J	5	25	5	14	0	17	35	20	5	25	0
J	8	16	19	8	3	11	42	8	3	22	2
A	6	13	21	11	3	2	26	15	6	27	4
S	12	7	20	6	10	3	6	30	3	19	3
O	23	2	9	5	6	1	1	50	6	19	10
N	.	.	13	2	.	.	.	.	.	.	.

TABLE 4.19 (*continued*)

	Variables (and industry stages)											
	selling prices (*II*)		*selling prices planned* (*II*)		*sales* (*III*)		*sales expected* (*III*)		*purchases* (*III*)		*purchases planned* (*III*)	
	x^1	x^3	x^1	x^3	x^1	x^3	x^1	x^3	x^1	x^3	x^1	x^3
1951, J	90	0	58	0	83	0	.	.	58	17	.	.
F	69	0	48	0	0	77	33	17	18	59	25	17
M	28	5	63	0	5	90	12	35	11	61	6	35
A	6	31	24	2	0	88	10	45	12	76	0	39
M	1	73	3	39	4	75	6	53	0	79	6	35
J	5	59	4	27	26	24	21	29	17	20	17	16
J	0	43	7	5	4	63	17	26	8	44	17	15
A	0	84	0	42	36	32	50	21	32	18	50	13
S	21	36	2	13	62	9	68	0	50	5	50	0
O	29	2	32	1	62	0	67	0	52	15	43	0
N	3	35	9	3	35	15	28	0	25	10	14	10
D	0	32	0	24	5	64	0	61	0	45	0	47
1952, J	0	71	4	35	37	26	19	45	31	32	18	50
F	0	97	0	45	15	60	37	21	10	50	32	10
M	0	92	0	66	6	59	35	10	11	42	35	20
A	0	72	0	28	9	72	41	24	9	62	29	29
M	4	66	0	44	6	50	14	27	6	44	5	19
J	40	15	10	10	42	16	28	33	53	10	22	39
J	31	2	30	1	27	18	26	26	23	18	26	29
A	30	0	46	0	36	12	65	0	28	12	50	0
S	6	13	2	0	64	8	60	4	36	24	48	4
O	3	8	0	9	24	28	40	4	14	28	20	4
N	67	2	4	7	14	14	29	0	0	14	9	5
D	60	0	35	0	13	39	0	20	26	44	0	40
1953, J	17	7	37	2	42	37	32	23	32	26	23	23
F	9	18	5	13	14	62	29	11	10	42	28	6
M	4	16	5	10	37	32	55	5	21	16	24	10
A	0	21	0	9	10	69	47	8	0	66	21	24
M	11	13	0	10	10	50	26	24	10	45	21	34
J	6	12	10	2	35	45	26	48	15	43	32	32
J	2	6	7	4	44	35	30	9	21	25	30	4
A	11	9	0	6	63	15	61	0	36	12	57	0
S	8	6	3	5	56	7	88	0	46	15	75	0
O	9	14	7	5	50	24	60	0	30	19	46	0
N	.	.	1	3	.	.	26	18	.	.	11	6

TABLE 4.19 (*continued*)

	Variables (and industry stages)											
	stocks (*III*)		*stocks expected* (*III*)		*buying prices* (*III*)		*buying prices expected* (*III*)		*selling prices* (*III*)		*selling prices planned* (*III*)	
	x^1	x^3	x^1	x^3	x^1	x^3	x^1	x^3	x^1	x^3	x^1	x^3
1951, J	8	50	.	.	100	0	.	.	92	0	.	.
F	30	29	33	0	94	0	83	9	89	0	75	8
M	17	17	0	6	22	6	53	6	6	5	38	6
A	18	29	0	33	0	63	0	22	0	63	0	22
M	4	29	6	29	0	87	0	68	0	92	0	68
J	0	33	16	17	10	40	13	15	5	52	9	15
J	13	31	9	13	0	79	13	2	0	79	4	7
A	23	36	4	35	0	86	0	50	0	84	0	52
S	14	19	32	13	43	5	5	13	29	4	5	13
O	40	25	10	23	81	0	55	0	64	0	50	0
N	21	16	0	19	10	5	10	4	10	5	10	4
D	9	34	11	21	0	19	5	35	0	14	5	32
1952, J	5	42	9	27	0	95	0	61	0	95	0	66
F	15	35	16	21	0	95	0	50	0	95	0	55
M	18	35	20	20	0	88	0	80	0	97	0	80
A	24	43	24	26	0	100	0	32	0	100	0	41
M	17	50	9	39	0	81	0	65	0	81	0	65
J	47	6	11	33	68	0	6	31	47	0	6	39
J	23	32	32	16	55	0	42	0	27	10	42	0
A	12	16	29	4	56	4	29	0	24	8	33	0
S	20	32	28	12	16	12	20	0	4	12	16	0
O	9	24	12	44	16	16	8	20	5	17	12	20
N	0	43	9	29	57	0	0	0	14	0	5	0
D	17	26	0	20	41	0	20	0	23	0	20	0
1953, J	32	32	19	14	11	5	2	0	5	5	4	0
F	33	19	21	0	0	5	0	30	0	7	0	18
M	16	24	5	24	0	7	5	14	0	3	9	14
A	16	29	5	21	0	29	5	5	5	34	5	9
M	10	30	5	24	0	15	0	29	0	10	0	24
J	23	32	32	32	0	2	5	3	0	10	5	3
J	27	39	17	9	0	8	0	13	0	2	0	13
A	14	38	23	13	2	0	0	12	6	0	0	2
S	37	17	28	31	0	0	0	0	8	0	0	0
O	10	40	27	38	8	3	0	0	4	3	0	0
N	.	.	10	25	.	.	0	12	.	.	0	19

TABLE 4.19 (*continued*)

	Variables (and industry stages)												
	position with regard to orders (*IV*)		*product-ion* (*IV*)		*product-ion planned* (*IV*)		*daily work-time* (*IV*)		*stocks* (*IV*)			*ap-praisal of stocks* (*IV*)	
	x^1	x^3	x^1	x^3	x^1	x^3	x^1	x^3	x^1	x^3	0	x^1	x^3
1951, J	14	5	36	5	.	.	0	7	17	12	7	5	49
F	2	25	8	3	19	4	1	1	9	16	6	3	54
M	1	64	10	11	7	4	1	8	18	7	11	6	33
A	2	60	0	27	1	12	0	29	39	1	1	19	31
M	2	74	6	31	0	39	0	32	31	8	2	16	41
J	17	30	6	42	0	38	1	42	61	8	3	21	2
J	27	20	2	30	0	20	5	27	49	17	10	41	9
A	48	8	12	20	11	46	12	13	30	32	5	49	5
S	16	6	10	12	9	13	11	12	15	12	4	44	3
O	37	5	22	0	6	8	21	7	2	25	8	32	13
N	47	13	22	35	12	26	29	32	7	17	3	38	3
D	22	17	2	12	5	4	3	7	14	18	3	34	3
1952, J	20	27	10	48	4	12	1	40	51	14	9	39	1
F	20	29	8	11	11	3	7	8	56	9	3	55	2
M	9	35	13	12	11	1	10	8	21	11	2	56	4
A	53	21	18	14	4	15	11	11	7	49	1	46	12
M	47	19	25	4	9	2	23	3	6	69	3	39	13
J	24	19	3	18	0	23	2	23	3	60	1	33	6
J	47	5	25	4	11	7	8	4	4	38	10	38	13
A	38	3	58	1	58	2	32	0	15	24	2	32	16
S	17	19	62	1	48	0	46	0	2	44	7	30	22
O	19	20	42	0	47	0	38	0	4	70	3	4	19
N	28	13	42	2	13	2	6	1	3	57	17	5	28
D	22	16	25	11	41	8	5	7	15	53	7	8	16
1953, J	14	28	25	23	24	9	2	22	37	13	5	13	5
F	5	44	11	11	13	1	2	8	16	12	8	6	12
M	28	38	20	7	15	4	8	3	12	43	4	11	9
A	28	28	22	8	13	5	17	7	11	49	6	10	23
M	5	59	4	25	9	10	5	25	17	37	10	16	19
J	37	10	1	32	11	25	0	29	35	27	6	14	12
J	41	16	36	5	23	4	17	5	39	19	8	11	8
A	21	46	25	1	20	2	12	1	19	30	10	20	7
S	12	47	26	1	26	0	6	5	12	51	12	13	18
O	24	43	11	8	18	0	2	5	19	33	11	19	12
N	.	.	.	.	8	9	.	.	.	.	.	.	.

TABLE 4.19 (*continued*)

	Variables (and industry stages)											
	selling prices (*IV*)		*selling prices planned* (*IV*)		*sales* (*V*)		*sales expected* (*V*)		*purchases* (*V*)		*purchases planned* (*V*)	
	x^1	x^3	x^1	x^3	x^1	x^3	x^1	x^3	x^1	x^3	x^1	x^3
1951, J	85	0	79	0	25	62	.	.	50	25	.	.
F	85	0	85	0	33	50	50	13	67	8	43	0
M	18	0	70	1	38	38	50	25	46	15	0	37
A	11	5	23	1	18	37	30	30	37	63	10	40
M	2	27	2	12	12	41	50	10	18	64	9	82
J	2	27	0	18	11	52	18	53	15	70	0	82
J	0	34	0	2	6	72	0	60	6	88	0	84
A	0	21	0	12	20	47	17	55	27	30	22	39
S	0	64	0	38	53	6	57	0	41	24	53	7
O	1	6	1	4	59	0	56	6	56	13	38	19
N	10	32	3	0	27	13	56	0	13	20	19	25
D	0	1	0	1	55	25	57	22	20	60	7	73
1952, J	0	35	0	37	0	93	14	70	0	100	17	61
F	0	44	0	34	17	50	21	15	53	26	71	15
M	0	66	6	61	55	12	66	5	28	33	37	5
A	0	47	0	29	68	6	59	12	26	26	29	18
M	7	22	0	13	38	8	32	10	27	23	21	11
J	0	51	0	26	5	81	0	50	4	73	0	64
J	0	7	1	1	52	11	14	27	22	41	14	50
A	3	4	4	1	38	29	24	36	62	24	56	12
S	16	1	15	0	61	13	80	0	52	5	57	0
O	16	0	21	0	77	0	55	5	54	14	30	10
N	13	1	23	0	54	14	52	6	41	27	10	35
D	12	2	6	0	54	14	38	14	25	46	17	52
1953, J	12	4	28	3	0	100	11	85	27	68	21	54
F	9	3	11	4	43	24	66	4	74	14	90	5
M	1	2	4	1	76	12	90	0	33	17	53	5
A	9	3	8	0	27	31	72	4	31	31	31	26
M	2	3	0	1	44	40	67	8	12	52	10	47
J	1	2	3	2	17	65	5	45	7	70	9	67
J	0	8	0	2	20	45	0	51	21	65	29	56
A	0	3	0	1	65	21	31	23	81	0	76	9
S	0	2	0	2	83	6	85	0	59	26	42	18
O	0	5	0	6	29	36	89	5	21	51	30	34
N	.	.	2	9	.	.	74	18	.	.	20	58

TABLE 4.19 (*continued*)

	Variables (and industry stages)											
	stocks (*V*)		*stocks expected* (*V*)		*buying prices* (*V*)		*buying prices expected* (*V*)		*selling prices* (*V*)		*selling prices planned* (*V*)	
	x^1	x^3	x^1	x^3	x^1	x^3	x^1	x^3	x^1	x^3	x^1	x^3
1951, J	38	37	.	.	.	.	.	.	87	0	.	.
F	91	9	13	0	100	0	87	0	100	0	75	0
M	62	7	0	27	69	0	67	8	45	0	67	8
A	36	28	17	25	18	0	33	22	14	0	33	12
M	18	29	10	70	0	29	0	9	0	25	0	27
J	10	45	0	71	0	30	0	53	0	30	0	53
J	0	67	0	79	0	58	0	16	0	64	0	25
A	7	43	17	50	0	57	0	27	0	70	0	33
S	12	17	33	20	0	18	7	23	0	18	0	30
O	31	13	19	19	6	0	12	19	0	0	6	19
N	7	20	6	44	0	7	19	0	0	0	6	0
D	10	75	0	80	0	5	0	0	0	0	0	0
1952, J	0	37	26	21	0	19	0	21	0	37	0	21
F	47	16	57	7	0	58	0	36	0	60	0	36
M	28	33	16	44	0	74	0	60	0	74	0	60
A	0	56	12	41	0	79	0	53	0	79	0	53
M	0	56	0	42	0	44	0	58	0	41	0	68
J	9	41	0	52	0	36	0	48	0	36	0	50
J	22	41	14	45	0	26	4	9	0	26	4	14
A	48	14	48	4	0	10	0	8	0	10	0	8
S	30	22	24	38	0	5	10	0	0	5	5	0
O	9	27	5	37	7	0	5	0	5	0	0	0
N	14	41	5	50	9	0	15	0	5	0	10	0
D	8	63	9	62	9	0	19	0	2	0	14	0
1953, J	39	26	25	29	9	0	9	0	4	0	9	0
F	76	5	55	0	0	0	5	0	0	5	5	0
M	36	28	37	31	0	0	0	0	0	4	0	0
A	23	27	14	43	0	12	0	0	0	8	0	0
M	8	48	4	63	0	4	0	29	0	0	0	25
J	10	65	5	57	0	5	0	14	0	5	0	14
J	24	50	36	41	0	6	0	7	0	6	0	0
A	75	0	54	14	0	0	0	0	0	0	0	0
S	47	29	27	26	0	6	0	0	0	6	0	0
O	17	23	10	47	5	0	0	0	0	0	0	0
N	.	.	0	75	.	.	0	0	.	.	0	0

TABLE 4.19 (*continued*)

	Variables (and industry stages)											
	sales (*VI*)		*sales expected* (*VI*)		*purchases* (*VI*)		*purchases planned* (*VI*)		*stocks* (*VI*)		*stocks expected* (*VI*)	
	x^1	x^3	x^1	x^3	x^1	x^3	x^1	x^3	x^1	x^3	x^1	x^3
1951, J	20	79	3	86	34	54	5	55	39	47	5	42
F	6	90	10	28	58	17	28	24	66	3	36	20
M	61	19	80	1	66	16	18	30	66	13	7	21
A	24	70	59	5	47	29	28	22	73	9	17	33
M	79	18	75	10	20	44	26	47	13	35	8	59
J	8	72	27	39	6	85	12	68	8	73	5	71
J	14	68	4	82	1	98	0	86	0	94	0	92
A	15	75	17	54	43	40	18	60	21	72	4	71
S	26	62	32	32	69	23	53	16	70	19	43	43
O	73	13	67	2	76	5	31	8	79	5	21	12
N	36	36	34	10	48	13	8	21	72	6	23	26
D	99	1	100	0	25	57	9	51	11	83	4	78
1952, J	2	98	0	90	31	62	23	60	21	63	27	50
F	2	85	16	35	47	31	55	2	59	9	53	10
M	66	28	93	0	73	17	66	11	70	3	27	22
A	97	2	96	0	39	26	23	44	30	28	8	53
M	71	16	50	3	58	20	12	41	37	32	2	65
J	3	93	4	62	2	96	0	96	4	65	0	91
J	85	2	6	33	7	91	1	87	2	94	1	90
A	3	85	4	78	74	11	63	16	73	17	59	24
S	65	21	53	18	95	3	87	2	92	3	91	1
O	92	4	96	0	53	21	44	12	66	12	54	12
N	88	7	48	10	41	15	14	38	38	22	16	49
D	100	0	88	2	23	60	13	69	4	80	5	91
1953, J	14	86	0	96	29	64	21	68	32	53	42	30
F	5	85	20	55	63	29	92	3	77	8	88	2
M	99	1	99	1	84	5	71	6	72	5	45	25
A	66	25	69	7	30	55	31	29	37	43	12	51
M	89	8	83	0	37	46	12	70	15	64	3	87
J	4	87	15	75	13	76	0	94	20	66	0	96
J	74	16	48	19	11	81	24	65	6	80	27	62
A	12	79	6	79	84	13	80	13	80	17	76	14
S	51	32	63	16	82	5	79	2	91	5	80	3
O	92	4	91	1	52	35	45	24	64	12	37	34
N	.	.	80	4	.	.	18	50	.	.	11	84

TABLE 4.19 (*concluded*)

	Variables (and industry stages)							
	buying prices (VI)		buying prices expected (VI)		selling prices (VI)		selling prices planned (VI)	
	x^1	x^3	x^1	x^3	x^1	x^3	x^1	x^3
1951, J	96	0	84	0	88	0	69	0
F	98	0	99	0	97	0	99	0
M	96	0	74	0	83	0	72	0
A	73	0	28	9	47	1	17	3
M	13	2	6	20	11	3	7	11
J	0	23	0	41	2	15	0	30
J	0	45	1	45	0	46	1	37
A	0	63	0	54	0	64	0	63
S	0	75	0	59	0	79	0	50
O	0	15	0	20	0	22	0	26
N	1	2	10	1	0	4	10	1
D	0	1	0	6	0	3	0	7
1952, J	0	18	0	6	0	22	0	8
F	0	27	0	30	0	25	0	27
M	0	66	0	57	0	59	0	57
A	0	78	0	76	0	67	0	69
M	0	56	0	66	0	64	0	61
J	0	57	0	61	0	53	0	65
J	0	59	0	44	0	70	0	47
A	5	9	1	11	0	19	0	17
S	20	7	8	4	1	9	0	4
O	21	4	44	0	4	4	23	0
N	44	0	46	0	11	0	32	0
D	43	0	48	0	13	4	36	0
1953, J	36	0	38	0	4	2	26	2
F	13	1	28	2	4	4	17	2
M	17	1	12	1	2	1	6	2
A	2	3	3	3	1	2	1	4
M	7	0	3	10	3	0	0	10
J	4	0	7	1	0	0	7	1
J	2	3	7	0	1	10	0	0
A	1	2	1	0	1	3	1	0
S	0	0	2	0	0	0	0	0
O	1	1	4	4	1	0	4	2
N	.	.	0	0	.	.	0	0

TABLE 4.20

MEANS, STANDARD DEVIATIONS, AND CORRELATION AND INEQUALITY COEFFICIENTS AND PROPORTIONS (ALL MULTIPLIED BY 100) OF TEST VECTOR TIME SERIES OF PREDICTIONS AND ACTUAL DEVELOPMENT: GERMAN LEATHER AND SHOE INDUSTRY, 1951–1953

Stage	Variable and test variate		$\bar{P}$	$\bar{A}$	s_P	s_A	r	U	U_M	U_S	U_C	U^M	U^S	U^C
I	T	x^1	20	22	19	16	53	32	−4	6	31	1	4	95
		x^2	58	47	23	20	22	26	10	3	24	14	1	84
		x^3	22	31	22	25	51	36	−13	−4	33	13	1	86
		b	−2	−9	34	37	62	44	10	−3	43	5	1	95
		d	30	39	16	16	22	29	−12	−0	26	16	0	84
	I	x^1	19	22	12	16	44	31	−6	8	30	4	7	90
		x^2	63	50	16	17	37	19	11	−1	16	34	0	65
		x^3	18	28	15	17	43	35	−18	−3	30	27	1	73
		b	1	−6	22	28	46	54	14	−12	51	7	5	88
		d	33	42	15	14	30	25	−12	2	21	23	0	76
	S	x^1	16	17	11	13	15	39	−3	−4	39	1	1	98
		x^2	65	54	14	15	27	17	9	−1	14	30	0	69
		x^3	19	29	13	15	38	33	−18	−5	28	28	2	70
		b	−3	−12	20	24	29	59	18	−9	56	9	3	88
		d	31	39	12	13	45	21	−11	−1	18	27	0	73
	p_b	x^1	22	30	24	34	63	36	−10	−13	32	8	13	79
		x^2	49	30	22	26	17	39	20	−4	33	27	1	72
		x^3	29	40	30	38	54	36	−11	−8	33	10	5	85
		b	−7	−10	50	68	65	44	2	−15	41	0	12	88
		d	26	23	13	19	−23	43	5	−11	42	1	6	93
	p_s	x^1	21	29	24	34	57	38	−10	−13	35	7	12	82
		x^2	50	29	23	25	8	40	22	−3	33	30	0	70
		x^3	29	42	30	39	57	36	−13	−9	32	13	6	81
		[illegible]	[illegible]	[illegible]	50	69	64	44	4	−16	42	1	13	87

			[illegible]	[illegible]	[illegible]	[illegible]	[illegible]	[illegible]	[illegible]	−11	23	23	16	62
		b	−3	−5	14	22	72	43	7	−23	35	2	28	69
		d	18	22	7	5	20	22	−10	4	19	19	3	77
	p_s	x^1	12	15	17	19	60	37	−6	−6	36	2	2	95
		x^2	74	56	17	25	63	19	13	−6	13	44	10	46
		x^3	14	29	17	30	91	34	−24	−20	15	47	35	18
		b	−2	−15	29	43	82	38	17	−19	28	19	25	55
		d	18	23	7	10	10	29	−12	−6	26	16	4	80
III	T	x^1	35	27	21	20	73	23	11	1	20	22	0	78
		x^2	46	33	14	14	34	24	15	0	19	39	0	61
		x^3	19	40	17	25	57	41	−28	−11	27	49	8	43
		b	16	−13	36	44	67	52	34	−9	38	43	3	54
		d	39	46	15	17	30	22	−8	−2	21	13	1	86
	I	x^1	27	21	18	15	63	26	10	5	24	13	3	83
		x^2	55	45	14	15	37	18	9	−1	15	28	0	72
		x^3	18	34	15	20	56	36	−24	−8	26	45	5	50
		b	8	−13	30	33	62	52	32	−4	41	37	0	62
		d	35	43	14	12	27	21	−9	2	19	18	1	81
	S	x^1	15	19	11	11	21	35	−8	−1	34	6	0	94
		x^2	63	52	13	11	28	16	10	2	12	40	1	59
		x^3	21	30	11	9	25	27	−15	3	23	31	1	68
		b	−6	−11	17	17	21	57	13	1	56	5	0	95
		d	33	44	13	12	16	24	−14	2	20	32	0	68
	p_b	x^1	11	18	19	27	74	35	−12	−13	30	11	15	74
		x^2	68	53	24	39	69	21	11	−7	16	28	11	61
		x^3	20	29	23	36	77	33	−11	−17	25	12	28	60
		b	−9	−11	35	55	78	38	2	−21	31	0	31	69
		d	19	16	10	11	20	33	6	−2	32	4	1	95
	p_s	x^1	11	11	17	20	81	27	−1	−6	26	0	5	95
		x^2	69	59	23	34	77	17	7	−8	14	17	20	62
		x^3	20	30	31	48	81	31	−12	−17	23	15	29	56
		b	−10	−19	34	49	82	34	10	−16	28	9	23	68
		d	18	14	10	10	24	33	11	0	31	11	0	88

TABLE 4.20 (*concluded*)

Stage	Variable and test variate		$\bar{P}$	$\bar{A}$	s_P	s_A	r	U	U_M	U_S	U_C	U^M	U^S	U^C
IV	P	x^1	15	19	14	15	82	22	-8	-2	20	13	1	86
		x^2	74	67	14	13	61	10	5	1	8	26	0	74
		x^3	11	14	12	13	70	29	-10	-2	27	13	1	87
		b	5	4	23	25	82	30	0	-5	29	0	3	97
		d	21	26	8	9	52	21	-12	-1	17	31	0	68
	p_s	x^1	10	7	19	15	86	27	7	11	24	6	16	78
		x^2	81	77	21	21	73	10	2	0	9	7	0	93
		x^3	9	16	15	20	89	27	-15	-11	19	33	18	49
		b	0	-9	27	28	91	26	16	-2	21	38	1	61
		d	12	15	9	9	53	28	-8	1	27	9	0	91
V	T	x^1	43	38	27	23	66	22	5	4	22	5	3	92
		x^2	35	29	15	13	46	23	8	2	21	13	1	86
		x^3	20	33	23	26	84	24	-14	-4	19	34	3	62
		b	20	5	48	48	77	36	15	-0	33	18	0	82
		d	39	48	15	19	27	25	-10	-5	22	17	3	80
	I	x^1	29	34	23	21	77	20	6	3	19	9	2	89
		x^2	37	27	17	15	64	23	13	2	19	30	1	69
		x^3	35	39	26	25	87	15	-5	0	14	10	0	89
		b	-6	-5	46	44	85	27	-0	2	27	0	1	99
		d	42	53	15	18	33	22	-11	-3	19	24	2	73
	S	x^1	18	26	17	23	58	35	-13	-11	31	14	10	76
		x^2	43	41	15	16	1	24	3	-1	24	1	0	99
		x^3	39	33	21	19	79	17	7	3	16	14	3	83
		b	-21	-7	35	40	78	35	-16	-5	31	21	2	77
		d	40	43	15	14	47	17	-3	1	17	3	0	97
	p_b	x^1	9	7	19	20	96	14	4	-4	13	9	6	86
		x^2	75	75	24	27	79	11	0	-2	10	0	4	96
		x^3	16	18	19	23	77	30	-4	-8	29	2	8	91

		[illegible]	[illegible]	18	20	25	79	27	− 3	− 8	26	1	8	91
		b	−10	−13	30	34	88	24	5	− 6	23	4	6	89
		d	14	11	11	9	65	29	11	7	27	14	5	82
VI	T	x^1	47	49	35	37	85	17	− 2	− 2	16	1	1	98
		x^2	24	9	17	7	51	53	38	25	26	52	23	25
		x^3	29	42	31	35	82	25	−14	− 4	20	31	3	66
		b	18	7	63	71	86	28	8	− 6	26	9	4	87
		d	32	45	20	15	20	30	−15	6	26	24	5	72
	I	x^1	33	45	27	26	80	22	−13	1	18	34	0	66
		x^2	28	16	17	11	73	33	23	12	19	51	14	35
		x^3	39	39	29	29	89	14	− 0	0	14	0	0	100
		b	− 6	6	53	54	86	29	−11	− 0	26	15	0	85
		d	43	55	19	23	60	21	−11	− 3	17	27	3	70
	S	x^1	28	45	27	30	76	28	−18	− 3	21	41	1	58
		x^2	27	19	18	12	44	33	14	11	28	18	11	71
		x^3	45	36	30	31	88	17	9	− 1	14	27	0	73
		b	−17	8	54	60	86	34	−22	− 4	26	40	2	58
		d	41	44	22	19	40	24	− 4	4	24	3	2	95
	Γ_b	x^1	14	15	24	27	92	18	− 1	− 5	17	1	8	92
		x^2	67	66	25	29	92	8	0	− 3	7	0	11	88
		x^3	19	19	24	26	96	12	1	− 3	11	0	6	93
		b	− 5	− 4	41	44	95	17	− 1	− 4	16	1	5	93
		d	17	14	9	9	78	18	7	0	17	14	0	85
	p_s	x^1	11	9	22	22	90	20	5	− 1	20	5	1	95
		x^2	71	71	25	29	91	8	− 0	− 2	8	0	9	90
		x^3	18	20	23	26	94	14	− 2	− 4	13	8	3	89
		b	− 7	−11	37	39	94	18	5	− 2	17	7	1	93
		d	15	12	8	8	76	20	8	0	18	15	0	85

V. Underestimation of Changes

5.1. Why are Changes Generally Underestimated?

5.1.1. Both in Chapter III and in Chapter IV we observed that the predicted changes analysed there show a bias in relation to the corresponding actual changes in the sense that they are on the average smaller. This phenomenon, which amounts to an underestimation of the level of the variable to be predicted in times of rises and to an overestimation of this level in times of falls, is not entirely unknown; but its general occurrence is not sufficiently realised. A few further examples are instructive. Table 5.1 below, derived from MODIGLIANI's and SAUERLENDER's analysis of surveys conducted by the *Fortune* magazine and by Dun & Bradstreet, suggests an underestimation of the dollar volume of sales of different categories in periods of rising activity (indicated by negative forecasting errors); and an overestimation or little or no bias in times of level or falling activity.[1] Similarly, Table 5.2, dealing with sales forecasts according to the surveys conducted by the Office of Business Economics of the American Department of Commerce and by the Securities and Exchange Commission suggests that changes in sales are generally underestimated, both by larger and by smaller firms.[2] It is of some interest to add that econometricians can be said to be implicitly aware of this error when they use present values of variables as approximations of expected future values; cf. the third paragraph of 2.3.4.

It is the purpose of this chapter to analyse this phenomenon more closely. The present section is devoted to theoretical aspects, the re-

[1] F. MODIGLIANI and O. H. SAUERLENDER, "Economic Expectations and Plans of Firms in Relation to Short-Term Forecasting," in: *Short-Term Economic Forecasting*, Vol. 17 of Studies in Income and Wealth (Princeton, 1955), pp. 288–289.

[2] *Ibidem*, p. 305. Still another example is that of the panel conducted by J. A. LIVINGSTON (quoted by V LEWIS BASSIE in *Short-Term Economic Forecasting*, pp. 19–20). He analysed the opinions of 38 of America's "top-ranking economists" on future economic trends and found that they showed a very close resemblance to the actual conditions at the moment of prediction.

TABLE 5.1

AVERAGE PERCENTAGE FORECASTING ERRORS IN TOTAL SALES OF THE FORTUNE AND THE DUN & BRADSTREET SURVEYS (Modigliani and Sauerlender, 1955)

Period	*Commodity or industry*	*Periods of rising activity*	*Periods of level or falling activity*
	Fortune Surveys		
1947–50	durable manuf.	−9 (6)	0 (2)
1947–50	nondurable manuf.	−6 (5)	0 (3)
1948–50	wholesale trade	−8 (4)	1 (3)
1948–50	retail trade	−6 (4)	−2 (3)
	Dun & Bradstreet Surveys		
1948–50	durable manuf.	−17 (4)	9 (4)
1948–50	nondurable manuf.	−7 (4)	6 (4)
1948–50	retail trade	−6 (4)	−1 (3)

Note: Figures in brackets indicate the relevant number of observations.

TABLE 5.2

AVERAGE PREDICTED AND ACTUAL PERCENTAGE CHANGES IN SALES OF MANUFACTURING FIRMS RESPONDING TO OBE-SEC SURVEYS (Modigliani and Sauerlender, 1955)

Year	*Asset size of firms*	*Number of observations*	*Average predicted change*	*Average actual change*
1948	above $50 million	26	7.8	14.2
1948	$10–$50 million	58	4.4	11.9
1948	below $10 million	39	0.5	5.8
1949	above $50 million	57	1.8	−2.1
1949	$10–$50 million	208	−4.5	−8.6
1949	below $10 million	211	−1.9	−7.0

maining sections (where we shall lean heavily upon work done by others) to further empirical evidence. The theoretical points will be confined to expectations, plans being disregarded. A separate analysis of plans seems largely superfluous in this connection, because it seems intuitively clear that an underestimation of changes in those exogenous variables which affect behaviour will in general lead to instrument changes that are too small. Certain subtle points are, however, involved here, which will be dealt with more extensively in Chapter VIII; but some empirical indications justifying this neglect have already been obtained in Section 4.5, where it was observed that a close similarity exists between corresponding plans and expectations.

5.1.2. Underestimation of changes is presumably an error of forecasting which is not confined to economic predictions. General Staffs, for example, are often suspected to be prepared for the last war, not for the next. Another example is Hitler's rise in Germany, which induced many important changes in that country. Their underestimation by foreign powers resulted in counter-measures that were too small and too late, with a major war as ultimate consequence. Less dramatic, though perhaps equally sizable in their own way, are, according to KEYNES, similar errors of long-term economic forecasts:[1] "The facts of the existing situation enter, in a sense disproportionately, into the formation of our long-term expectations; our usual practice being to take the existing situation and to project it into the future, modified only to the extent that we have more or less definite reasons for expecting a change." This is clearly related to what has been said in 2.3.3 for expectations in general, viz., that they are derived by means of the assumption of a partial stability of determining factors.

As will be argued below, this feature is one of the causes of the underestimation of changes. It should perhaps be noted beforehand that the "economic" analysis which follows has, in a sense, a "psychological" competitor. For, if a man predicts large but not very large changes, the public will regard him as a man of imagination; but if he predicts extremely large changes, his audience will replace imagination by phantasy. Thus, there is some kind of social pressure in the direction of the bias which we have observed; and in the case of the Netherlands Central Planning Bureau, for example, this pressure was unmistakable at many occasions. This "theory" is, however, not very satisfactory, for it can explain only why forecasters underestimate changes when other forecasters do.

5.1.3. In general, the phenomenon to be predicted can approximately be described as a function of three types of determining factors; viz., those which are supposed to remain unchanged (though in fact they may change), those which are supposed to change, and certain random elements. Let us write, therefore,

$$f_t^A = f(S_t, V_t) + u_t, \tag{5.1}$$

where f_t^A is the actual value to be predicted in t, u_t a random disturb-

[1] J. M. KEYNES, *The General Theory of Employment, Interest, and Money* (London, 1936), p. 148.

ance with zero mean, and S_t and V_t the more "systematic" factors, the latter of which is one of the forecaster's objects of prediction, the former his "constant." We assume that all quantities are real-valued, and that u is distributed independently of S and V. Taking first differences, we find for the actual change:

$$\Delta f_t^A = f^S \Delta S_t + f^V \Delta V_t + \Delta u_t, \tag{5.2}$$

where f^S and f^V are the partial derivatives of f with respect to S and V, respectively, in the point S_{t-1}, V_{t-1}.[1] This implies that we assume differentiability and neglect higher-order differentials.

Next, we turn to the prediction, f_t^P. To simplify the discussion, we shall assume that the forecaster knows (approximately) the general form of the function f. The analysis is then confined to the prediction of the three quantities S_t, V_t, u_t. As to S_t, the fact that the forecaster supposes this part to remain unchanged suggests that its predicted value is S_{t-1}. For the prediction of V_t (which is a forecast of higher order)[2] we shall write

$$V_{t-1} + h_t \Delta V_t,$$

which means simply that we postpone the answer to the question what value is predicted. If $h_t > 1$, the change in V is overestimated; if $0 < h_t < 1$, it is underestimated; if $h_t < 0$, there is a turning point error.[3] As to the disturbances, finally, here their probability characteristics become important. We shall suppose that they satisfy the first-order Markov-scheme

$$u_t = \varrho u_{t-1} + u'(t), \qquad 0 < \varrho < 1, \tag{5.3}$$

$u'(t)$ being a series of independent random variables with zero mean and constant variance. This assumption is simple and not altogether unrealistic. Clearly, the forecaster's "best" estimate of u_t is ϱu_{t-1}; it is "best" in the sense that this is the conditional mean value of u_t, given u_{t-1}. On the other hand, it is far from sure whether the forecaster is able or willing to take ϱu_{t-1} as a prediction of u_t. Not only should he know ϱ, but he should also be able to specify the numerical value of the disturbance associated with f_{t-1}^A. In the Netherlands Central Planning Bureau, for example, this is "solved" by assuming that the

[1] If there are several factors which fall under S and V, we should interpret S, V, ΔS, ΔV as column vectors and f^S and f^V as row vectors of first-order derivatives.
[2] Compare Section 2.3.
[3] If V is a vector (cf. footnote 1), we should interpret h_t as a diagonal matrix.

last term of (5.2), viz. Δu_t, vanishes on the average. This "first-difference" procedure is equivalent to (5.3) for $\varrho = 1$. We shall assume, therefore, that u_t is predicted as $k_t u_{t-1}$ with

$$0 \leq k_t \leq 1, \tag{5.4}$$

$k_t = \varrho$ being "best" according to the above-mentioned criterion. It follows that

$$f_t^P = f(S_{t-1}, V_{t-1} + h_t \Delta V_t) + k_t u_{t-1}, \tag{5.5}$$

so that the predicted change becomes approximately

$$\Delta f_t^P = f_t^P - f_{t-1}^A = h_t f^V \Delta V_t - (1 - k_t) u_{t-1}. \tag{5.6}$$

5.1.4. Let us now suppose that time series of predicted and actual changes are available. Such a pair of series can be represented by a scatter in a Δf^P, Δf^A-diagram of the type considered earlier in the Chapters II and III. We proceed to consider three regressions, viz., that of Δf^P on Δf^A, the orthogonal regression, and the regression of Δf^A on Δf^P. The first and the third have been considered in Chapter III, the second—which treats predictions and actual changes symmetrically—was one of the objects of the geometrical discussion of Section 2.5; we may also say that the orthogonal regression corresponds conceptually with the analysis of Chapter IV, because our use of Business Test data was such that actual and planned or expected changes were treated symmetrically.

In order to find the coefficients corresponding to these regressions, we have to derive the variances and the covariance of Δf^A and Δf^P. Writing s^2 for the variance of $f^S \Delta S$, v^2 for the variance of $f^V \Delta V$, rsv for their covariance, σ^2 for the variance of u, and neglecting the variation of h_t and $(1 - k_t)$ over time—the former approximation amounting to the assumption of proportional over or underestimation of ΔV—, we obtain:

$$\text{var}\,(\Delta f^A) = s^2 + v^2 + 2rsv + 2(1 - \varrho)\sigma^2; \tag{5.7}$$

$$\text{var}\,(\Delta f^P) = h^2 v^2 + (1 - k)^2 \sigma^2; \tag{5.8}$$

$$\text{cov}\,(\Delta f^A, \Delta f^P) = hv^2 + hrsv + (1 - k)(1 - \varrho)\sigma^2. \tag{5.9}$$

Consider then the regression of Δf^P on Δf^A. Its coefficient equals the ratio of the covariance (5.9) to the variance (5.7). If this ratio is below unity—or alternatively, if (5.7) shows a positive excess over (5.9)—, there is a bias towards underestimation of changes in the sense of this regression, *provided* the regression goes through the origin. If this proviso is not fulfilled, e.g., if the regression line meets the horizontal Δf^A-axis in a point with negative Δf^A-value, there is a bias towards overestimation of changes for small actual increases and a bias towards turning point errors for small actual decreases, the tendency towards underestimation being confined to larger increases and decreases. The findings of Chapter III suggest that, in that case, the proviso plays no important rôle; but, as will be indicated later in this chapter, this is not the law of the Medes and the Persians, and a qualification of this kind must be made in the further analysis of all three regressions.

For the excess of the variance (5.7) over the covariance (5.9) we find

$$s^2 + (1 - h)v^2 + (2 - h)rsv + (1 + k)(1 - \varrho)\sigma^2. \tag{5.10}$$

The first and the last terms are always positive. As to the second and the third, consider first the case $h = 1$ corresponding to no bias towards under or overestimation of the changes in the predicted factors V. The first three terms of (5.10) become then $s^2 + rsv$, which is negative only if r, the correlation between the predicted components $f^V \Delta V_t$ and the nonpredicted components $f^S \Delta S_t$, is negative and larger than s/v in absolute value. There is hence more "room" for a positive sum of the first three terms in the case $h = 1$.[1] Still, $r < -s/v$ is not sufficient to make (5.10) negative because of the positive fourth term. Furthermore, as long as $0 \leq h < 2$—which excludes a negative association between forecasts and actual changes ΔV as well as an overestimation by 100 per cent or more—, the correlation r is confined to less than one half of its range if the first and the third terms combined are to be negative. Since the second term, finally, is positive if ΔV is underestimated ($h < 1$) and negative in the opposite case, our conclusion should be that there is a bias towards underestimation of changes in the sense of the regression of Δf^P on Δf^A unless at least one of the following conditions is satisfied: either r is sufficiently negative, or there is a considerable bias towards overestimating the changes in the determining factor V. These conditions are rather drastic, so that underestimation in this sense seems indeed a plausible feature of predictions.

[1] Note that this argument is formally the same as that used for mixtures of forecasting and observational errors in 2.4.3.

For the underestimation of changes in the orthogonal sense we must consider the excess of the variance (5.7) over the variance (5.8):

$$s^2 + (1 - h^2)v^2 + 2rsv + (1 - 2\varrho + 2k - k^2)\sigma^2. \tag{5.11}$$

The first term is again positive. The fourth is also positive if the forecaster uses the "best" estimate $k = \varrho$; in that case it is equal to the corresponding term in (5.10). If he uses the first-difference approach $k = 1$, then the term becomes $2(1 - \varrho)\sigma^2$, which is still larger, though again equal to the corresponding term of (5.10) in the case $k = 1$. However, whereas in (5.10) the term is always positive, it may be negative here, viz., when $k < 1 - \sqrt{2(1 - \varrho)}$.[1] Since the second and the third terms are similar to those of (5.10), except that the replacement of $(2 - h)$ by 2 allows a somewhat larger range for r to make the first and third terms combined negative and that the h^2 in the second term implies a more considerable effect of deviations of h from 1, we should conclude that the underestimation of changes in the orthogonal sense takes place, qualitatively at least, under conditions which are about the same as those of the previous paragraph; the qualifications being that the quantitative conditions under which the opposite is true are somewhat less restrictive and that the disturbance term (the fourth) will contribute to the opposite effect when the autocorrelation is both sufficiently large and sufficiently underestimated.

For the underestimation in the sense of the regression of Δf^A on Δf^P, finally, we have to analyse under what conditions the excess of the covariance (5.9) over the variance (5.8):

$$h(1 - h)v^2 + hrsv + (1 - k)(k - \varrho)\sigma^2, \tag{5.12}$$

is positive. The third term vanishes when either $k = \varrho$ or $k = 1$; it is negative when $k < \varrho$, positive when $\varrho < k < 1$. As to the second, we can no longer use the argument of a restricted range for r, since the term in s^2 is absent. The sign of the first term is, if $h > 0$, determined by the question whether ΔV is over or underestimated. As a whole, therefore, it seems clear that underestimation of changes according to the third criterion is not self-evident.

5.1.5. Thus, the phenomenon of underestimation suggests itself as the result of a mechanism in which the following quantities are involved:

[1] This inequality makes obviously only sense when the right-hand side is positive. This implies $\varrho > \frac{1}{2}$.

three variances (s^2, v^2, σ^2), an autocorrelation and its estimate (ϱ, k), a "current" correlation about which it is not easy to generalise (r), and an h which describes the degree of over or underestimation of higher-order predictions; and we have found that, at least according to the first two criteria, underestimation is more plausible than overestimation even when there is no bias of this kind for the higher-order predictions.

This result suggests another useful hypothesis. So far, we have considered the determining factors which come under S and V as fixed. It is clear, however, that if there are two different forecasters, one of whom is much more intelligent and sophisticated than the other, the former will have fewer factors under S and more under V. This implies that the ratio s/v is smaller for the intelligent forecaster than for his less gifted colleague and hence, from (5.10) and (5.11), that the underestimation of changes will in general play a smaller rôle in the former's forecasts. It seems interesting, therefore, to test the hypothesis that the degree of underestimation is a decreasing function of the general quality of the forecasts. It is necessary, of course, to interpret this expression cautiously, for underestimation is simply one of the components of this "general quality." But one promising result in this direction has already been obtained: the results in 4.4.3 (Table 4.14) suggested a negative rank correlation between the underestimation of changes and the degree to which the ups and downs of actual development are reflected in the forecasters' predictions. Also, it is of some interest to add that higher-order predictions are frequently not much more than guesses, in which case they will be characterised by rather considerable underestimation if this hypothesis is correct. Since this corresponds to $0 < h < 1$ in 5.1.5, it is easily seen that this feature contributes to underestimation of changes, even in the strongest sense (viz., that of the regression of Δf^A on Δf^P), for the lower-order predictions.

5.2. Further Results on Macroeconomic Forecasts in The Netherlands

5.2.1. Our first piece of additional empirical evidence on the underestimation of changes is LIPS' and SCHOUTEN's analysis of the Dutch forecasts which were considered earlier in Chapter III.[1] This analysis,

[1] J. LIPS and D. B. J. SCHOUTEN, "The Reliability of the Policy Model Used by the Central Planning Bureau of the Netherlands." Paper read at the Hindsgavl Meeting

which has been carried out for the period 1949–1954, is based on approach (*ii*) of 3.2.1; that is, the observed changes in exogenous variables are inserted in the model, and the corresponding computed changes in the endogenous variables (i.e., their conditional forecasts) are then compared with the observed changes in these variables.

A few remarks should be made on the derivation of these conditional predictions. First, the model used is the one described in Section 3.1. This model was actually used for the 1955-forecasts only. Hence the analysis is concerned with the forecasting power of this particular model, not with that of the earlier models on which the forecasts of Chapter III are based. Second, the numerical coefficients of the linearised model of Section 3.1 are not immediately applicable to the earlier years, just because of this linearisation. Thus, when going back to the example of 3.1.3, the change in the product xy can be approximately written as $\Delta(xy) = \bar{x}\Delta y + \bar{y}\Delta x$, $\bar{x}$ and $\bar{y}$ being last year's values; and these values change from year to year. Third, there is a difficulty as to the autonomous term of the export equation (3.21). Its numerical specification afterwards is no easy matter, and alternative values have a rather considerable effect on the conditional forecasts. However, such autonomous terms are exogenous; and since the price term of the

TABLE 5.3

LIST OF DUTCH MACROVARIABLES ANALYSED
(Lips and Schouten, 1955)

Price indices of:	*Quantities and volumes:*
commodity exports consumption investment goods inventories Government commodity purchases	commodity imports consumption gross fixed investment gross national product employment in private sector
Money values:	*Exogenous variables:*
indirect taxes minus subsidies income taxes paid by wage-earners income taxes paid by others non-wage income	commodity exports (volume) import prices depreciation allowances (volume) available labour force Government wage bill (value) Government commodity purchases (value) exports of services (value) imports of services (value)

of the International Association for Research in Income and Wealth (1955). The present analysis is based on a slightly revised version of this paper.

export equation was generally small compared with this term, the most satisfactory procedure is then to take the whole of exports as exogenous. For further details we refer to the Appendix of this chapter (Section 5.A), which also contains a survey of underlying data.

5.2.2. The variables analysed are listed in Table 5.3. It is seen that, contrary to the corresponding Table 3.1 of Chapter III, the table contains no value variables if the corresponding volume and price variables are listed. This reduces the number of identities connecting the separate forecasts and the actual changes, so that it may seem that

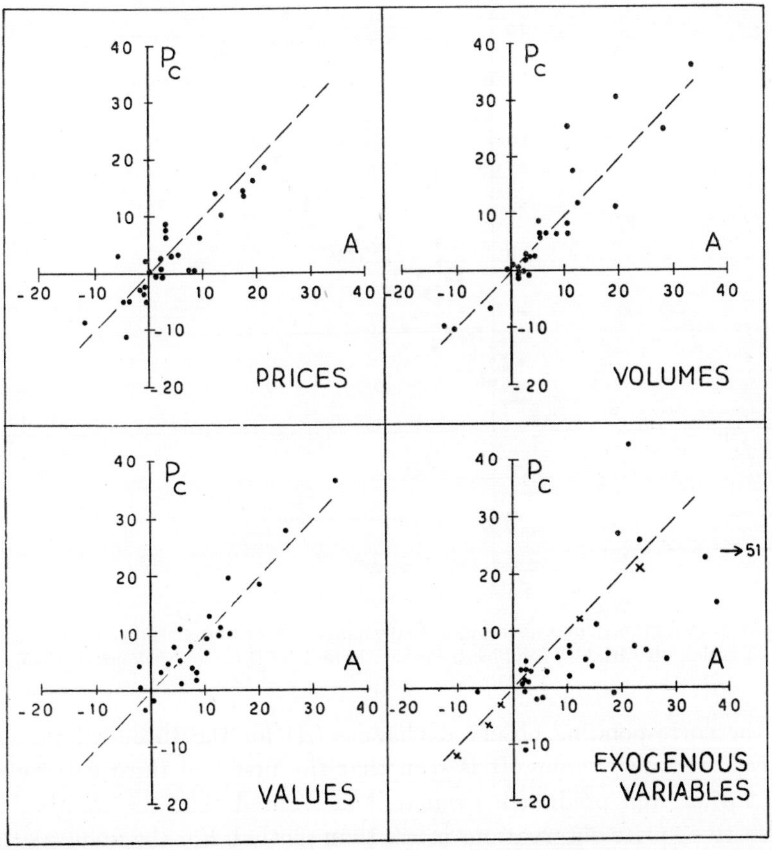

Fig. 5.1. Conditional forecasts and actual changes of 14 Dutch endogenous macro-variables, for prices, volumes and values separately; and unconditional forecasts and actual changes of 8 exogenous variables. Period: 1949–1954. Observations on the import price level are indicated by crosses (Lips and Schouten, 1955)

there is more independence in the present case than in that of Chapter III. However, the rather large number of price variables, most of which are supposed to be mainly determined by wage and import price level (though with different coefficients—cf. the end of 3.1.3), leads to more dependence, at least for these variables. This should be borne in mind when the results are interpreted.

Fig. 5.1 gives a picture of the conditional predictions (P_C) in relation

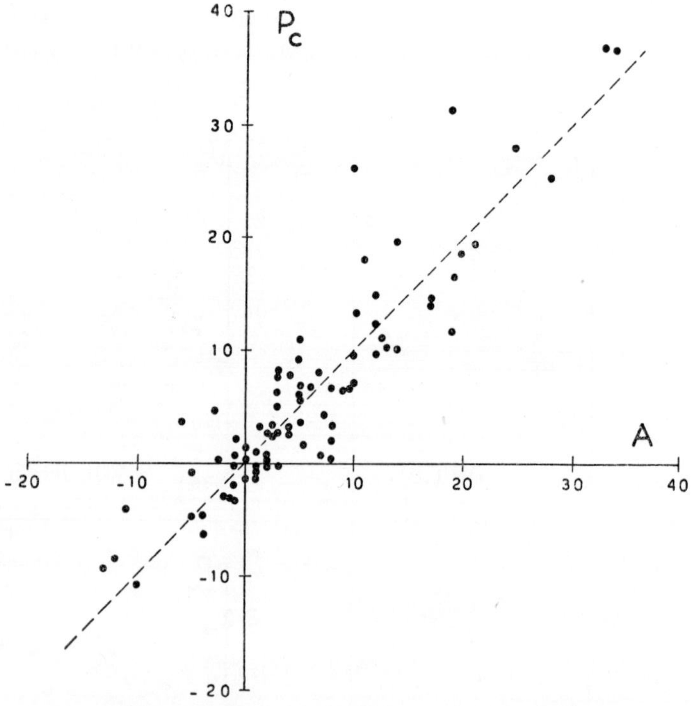

Fig. 5.2. Conditional forecasts and actual changes of 14 Dutch endogenous macro-variables, all variables combined. Period: 1949–1954 (Lips and Schouten, 1955)

to the corresponding observed changes (A) for the three categories: prices, volumes, values. It is seen that the first and third categories are rather well predicted, even if it is realised that the number of "effective" price observations is less than plotted. For the volumes the result seems to be somewhat worse, which is largely due to the imports of commodities; all four points with P_C's above 20 per cent belong to this variable. This, in turn, is presumably due to the rather erratic inventory policy of Dutch firms in those years, which is not well described by the equation system.

Fig. 5.2 gives a summarising picture for all three categories combined. There is no evidence of underestimation of changes, which stands in sharp contrast to the result for the (unconditional) predictions of exogenous changes—cf. the lower right-hand scatter of Fig. 5.1. This is in accordance with the remarks made at the end of 5.1.5, for the latter forecasts are much more primitive and less sophisticated than

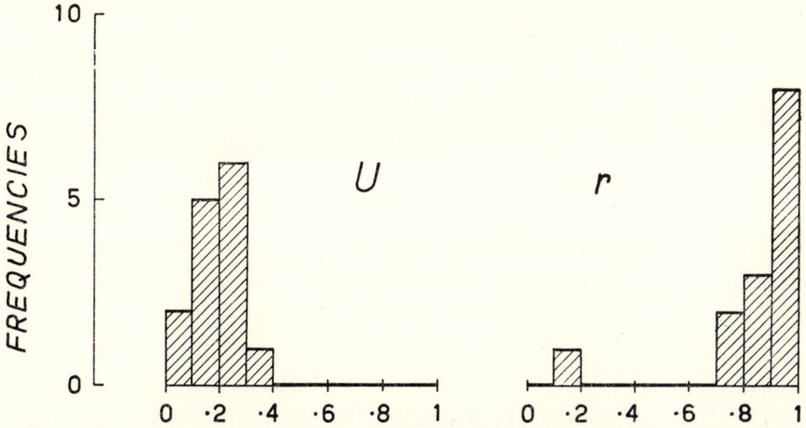

Fig. 5.3. Frequency distributions of the (total) inequality coefficients (U) of the conditional Dutch predictions and actual changes, and of their correlation coefficients (r)

the conditional predictions. The only exception is the import price level. This exogenous variable, the observations on which are marked by crosses rather than dots in Fig. 5.1, was not characterised by any forecasting bias of the kind under consideration. However, this "exception" should be regarded as corroboration of the hypothesis of 5.1.5, because, as observed earlier at several places (see e.g. 2.3.2), this variable can be predicted rather accurately. But in general we should expect, in accordance with the over-all results of this section, exogenous predictions to be worse and characterised by more underestimation bias than conditional endogenous predictions.

5.2.3. In the Appendix, Section 5.A (Table 5.10), the various correlation and inequality coefficients and proportions of these conditional forecasts are presented. Here, we confine ourselves to a brief summary of the aggregate outcomes.

Fig. 5.3 contains the frequency distributions of the inequality coefficients and correlation coefficients of the fourteen pairs of time series. All correlations except one exceed the value 0.75, and more than one half exceeds 0.9. The average of the inequality coefficients is 0.20.[1] This is clearly better than the corresponding result of Chapter III; but it should be admitted that neither the period covered, nor the variables themselves, are the same as those of the earlier analysis, so that this comparison cannot be fully satisfactory.

The three inequality proportions U^M, U^S, U^C are illustrated in Fig. 5.4; they are indicated by dots. It is seen that, contrary to our findings in Chapter III for the unconditional forecasts, the covariance proportion plays a dominant rôle. Its average over all fourteen observations is about 0.7, and the two other proportions (U^M and U^S) are on the average approximately equal. The errors of the conditional forecasts are hence largely "unsystematic" in the sense of the analysis of 2.5.3. As to the partial coefficient of unequal central tendency (U_M), its sign is positive in six, negative in eight cases. This suggests that there is no appreciable bias towards underestimation of changes, which was also illustrated by Fig. 5.2.

Fig. 5.4 contains also a triangular representation of the inequality proportions U^M, U^R, U^D, corresponding to the second decomposition of U (cf. 2.5.4); they are indicated by small circles. In the present analysis there is indeed much to say in favour of the application of this alternative decomposition, since the equation system yields conditional forecasts which are mean values of the corresponding actual outcomes; at least, it would yield such estimates if the usual assumptions underlying such systems are satisfied and if the coefficients of the system coincide with the "true" parameters. We shall come back to these statistical problems in Chapter VI (Section 6.2); we note here that, even if the above-mentioned conditions are only satisfied to a limited extent, it is nevertheless interesting to analyse the magnitude of the proportions U^M, U^R, U^D in view of the conceptual applicability of the stochastic theory of 2.5.4. It appears then that the disturbance proportion is dominant, viz., about two thirds on the average, just as the covariance proportion of the first decomposition. This suggests that

[1] Note that the inequality coefficient for the volume of imports of commodities is relatively small, viz. 0.19, whereas its errors in Fig. 5.1 appeared rather large. This is due to the fact that the inequality coefficient takes account, *via* its denominator, of the size of the changes predicted and observed. These changes are substantial in this case, their algebraic average being of the order of 15 per cent. The dependence on forecasts in the denominator can be regarded as a disadvantage of U; we shall come back to this point in Chapter VIII (Section 8.4).

the greater part of the errors is due to the disturbances of the equation system. It is also interesting to note that 9 of the 14 partial inequality coefficients U_R are positive, whereas this holds for only 5 of the U_S's. The latter feature implies that in most cases the variance of the predicted changes is smaller than that of the observed changes; hence,

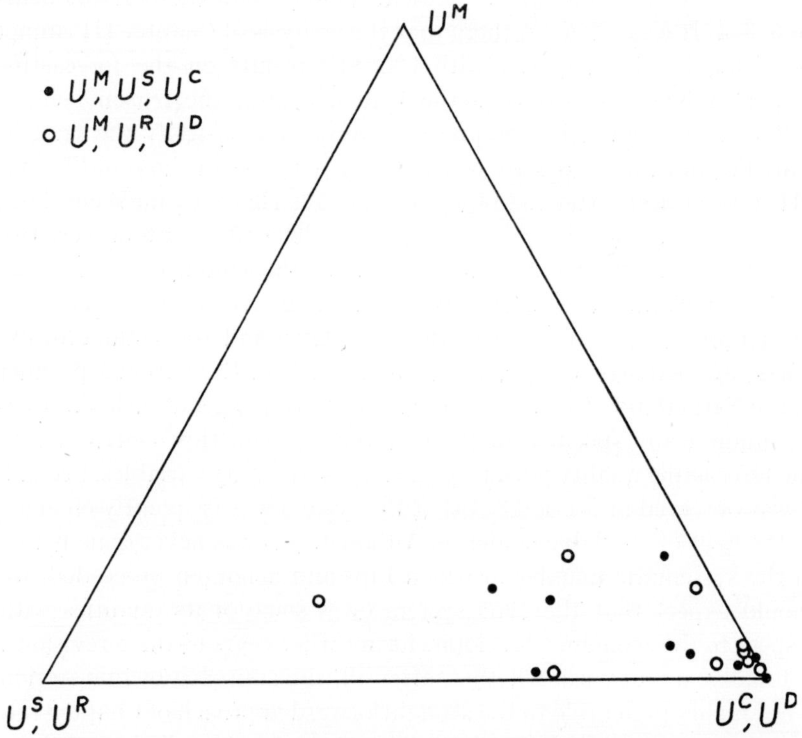

Fig. 5.4. Triangular illustration of the inequality proportions U^M, U^S, U^C and U^M, U^R, U^D of the conditional Dutch predictions and actual changes

confining ourselves to our small sample, we can say that there is "too little variation" in the forecasts. On the other hand, when following the stochastic theory, we should conclude from the majority of positive U_R's that there is too much variation, because a positive U_R implies an excess of s_P over rs_A (s_P and s_A being the standard deviations of predicted and actual changes, respectively, and r their correlation), and hence a slope of the regression of A on P which exceeds unity. Needless to say, the limited and interdependent material of this analysis is hardly sufficient for valid conclusions of this kind; it is merely instructive to show that differences of appraisal result from the adoption of different criteria. We shall come back to this point in Chapter VIII (Section 8.4).

5.2.4. Two other points should be raised before concluding this section. First, we should compare the present findings with the remarks made in 3.3.4. It was observed there that the analysis of Chapter III cannot be immediately compared with CHRIST's results on the forecasting power of KLEIN's models of the United States, the reason being a difference in approach. The present approach is basically the same as Christ's, and the results are considerably better than those of Chapter III and *a fortiori* better than those of Christ's. This outcome seems both surprising and encouraging for future model building; however, two qualifications are of importance. First, in the Dutch case there are more important exogenous variables than in Klein's case. The two most prominent examples are the wage level and the volume of exports; and exports amount to about one half of the national product in the Netherlands. Clearly, when the observed changes of such variables are numerically specified in the equation system, this contributes to the forecasting quality with respect to the remaining variables. Second, it was observed in Section 3.1 that the system was frequently changed in the light of available evidence. Although this was never done before in the systematic manner in which Lips and Schouten proceeded, we should expect that the 1955 system owes some of its qualities with respect to the economic development in earlier years to these revisions.

Finally, we may ask whether, after all, the approach of this section is not highly preferable to the straightforward approach of Chapter III. Isn't it better to test the model, which pretends to be the kernel of the prediction procedure—cf. 3.1.4?[1]

The answer can be conveniently given in three steps, the second of which is a qualification on the first, and the third on the second. First, if a macroeconomic forecaster hands over his predictions to a policy-maker, who uses them for certain decisions, it is a meagre consolation for the latter when these predictions, though derived from a correct model, are bad due to bad exogenous forecasts. If the policy-maker's picture of the future is incorrect, in one way or another, this will affect

[1] For an analysis of the possibility of separating the prediction errors in terms of its two components—viz., imperfect exogenous forecasts and an incorrect model—, cf. the Appendix to this chapter, Section 5.B.

his decisions unfavourably. However (and this is the second step), if the model is correct in the sense that all coefficients by which the variables are multiplied in the separate equations are correct, this as such is favourable because it enables the policy-maker to draw correct conclusions as to the effects of his measures on the endogenous variables; where "measures" are to be interpreted as changes in those exogenous variables over which he has control. The favourable picture of Fig. 5.2 may be regarded as a *prima facie* indication that this is at least approximately the case. But again—and this is the third step—this is not more than *prima facie*, for we may have a problem of the following kind. Suppose that investment is a function of profits after taxes and of the volume of sales. Suppose also that the time series of the latter variables, on which the numerical specification of the function is based, are highly correlated. In that case the possibility of estimating the influence of these variables separately is limited, but for forecasting purposes of the type of Fig. 5.2 this is not very important as long as the correlation is maintained in the prediction period. So, the quality of the picture of this diagram is then not seriously affected if part of the influence of the volume of sales on investment is wrongly attributed to profits after taxes, or *vice versa*; but for the policy-maker it is highly important to know the effect of changes in profits after taxes on investment, for this is one of the bases of his taxation policy.

We shall come back to these topics in later chapters. For the present it is sufficient to conclude that the arguments are so involved that a twofold analysis of the type carried out in this section and in Chapter III is not entirely superfluous.

5.3. Business Test Forecasts of the German Textile Industry

5.3.1. O. ANDERSON, R. K. BAUER and E. FELS made an analysis of the Business Test forecasts of firms of the German textile industry.[1] They did not use the test variates considered in the preceding chapter, but counted the number of times in which firms predicted an increase in a certain variable and reported an increase afterwards, predicted

[1] "On the Accuracy of Short-Term Entrepreneurial Expectations," *Proceedings of the Business and Economic Statistics Section of the American Statistical Association*, September 1954, pp. 124–147.

an increase but reported no change afterwards, etc. This leads to nine possibilities, the frequencies of which can be arranged as follows:

$$\begin{matrix} f_{11} & f_{12} & f_{13} \\ f_{21} & f_{22} & f_{23} \\ f_{31} & f_{32} & f_{33} \end{matrix}$$

The indices 1, 2, 3 correspond—as in the preceding chapter—to increase, no change and decrease, respectively, and the first index refers to predictions, the second to actual development. Hence f_{12} is the number of cases in which an entrepreneur predicts an increase but reports no change afterwards; etc.

Obviously, perfect forecasting requires that this square array has zeros outside the main diagonal: $f_{rs} = 0$ if $r \neq s$. If such an f_{rs} is $\neq 0$, then there are prediction errors of various kinds, and the underestimation of changes may be one of them. A convenient measure for this error is the ratio of the frequency of incorrect no-change predictions to the frequency of cases in which no change is incorrectly not predicted:

$$u = \frac{f_{21} + f_{23}}{f_{12} + f_{32}}. \tag{5.13}$$

This ratio (which should exceed unity before we are allowed to con-

TABLE 5.4

UNDERESTIMATION RATIOS (5.13) FOR FIRMS AND VARIABLES OF THE GERMAN TEXTILE INDUSTRY, 1950–1953 (Anderson c.s., 1954)

Industry	*Size of firms*	*Variables*		
		production	*employees*	*selling prices*
spinning & weaving	small	1.7	1.4	1.5
	medium	1.4	1.3	1.8
	large	1.6	2.0	2.1
confection	small	2.5	1.9	1.1
	medium	1.9	1.4	1.0
	large	2.4	1.7	0.8
		sales	*buying prices*	*selling prices*
textile wholesalers	small	2.5	1.1	0.9
	medium	2.6	0.6	0.8
	large	1.7	1.1	0.9
textile retailers	small	2.2	1.3	0.9
	medium	3.1	1.1	0.8
	large	3.4	1.0	0.7

clude to a bias towards underestimation) is presented in Table 5.4 for certain sets of firms and variables considered by Anderson c.s. The firms belong to the spinning and weaving industry, the confection industry, and the textile wholesale and retail trade; the available variables are production, employees and selling prices for the manufacturers, sales value and buying and selling prices for the traders. The firms of each industry are divided into three groups according to their size. The results suggest a general underestimation of changes for all variables and all firms of each size, except for the buying and selling prices of those firms which are not far from the ultimate consumer—just as we found in Section 4.4 for the leather and shoe industry.

5.3.2. It is of some interest to note that the underestimation ratio u is not uncorrelated with the degree to which increases are predicted as decreases, and *vice versa*. A convenient measure for the relative frequency of these turning point errors is

$$t = \frac{f_{13} + f_{31}}{f_{11} + f_{33}}, \tag{5.14}$$

TABLE 5.5

RATIOS (5.14) OF TURNING POINT ERRORS OF THE FIRMS AND VARIABLES OF TABLE 5.4

Industry	*Size of firms*	*Variables*		
		production	*employees*	*selling prices*
spinning & weaving	small	0.03	0.00	0.08
	medium	0.05	0.02	0.05
	large	0.02	0.02	0.07
confection	small	0.07	0.00	0.07
	medium	0.15	0.04	0.04
	large	0.11	0.12	0.03
		sales	*buying prices*	*selling prices*
textile wholesalers	small	0.22	0.04	0.04
	medium	0.22	0.00	0.00
	large	0.12	0.00	0.00
textile retailers	small	0.32	0.05	0.03
	medium	0.27	0.02	0.02
	large	0.26	0.03	0.02

i.e., the ratio of the frequency of these errors to the frequency of correct predictions of increases and decreases.[1] These ratios are given in Table 5.5, and Fig. 5.5 gives a picture of u and t jointly. There is, for obvious reasons, a large amount of scatter in the diagram, but the

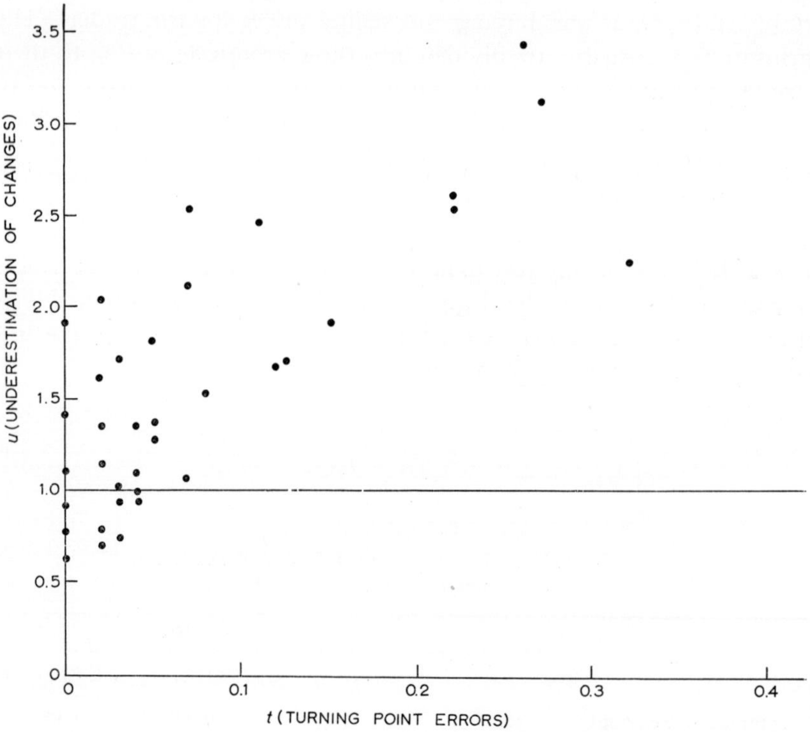

Fig. 5.5. Underestimation of changes and turning point errors: thirty-six variables of the German textile industry, 1950–53

results as a whole suggest nevertheless that underestimation of changes is absent only if there is a negligible number of turning point errors; which may be regarded as a further corroboration of the hypothesis suggested in 5.1.5.

[1] Note that t is defined such that its components f_{rs} are all different from the components of u (and that f_{22} is absent in both t and u). If this were not the case, we would have the danger of spurious correlation (cf. 5.1.5).

5.4. On the Interpretation of the Concept of Changes; Forecasts of Investment and of Railroad Shipments

5.4.1. It will be clear that the concept of change is only unique with respect to a well-defined variable. In particular, it is not invariant against a replacement of such a variable by (e.g.) its integral over time. To take an example, consider the stock of capital goods and net investment. If we say that changes in the former variable are underestimated, then—assuming the changes to be positive—the investment forecasts corresponding to them are generally below the actual investment *level*. But if we take investment rather than capital stock and say that the changes in this variable are underestimated, this implies that next year's investment level is farther from last year's level than the prediction indicates, which may be either in positive or in negative direction.

So it appears to be necessary to specify unambiguously what kind of variable is under consideration. In Section 5.1 this was done formally by specifying a particular variable, f^A; and we find here that the idea of underestimation of changes cannot be applied to arbitrary transformations of f^A as a function of time. In practical applications, the most convenient procedure to find the appropriate variable is to ask in what manner "no change" is interpreted by the forecaster. For instance, "no change" with respect to the prediction of exports, consumption, price levels, etc., of Chapter III is to be interpreted as an unchanged level of exports (consumption, etc.) in two successive years, not as (e.g.) an unchanged rate of change of exports; the reason being that the Governments for whom the forecasts were prepared are interested in the future levels of exports, consumption, etc., rather than in their rates of change or in any other derived functions. Similarly, when analysing investment forecasts according to surveys among entrepreneurs, we should ask ourselves (or the entrepreneurs) what is the relevant f^A. It seems then rather plausible that f^A is the size of the firm (the stock of capital goods), for "no change" means presumably —from the entrepreneur's standpoint—that the firm's size remains unchanged. So we should expect the investment forecasts of these surveys to be such that the change in capital stock is underestimated. It may very well be that this situation would be different if the survey were held among academic economists, who consider investment as an important component of the national product but the stock of capital goods largely as a derived variable, and who regard the fluctuations of investment through time as much more interesting in the short run than the fluctuations of capital. Such a survey, we might guess, would be characterised by an underestimation of investment changes; but for entrepreneurs the size of their firms seems a "primary" variable, and investment a derived one.

To test this proposition empirically, it is necessary to know whether the capital stock is increasing or decreasing over time. If it is decreasing and if its change is underestimated, net investment is negative and its forecast is algebraically larger than actual investment. Consequently, if depreciation is a predetermined variable (which is a reasonable assumption), predicted gross investment exceeds then actual gross investment. But if the capital stock is increasing over time, then, all other assumptions being fulfilled, the conclusion is the reverse and the predicted investment level is below the actual level. In the case of the surveys mentioned below, no accurate data on the development of capital are available. However, it is very unplausible that decreasing capital stocks played a significant rôle during the period of these surveys. We shall therefore neglect this possibility and say that underestimation of the change in capital stock is equivalent to underestimation of the level of investment. Table 5.6 below gives then some results

TABLE 5.6

RELATIVE FREQUENCIES OF UNDER AND OVERESTIMATION WITH RESPECT TO INVESTMENT IN SIX AMERICAN AND SIX CANADIAN INDUSTRIES, 1947–1951 (Firestone, 1955)

Types of forecasting errors	*United States*	*Canada*
Estimation of investment levels		
underestimation	0.7	0.8
overestimation	0.3	0.2
Estimation of investment changes		
turning point errors	0.1	0.1
underestimation	0.4	0.7
overestimation	0.5	0.2

on about 60 survey forecasts for six American and six Canadian industry groups (manufacturing, mining, railroads, other transportation, electric and gas utilities, commercial and miscellaneous) for the years 1947–1951.[1] It appears that about 70–80 per cent of the investment predictions are below the corresponding actual levels, both for Canada and the United States. In the case of the American industries there is no evidence of a tendency towards underestimation of investment changes, the frequency of underestimation being about equal to that of overestimation. For Canada it is impossible to distinguish between the two types of underestimation because of strong upward trends. So, when viewed as a whole, there seems to be more evidence in the direction of underestimation of investment levels than in that of underestimation of investment changes. Although it is possible to ascribe the former effect to several specific causes,[2] it is clearly more instructive to see it also in the light of the general bias towards change underestimation (in this case: of capital stock).

5.4.2. Some further results can be obtained by means of similar Dutch investment surveys, conducted by the Netherlands Central Bureau of Statistics.[3] Table 5.7 is a bivariate frequency table containing observations for 96 industrial classifications in the three consecutive years 1952, 1953, 1954. The variables observed are predicted and actual investment, both measured as percentage deviations from the corresponding actual investment level in the preceding year. The frequencies of Table 5.7 are indicated only if they are not zero, except when a zero occurs in the main diagonal; all entries of the main diagonal are printed in italics. Several conclusions can be drawn from this table. First, there is a clear positive correlation between predicted and actual investment changes, though the forecasts are evidently far from perfect. Second, the table shows some heteroskedasticity: the variance of predicted changes for highly negative actual changes tends to be smaller than that for highly positive actual changes, and the same holds when predicted and actual changes are interchanged. This effect is rather

[1] The data are derived from O. J. FIRESTONE's article "Investment Forecasting in Canada" in *Short-Term Economic Forecasting*, pp. 190–191, 231; we refer to this article for more detailed information. The frequencies for investment changes in the United States refer to the years 1948–1951 only. Investment is to be understood as gross investment.

[2] Like "the omission of many small items of capital outlay and the exclusion of items whose acquisition is uncertain." Cf. I. FRIEND and J. BRONFENBRENNER, "Plant and Equipment Programs and their Realization" in *Short-Term Economic Forecasting*, p.55.

[3] The analysis reported below has been communicated to me by Mr. A. RUSSCHEN in private correspondence. I am indebted to him for his permission to quote the results. Data for the separate years 1952, 1953, 1954 are presented in the Appendix to this chapter, Section 5.C.

TABLE 5.7

BIVARIATE FREQUENCY TABLE OF ACTUAL AND PREDICTED PERCENTAGE INVESTMENT CHANGES RELATIVE TO ACTUAL INVESTMENT IN THE PRECEDING YEAR, FOR 96 DUTCH INDUSTRIES IN THE YEARS 1952, 1953 AND 1954 (Russchen, 1956)

Predicted change	*Actual change (percentage intervals)*														*Sum*
	−100/−81	*−80/−61*	*−60/−41*	*−40/−21*	*−20/−1*	*0/19*	*20/39*	*40/59*	*60/79*	*80/99*	*100/119*	*120/139*	*140/159*	*≧160*	
−100/−81	*0*	3	2	.	.	.	2	.	.	.	.	.	.	1	8
−80/−61	.	*5*	6	7	2	1	3	2	.	.	.	.	.	.	26
−60/−41	1	2	*7*	12	6	3	1	1	1	.	.	1	.	1	36
−40/−21	.	1	1	*14*	14	9	3	.	1	1	.	.	.	1	45
−20/−1	.	2	4	6	*16*	11	7	6	2	1	1	.	.	.	56
0/19	.	.	1	3	4	*8*	9	6	1	2	1	2	1	2	40
20/39	.	.	1	1	2	3	*7*	4	2	1	2	.	.	1	24
40/59	.	.	.	.	1	.	5	*0*	1	.	1	1	.	1	10
60/79	.	.	.	.	1	2	3	4	*6*	1	.	2	.	.	19
80/99	.	.	.	.	1	.	.	1	1	*0*	.	.	.	1	4
100/119	.	.	.	.	.	.	.	.	1	1	*0*	1	.	.	3
120/139	.	.	.	.	.	.	.	.	1	1	.	*0*	1	2	5
140/159	.	.	.	.	.	1	.	.	.	.	.	.	*0*	.	1
≧ 160	.	.	.	.	.	.	1	.	1	.	.	.	1	*7*	10
Sum	1	13	22	43	47	38	41	24	18	8	5	7	3	17	

easy to understand, for considerable positive changes in predicted and actual investment will frequently occur when the original investment level is small, in which case the variance of the changes will generally be considerable, too.

More interesting from our present point of view is that the table gives no indication of an underestimation of investment changes, but that it shows a clear underestimation of investment levels. The former type of underestimation would imply a difference between the marginal distribution of predictions and that of realisations in the sense that the former has smaller frequencies both for highly negative and for highly positive changes. The table reveals that this is true for positive, not for negative changes. Indeed, actual decreases have generally been predicted still more negatively than the outcomes justified: there are 126 cases of a reported decrease in investment, 52 of which are above the main diagonal in Table 5.7 and 32 are below. The median of all actual changes is an increase of about 9 per cent, whereas the median of the predicted changes is a decrease of about 10 per cent; which amounts to a "turning point error" in the aggregate. Similar median differences can be observed for the separate years. It is also interesting to note that, if we would increase all predicted changes by 20 per cent, the resulting marginal distribution of predictions is closer to that of the realisations in the sense that the sum of squares of the differences between corresponding frequencies is reduced by almost 40 per cent.[1]

5.4.3. Another problem of interpretation of changes arises when the analysis covers variables which are subject to seasonal fluctuations. An example is that of the quarterly forecasts of American railroad shippers, which have recently been analysed by several authors.[2] Since 1927,

[1] Note that predicted and actual investment have been taken here at the prices of the period of prediction. If it is assumed that the entrepreneurs forecast in real terms (i.e., that they give their investment predictions at the prices of the moment of the prediction), this affects the outcomes, though the conclusions remain qualitatively the same. Note further that the aggregate outcomes for predicted national investment may be influenced to a considerable degree by the way in which the individual forecasts are weighted. Since large firms tend to be more successful in forecasting (see e.g. FRIEND and BRONFENBRENNER, *loc. cit.*, p. 55), the underestimation at the national level is often of moderate size. The Dutch forecasts considered above are quite interesting in this connection. Although there can be no doubt about the general underestimation of future investment levels throughout the economy, the aggregate figures showed sometimes an overestimation; see the Central Bureau's publication *Investeringen in vaste activa, 1954 en 1955* (Utrecht, 1955), p. 11. This effect is largely due to the relatively substantial overestimation of the large investments of the public utilities. Also cf. Section 5. C of the Appendix.

[2] Cf. R. FERBER, *The Railroad Shippers' Forecasts* (Urbana, Ill., 1953); F. MODIGLIANI

these shippers have made predictions of the number of carloadings required for the next quarter, after which the results were aggregated by "commodity chairmen" to macropredictions for separate areas and commodity classifications. There is a seasonal problem in general; and accordingly predicted (and actual) percentage changes are given in the form

$$(5.15) \qquad P_t = \frac{p_t - a_{t-4}}{a_{t-4}} 100; \qquad A_t = \frac{a_t - a_{t-4}}{a_{t-4}} 100,$$

respectively, where p_t is the required number of carloadings predicted at the end of the quarter $t - 1$ for quarter t, a_{t-4} the actual number of carloadings used in the same quarter of the preceding year, etc. Further, it has been argued that the shippers base their predictions largely upon the changes observed in the quarter before $(t - 1)$ with respect to the corresponding quarter of the previous year;[1] this amounts to an equation of the form $P_t = g(A_{t-1})$ describing the generation of the forecasts. Some empirical evidence is presented in Fig. 5.6, which contains twenty-one scatters for the pairs of variables P_t and A_t, P_t and A_{t-1}, and A_t and A_{t-1}, and for several commodity classifications. The first pair (P_t and A_t) corresponds with the accuracy analysis; the second (P_t and A_{t-1}) with the suggested relation $P_t = g(A_{t-1})$ for the generation of the predictions; and the third pair (A_t and A_{t-1}) is chosen in order to see whether the correlation between P_t and A_{t-1} is merely the result of a combined effect of the autocorrelation of the A's and the accuracy of forecasting. Fig. 5.6 suggests that this combined effect is not sufficient to explain the correlation between P_t and A_{t-1}, for this correlation is in general higher than that between A_t and A_{t-1}. On the other hand, the former correlations tend to be somewhat below the level of the scatters of P_t and A_t, so that the shippers' achievements are presumably better than this simple extrapolation theory suggests.

The seven scatters for P_t and A_t suggest a general underestimation of changes; where, of course, "change" should be interpreted here as the deviation from the level of the corresponding quarter of the preceding year. When confining ourselves to the first criterion of Section 5.1 (underestimation in the sense of the regression of P on A), we can

and O. H. SAUERLENDER, "Economic Expectations and Plans in Relation to Short-Term Forecasting;" T. HULTGREN, "Forecasts of Railway Traffic." The last two papers are published in *Short-Term Economic Forecasting*. The data underlying Fig. 5.6 below are derived from Ferber's Appendix, Table 1, pp. 138–139.

[1] Cf. Ferber, *loc. cit.*, pp. 68–71.

describe the situation for total shipments in a simple manner by means of the following three least-squares regressions:

$$\underset{(0.5)}{P_t = 3.2} + \underset{(0.03)}{0.50}\, A_t; \qquad \underset{(0.7)}{P_t = 3.6} + \underset{(0.04)}{0.48}\, A_{t-1};$$

(5.16)

$$A_t = \underset{(1.3)}{0.6} + \underset{(0.08)}{0.82}\, A_{t-1}.$$

The first two regressions are characterised by multiplicative coefficients of about $\frac{1}{2}$. This suggests that the bias towards underestimation could be eliminated by doubling the influence of the change observed in the quarter before, the coefficient in the regression of A_t on A_{t-1} being hardly significantly different from unity. The constant terms in the first two regressions are significantly positive, and the same is not true for the third. This implies that two types of systematic errors are made, viz., an overestimation of the level of shipments by 2–4 per cent, and an underestimation of its changes by about 50 per cent; which means a general underestimation of large increases and decreases and a slight tendency towards turning point errors (overestimation) when actual development shows small decreases (increases).[1] But the underestimation of changes is evidently predominant.

5.4.4. Summarising our results, we may say that the answer to the question whether there is any tendency towards underestimation of changes depends on the criterion chosen; but that, in fact, we have observed this bias even under the "strongest" of the criteria which we considered, viz., in the sense of the regression of actual on predicted changes. This is especially clear for the macroeconomic forecasts analysed in Chapter III, and it is now obvious from its sequel in Section 5.2 that this phenomenon has been primarily caused by the underestimation of the "higher-order" exogenous changes—which is in accordance with the theoretical result of the last paragraph of 5.1.4 when we take $0 < h < 1$. Underestimation of changes seems to be absent only if the forecaster has a rather good prediction mechanism at his disposal—cf. the price forecasts of firms near the consumer, and the conditional predictions of endogenous macrovariables.

We conclude this chapter with a slightly different interpretation of its subject. The argument is as follows. In most cases we can approxi-

[1] Cf. the second paragraph of 5.1.4.

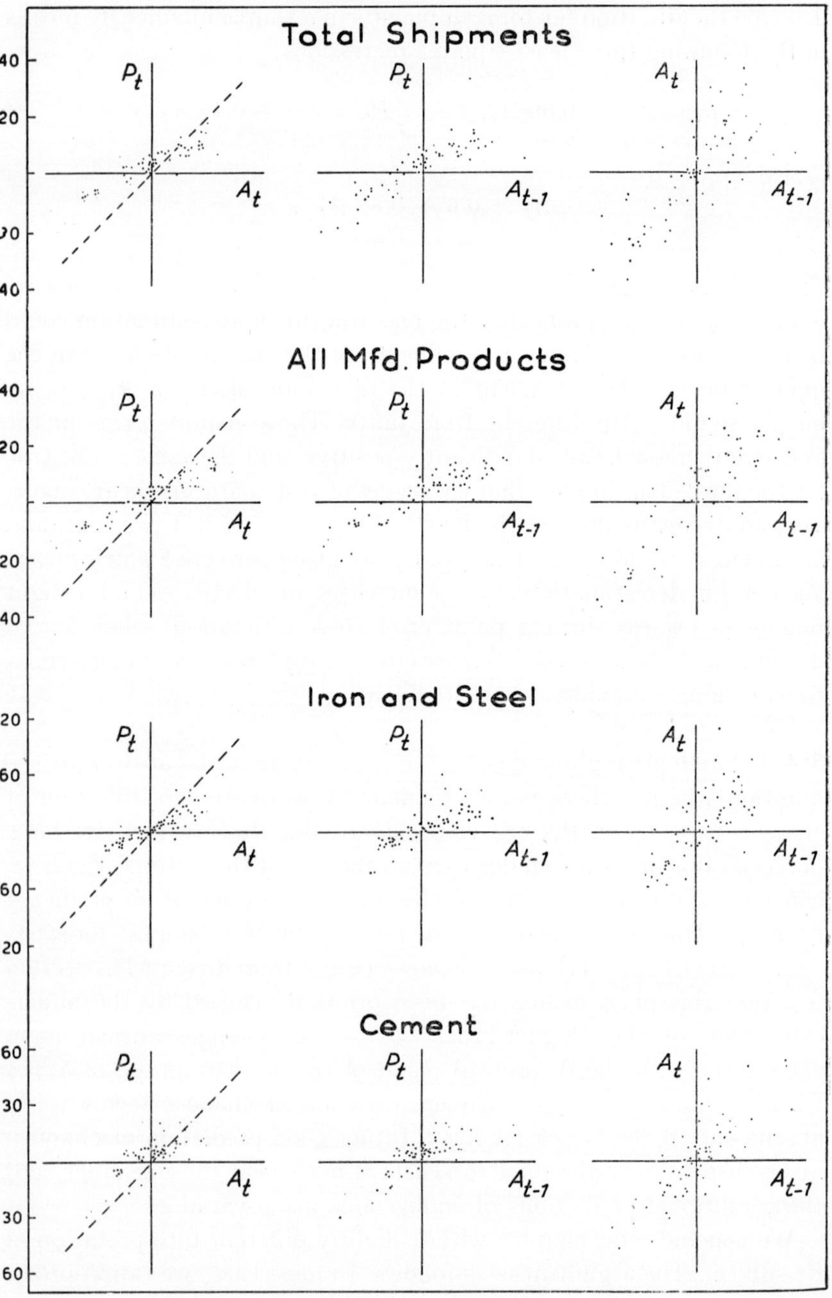
Total Shipments
40
20
-40
All Mfd. Products
40
20
-20
-40
Iron and Steel
120
60
-60
.120
Cement
60
30
-30
-60
P_t
A_t
A_{t-1}

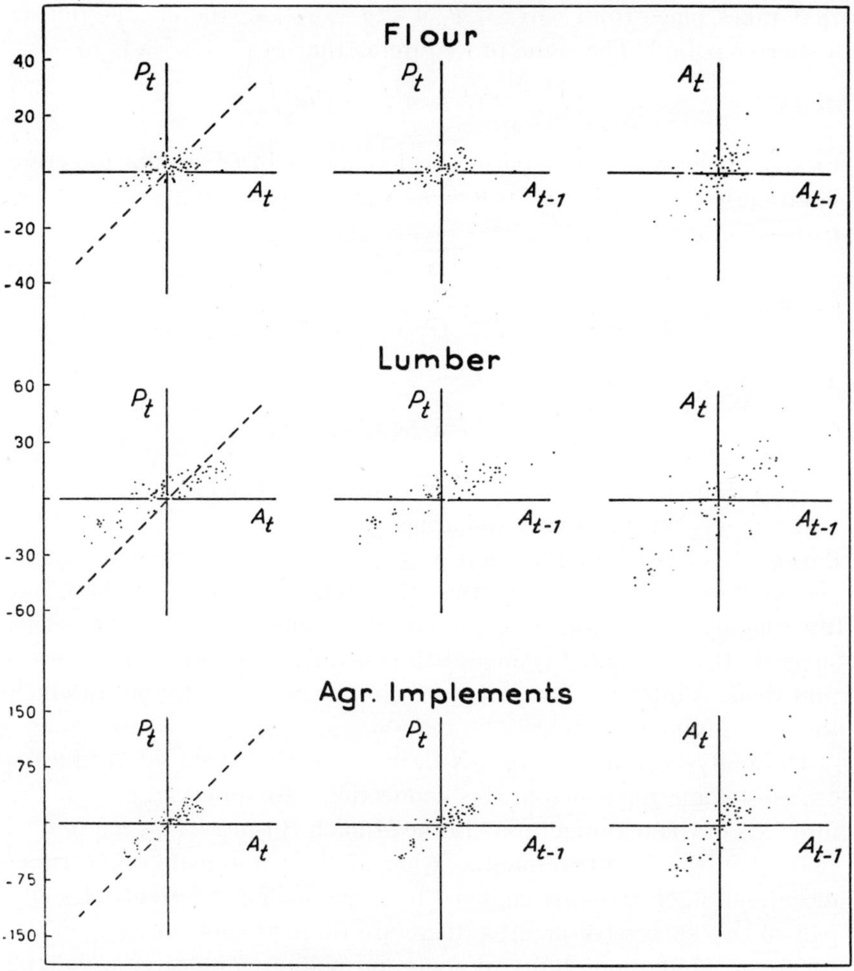

Fig. 5.6. Scatter diagrams connecting, for the aggregate American railroad shipments and for several sub-classifications, the predicted percentage change in relation to the corresponding quarter in the previous year (P_t), the actual change defined similarly (A_t), and the actual change lagged one quarter (A_{t-1}). Period: 1927–1941, 1946–1950

mate the time path of the variable to be predicted—f^A in the notation of Section 5.1—by a smooth curve. Hence

$$f_{t+1}^A - f_t^A = \dot{f}_t^A + \tfrac{1}{2}\ddot{f}_t^A, \tag{5.17}$$

$\dot{f}_t^A$ and $\ddot{f}_t^A$ being the first and second-order time derivatives, respectively, of f^A in t, is approximately true. Now consider also the change in f^A

that takes place from t to $t + \theta$, $0 < \theta < 1$; i.e., the change during a shorter period. The same procedure as that of (5.17) leads to

$$(5.18) \qquad f^A_{t+\theta} - f^A_t = \theta \dot{f}^A_t + \tfrac{1}{2}\theta^2 \ddot{f}^A_t .$$

Clearly, as long as the higher-order derivatives of f^A are not too large in absolute value—that is, as long as a linear approximation is not too bad—, we have

$$(5.19) \qquad \begin{aligned} 0 &< f^A_{t+\theta} - f^A_t < f^A_{t+1} - f^A_t \text{ if } f^A_{t+1} > f^A_t ; \\ 0 &> f^A_{t+\theta} - f^A_t > f^A_{t+1} - f^A_t \text{ if } f^A_{t+1} < f^A_t , \end{aligned}$$

and even

$$(5.20) \qquad f^A_{t+\theta} - f^A_t \approx \theta (f^A_{t+1} - f^A_t),$$

which means that the change during a fixed smaller interval of time tends to be smaller than, and roughly proportional to, the change during the original interval. But we found earlier that predicted changes have exactly these properties: they tend to be smaller than, but are roughly proportional to, the corresponding actual changes. This suggests that predicted changes will generally look better if we interpret them as referring to a period which is smaller than the one to which they are supposed to refer.

The analysis of the German textile industry carried out by ANDERSON c.s. is of some relevance in this connection.[1] As observed earlier, the forecasts of the manufacturers in the Munich Business Test referred to changes in the next two months, whereas their statements concerning recent actual changes are confined to only one month.[2] Hence, for any pair of two successive months, there are three possible answers in the sphere of predictions (viz., increase, no change, or decrease for the two-month period as a whole), but nine as to actual development: increase in both months, increase in the first month and no change in the second, etc. Let us denote these nine possibilities by (11), (12), (13), (21), . . ., (33), where the first number refers to the first month, the second to the second month, and 1, 2, 3 to increase, no change, and decrease respectively. Consider then (12) and (21), i.e., an increase in one month and no change in the other, in either order. As long as we know nothing about the magnitude of the change involved, we should

[1] Cf. p. 169 n.
[2] Cf. the Appendix to Chapter IV.

conclude that both categories are characterised by the same *a priori* probabilities of being predicted as increases, provided it is true that the forecaster gives equal weights to both months. If, however, the forecaster underestimates changes in the sense of the preceding paragraph, i.e., in the sense that his predictions are generally closer to the actual changes during a period from now till an earlier date, then we should expect the category (12) to be characterised by a larger frequency of being predicted as an increase than (21). Some results are presented in Table 5.8, both for (12), (21) and for (32), (23). It appears that the frequency of predicted increases is consistently larger in the case of an actual increase in the first month than in that in the second, and similarly for decreases; which is as we expected. It is also seen that the effect exists even for the prices of firms which are not far from the ultimate consumer. To go back to Keynes' quotation, we may say that not only the facts of the existing situation enter disproportionately into the formation of long-term predictions, but also that a similar rôle is played by those changes in this situation which will occur (and are presumed to occur) in the near future. At least, this is what is suggested by the results of Table 5.8.

TABLE 5.8

FREQUENCY OF PREDICTED INCREASES CORRESPONDING TO AN ACTUAL INCREASE IN THE FIRST AND NO-CHANGE IN THE SECOND MONTH (12) AND TO ACTUAL NO-CHANGE IN THE FIRST AND AN INCREASE IN THE SECOND MONTH (21) — AND SIMILARLY WITH INCREASES REPLACED BY DECREASES [(32) AND (23), RESPECTIVELY] —, FOR FIRMS AND VARIABLES OF THE GERMAN TEXTILE INDUSTRY, 1950–1953 (Anderson c.s., 1954)

Industry	*Actual development*	*Variables**		
		production	*employees*	*selling prices*
spinning and weaving	(12)	0.27 (188)	0.27 (75)	0.55 (197)
	(21)	0.12 (162)	0.11 (63)	0.31 (168)
	(32)	0.38 (143)	0.33 (72)	0.33 (207)
	(23)	0.14 (156)	0.16 (74)	0.16 (205)
confection	(12)	0.37 (241)	0.35 (101)	0.53 (93)
	(21)	0.22 (167)	0.21 (80)	0.34 (101)
	(32)	0.37 (93)	0.39 (59)	0.35 (112)
	(23)	0.14 (152)	0.19 (81)	0.15 (137)

* Figures in brackets indicate the relevant number of observations.

Appendix to Chapter V

5.A. Further Figures on Dutch Macroeconomic Forecasts

Table 5.9 below contains the figures underlying the analysis of Section 5.2, in so far as they are not contained in Section 3.A of the Appendix of Chapter III. The second column indicates whether the relevant row refers to conditional predictions (P_C), actual changes (A) or unconditional forecasts (P). The figures in the final column refer to observed changes in 1954; they have not been given in Chapter III, and their inclusion in P_C- or P-rows (where they do not belong, strictly speaking) serves to condense the table. Naturally, these 1954 changes are mostly preliminary and must be expected to have relatively sizable errors of measurement. Table 5.10 contains the means and the standard deviations of these series, all multiplied by 10, and their correlation and inequality measures, all multiplied by 100.

It is interesting, furthermore, to note that the depreciation allowances form a variable for which, at least from 1950 onwards, the systematic U_S-error mentioned in 2.5.3 has been made: the predicted changes are almost constant, whereas the observed changes show much more variation. Again, it should be admitted that such observed changes are subject to uncertainties.

Two further remarks should be made on the application of the equation system. First, the autonomous tax term of the price equations was neglected in all cases except for the equation describing the price level of consumption goods. Second, the investment equation of the model-1955 was abandoned and replaced by a relation of the following form:

$$(5.21) \qquad i = \delta \left\{ \theta \frac{(v-k) + (v-k)_{-1}}{2} - (\bar{\imath} - \bar{\imath}_h) \right\} + i_h,$$

where i is the change in net investment, i_h the change in net investment in housing (an exogenous variable), $\bar{\imath}$ and $\bar{\imath}_h$ the level of these variables in the preceding year, v the change in output of enterprises, k the sum of the changes in house rents (r in the notation of Section

TABLE 5.9

CONDITIONAL PREDICTED PERCENTAGE CHANGES AND FURTHER DATA ON DUTCH MACROECONOMIC VARIABLES, 1949–1954 (Lips and Schouten, 1955)

Variables	P_C, *A or P*	*1949*	*1950*	*1951*	*1952*	*1953*	*1954*	*1954 (A)*
(a) *Price indices of:*								
commodity exports	P_C	+ 3.4	+ 6.2	+16.5	+2.6	− 4.2	− 0.8	− 5
consumption	P_C	+ 3.6	+ 6.3	+14.6	+2.0	− 3.5	+ 2.9	+ 4
investment goods	P_C	− 0.5	+ 7.8	+14.0	+0.5	− 4.8	+ 0.3	.
	A	+ 1	+ 3	+17	+8	− 5	+ 0	.
inventories	P_C	− 2.0	+10.3	+19.4	−0.4	− 8.5	− 2.9	.
	A	− 1	+13	+21	+1	−12	− 2	.
Government commodity purchases	P_C	− 0.3	+ 8.1	+14.5	+0.7	− 4.6	+ 0.8	.
	A	+ 2	+ 3	+17	+7	− 4	+ 2	.
(b) *Quantities and volumes:*								
commodity imports	P_C	+26.0	+36.9	− 0.6	−9.3	+31.3	+25.4	+28
consumption	P_C	+ 1.3	+ 1.0	− 6.4	−0.1	+ 9.1	+ 6.9	+ 5
gross fixed investment	P_C	+18.1	+12.3	−10.9	−1.3	+ 6.8	+11.7	.
	A	+11	+12	−10	+1	+ 6	+19	.
gross national product	P_C	+ 7.0	+ 6.7	+ 0.7	−0.3	+ 8.5	+ 6.0	.
	A	+10	+ 8	− 1	+3	+10	+ 5	.
employment in private sector	P_C	+ 2.8	+ 2.7	+ 0.3	−0.1	+ 3.4	+ 2.4	+ 2.5
(c) *Money values:*								
indirect taxes minus subsidies	P_C	+36.5	+19.7	+27.9	−1.5	+ 4.9	+11.1	+12.5
income taxes paid by wage-earners	P_C	+ 6.7	+13.2	− 3.2	+3.2	+ 8.0	+ 5.6	.
	A	+ 9.8	+10.4	− 1.4	+1.4	+ 6.8	+ 5.1	.
income taxes paid by others	P_C	+ 1.5	+18.7	+ 4.6	+4.2	+ 3.3	+ 0.2	.
	A	+ 5.4	+19.8	− 2.8	+7.3	+ 8.1	− 2.5	.
non-wage income	P_C	+10.0	+ 9.7	+10.9	+1.8	+ 9.3	+ 7.8	.
	A	+14	+12	+ 5	+8	+10	+ 4	.
(d) *Exogenous variables:*								
commodity exports	*P*	.	.	.	.	.	+ 6.0	+17
import prices	*P*	.	.	.	.	.	− 6.7	− 5
depreciation allowances	*P*	+ 4.7	+ 2.8	+ 2.9	.	+ 3.2	+ 3.0	.
	A	+ 2	+ 6	+ 3	.	+ 2	+ 1	.
available labour force	*P*	.	.	.	.	.	+ 1.3	+ 1.8
Government wage bill	*P*	.	.	.	.	.	+11.5	+15
Government commodity purchases	*P*	.	.	.	.	.	− 0.5	+ 2
exports of services	*P*	.	.	.	.	.	− 1.8	+ 5
imports of services	*P*	.	.	.	.	.	+ 6.3	+10

TABLE 5.10

MEANS AND STANDARD DEVIATIONS (MULTIPLIED BY 10), AND CORRELATION AND INEQUALITY COEFFICIENTS AND PROPORTIONS (MULTIPLIED BY 100) CORRESPONDING TO TABLE 5.9

Variables	$\bar{P}$	$\bar{A}$	s_P	s_A	r	U	U_M	U_S	U_C	U_R	U_D	U^M	U^S	U^C	U^R	U^D
(a) *Price indices of:*																
commodity exports	39	3	65	96	96	31	21	–18	13	–16	16	47	35	18	27	26
consumption	43	47	55	48	91	17	– 3	5	16	8	15	2	9	89	23	75
investment goods	29	40	62	70	85	26	– 8	– 5	24	2	25	8	4	88	1	91
inventories	26	33	94	107	99	10	– 3	– 7	6	– 6	7	11	46	43	40	49
Government commodity purchases	32	45	63	64	86	24	– 9	– 1	23	5	22	13	0	87	4	83
(b) *Quantities and volumes:*																
commodity imports	183	130	171	158	92	19	12	3	15	6	14	38	2	60	9	53
consumption	20	15	50	31	95	26	5	22	14	23	11	4	68	28	79	17
gross fixed investment	81	65	67	92	76	29	7	–12	25	– 1	28	7	16	77	0	93
gross national product	48	58	34	37	94	13	– 8	– 1	10	– 1	10	42	1	57	0	58
employment in private sector	19	22	13	15	77	20	– 5	– 5	19	2	20	6	5	89	1	93
(c) *Money values:*																
indirect taxes minus subsidies	164	147	131	118	98	8	4	3	6	3	5	33	16	51	20	47
income taxes paid by wage-earners	56	53	50	43	91	14	2	5	13	8	12	1	12	87	28	71
income taxes paid by others	54	59	61	76	83	24	– 3	– 8	23	– 1	24	1	12	87	0	99
non-wage income	82	88	30	36	19	23	– 3	– 3	23	13	19	2	2	96	30	68

3.1), in exports of services (e_s) and in inventory changes (n). Further, θ stands for the normal capital-output ratio of the aggregate enterprise system; and δ is an adjustment coefficient, the dimension of which is that of the inverse of a year. Hence (5.21) describes investment outside the dwelling sector as proportional to the difference between the stock of capital goods in the beginning of the year and the capital stock which corresponds in the long run with the average of this year's and last year's output; except, of course, for a first-difference transformation.

5.B. On the Allocation of the Errors of Forecasting Made by Means of Econometric Models

5.B.1. When an equation system is used for prediction purposes, the errors of forecasting are always due to the following pair of causes: the equation system may be different from the "true" system, and erroneous values of exogenous variables may have been used. The results of Chapter III and Section 5.2 are such that there can be little doubt about the relative magnitude of these sources in the Dutch case; a further analysis of that case is therefore not very urgent. Nevertheless, this subject is of some general interest.

Confining ourselves to linear equation systems, we can write for the unconditional point prediction of the vector of endogenous values ($\mathbf{y}^P$)

$$\mathbf{y}^P = \mathbf{\Pi}_e \mathbf{z}^P, \tag{5.22}$$

where $\mathbf{z}^P$ is the unconditional point prediction of the vector of exogenous values and $\mathbf{\Pi}_e$ the coefficient matrix of the equation system used. Supposing that the "true" system is also linear, we can write for the "true" value of the endogenous vector

$$\mathbf{y} = \mathbf{\Pi z}, \tag{5.23}$$

$\mathbf{z}$ being the "true" exogenous vector. The error in $\mathbf{y}$ is then

$$\begin{aligned} \mathbf{y}^P - \mathbf{y} &= (\mathbf{\Pi}_e - \mathbf{\Pi})\mathbf{z} + \mathbf{\Pi}(\mathbf{z}^P - \mathbf{z}) + (\mathbf{\Pi}_e - \mathbf{\Pi})(\mathbf{z}^P - \mathbf{z}) \\ &= \mathbf{a} + \mathbf{b} + \mathbf{c}, \text{ say.} \end{aligned} \tag{5.24}$$

The first term ($\mathbf{a}$) can be regarded as being due to the incorrectly specified model; the second ($\mathbf{b}$) to the imperfect exogenous prediction; and the third ($\mathbf{c}$) is a mixture of both errors. However, this last term is of the second order of smallness and hence small if $\mathbf{a}$ and $\mathbf{b}$ are moderate. So we have:

$$\mathbf{y}^P - \mathbf{y} \approx \mathbf{a} + \mathbf{b}. \tag{5.25}$$

It will be noted that the specification (5.22)–(5.23) includes the case where we have a constant term in the equations; one of the components of $\mathbf{z}$ and of $\mathbf{z}^P$ is then put equal to 1. Also, this specification can be easily generalised for additive disturbances: we should add $\mathbf{u}^P$ and $\mathbf{u}$ in the right-hand sides of (5.22) and (5.23), respectively, and replace $\mathbf{b}$ of (5.24) by

$$\mathbf{b}^* = \mathbf{\Pi}(\mathbf{z}^P - \mathbf{z}) + \mathbf{u}^P - \mathbf{u}.$$

This implies simply that the disturbances are interpreted as values assumed by (unspecified) exogenous variables.

5.B.2. Suppose then that a series of successive observations $\overset{P}{\mathbf{y}_t}$, $\mathbf{y}_t$, $\mathbf{a}_t, \ldots$ $(t = 1, 2, \ldots)$ is available. Suppose further that the criterion used for judging the quality of the forecasts is a quadratic expression in the forecasting errors $\overset{P}{\mathbf{y}_1} - \mathbf{y}_1$, $\overset{P}{\mathbf{y}_2} - \mathbf{y}_2, \ldots$ This device has been applied in Section 2.5 for the definition of the inequality coefficient, and its relevance will be further illustrated in Chapter VIII. Applying (5.25), we then find that this expression is approximately equal to a quadratic function of $\mathbf{a}_1, \mathbf{a}_2, \ldots$ plus a quadratic function of $\mathbf{b}_1, \mathbf{b}_2, \ldots$ plus a bilinear function of both sets of vectors. The first two quadratic forms can be uniquely allocated, viz., to model errors and to exogenous errors, respectively; but the bilinear form is due to the joint operation of both error types and cannot be divided among them. It will be observed that this situation is comparable with the rôle of $\mathbf{c}$ in (5.24); except, however, for the important difference that the bilinear form is not of the second order of smallness as compared with the two quadratic forms.

Further, it should be noted that the three terms of (5.24) can be computed only if $\mathbf{\Pi}$ is known. In general this is not true. If the knowledge of the structure of the constraints does not go beyond $\mathbf{\Pi}_e$, one must replace (5.24) by

$$\mathbf{y}^P - \mathbf{y} = (\mathbf{\Pi}_e\mathbf{z} - \mathbf{y}) + \mathbf{\Pi}_e(\mathbf{z}^P - \mathbf{z}), \tag{5.26}$$

which means that $\mathbf{b}$ and $\mathbf{c}$ are combined. When there are additive disturbances ($\mathbf{u}$ and $\mathbf{u}^P$), we have the problem that $\mathbf{u}$ can no longer be determined, since $\mathbf{u} = \mathbf{y} - \mathbf{\Pi z}$, $\mathbf{\Pi}$ being unknown. The best procedure is then to include them in the first term of (5.26) by replacing this by $(\mathbf{\Pi}_e \mathbf{z} + \mathbf{u}^P - \mathbf{y})$.

5.C. Further Data on Dutch Investment Surveys

The data underlying Table 5.7 are not free from sampling errors, and the successive samples drawn from the population of all firms in each industrial classification are not identical. However, in most of the cases participation took place by more than one half of the firms, especially the larger ones. In order to obtain figures for the separate classifications as a whole, all predicted and actual investment amounts in each group have been multiplied by the ratio of the total number of workers in the classification to the total number in the sample.[1]

Table 5.11 gives a survey of all quartiles of the marginal distributions of predicted and actual changes; the Tables 5.12–5.14 give the same data as Table 5.7, but for separate years. It appears that the underestimation of investment levels is persistent. If we would increase all predicted investment changes by 20 per cent, the sum of squares of the differences between the corresponding frequencies of the two marginal distributions of Table 5.12 would decrease by about 70 per cent; and in the case of Table 5.13 and 5.14, by about 30 and 50 per cent, respectively.

TABLE 5.11

QUARTILES OF THE MARGINAL DISTRIBUTIONS OF PREDICTED AND ACTUAL INVESTMENT CHANGES, RELATIVE TO ACTUAL INVESTMENT IN THE PRECEDING YEAR, FOR 96 DUTCH INDUSTRIES IN 1952–1954 (Russchen, 1956)

Quartiles	*1952*		*1953*		*1954*	
	forecast	*actual*	*forecast*	*actual*	*forecast*	*actual*
lower quartile	−56	−37	−31.5	−22.5	−18.5	4.5
median	−32	−17	−14	6.5	4.5	32.5
upper quartile	2	18	20.5	53	44.5	66

[1] We should also mention that different questions asked on the same topic may easily lead to significantly different answers. The Dutch investment survey, for example, asks for the total amount invested in those projects that are expected to be completed in the next year; and if the projects are sizable, part of that amount has been invested in earlier years, but it is considered in the survey as falling under the investment of next year. This procedure is not followed in all other countries. Further, there are sometimes other phenomena which conceal the phenomenon of underestimation of investment levels. At present (winter 1957–1958) many industries work close to their capacity ceiling, which implies that the supply of investment goods is below their demand; and many firms failed to predict this change from buyers' to sellers' markets.

TABLE 5.12

BIVARIATE FREQUENCY TABLE OF ACTUAL AND PREDICTED PERCENTAGE INVESTMENT CHANGES RELATIVE TO ACTUAL INVESTMENT IN THE PRECEDING YEAR, FOR 95 DUTCH INDUSTRIES IN 1952 (Russchen, 1956)

Predicted change	*Actual change (percentage intervals)*														*Sum*
	−100/−81	*−80/−61*	*−60/−41*	*−40/−21*	*−20/−1*	*0/19*	*20/39*	*40/59*	*60/79*	*80/99*	*100/119*	*120/139*	*140/159*	*≥160*	
−100/−81	*0*	2	2	.	.	.	1	.	.	.	.	.	.	.	5
−80/−61	.	*2*	5	4	2	.	2	.	.	.	.	.	.	.	15
−60/−41	.	.	*3*	10	5	1	1	.	.	.	.	.	.	.	20
−40/−21	.	1	1	*7*	3	4	.	.	.	.	.	.	.	.	16
−20/−1	.	2	2	1	*4*	2	1	1	.	.	.	.	.	.	13
0/19	.	.	.	1	3	*2*	3	.	.	.	.	1	.	.	10
20/39	.	.	.	.	1	2	*2*	.	.	.	1	.	.	.	6
40/59	.	.	.	.	.	.	.	*0*	.	.	1	.	.	.	1
60/79	.	.	.	.	.	.	2	2	*2*	.	.	.	.	.	6
80/99	.	.	.	.	.	.	.	.	.	*0*	.	.	.	.	0
100/119	.	.	.	.	.	.	.	.	.	.	*0*	.	.	.	0
120/139	.	.	.	.	.	.	.	.	.	.	.	*0*	.	.	0
140/159	.	.	.	.	.	.	.	.	.	.	.	.	*0*	.	0
≥160	.	.	.	.	.	.	.	.	1	.	.	.	.	*2*	3
Sum	0	7	13	23	18	11	12	3	3	0	2	1	0	2	

TABLE 5.13

SAME AS TABLE 5.12, FOR 96 DUTCH INDUSTRIES IN 1953 (Russchen, 1956)

Predicted change	*Actual change (percentage intervals)*														*Sum*
	-100/-81	*-80/-61*	*-60/-41*	*-40/-21*	*-20/-1*	*0/19*	*20/39*	*40/59*	*60/79*	*80/99*	*100/119*	*120/139*	*140/159*	*≧160*	
-100/-81	*0*	1	.	.	.	.	1	.	.	.	.	.	.	1	3
-80/-61	.	*2*	1	1	.	1	1	2	.	.	.	.	.	.	8
-60/-41	1	1	*4*	1	1	1	.	.	1	.	.	.	.	1	11
-40/-21	.	.	.	*6*	7	1	1	.	1	.	.	.	.	.	16
-20/-1	.	.	1	3	*6*	8	1	1	1	.	1	.	.	.	22
0/19	.	.	.	2	1	*3*	1	2	.	1	.	.	1	1	12
20/39	.	.	1	1	.	.	*1*	3	.	.	1	.	.	1	8
40/59	.	.	.	.	.	.	1	*0*	.	.	.	1	.	.	2
60/79	.	.	.	.	1	1	1	.	*0*	.	.	1	.	.	4
80/99	.	.	.	.	1	.	.	.	.	*0*	.	.	.	1	2
100/119	.	.	.	.	.	.	.	.	.	.	*0*	1	.	.	1
120/139	.	.	.	.	.	.	.	.	.	1	.	*0*	.	1	2
140/159	.	.	.	.	.	1	.	.	.	.	.	.	*0*	.	1
≧160	.	.	.	.	.	.	.	.	.	.	.	.	1	*3*	4
Sum	1	4	7	14	17	16	8	8	3	2	2	3	2	9	

TABLE 5.14

SAME AS TABLE 5.12, FOR 96 DUTCH INDUSTRIES IN 1954 (Russchen, 1956)

Predicted change	*Actual change (percentage intervals)*														*Sum*
	-100/-81	*-80/-61*	*-60/-41*	*-40/-21*	*-20/-1*	*0/19*	*20/39*	*40/59*	*60/79*	*80/99*	*100/119*	*120/139*	*140/159*	*≧160*	
-100/-81	*0*	.	.	.	.	.	.	.	.	.	.	.	.	.	0
-80/-61	.	*1*	.	2	.	.	.	.	.	.	.	.	.	.	3
-60/-41	.	1	*0*	1	.	1	.	1	.	.	.	1	.	.	5
-40/-21	.	.	.	*1*	4	4	2	.	.	1	.	.	.	1	13
-20/-1	.	.	1	2	*6*	1	5	4	1	1	.	.	.	.	21
0/19	.	.	1	.	.	*3*	5	4	1	1	1	1	.	1	18
20/39	.	.	.	.	1	1	*4*	1	2	1	.	.	.	.	10
40/59	.	.	.	.	1	.	4	*0*	1	.	.	.	.	1	7
60/79	.	.	.	.	.	1	.	2	*4*	1	.	1	.	.	9
80/99	.	.	.	.	.	.	.	1	1	*0*	.	.	.	.	2
100/119	.	.	.	.	.	.	.	.	1	1	*0*	.	.	.	2
120/139	.	.	.	.	.	.	.	.	1	.	.	*0*	1	1	3
140/159	.	.	.	.	.	.	.	.	.	.	.	.	*0*	.	0
≧160	.	.	.	.	.	.	1	.	.	.	.	.	.	*2*	3
Sum	0	2	2	6	12	11	21	13	12	6	1	3	1	6	

VI. Analysis of Interrelationships Among Expected, Planned, and Actual Prices

6.1. Problems of Business Test Methodology

6.1.1. This chapter is devoted to the second type of forecasting problems mentioned in Section 2.3, viz., that of the factors determining predictions. The object of our analysis will be the buying and selling prices of the German leather and shoe industry, considered earlier in Chapter IV; we may refer to that chapter for the underlying data.

There are several reasons for the choice of just these variables. First, they are reasonably complete in the sense that they comprise almost all predicted and actual buying and selling prices of the six stages of the industry, the only exceptions being the expected and actual buying prices of the manufacturers (tanners and shoe manufacturers). Second, the prices are not so much characterised by seasonal fluctuations as the other, non-price variables, which facilitates their analysis. Third, it appeared in Chapter IV that their predictions are in general better than those of the other variables. This does not mean, however, that no interesting conclusions can be drawn about their forecasting errors. On the contrary, it seems that these errors, when defined as the fractions of predicted increases (no change, decreases) minus the corresponding fractions for actual development, are not entirely random but have some positive association through time. Table 6.1 below shows indeed that the Von Neumann ratios of the forecasting errors of the traders' buying prices [defined as $T\Sigma(e_t - e_{t-1})^2/(T-1)\Sigma e_t^2$, T being the number of observations and e_t the error in month t] are frequently below the mean value under the independence hypothesis, especially for those sets of traders which are rather successful in forecasting according to Chapter IV. Fourth, not only the predictions, but also the actual values of these prices show interesting and plausible

TABLE 6.1

VON NEUMANN RATIOS OF THE FORECASTING ERRORS OF THE TRADERS' BUYING PRICES: GERMAN LEATHER AND SHOE INDUSTRY, 1951–1953

Industry stages	*Test variates*		
	x^1	x^2	x^3
traders in hides	2.17	2.75	2.73
traders in leather	1.57	1.62	1.46
wholesalers in shoes	1.57	2.11	2.17
retailers in shoes	1.46	1.79	1.63

TABLE 6.2

AVERAGES OF BASIC TEST VARIATES OF THE TRADERS' AND MANUFACTURERS' ACTUAL PRICES: GERMAN LEATHER AND SHOE INDUSTRY, 1951–1953

Industry stages	*Prices variables*	*Test variates*		
		x^1	x^2	x^3
traders in hides	p_b	0.30	0.30	0.40
	p_s	0.29	0.29	0.42
tanneries	p_s	0.15	0.56	0.29
traders in leather	p_b	0.18	0.53	0.29
	p_s	0.11	0.59	0.30
shoe manufacturers	p_s	0.07	0.77	0.16
wholesalers in shoes	p_b	0.07	0.71	0.22
	p_s	0.06	0.72	0.22
retailers in shoes	p_b	0.15	0.66	0.19
	p_s	0.09	0.71	0.20

patterns, as is seen from Table 6.2. This table contains the averages through time of their basic test variates, and shows that transitions to lower stages are characterised by increased no-change fractions if the lower stage consists of manufacturers, but by roughly the same (or even slightly smaller) average no-change fractions if the lower stage consists of traders. The exact implications of this effect depend on the size of the indifference intervals involved—to which we shall return below—, but even if these intervals are all identical the effect is not unplausible, since manufacturers may be expected to show more inertia in their pricing behaviour than traders do.

Finally, it was observed in Section 4.2 that prices show less disconformity than other variables do. Although the extreme case of absence of disconformity is obviously unfavourable for our present analysis, since this would reduce the possible test results to only three alternatives ($x^1 = 1$, $x^2 = 1$, or $x^3 = 1$), the other extreme case of maximum disconformity is almost equally unfavourable; for it would then be impossible to say anything about facts and forecasts of our sets of firms—except that the elements of the sets are highly different. Much of the analysis will be based on balances and, clearly, such a measure of central tendency of microchanges loses its value when these changes are hardly characterised by any central tendency.

This section and Section 6.2 are devoted to problems of methodology, the latter to problems of statistical estimation and testing of hypotheses, the former to those which are inherent to the use of Business Test data. The remainder of this chapter deals with the statistical analysis of the formation of predictions and behaviour. First, the traders are considered: their expected buying prices (Section 6.3), their planned and actual selling prices (Section 6.4), and their actual buying prices (Section 6.5); second, the manufacturers' planned and actual selling prices (Section 6.6); third, the expected and actual buying prices of the traders in hides, who play a special rôle because they form the first stage (Section 6.7); and, finally, a summarising picture is given in Section 6.8.

6.1.2. It is convenient, when discussing the problem of the use of Business Test data for the analysis of behaviour and other relations, to start with some remarks on the way in which conventional data are generally used for this purpose.[1] The latter type is usually given in the form of aggregates which are linear combinations of microvariables (national totals, averages, fixed-weights indices, etc.). On the other hand, the relationships that are postulated between such aggregates are derived from *micro*economic theory. For instance, the macrorelation connecting the aggregate sugar consumption in some country with total disposable income and the average price of sugar is *not* derived from a macrotheory which tells us that some authority bases his decisions as to the first aggregate on numerical values of the other two; but it is simply postulated on the ground that economic microtheory states that individual sugar consumption is a function of the income of this individual and of the sugar price which this individual has to pay, after

[1] Cf. also H. Theil, *Linear Aggregation of Economic Relations* (Amsterdam, 1954), Sections 1.3 and 8.2.

which it is believed that a similar relation should exist between the aggregates.

Now, if we are prepared to accept this line of argument, there is in principle no objection to an application of the same procedure to balances of test variates. This would simply mean the replacement of one measure of central tendency of microchanges (viz., the mean of the distribution of first microdifferences) by another (viz., the mean of the signum distribution); and it is exactly this central-tendency character of macrovariables that is the main intuitive justification of conventional aggregation. Moreover, in view of the high correlations obtained by ANDERSON for balance series and first differences of indices (cf. 4.2.2), it seems plausible that relations among balances are comparable with relations among indices. This comparability cannot, of course, be perfect, but we may hope that it applies at least to the variables and to their lags that should be introduced into the equations. For this reason, and because of the novelty of the data which justifies some experimentation, we shall sometimes work in this chapter with relationships that can only be justified by means of analogy considerations of the above-mentioned type. On the other hand, it is clearly desirable to give somewhat more insight into the exact implications of this procedure. This is the purpose of the remainder of this section; 6.1.3 is devoted to a refinement of the theory which relates balances to first differences of indices, 6.1.4 to a simple approach which can be adequate when there is only one explanatory variable, and 6.1.5 to relationships in balances. A summarising conclusion is given in 6.1.6.

6.1.3. The assumption of a fixed indifference interval, introduced in Section 4.2, is clearly restrictive. The following analysis, mainly due to J. PFANZAGL, may therefore be regarded as a convenient generalisation.[1]

Consider the production (or any other microvariable) of each of a certain set of firms participating in the Business Test. We denote the production of a firm i in month $t-1$ by u_i and its relative increase in t by δ_i. Hence the production index in t for all firms combined (base: previous month) is

$$(6.1) \qquad P = \sum_i w_i(1+\delta_i) \qquad (w_i = u_i/\Sigma u).$$

[1] "Zur Methodik des Konjunkturtest-Verfahrens," *Statistische Vierteljahresschrift*, Vol. 5 (1952), pp. 161–173.

We do not assume that there is a fixed interval for δ which determines the M.B.T. answers completely, but introduce, instead, the *probability* p that an entrepreneur reports an increase in the Test. When supposing (*i*) that this probability is, for each firm i, a function of the relative increase δ_i alone, and (*ii*) that this function is the same for all firms and all months, we obtain a "response function" $p(\delta)$, which determines stochastically—given the δ's of the separate firms—the fraction of increases, x^1. A similar set of assumptions for decreases leads to a second response function, $q(\delta)$, which determines x^3; we have, of course, $0 \leq p(\delta)$, $q(\delta)$ and $p(\delta) + q(\delta) \leq 1$ for any δ. Furthermore, under the plausible assumptions that p and $-q$ are monotonically non-decreasing functions of δ and that $p(-\infty) = q(\infty) = 0$ and $p(\infty) = q(-\infty) = 1$, we may regard both p and $1 - q$ as cumulative frequency functions.[1] The case of a fixed indifference interval may hence be considered as the "zero-variance case" of both response functions. In the more general case (that of "stochastic indifference intervals") it is not necessary to exclude the possibility that an entrepreneur is confronted with an increase but reports a decrease. Fig. 6.1 provides an example.

The fractions published as test variates are

$$(6.2)\qquad \begin{aligned} x^1 &= \Sigma w_i r_i, & r_i &= 1, \text{ if } i \text{ reports an increase; 0, otherwise;} \\ x^3 &= \Sigma w_i s_i, & s_i &= 1, \text{ if } i \text{ reports a decrease; 0, otherwise.} \end{aligned}$$

We consider a linear function of x^1 and x^3,

$$(6.3)\qquad Z = \alpha + \beta x^1 + \gamma x^3,$$

the parameters α, β, γ being such that Z is an unbiased estimator of P. This implies $P = \mathscr{E}Z$, where $\mathscr{E}$ stands for the mean-value operator; or

$$(6.4)\qquad \Sigma w_i(1 + \delta_i) = \alpha + \beta\Sigma w_i p(\delta_i) + \gamma\Sigma w_i q(\delta_i).$$

In order that parameters α, β, γ exist for which (6.4) is fulfilled, it is sufficient that

$$(6.5)\qquad 1 + \delta \equiv \alpha + \beta p(\delta) + \gamma q(\delta) \quad \text{for any } \delta \text{ and some } \alpha, \beta, \gamma.$$

There is no need to stress that (6.5) is a strong condition, but it will often be approximately fulfilled. In Fig. 6.1 both response functions are approximated by the broken straight lines through the origin, with

[1] If the variables considered cannot be negative (like production), we should replace $-\infty$ by -1.

equal slopes apart from sign. This implies, first, $p(0) = q(0) = 0$ and hence, when putting $\delta = 0$ in (6.5), $\alpha = 1$; second, $p(\delta) = q(-\delta)$ for any nonnegative δ, so that $\gamma = -\beta$, β being positive and equal to one half of the reciprocal of the slope of the straight line. In that case the use of Z [equation (6.3)] means simply that the first differences of the index are associated with the balances.

(6.5) cannot hold for arbitrarily large values of δ, for its right-hand side is bounded, whereas its left-hand side is not. Put more simply,

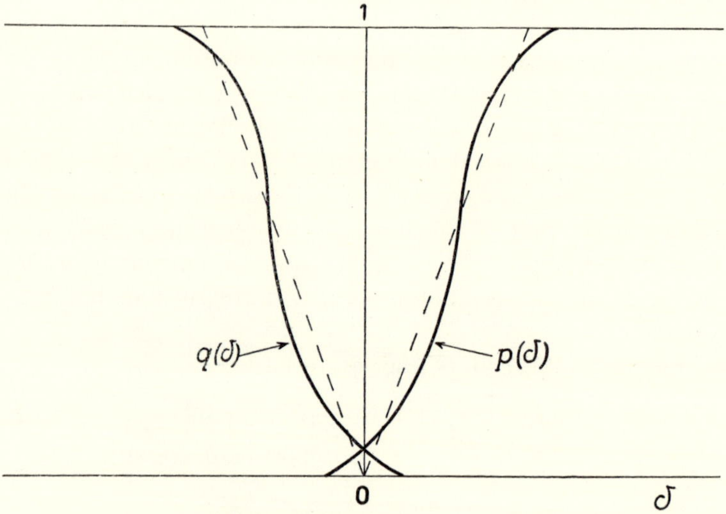

Fig. 6.1. Hypothetical response functions in Business Test analysis

when all firms report increases, there is no way to transform test variates into conventional indices. Similarly, if $p(\delta) = q(\delta) = 0$ for an appreciable range of δ around zero, i.e., if all firms are "silent" about considerable changes by reporting simply "no change;" and if, furthermore, the δ's of these firms are frequently within this range, we run into difficulties too, because there is then no information about an important range of variability. But otherwise it is clear, first, that stochastic indifference intervals are not necessarily an impediment to a close association between balances and first differences of indices, and that even "false" reports (increases in reality, but reported decreases, and *vice versa*) do not necessarily disturb this feature to a large extent; second, that the numerical specification of this association depends on the entrepreneurs' pattern of answering the questionnaires.

In the simple case of the straight-line approximation of the preceding paragraph, for example, the ratio of the balance to the first difference of the index is equal to twice the slope of the reponse functions (apart from sampling errors). For a further analysis we refer to the Appendix of this chapter, Section 6.A.

6.1.4. The generalisation of 6.1.3 may be regarded as a certain justification of the use of balance series in behaviour and other equations. If, however, such equations contain only one explanatory variable, there exists a method which is considerably simpler.

Suppose we have two related variables, e.g. buying and selling prices, or sales and purchases, the former determining the latter; and suppose that we are interested in the hypothesis that every entrepreneur who observes an increase (decrease, no change) in the former variable raises (lowers, keeps constant) the latter. For instance, every firm will raise (lower) its selling price if, and only if, it is confronted with an increase (decrease) of its buying price. Obviously, a necessary condition for the tenability of this hypothesis is

$$\mathbf{y} = \mathbf{x} \tag{6.6}$$

or in a scalar notation: $y^1 = x^1$, $y^2 = x^2$, $y^3 = x^3$, where the y's stand for the test variates of the dependent variable and the x's for those of the explanatory variable. A convenient method for testing condition (6.6) is to insert an arbitrary 3×3 matrix $\mathbf{A}$,

$$\mathbf{y} = \mathbf{A}\mathbf{x}, \tag{6.7}$$

to estimate the elements of $\mathbf{A}$,

$$\mathbf{A} = \begin{bmatrix} a_{11} & a_{12} & a_{13} \\ a_{21} & a_{22} & a_{23} \\ a_{31} & a_{32} & a_{33} \end{bmatrix},$$

and to see whether $\mathbf{A}$ differs significantly from the unit matrix. If no significant differences exist, we cannot reject (6.6), and the same applies to the corresponding equation in balances, $b(\mathbf{y}) = b(\mathbf{x})$. Another interesting case occurs when only part of the firms confronted with increased x-values react by raising their y-variables, the remainder keeping the latter constant. We then have $a_{11} < 1$, $a_{21} > 0$. If the same is true for decreased x-values, *mutatis mutandis*, we have $a_{33} < 1$,

$a_{23} > 0$. If, furthermore, the first and the third row of $\mathbf{A}$ are symmetric with respect to the middle element a_{22}, i.e., if $a_{11} = a_{33}$, $a_{12} = a_{32}$, $a_{13} = a_{31}$, then we have $b(\mathbf{y}) = kb(\mathbf{x})$ with $k = a_{11} - a_{31} = a_{33} - a_{13}$.[1] The balances of the two variables are then proportional to each other, but no longer equal; and the proportionality constant k will be below unity if a_{31}, a_{13} are nonnegative. As to the sign of the elements of $\mathbf{A}$, negative values are not very plausible, since this would lead, *via* (6.7), to test variates of the dependent variable which lie outside the range (0, 1) for certain values of the x-test variates. This argument is not applicable if we restrict the range of variation of the latter variates sufficiently, but even then the occurrence of negative elements would certainly be remarkable and interesting. Suppose e.g. that we deal with buying and selling prices and that $a_{11} = 1 + \varepsilon$, $a_{31} = -\varepsilon$, $\varepsilon > 0$; and, as to the other elements, $a_{rs} = 1$ if $r = s$, 0 if $r \neq s$. Then it is easy to see that the mere presence of some entrepreneurs who are confronted with increased buying prices ($x^1 > 0$) reduces the fraction of firms lowering their selling prices (y^3) below the size of the set of firms confronted with decreased buying prices (x^3). Such an effect will occur only if there is a considerable degree of interconnection between the price decisions of individual firms. We shall not go deeper into this matter here, since no significant negative values have been found in the empirical analysis.

When least-squares is applied to time series of test vectors in order to estimate $\mathbf{A}$, the sum of the rows of the resulting matrix is a row vector of units, as will be shown in the Appendix (6.A.3).[2] It is impossible to introduce constant terms into the equations (6.7), since this would lead to linear dependence of the explanatory variables.

6.1.5. When there are several explanatory variables, it is no longer possible to use this "matrix method" in its simple form, again because of linear dependence. For such cases, therefore, we shall use the "balance method," which is our next topic. The attention will be confined, first, to the case of a variable y which is determined by two variables x_1 and x_2 (for example, y = selling price, x_1 = current buying price, x_2 = lagged buying price); furthermore, to the case of functions that are monotonic with respect to both x_1 and x_2. Without loss of

[1] The symmetry condition can be weakened if we allow a constant term in the equation connecting the balances.
[2] This has been used as a check on the computations of the subsequent sections.

generality we may then assume that y increases monotonically with x_1 and x_2; viz., by interchanging, if necessary, the fractions of increases and those of decreases for one or both of the explanatory variables.

It will prove useful to introduce the (unknown) fractions of firms reporting increases in both x_1 and x_2, an increase in x_1 but a decrease in x_2, etc. They will be denoted by x^{rs}, where the superscripts r and s (belonging to x_1 and x_2, respectively) assume the three values 1 (increase), 2 (no change), 3 (decrease) in accordance with the notation x^1, x^2, x^3 for one variable. Table 6.3 gives these fractions more fully; it contains also the "marginal" fractions $x_1^r = \sum_s x^{rs}$ and $x_2^s = \sum_r x^{rs}$. We have, of course, $\Sigma\Sigma x^{rs} = 1$ for all nine fractions together.

TABLE 6.3

NOTATION OF FRACTIONS IN BIVARIATE BUSINESS TEST ANALYSIS

Changes with respect to x_1	*Changes with respect to* x_2			*Marginal*
	increase	*no change*	*decrease*	
increase	x^{11}	x^{12}	x^{13}	x_1^1
no change	x^{21}	x^{22}	x^{23}	x_1^2
decrease	x^{31}	x^{32}	x^{33}	x_1^3
Marginal	x_2^1	x_2^2	x_2^3	1

Now let us suppose that a fraction η'_{rs} of the firms falling under x^{rs} report an increase in y, and similarly η''_{rs} for those reporting a decrease in y. This implies

$$(6.8) \qquad y^1 = \sum_r \sum_s \eta'_{rs}\, x^{rs}, \qquad y^3 = \sum_r \sum_s \eta''_{rs}\, x^{rs};$$

and hence, writing $\eta_{rs} = \eta'_{rs} - \eta''_{rs}$, for the balance:

$$(6.9) \qquad b(\mathbf{y}) = \sum_r \sum_s \eta_{rs}\, x^{rs} = \eta_{22} + \sum_r \sum_s (\eta_{rs} - \eta_{22})\, x^{rs} =$$

$$= \eta_{22} + \sum_r \sum_s \bar{\eta}_{rs} x^{rs},$$

where x^{22}—the middle element of Table 6.3—is eliminated from the double sum by means of $\Sigma\Sigma x^{rs} = 1$, and $\bar{\eta}_{rs} = \eta_{rs} - \eta_{22}$. Obviously, a linear equation in balances,

$$(6.10) \qquad b(\mathbf{y}) = a + \beta_1\, b(\mathbf{x}_1) + \beta_2\, b(\mathbf{x}_2)$$

is considerably simpler and more restrictive than the equation (6.9) in bivariate fractions. Indeed, when identifying a with η_{22} and writing $b(\mathbf{x}_1) = x_1^1 - x_1^3 = \Sigma x^{1s} - \Sigma x^{3s}$ and similarly for $b(\mathbf{x}_2)$, we find that (6.9) and (6.10) are identical if, and only if,

$$(6.11) \qquad [\bar{\eta}_{rs}] = \begin{bmatrix} \beta_1 + \beta_2 & \beta_1 & \beta_1 - \beta_2 \\ \beta_2 & 0 & -\beta_2 \\ -\beta_1 + \beta_2 & -\beta_1 & -\beta_1 - \beta_2 \end{bmatrix}.$$

In order to facilitate the discussion of these conditions, we shall suppose that, when firms report no change in both determining variables, they always report no change in y as well, or at least report increased and decreased y-values with equal frequencies. In the former case we have $\eta'_{22} = \eta''_{22} = 0$, in the latter $\eta'_{22} = \eta''_{22} > 0$, but in both cases $\eta_{22} = 0$ and hence $a = 0$ and $\bar{\eta}_{rs} = \eta_{rs}$. The matrix of coefficients (6.11) may then be regarded as measuring the contributions of the bivariate fractions x^{rs} to the excess of the fraction of y-increases over that of y-decreases, viz. $b(\mathbf{y})$. It follows from (6.11) that negative symmetry around the middle term is one of the conditions. Hence, if 40 per cent of the firms reporting x_1-increases and x_2-decreases (x^{13}) report increased y-values (i.e., $\eta'_{13} = 0.4$) and if 30 per cent of them report decreased y's (i.e., $\eta''_{13} = 0.3$), so that their contribution to $b(\mathbf{y})$ is measured by $\eta_{13} = 0.1$, then the contribution of the firms reporting x_1-decreases and x_2-increases (x^{31}) to this balance should be $\eta_{31} = -0.1$. A sufficient condition is that 40 per cent of the latter set report decreased and 30 per cent increased y-values (i.e., $\eta''_{31} = 0.4$, $\eta'_{31} = 0.3$), but the difference alone is relevant. Negative symmetry around the middle term, therefore, is surely a restrictive condition, but it is not altogether unplausible. The other condition is the following: Consider one of the three change types of one of the determining variables; take e.g. increases in x_1, so that we remain in the first row of (6.11). Then the contribution η_{12} of the bivariate fraction with no change in the other variable (x^{12}) to $b(\mathbf{y})$ should lie half-way between the contributions of the fractions with increases (x^{11}) and those with decreases (x^{13}), respectively, in this variable; i.e., $\eta_{12} = \frac{1}{2}(\eta_{11} + \eta_{13})$. This condition, too, is restrictive but not unplausible.

Similar results can be easily obtained for relationships containing more determining variables $x_3, x_4, \ldots$ They all refer to negative symmetry around the middle element $x^{222\cdots}$ and to "half-way contributions" of arrays of coefficients $\eta_{rst\ldots}$ in three or more dimensions.

6.1.6. Our conclusion must be that the matrix method for the case of one explanatory variable and the balance method for more variables are worth trying, and that our final appraisal must depend on the plausibility of the results obtained. However, there are two further points which should be mentioned here.

First, if we accept the assumption $\eta'_{22} = \eta''_{22} = 0$ of 6.1.5, it is tempting to go on and to assume also $\eta'_{11} = \eta''_{33} = 1$ and $\eta''_{11} = \eta'_{33} = 0$. This amounts to supposing that all firms reporting increases (decreases) in both x_1 and x_2 report increased (decreased) y-values as well, simply because of the earlier assumption that no change in both x_1 and x_2 always leads to no change in y. It follows then that the matrix (6.11) has 1, 0, -1 in its main diagonal, so that equation (6.10) in balances has, not only a zero constant term ($\alpha = 0$), but also multiplicative coefficients with sum unity. It is rather easy to impose these restrictions *a priori* in the statistical estimation, but it is questionable whether it is good to do so—for several reasons. First, the assumptions $\eta'_{11} = 1$, etc., imply certain restrictions, *i.a.* on the indifference intervals of y, x_1 and x_2. Actually, these restrictions are closely related to those which lead to $\mathbf{A} = \mathbf{I}$ in the matrix approach of one single explanatory variable; and we saw in 6.1.4 that $\mathbf{A} \neq \mathbf{I}$ represents at least an interesting possibility. Second, the η's are in general not constant through time, so that equation (6.10) is not more than an idealisation. Third, the analysis of 6.1.5 is carried out under the assumption that all variables refer to one set of firms. In practice, however, we shall frequently be forced to introduce test variates of different sets of firms into one equation. All this suggests that it is better not to base the statistical estimation on too many restrictions; indeed, they have not been adopted in the computations which follow.

The other point deals with the numerical interpretation of the β's. Going back to (6.11), we find that these coefficients are related (as they should be) to the influence of the variables to which they belong, in the following sense. Take β_1; it is concerned with the entrepreneurs who report an increase in x_1 but no change in x_2, and it measures the fraction of this group which raises y minus the fraction which lowers y. A similar interpretation holds for $-\beta_1$ in the third row of the square array (6.11), and also for β_2 and $-\beta_2$ in the first and third columns, respectively. In other words, the β's measure the influence of their variables under *ceteris paribus* conditions (in terms of indifference intervals) on the other variables. It must be admitted, though, that the exact meaning of such *ceteris paribus* clauses is not known, since the intervals themselves are unknown. Again, this is a problem that can only be analysed satisfactorily when empirical results have been obtained.

6.2. Problems of Statistical Methodology

6.2.1. A discussion of problems of statistical inference is not only justified by the extensive empirical analysis of this chapter, but also by the fact that we shall meet these problems again in later chapters.[1] Moreover, the subject has been under debate for several years, so that an analysis of this kind can hardly be avoided.

In this section we shall confine ourselves largely to those subjects which are relevant to the empirical sections 6.3–6.8; and in order not to make this section too lengthy, certain more technical problems will be discussed in the Appendix (Sections 6.B, 6.C and 6.D). We shall start (in 6.2.2) with certain basic principles of econometric model construction. After this we will consider least-squares under its classical assumptions (in 6.2.3), which is followed by a discussion of its numerous complications. First, in 6.2.4, we shall consider specification errors and the criterion of maximum correlation for the choice of the specification; second, in 6.2.5, we shall consider the problems of multicollinearity and distributed lags; third, in 6.2.6, the problems of autocorrelation of disturbances; fourth, in 6.2.7, simultaneous equations complications. In 6.2.8 the method of mixed estimation will be considered, which is a device for using uncertain *a priori* information. A conclusion is given in 6.2.9.

In Chapter VIII (in particular Section 8.5 and the Appendix of that chapter) the subject of statistical estimation of economic relations will be considered again. At that place we will have gained insight into the decision consequences of the sampling errors of our estimation methods, and this will enable us to see certain properties of these methods in a more fundamental light.

[1] We may even say that statistical estimation falls under forecasting, since it deals with statements about unknown (though usually not future) events. However, statistical estimators do not fall into the category of "scientific forecasts" as defined in Section 2.3, because it is in general impossible to give a conclusive answer to the question whether the statement has come true or not. The reason for this is the "latent" character of statistical parameters, which exist only in the statistician's imagination.

6.2.2. "The" criterion for a good econometric model is that it *predicts* well—the very subject of this book. Suppose, for example, that the model describes some variable y as a (numerically specified) function of certain other variables $x_1, x_2, \ldots$ Then, if a number of observations on the latter variables is available, we can use the model to predict the corresponding y-values and compare these (conditional) forecasts with the observed y-values. This idea was applied in Section 5.2, and it will be applied again at the end of this chapter; but it should be stressed that it is neither always conclusive nor always feasible. For one thing, such a straightforward accuracy analysis does not necessarily take account of the way in which the predictions are used for policy purposes; this is the subject of later chapters, to which we may therefore refer. For another, almost always the number of observations is limited, and part of them have to be used to specify the model itself. The temptation is then great to use all or most of the observations for this purpose, so that the possibility of testing the model by means of observations outside the sample used is considerably reduced. The econometrician is then forced to retreat from the prediction criterion, and he can do no more than choose his model in such a way as to maximise the chance that it predicts well. The criteria for this—rather subjective—procedure are those of *plausibility* and *simplicity*. The former criterion (that of plausibility) serves to raise the probability of forecasting success, the latter to apply Occam's razor in the case when competing models with equal chance are available, or to rule out plausible models which are so unwieldy as to exclude the possibility of prediction. Usually, these two requirements are contradictory. For instance, it can often be argued that a great many variables affect the phenomenon to be analysed, and plausibility requires then the introduction of numerous explanatory factors; but the resulting picture will be far from simple, so that it may be rejected because it cannot be handled for practical purposes. Similarly, it may be argued on rather firm grounds that the relationship to be analysed is characterised by particular curvatures. An example is a consumer's Engel curve in the case of a quadratic utility function, when account is taken of the fact that no negative quantities can be bought. It can be shown that these assumptions lead to Engel curves consisting of a series of straight line segments with slopes that decrease in general with increasing income.[1]

[1] Cf. H. S. Houthakker, "La forme des courbes d'Engel," *Cahiers du Séminaire d'Econométrie*, No. 2 (1953), pp. 59–66.

However, this form is not very suitable for statistical prediction purposes, so that requirements of simplicity compel the econometrician to use a smoother form. Conversely, by far the simplest picture is obtained when it is assumed that the phenomenon considered is not affected in a systematic way by any factor, and that its fluctuations are all random. But this picture is usually far from plausible, so that a compromise between simplicity and plausibility is a preferable solution.

The way in which this compromise is obtained in the analysis of behaviour and other equations can be sketched as follows. First, some general properties of the equation to be analysed are postulated; for example, that the variable "to be explained," y, is a linear function of two other variables, x_1, and x_2, except for certain disturbances u:

$$y = \alpha + \beta_1 x_1 + \beta_2 x_2 + u;$$

furthermore, that the disturbances obey the following probability rules: they have constant variance and are correlated, neither among themselves, nor with x_1 or x_2. Economic theory is supposed to guarantee the correctness of this hypothesis. It is called a "maintained hypothesis," because in the second step it is fully accepted and no longer questioned. This second step consists of the testing of hypotheses about parameters like α, β_1, β_2 ("tested hypothesis") or of the estimation of such parameters.

In practice, however, the picture of the preceding paragraph greatly overestimates the economic theorist's knowledge and intellectual power. Economic theory can give some indications as to the variables that are possibly relevant; it may even give some vague indications as to curvature and as to the numerical magnitude of some coefficients, although less frequently for macro than for microrelationships; but it rarely gives any indication about probability properties of disturbances. The obvious result is that, if a "maintained" hypothesis gives unsatisfactory results, it is not maintained but rejected, and replaced by another "maintained" hypothesis; etc. It is hardly reasonable to say that this kind of experimentation is incorrect, even if it affects the superstructure built on such "maintained" hypotheses.[1] It is especially

[1] In particular, the standard errors derived according to the classical formulae tend then to overestimate the accuracy of the point estimates obtained. An example is the simultaneous-equations case (cf. below) where the specification of the equations is made dependent on the outcome of a test on over-identifying restrictions.

It should also be noted that the division of the statistical procedure in terms of maintained and tested hypotheses is justified by its convenience, not by its fundamental nature. The problem is to select a satisfactory model (or set of models) which is fully

unreasonable to reject such an experimental approach, because—as will become clear after a few pages—the statistical theory which forbids the rejection of a "maintained" hypothesis is not fully satisfactory either in view of the difficulty of its application.

What *is* incorrect, however, is to act as if the final hypothesis presented is the first one, whereas in fact it is the result of much experimentation. Since every econometric analysis is an essay in persuasion—just as is true for any other branch of science—, the line of thought leading to the finally accepted result must be expounded. It is not true that analyses which are in the end not accepted are useless. The mere fact that a certain "maintained" hypothesis can be excluded raises the plausibility of its rivals. This can be compared to a large extent with the function of standard errors of parameter estimates. Just as the standard errors contribute to an appraisal of numerical outcomes within a certain "maintained" hypothesis, in just the same way alternative analyses of separate "maintained" hypotheses contribute to an appraisal of the hypothesis which is finally preferred. It is conceivable, of course, that it is impossible to decide between two or three hypotheses. In such a case a class of acceptable hypotheses remains, and further analyses (the derivation of point estimates of certain parameters) can be made for each of them; but this, too, is not different from the function of standard errors, which lead to a class of empirically acceptable parameter values.

So much for problems of principles. As to the statistical method which is to be employed in order to carry out the program, here again it is possible and useful to set up certain criteria for an adequate choice: *simplicity, validity* and "*sharpness.*" Simplicity refers to the computations necessary for applying the method and is decisive for its cheapness. This criterion is obviously related to the corresponding criterion for the choice of models; the two others serve to contribute to the forecasting quality, just as the plausibility criterion does. Validity refers to the size of the (maintained) class of admissible hypotheses. If this class is larger for one method than for another, the former has greater validity; but sometimes the classes overlap each other partially, so that either method has then greater validity in some particular respects. "Sharpness," finally, indicates the discriminating power

numerically specified; and there is no reason—except that of convenience—why this should be carried out in two separate steps. (I am indebted to Professor MILTON FRIEDMAN of The University of Chicago, with whom I had a discussion on this subject.)

of the method and stands for efficiency (or any similar concept) in the case of point estimation, for the average size of confidence intervals for given confidence coefficients in the case of interval estimation, and for the power of the test in hypothesis testing.[1] The predominant use of the maximum-likelihood method and the virtual absence of rank correlation methods in recent statistical contributions to econometrics suggest that the third of these desirable properties has been taken more seriously than the others. This seems natural, for econometric work is frequently based on a rather small number of observations, and "sharp" methods are then necessary to achieve anything of value. Nevertheless, it is good not to forget the other criteria.

6.2.3. The method of least-squares, which goes back to GAUSS and LAPLACE, and practically all related methods of estimating economic relationships are based upon two fundamental ideas:[2] first, the variable of which the fluctuations are to be analysed contains a *systematic* part that depends *linearly* on certain other variables; second, about the other, *nonsystematic*, part it is possible to make certain *probability* statements. Hence, when denoting the former variable by y and its values by $y(1), \ldots, y(t), \ldots, y(T)$, the latter variables by $x_1, \ldots, x_\lambda, \ldots, x_\Lambda$ and their values by $x_\lambda(t)$, and the nonsystematic disturbances by $u(t)$, we have

$$y(t) = \sum_{\lambda=1}^{\Lambda} \beta_\lambda x_\lambda(t) + u(t) \qquad (t = 1, \ldots, T) \tag{6.12}$$

or in matrix notation

$$\mathbf{y} = \mathbf{X}\boldsymbol{\beta} + \mathbf{u}, \tag{6.13}$$

[1] The term "sharpness" is borrowed from I. D. J. BROSS, *Design for Decision* (New York, 1953).

[2] An exception is FRISCH' bunch map analysis, which is not based on the probability concept. Cf. R. Frisch, *Statistical Confluence Analysis by Means of Complete Regression Systems* (Oslo, 1934).

For a brief account of the history of the method of least-squares, cf. R. L. PLACKET, "A Historical Note on the Method of Least-Squares," *Biometrika*, Vol. 36 (1949), pp. 458–460. For a more extensive account, cf. E. T. WHITTAKER and G. ROBINSON, *The Calculus of Observations* (London-Glasgow, fourth ed., 1944), Chapter IX. These publications deal also with the well-known Gauss-Markov theorem of least-squares; the treatment of this subject will be postponed till Chapter VIII, where it will be considered in a more general context.

where

$$\mathbf{y} = \begin{bmatrix} y(1) \\ \vdots \\ y(T) \end{bmatrix}; \quad \mathbf{X} = \begin{bmatrix} x_1(1) \dots x_\Lambda(1) \\ \vdots \qquad \vdots \\ x_1(T) \dots x_\Lambda(T) \end{bmatrix}; \quad \mathbf{u} = \begin{bmatrix} u(1) \\ \vdots \\ u(T) \end{bmatrix}; \quad \boldsymbol{\beta} = \begin{bmatrix} \beta_1 \\ \vdots \\ \beta_\Lambda \end{bmatrix}.$$

The linearity assumption is not as restrictive as it may seem, for our variables may be squares, logarithms, etc., of other variables, and one of them may be constant (e.g., unity), so that the corresponding component of $\boldsymbol{\beta}$ represents then the constant term of the equation.

Least-squares is usually based upon the following assumptions:

(*i*) *The disturbances of* (6.13) *have zero mean value*: $\mathscr{E}\mathbf{u} = \mathbf{0}$.

(*ii*) *The disturbances of* (6.13) *have constant variance and are not correlated*: $\mathscr{E}(\mathbf{uu}') = \sigma^2\mathbf{I}$, $\sigma^2 < \infty$.

In more detail, this means

$$(6.14) \quad \begin{bmatrix} \operatorname{var} u(1) & \operatorname{cov}\{u(1), u(2)\} & \dots & \operatorname{cov}\{u(1), u(T)\} \\ \operatorname{cov}\{u(2), u(1)\} & \operatorname{var} u(2) & \dots & \operatorname{cov}\{u(2), u(T)\} \\ \vdots & \vdots & & \vdots \\ \operatorname{cov}\{u(T), u(1)\} & \operatorname{cov}\{u(T), u(2)\} & \dots & \operatorname{var} u(T) \end{bmatrix} =$$

$$= \begin{bmatrix} \sigma^2 & 0 & \dots & 0 \\ 0 & \sigma^2 & \dots & 0 \\ \vdots & \vdots & & \vdots \\ 0 & 0 & \dots & \sigma^2 \end{bmatrix},$$

and the equal diagonal elements imply that all disturbances have the same variance, while the zero off-diagonal elements imply zero correlations for all pairs of disturbances.

(*iii*) *The* ΛT *values* $x_\lambda(t)$ *of* (6.13) *are nonstochastic real numbers.*

These three assumptions in relation to the T equations (6.13) form the "maintained hypothesis." The method of least-squares is then the method which provides that estimator $\mathbf{b}$ of $\boldsymbol{\beta}$ which minimises the sum of squares of the estimated disturbances. The vector of estimated disturbances is $\mathbf{y} - \mathbf{Xb}$, and so the sum of squares is

$$(6.15) \quad Ts^2 = (\mathbf{y} - \mathbf{Xb})'(\mathbf{y} - \mathbf{Xb}) = \mathbf{y}'\mathbf{y} - 2\mathbf{y}'\mathbf{Xb} + \mathbf{b}'\mathbf{X}'\mathbf{Xb},$$

where s^2 is the second moment of the estimated disturbances. If we differentiate (6.15) with respect to $\mathbf{b}$, we obtain the Λ "normal equations"[1]

$$(6.16) \qquad \mathbf{X}'\mathbf{y} = \mathbf{X}'\mathbf{Xb},$$

from which

$$(6.17) \qquad \mathbf{b} = (\mathbf{X}'\mathbf{X})^{-1}\mathbf{X}'\mathbf{y},$$

provided $\mathbf{X}'\mathbf{X}$ is nonsingular, i.e., provided the Λ vectors of values assumed by the explanatory variables are not linearly dependent. Upon combining (6.13) and (6.17), we find

$$(6.18) \qquad \mathbf{b} = \boldsymbol{\beta} + (\mathbf{X}'\mathbf{X})^{-1}\mathbf{X}'\mathbf{u},$$

so that $\mathscr{E}\mathbf{b} = \boldsymbol{\beta}$ from assumptions (*i*) and (*iii*), i.e., the least-squares estimator is unbiased; it will be observed that this result is independent of assumption (*ii*). From (6.18) it follows that

$$(6.19) \qquad \begin{aligned} \mathscr{E}\{(\mathbf{b} - \boldsymbol{\beta})(\mathbf{b} - \boldsymbol{\beta})'\} &= \mathscr{E}\{(\mathbf{X}'\mathbf{X})^{-1}\mathbf{X}'\mathbf{uu}'\mathbf{X}(\mathbf{X}'\mathbf{X})^{-1}\} \\ &= \sigma^2(\mathbf{X}'\mathbf{X})^{-1}. \end{aligned}$$

Here we made use of assumption (*ii*). We have now obtained the covariance matrix of the least-squares estimator, which turns out to be equal to the inverse of the matrix of the sums of squares and products of the explanatory variables, apart from a scalar, σ^2. It follows immediately that the estimator is consistent, provided the increase of the sample size, T, takes place in such a way that these sums increase indefinitely.

The covariance matrix (6.19) cannot be determined exactly because σ^2 is unknown, but it can be estimated unbiasedly, for under the above assumptions we have

$$(6.20) \qquad \frac{T}{T - \Lambda}\mathscr{E}s^2 = \sigma^2,$$

where s^2 has been defined in (6.15).

[1] The following simple rules for taking the derivative with respect to some vector $\mathbf{x}$ are used: $\partial(\mathbf{a}'\mathbf{x})/\partial\mathbf{x} = \mathbf{a}$ and $\partial(\mathbf{x}'\mathbf{Ax})/\partial\mathbf{x} = 2\mathbf{Ax}$, where $\mathbf{a}$ is a column vector and $\mathbf{A}$ a symmetric matrix of constant coefficients.

This can be shown as follows. Using (6.17), we have

$$
\begin{aligned}
Ts^2 &= (\mathbf{y} - \mathbf{Xb})'(\mathbf{y} - \mathbf{Xb}) \\
&= \mathbf{y}'[\mathbf{I} - \mathbf{X}(\mathbf{X}'\mathbf{X})^{-1}\mathbf{X}']'[\mathbf{I} - \mathbf{X}(\mathbf{X}'\mathbf{X})^{-1}\mathbf{X}']\mathbf{y} \\
&= \mathbf{y}'[\mathbf{I} - \mathbf{X}(\mathbf{X}'\mathbf{X})^{-1}\mathbf{X}']\mathbf{y} \qquad (6.21) \\
&= (\mathbf{X}\boldsymbol{\beta} + \mathbf{u})'[\mathbf{I} - \mathbf{X}(\mathbf{X}'\mathbf{X})^{-1}\mathbf{X}'](\mathbf{X}\boldsymbol{\beta} + \mathbf{u}) \\
&= \mathbf{u}'[\mathbf{I} - \mathbf{X}(\mathbf{X}'\mathbf{X})^{-1}\mathbf{X}']\mathbf{u}.
\end{aligned}
$$

Taking mean values and writing $\mathbf{M} = [m_{tt'}] = \mathbf{I} - \mathbf{X}(\mathbf{X}'\mathbf{X})^{-1}\mathbf{X}'$, we find

$$T\mathscr{E}s^2 = \sum_t \sum_{t'} m_{tt'}\mathscr{E}\{u(t)u(t')\} = \sigma^2 \sum_t m_{tt},$$

which is σ^2 times the trace of $\mathbf{M}$.[1] Hence

$$
\begin{aligned}
T\mathscr{E}s^2 &= \sigma^2 \operatorname{tr} \mathbf{M} = \sigma^2[\operatorname{tr} \mathbf{I} - \operatorname{tr} \mathbf{X}(\mathbf{X}'\mathbf{X})^{-1}\mathbf{X}'] = \qquad (6.22) \\
&= \sigma^2[\operatorname{tr} \mathbf{I} - \operatorname{tr} (\mathbf{X}'\mathbf{X})^{-1}\mathbf{X}'\mathbf{X}] = \sigma^2(T - \Lambda).
\end{aligned}
$$

This leads immediately to (6.20); it is clear that this result requires condition (*ii*).

In all analyses of the subsequent sections both **b** and its standard errors (the square roots of the elements along the main diagonal of the estimated covariance matrix) are given.

6.2.4. As stated in 6.2.2, it is in general not known with certainty whether a particular "maintained" hypothesis is correct. So there is the problem of choice between two or more alternative specifications. A well-known criterion is that of the highest multiple correlation coefficient. This coefficient can be defined as the zero-order correlation R between the observed y-values, $y(1), \ldots, y(T)$, and the corresponding values obtained according to the regression equation,

$$y^*(t) = \sum_{\lambda=1}^{\Lambda} b_\lambda x_\lambda(t) \qquad \text{for } t = 1, \ldots, T. \qquad (6.23)$$

[1] The trace of a square matrix is the sum of its diagonal elements. The following simple properties are used in (6.22): $\operatorname{tr} (\mathbf{A} - \mathbf{B}) = \operatorname{tr} \mathbf{A} - \operatorname{tr} \mathbf{B}$ if $\mathbf{A}$ and $\mathbf{B}$ are square of the same order; and $\operatorname{tr} \mathbf{AB} = \operatorname{tr} \mathbf{BA}$ if both product matrices exist. Note that before the last equality sign of (6.22) we have the traces of two different unit matrices: the first is of order T (so that its trace is also T), the second is $\mathbf{X}'\mathbf{X}$ premultiplied by its inverse and hence a unit matrix of order Λ.

It can be easily shown that $1 - R^2$ equals the ratio of s^2 to the sample variance of y. Since s^2 is a biased estimator of σ^2 [cf. (6.20)], we shall replace R by $\bar{R}$, defined according to

$$1 - \bar{R}^2 = \frac{T}{T - \Lambda}(1 - R^2). \tag{6.24}$$

The relevance of this correction will become clear immediately. In all empirical analyses of this chapter the value of $\bar{R}^2$ is given.

The criterion of maximum multiple correlation is frequently based on rather primitive grounds: the investigator feels that the work he has done is of better quality if he can point out that he left only little of the variance of his dependent variable "unexplained." Certainly, such a feature has a good deal of intuitive appeal, and efforts to find "good" explanatory variables should be appreciated. It might even be argued that such a procedure has the virtue of maximising the quality of the forecasts, for small residuals in the sample analysed are *prima facie* indicators of small prediction errors in the future. However, this argument is not very satisfactory, since it is far from sure whether the small residuals are due to the characteristics of the population or to the investigator's tenacity. Small errors in the sample are not indicators of plausibility, there being no fundamental law in economics stating that disturbances are small or "as small as possible," nor are they indicators of simplicity. Fortunately, it can be shown that better arguments are available. We shall not consider the correlation criterion itself, but the residual variation criterion [that of minimising $s^2T/(T - \Lambda)$]; both are equivalent when the competing approaches deal with the same sample of y-values.[1] Further, we shall confine ourselves to alternative approaches which are characterised by the same dependent variable. In particular, we exclude the case in which one specification has y and another $\log y$ (say) as left-hand variable.[2]

Suppose then that there are two competing specifications, viz.:

$$\mathbf{y} = \mathbf{X}_1\boldsymbol{\beta}_1 + \mathbf{u}_1 \tag{6.25}$$

$$\mathbf{y} = \mathbf{X}_2\boldsymbol{\beta}_2 + \mathbf{u}_2; \tag{6.26}$$

[1] This proviso is not fulfilled when different lags in the alternative equations lead to unequal sample size because of the omission of some observations in those equations which contain the largest number of lag periods. An adjustment is then necessary.

[2] Even in this case it is possible to obtain certain results; cf. H. THEIL, "Specification Errors and the Estimation of Economic Relationships," *Review of the International Statistical Institute*, Vol. 25 (1957), pp. 41–51.

suppose further that one of them, say (6.25), is "true" in the sense that condition (*iii*) is satisfied for $\mathbf{X}_1$ and conditions (*i*) and (*ii*) for $\mathbf{u}_1$. Our first problem is: what is then the meaning of (6.26)? As long as we do not specify anything about its disturbance vector $\mathbf{u}_2$, there is no erroneous specification; actually, there is then hardly any specification at all. However, let us postpone this problem for a moment, and let us confine ourselves to the sample variance of the residuals which are obtained when least-squares is applied to (6.26), i.e., to the residual variance of the regression with $\mathbf{y}$ as dependent vector and $\mathbf{X}_2$ as explanatory matrix. Writing $\mathbf{b}_2 = (\mathbf{X}_2'\mathbf{X}_2)^{-1}\mathbf{X}_2'\mathbf{y}$ for the vector of least-squares regression coefficients, we find for T times the sample variance of the residuals $\mathbf{y} - \mathbf{X}_2\mathbf{b}_2$:

$$
\begin{aligned}
(\mathbf{y} - \mathbf{X}_2\mathbf{b}_2)'(\mathbf{y} - \mathbf{X}_2\mathbf{b}_2) &= \mathbf{y}'[\mathbf{I} - \mathbf{X}_2(\mathbf{X}_2'\mathbf{X}_2)^{-1}\mathbf{X}_2']\mathbf{y} = \\
&= (\mathbf{X}_1\boldsymbol{\beta}_1 + \mathbf{u}_1)'[\mathbf{I} - \mathbf{X}_2(\mathbf{X}_2'\mathbf{X}_2)^{-1}\mathbf{X}_2'](\mathbf{X}_1\boldsymbol{\beta}_1 + \mathbf{u}_1).
\end{aligned} \tag{6.27}
$$

Suppose then that $\mathbf{X}_2$ is nonstochastic, just as $\mathbf{X}_1$. The mean value of the sample variance is then

$$
\begin{aligned}
\mathscr{E}\left[\frac{1}{T}(\mathbf{y} - \mathbf{X}_2\mathbf{b}_2)'(\mathbf{y} - \mathbf{X}_2\mathbf{b}_2)\right] &= \frac{1}{T}(\mathbf{X}_1\boldsymbol{\beta}_1)'[\mathbf{I} - \mathbf{X}_2(\mathbf{X}_2'\mathbf{X}_2)^{-1}\mathbf{X}_2']\mathbf{X}_1\boldsymbol{\beta}_1 + \\
&+ \mathscr{E}\left\{\frac{1}{T}\mathbf{u}_1'[\mathbf{I} - \mathbf{X}_2(\mathbf{X}_2'\mathbf{X}_2)^{-1}\mathbf{X}_2']\mathbf{u}_1\right\} \\
&\geq \mathscr{E}\left\{\frac{1}{T}\mathbf{u}_1'[\mathbf{I} - \mathbf{X}_2(\mathbf{X}_2'\mathbf{X}_2)^{-1}\mathbf{X}_2']\mathbf{u}_1\right\} = \sigma_1^2\frac{T - \Lambda_2}{T},
\end{aligned} \tag{6.28}
$$

σ_1^2 being the variance of the components of $\mathbf{u}_1$, and Λ_2 the number of columns of $\mathbf{X}_2$. The inequality (6.28) follows from the fact that the first term behind the first equality sign is nothing else than the second moment of a regression in which $\mathbf{X}_1\boldsymbol{\beta}_1$ plays the role of the vector of values taken by the dependent variable and $\mathbf{X}_2$ that of the matrix of values taken by the explanatory variables; and such a second moment is necessarily nonnegative. It is then easily seen that (6.28) implies

$$
\begin{aligned}
\mathscr{E}\left[\frac{1}{T - \Lambda_2}(\mathbf{y} - \mathbf{X}_2\mathbf{b}_2)'(\mathbf{y} - \mathbf{X}_2\mathbf{b}_2)\right] &\geq \\
\geq \mathscr{E}\left[\frac{1}{T - \Lambda_1}(\mathbf{y} - \mathbf{X}_1\mathbf{b}_1)'(\mathbf{y} - \mathbf{X}_1\mathbf{b}_1)\right]&,
\end{aligned} \tag{6.29}
$$

where Λ_1 is the number of explanatory variables in the correct specification. In other words, the residual variance of the incorrect specification, when corrected for loss of degrees of freedom by multiplying by $T/(T-\Lambda_2)$, is on the average larger (at least not smaller) than the residual variance of the correct specification. Similarly, the corrected multiple correlation $\bar{R}$ is then smaller on the average. In this sense, therefore, the criterion of maximum multiple correlation leads "on the average" to the correct choice.[1]

Suppose, however, that assumption (*iii*) must be replaced by:

(*iv*) *For each* $t = 1, \ldots, T$, *the* Λ *values* $x_\lambda(t)$ *of* (6.13) *are stochastic and distributed jointly independently of* $u(t)$ *for the same value of* t.

This assumption is important in view of the fact that lagged values of the dependent variable enter frequently as explanatory variables. But for most purposes this alteration is not essential because the second half of the assumption permits the x's then to be treated as if they are fixed and nonstochastic, at least for large samples.[2] In our present case, of course, assumption (*iv*) refers to $\mathbf{X}_1$ and $\mathbf{u}_1$. We shall also assume that $\mathbf{X}_2$ is stochastic; but it is then no longer self-evident that each row of $\mathbf{X}_2$ is independent of the corresponding component of $\mathbf{u}_1$.[3] It is easy to see that the derivation (6.28) is then no longer applicable, and hence that the criterion of maximum multiple correlation is not necessarily adequate on the average. More detailed results can be obtained only if at least something of the correct specification is known.

[1] The problem of the significance of the difference between correlation coefficients has been considered by H. HOTELLING in "The Selection of Variates for Use in Prediction with some Comments on the General Problem of Nuisance Parameters," *Annals of Mathematical Statistics*, Vol. 11 (1940), pp. 271–283. Hotelling's approach is, however, different from the approach described in the text, because his null-hypothesis amounts to equal parent correlations of the two competing specifications; hence a combination of all explanatory variables of the two specifications combined gives then in general a higher multiple parent correlation. Here, we assume that (6.25) is correct in the sense that addition of the variables of $\mathbf{X}_2$ to the set of explanatory variables of $\mathbf{X}_1$ leads to zero parent coefficients for the former variables.

[2] See J. DURBIN, "Estimation of Parameters in Time-Series Regression Models." Mimeographed report of the Research Techniques Division of the London School of Economics.

[3] In a sense, one might argue that there should be independence. For suppose—as is frequently done—that the disturbances are combinations of neglected explanatory variables which are not worth-while to be considered separately, although combined they are of importance. Then, if it is possible to specify a (neglected) variable which is associated with the disturbances, this is an indication that the original specification is not correct; the reason being that the variable added is separately important. It is difficult, however, to appraise such arguments as long as so little is really known about the nature of disturbances. Also, the argument is not applicable in the case of simultaneous equations (cf. below, 6.2.7).

The above analysis belongs to the more general topic of *specification analysis*. Further results are presented in the Appendix to this chapter, Section 6.B; the following should, however, be mentioned here. First, it was observed that the specification (6.26) as such has been hardly defined; in particular, $\boldsymbol{\beta}_2$ is not defined. So we are entirely free in defining; and we shall interpret $\boldsymbol{\beta}_2$ as the mean value of the least-squares expression $\mathbf{b}_2 = (\mathbf{X}_2'\mathbf{X}_2)^{-1}\mathbf{X}_2'\mathbf{y}$. In that case $\boldsymbol{\beta}_2$ can be easily shown to be equal to

$$\boldsymbol{\beta}_2 = \mathbf{P}\boldsymbol{\beta}_1, \tag{6.30}$$

where $\mathbf{P}$ is the coefficient matrix of the least-squares regressions of the correct explanatory variables on the erroneous ones:

$$\mathbf{X}_1 = \mathbf{X}_2\mathbf{P} + \text{least-squares residuals}; \tag{6.31}$$

that is,

$$\mathbf{P} = (\mathbf{X}_2'\mathbf{X}_2)^{-1}\mathbf{X}_2'\mathbf{X}_1. \tag{6.32}$$

This result pre-supposes that both $\mathbf{X}_1$ and $\mathbf{X}_2$ are nonstochastic. It will be used in one of the empirical sections of this chapter.

Secondly, specification analysis can be used for the treatment of *errors of measurement* (or errors of observation). When there are errors of this kind in the x's such that the correct specification is in terms of "pure" x's and the specification used is in terms of observed values, then—under certain assumptions—the following two results emerge: if there is no correlation among the explanatory variables, the least-squares parameter estimates are biased towards zero; and if there is such a correlation, this effect tends to be even worse, and it is combined with a second effect, which implies that the influence of x_λ on y is partly allocated to $x_{\lambda'}$, for all pairs λ, λ' ($\lambda \neq \lambda'$). For details we refer to Section 6.B of the Appendix.

6.2.5. That we do not know the "true" specification in general and that it is our task to find or at least approximate it, and that there are errors of measurement—these complications are simply the first two of the list of difficulties associated with least-squares and its classical assumptions. We proceed to the third, viz., that of *multicollinearity*. It is related both to the last remarks of 6.2.4 and to the nonsingularity of $\mathbf{X}'\mathbf{X}$ that was assumed in (6.17) for the existence of the least-squares estimator. This nonsingularity involves the following assumption:

(*v*) *The matrix* **X** *of* (6.13) *has rank* Λ.

In general, multicollinearity is not present in its extreme form in the sense that the rank of **X** is smaller than Λ,[1] but this situation is often approached. In geometric terms, and using the $(\Lambda + 1)$-dimensional $y, x_1, \ldots, x_\Lambda$-space of variables, we find that the T sample points are no longer evenly spread around a Λ-dimensional hyperplane, but that they are clustered around a plane or line of a smaller number of dimensions. It is then intuitively clear that the former hyperplane cannot be determined accurately. Indeed, it follows from (6.19) that the sampling variances of the least-squares coefficients must be considerable, for the covariance matrix of the estimator, being equal to $(\mathbf{X}'\mathbf{X})^{-1}$ apart from a scalar, must have large elements if the columns of **X** are "almost" dependent. In principle, nothing can be done about this situation, for it can be shown that least-squares has optimal properties under the assumptions mentioned so far; and this holds even in the case of a high degree of multicollinearity.[2] But the seriousness of a multicollinear situation should not be underestimated; it goes beyond the immediate fact of increased standard errors. For example, take the "true" equation

$$y(t) = \alpha + \beta_1 x_1(t) + \beta_2 x_2(t) + u(t); \tag{6.33}$$

and suppose that, first, y is considered as a linear function of x_1 (which leads to a significant regression, say), after which y is written as a linear function of both x_1 and x_2. This kind of experimentation is quite usual in econometric research and will be illustrated on a large scale in the next sections. It would be preferable, of course, to use the "true" form immediately; but, since this is unknown, the procedure is normally to add explanatory variables one after another and to appraise their adequacy *inter alia* on the basis of their statistical significance. Suppose now that x_1 and x_2 are highly correlated. In such a case the introduction of x_2 will frequently not lead to significance, so that the

[1] But compare the remarks made at the end of 6.1.4 and at the beginning of 6.1.5.

[2] The least-squares estimator is, under the assumptions (*i*), (*ii*), (*iii*) and (*v*), "best linear unbiased;" i.e., among all estimators of $\boldsymbol{\beta}$ which are also unbiased and linear in the dependent variable, the covariance matrix of the least-squares estimator has certain minimum properties. We shall come back to this point in Chapter VIII (Section 8.5).

statistician, when applying the simplicity criterion, may wrongly decide that x_2 should be dropped. If there are more variables, the situation may be even worse, because the correlations need not be large in order to produce this effect.[1]

It is conceivable, however, that we can re-arrange our problem in such a way that the multicollinearity difficulty is avoided. Let us go back to the $(\Lambda + 1)$-dimensional space, and suppose that it is plausible on *a priori* grounds that the Λ-plane in which we are interested goes through a certain fixed point, or that its slopes in two different directions should be equal, or have a known ratio, etc. It will be intuitively clear that this *a priori* information—if valid—will restrict the indeterminacy of the plane; indeed, it is shown in the Appendix (Section 6.B) that this is the case. Here, we shall consider one important special case, viz., the determination of *distributed lags*:

$$(6.34) \qquad y(t) = \alpha + \beta_1 x(t) + \beta_2 x(t-1) + \ldots + u(t).$$

It is well-known that successive lagged values of economic variables are often highly correlated, so that the least-squares estimators of $\beta_1, \beta_2, \ldots$ must be expected to have large standard errors. Consider then the following approach, which is due to L. M. KOYCK.[2] It is often reasonable to assume that, from a certain point onwards, the influence of successive lagged values of x decreases regularly, say in geometric proportion. When supposing, first, that this geometric series begins with the first lag, we can replace (6.34) by

$$(6.35) \qquad y(t) = \alpha + \beta x(t) + \varrho\beta x(t-1) + \varrho^2\beta x(t-2) + \ldots + u(t),$$

where $0 < \varrho < 1$. We shift the equation one period backwards, multiply it by ϱ and subtract the result from (6.35):

$$(6.36) \qquad y(t) = \alpha(1-\varrho) + \beta x(t) + \varrho y(t-1) + [u(t) - \varrho u(t-1)].$$

This reduces the estimation problem to one of two explanatory variables plus a constant term, which is a considerable advantage because $x(t)$ and $y(t-1)$ are usually not so highly correlated as the successive

[1] Suppose that $+\beta_3 x_3(t)$ has to be added in order to obtain the "true" specification; that first y is correlated with x_1, then with x_1 and x_2; and that both x_1 and x_2 are uncorrelated with $\beta_2 x_2 + \beta_3 x_3$. Then the regression of y on x_1 and x_2 gives no significance for x_2. The condition for x_2 to be uncorrelated with $\beta_2 x_2 + \beta_3 x_3$ is that the correlation between x_2 and x_3 equals $-\beta_2/\beta_3$, both variables being measured with the standard deviation as unit. This correlation is not necessarily large.

[2] *Distributed Lags and Investment Analysis* (Amsterdam, 1954), Chapter II.

lagged series $x(t)$, $x(t-1)$,... are. It should be noted, however, that the applicability of least-squares to (6.36) under its classical assumptions requires that all explanatory variables, including the "new" one, $y(t-1)$, are uncorrelated with the new disturbance, $u(t) - \varrho u(t-1)$. This implies that u should satisfy the Markov-scheme

$$u(t) = \varrho u(t-1) + u^*(t), \tag{6.37}$$

where u^* satisfies the earlier assumptions (*i*), (*ii*) and (*iv*) [zero mean, constant variance, absence of correlation and independence of the explanatory variables $x(t)$ and $y(t-1)$]. In most cases this condition is, although restrictive, not unplausible, for positive association between the successive disturbances of (6.35) is often more plausible than the absence of any association.

The same operation can be used when the geometric series starts with the second lag:

$$y(t) = \alpha + \beta_1 x(t) + \beta_2 x(t-1) + \varrho\beta_2 x(t-2) + \ldots + u(t). \tag{6.38}$$

The result is

$$\begin{aligned} y(t) = \alpha(1-\varrho) &+ \beta_1 x(t) + (\beta_2 - \varrho\beta_1)x(t-1) + \\ &+ \varrho y(t-1) + [u(t) - \varrho u(t-1)]. \end{aligned} \tag{6.39}$$

This is a three-variable regression, and we may analyse the significance of the coefficient of $x(t-1)$ in order to appraise the plausibility of the approach (6.38) in relation to the simpler alternative (6.35). The multicollinearity complication is avoided here less adequately because of the presence of both $x(t)$ and $x(t-1)$.

When there are several explanatory variables with distributed lags, a similar procedure can be applied. Take for example

$$\begin{aligned} y(t) = \alpha &+ \beta_1 x_1(t) + \varrho_1\beta_1 x_1(t-1) + \ldots \\ &+ \beta_2 x_2(t) + \varrho_2\beta_2 x_2(t-1) + \ldots + u(t). \end{aligned} \tag{6.40}$$

Shifting the equation one period backward, multiplication by ϱ_1 and substraction of the result from (6.40) lead to

$$\begin{aligned} y(t) - \varrho_1 y(t-1) = \alpha(1-\varrho_1) &+ \beta_1 x_1(t) + \beta_2 x_2(t) + \\ &+ (\varrho_2 - \varrho_1)\beta_2[x_2(t-1) + \varrho_2 x_2(t-2) + \ldots] + \\ &+ [u(t) - \varrho_1 u(t-1)]. \end{aligned} \tag{6.41}$$

Application of the same operation to (6.41) with ϱ_2 instead of ϱ_1 gives

$$\begin{aligned} y(t) - (\varrho_1 + \varrho_2)y(t-1) + \varrho_1\varrho_2 y(t-2) = \\ = \alpha(1-\varrho_1)(1-\varrho_2) + \beta_1[x_1(t) - \varrho_2 x_1(t-1)] + \\ + \beta_2[x_2(t) - \varrho_1 x_2(t-1)] + \\ + [u(t) - (\varrho_1+\varrho_2)u(t-1) + \varrho_1\varrho_2 u(t-2)]. \end{aligned} \tag{6.42}$$

This result is considerably more complicated than the corresponding equation (6.36) in the one-variable case. First, three additional lagged variables are involved, viz., $y(t-2)$, $x_1(t-1)$, $x_2(t-1)$. Second, the number of multiplicative coefficients (= the number of explanatory variables) is six, but they are all determined by the four parameters β_1, β_2, ϱ_1, ϱ_2, the two resulting restrictions being of a nonlinear type.[1] Third, independence of the disturbances of (6.42) requires a second-order Markov-scheme for the original disturbances u. Therefore, no computations based on (6.42) are presented in the next empirical sections. If relationships of the type (6.40) are considered adequate, their estimation is based upon

$$y(t) = \alpha' + \beta_1' x_1(t) + \beta_2' x_2(t) + \varrho' y(t-1) + u'(t), \tag{6.43}$$

which amounts to taking (6.41) and neglecting the difference $\varrho_2 - \varrho_1$. In the Appendix to this chapter, Section 6.B, this approximation is further analysed.

6.2.6. Our fourth problem is that of *autocorrelated disturbances*. It arises mainly because of the fact that the values assumed by our variables refer usually to successive points or intervals of time. Since the disturbances **u** are generally interpreted as combinations of "neglected" variables[2] and, furthermore, these variables are not independent through time, it is plausible that assumption (*ii*) of 6.2.3 is not always realistic. Much more general is the following assumption:

(*vi*) *The disturbances of* (6.13) *have a finite and nonsingular covariance matrix,* $\mathscr{E}(\mathbf{uu}') = \mathbf{\Omega}$.

This generalization can be reduced to the original least-squares case in the following manner. It follows from assumption (*vi*) that $\mathbf{\Omega}$ and

[1] Linear restrictions are easier to handle; cf. the Appendix, Section 6.B.
[2] Cf. p. 214, n. 3.

hence also $\mathbf{\Omega}^{-1}$ are positive-definite;[1] and any such matrix can be written as the product of a matrix $\mathbf{\Psi}$ and its transpose:

$$\mathbf{\Omega}^{-1} = \mathbf{\Psi}'\mathbf{\Psi}, \tag{6.44}$$

where $\mathbf{\Psi}$ is square and nonsingular. Let us then premultiply (6.13) by this $\mathbf{\Psi}$:

$$\mathbf{\Psi y} = (\mathbf{\Psi X})\boldsymbol{\beta} + \mathbf{\Psi u}, \tag{6.45}$$

then $\mathbf{\Psi u}$ is a transformed disturbance vector with zero mean and covariance matrix

$$\mathscr{E}(\mathbf{\Psi uu}'\mathbf{\Psi}') = \mathbf{\Psi\Omega\Psi}' = \mathbf{\Psi\Psi}^{-1}\mathbf{\Psi}'^{-1}\mathbf{\Psi}' = \mathbf{I}, \tag{6.46}$$

which is the covariance matrix of assumption (*ii*) for the special case $\sigma^2 = 1$. In other words, we are able to reduce the case of assumption (*vi*) to that of (*ii*) by replacing (6.13) by (6.45), which is characterised by the same coefficient vector $\boldsymbol{\beta}$. This suggests that we should apply ordinary least-squares to (6.45). The normal equations are then

$$(\mathbf{\Psi X})'\mathbf{\Psi y} = (\mathbf{\Psi X})'\mathbf{\Psi X b}^*, \tag{6.47}$$

or, applying (6.44):

$$\mathbf{X}'\mathbf{\Omega}^{-1}\mathbf{y} = \mathbf{X}'\mathbf{\Omega}^{-1}\mathbf{X b}^*, \tag{6.48}$$

where $\mathbf{b}^*$ is the *generalised least-squares* estimator. This method was proposed by A. C. AITKEN.[2]

We have

$$\begin{aligned} \mathbf{b}^* &= (\mathbf{X}'\mathbf{\Omega}^{-1}\mathbf{X})^{-1}\mathbf{X}'\mathbf{\Omega}^{-1}\mathbf{y} \\ &= \boldsymbol{\beta} + (\mathbf{X}'\mathbf{\Omega}^{-1}\mathbf{X})^{-1}\mathbf{X}'\mathbf{\Omega}^{-1}\mathbf{u}, \end{aligned} \tag{6.49}$$

[1] Proof: for any column vector $\mathbf{p}$ of T nonstochastic elements, we have $0 \leqq \mathscr{E}(\mathbf{p}'\mathbf{u})^2 = \mathscr{E}(\mathbf{p}'\mathbf{u} \cdot \mathbf{u}'\mathbf{p}) = \mathbf{p}'\mathbf{\Omega p}$; and $\leqq$ can be replaced by $<$ because $\mathscr{E}(\mathbf{p}'\mathbf{u})^2 = 0$ would imply that the elements of $\mathbf{u}$ are linearly dependent and so have a singular covariance matrix, contrary to assumption (*vi*).

[2] Cf. "Least Squares and Linear Combination of Observations," *Proceedings of the Royal Society of Edinburgh*, Vol. 55 (1934–1935), pp. 42–48. It will also be noted that assumption (*vi*) covers the case of heteroskedasticity (unequal elements on the main diagonal of $\mathbf{\Omega}$), which is important *inter alia* in family budget studies. For an analysis of the consequences of the application of least-squares in the case of heteroskedasticity, cf. H. THEIL, "Estimates and their Sampling Variance of Parameters of Certain Heteroskedastic Distributions," *Review of the International Statistical Institute*, Vol. 19 (1951), pp. 141–147; and S. J. PRAIS and H. S. HOUTHAKKER, *The Analysis of Family Budgets* (Cambridge, Engl., 1955), pp. 57–58

so that $\mathscr{E}\mathbf{b}^* = \mathscr{E}\mathbf{b} = \boldsymbol{\beta}$; that is, the generalised and the ordinary least-squares estimators are both unbiased. The covariance matrix of $\mathbf{b}^*$ is

$$\begin{aligned}&\mathscr{E}\{(\mathbf{b}^* - \boldsymbol{\beta})(\mathbf{b}^* - \boldsymbol{\beta})'\} = \\ &= \mathscr{E}\{(\mathbf{X}'\boldsymbol{\Omega}^{-1}\mathbf{X})^{-1}\mathbf{X}'\boldsymbol{\Omega}^{-1}\mathbf{u}\mathbf{u}'\boldsymbol{\Omega}^{-1}\mathbf{X}(\mathbf{X}'\boldsymbol{\Omega}^{-1}\mathbf{X})^{-1}\} \\ &= (\mathbf{X}'\boldsymbol{\Omega}^{-1}\mathbf{X})^{-1}.\end{aligned} \tag{6.50}$$

It is easily seen that the special case $\boldsymbol{\Omega} = \sigma^2\mathbf{I}$, (6.48) and (6.50) reduce to (6.16) and (6.19), respectively. A multiple correlation coefficient R^* corresponding to this method, which we shall meet again in another connection, is the one determined by

$$1 - R^{*2} = \frac{\hat{\mathbf{u}}^{*\prime}\boldsymbol{\Omega}^{-1}\hat{\mathbf{u}}^*}{\mathbf{y}'\boldsymbol{\Omega}^{-1}\mathbf{y}}, \tag{6.51}$$

where $\hat{\mathbf{u}}^* = \mathbf{y} - \mathbf{X}\mathbf{b}^*$ is the vector of estimated disturbances. Since $\mathscr{E}(\mathbf{u}'\boldsymbol{\Omega}^{-1}\mathbf{u}) = T$,[1] the parent value of $1 - R^{*2}$ equals the reciprocal of $(1/T)\mathscr{E}(\mathbf{y}'\boldsymbol{\Omega}^{-1}\mathbf{y})$. If $\boldsymbol{\Omega} = \sigma^2\mathbf{I}$, then R and R^* are equivalent, provided R is based on the second moment of the y's around zero (not about the mean). If there is only one explanatory variable ($\Lambda = 1$), R^* reduces to the zero-order correlation

$$r^* = \frac{\mathbf{x}'\boldsymbol{\Omega}^{-1}\mathbf{y}}{\sqrt{\mathbf{x}'\boldsymbol{\Omega}^{-1}\mathbf{x}.\mathbf{y}'\boldsymbol{\Omega}^{-1}\mathbf{y}}}, \tag{6.52}$$

which may be positive or negative, contrary to R^*.

A serious difficulty in the application of generalised least-squares is that we do not know $\boldsymbol{\Omega}$ in most cases. Three alternative approaches are then available. First, we can try to estimate $\boldsymbol{\Omega}$. One might think that this can be done by applying first least-squares (i.e., by replacing $\boldsymbol{\Omega}$ by $\sigma^2\mathbf{I} = \boldsymbol{\Omega}_1$, say), computing the moment matrix $\boldsymbol{\Omega}_2$ of the resulting estimated disturbances $\hat{\mathbf{u}}$, applying generalised least-squares based upon $\boldsymbol{\Omega}_2$, etc. This iterative method is not possible, however, because $\boldsymbol{\Omega}_2 = \hat{\mathbf{u}}\hat{\mathbf{u}}'$ is singular. It is preferable to make some *a priori* assumptions about the unknown $\boldsymbol{\Omega}$; for example, that the disturbances satisfy the first-order Markov-scheme (6.37) for unknown ϱ. The (t, t')-th element of $\boldsymbol{\Omega}$ becomes then $\sigma^2\varrho^{|t-t'|}$, σ^2 being the common variance of the

[1] Proof: Since $\mathbf{u}'\boldsymbol{\Omega}^{-1}\mathbf{u}$ is a scalar, it is equal to its own trace and hence also equal to the trace of $\boldsymbol{\Omega}^{-1}\mathbf{u}\mathbf{u}'$ (see p. 211 n.). But the mean value of the trace of a matrix is equal to the trace of the mean value, and the mean value of $\boldsymbol{\Omega}^{-1}\mathbf{u}\mathbf{u}'$ is the unit matrix of order T.

$u(t)$; and it is possible in principle to estimate both ϱ and $\boldsymbol{\beta}$.[1] The second approach goes even further by applying a transformation to the variables without introducing another unknown parameter. This transformation must be such that the disturbances associated with the transformed variables can be regarded as independent (more precisely: as having a scalar covariance matrix), or at least approximately so. A well-known procedure is that of taking first differences, which amounts to replacing (6.12) by

$$\Delta y(t) = \sum_{\lambda=1}^{\Lambda} \beta_\lambda \Delta x_\lambda(t) + \Delta u(t), \tag{6.53}$$

where $\Delta y(t) = y(t) - y(t-1)$, etc.[2] The new assumption is then that Δu satisfies assumption (*ii*). No doubt, this first-difference approach may be valuable for our present empirical analysis, since the small time units used (months) may be expected to lead to a considerable positive correlation between successive disturbances. Nevertheless, it has not been applied, because (as mentioned earlier) the underlying data themselves have a first-difference character, so that we may guess that it is appropriate to leave them as they are. Also, it will be clear that small errors in the choice of the transformation lead to a loss of efficiency (= sampling variance in excess of the minimum attainable) which is small of a higher order.[3]

The third approach takes the transformation as given (or does not apply any transformation at all), but tests the independence of the disturbances. The most widely used statistic is the Von Neumann ratio (mentioned already in 6.1.1) of the estimated disturbances. It is defined as

$$Q = \frac{T}{T-1} \, \frac{\Sigma\{\hat{u}(t) - \hat{u}(t-1)\}^2}{\Sigma\{\hat{u}(t)\}^2}, \tag{6.54}$$

where $\hat{u}(t)$ is an estimated disturbance according to least-squares:

$$\hat{u}(t) = y(t) - \sum_{\lambda=1}^{\Lambda} b_\lambda x_\lambda(t). \tag{6.55}$$

[1] See e.g. L. R. KLEIN, *A Textbook of Econometrics* (New York-Evanston, 1953), pp. 86–89.

[2] This procedure was followed by J. R. N. STONE in his recent work *The Measurement of Consumers' Expenditure and Behaviour in the United Kingdom, 1920–1938*, Vol. I (Cambridge, Engl., 1954), pp. 287–291; and, for prediction purposes, by the Netherlands Central Planning Bureau (cf. 5.1.3).

[3] This has been proved by J. VAN IJZEREN in "De theoretische zijde van de methode der kleinste kwadraten" (Theoretical Aspects of Least-Squares), *Statistica*, Vol. 8 (1954), pp. 21–45.

If the parent disturbances u are independently distributed, Q should lie in the neighbourhood of 2; positive association between successive disturbances (the usual alternative) reduces Q with zero as lower bound, negative association leads to larger Q's. The distribution of Q under the null-hypothesis that the parent disturbances are normally and independently distributed with constant variance (and that the explanatory variables are all nonstochastic) has been analysed by DURBIN and WATSON.[1] It appears impossible to give exact confidence limits, but approximate upper and lower bounds (Q_U and Q_L) for these limits in the one-tailed test against positive serial correlation are available. They are given in Table 6.4 below for $T = 30$ (which corresponds approximately with the number of months in the empirical analysis of this chapter) and for alternative values of Λ, one of the explanatory variables being a constant term. If $Q < Q_L$, we should reject the hypothesis of independence of the u's; if $Q > Q_U$, we should not reject it at the chosen level of significance; if $Q_L \leq Q \leq \leq Q_U$, the test is inconclusive. A one-tailed test against negative serial correlation is obtained by replacing Q by $4 - Q$. Q is computed for all empirical analyses of this chapter which are finally preferred.

TABLE 6.4

LOWER AND UPPER BOUNDS FOR THE SIGNIFICANCE POINTS OF THE VON NEUMANN RATIO OF ESTIMATED REGRESSION DISTURBANCES FOR 30 OBSERVATIONS
(Durbin and Watson, 1951)

Λ	*Significance level*					
	5%		$2\frac{1}{2}$%		1%	
	Q_L	Q_U	Q_L	Q_U	Q_L	Q_U
2	1.40	1.54	1.29	1.43	1.17	1.30
3	1.32	1.62	1.22	1.51	1.11	1.39
4	1.25	1.71	1.16	1.59	1.04	1.47
5	1.18	1.80	1.09	1.69	0.97	1.56
6	1.11	1.89	1.01	1.79	0.91	1.67

The question arises what to do with analyses leading to Q's that are far from 2. The unbiasedness of the least-squares estimator **b** is not affected, of course, but that of its variance estimator is, and the question arises to what extent. We shall consider this problem under certain simplifying assumptions.

[1] J. Durbin and G. S. Watson, "Testing for Serial Correlation in Least Squares Regression," I and II, *Biometrika*, Vol. 37 (1950), pp. 409–428, and *ibidem*, Vol. 38 (1951), pp. 159–178. The authors consider the slightly different coefficient $d = (1/T)(T - 1)Q$.

Under assumptions (*i*), (*iii*), (*v*), (*vi*) the covariance matrix of the least-squares estimator is

$$\mathscr{E}\{(\mathbf{b}-\boldsymbol{\beta})(\mathbf{b}-\boldsymbol{\beta})'\} = (\mathbf{X}'\mathbf{X})^{-1}\mathbf{X}'\boldsymbol{\Omega}\mathbf{X}(\mathbf{X}'\mathbf{X})^{-1}. \tag{6.56}$$

Suppose then that all correlations between disturbances can be neglected except those between successive values, that the latter correlations are all equal (to θ, say), and that the disturbances have constant variance. Hence

$$\boldsymbol{\Omega} = \sigma^2 \begin{bmatrix} 1 & \theta & 0.\,.\,.\,.\,.0 \\ \theta & 1 & \theta.\,.\,.\,.\,.0 \\ 0 & \theta & 1.\,.\,.\,.\,.0 \\ \vdots & \vdots & \vdots \quad\;\; \vdots \\ 0 & 0 & 0.\,.\,.\,.\,.1 \end{bmatrix}, \tag{6.57}$$

or

$$\boldsymbol{\Omega} = \sigma^2(\mathbf{I} + \theta\mathbf{J}), \tag{6.58}$$

where

$$\mathbf{J} = \begin{bmatrix} 0 & 1.\,.\,.\,.\,.0 \\ 1 & 0.\,.\,.\,.\,.0 \\ \vdots & \vdots \quad\;\; \vdots \\ 0 & 0.\,.\,.\,.\,.0 \end{bmatrix}. \tag{6.59}$$

Substituting (6.58) into (6.56), we obtain

$$\begin{aligned} \mathscr{E}\{(\mathbf{b}-\boldsymbol{\beta})(\mathbf{b}-\boldsymbol{\beta})'\} &= \sigma^2(\mathbf{X}'\mathbf{X})^{-1}\mathbf{X}'(\mathbf{I}+\theta\mathbf{J})\mathbf{X}(\mathbf{X}'\mathbf{X})^{-1} \\ &= \sigma^2(\mathbf{X}'\mathbf{X})^{-1}[\mathbf{I}+\theta\mathbf{X}'\mathbf{J}\mathbf{X}(\mathbf{X}'\mathbf{X})^{-1}], \end{aligned} \tag{6.60}$$

so that we may regard

$$\theta\mathbf{X}'\mathbf{J}\mathbf{X}(\mathbf{X}'\mathbf{X})^{-1} \tag{6.61}$$

as the relative error that is committed when the classical expression $\sigma^2(\mathbf{X}'\mathbf{X})^{-1}$ is used; it is seen immediately that this error is proportional to θ, given $\mathbf{X}$. The product $\mathbf{X}'\mathbf{J}\mathbf{X}$ is the $\Lambda \times \Lambda$ matrix

$$\mathbf{X}'\mathbf{J}\mathbf{X} = [\sum_t x_\lambda(t)x_{\lambda'}(t-1) + \sum_t x_\lambda(t-1)x_{\lambda'}(t)]. \tag{6.62}$$

If we measure the explanatory variables as deviations from their means, and if we make the simplifying assumption that different explanatory variables have no lagged correlations of the first order, $\mathbf{X'JX}$ is a diagonal matrix. When assuming, furthermore, that all explanatory variables have the same first-order autocorrelation[1] (θ_x, say), we have

$$\text{(6.63)} \quad \mathbf{X'JX} = 2\theta_x \begin{bmatrix} \Sigma\{x_1(t)\}^2 & 0 & \cdots & 0 \\ 0 & \Sigma\{x_2(t)\}^2 & \cdots & 0 \\ \cdots & \cdots & \cdots & \cdots \\ 0 & 0 & \cdots & \Sigma\{x_\Lambda(t)\}^2 \end{bmatrix}.$$

If, moreover, all current explanatory variables are uncorrelated, $\mathbf{X'X}$ is diagonal too, and the relative error (6.61) turns out to be $2\theta\theta_x\mathbf{I}$.[2] The variances are then underestimated if θ and θ_x have the same sign—which will usually be true. A plausible numerical example: $\theta = 0.3$, $\theta_x = 0.7$, and hence $2\theta\theta_x = 0.42$, so that the classical standard errors should be increased by about 20 per cent.

The alternative assumption that current explanatory variables are correlated will often lead to larger errors. For $\Lambda = 2$, for example, we obtain $2\theta\theta_x/(1 - \varrho^2)$ as the relative error of the variance estimators, ϱ being the correlation between x_1 and x_2. This suggests that multicollinearity does not only lead to large standard errors according to the classical expression $\sigma^2(\mathbf{X'X})^{-1}$, but in this special case also to a large relative underestimation of just these standard errors when the classical expression is used. This unfavourable effect of multicollinearity is to some extent comparable with the consequences of errors of measurement; cf. the end of 6.2.4.

6.2.7. Our fifth problem is that of the celebrated *simultaneous equations*. It arises because the interdependence of economic phenomena sometimes leads to a situation in which explanatory variables do not only influence the dependent variable analysed, but are also influenced by it, directly of indirectly, in a manner to be considered below. Such a situation may occur in the price behaviour to be analysed in this chapter, as for instance prices may both affect and be affected by other variables like stocks. In that case the equation describing the fluctua-

[1] This assumption has been justified to some extent by G. H. ORCUTT in "A Study of the Autoregressive Nature of the Time Series Used for Tinbergen's Model of the Economic System of the United States, 1919–1932," *Journal of the Royal Statistical Society*, Series B, Vol. 10 (1948), pp. 1–53.

[2] For the case of one explanatory variable (plus constant term) H. WOLD has given a similar expression involving fewer approximations; cf. his *Demand Analysis* (New York-Stockholm, 1953), pp. 212–213.

tions of the variable analysed contains two types of explanatory variables, viz., variables for which such a mutual relationship exists, and variables for which this is not true. Under linearity assumptions we may write the equation then in the form

$$y(t) = \sum_{\mu=1}^{m} \gamma_\mu y_\mu(t) + \sum_{\lambda=1}^{l} \beta_\lambda x_\lambda(t) + u(t) \tag{6.64}$$

or in matrix notation:

$$\mathbf{y} = \mathbf{Y}\boldsymbol{\gamma} + \mathbf{X}_1\boldsymbol{\beta} + \mathbf{u}, \tag{6.65}$$

where $\mathscr{E}\mathbf{u} = \mathbf{0}$, $\mathscr{E}(\mathbf{uu}') = \sigma^2\mathbf{I}$. The variables $y, y_1, \ldots, y_m$ are those which exhibit mutual relationships; they are called "jointly dependent." The other variables $(x_1, \ldots, x_l)$ are called "predetermined;" the subscript 1 of their matrix $\mathbf{X}_1$ will be explained below. The latter category consists in general of two groups, viz., exogenous and lagged endogenous variables, the values of the latter being identical with those of certain jointly dependent variables except for a lag transformation. An example: we may have a demand equation which describes the quantity bought and sold in period t (q_t) as a linear function of the price p_t of that period, of the same price lagged (p_{t-1}), and of income (M_t):

$$q_t = \alpha + \beta_1 p_t + \beta_2 p_{t-1} + \beta_3 M_t + u_t, \tag{6.66}$$

u_t being a random disturbance. If we assume price and quantity to be interrelated by a demand and supply mechanism, while income is determined by outside factors, then p_t is a current endogenous, p_{t-1} a lagged endogenous, and M_t a current exogenous variable. Hence p_t and q_t are jointly dependent, whereas p_{t-1} and M_t are predetermined. Here, we shall assume that all predetermined variables are of the exogenous type, so that their values can be regarded as nonstochastic; the necessary generalisation will be presented in the Appendix to this chapter, Section 6.C.

It is now no longer correct to assume that the disturbance vector is independent of all explanatory variables, since this cannot be true in general for all y's on the right of (6.64). This reduces the possibility of estimation, for it is this independence which underlies the estimation methods of the preceding pages. However, the possibility may be restored just because of the mutual relationships which are the cause of the complication. Let us assume that these relations, together with (6.64), form a *system* of "simultaneous" linear equations. For example, we can imagine that the demand and supply mechanism considered in the preceding paragraph is described by a system of two equations, one of which is the demand relation (6.66) and the other a supply relation of the form

$$q_t = \gamma + \delta_1 p_t + \delta_2 p_{t-1} + \delta_3 k_t + v_t, \tag{6.67}$$

where k_t is the price of a production factor and v_t a random disturbance. Combining (6.66) and (6.67), we have a system of two linear equations; and it is the function of this system to describe jointly or "simultaneously" p_t and q_t (the jointly dependent variables) in terms of the predetermined variables. If we assume k_t to be determined by outside factors, the predetermined variables in the system as a whole are p_{t-1}, M_t and k_t. It will be noted that there are as many equations as jointly dependent variables (two in this case); the system is then said to be *complete*.[1]

In general, we will have more predetermined variables in the whole system than in any of its separate equations like (6.65). Now the basic idea in the estimation of the coefficients of such equations is that the excess of the number of predetermined variables in the system over that in any particular equation can be used in order to replace the right-hand y's about which we cannot assume that they are independent of the disturbance vector of that equation. But it will be intuitively clear (and it will be made clearer below) that the excess just-mentioned $(\Lambda - l)$ should then at least be equal to the number of these y's (m):

$$\Lambda \geq m + l. \tag{6.68}$$

More precisely, we introduce the following assumption:

(*vii*) *Equation* (6.64) [*or* (6.65)] *is one of a complete system of* $M \geq m + 1$ *stochastic linear equations in* M *jointly dependent and* $\Lambda \geq m + l$ *predetermined variables.*[2] *This system can be solved for the jointly dependent variables.*

Under this and some of the earlier assumptions—which refer now, of course, to (6.65), not to (6.13)—, it is possible to derive estimators

[1] Another example is the 27-equation system of the Dutch economy considered in Section 3.1.

[2] As mentioned above, it is assumed in the text that the predetermined variables are all exogenous; the generalisation for lagged endogenous variables is considered in Section 6.C of the Appendix.

with certain desirable properties. But a price has to be paid: these properties do not refer to finite samples, but to infinite ones, just as in the case of the sampling variances of the inequality coefficient and proportions of Section 2.5.

It follows from the second part of assumption (*vii*) that the jointly dependent variables can be written explicitly in terms of the predetermined variables. This is the *reduced form* of the system, which consists of M reduced-form equations (one for each jointly dependent variable); in contrast to this, the M equations of the original system are called *structural equations*. Now if the latter equations are all linear, this must also be true for the former. Consider then in particular that part of the reduced form that corresponds with the right-hand jointly dependent variables of (6.65). Estimating it by least-squares, we obtain

$$\mathbf{Y} = \mathbf{X}(\mathbf{X}'\mathbf{X})^{-1}\mathbf{X}'\mathbf{Y} + \mathbf{V}, \tag{6.69}$$

where $(\mathbf{X}'\mathbf{X})^{-1}\mathbf{X}'\mathbf{Y}$ is the matrix of the least-squares reduced-form coefficients, and $\mathbf{V}$ the matrix of estimated reduced-form disturbances. Let us then write (6.65) in the form

$$\mathbf{y} = (\mathbf{Y} - \mathbf{V})\boldsymbol{\gamma} + \mathbf{X}_1\boldsymbol{\beta} + (\mathbf{u} + \mathbf{V}\boldsymbol{\gamma}), \tag{6.70}$$

and apply least-squares to this equation. In other words, let us apply ordinary least-squares to (6.65) after the dependent explanatory variables are corrected by subtracting the estimated reduced-form disturbances. We shall call this the method of *two-stage least-squares*: the first stage consists of applying least-squares to the reduced form in order to find $\mathbf{V}$, the second amounts to applying the same method to (6.65) after replacing $\mathbf{Y}$ by $\mathbf{Y} - \mathbf{V}$. This approach can be justified in the following heuristic manner. If we would know the parent reduced-form disturbances corresponding to $\mathbf{Y}$, $\overline{\mathbf{V}}$ say, we could apply least-squares to

$$\mathbf{y} = (\mathbf{Y} - \overline{\mathbf{V}})\boldsymbol{\gamma} + \mathbf{X}_1\boldsymbol{\beta} + (\mathbf{u} + \overline{\mathbf{V}}\boldsymbol{\gamma}), \tag{6.71}$$

since the objection that some of the right-hand variables are not independent of the disturbances is no longer valid, $\mathbf{Y} - \overline{\mathbf{V}}$ being an exact linear function of $\mathbf{X}$ and hence nonstochastic. We do not know $\overline{\mathbf{V}}$, but we can estimate it by means of $\mathbf{V}$, and the sampling error tends to zero for increasing T under appropriate conditions. So let us apply least-squares:

$$(6.72)\qquad \begin{bmatrix} \mathbf{Y}' - \mathbf{V}' \\ \mathbf{X}_1' \end{bmatrix} \mathbf{y} = \begin{bmatrix} \mathbf{Y}' - \mathbf{V}' \\ \mathbf{X}_1' \end{bmatrix} [\mathbf{Y} - \mathbf{V} \quad \mathbf{X}_1] \begin{pmatrix} \mathbf{c} \\ \mathbf{b} \end{pmatrix},$$

$\mathbf{c}$, $\mathbf{b}$ being an estimator of $\boldsymbol{\gamma}$, $\boldsymbol{\beta}$. (6.72) can also be written as

$$(6.73)\qquad \begin{bmatrix} (\mathbf{Y} - \mathbf{V})'\mathbf{y} \\ \mathbf{X}_1'\mathbf{y} \end{bmatrix} = \begin{bmatrix} \mathbf{Y}'\mathbf{Y} - \mathbf{V}'\mathbf{V} & \mathbf{Y}'\mathbf{X}_1 \\ \mathbf{X}_1'\mathbf{Y} & \mathbf{X}_1'\mathbf{X}_1 \end{bmatrix} \begin{pmatrix} \mathbf{c} \\ \mathbf{b} \end{pmatrix},$$

because we have

$$\mathbf{X}'\mathbf{V} = \mathbf{X}'[\mathbf{Y} - \mathbf{X}(\mathbf{X}'\mathbf{X})^{-1}\mathbf{X}'\mathbf{Y}] = \mathbf{0},$$

so that $\mathbf{X}_1'\mathbf{V}$, being a submatrix of $\mathbf{X}'\mathbf{V}$, must also be a zero matrix; and because

$$(\mathbf{Y} - \mathbf{V})'(\mathbf{Y} - \mathbf{V}) = \mathbf{Y}'\mathbf{Y} - \mathbf{Y}'\mathbf{V} - \mathbf{V}'\mathbf{Y} + \mathbf{V}'\mathbf{V},$$

where

$$\mathbf{V}'\mathbf{Y} = \mathbf{V}'[\mathbf{X}(\mathbf{X}'\mathbf{X})^{-1}\mathbf{X}'\mathbf{Y} + \mathbf{V}] = \mathbf{V}'\mathbf{V} = \mathbf{Y}'\mathbf{V}.$$

Combining (6.65) and (6.73), and writing

$$(6.74)\qquad \mathbf{e} = \begin{pmatrix} \mathbf{c} \\ \mathbf{b} \end{pmatrix} - \begin{pmatrix} \boldsymbol{\gamma} \\ \boldsymbol{\beta} \end{pmatrix}$$

for the sampling error, we obtain

$$(6.75)\qquad \mathbf{e} = \begin{bmatrix} \mathbf{Y}'\mathbf{Y} - \mathbf{V}'\mathbf{V} & \mathbf{Y}'\mathbf{X}_1 \\ \mathbf{X}_1'\mathbf{Y} & \mathbf{X}_1'\mathbf{X}_1 \end{bmatrix}^{-1} \begin{bmatrix} \mathbf{Y}' - \mathbf{V}' \\ \mathbf{X}_1' \end{bmatrix} \mathbf{u},$$

provided that the inverse matrix exists. It is easily seen that this proviso requires that inequality (6.68) be fulfilled, because the matrix to be inverted can be written as the product of $[\mathbf{Y} - \mathbf{V} \quad \mathbf{X}_1]$ and its transpose [cf. (6.72)–(6.73)]; and this matrix, in turn, can be written as

$$(6.76)\qquad [\mathbf{Y} - \mathbf{V} \quad \mathbf{X}_1] = \mathbf{X} \begin{bmatrix} (\mathbf{X}'\mathbf{X})^{-1}\mathbf{X}'\mathbf{Y} & \begin{matrix} \mathbf{I} \\ \cdots \\ \mathbf{0} \end{matrix} \end{bmatrix}$$

[where $\mathbf{I}$ is the $l \times l$ unit matrix and $\mathbf{0}$ the $(\Lambda - l) \times l$ zero matrix], so that the rank of our matrix can never be larger than the rank of **X**, that is, Λ. If we have $\Lambda < m + l$, the parameters of (6.65) are said to be "not identifiable;" if we have $\Lambda = m + l$, there is "just-identification," which is a special case considered in more detail in Section 6.C of the Appendix; if $\Lambda > m + l$, there is "over-identification."[1]

It is also seen that, under the assumptions (*i*), (*ii*), (*iii*), (*v*) and (*vii*) on **u** and **X**, the estimator is not unbiased for finite samples, owing to the precence of the matrix **Y** which consists of stochastic elements. But it is asymptotically unbiased, lim $\mathscr{E}\mathbf{e} = \mathbf{0}$, provided that each row of $\mathbf{Y} - \mathbf{V}$ is asymptotically an exact nonstochastic linear function of the corresponding row of **X**. This involves the assumption of consistent reduced-form estimation; and hence, following assumption (*ii*) of 6.2.3, we suppose:

(*viii*) *For each pair t, t' (= 1, . . ., T) and for each pair μ, μ' (= 1, . . ., m), the parent reduced-form disturbances $\bar{v}_\mu(t)$ and $\bar{v}_{\mu'}(t')$ corresponding to the right-hand variables y_μ and $y_{\mu'}$, respectively, of* (6.65) ***have zero*** *mean and satisfy*

$$\begin{aligned} \mathscr{E}[\bar{v}_\mu(t)\,\bar{v}_{\mu'}(t')] &= \sigma_{\mu\mu'} \quad \text{if } t = t' \\ &= 0 \qquad \text{if } t \neq t', \end{aligned} \tag{6.77}$$

$\sigma_{\mu\mu'}$ being independent of t and t'.

This assumption is satisfied as soon as the disturbances of each of the M structural equations satisfy the analogous condition. Note that this does not exclude the possibility that the disturbances of different equations for the same t are correlated. There may be nonzero "contemporaneous" correlations; but there should be no correlation between disturbances of different t's, irrespective of whether they belong to the same or to different equations. Also, contemporaneous covariances and variances should be constant through time, i.e., independent of t. Note further that assumption (*viii*), which is of the same type as (*ii*) of 6.2.3, is required for the asymptotic unbiasedness of our present estimator, whereas (*ii*) was not necessary for the un-

[1] For a more detailed analysis, cf. T. C. KOOPMANS, H. RUBIN and R. B. LEIPNIK, "Measuring the Equation Systems of Dynamic Economics," Chapter II of *Statistical Inference in Dynamic Economic Models* (edited by T. C. Koopmans; New York-London, 1950); and T. C. KOOPMANS, "Identification Problems in Economic Model Construction," Chapter II of *Studies in Econometric Method* (edited by W. C. Hood and T. C. Koopmans; New York-London, 1953).

biasedness for finite samples in the least-squares case considered in 6.2.3.

Postmultiplying (6.75) by its transpose, multiplying by T and taking the mean value gives, for large samples,

$$\lim_{T\to\infty} \mathscr{E}(T\mathbf{e}\mathbf{e}') = \sigma^2 \operatorname*{plim}_{T\to\infty} T \begin{bmatrix} \mathbf{Y}'\mathbf{Y} - \mathbf{V}'\mathbf{V} & \mathbf{Y}'\mathbf{X}_1 \\ \mathbf{X}_1'\mathbf{Y} & \mathbf{X}_1'\mathbf{X}_1 \end{bmatrix}^{-1}, \tag{6.78}$$

provided the probability limit exists. The variance σ^2 is consistently estimated by the sample variance of the estimated disturbances, if the assumptions (*i*), (*ii*), (*iii*), (*v*), (*vii*) and (*viii*) are satisfied. Hence it is possible to compute asymptotic standard errors.

More generally, let us replace the estimation equations (6.73) by

$$\begin{bmatrix} (\mathbf{Y} - k\mathbf{V})'\mathbf{y} \\ \mathbf{X}_1'\mathbf{y} \end{bmatrix} = \begin{bmatrix} \mathbf{Y}'\mathbf{Y} - k\mathbf{V}'\mathbf{V} & \mathbf{Y}'\mathbf{X}_1 \\ \mathbf{X}_1'\mathbf{Y} & \mathbf{X}_1'\mathbf{X}_1 \end{bmatrix} \begin{pmatrix} \mathbf{c} \\ \mathbf{b} \end{pmatrix}_k, \tag{6.79}$$

where k is any scalar, stochastic or nonstochastic, which may depend on the sample. Clearly, (6.79) defines a class of estimators, to be called the *k-class*, of which two-stage least-squares is one member ($k = 1$), and least-squares with y treated as sole dependent variable another ($k = 0$); we shall indicate the latter method as "single-stage least-squares," because the first stage (that of determining $\mathbf{V}$) is omitted. A third member of the k-class is the limited-information maximum-likelihood estimator, which was derived by T. W. Anderson and H. Rubin.[1] The maximum-likelihood variant is the case $k = 1 + \nu$, ν being the smallest root of the determinantal equation

$$|\mathbf{M}_1 - (1 + \nu)\mathbf{M}| = 0, \tag{6.80}$$

where $\mathbf{M}_1$ and $\mathbf{M}$ are the moment matrices of the estimated disturbances in the least-squares regressions of $y, y_1, \ldots, y_m$ on $x_1, \ldots, x_l$ and on $x_1, \ldots, x_A$, respectively:

[1] "Estimation of the Parameters of a Single Equation in a Complete System of Stochastic Equations," *Annals of Mathematical Statistics*, Vol. 20 (1949), pp. 46–63; "The Asymptotic Properties of Estimates of the Parameters of a Single Equation in a Complete System of Stochastic Equations," *ibidem*, Vol. 21 (1950), pp. 570–582. Cf. also T. C. Koopmans and W. C. Hood, "The Estimation of Simultaneous Linear Economic Relationships," Chapter VI of *Studies in Econometric Method*.

$$(6.81) \qquad \mathbf{M}_1 = \begin{bmatrix} \mathbf{y}' \\ \mathbf{Y}' \end{bmatrix} [\mathbf{y} \quad \mathbf{Y}] - \begin{bmatrix} \mathbf{y}' \\ \mathbf{Y}' \end{bmatrix} \mathbf{X}_1(\mathbf{X}_1'\mathbf{X}_1)^{-1}\mathbf{X}_1'[\mathbf{y} \quad \mathbf{Y}]$$

$$(6.82) \qquad \mathbf{M} = \begin{bmatrix} \mathbf{y}' \\ \mathbf{Y}' \end{bmatrix} [\mathbf{y} \quad \mathbf{Y}] - \begin{bmatrix} \mathbf{y}' \\ \mathbf{Y}' \end{bmatrix} \mathbf{X}(\mathbf{X}'\mathbf{X})^{-1}\mathbf{X}'[\mathbf{y} \quad \mathbf{Y}].$$

It can be shown that ν is always zero if $\Lambda = m + l$ (the case of just-identification), so that the maximum-likelihood variant is then identical with two-stage least-squares. For $\Lambda > m + l$ we have $\nu \geq 0$.

The following results for members of the k-class can be easily proved. First, if plim $(k - 1) = 0$, then they are consistent under the above-mentioned assumptions. Second, if plim $\sqrt{T}(k - 1) = 0$, then their sampling errors

$$\mathbf{e}_k = \begin{pmatrix} \mathbf{c} \\ \mathbf{b} \end{pmatrix}_k - \begin{pmatrix} \boldsymbol{\gamma} \\ \boldsymbol{\beta} \end{pmatrix}$$

have the asymptotic covariance matrix (6.78). It follows that the single-stage least-squares estimator ($k = 0$) is not consistent—except accidentally—, but that the maximum-likelihood estimator is, its asymptotic covariance matrix being given by (6.78), because the latent root ν is of the order of $1/T$ in probability. Furthermore, since the latter estimator is asymptotically efficient under normality conditions on the disturbances, the same must be true for the other estimators of the k-class for which plim $\sqrt{T}(k - 1) = 0$, like two-stage least-squares.

6.2.8. By now, we have considered a series of difficulties associated with the method of least-squares as well as a number of methods to handle these difficulties. This list is not exhaustive; reference is made to the Appendix (Sections 6.B–6.D) in which certain topics are considered in more detail. Here, attention will be paid to one particular, more basic, aspect which will take us back to the introductory considerations of 6.2.2.

Let us consider the linear relationship which is to be estimated in its simplest form, $\mathbf{y} = \mathbf{X}\boldsymbol{\beta} + \mathbf{u}$ with the $\mathbf{X}$-elements nonstochastic and $\mathscr{E}\mathbf{u} = \mathbf{0}$, $\mathscr{E}(\mathbf{uu}') = \sigma^2\mathbf{I}$. This set of assumptions implies that we know which variables are to be introduced as explanatory variables and in which form (linear, linear in the logarithms, etc.). But since the research worker frequently does not know this with certainty he will experiment with alternative sets of explanatory variables until he finds a result which satisfies him; frequently such that certain coefficients (or coefficient combinations) have "correct" signs and are of a plausible order of magnitude. Evidently, the problem has a twofold character: on the one hand, the analyst has at his disposal certain *a priori* information, usually of a qualitative rather than of a quantitative type, which he does not include in his maintained hypothesis (such as signs and orders of magnitude of coefficients); on the other hand, he does include in his maintained hypothesis information about which he is not entirely sure, such as the introduction of certain explanatory variables. And the result is that if the numerical outcomes violate the *a priori* information not included in the maintained hypothesis, this is in many cases ascribed to invalid information which is erroneously included in the maintained hypothesis.

In principle, the obvious way out is not to include information the validity of which is dubious, and to include the information about which the analyst is so sure that he is willing to sacrifice his "maintained" hypothesis if the contents of this information are violated. An attempt to handle at least the second part of this program is the method of *mixed estimation*, which can be described as follows.[1] Suppose we have the specification $\mathbf{y} = \mathbf{X}\boldsymbol{\beta} + \mathbf{u}$ where $\mathbf{X}$ and $\mathbf{u}$ satisfy assumptions (*i*), (*iii*), (*v*), (*vi*). Suppose also that we know something about one of the components of $\boldsymbol{\beta}$, β_1 say; e.g. that it is of the order of 0.5 and that it is very unplausible that it lies outside the interval (0.3, 0.7). This may e.g. be the case when β_1 represents the income elasticity of the demand for food. We can then apply the methods of the preceding pages and find an estimate for β_1 inside the interval (in which case the specification is accepted) or outside (in which case a new specification is formulated). But we can also say that our *a priori* information is equivalent with a point estimate of β_1 of 0.5 whose standard error is 0.1; for this ensures a β_1-value which is unlikely to lie outside the interval $0.5 \pm 2 \times 0.1$. Now the method of mixed estimation is a method which handles such qualitative or uncertain *a priori* information in the same way as observational information; it stands in contrast to *pure estimation* which (by definition) is confined to the latter type of information—and it will be clear that all estimation methods of the preceding pages fall under that category. We

[1] For more details, cf. H. THEIL and A. S. GOLDBERGER, "On Pure and Mixed Statistical Estimation in Economics" (to be published in the *International Economic Review*).

might also put it this way: whereas in the case of pure estimation the analyst relies solely on observations as far as his numerical estimates are concerned, he will use in the case of mixed estimation both observations and his own *a priori* ideas about how the estimates should look like. In still other words: mixed estimation is a method to make such preliminary ideas more precise on the basis of observations. One may object to the subjectivity of such an approach; on the other hand, one should not forget that the approach of successive rejection of "maintained" hypotheses is not objective either. Also, the method of mixed estimation enables us to use the *a priori* information in judging the reliability of the estimates, whereas this is much more difficult when this information is used in terms of a sequence of successive specifications.

Suppose then, more generally, that we have *a priori* information about a number of linear combinations of the unknown coefficients; in other words, that we have a vector estimate **r** of $\mathbf{R}\boldsymbol{\beta}$, where **R** is a given matrix. Writing **v** for the vector of estimation errors and supposing that this vector has zero mean and a nonsingular covariance matrix $\boldsymbol{\Psi}$, we have

$$\text{(6.83)} \qquad \mathbf{r} = \mathbf{R}\boldsymbol{\beta} + \mathbf{v}; \qquad \mathscr{E}\mathbf{v} = \mathbf{0}; \qquad \mathscr{E}(\mathbf{v}\mathbf{v}') = \boldsymbol{\Psi}.$$

Upon combining this with the observational information, we write

(6.84)

$$\begin{bmatrix} \mathbf{y} \\ \mathbf{r} \end{bmatrix} = \begin{bmatrix} \mathbf{X} \\ \mathbf{R} \end{bmatrix} \boldsymbol{\beta} + \begin{bmatrix} \mathbf{u} \\ \mathbf{v} \end{bmatrix}; \; \mathscr{E}\begin{bmatrix} \mathbf{u} \\ \mathbf{v} \end{bmatrix} = \mathbf{0}; \; \mathscr{E}\left(\begin{bmatrix} \mathbf{u} \\ \mathbf{v} \end{bmatrix} [\mathbf{u}' \quad \mathbf{v}']\right) = \begin{bmatrix} \boldsymbol{\Omega} & \mathbf{0} \\ \mathbf{0} & \boldsymbol{\Psi} \end{bmatrix},$$

the assumption being made that the random errors in the observational and the non-observational information are uncorrelated. If we apply generalised least-squares to this combination of two types of information, we obtain the estimator

$$\hat{\boldsymbol{\beta}} = \left([\mathbf{X}' \quad \mathbf{R}'] \begin{bmatrix} \boldsymbol{\Omega} & \mathbf{0} \\ \mathbf{0} & \boldsymbol{\Psi} \end{bmatrix}^{-1} \begin{bmatrix} \mathbf{X} \\ \mathbf{R} \end{bmatrix} \right)^{-1} [\mathbf{X}' \quad \mathbf{R}'] \begin{bmatrix} \boldsymbol{\Omega} & \mathbf{0} \\ \mathbf{0} & \boldsymbol{\Psi} \end{bmatrix}^{-1} \begin{bmatrix} \mathbf{y} \\ \mathbf{r} \end{bmatrix},$$

or more simply:

$$\text{(6.85)} \qquad \hat{\boldsymbol{\beta}} = (\mathbf{X}'\boldsymbol{\Omega}^{-1}\mathbf{X} + \mathbf{R}'\boldsymbol{\Psi}^{-1}\mathbf{R})^{-1}(\mathbf{X}'\boldsymbol{\Omega}^{-1}\mathbf{y} + \mathbf{R}'\boldsymbol{\Psi}^{-1}\mathbf{r});$$

and the covariance matrix is

$$(6.86)\qquad \mathscr{E}\{(\hat{\boldsymbol{\beta}} - \boldsymbol{\beta})(\hat{\boldsymbol{\beta}} - \boldsymbol{\beta})'\} = (\mathbf{X}'\boldsymbol{\Omega}^{-1}\mathbf{X} + \mathbf{R}'\boldsymbol{\Psi}^{-1}\mathbf{R})^{-1}.$$

The application of this method requires knowledge of $\boldsymbol{\Psi}$ and $\boldsymbol{\Omega}$. As to $\boldsymbol{\Psi}$, here we need variances and covariances of the errors in the *a priori* estimates and this can be done, at least approximately, in the way indicated in the example given above (0.01 as the variance of the β_1-estimate). As to $\boldsymbol{\Omega}$ and in the case $\boldsymbol{\Omega} = \sigma^2\mathbf{I}$, we can estimate σ^2 in the ordinary least-squares manner on the basis of observational information alone. This yields estimates of $\boldsymbol{\Omega}$ and $\boldsymbol{\Psi}$, so that $\hat{\boldsymbol{\beta}}$ as defined in (6.85) can be approximated. On the basis of this approximation we can derive a new estimate of σ^2, and so on. For example, suppose that the only *a priori* information which we have is an estimate b_1 of β_1 with variance σ_*^2. Then the normal equations corresponding to (6.85) become

$$\mathbf{X}'\mathbf{y} + \begin{bmatrix} b_1\sigma^2/\sigma_*^2 \\ 0 \\ \vdots \\ 0 \end{bmatrix} = \left(\mathbf{X}'\mathbf{X} + \begin{bmatrix} \sigma^2/\sigma_*^2 & 0 & \dots & 0 \\ 0 & 0 & \dots & 0 \\ \vdots & \vdots & & \vdots \\ 0 & 0 & \dots & 0 \end{bmatrix} \right) \hat{\boldsymbol{\beta}},$$

that is, the only things that change compared with the classical normal equations is the addition of $b_1\sigma^2/\sigma_*^2$ to the top element of the left-hand vector and the addition of σ^2/σ_*^2 to the leading element of the right-hand square matrix. In the initial round of the iteration we apply ordinary least-squares, i.e., we put $\sigma^2 = 0$ in the above equation; this leads to a positive estimate of σ^2 (in the manner described at the end of 6.2.3), which when inserted into the same estimation equations leads to new estimates of $\boldsymbol{\beta}$ and σ^2, and so on.

6.2.9. Summarizing our results, we should conclude that there is a general tendency for estimation methods to increase in difficulty when they are supposed to handle more delicate situations. One of the difficulties sometimes is that the price of unbiasedness is an increase in variance. There are some indications that this is the case in simultaneous equations estimation. Table 6.5 and Fig. 6.2 illustrate this for GIRSHICK's and HAAVELMO's model of the U.S. food market;[1] in

[1] M. A. GIRSHICK and T. HAAVELMO, "Statistical Analysis of the Demand for Food: Examples of Simultaneous Estimation of Structural Equations," *Econometrica*, Vol. 15 (1947), pp. 79–110. This paper has been partly reprinted as Chapter V of *Studies in Econometric Method*. We refer to these publications for further details.

Fig. 6.2 the point estimates of the parameters of this model according to the k-class are shown as functions of k.[1] It is seen that in many cases the estimates "explode" for k-values slightly above 1, which means that the matrix which is to be inverted for deriving the estimate,

$$\begin{bmatrix} \mathbf{Y'Y} - k\mathbf{V'V} & \mathbf{Y'X_1} \\ \mathbf{X_1'Y} & \mathbf{X_1'X_1} \end{bmatrix},$$

is singular for such a k-value. It will therefore be intuitively clear that in such a case at least, a k-class estimator whose k is about 1 must be much more unstable than an estimator whose k is about zero like single-stage least-squares. In fact, in the case of Girshick's and Haavelmo's model it is far from sure whether two-stage least-squares is preferable to single-stage least-squares because the smaller variance of the latter may outweigh the asymptotic unbiasedness of the former.

TABLE 6.5

SUMMARY OF GIRSHICK'S AND HAAVELMO'S MODEL OF THE U.S. FOOD MARKET

Structural equations	
Demand for food	$y_1 = \alpha_0 + \alpha_1 y_2 + \alpha_2 y_3 + \alpha_3 x_3 + \alpha_4 x_4$
Supply of food by retailers	$y_2 = \beta_0 + \beta_1 y_2 + \beta_2 y_4 + \beta_3 x_3$
Income equation	$y_3 = \gamma_0 + \gamma_1 x_2 + \gamma_2 x_4$
Supply of food by farmers	$y_4 = \delta_0 + \delta_1 y_5 + \delta_2 x_1 + \delta_3 x_3$
Farm price equation	$y_5 = \varepsilon_0 + \varepsilon_1 y_2 + \varepsilon_2 x_3$

Jointly dependent variables	*Predetermined variables*
y_1 per capita food consumption	x_1 farm price index lagged 1 year
y_2 retail food price index (defl.)	x_2 per capita real net investment
y_3 per capita real income	x_3 time (calendar years)
y_4 per capita food production	x_4 per capita real income lagged 1 year
y_5 farm price index (defl.)	

The question arises which estimation method is to be considered as appropriate for the purpose of establishing relationships among test variates. In this connection, it is worth-while to realise that although the results of Chapter IV are encouraging, any regression based on

[1] The scales of Fig. 6.2 are chosen such that all variables have the same standard deviation over time. The vertical line segments drawn at $k = 0$ and $k = 1$ above and below the curves indicate the standard errors of single-stage and two-stage least-squares respectively. For single-stage least-squares they are based on the classical formula (6.19) which cannot claim validity in the present case; so these vertical lines serve only to give a rough impression of the reliability of the point estimates.

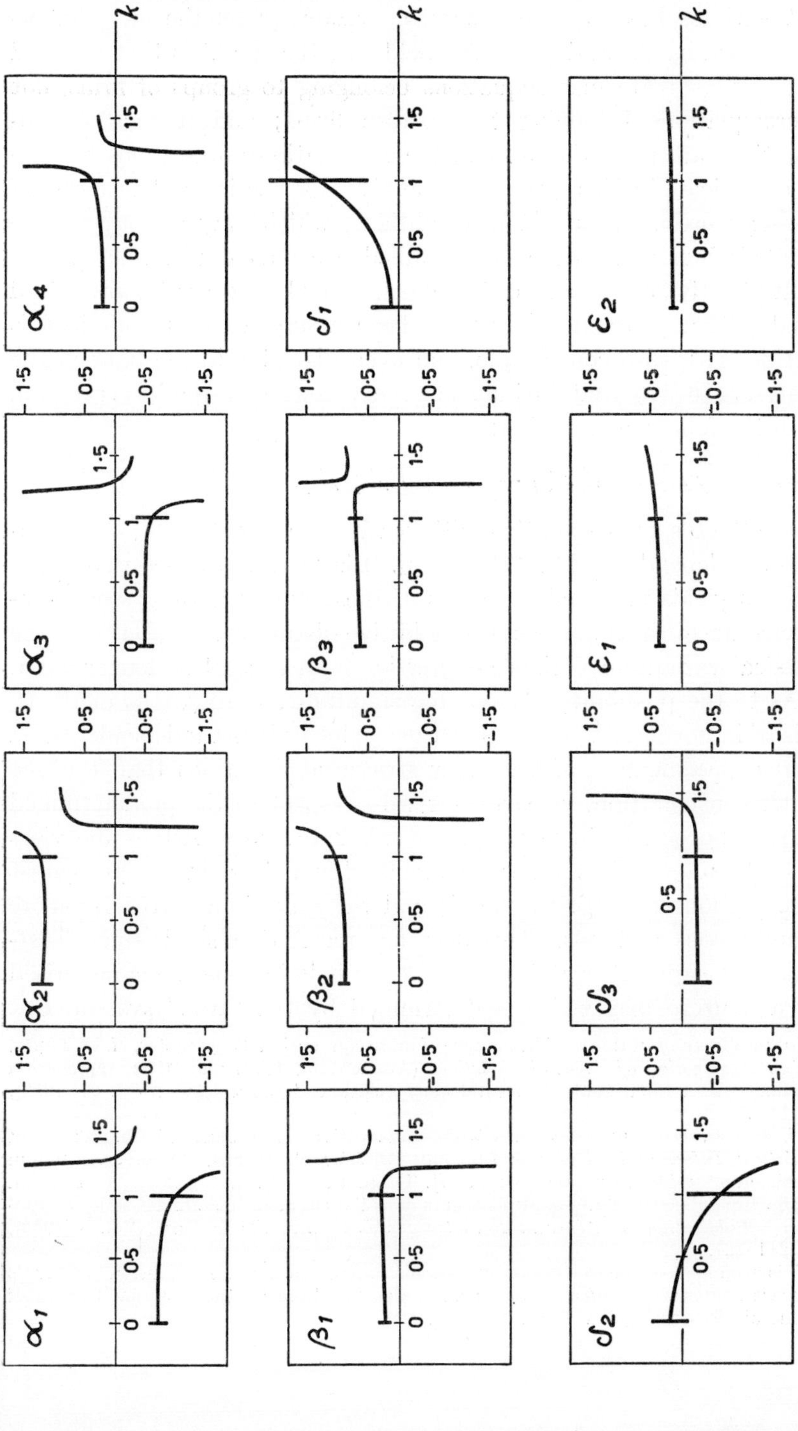

Fig. 6.2. Parameter estimates according to the k-class of Girshick's and Haavelmo's model of the U.S. food market

test variates has an experimental character, given the fact that so little work has been done in this field. Another point is that we shall test and estimate macroequations belonging to groups of firms, not microequations belonging to separate firms; and if such macroequations are part of a system, the aggregation implications tend to be complicated.[1] The aggregation analysis of Section 6.1 in terms of balances presupposes certain conditions, which may or may not be fulfilled; but even if they are fulfilled, we may doubt whether the multiplicative coefficients of the explanatory balance series are indeed fixed (although unknown), as has been assumed throughout in this section. It is also conceivable, and even plausible in the light of the analysis of 6.1.5, that the influence of explanatory variables is random, as in the following equation:[2]

$$(6.87) \qquad y(t) = B_1(t)x_1(t) + \ldots + B_A(t)x_A(t), \qquad (t = 1, \ldots, T)$$

where the B's are stochastic multiplicative coefficients with, say, mean values independent of $t : \mathscr{E}B_\lambda(t) = \beta_\lambda$. It is then easy to see that least-squares yields unbiased estimates of these means if the x's are non-stochastic—just as in the case of additive disturbances—, but that the classical variance-covariance expression is in general no longer valid.

As to the possibility of applying simultaneous equations methods, it is of importance to stress that their validity is not independent of a correct specification of the other structural equations than the one under consideration, in particular with respect to the predetermined variables occurring in such equations. Whatever the virtues and vices of single-stage least-squares, this method is at least invariant against specification errors of this kind; and the same is not true for more simultaneous methods.[3] This does not mean that single-stage least-squares has greater validity (cf. 6.2.2); it is in general characterised by a nonzero bias which is determined by the "true" system. But

[1] For implications of this kind in the case of more conventional aggregates, cf. H. Theil, *Linear Aggregation of Economic Relations* (Amsterdam, 1954) and "The Aggregation Implications of Identifiable Structural Macrorelations," *Econometrica*, Vol. 27 (1959), pp. 14–29.

[2] Cf. also L. Hurwicz, "Systems with Nonadditive Disturbances," Chapter 18 of *Statistical Inference in Dynamic Economic Models;* H. Rubin, "Note on Random Coefficients" (*ibidem*, Chapter 19); and H. Theil and L. B. M. Mennes, "Conception stochastique de coefficients multiplicateurs dans l'ajustement linéaire des séries temporelles," *Publications de l'Institut de Statistique de l'Université de Paris*, Vol. 8 (1959), pp. 211–227.

[3] This argument is due to Tinbergen; see his contribution to the discussion of Christ's forecast analysis in *Conference on Business Cycles*, edited by the National Bureau of Economic Research (New York, 1951), p. 129.

two-stage least-squares will also be characterised by a bias—even asymptotically—, if the other equations are specified incorrectly; and this feature was disregarded in 6.2.7, simply because we assumed all specifications to be correct. Also, it has been argued that the simultaneity of economic relations is primarily the result of aggregation over time.[1] Since the analyses of the next sections are in terms of monthly periods, we may doubt whether our relations are indeed of a simultaneous type. It will not be possible to test this empirically, because these relations are confined to the generation of prices—for which a recursive system is rather plausible[2]—, the generation of quantity and value variables being outside the scope of this chapter.

As stated 6.2.8, the method of mixed estimation may be supposed to yield a valuable addition to the precision of our estimates if we have some *a priori* knowledge of the parameters; but given the kind of our data, it seems that such knowledge is rather meagre in the present case.[3] Therefore, after reviewing all arguments, we should conclude that although the method of least-squares can no longer claim to have the brilliant properties which earlier econometricians thought it had, it can be regarded as one of the few one-eyed men who are eligible for king in the country of the blind—at least, as far as experimental small-sample estimation unaided by significant *a priori* information is concerned. Since the validity and the sharpness criteria do not give a clear answer to the question which method is to be chosen, the simplicity criterion should convince us to use least-squares. But there are good reasons to believe that the classical least-squares standard errors tend to overestimate to accuracy of the point estimates. "Not significant" is, therefore, an expression which may be pronounced with louder voice than "significant."

This completes our account of estimation methods as far as these are relevant for the empirical analysis of this chapter. In the Appendix

[1] Cf. R. Bentzel and B. Hansen, "On Recursiveness and Interdependence in Economic Models," *Review of Economic Studies*, Vol. 22 (1954–1955), pp. 153–168.

[2] A recursive system is a system of simultaneous relations in which the simultaneity is degenerated in the following way: the equations can be arranged such that the first contains only one dependent variable, the second two of which one is the dependent variable of the first equation, etc.; and the disturbances of the different equations for each t are independent. In such a case we can regard the system as a hierarchy of one-equation systems, each of which can be estimated by least-squares in the classical manner. See e.g. H. Wold, *Demand Analysis* (New York – Stockholm, 1953), pp. 64–71.

[3] Moreover, the mixed estimation method was found after the computations reported in this chapter had been carried out.

we consider a number of technical points in more detail, and in Chapter VIII (Section 8.5) we shall take up this topic again; there, it will be considered from the standpoint of decision theory in the light of the use which is made of the estimates.

6.3. The Traders' Expected Buying Prices

6.3.1. In accordance with the methodological observations of Section 2.3, we start our empirical analysis with that of the formation of expectations, after which we shall consider the factors determining plans and actual behaviour.

Since expectation data (in the form of test variates for expected buying prices) are only available for the traders in the leather and shoe industry, not for the manufacturers, we are forced to confine ourselves to the former group. This as such is clearly unfavourable. On the other hand, the fact that still as many as four sets of traders are available and can be compared has considerable advantages. We found in Chapter IV that the forecasting results of these firms are, although certainly not identical, rather regular when we arrange them according to decreasing distance from the ultimate consumer; and hence, we may hope that the formation of their buying price expectations is characterised by a similar regularity. Such a hope, if justified, contributes to a specification of the plausibility criterion mentioned in 6.2.2.

Let us take first the simplest explanation of expectation formation that can be imagined. This is the theory which assumes that the forecaster bases his predictions entirely on the present conditions of the phenomenon to be predicted. When applied to our traders, this theory in its extreme form would mean that no entrepreneur ever expects any change to occur, and as such it is obviously false. Still, the evidence of the M.B.T. data suggests that it is not altogether irrelevant, because—as observed earlier in Section 4.4—the traders in raw hides and those in leather expected no change in buying prices more frequently than their reports afterwards justified. Thus, the monthly differences between the expected and the actual no-change fractions of the former traders are distributed about a mean of 0.19 with a standard deviation of 0.31, and for the leather traders these figures are 0.15 and 0.24, respectively. No such effect exists for the lower stages. It is clear that large values of no-change fractions of expectations restrict the range of their balances, so that, when regression analysis is applied to these quantities, the regression coefficients will also be relatively small.

6.3.2. We proceed with the simple "extrapolation theories," which connect expected future changes with present and recent actual changes in the same variable. In view of the results of the Sections 6.1 and 6.2, the obvious approach is to take the balances of the expectations and to compute their least-squares regressions on the balances of previous realisations. This leads to equations of the following types:

$$b(\bar{\mathbf{p}}_\mathbf{b}) = \alpha + \beta_1 b(\mathbf{p}_\mathbf{b})_{-1}$$

$$b(\bar{\mathbf{p}}_\mathbf{b}) = \alpha + \beta_1 b(\mathbf{p}_\mathbf{b})_{-1} + \beta_2 b(\mathbf{p}_\mathbf{b})_{-2}$$

$$b(\bar{\mathbf{p}}_\mathbf{b}) = \alpha + \beta_1 b(\mathbf{p}_\mathbf{b})_{-1} + \beta_2 b(\mathbf{p}_\mathbf{b})_{-2} + \beta_3 b(\mathbf{p}_\mathbf{b})_{-3}.$$

The results are gathered in Table 6.6. This table, as well as most of the other tables in the remainder of this chapter, contains in its first column the square of the multiple correlation coefficient, adjusted for degrees of freedom; in the next columns regression coefficients with their standard errors in parentheses, and in the last the constant term.[1] A serial number is attached to each analysis for reference purposes.

It appears that, as a whole, the fit cannot be said to be excellent. With one explanatory variable the correlations $\bar{R}$ are of the order of 0.6–0.7 and 0.8 in only one case (shoe wholesalers); and they increase to 0.7–0.8 when a second variable is added.[2] The introduction of the balance of actual selling prices lagged 3 months is not a success for the

[1] The following abbreviations are used in the tables. "Own buying, lagged" means the actual buying prices, lagged 1 month, of the same set of firms of which some variable is the dependent one in the regression. If no lag is involved, this will not be mentioned explicitly (e.g., "own buying," "own selling"); if lags of 2 or more months are involved, the number of months is mentioned (e.g., "own buying, lagged 2 months"). If the variable refers to another set of firms, this is indicated by its roman numeral ("selling II, lagged"). Planned or expected variables are denoted in this way: "own selling planned," "buying I expected, lagged," "selling IV planned, lagged 2 months," etc.

[2] These and the following estimates are based on the 33-month period beginning in February 1951. If lagged variables are introduced, the period is somewhat reduced, so that the correlation coefficients of different equations can then not always be exactly compared. The third decimals of these coefficients should merely be regarded as weak indications that are useful when the correlations are close to unity; they may be subject to small errors of rounding.

upper stages I and III, and the results of the analyses 3 and 6 as compared with 2 and 5, respectively, are indeed such that the simplicity criterion requires that this variable be dropped. On the other hand, if we confine ourselves to the first two variants [$b(\mathbf{p_b})_{-3}$ omitted], the regression coefficients exhibit a certain degree of regularity in accordance with the plausibility criterion: with one explanatory variable they are all of order of 0.5, and with two variables the coefficients of the buying prices lagged one month increase regularly from 0.5 to about unity

TABLE 6.6

FIRST SET OF ALTERNATIVE REGRESSIONS FOR THE BALANCES OF THE TRADERS' EXPECTED BUYING PRICES: $b(\bar{\mathbf{p}}_\mathbf{b})^K$ FOR K = I, III, V, VI (GERMAN LEATHER AND SHOE INDUSTRY, 1951–1953)

Industry stages	$\bar{R}^2$	*Coefficients of price variables*			*Constant term*	
		own buying, lagged	*own buying, lagged 2 months*	*own buying, lagged 3 months*		
traders in hides	0.341	0.45 (0.10)	.	.	−0.06	1
(I)	0.506	0.51 (0.11)	−0.30 (0.11)	.	−0.08	2
	0.495	0.55 (0.10)	−0.33 (0.09)	0.08 (0.09)	−0.07	3
traders in leather	0.500	0.43 (0.07)	.	.	−0.06	4
(III)	0.654	0.60 (0.08)	−0.29 (0.08)	.	−0.08	5
	0.641	0.59 (0.08)	−0.26 (0.10)	−0.03 (0.08)	−0.08	6
wholesalers in	0.653	0.59 (0.08)	.	.	−0.03	7
shoes (V)	0.672	0.99 (0.14)	−0.40 (0.12)	.	−0.02	8
	0.699	0.86 (0.17)	−0.05 (0.23)	−0.21 (0.14)	−0.01	9
retailers in shoes	0.513	0.68 (0.12)	.	.	−0.04	10
(VI)	0.657	1.18 (0.17)	−0.55 (0.15)	.	−0.03	11
	0.684	1.03 (0.18)	−0.15 (0.25)	−0.30 (0.16)	−0.03	12

when we approach the consumer, the coefficients of the buying prices lagged two months being of the order of −0.3 to −0.5. To interpret these negative values, we write the result of analysis 5 as

$$b(\bar{\mathbf{p}}_\mathbf{b})^{\mathrm{III}} = 0.6\, b(\mathbf{p_b})_{-1}^{\mathrm{III}} - 0.3\, b(\mathbf{p_b})_{-2}^{\mathrm{III}} =$$

$$= 0.3\, b(\mathbf{p_b})_{-1}^{\mathrm{III}} + 0.3\{b(\mathbf{p_b})_{-1}^{\mathrm{III}} - b(\mathbf{p_b})_{-2}^{\mathrm{III}}\},$$

the constant term being omitted; the superscript III refers to the relevant stage of the industry (leather traders in this case). Since the balances have the character of first differences, we may say that their successive differences are to be regarded as second differences. The interpretation of the above equation is then that prices are expected to rise (*i*) if they rose last month and (*ii*) if this rise was more widespread in last month than in the month before. It is not at all unplausible that such a twofold effect exists, although it does not seem plausible that the two coefficients should be of the same order of magnitude; and that is suggested by the relevant point estimates. However, we are not yet entitled to go as far as this, since there are important variables which we have not yet included. The analyses of Table 6.6 are experimental at a primitive level, and their main use is that they enable us to see how much farther we come by the adoption of more satisfactory specifications.

6.3.3. Our next approach is to take the extrapolation theory of 6.3.2, but supplemented by the idea of approaching price movements in the higher stages of the industry. The theory becomes then that, say, the shoe retailers' expected changes in buying prices are determined by recent actual changes in the same prices and (e.g.) by recent actual price changes in the leather market. Naturally, we cannot apply this idea directly to the first stage (that of the traders in hides), because for this there is no higher stage. So we leave these firms out of consideration, and shall come back to them in Section 6.7.

Table 6.7 contains a number of alternative analyses for the other three sets of trading firms. One variable is retained in all regressions, viz.

$$b(\mathbf{p_b})_{-1} \qquad \text{(``own buying, lagged'')}.$$

Experimentation takes place with several other variables. The first is

$$b(\mathbf{p_b})_{-2} \qquad \text{(``own buying, lagged 2 months'')},$$

because of the result of the analyses described in 6.3.2. Other experimental variables refer to observed price changes in higher stages. Ideally, we should have test variates for all sets of traders describing their opinions of what happens "above them." Such data are not available; the best thing we can do, therefore, is to accept the corresponding test variates of the higher stages as substitutes. Consequently, we introduce for the expected price changes of the leather traders (III):

TABLE 6.7

SECOND SET OF ALTERNATIVE REGRESSIONS FOR THE BALANCES OF THE TRADERS' EXPECTED BUYING PRICES: $b(\mathbf{p_b})^K$ FOR K = III, V, VI
(GERMAN LEATHER AND SHOE INDUSTRY, 1951–1953)

Industry stages	$\bar{R}^2$	*Coefficients of price variables*								*Con-stant term*	
		own buying, lagged	*own buying, lagged 2 months*	*selling I, lagged*	*selling II, lagged*	*selling III, lagged*	*selling IV, lagged*	*selling V, lagged*	*selling H, lagged 2 months**		
traders in leather (III)	0.696	0.14 (0.09)	.	0.31 (0.07)	.	.	.	.	.	−0.07	13
	0.506	0.66 (0.18)	.	.	−0.32 (0.23)	.	.	.	.	−0.09	14
	0.737	0.32 (0.13)	−0.14 (0.08)	0.23 (0.08)	.	.	.	.	.	−0.06	15
	0.722	0.34 (0.13)	−0.11 (0.10)	0.21 (0.08)	.	.	.	.	−0.06 (0.07)	−0.07	16
wholesalers in shoes (V)	0.741	0.51 (0.08)	.	0.12 (0.04)	.	.	.	.	.	−0.03	17
	0.808	0.29 (0.08)	.	.	0.33 (0.06)	.	.	.	.	−0.02	18
	0.839	0.30 (0.07)	.	.	.	0.30 (0.06)	.	.	.	−0.01	19
	0.650	0.48 (0.14)	.	.	.	.	0.16 (0.18)	.	.	−0.03	20
	0.842	0.27 (0.08)	.	.	0.12 (0.10)	0.22 (0.09)	.	.	.	−0.01	21
	0.773	0.51 (0.17)	−0.20 (0.11)	.	0.27 (0.07)	.	.	.	.	−0.02	22
	0.774	0.50 (0.17)	−0.25 (0.12)	.	0.24 (0.08)	.	.	.	0.08 (0.08)	−0.02	23
	0.784	0.39 (0.19)	−0.07 (0.13)	.	.	0.28 (0.07)	.	.	.	−0.01	24
	0.782	0.37 (0.19)	−0.11 (0.13)	.	.	0.26 (0.07)	.	.	0.05 (0.07)	−0.01	25
retailers in shoes (VI)	0.621	0.61 (0.09)	.	0.19 (0.06)	.	.	.	.	.	−0.04	26
	0.757	0.31 (0.08)	.	.	0.48 (0.08)	.	.	.	.	0.00	27
	0.761	0.47 (0.08)	.	.	.	0.40 (0.07)	.	.	.	0.02	28
	0.577	0.16 (0.14)	.	.	.	.	0.98 (0.25)	.	.	0.03	29
	0.718	0.08 (0.15)	.	.	.	.	.	0.83 (0.20)	.	0.03	30
	0.839	0.41 (0.08)	.	.	0.25 (0.17)	0.22 (0.14)	.	.	.	0.02	31
	0.804	0.15 (0.11)	.	.	0.38 (0.18)	.	0.58 (0.21)	.	.	0.04	32
	0.825	0.21 (0.10)	.	.	.	0.33 (0.06)	0.65 (0.19)	.	.	0.06	33
	0.869	0.21 (0.10)	.	.	0.19 (0.16)	0.18 (0.12)	0.46 (0.17)	.	.	0.03	34
	0.831	0.57 (0.20)	−0.16 (0.16)	.	0.44 (0.10)	.	.	.	.	0.01	35
	0.763	0.47 (0.22)	−0.18 (0.16)	.	0.35 (0.11)	.	.	.	0.15 (0.13)	0.00	36
	0.834	0.66 (0.18)	−0.17 (0.15)	.	.	0.36 (0.08)	.	.	.	0.02	37
	0.757	0.57 (0.20)	−0.15 (0.16)	.	.	0.31 (0.09)	.	.	0.08 (0.10)	−0.04	38
	0.861	0.29 (0.21)	−0.10 (0.14)	.	0.36 (0.09)	.	0.47 (0.14)	.	.	0.03	39
	0.864	0.36 (0.20)	−0.10 (0.14)	.	.	0.29 (0.07)	0.47 (0.17)	.	.	0.03	40

* H = I in analysis 16, II in analyses 23 and 36, III in analyses 25 and 38.

$b(\mathbf{p_s})^{\mathrm{I}}_{-1}$ ("selling I, lagged")

$b(\mathbf{p_s})^{\mathrm{II}}_{-1}$ ("selling II, lagged");

for those of the shoe wholesalers (V):

$b(\mathbf{p_s})^{\mathrm{I}}_{-1}$ ("selling I, lagged")

$b(\mathbf{p_s})^{\mathrm{II}}_{-1}$ ("selling II, lagged")

$b(\mathbf{p_s})^{\mathrm{III}}_{-1}$ ("selling III, lagged")

$b(\mathbf{p_s})^{\mathrm{IV}}_{-1}$ ("selling IV, lagged");

and similarly for the retailers in shoes. Finally, in five analyses

$b(\mathbf{p_s})^{H}_{-2}$ ("selling H, lagged 2 months")

is introduced (for H = I, II, or III), because this variable plays the same "second-difference" rôle with respect to $b(\mathbf{p_s})^{H}_{-1}$ as $b(\mathbf{p_b})_{-2}$ does with respect to $b(\mathbf{p_b})_{-1}$. The value H is always chosen in such a way that $b(\mathbf{p_s})^{H}_{-2}$ refers to the same stage as the other lagged selling price in the equation, $b(\mathbf{p_s})^{H}_{-1}$.

It appears from Table 6.7 that the correlations obtained are larger than the corresponding values of Table 6.6. For the leather traders $\bar{R}$ increases from about 0.8 to 0.85, for the shoe wholesalers from 0.8 to about 0.9, and for the retailers from 0.8 to more than 0.9. If we would decide to accept only two explanatory variables in each equation, viz., $b(\mathbf{p_b})_{-1}$ and $b(\mathbf{p_s})^{H}_{-1}$ for some higher stage H, our choice would be H = I for the leather traders (cf. the analyses 13 and 14), H = II or III for the shoe wholesalers (cf. 17–20), and H = II or III for the retailers (cf. 26–30). It is difficult to decide between $b(\mathbf{p_s})^{\mathrm{II}}_{-1}$ and $b(\mathbf{p_s})^{\mathrm{III}}_{-1}$, for these variables show a high correlation (about 0.9); the introduction of both variables together leads to considerable sampling variances (cf. 21 and 31). The use of only one explanatory selling price is, however, rather restrictive, and for the retailers especially it seems appropriate to introduce another selling price, viz., $b(\mathbf{p_s})^{\mathrm{IV}}_{-1}$ of the shoe manufacturers. In all cases where this variable is introduced the point estimates and standard errors suggest significance, and the correlation is larger than in the corresponding analysis where this variable is omitted (32 vs. 27, 33 vs. 28, 34 vs. 31, 39 vs. 35, 40 vs. 37).

The variable $b(\mathbf{p_s})^{H}_{-2}$ has nowhere a significant influence; and the point estimates have not the same sign in all cases. So the simplicity criterion suggests that it should be dropped. The coefficients of $b(\mathbf{p_b})_{-2}$ are not significant either (except for one or two cases), most of the standard errors being of the same order of magnitude as the estimates themselves; and the point estimates are all closer to zero than the corresponding estimates in Table 6.6 (cf. analyses 2, 5, 8, 11). However, the sign of the estimates is persistently negative; and to find a point estimate with a distance from zero equal to the standard error three times is a moderately significant event under classical standards.[1] There can be no doubt that the usual underestimation of inaccuracy by the standard errors is not favourable for our appraisal of this significance; but, as observed earlier in 6.3.2, the effect under consideration is not unplausible, so that we may accept the variable $b(\mathbf{p_b})_{-2}$ with a small coefficient, -0.1, say.

The final question to be settled is whether we should introduce $b(\mathbf{p_s})_{-1}^{\mathrm{II}}$ into the equations for the shoe wholesalers and retailers, or $b(\mathbf{p_s})_{-1}^{\mathrm{III}}$, or both. It was noted before (cf. 4.1.4) that the shoes which these traders buy and sell are manufactured by means of leather which is in general bought from the tanneries directly, not from the leather traders. At first sight it may seem, therefore, that it is appropriate to take $b(\mathbf{p_s})_{-1}^{\mathrm{II}}$ and to drop $b(\mathbf{p_s})_{-1}^{\mathrm{III}}$. Upon closer inspection, however, it becomes clear that this argument is hardly valid, since the traders may use other sources of information for prediction purposes than the prices of industry branches with which they are indirectly connected. Since, furthermore, the variables $b(\mathbf{p_s})_{-1}^{\mathrm{II}}$ and $b(\mathbf{p_s})_{-1}^{\mathrm{III}}$ have about the same coefficients when they are both introduced, $\bar{R}$ being somewhat larger than in the corresponding analyses containing only one of these variables, the best solution is presumably to give them equal coefficients. This leads to the following equations which we finally prefer:

$$(6.88)\qquad b(\bar{\mathbf{p}}_{\mathbf{b}})^{\mathrm{III}} = 0.3\, b(\mathbf{p_b})_{-1}^{\mathrm{III}} - 0.1\, b(\mathbf{p_b})_{-2}^{\mathrm{III}} + 0.25\, b(\mathbf{p_s})_{-1}^{\mathrm{I}};$$

$$(6.89)\qquad b(\bar{\mathbf{p}}_{\mathbf{b}})^{\mathrm{V}} = 0.35\, b(\mathbf{p_b})_{-1}^{\mathrm{V}} - 0.1\, b(\mathbf{p_b})_{-2}^{\mathrm{V}} + 0.15\, b(\mathbf{p_s})_{-1}^{\mathrm{II}} + 0.15\, b(\mathbf{p_s})_{-1}^{\mathrm{III}};$$

$$(6.90)\qquad b(\bar{\mathbf{p}}_{\mathbf{b}})^{\mathrm{VI}} = 0.4\, b(\mathbf{p_b})_{-1}^{\mathrm{VI}} - 0.1\, b(\mathbf{p_b})_{-2}^{\mathrm{VI}} + 0.15\, b(\mathbf{p_s})_{-1}^{\mathrm{II}} + 0.15\, b(\mathbf{p_s})_{-1}^{\mathrm{III}} + 0.5\, b(\mathbf{p_s})_{-1}^{\mathrm{IV}},$$

[1] It is to be noted that the lower correlations in the regressions with $b(\mathbf{p_b})_{-2}^{\mathrm{V}}$ included are due to the omission of the first observation. Thus, if we take analysis 19 and disregard the first observation, the resulting $\bar{R}$ is reduced to about the same value as that of the $\bar{R}$ of analysis 24.

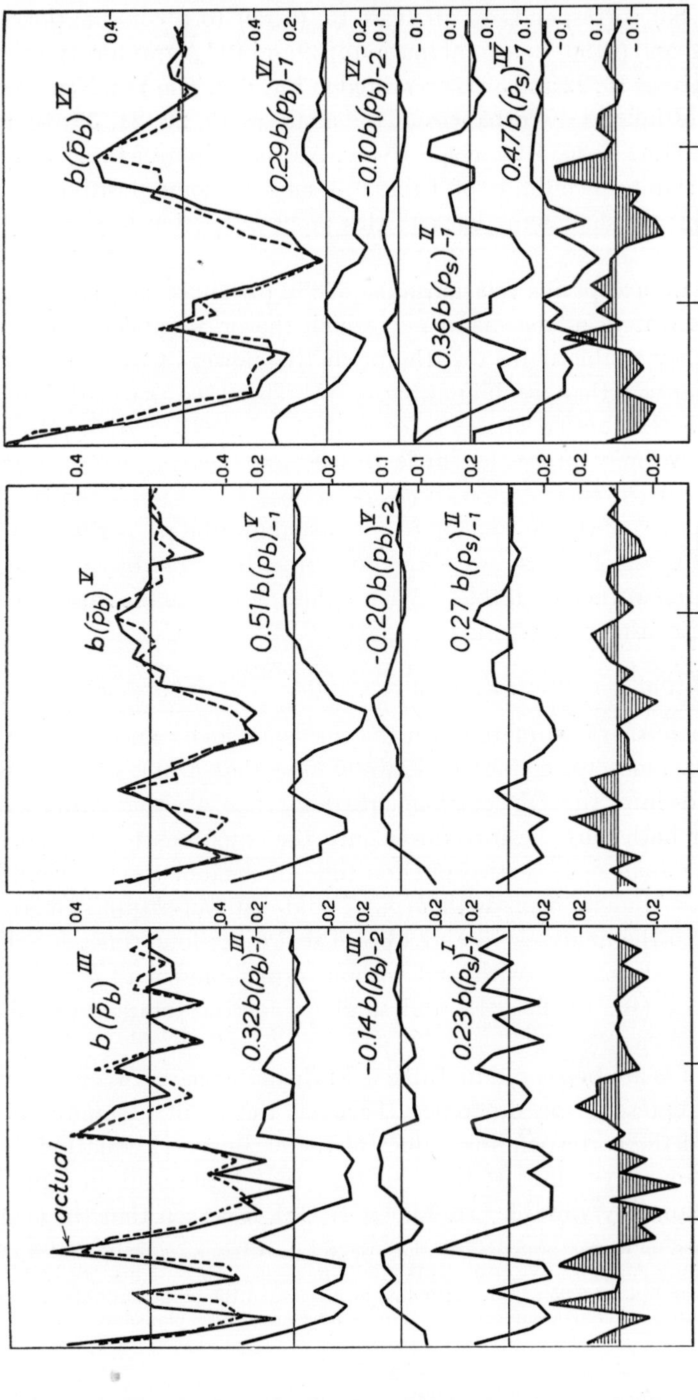

Fig. 6.3. Regressions describing the balances of the expected buying prices of the traders in leather, of the wholesalers in shoes, and of the retailers in shoes: analyses 15, 22 and 39 (German leather and shoe industry, 1951–1953)

where (6.88) corresponds to analysis 15, (6.89) to a combination of 22 and 24, and (6.90) to a combination of 39 and 40.[1] A graphical picture of the analyses 15, 22 and 39 is presented in Fig. 6.3. The Von Neumann ratios of estimated disturbances of the analyses 15, 22, 24, 39, 40 are 1.98, 1.62, 1.52, 1.25, 1.21, respectively. A comparison of these values with the significance limits of Table 6.4 suggests some positive autocorrelation; we shall come back to this point in Section 6.8.

6.3.4. If we accept the relationships (6.88), (6.89), (6.90) as an adequate description of the manner in which the price expectations are formed, they enable us to test the predictive power of the traders in yet another way than we did in Chapter IV. There, we analysed simply to what extent actual changes correspond with expectations. Here, however, we may proceed a little further and analyse whether the entrepreneurs, if their expectations are indeed based upon the right-hand variables of (6.88), (6.89), (6.90), attribute the proper influence to each of these. To do so, we should describe the *actual* buying prices as a function of these variables. When following the balance approach, we should consider therefore

$$b(\mathbf{p_b})^{\text{III}} = \alpha + \beta_1 b(\mathbf{p_b})^{\text{III}}_{-1} + \beta_2 b(\mathbf{p_b})^{\text{III}}_{-2} + \beta_3 b(\mathbf{p_s})^{\text{I}}_{-1},$$

and compare the β-estimates with the corresponding values of (6.88); and so on. Since we cannot be entirely sure that $b(\mathbf{p_b})_{-2}$ should be introduced into the expectation equations, nor whether $b(\mathbf{p_s})^{\text{II}}_{-1}$ or $b(\mathbf{p_s})^{\text{III}}_{-1}$ or both must be introduced into the equations for the lower stages, the analysis is carried out ten times instead of three; twice for the leather traders, viz., with $b(\mathbf{p_b})^{\text{III}}_{-2}$ and without $b(\mathbf{p_b})^{\text{III}}_{-2}$ (corresponding to the analyses 15 and 13 of Table 6.7); four times for the shoe wholesalers, viz., with and without $b(\mathbf{p_b})^{\text{V}}_{-2}$ and with $b(\mathbf{p_s})^{\text{II}}_{-1}$ or with $b(\mathbf{p_s})^{\text{III}}_{-1}$ (18, 19, 22, 24); and similarly for the retailers (32, 33, 39, 40).

The results are presented in Table 6.8; the numbers between square brackets represent the differences between the point estimates obtained and the corresponding values of the expectation equations. If we confine ourselves, first, to those analyses that do not contain $b(\mathbf{p_b})_{-2}$ as an explanatory variable (41, 43, 44, 47, 48), it is seen that the coef-

[1] In these and all further preferred relations the constant terms are omitted, and the estimates of the multiplicative coefficients are rounded off. This rounding is usually to the nearest multiple of 0.05 or 0.1, depending on the size of the point estimate, except when a (slightly) different rounding procedure is considered more plausible.

TABLE 6.8

REGRESSIONS FOR THE BALANCES OF THE TRADERS' ACTUAL BUYING PRICES CORRESPONDING TO SOME OF THE REGRESSIONS OF TABLE 6.7: $b(\mathbf{p_b})^K$ FOR K = III, V, VI (GERMAN LEATHER AND SHOE INDUSTRY, 1951–1953)

Industry stages	*Corresponding analysis in Table 6.7*	$\bar{R}^2$	*Coefficients of price variables [and differences with corresponding coefficients in Table 6.7]*						*Constant term*	
			own buying, lagged	*own buying, lagged 2 months*	*selling I, lagged*	*selling II, lagged*	*selling III, lagged*	*selling IV, lagged*		
traders in leather (III)	13	0.320	0.34[+0.20]	.	0.25[−0.06]	.	.	.	−0.07	41
	15	0.360	0.73[+0.41]	−0.35[−0.21]	0.05[−0.18]	.	.	.	−0.08	42
wholesalers in shoes (V)	18	0.740	0.42[+0.13]	.	.	0.29[−0.04]	.	.	−0.05	43
	19	0.759	0.42[+0.13]	.	.	.	0.27[−0.02]	.	−0.04	44
	22	0.705	0.80[+0.28]	−0.33[−0.13]	.	0.19[−0.09]	.	.	−0.06	45
	24	0.696	0.77[+0.38]	−0.28[−0.20]	.	.	0.16[−0.11]	.	−0.05	46
retailers in shoes (VI)	32	0.832	0.41[+0.26]	.	.	0.35[−0.03]	.	0.33[−0.25]	0.02	47
	33	0.825	0.46[+0.25]	.	.	.	0.28[−0.05]	0.41[−0.23]	0.05	48
	39	0.822	0.40[+0.11]	0.01[+0.11]	.	0.36[−0.00]	.	0.33[−0.14]	0.03	49
	40	0.817	0.42[+0.06]	0.03[+0.13]	.	.	0.29[−0.00]	0.43[−0.04]	0.05	50

ficients of $b(\mathbf{p_b})_{-1}$ in the expectation equations are all smaller than the corresponding coefficients in the equations describing actual buying prices, and that the opposite is true for the coefficients of the selling prices of higher stages. This suggests that the traders' price expectations are influenced too much by their observations of price changes in higher markets, and too little by price changes in their own markets. When $b(\mathbf{p_b})_{-2}$ is included (analyses 42, 45, 46, 49, 50) the same result emerges if we take the combined influence of this variable and of $b(\mathbf{p_b})_{-1}$. In analysis 15, e.g., the sum of their coefficients equals 0.18, and in the corresponding analysis 42 of actual prices it is 0.38.

Our tentative conclusion is, therefore, that the traders pay insufficient attention to the inertia of their own market, and too much attention to price changes in higher markets. The necessary qualifications are obvious—they refer both to sampling errors and to the type of data employed—, but it is interesting to note that effects of this kind are not unplausible. It is indeed a more obvious procedure for, say, a retailer in shoes to base his price predictions on observable price movements in the leather market than to rely on trends in his own market which are more or less abstract for him. Still, it appears that these traders do rely on such trends. But they should double approximately their "weight" and reduce the weights of "higher" prices in order to get better predictions—at least, in so far as we are allowed to use point estimates and test variates for statements like these.

6.3.5. There can be no doubt that entrepreneurs are sometimes in a position to take factors into account which cannot be represented in equations like (6.88)–(6.90). The possibilities of analysing such effects are obviously limited, but this does not exclude an analysis of the adequacy of their use in the forecasting process. For, if this use is indeed adequate, we should expect the disturbances of the expectation equations to be positively correlated with the disturbances of the corresponding equations describing the actual phenomena.

For the expected and actual buying price analyses of the Tables 6.8 and 6.7, the estimated residual correlations are given in Table 6.9. It appears that the correlations are all positive, some of them being even significant under classical conditions. Although these conditions are unlikely to be fulfilled, the results suggest nevertheless that the traders—at least some of them—do have the disposal of some additional information that has indeed a positive value.

6.3.6. When reviewing the arguments used in this section and comparing them with the methodological remarks of 6.2.2, the conclusion is tempting that the procedure followed is not fully in accordance with our earlier requirements. The tables contain several analyses which have not been discussed separately; and many additional remarks could have been made about others as well. The reason for this austerity is, of course, that a more elaborate account is not very exciting; and for this same reason we shall proceed in the same fashion in the foll-

TABLE 6.9

CORRELATIONS BETWEEN ESTIMATED DISTURBANCES OF THE ANALYSES OF TABLE 6.8 AND THOSE OF THE CORRESPONDING ANALYSES OF TABLE 6.7

Industry stages	*analyses*			
	13/41	15/42		
traders in leather (III)	0.59	0.52		
	analyses			
	18/43	19/44	22/45	24/46
wholesalers in shoes (V)	0.31	0.23	0.18	0.20
	analyses			
	32/47	33/48	39/49	40/50
retailers in shoes (VI)	0.62	0.61	0.62	0.60

owing pages. In the Appendix (Section 6.E) an attempt is made to approach the ideal more closely; it is confined to the analysis of the traders' expected buying prices, the corresponding elaborations of the next sections being left to the reader's imagination. No doubt, the reader will find several places in Section 6.E where he feels that he can reasonably disagree. He will also find that the arguments used become less and less cogent when the analysis proceeds. Both features are natural; the former because of the subjective nature of the choice between plausibility and simplicity, the latter because of the increasing number of questions asked when the number of variables accumulates. Again, it is to be stressed that the statistical calculations with their biased estimates and optimistic standard errors are not the only basis for the choice of a preferred relation. Economic intuition is another basis; and the primary function of the statistical results is to guide this intuition.

6.4. The Traders' Planned and Actual Selling Prices

6.4.1. We proceed with the traders' selling prices. There is no need to exclude the traders in hides here, since the fact that they form the first stage has no particular implications for their selling prices.

A considerable advantage is obtained when planned and actual selling prices are analysed side by side, because—as observed earlier in Section 2.3—similar variables are likely to determine these two phenomena. For instance, if the traders' behaviour pattern is such that a certain variable A in month t affects the actual selling prices in t, it is reasonable to assume that their expectations about A for t show a relationship with the selling price plans for t. This, together with the fact that four sets of firms are available, implies that we have eight sets of data for analysing related processes; a circumstance which obviously facilitates the use of the plausibility criterion. And this, together with the importance of the subject, justifies elaborate experimentation.

The first part of this section is based on balances, and it is carried out on three distinct levels:

(*i*) The influence of possibly relevant expectations and other data on planned selling prices is considered.

(*ii*) Actual selling prices are described as functions of actual predetermined and other variables.

(*iii*) Actual behaviour as a correction on the intentions is described as a function of similar explanatory differences.

Of these three types of analysis, the second corresponds with the familiar procedure, according to which behaviour is directly related to predetermined data. It has been argued before (cf. 2.3.5) that this procedure is permissible under special circumstances only, so that it is interesting to test these by means of a combination of the analyses sub (*i*) and (*iii*). This will be done in 6.4.3.

6.4.2. First, we take up the analyses sub (*i*) and (*ii*) of 6.4.1. In view of the very small inequality coefficients obtained earlier for the test vector series of planned selling and expected buying prices, and of actual selling and actual buying prices (cf. Table 4.10 in Section 4.4), our initial approach should obviously be to describe the balance of planned selling prices as a function of the balance of the expected buying prices of the same set of firms,

$b(\bar{\mathbf{p}}_\mathbf{b})$ ("own buying expected");

and, similarly, the balance of actual selling prices as a function of

$b(\mathbf{p}_\mathbf{b})$ ("own buying").

These two variables are retained in all regressions that are summarised in the Tables 6.10 and 6.11, respectively.

Experimentation takes place with five variables for intentions, with seven for actual prices. As to the latter category, we may first think of

$b(\bar{\mathbf{p}}_\mathbf{s})$ ("own selling planned")

because of the possibility that plans have a separate influence on behaviour. This may seem superfluous in view of the correction approach which follows in 6.4.3; however, a preliminary analysis may be valuable. Secondly, we should think of a possible lagged influence of changes in buying prices. For the actual selling prices an adequate additional variable may therefore be

$b(\mathbf{p}_\mathbf{b})_{-1}$ ("own buying, lagged");

or perhaps

$b(\mathbf{p}_\mathbf{s})_{-1}$ ("own selling, lagged"),

which amounts to Koyck's treatment of distributed lags:

$$b(\mathbf{p}_\mathbf{s}) = \alpha + \beta b(\mathbf{p}_\mathbf{b}) + \varrho\beta b(\mathbf{p}_\mathbf{b})_{-1} + \ldots + u,$$

implying:

$$b(\mathbf{p}_\mathbf{s}) = \alpha(1 - \varrho) + \beta b(\mathbf{p}_\mathbf{b}) + \varrho b(\mathbf{p}_\mathbf{s})_{-1} + (u - \varrho u_{-1}).$$

Similarly, for intentions, it is conceivable that their balances are positively affected by a failure to react to buying price increases in the preceding month; negatively by a recent raise of selling prices if this was not accompanied by a similar change of buying prices; etc. Hence, a plausible lag variable in the intention equation is

$b(\mathbf{p}_\mathbf{b})_{-1} - b(\mathbf{p}_\mathbf{s})_{-1}$ ("own buying minus selling, lagged").

TABLE 6.10

ALTERNATIVE REGRESSIONS FOR THE BALANCES OF THE TRADERS' PLANNED SELLING PRICES: $b(\bar{\mathbf{p}}_{\mathbf{s}})^{\mathrm{K}}$ FOR K = I, III, V, VI (GERMAN LEATHER AND SHOE INDUSTRY, 1951–1953)

Industry stages	$\overline{R}^2$	Coefficients of price variables		Coefficients of other variables				Constant term	
		own buying expected	own buying minus selling, lagged	sales expected	sales expected, distributed lag	stocks expected	stocks expected, distributed lag		
traders in hides (I)	0.985	0.99 (0.02)	.	.	.	.	.	−0.01	51
	0.987	0.99 (0.02)	0.11 (0.14)	.	.	.	.	−0.01	52
	0.987	0.94 (0.05)	.	0.08 (0.06)	.	.	.	−0.01	53
	0.989	0.98 (0.02)	.	.	0.06 (0.05)	.	.	−0.01	54
	0.987	1.00 (0.03)	.	.	.	0.04 (0.06)	.	−0.00	55
	0.989	0.99 (0.02)	.	.	.	.	−0.02 (0.08)	−0.01	56
traders in leather (III)	0.968	0.97 (0.03)	.	.	.	.	.	−0.01	57
	0.967	0.96 (0.04)	0.04 (0.09)	.	.	.	.	−0.02	58
	0.969	0.95 (0.03)	.	0.05 (0.03)	.	.	.	−0.02	59
	0.973	0.97 (0.03)	.	.	0.06 (0.04)	.	.	−0.02	60
	0.967	0.95 (0.03)	.	.	.	0.09 (0.07)	.	−0.01	61
	0.973	0.97 (0.03)	.	.	.	.	0.24 (0.12)	0.01	62
wholesalers in shoes (V)	0.950	1.00 (0.04)	.	.	.	.	.	−0.03	63
	0.949	1.00 (0.04)	0.01 (0.17)	.	.	.	.	−0.03	64
	0.950	1.01 (0.04)	.	−0.02 (0.02)	.	.	.	−0.02	65
	0.939	0.97 (0.05)	.	.	0.01 (0.04)	.	.	−0.04	66
	0.952	1.00 (0.04)	.	.	.	0.04 (0.03)	.	−0.02	67
	0.944	0.96 (0.04)	.	.	.	.	0.07 (0.05)	−0.02	68
retailers in shoes (VI)	0.968	0.87 (0.03)	.	.	.	.	.	−0.04	69
	0.969	0.91 (0.03)	−0.19 (0.10)	.	.	.	.	−0.02	70
	0.965	0.87 (0.03)	.	0.01 (0.02)	.	.	.	−0.04	71
	0.956	0.84 (0.03)	.	.	0.05 (0.03)	.	.	−0.05	72
	0.965	0.88 (0.03)	.	.	.	−0.02 (0.02)	.	−0.04	73
	0.965	0.85 (0.03)	.	.	.	.	0.01 (0.03)	−0.04	74

ALTERNATIVE REGRESSIONS FOR THE BALANCES OF THE TRADERS' ACTUAL SELLING PRICES: $b(\mathbf{p_s})^K$ FOR K = I, III, V, VI
(GERMAN LEATHER AND SHOE INDUSTRY, 1951–1953)

Industry stages	$\bar{R}^2$	*Coefficients of price variables*				*Coefficients of other variables*				*Con-stant term*	
		own buying	*own selling planned*	*own buying, lagged*	*own selling, lagged*	*sales*	*sales, distributed lag*	*stocks*	*stocks, distributed lag*		
traders in hides (I)	0.992	1.01 (0.02)	.	.	.	.	.	.	.	–0.03	75
	0.990	1.00 (0.02)	0.02 (0.03)	.	.	.	.	.	.	–0.02	76
	0.989	1.01 (0.02)	.	0.01 (0.02)	.	.	.	.	.	–0.01	77
	0.989	1.01 (0.03)	.	.	0.01 (0.02)	.	.	.	.	–0.02	78
	0.991	0.99 (0.02)	.	.	.	0.04 (0.04)	.	.	.	–0.03	79
	0.993	0.99 (0.01)	.	.	.	.	0.12 (0.04)	.	.	–0.01	80
	0.991	1.01 (0.02)	.	.	.	.	.	0.02 (0.05)	.	–0.03	81
	0.991	1.01 (0.02)	.	.	.	.	.	.	0.01 (0.07)	–0.02	82
traders in leather (III)	0.952	0.87 (0.03)	.	.	.	.	.	.	.	–0.09	83
	0.950	0.85 (0.06)	0.04 (0.10)	.	.	.	.	.	.	–0.09	84
	0.950	0.85 (0.04)	.	0.04 (0.04)	.	.	.	.	.	–0.09	85
	0.954	0.83 (0.04)	.	.	0.07 (0.04)	.	.	.	.	–0.08	86
	0.950	0.87 (0.04)	.	.	.	0.00 (0.05)	.	.	.	–0.09	87
	0.949	0.81 (0.05)	.	.	.	.	0.12 (0.08)	.	.	–0.09	88
	0.954	0.84 (0.04)	.	.	.	.	.	0.23 (0.12)	.	–0.07	89
	0.954	0.80 (0.04)	.	.	.	.	.	.	0.52 (0.23)	–0.04	90
wholesalers in shoes (V)	0.952	0.93 (0.04)	.	.	.	.	.	.	.	–0.03	91
	0.952	1.00 (0.08)	–0.09 (0.09)	.	.	.	.	.	.	–0.04	92
	0.952	1.00 (0.06)	.	–0.07 (0.05)	.	.	.	.	.	–0.03	93
	0.953	1.00 (0.07)	.	.	–0.07 (0.06)	.	.	.	.	–0.03	94
	0.956	0.94 (0.04)	.	.	.	–0.04 (0.02)	.	.	.	–0.03	95
	0.963	0.97 (0.04)	.	.	.	.	0.07 (0.04)	.	.	–0.03	96
	0.950	0.94 (0.07)	.	.	.	.	.	–0.01 (0.03)	.	–0.03	97
	0.961	0.98 (0.04)	.	.	.	.	.	.	0.06 (0.05)	–0.02	98
retailers in shoes (VI)	0.935	0.85 (0.04)	.	.	.	.	.	.	.	–0.08	99
	0.933	0.94 (0.12)	–0.10 (0.13)	.	.	.	.	.	.	–0.08	100
	0.935	0.70 (0.07)	.	0.12 (0.06)	.	.	.	.	.	–0.09	101
	0.950	0.69 (0.06)	.	.	0.21 (0.06)	.	.	.	.	–0.07	102
	0.935	0.85 (0.04)	.	.	.	–0.02 (0.02)	.	.	.	–0.08	103
	0.915	0.79 (0.04)	.	.	.	.	–0.05 (0.05)	.	.	–0.09	104
	0.933	0.85 (0.04)	.	.	.	.	.	0.02 (0.03)	.	–0.08	105
	0.917	0.75 (0.04)	.	.	.	.	.	.	0.07 (0.05)	–0.10	106

The other variables are all outside the price sector proper. A rather obvious one would be the appraisal of stocks. Unfortunately, no time series of such a variable of sufficient length are available for our traders. Expected and actual sales and stocks are perhaps suitable substitutes. For actual selling prices this leads to

$b(\mathbf{T})$ ("sales")

$b(\mathbf{S})$ ("stocks")

as explanatory variables, for planned selling prices to

$b(\overline{\mathbf{T}})$ ("sales expected")

$b(\overline{\mathbf{S}})$ ("stocks expected").

Introduction of these variables in this form implies that they are supposed to determine the selling prices without lag. Since it is conceivable that entrepreneurs react after some distributed lag on variables like sales and stocks, whereas no such lag exists with respect to buying prices, a form

$$b(\mathbf{T}^*) = \frac{4b(\mathbf{T}) + 3b(\mathbf{T})_{-1} + 2b(\mathbf{T})_{-2} + b(\mathbf{T})_{-3}}{10}$$

may be useful. This smoothing has the additional advantage that it eliminates seasonal fluctuations to some extent. Consequently, the four variables

$b(\mathbf{T}^*)$ ("sales, distributed lag")

$b(\mathbf{S}^*)$ ("stocks, distributed lag")

$b(\overline{\mathbf{T}}^*)$ ("sales expected, distributed lag")

$b(\overline{\mathbf{S}}^*)$ ("stocks expected, distributed lag"),

all defined in accordance with $b(\mathbf{T}^*)$ above, are used as explanatory variables in the equations for $b(\mathbf{p_s})$ and $b(\bar{\mathbf{p}}_\mathbf{s})$. The introduction of $b(\overline{\mathbf{T}}^*)$ and $b(\overline{\mathbf{S}}^*)$ into the intention equations may be justified by the argument that, when entrepreneurs expect in successive months, again and again, an increase in sales (stocks), this will eventually lead some of them to plan a raise (fall) in their selling prices, even apart from their expectations as to buying prices.

The regressions of the Tables 6.10 and 6.11 show very high correlations ($\bar{R}$), all between 0.96 and 1.00. This is not, however, due to the above-mentioned additional explanatory variables, for the eight zero-order correlations between buying and selling prices, without lags, are between 0.97 and 1.00. Indeed, the regression coefficients of the other variables are almost all both close to zero and insignificant. Planned selling prices, when introduced into the equations for actual selling prices, have small coefficients, some of them being even negative, but none of them significantly different from zero; and their introduction tends to depress the correlation coefficient (cf. the analyses 76, 84, 92, 100). Similarly, lagged buying prices do not contribute very much to the "explanation" of the fluctuations of the balances of actual selling prices. In only one case there is some indication of a lagged determination, viz., that of the shoe retailers (analyses 101 and 102); but its plausibility is suppressed by the negative point estimate of the coefficient of $b(\mathbf{p_b})_{-1} - b(\mathbf{p_s})_{-1}$ in the intention equation (70). Such a negative value is unacceptable and, to make it positive, we should increase it by at least twice the standard error. So the best thing we can reasonably do is to replace it by zero; and this is hardly compatible with a lagged determination of actual prices, for it means that plans for these prices are made without such lags. In the same way, sales and stocks are no successful variables. The coefficients of stocks have almost all unacceptable signs, both in Table 6.10 and in Table 6.11; but most of these signs are not significant. For sales the picture is somewhat less unfavourable: only four of the sixteen relevant analyses give "wrong" signs, and in one or two cases there is significance at the 5 per cent level under classical standards. Still, there is no cogent reason why this variable, in whatever form (T, T^*, $\bar{T}$, $\bar{T}^*$), should be accepted.

6.4.3. The correction approach is considered in Table 6.12. Again, one variable is retained systematically in the regressions of $b(\mathbf{p_s}) - b(\bar{\mathbf{p}}_\mathbf{s})$, viz., the corresponding quantity at the demand side:

$$b(\mathbf{p_b}) - b(\bar{\mathbf{p}}_\mathbf{b}) \qquad \text{("own buying, actual minus expected").}$$

Six variables play an experimental rôle. Following the line of thought of Section 2.3, we should first think of the buying price expected for next month:

$$b(\bar{\mathbf{p}}_\mathbf{b})_{+1} \qquad \text{("own buying expected, next month").}$$

TABLE 6.12

ALTERNATIVE REGRESSIONS FOR THE DIFFERENCES BETWEEN THE BALANCES OF THE TRADERS' ACTUAL AND THOSE OF THEIR PLANNED SELLING PRICES (CORRECTION APPROACH): $b(\mathbf{p_s})^K - b(\bar{\mathbf{p}}_\mathbf{s})^K$ FOR K = I, III, V, VI (GERMAN LEATHER AND SHOE INDUSTRY, 1951–1953)

Industry stages	$\bar{R}^2$	Coefficients of price variables: own buying, actual minus expected	own buying expected, next month	"incomplete correction last month"	Coefficients of other variables: sales, actual minus expected	sales expected, next month	stocks, actual minus expected	stocks expected, next month	Constant term	
traders in hides (I)	0.979	1.02(0.03)	.	.	.	.	.	.	−0.02	107
	0.980	1.03(0.03)	−0.01(0.04)	.	.	.	.	.	−0.02	108
	0.978	1.02(0.03)	.	−0.05(0.18)	.	.	.	.	−0.02	109
	0.978	1.02(0.03)	.	.	0.04(0.05)	.	.	.	−0.02	110
	0.980	1.01(0.04)	.	.	0.06(0.05)	0.01(0.05)	.	.	−0.02	111
	0.978	1.02(0.03)	.	.	.	.	−0.01(0.05)	.	−0.02	112
	0.977	1.02(0.03)	.	.	.	.	−0.01(0.06)	−0.01(0.08)	−0.02	113
traders in leather (III)	0.849	0.76(0.06)	.	.	.	.	.	.	−0.07	114
	0.847	0.83(0.08)	−0.10(0.09)	.	.	.	.	.	−0.08	115
	0.874	0.77(0.05)	.	−0.35(0.12)	.	.	.	.	−0.05	116
	0.841	0.77(0.06)	.	.	−0.02(0.06)	.	.	.	−0.07	117
	0.837	0.75(0.06)	.	.	0.01(0.07)	−0.02(0.05)	.	.	−0.07	118
	0.864	0.74(0.05)	.	.	.	.	0.19(0.09)	.	−0.06	119
	0.872	0.73(0.05)	.	.	.	.	0.24(0.08)	−0.07(0.14)	−0.07	120
wholesalers in shoes (V)	0.655	0.83(0.10)	.	.	.	.	.	.	−0.01	121
	0.649	0.86(0.11)	−0.06(0.08)	.	.	.	.	.	−0.01	122
	0.643	0.83(0.11)	.	0.01(0.19)	.	.	.	.	−0.01	123
	0.642	0.83(0.11)	.	.	0.01(0.05)	.	.	.	0.00	124
	0.649	0.81(0.10)	.	.	−0.02(0.05)	−0.04(0.03)	.	.	0.00	125
	0.644	0.83(0.10)	.	.	.	.	0.02(0.07)	.	−0.01	126
	0.706	0.82(0.10)	.	.	.	.	−0.05(0.06)	−0.12(0.05)	−0.03	127
retailers in shoes (VI)	0.657	0.77(0.09)	.	.	.	.	.	.	−0.05	128
	0.619	0.75(0.09)	−0.09(0.04)	.	.	.	.	.	−0.05	129
	0.648	0.78(0.10)	.	−0.06(0.17)	.	.	.	.	−0.05	130
	0.710	0.68(0.09)	.	.	−0.10(0.04)	.	.	.	−0.06	131
	0.704	0.65(0.10)	.	.	−0.11(0.04)	−0.02(0.02)	.	.	−0.06	132
	0.649	0.75(0.10)	.	.	.	.	0.03(0.05)	.	−0.05	133
	0.664	0.74(0.10)	.	.	.	.	−0.03(0.06)	−0.05(0.03)	−0.05	134

Also, we should think in terms of lagged corrections. Let us write

$$C^s = b(\mathbf{p_s}) - b(\bar{\mathbf{p}}_\mathbf{s});\ C^b = b(\mathbf{p_b}) - b(\bar{\mathbf{p}}_\mathbf{b})$$

for selling and buying price corrections, respectively. The analyses that do not include experimental variables are of the form $C^s = \alpha + \beta C^b$, the case $\alpha = 0$, $\beta = 1$ being that of complete and immediate adjustment. It is conceivable, however, that

$$C^s = \alpha + \beta_1 C^b + \beta_2 (C^b_{-1} - C^s_{-1})$$

is a preferable specification, since it enables us to take account of the possibility that incomplete selling price corrections in the preceding month are corrected for in the present month. We should obviously expect $\beta_2 \geqq 0$. So we introduce this additional explanatory variable,

$$[b(\mathbf{p_b})_{-1} - b(\bar{\mathbf{p}}_\mathbf{b})_{-1}] - [b(\mathbf{p_s})_{-1} - b(\bar{\mathbf{p}}_\mathbf{s})_{-1}],$$

the coefficients of which are to be found in Table 6.12 under "incomplete correction last month."

Other variables, finally, are sales and inventories, both in the correction form and the expectation for the next month:

$b(\mathbf{T}) - b(\bar{\mathbf{T}})$	("sales, actual minus expected")
$b(\bar{\mathbf{T}})_{+1}$	("sales expected, next month")
$b(\mathbf{S}) - b(\bar{\mathbf{S}})$	("stocks, actual minus expected")
$b(\bar{\mathbf{S}})_{+1}$	("stocks expected, next month").

The correlations obtained are, although still substantial for the higher stages, lower than those of the Tables 6.10 and 6.11. For the traders in hides they are of the order of 0.99, those of the leather traders are somewhat above 0.9, and those of the wholesalers and retailers in shoes about 0.8. The experimental variables are again not successful. When taking e.g. $b(\bar{\mathbf{p}}_\mathbf{b})_{+1}$, it is seen that this variable has coefficients of negative and hence unacceptable sign (analyses 108, 115, 122, 129). The same holds for the other price variable, "no correction last month," in three cases out of four (109, 116, 123, 130). Regressions with sales variables are presented in two alternative forms, viz., with one additional variable, $b(\mathbf{T}) - b(\bar{\mathbf{T}})$, and with two additional variables, $b(\mathbf{T}) - b(\bar{\mathbf{T}})$ and $b(\bar{\mathbf{T}})_{+1}$. Neither shows significant outcomes that are at the same time acceptable from an economic point of view. A similar procedure applied to stocks leads to more or less the same results. The coefficients of $b(\bar{\mathbf{S}})_{+1}$ have all four correct signs, but it is not difficult to ascribe this to chance; and it seems reasonable to do so for two distinct reasons. First, because of the bad results of stocks in the analyses of plans and behaviour in the Tables 6.10 and 6.11; second, because the sole analysis with stocks in Table 6.12 that gives a somewhat appreciably larger $\bar{R}^2$, viz. 120, does so at the cost of a positive point estimate of the coefficient of $b(\mathbf{S}) - b(\bar{\mathbf{S}})$.

These results suggest that, if the correction approach is adequate, one explanatory variable, viz., $b(\mathbf{p_b}) - b(\bar{\mathbf{p}}_\mathbf{b})$, must be considered sufficient; the argument being that the introduction of other variables would violate the requirements of simplicity without contributing very much to plausibility. The question then arises whether the correction approach is indeed adequate in the sense that it yields a more accurate picture of behaviour patterns than the direct attack of Table 6.11 does. If the answer is negative, we should reject the correction approach because its rival is simpler. Going back to the empirical findings, it is then seen that the answer has to be negative for the traders in hides: both in Table 6.10 and in Table 6.12 their group is characterised by coefficients of buying price variables which are about 1, with standard errors that are so small that the corresponding parameters cannot differ too much from unity even if the inaccuracy of the point estimates is, say, 50 percent larger than what is suggested by these errors. Addition of the intention equation and the correction equation gives then a behaviour equation—also with a coefficient of about unity—, which contains "actual" variables only. The situation is somewhat, but not much, different for the lowest stages of the industry: both for the wholesalers and for the retailers in shoes the coefficient in the intention equation exceeds the coefficient in the correction equation by 0.1–0.15. As observed earlier, this indicates an independent influence of plans on actual behaviour. It should be stressed, however, that the excess is not significantly different from zero. For stage III (leather traders) the difference is slightly larger, and even significant under classical conditions. But it should be added immediately that planned selling prices introduced into the behaviour equation for actual selling prices appeared to have an insignificant influence in all cases (cf. analyses 76, 84, 92, 100). We must conclude that we have not completed our work.

TABLE 6.13

MATRIX REGRESSIONS CONNECTING THE TRADERS' PLANNED SELLING PRICES WITH THEIR EXPECTED BUYING PRICES: $\bar{\mathbf{p}}_{\mathbf{s}} = \mathbf{A}\bar{\mathbf{p}}_{\mathbf{b}}$
(GERMAN LEATHER AND SHOE INDUSTRY, 1951–1953)

Industry stages	$\bar{R}^2$	$\bar{R}'^2$	Q	*Elements of* **A**			
traders in	0.989	0.987	2.05	0.988 (0.022)	−0.011 (0.014)	0.011 (0.015)	135
hides	0.993	0.963	2.57	0.018 (0.031)	1.013 (0.020)	−0.016 (0.022)	136
(I)	0.993	0.967	2.08	−0.005 (0.023)	−0.002 (0.015)	1.005 (0.016)	137
traders in	0.961	0.944	1.32	0.862 (0.035)	0.013 (0.009)	−0.010 (0.020)	138
leather	0.998	0.944	1.86	0.128 (0.046)	0.988 (0.012)	−0.009 (0.027)	139
(III)	0.987	0.965	2.15	0.010 (0.049)	−0.000 (0.013)	1.018 (0.028)	140
wholesalers	0.974	0.970	1.36	0.897 (0.026)	−0.015 (0.008)	0.017 (0.024)	141
in shoes	0.995	0.947	2.36	0.135 (0.046)	1.004 (0.014)	−0.050 (0.043)	142
(V)	0.966	0.943	2.49	−0.032 (0.042)	0.011 (0.012)	1.034 (0.038)	143
retailers in	0.946	0.933	1.44	0.795 (0.035)	−0.020 (0.011)	0.018 (0.025)	144
shoes	0.993	0.931	1.96	0.221 (0.053)	1.014 (0.017)	0.035 (0.037)	145
(VI)	0.978	0.965	1.93	−0.016 (0.040)	0.006 (0.013)	0.947 (0.028)	146

TABLE 6.14

MATRIX REGRESSIONS CONNECTING THE TRADERS' ACTUAL SELLING PRICES WITH THEIR ACTUAL BUYING PRICES: $\mathbf{p}_{\mathbf{s}} = \mathbf{B}\mathbf{p}_{\mathbf{b}}$
(GERMAN LEATHER AND SHOE INDUSTRY, 1951–1953)

Industry stages	$\bar{R}^2$	$\bar{R}'^2$	Q	*Elements of* **B**			
traders in	0.989	0.985	2.80	0.981 (0.019)	0.006 (0.023)	−0.010 (0.016)	147
hides	0.965	0.916	2.05	0.033 (0.031)	0.950 (0.037)	−0.010 (0.025)	148
(I)	0.991	0.980	1.50	−0.014 (0.023)	0.045 (0.028)	1.021 (0.018)	149
traders in	0.880	0.841	1.30	0.684 (0.046)	−0.018 (0.024)	0.003 (0.031)	150
leather	0.985	0.940	1.77	0.292 (0.049)	1.019 (0.026)	−0.023 (0.033)	151
(III)	0.993	0.987	2.46	0.025 (0.024)	−0.001 (0.013)	1.021 (0.016)	152
wholesalers	0.959	0.956	2.41	0.882 (0.032)	−0.016 (0.009)	0.017 (0.025)	153
in shoes	0.994	0.951	2.10	0.117 (0.050)	1.018 (0.015)	−0.059 (0.039)	154
(V)	0.977	0.964	1.97	0.001 (0.038)	−0.002 (0.011)	1.043 (0.030)	155
retailers in	0.870	0.851	0.67	0.761 (0.051)	−0.053 (0.023)	0.039 (0.050)	156
shoes	0.985	0.889	1.07	0.236 (0.057)	1.032 (0.026)	−0.023 (0.056)	157
(VI)	0.980	0.978	1.86	0.003 (0.028)	0.021 (0.013)	0.984 (0.027)	158

6.4.4. It is clear that the results obtained do not go very far beyond the simple approach according to which planned and actual selling prices are supposed to be determined by expected and actual buying prices, respectively, of the same month; cf. the analyses 51, 57, 63, 69, 75, 83, 91, 99. Furthermore, these analyses show multiplicative coefficients of the order of 0.8–1 and negative constant terms. The fact that one variable is the main determinant suggests that a matrix approach

$$\bar{\mathbf{p}}_{\mathbf{s}} = \mathbf{A}\bar{\mathbf{p}}_{\mathbf{b}}, \qquad \mathbf{p}_{\mathbf{s}} = \mathbf{B}\mathbf{p}_{\mathbf{b}},$$

may be valuable; the fact that the multiplicative coefficients are not all unity and the constant terms not all zero suggests that the result will not be $\mathbf{A} = \mathbf{B} = \mathbf{I}$ in all cases.

Least-squares estimates of $\mathbf{A}$ and $\mathbf{B}$ are given in the Tables 6.13 and 6.14, respectively. It appears that the correlations $\bar{R}$ are practically all extremely close to unity. This is, however, partly due to the absence of constant terms in the equations, which implies that $1 - \bar{R}^2$ is the ratio—adjusted for degrees of freedom—of the variance of the residuals to the second moment about zero of the dependent variable. Therefore, squares of "revised" correlations, $\bar{R}'^2$, are given in the second column, such that $1 - \bar{R}'^2$ is the familiar ratio of the variance of the residuals to the variance of the dependent variable. Although smaller than $\bar{R}$, the coefficients $\bar{R}'$ are still close to unity, their median being about 0.98 for plans and 0.97 for behaviour.

As to the elements of $\mathbf{A}$ and $\mathbf{B}$, it follows from the tables that most of the diagonal values are close to unity, and most of the off-diagonal values close to zero, with very small standard errors in general. The only exceptions are found in the first columns, where the α_{11}- and β_{11}-estimates tend to be smaller than unity (and significantly so in most of the cases except for the traders in hides), and the α_{21}- and β_{21}-estimates are mostly positive. It seems, therefore, that—if we accept the matrix approach for these price relations—the matrices $\mathbf{A}$ and $\mathbf{B}$ are not all of the unit form, but of the slightly different type

$$\begin{bmatrix} 1-\delta & 0 & 0 \\ \delta & 1 & 0 \\ 0 & 0 & 1 \end{bmatrix},$$

δ being zero for the traders in raw hides, but positive in most of the other cases.

6.4.5. The matrix result is decidedly simpler than that of the correction approach. It will be argued in 6.4.6 that it is also rather plausible —after some amendments—on economic grounds. The question remains how it can be explained that, under the assumption that the matrix result gives a correct description of selling price planning and behaviour, we obtained the balance results of the Tables 6.10, 6.11 and 6.12. The answer to this question amounts to an application of specification analysis and will be considered here. It will be noted, parenthetically, that our matrix result violates the negative-symmetry postulate of 6.1.5, for this would require $\alpha_{11} = \alpha_{33}$, $\beta_{11} = \beta_{33}$, etc.

First, we take the balance relations of the Tables 6.10 and 6.11. Since there are no mathematical differences between the analyses of planned and of actual selling prices of these tables, we may confine ourselves to either of these categories; say, actual selling prices. The matrix approach implies then that the "true" specification is

$$b(\mathbf{p_s}) = (1 - \delta)\overset{1}{p_b} - \overset{3}{p_b} + u,$$

u being a disturbance. The balance approach specifies

$$b(\mathbf{p_s}) = \alpha + \beta b(\mathbf{p_b}) + u'.$$

Returning to the specification analysis of 6.2.4, we observe that $\mathbf{X}_1$ of (6.25) corresponds to the values assumed by the variables $\overset{1}{p_b}$ and $\overset{3}{p_b}$, and $\mathbf{X}_2$ of (6.26) to those assumed by the fixed variable 1 and the variable $b(\mathbf{p_b})$. So the parameters α, β are given by [cf. (6.30)]

$$\begin{bmatrix} \alpha \\ \\ \beta \end{bmatrix} = \mathbf{P} \begin{bmatrix} 1 - \delta \\ \\ -1 \end{bmatrix},$$

where $\mathbf{P}$ is the coefficient matrix of the regression of $\mathbf{X}_1$ on $\mathbf{X}_2$:

$$\mathbf{P} = (\mathbf{X}_2'\mathbf{X}_2)^{-1}\mathbf{X}_2'\mathbf{X}_1 = \begin{bmatrix} a_1 & a_3 \\ \\ b_1 & b_3 \end{bmatrix}$$

with

$$\overset{1}{p_b} = a_1 + b_1 b(\mathbf{p_b})$$

$$\overset{3}{p_b} = a_3 + b_3 b(\mathbf{p_b}),$$

the residuals being omitted. Writing s_{11} for the variance of $\overset{1}{p}_b$, s_{33} for that of $\overset{3}{p}_b$, and s_{13} for the covariance, we find

$$b_1 = \frac{s_{11} - s_{13}}{s_{11} + s_{33} - 2s_{13}}\,; \qquad b_3 = b_1 - 1$$

$$a_1 = a_3 = b_1\hat{\overset{3}{p}}_b - b_3\hat{\overset{1}{p}}_b = \frac{s_{11}\hat{\overset{3}{p}}_b + s_{33}\hat{\overset{1}{p}}_b - s_{13}(\hat{\overset{1}{p}}_b + \hat{\overset{3}{p}}_b)}{s_{11} + s_{33} - 2s_{13}}\,,$$

$\hat{\overset{1}{p}}_b$ and $\hat{\overset{3}{p}}_b$ being the averages of $\overset{1}{p}_b$ and $\overset{3}{p}_b$, respectively, over time. Hence

$$\beta = b_1(1 - \delta) - b_3 = 1 - \delta\frac{s_{11} - s_{13}}{s_{11} + s_{33} - 2s_{13}}$$

$$\alpha = a_1(1 - \delta) - a_3 = -\delta\,\frac{s_{11}\hat{\overset{3}{p}}_b + s_{33}\hat{\overset{1}{p}}_b - s_{13}(\hat{\overset{1}{p}}_b + \hat{\overset{3}{p}}_b)}{s_{11} + s_{33} - 2s_{13}}\,.$$

Since the fractions of increases and of decreases are negatively correlated over time (i.e., $s_{13} < 0$), we have

$$1 - \delta < \beta < 1 \text{ and } \alpha < 0,$$

which is in accordance with our findings. It can also be shown that the balance specification may be characterised by a considerable correlation in spite of its incorrectness. To see this, let us write the disturbance of the balance equation in terms of the disturbance u of the matrix specification and the relevant explanatory variables:

$$u' = u + (1 - \delta)\overset{1}{p}_b - \overset{3}{p}_b - [\alpha + \beta(\overset{1}{p}_b - \overset{3}{p}_b)]$$

$$= u - \delta\,\frac{(s_{33} - s_{13})(\overset{1}{p}_b - \hat{\overset{1}{p}}_b) + (s_{11} - s_{13})(\overset{3}{p}_b - \hat{\overset{3}{p}}_b)}{s_{11} + s_{33} - 2s_{13}}\,.$$

Its variance equals

$$\operatorname{var} u' = \operatorname{var} u + \delta^2\,\frac{s_{11}s_{33} - s_{13}^2}{s_{11} + s_{33} - 2s_{13}}\,,$$

and this will be small compared with the variance of the dependent variable of the balance specification,

$$\operatorname{var} b(\mathbf{p_s}) = (1 - \delta)^2 s_{11} + s_{33} - 2(1 - \delta)\, s_{13} + \operatorname{var} u,$$

especially when δ and var u are small, and when s_{13} is sufficiently negative.

Next, we take the correction approach of Table 6.12. Since the corresponding equations of the Tables 6.10 and 6.11—which themselves are not more than incorrectly specified superstructures built upon matrix relations—have rather small disturbances, we take these as our starting point:

$$b(\mathbf{p_s}) = \alpha + \beta b(\mathbf{p_b}) + u'$$
$$b(\bar{\mathbf{p}}_\mathbf{s}) = \alpha' + \beta' b(\bar{\mathbf{p}}_\mathbf{b}) + u''.$$

Hence:

$$b(\mathbf{p_s}) - b(\bar{\mathbf{p}}_\mathbf{s}) = \alpha_1 + \beta b(\mathbf{p_b}) - \beta' b(\bar{\mathbf{p}}_\mathbf{b}) + u_1$$

with $\alpha_1 = \alpha - \alpha'$, $u_1 = u' - u''$. On the other hand, the specification according to the correction approach is

$$b(\mathbf{p_s}) - b(\bar{\mathbf{p}}_\mathbf{s}) = \alpha_2 + \beta_2\{b(\mathbf{p_b}) - b(\bar{\mathbf{p}}_\mathbf{b})\} + u_2.$$

The analysis is then entirely analogous to the preceding one, if we give $b(\mathbf{p_b})$ the rôle of $\overset{1}{p}_b$, $b(\bar{\mathbf{p}}_\mathbf{b})$ that of $\overset{3}{p}_b$, β that of $(1 - \delta)$, etc. The sole difference is that the first specification contains a nonzero constant term (α_1) in the present case; but this difference is removed if we agree to measure all variables as deviations from their average. So we find after some rearrangements:

$$\beta_2 = \frac{(t_{11} - t_{12})\,\beta + (t_{22} - t_{12})\,\beta'}{t_{11} + t_{22} - 2t_{12}},$$

where t_{11} is the variance of $b(\mathbf{p_b})$, t_{22} that of $b(\bar{\mathbf{p}}_\mathbf{b})$, and t_{12} the covariance. Hence β_2 is a weighted average of the underlying parameters β and β', the sum of the weights being unity. But the weights are not necessarily nonnegative. Indeed, in all three cases for which $\delta > 0$ is plausible (viz., the stages III, V and VI), we find that the β_2-estimate lies to the left of the (β, β')-interval. This is the result of a negative weight, $t_{22} - t_{12} < 0$; and this, in turn, is due to the small variance of the balances of expected buying prices relative to that of the "actual" balances, $t_{22} < t_{11}$, and to the considerable positive correlation between both, $t_{12} > 0$; cf. Chapter IV. Finally, the fact that t_{12} does not have the negative sign of s_{13} in the preceding case implies that the correlation of the correction regression is affected more seriously.

6.4.6. Our final problem is that of the interpretation of the asymmetric matrix result. The immediate interpretation is rather simple: only part of the traders reacted to buying price increases by raising their selling prices—a statement which holds both for behaviour and for plans and expectations—, but all of them reacted to buying price decreases by lowering their selling prices. In principle, it is possible to ascribe this observed result to three entirely different causes; viz., to peculiar characteristics and deficiencies of Business Test data, to incorrect information supplied by some of the participants, or to a more "real" economic phenomenon.[1] The first possibility will occur if the indifference intervals for selling prices have a higher upper bound than those of the buying prices, their lower bounds being the same. The second possibility can be formally described in the same manner, though in the case of conscious misinformation it is not very satisfactory to do so. Now it is clearly not easy to test the validity of either of these possibilities; but there are some arguments against them. First, the objection of these deficiencies can be used against all of the results obtained from Business Test data; so far, however, we found no reason to do so. In particular, we considered this earlier in connection with the underestimation of changes (cf. 4.4.3), but the subsequent analysis in Chapter V did not support the idea that the results should be rejected. Second, there is some independent information to the effect that, owing to sharp competition, the traders under consideration were forced to follow falling buying prices, whereas they were not always in a position to follow increasing buying prices.[2] On the other hand, we should also mention that in recent years raising selling prices has become a more or less anti-social deed—at least in several European countries—; and this may induce entrepreneurs to conceal such plans and behaviour. The organisers of the Business Test tried to avoid this effect by a careful formulation of the question. They asked: "Did you have to raise your selling prices?" Not: "Did you raise your selling prices?" In so far as the phenomenon considered affects the reports of the participants, it contributes to a trivial explanation of the asymmetric matrix results; in so far as the organisers of the survey were

[1] There is a fourth possibility; viz., that selling prices are increased less frequently than buying prices, but that the size of the raise is relatively larger. This variant is not very plausible, however, for if it were true, we should have obtained some significance for lagged buying prices; cf. the Tables 6.10 and 6.11.

[2] See the *Branchenhandbuch* for leather and shoes, edited by the IFO-Institute (München, 1954), p. R 36.

successful in their formulation, this contribution is reduced. It is clearly difficult to make a discrimination of the competing theories by means of the available data.

Another approach to this problem of asymmetry is to assume that it is a "real" economic phenomenon (i.e., not due to the first two possibilities of the preceding paragraph), and to see how it can be explained. The independent information mentioned above may be regarded as a justification for this alternative line of attack. The most fruitful approach is presumably that of the basis underlying the theory of the kinked demand curve.[1] As is well-known, this theory states that the individual seller expects, *ceteris paribus*, his competitors to follow suit if he lowers his selling price, whereas the converse is true if he raises the price. Let us assume that this is true; and let us consider what happens if a set of firms is confronted with changes in their buying prices. Suppose first that these changes are decreases. Since everybody knows (or thinks he knows) that one man is sufficient to cause a general downward movement of all selling prices of the group; since, furthermore, everybody considers it plausible that at least one such individual can be found; given these two reasons, there is no point in waiting very long. So a general reduction of selling prices is a very likely result, even if the group under consideration is not more than a subset of the set of all competitors. This is in accordance with the matrix results $\alpha_{33} = \beta_{33} = 1$. Consider then the case in which the buying price changes are increases rather than decreases. Presumably everyone would be inclined to raise his selling price, provided he is reasonably sure that he would be followed; but nobody is really certain about this point. Now it seems likely that the degree to which this picture is a correct description of the situation depends on the size of the group considered relative to the set of all competitors. For, if the group which is confronted with increased buying prices covers all traders of a certain stage, the reluctance to raise selling prices will be less than in the case where this group covers only part of the stage. We should therefore expect that the fraction of this group which raises the price is smaller if the group itself is a smaller fraction of the total group; in other words, that the ratio $\overset{1}{p_s}/\overset{1}{p_b}$ is an increasing function of $\overset{1}{p_b}$. When inspecting the scatters of the Figs. 6.4 and 6.5, we see that this is indeed

[1] Cf. R. L. HALL and C. J. HITCH, "Price Theory and Business Behaviour," *Oxford Economic Papers*, No. 2 (1939), pp. 12–45; P. M. SWEEZY, "Demand Under Conditions of Oligopoly," *Journal of Political Economy*, Vol. 47 (1939), pp. 568–573.

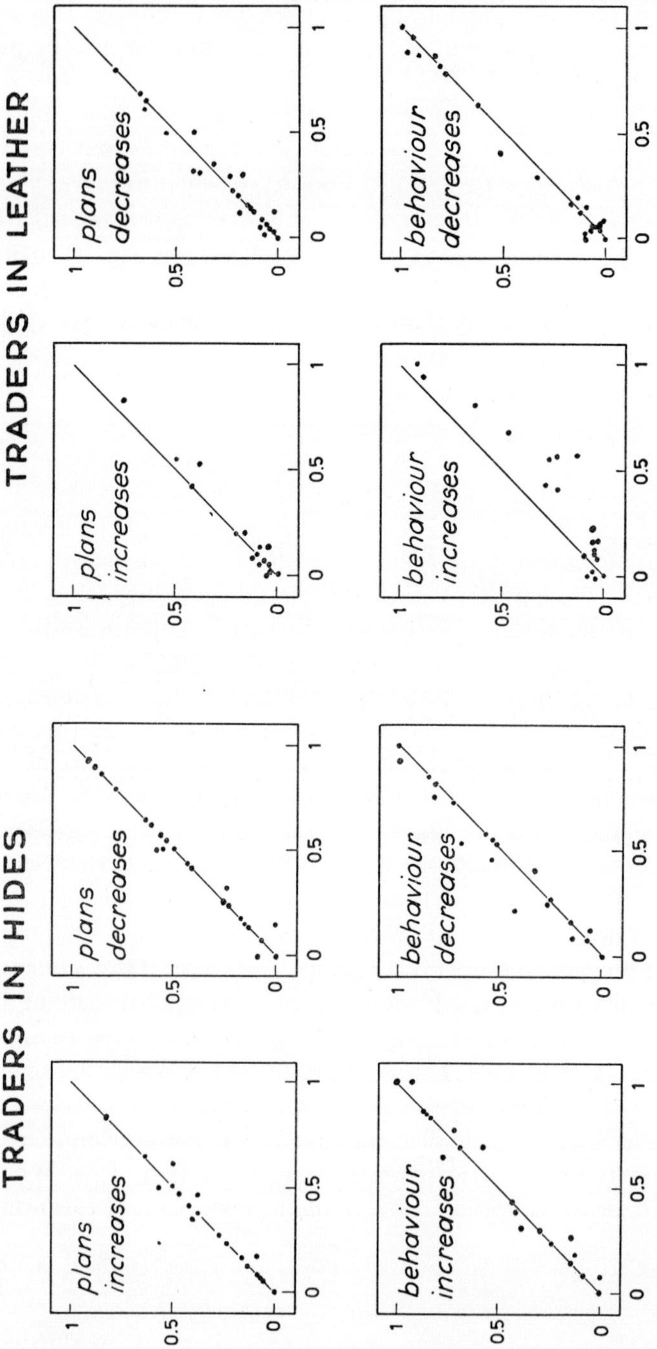

Fig 6.4. Scatter diagrams for the fractions of increases (and decreases), planned-expected and actual, of the buying and selling prices of the traders in hides and the traders in leather (German leather and shoe industry, 1951–1953)

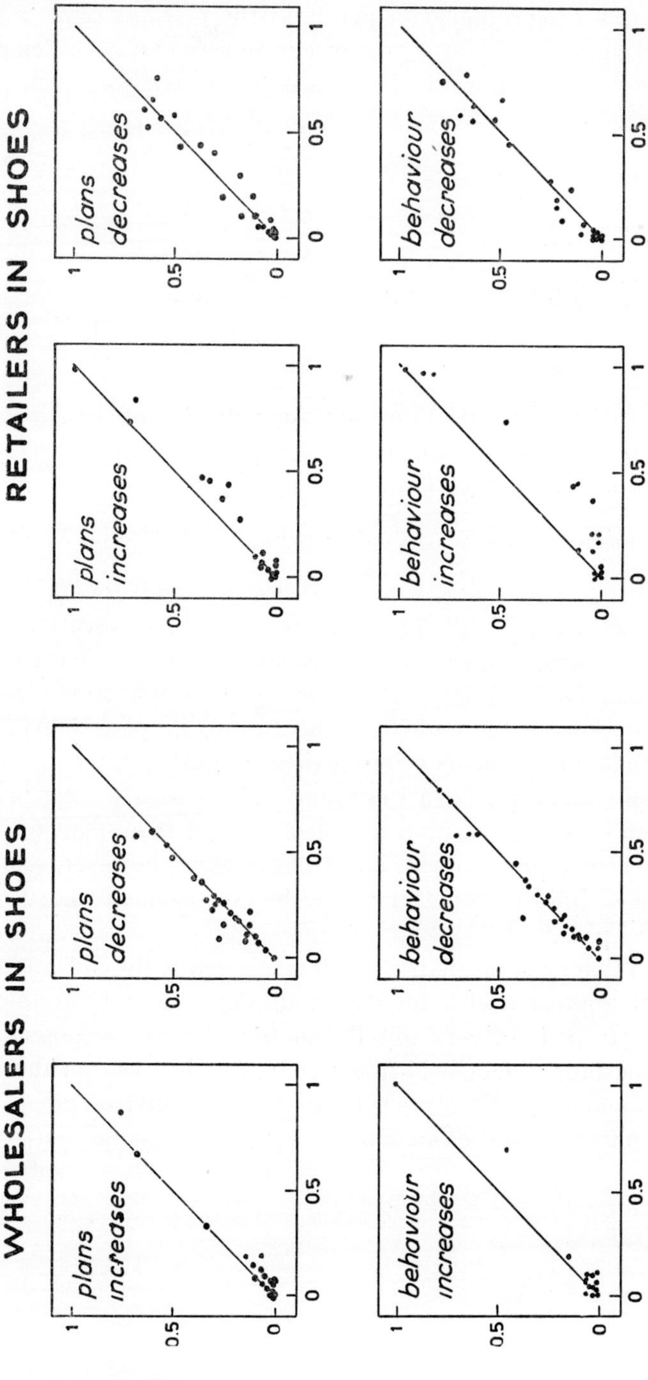

Fig. 6.5. Scatter diagrams for the fractions of increases (and decreases), planned-expected and actual, of the buying and selling prices of the wholesalers and retailers in shoes (German leather and shoe industry, 1951–1953)

the case. Even if the number of points in the relevant range is not always very large, a certain degree of curvilinearity can be detected for the stages III, V and VI. This leads to the relations which we finally prefer:

$$(6.91) \qquad \overset{-1}{p}_s = (\overset{-1}{p}_b)^{\varepsilon} \qquad \text{with } \varepsilon = 1 \text{ for stage I,} \quad = 1.5 \text{ for the stages III, V, VI;}$$

$$\overset{-3}{p}_s = \overset{-3}{p}_b.$$

$$(6.92) \qquad \overset{1}{p}_s = (\overset{1}{p}_b)^{\varepsilon} \qquad \text{with } \varepsilon = 1 \text{ for stage I,} \quad = 2 \text{ for the stages III, V, VI;}$$

$$\overset{3}{p}_s = \overset{3}{p}_b.$$

These constant-elasticity relations fulfil the requirement that the ratio of the fraction of selling price increases to that of buying price increases should be an increasing function of the latter fraction:

$$\overset{-1}{p}_s/\overset{-1}{p}_b = (\overset{-1}{p}_b)^{\frac{1}{2}}; \qquad \overset{1}{p}_s/\overset{1}{p}_b = \overset{1}{p}_b \text{ for the stages III, V, VI;}$$

and they give $\overset{1}{p}_s = \overset{1}{p}_b$ if $\overset{1}{p}_b = 0$ or 1 (and similarly for plans and expectations), in accordance with the Figs. 6.4 and 6.5. The scatters give some, but not much, evidence that the elasticity ε is somewhat smaller for plans than for behaviour. This feature has been accepted in the preferred relations (6.91) and (6.92) because of its plausibility. For it is likely that entrepreneurs feel that their interest requires that they do raise their selling prices in the event of increasing buying prices. Hence, when expecting such an increase, most of them plan to raise the price; when confronted with an actual increase, however, some of them become afraid of being alone at the last moment and do not carry out the plan.[1]

So we find that even the matrix result is rejected at the end, and that the original approach with its numerous experimental variables is boiled down to pairs of very simple equations. It will be noted that these relationships cannot hold indefinitely, for they lead in the long run to lower and lower selling prices compared with purchase prices, and hence to bankruptcy in the end. But for a limited period of sharp com-

[1] Although this curvilinearity is a point in favour of the theory which states that the asymmetric result is a real economic phenomenon, we should add that this feature may also be explained by the theory of the fear of anti-social attitudes. For, if all or almost all of the competitors are confronted with increased buying prices, it becomes easier for each of them to apologise his act of raising the selling price by pointing out that all purchase prices are rising.

petition their description may well be realistic. Since the survey of 4.1.4 of the situation of the firms under consideration suggests that there was indeed sharp competition, this may be regarded as a certain corroboration of the explanation given. However, the curvilinearity will be much less pronounced (or even wholly absent) when there is an open or tacit understanding among entrepreneurs, or when they operate close to their capacity ceiling, in which case competitive stimuli tend to lose their power.[1]

6.5. Analysis of Market Relationships: The Traders' Actual Buying Prices

6.5.1. Our next topic is that of the traders' actual buying prices. This subject is no longer entirely new, since we presented a number of regressions for these variables in an earlier stage, viz., in 6.3.4. It is clear, however, that the analyses reported there should not be regarded as attempts to give an adequate description of the process by which these prices are numerically determined; the reason being that we confined ourselves to those explanatory variables which appeared to be relevant for expected prices, not for the actual ones.

Instead, it might seem that the traders' actual buying prices form a trivial problem from our present point of view. To see this, suppose first for a moment that we had conventional indices instead of test variates at our disposal. Then the buying price index should always be identical with the selling price index of the supplying firms, provided weighting takes place conformably. The same seems to apply to test variates, provided also unequal indifference intervals do not give rise to difficulties. At first sight, therefore, one might think that an analysis of the determination of the traders' actual buying prices

[1] It should be stressed that a straightforward test of the theory of the kinked demand curve in the form implied by the question, Do competitors actually follow price raises?, is not conclusive; cf. G. J. STIGLER, "The Kinky Oligopoly Demand Curve and Rigid Prices," *Journal of Political Economy*, Vol. 55 (1947), pp. 432–447. For suppose that it is true, as the theory says, that entrepreneurs are indeed afraid of not being followed by their competitors under all circumstances. Then they may abstain from action unless these circumstances are such that they can be reasonably sure that they will be followed; and, if this is true and if these guesses are usually correct, the actual and observed price raises will in most cases be followed by competitors' raises. A satisfactory analysis of the asymmetry postulated by the theory of the kinked demand curve should be based, not exclusively on selling price changes, but also on the factors which determine them, like changes in buying prices.

is suitable for testing the adequacy of test variate data, but not very interesting from an economic point of view. Although the former purpose is sufficient in itself to justify a number of computations, it should be stressed that more may be involved than a basic identity of buying and selling prices. It is conceivable that buyers report changes in their purchase prices only when buying, whereas sellers report changes in their selling prices immediately when charging them. This possibility may lead to certain lags, the analysis of which is another purpose of this section. We shall confine ourselves to the stages III, V, VI; the traders in hides will be considered separately in Section 6.7.

6.5.2. Table 6.15 contains a number of alternative regressions in balances. The first explanatory variable is the selling price of the next higher stage,

$b(\mathbf{p_s})^{K-\mathrm{I}}$ ("selling, next higher stage"),

which is retained in all regressions; the superscript $K - \mathrm{I}$ should be read as II when the buying prices of III are considered, as IV when those of V are considered, etc. A further variable is the same selling price lagged,

$b(\mathbf{p_s})_{-1}^{K-\mathrm{I}}$ ("selling, next higher stage, lagged"),

and the lagged dependent variable,

$b(\mathbf{p_b})_{-1}$ ("own buying, lagged")

because of a possible suitability of Koyck's approach. There is an additional complication for the retailers in shoes, since they may buy their shoes from the wholesalers (their next higher stage) as well as from the manufacturers directly. Hence, for these firms the following variables are also included:

$b(\mathbf{p_s})^{\mathrm{IV}}$ ("selling IV")

$b(\mathbf{p_s})_{-1}^{\mathrm{IV}}$ ("selling IV, lagged").

Table 6.15 suggests that there is no need to assume a lagged determination of the leather traders' buying prices. The coefficients of the alternative lagged variables (analyses 160–161) are both negative, although not significant. Since negative parameters are unplausible here, we should prefer analysis 159; and, since the multiplicative co-

TABLE 6.15

ALTERNATIVE REGRESSIONS FOR THE BALANCES OF THE TRADERS' ACTUAL BUYING PRICES: $b(\mathbf{p_b})^K$ FOR K = III, V, VI (GERMAN LEATHER AND SHOE INDUSTRY, 1951–1953)

Industry stages	$\bar{R}^2$	*Coefficients of price variables*					*Constant term*	
		selling, next higher stage	*selling, next higher stage, lagged*	*own buying, lagged*	*selling IV*	*selling IV, lagged*		
traders in leather (III)	0.806	1.16(0.09)	.	.	.	.	0.06	159
	0.816	1.31(0.12)	−0.20(0.11)	.	.	.	0.06	160
	0.802	1.21(0.13)	.	−0.08(0.09)	.	.	0.06	161
wholesalers in shoes (V)	0.570	0.99(0.15)	.	.	.	.	−0.02	162
	0.752	0.61(0.14)	0.53(0.11)	.	.	.	−0.02	163
	0.764	0.54(0.14)	.	0.46(0.09)	.	.	−0.02	164
	0.778	0.52(0.14)	0.27(0.16)	0.29(0.14)	.	.	−0.02	165
retailers in shoes (VI)	0.678	1.22(0.15)	.	.	.	.	0.14	166
	0.872	0.39(0.15)	0.84(0.12)	.	.	.	0.11	167
	0.894	0.75(0.10)	.	0.51(0.06)	.	.	0.08	168
	0.904	0.55(0.14)	0.36(0.18)	0.34(0.11)	.	.	0.09	169
	0.718	0.83(0.22)	.	.	0.61(0.26)	.	0.14	170
	0.896	0.22(0.07)	0.44(0.07)	.	0.22(0.07)	0.44(0.07)	0.09	171
	0.918	0.49(0.12)	.	0.48(0.05)	0.44(0.15)	.	0.09	172
	0.920	0.29(0.07)	0.18(0.10)	0.34(0.11)	0.29(0.07)	0.18(0.10)	0.06	173

efficient of this analysis is not significantly different from unity, we should try the matrix approach,

$$(\mathbf{p_b})^{\mathrm{III}} = \mathbf{A}(\mathbf{p_s})^{\mathrm{II}}.$$

The result is presented in Table 6.16, which shows correlations lower than those of the matrix relations of the Tables 6.13 and 6.14, but no significant differences from the unit matrix. In view of its simplicity, we shall accept the hypothesis $\mathbf{A} = \mathbf{I}$, so that $(\mathbf{p_b})^{\mathrm{III}} = (\mathbf{p_s})^{\mathrm{II}}$.

TABLE 6.16

MATRIX REGRESSIONS CONNECTING THE LEATHER TRADERS' ACTUAL BUYING PRICES WITH THE TANNERS' ACTUAL SELLING PRICES: $(\mathbf{p_b})^{\mathrm{III}} = \mathbf{A}(\mathbf{p_s})^{\mathrm{II}}$ (GERMAN LEATHER AND SHOE INDUSTRY, 1951–1953)

$\bar{R}^2$	$\bar{R}'^2$	Q	Elements of **A**			
0.796	0.706	1.01	1.19(0.12)	0.01(0.05)	−0.00(0.07)	174
0.902	0.650	2.11	−0.12(0.17)	1.01(0.07)	−0.08(0.09)	175
0.891	0.822	2.23	−0.07(0.13)	−0.03(0.06)	1.08(0.07)	176

There is a rather strong indication of lagged determination for the buying prices of the traders in shoes. Koyck's variable $b(\mathbf{p_b})_{-1}$, e.g., has a coefficient of about 0.5 for the wholesalers (164) and also for the retailers, in the latter case both when the selling price of the next higher stage V alone is introduced as additional explanatory variable (168) and when the selling price of the shoe manufacturers is introduced as well (172). The selling prices of the stages IV and V are, however, highly correlated; and since, moreover, in those analyses (170 and 172) where they are both introduced without *a priori* restrictions they show about the same coefficients, it seems preferable to impose equal coefficients in those analyses (171 and 173) which contain more variables. Our final choice is

$$(6.93) \quad (\mathbf{p_b})^{\mathrm{III}} = (\mathbf{p_s})^{\mathrm{II}};$$

$$(6.94) \quad b(\mathbf{p_b})^{\mathrm{V}} = 0.5\, b(\mathbf{p_s})^{\mathrm{IV}} + 0.3\, b(\mathbf{p_s})^{\mathrm{IV}}_{-1} + 0.3\, b(\mathbf{p_b})^{\mathrm{V}}_{-1};$$

$$(6.95) \quad b(\mathbf{p_b})^{\mathrm{VI}} = 0.3[b(\mathbf{p_s})^{\mathrm{IV}} + b(\mathbf{p_s})^{\mathrm{V}}] + 0.2[b(\mathbf{p_s})^{\mathrm{IV}}_{-1} + b(\mathbf{p_s})^{\mathrm{V}}_{-1}] + {} + 0.35\, b(\mathbf{p_b})^{\mathrm{VI}}_{-1},$$

the last two of which correspond to the analyses 165 and 173, their Von Neumann ratios being 1.42 and 1.87, respectively. This choice is based upon the consideration that the lagged determination seems to become more pronounced when we approach the ultimate consumer, which is easily verified by a comparison of the matrix results of Table 6.16 with the balance specifications 165 and 173. The matrix relations are not characterised by any lag at all. For the shoe wholesalers the sum of the coefficients of the lagged selling prices $b(\mathbf{p_s})^{\mathrm{IV}}_{-1}$, $b(\mathbf{p_s})^{\mathrm{IV}}_{-2}, \ldots$ equals, according to 165,

$$\frac{0.27 + 0.29 \times 0.52}{1 - 0.29} = 0.6,$$

where use is made of the geometric series in (6.38). Comparing this with the point estimate 0.52 of the coefficient of the current variable $b(\mathbf{p_s})^{\mathrm{IV}}$, we conclude that all lagged variables combined have about the same influence on $b(\mathbf{p_b})^{\mathrm{V}}$ as the current variable has. A similar computation carried out for analysis 173 of the shoe retailers leads to the result that the influence of lagged selling prices exceeds that of the current prices by almost 50 per cent. Our conclusion from this and the preceding section must be, therefore, that all four sets of traders are characterised by the *idea* that their selling price reactions to buying price changes are immediate; but that there is a lagged association between the buying price changes reported by the lower stages and the selling prices to which these changes refer, so that *in fact* there is a lagged reaction of these stages.

The Figs. 6.6 and 6.7 give a picture of the relations (6.93), (6.94) and (6.95).

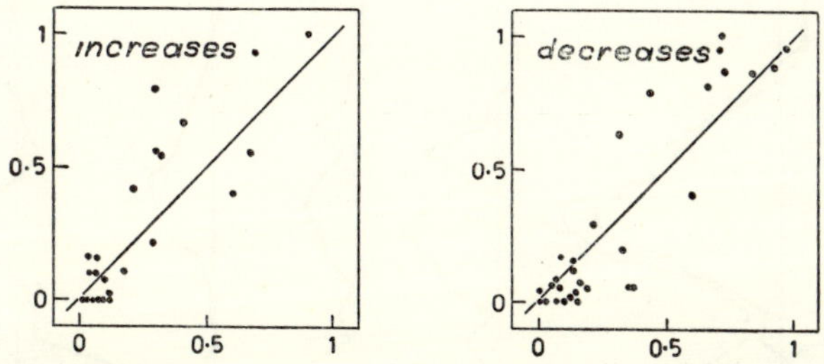

Fig. 6.6. Scatter diagrams for the fractions of increases (and decreases) of the actual buying prices of the leather traders and the actual selling prices of the tanners (German leather and shoe industry, 1951–1953)

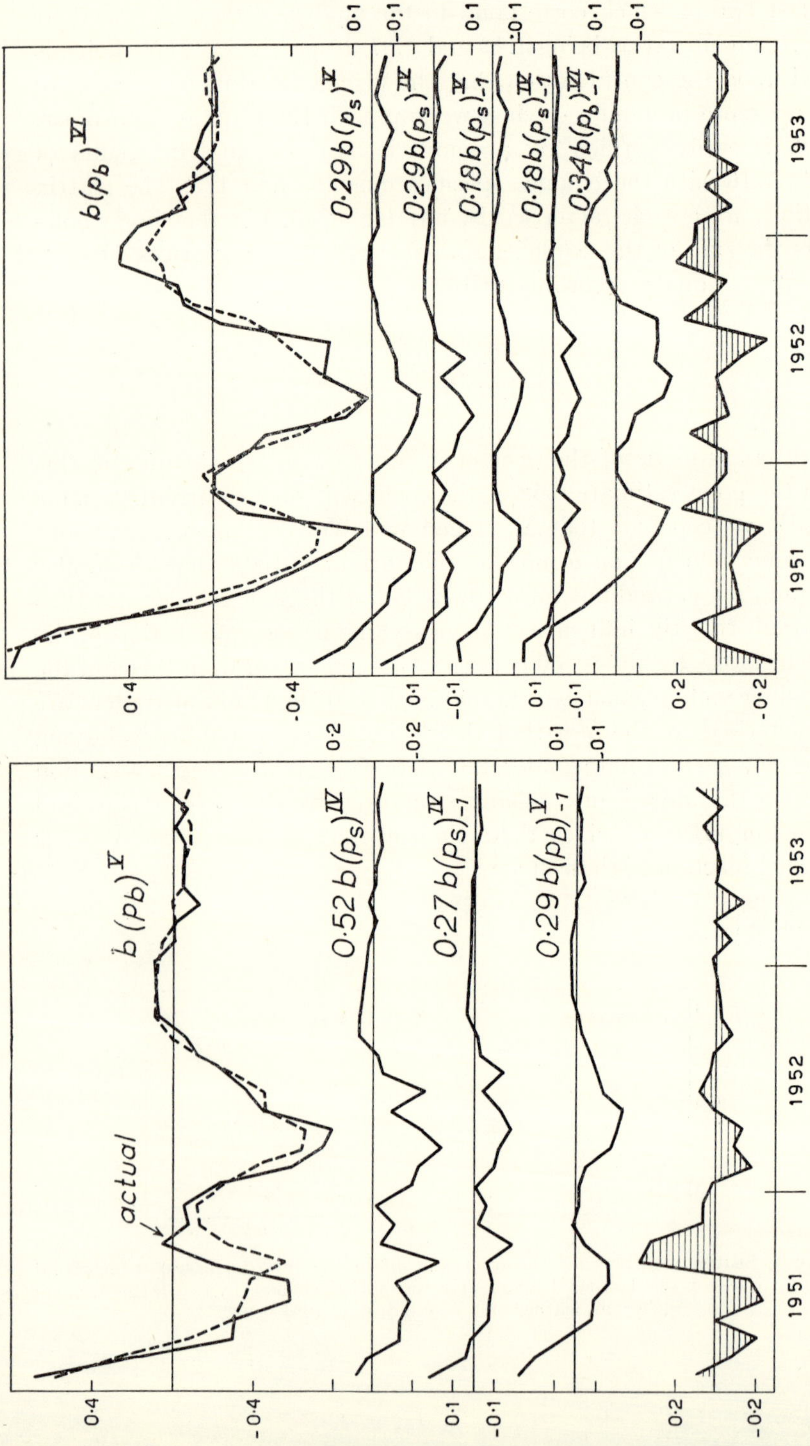

Fig. 6.7. Regressions describing the balances of the actual buying prices of the wholesalers in shoes and of the retailers in shoes: analyses 165 and 173 (German leather and shoe industry, 1951–1953)

6.6. The Manufacturers' Planned and Actual Selling Prices

6.6.1. It is a fortunate thing for the analysis of the manufacturers' selling prices that their raw material expenses form a very substantial part of their total cost (cf. 4.1.4), so that changes in other cost items—about which no test variate information exists—may be expected to have a minor influence on their pricing behaviour, at least in the short run. In so far as variations in labour cost affect selling prices, we may assume that their influence is mainly confined to the constant terms of the equations in balances, first because this influence will be largely of the long-run type compared with our monthly periods, secondly because wages showed a one-sided upward movement during the period under consideration. It is also fortunate that we can compare the processes leading to planned and those leading to actual prices, and that we can do so for two sets of manufacturers—although the advantage is less conspicuous than in the traders' case, where we had four sets at our disposal. It is unfortunate that no data about the manufacturers' buying prices are available. It will be necessary, therefore, to look for "substitutes" as is so usual in econometric work; and in the present case the obvious choice seems the selling price of the next higher stage. This means that we have to combine for the manufacturers what we did for the traders separately in the Sections 6.4 and 6.5.

6.6.2. First, however, we are faced with a preliminary problem of another kind, viz., that of the determination of the "next higher stage" for the shoe manufacturers. Our choice is between the tanneries (II) and the leather traders (III); and the former seems the better alternative, since it has been stated elsewhere (cf. 4.1.4 and also 6.3.3) that the greater part of the leather bought by the shoe manufacturers is supplied directly by the tanneries. Before accepting this choice, however, it is preferable to test this empirically; of course, such a test can equally well be regarded as an analysis of the adequacy of the material. Our procedure will be to take those explanatory variables the influence of which on the planned and actual selling prices of the shoe manufacturers seems most plausible, and to experiment with the stages II and III. For the actual selling price, our first choice should be the shoe manufacturers' actual buying price, which is substituted by the competing variables

$b(\mathbf{p_S})^{II}$ or $b(\mathbf{p_S})^{III}$ ["selling II (or III")].

Furthermore, we should take the same variable lagged:

$b(\mathbf{p_S})^{II}_{-1}$ or $b(\mathbf{p_S})^{III}_{-1}$ ["selling II (or III), lagged"],

and possibly

$b(\mathbf{p_S})^{IV}_{-1}$ ("own selling, lagged")

because of Koyck's treatment of distributed lags. Such lags can easily be justified by pointing to the lagged market relationships between corresponding buying and selling prices found in Section 6.5, and to the consideration that lagged selling price reactions are presumably even more realistic for manufacturers than for traders.

Similarly, for the shoe manufacturers' planned selling prices, we should first think of their expected buying prices, which are to be substituted by the following combination:

$b(\mathbf{p_S})^{II}_{-1}$ or $b(\mathbf{p_S})^{III}_{-1}$ ["selling II (or III), lagged"];

$b(\mathbf{p_S})^{II}_{-2}$ or $b(\mathbf{p_S})^{III}_{-2}$ ["selling II (or III), lagged 2 months"];

$b(\mathbf{p_S})^{IV}_{-1}$ ("own selling, lagged").

These variables are analogous to the finally preferred set of explanatory variables for the traders' expected buying prices (cf. Section 6.3); provided, however, we accept $b(\mathbf{p_S})^{IV}_{-1}$ as a substitute for lagged values of the shoe manufacturers' buying prices.

The results are presented in the Tables 6.17 and 6.18. It appears that in all cases the approach with $b(\mathbf{p_S})^{II}$ gives a higher correlation than the corresponding approach with $b(\mathbf{p_S})^{III}$. The best fit for planned selling prices is obtained when we take $b(\mathbf{p_S})^{II}_{-1}$ and $b(\mathbf{p_S})^{IV}_{-1}$ (analysis 181), the introduction of $b(\mathbf{p_S})^{II}_{-2}$ as additional explanatory variable being characterised by a small and insignificant coefficient (183). For actual selling prices the largest $\bar{R}^2$ is obtained when we introduce exactly the same pair of explanatory variables, $b(\mathbf{p_S})^{II}_{-1}$ and $b(\mathbf{p_S})^{IV}_{-1}$ (195); in this case $b(\mathbf{p_S})^{II}$, when introduced additionally, has an insignificant coefficient (191). This is used in Table 6.19 in the final test for the alternative "stage II versus stage III," where the lagged selling prices of both sets of firms together are introduced. It appears that $b(\mathbf{p_S})^{II}_{-1}$ has coefficients that are more significantly different from zero

TABLE 6.17

FIRST SET OF ALTERNATIVE REGRESSIONS FOR THE BALANCES OF THE SHOE MANUFACTURERS' PLANNED SELLING PRICES: $b(\bar{\mathbf{p}}_{\mathbf{s}})^{IV}$ (GERMAN LEATHER AND SHOE INDUSTRY, 1951–1953)

	Regressions based on Selling II					Regressions based on Selling III					
	Constant term	Coefficients of price variables: selling II, lagged	selling II, lagged 2 months	own selling, lagged	$\bar{R}^2$	$\bar{R}^2$	Coefficients of price variables: selling III, lagged	selling III, lagged 2 months	own selling, lagged	Constant term	
177	0.04	0.42 (0.05)	.	.	0.637	0.536	0.34 (0.06)	.	.	0.04	178
179	0.04	0.32 (0.07)	0.13 (0.07)	.	0.665	0.577	0.26 (0.07)	0.13 (0.06)	.	0.04	180
181	0.04	0.30 (0.07)	.	0.27 (0.10)	0.696	0.677	0.23 (0.05)	.	0.36 (0.10)	0.05	182
183	0.04	0.29 (0.07)	0.02 (0.09)	0.24 (0.14)	0.686	0.666	0.24 (0.06)	−0.01 (0.07)	0.37 (0.13)	0.05	184

TABLE 6.18

FIRST SET OF ALTERNATIVE REGRESSIONS FOR THE BALANCES OF THE SHOE MANUFACTURERS' ACTUAL SELLING PRICES: $b(\mathbf{p}_{\mathbf{s}})^{IV}$ (GERMAN LEATHER AND SHOE INDUSTRY, 1951–1953)

	Regressions based on Selling II					Regressions based on Selling III					
	Constant term	Coefficients of price variables: selling II	selling II, lagged	own selling, lagged	$\bar{R}^2$	$\bar{R}^2$	Coefficients of price variables: selling III	selling III, lagged	own selling, lagged	Constant term	
185	−0.03	0.43 (0.09)	.	.	0.401	0.255	0.31 (0.05)	.	.	−0.03	186
187	−0.02	0.08 (0.09)	0.44 (0.08)	.	0.672	0.546	0.06 (0.09)	0.38 (0.08)	.	−0.02	188
189	−0.03	0.27 (0.08)	.	0.43 (0.11)	0.578	0.366	0.19 (0.07)	.	0.49 (0.11)	−0.03	190
191	−0.03	0.09 (0.09)	0.35 (0.10)	0.18 (0.12)	0.685	0.624	0.06 (0.08)	0.25 (0.09)	0.32 (0.12)	−0.02	192
193	−0.03	.	0.50 (0.06)	.	0.673	0.555	.	0.41 (0.06)	.	−0.03	194
195	−0.03	.	0.41 (0.08)	0.18 (0.12)	0.685	0.630	.	0.29 (0.07)	0.32 (0.12)	−0.03	196

than those of $b(\mathbf{p_s})^{III}_{-1}$, both when $b(\mathbf{p_s})^{IV}_{-1}$ is introduced as additional explanatory variable into the behaviour equation (199) and when it is not (198). The difference of significance is not so pronounced in the intention equation (197), and it might be argued that this is due to the fact that the shoe manufacturers' expected buying prices (which may be presumed to determine the planned selling prices to a large extent) are partly based upon their information about the leather traders' recent selling price changes, even though they do not buy from these firms. But we prefer to follow the simplicity criterion by dropping $b(\mathbf{p_s})^{III}_{-1}$, since such a twofold determination is—because of the several substitutes—more uncertain in the present case than it was in that of the traders.[1] Our further analysis of the shoe manufacturers' selling prices will therefore be based upon the selling prices of the tanneries, not on those of the leather traders.

TABLE 6.19

SECOND SETS OF ALTERNATIVE REGRESSIONS FOR THE BALANCES OF THE SHOE MANUFACTURERS' PLANNED AND THOSE OF THEIR ACTUAL SELLING PRICES: $b(\bar{\mathbf{p}}_\mathbf{s})^{IV}$ AND $b(\mathbf{p_s})^{IV}$ (GERMAN LEATHER AND SHOE INDUSTRY, 1951–1953)

Dependent variable	$\bar{R}^2$	*Coefficients of price variables*			*Constant term*	
		selling II, lagged	*selling III, lagged*	*own selling, lagged*		
plans: $b(\bar{\mathbf{p}}_\mathbf{s})^{IV}$	0.761	0.19(0.14)	0.11(0.11)	0.36(0.10)	0.06	197
behaviour: $b(\mathbf{p_s})^{IV}$	0.662	0.48(0.15)	0.01(0.13)	.	−0.03	198
	0.675	0.37(0.16)	0.03(0.13)	0.18(0.13)	−0 03	199

6.6.3. The Tables 6.20 and 6.21 continue the series of analyses of the manufacturers' planned selling prices, the former for the tanneries, the latter for the shoe manufacturers. The variable which is retained in all regressions is, for the tanneries,

$$b(\mathbf{p_s})^{I}_{-1} \qquad \text{("selling I, lagged")};$$

and for the shoe manufacturers:

$$b(\mathbf{p_s})^{II}_{-1} \qquad \text{("selling II, lagged")}.$$

In every second regression the variable

$$b(\mathbf{p_s})_{-1} \qquad \text{("own selling, lagged")}$$

[1] The difference between $\bar{R}^2$ of analysis 197 and that of 181 is wholly due to the use of an unequal number of observations caused by the presence of $b(\mathbf{p_s})^{II}_{-2}$ in Table 6.17.

is introduced because of its partial success in Table 6.17. Experimentation takes place with

$$b(\mathbf{p_S})^{\mathrm{I}}_{-2} \qquad \text{("selling I, lagged 2 months")}$$

for the tanneries; the analogous variable in the shoe manufacturers' case, $b(\mathbf{p_S})^{\mathrm{II}}_{-2}$, seems superfluous in view of its results in Table 6.17. Further experimentation takes place with

$$b(\bar{\mathbf{p}}_{\mathbf{S}})_{-1} \qquad \text{("own selling planned, lagged")}$$

because of a possible adequacy of Koyck's method; with

$$b(\mathbf{S_A})_{-1} \qquad \text{("stock appraisal, lagged")}$$

because it is conceivable that, when stocks are considered too large, this leads to a plan of lowering (or of not raising) selling prices; and with

$$b(\mathbf{S}^*_{\mathbf{A}})_{-1} \qquad \text{("stock appraisal, distributed lag"),}$$

defined according to

$$b(\mathbf{S}^*_{\mathbf{A}}) = \frac{4b(\mathbf{S_A}) + 3b(\mathbf{S_A})_{-1} + 2b(\mathbf{S_A})_{-2} + b(\mathbf{S_A})_{-3}}{10}$$

[cf. the corresponding definitions of $b(\mathbf{S}^*)$ and $b(\mathbf{T}^*)$ in 6.4.2]. The variable $b(\mathbf{S}^*_{\mathbf{A}})_{-1}$ may be useful in view of the possibility that the appraisal of stocks has a slow and gradual influence upon planned selling prices, whereas changes in the other variables lead to a more immediate reaction.

Before proceeding to a discussion of the results, it is convenient to present the set-up for the actual selling prices. As to these, there is a difference between the two stages regarding the variable which is retained in all regressions. For the tanneries (in Table 6.22) it is

$$b(\mathbf{p_S})^{\mathrm{I}} \qquad \text{("selling I");}$$

but for the shoe manufacturers (cf. Table 6.23) we take the corresponding lagged variable:

$$b(\mathbf{p_S})^{\mathrm{II}}_{-1} \qquad \text{("selling II, lagged").}$$

This is because a lagged determination of selling prices seems to be

TABLE 6.20

ALTERNATIVE REGRESSIONS FOR THE BALANCES OF PLANNED SELLING PRICES OF THE TANNERIES: $b(\bar{\mathbf{p}}_{\mathbf{s}})^{\mathrm{II}}$ (GERMAN LEATHER AND SHOE INDUSTRY, 1951–1953)

$\bar{R}^2$	*Coefficients of price variables*				*Coefficients of other variables*		*Constant term*	
	selling I, lagged	*own selling, lagged*	*selling I, lagged 2 months*	*own selling planned, lagged*	*stock appraisal, lagged*	*stock appraisal, distributed lag*		
0.633	0.33 (0.04)	.	.	.	.	.	0.00	200
0.771	0.20 (0.05)	0.31 (0.07)	.	.	.	.	0.03	201
0.673	0.30 (0.04)	.	0.09 (0.04)	.	.	.	0.01	202
0.777	0.19 (0.05)	0.36 (0.10)	−0.03 (0.05)	.	.	.	0.04	203
0.728	0.28 (0.04)	.	.	0.31 (0.09)	.	.	0.00	204
0.763	0.20 (0.05)	0.32 (0.14)	.	−0.01 (0.17)	.	.	0.03	205
0.770	0.28 (0.04)	.	.	.	−0.50 (0.12)	.	0.08	206
0.781	0.23 (0.05)	0.18 (0.11)	.	.	−0.27 (0.18)	.	0.06	207
0.739	0.32 (0.04)	.	.	.	.	−0.34 (0.11)	0.05	208
0.790	0.21 (0.05)	0.26 (0.09)	.	.	.	−0.10 (0.13)	0.04	209

TABLE 6.21

THIRD SET OF ALTERNATIVE REGRESSIONS FOR THE BALANCES OF THE SHOE MANUFACTURERS' PLANNED SELLING PRICES: $b(\bar{\mathbf{p}}_{\mathbf{s}})^{\mathrm{IV}}$ (GERMAN LEATHER AND SHOE INDUSTRY, 1951–1953)

$\bar{R}^2$	*Coefficients of price variables*			*Coefficients of other variables*		*Constant term*	
	selling II, lagged	*own selling, lagged*	*own selling planned, lagged*	*stock appraisal, lagged*	*stock appraisal, distributed lag*		
0.769	0.30 (0.07)	.	0.39 (0.11)	.	.	0.03	210
0.765	0.29 (0.07)	0.13 (0.20)	0.27 (0.21)	.	.	0.04	211
0.746	0.34 (0.07)	.	.	−0.37 (0.12)	.	0.07	212
0.762	0.29 (0.07)	0.24 (0.14)	.	−0.18 (0.16)	.	0.07	213
0.748	0.37 (0.06)	.	.	.	−0.33 (0.11)	0.07	214
0.764	0.31 (0.07)	0.24 (0.14)	.	.	−0.17 (0.14)	0.06	215

more pronounced for the latter firms. Conversely, experimentation takes place with

$$b(\mathbf{p}_{\mathbf{s}})^{\mathrm{I}}_{-1} \qquad \text{("selling I, lagged")}$$

TABLE 6.22

ALTERNATIVE REGRESSIONS FOR THE BALANCES OF ACTUAL SELLING PRICES OF THE TANNERIES: $b(\mathbf{p_s})^{\mathrm{II}}$
(GERMAN LEATHER AND SHOE INDUSTRY, 1951–1953)

$\bar{R}^2$	*Coefficients of price variables*					*Coefficients of*	*Constant term*	
	selling I	*own selling, lagged*	*selling I, lagged*	*own selling planned*	*own selling, planned minus actual, lagged*	*stock appraisal*		
0.394	0.40(0.09)	.	.	.	.	.	–0.09	216
0.775	0.34(0.05)	0.58(0.08)	.	.	.	.	–0.03	217
0.670	0.32(0.06)	.	0.34(0.06)	.	.	.	–0.08	218
0.799	0.32(0.05)	0.44(0.10)	0.14(0.07)	.	.	.	–0.04	219
0.820	0.27(0.05)	.	.	1.03(0.12)	.	.	–0.09	220
0.837	0.29(0.05)	0.24(0.12)	.	0.70(0.20)	.	.	–0.06	221
0.721	0.25(0.06)	.	.	.	–1.02(0.15)	.	0.00	222
0.790	0.30(0.06)	0.41(0.12)	.	.	–0.41(0.23)	.	–0.01	223
0.752	0.28(0.06)	.	.	.	.	–1.27(0.18)	0.10	224
0.812	0.30(0.05)	0.36(0.11)	.	.	.	–0.65(0.25)	0.04	225
0.831	0.29(0.05)	0.24(0.12)	0.02(0.08)	0.66(0.26)	.	.	–0.07	226
0.850	0.27(0.05)	0.15(0.12)	.	0.58(0.20)	.	–0.44(0.23)	–0.01	227
0.834	0.28(0.05)	0.24(0.12)	0.13(0.06)	.	.	–0.62(0.23)	0.03	228
0.856	0.27(0.05)	0.14(0.12)	0.04(0.08)	0.48(0.26)	.	–0.46(0.24)	0.00	229

TABLE 6.23

THIRD SET OF ALTERNATIVE REGRESSIONS FOR THE BALANCES OF THE SHOE MANUFACTURERS' ACTUAL SELLING PRICES: $b(\mathbf{p_s})^{\mathrm{IV}}$
(GERMAN LEATHER AND SHOE INDUSTRY, 1951–1953)

$\bar{R}^2$	*Coefficients of price variables*					*Coefficients of*	*Constant term*	
	selling II, lagged	*own selling, lagged*	*selling II*	*own selling planned*	*own selling, planned minus actual, lagged*	*stock appraisal*		
0.829	0.14(0.08)	.	.	0.74(0.14)	.	.	–0.08	230
0.829	0.15(0.08)	–0.10(0.11)	.	0.82(0.16)	.	.	–0.08	231
0.825	0.12(0.09)	.	0.04(0.07)	0.73(0.14)	.	.	–0.07	232
0.662	0.50(0.06)	.	.	.	0.03(0.24)	.	–0.04	233
0.680	0.40(0.09)	0.22(0.13)	.	.	0.18(0.25)	.	–0.05	234
0.683	0.32(0.11)	0.23(0.13)	0.10(0.09)	.	0.23(0.26)	.	–0.04	235
0.783	0.31(0.07)	.	.	.	.	–0.52(0.13)	–0.00	236
0.780	0.33(0.07)	–0.10(0.13)	.	.	.	–0.59(0.16)	0.00	237
0.776	0.31(0.08)	.	0.01(0.08)	.	.	–0.51(0.13)	–0.00	238
0.849	0.14(0.08)	.	.	0.56(0.13)	.	–0.25(0.13)	–0 05	239
0.857	0.16(0.07)	–0.22(0.11)	.	0.65(0.16)	.	–0.36(0.14)	–0.02	240
0.836	0.13(0.08)	.	0.01(0.07)	0.56(0.17)	.	–0.24(0.14)	–0.05	241

for the tanneries, and for the shoe manufacturers:

$b(\mathbf{p_S})^{II}$ ("selling II").

Other variables are:

$b(\mathbf{p_S})_{-1}$ ("own selling, lagged")

because of Koyck's method;

$b(\bar{\mathbf{p}}_\mathbf{S})$ ("own selling planned")

because of a possible independent influence of plans on behaviour; the difference

$b(\bar{\mathbf{p}}_\mathbf{S})_{-1} - b(\mathbf{p_S})_{-1}$ ("own selling, planned minus actual, lagged"),

because it is possible that, if, for one reason or another, a plan was not carried out in the month before, this is a stimulus to carry it out now; and

$b(\mathbf{S_A})$ ("stock appraisal").

It is not necessary to introduce $b(\mathbf{S_A^*})$, since a distributed lag is already implied by the use of Koyck's variable $b(\mathbf{p_S})_{-1}$. The same is not true for the corresponding intention equations of the Tables 6.20 and 6.21, where the variables $b(\mathbf{S_A})_{-1}$ and $b(\bar{\mathbf{p}}_\mathbf{S})_{-1}$ are not introduced both at the same time.

6.6.4. A brief inspection of the Tables 6.20–6.23 is sufficient to show that the fits are in general satisfactory, especially when account is taken of the unavoidable substitutions. The correlations $\bar{R}$ exceed 0.9 in several of the analyses of the actual prices; and in those of the planned selling prices, they are not far below this level.

Considering first the planned prices, we must conclude that the lagged selling prices of the planners, $b(\mathbf{p_S})_{-1}$, is a variable which is to be accepted. Its coefficient is persistently positive and usually significant, especially for the tanneries. Our appraisal of the other experimental price variables must be much less favourable. This is especially clear for $b(\mathbf{p_S})^{I}_{-2}$ in the tanners' case, but the same is true for Koyck's variable $b(\bar{\mathbf{p}}_\mathbf{S})_{-1}$. Although the latter variable has a significant coefficient under the assumption that the planners' lagged actual selling price $[b(\mathbf{p_S})_{-1}]$ has no influence (cf. 204 and 210), this has little meaning in view of the success of $b(\mathbf{p_S})_{-1}$ in most cases when it is introduced.

Indeed, when $b(\bar{\mathbf{p}}_\mathbf{S})_{-1}$ and $b(\mathbf{p}_\mathbf{S})_{-1}$ are both introduced (cf. 205 and 211), the lagged plans become an insignificant variable; in the tanners' case it has even a negative coefficient, though far from significant. So the remaining variables for the manufacturers' plans are, apart from the retained variable (the lagged selling price of the suppliers), the planners' lagged actual selling prices and their appraisal of the size of their inventories.

Next, consider the factors determining the actual selling prices. A striking feature is the success of the corresponding plans. In Table 6.23, the first three analyses [with $b(\bar{\mathbf{p}}_\mathbf{S})$] have all rather considerably higher correlations than the next six analyses in which this variable is replaced. The same is true for the corresponding analyses for the tanneries in Table 6.22 (cf. 220–221 vs. 218–219, 222–225), although it should be added that the appraisal of stocks is not unpromising either. Since $b(\mathbf{S}_\mathbf{A})_{-1}$ and $b(\overset{*}{\mathbf{S}}_\mathbf{A})_{-1}$ in the intention equations of the earlier Tables 6.20 and 6.21 have persistently correct signs, it seems appropriate to keep both $b(\bar{\mathbf{p}}_\mathbf{S})$ and $b(\mathbf{S}_\mathbf{A})$ in the equations describing actual behaviour. But we shall disregard the lagged difference variable $b(\bar{\mathbf{p}}_\mathbf{S})_{-1} - b(\mathbf{p}_\mathbf{S})_{-1}$, for its coefficient is smaller than its standard error in all three relevant analyses (233–235) for the shoe manufacturers and even negative for the tanneries.

Various combinations are made in the final rows of the different tables. They lead us to the following choice: first, the intention equations corresponding to the analyses 207 and 213 (with Von Neumann ratios 1.87 and 1.93, respectively),

$$(6.96) \qquad b(\bar{\mathbf{p}}_\mathbf{S})^{\mathrm{II}} = 0.25\, b(\mathbf{p}_\mathbf{S})^{\mathrm{I}}_{-1} + 0.2\, b(\mathbf{p}_\mathbf{S})^{\mathrm{II}}_{-1} - 0.3\, b(\mathbf{S}_\mathbf{A})^{\mathrm{II}}_{-1}$$

$$(6.97) \qquad b(\bar{\mathbf{p}}_\mathbf{S})^{\mathrm{IV}} = 0.3\, b(\mathbf{p}_\mathbf{S})^{\mathrm{II}}_{-1} + 0.25\, b(\mathbf{p}_\mathbf{S})^{\mathrm{IV}}_{-1} - 0.2\, b(\mathbf{S}_\mathbf{A})^{\mathrm{IV}}_{-1};$$

second, the behaviour equations corresponding to the analyses 227 and 239 (with Von Neumann ratios 1.47 and 2.57, respectively),

$$(6.98) \qquad b(\mathbf{p}_\mathbf{S})^{\mathrm{II}} = 0.3\, b(\mathbf{p}_\mathbf{S})^{\mathrm{I}} + 0.15\, b(\mathbf{p}_\mathbf{S})^{\mathrm{II}}_{-1} + 0.6\, b(\bar{\mathbf{p}}_\mathbf{S})^{\mathrm{II}} - 0.4\, b(\mathbf{S}_\mathbf{A})^{\mathrm{II}}$$

$$(6.99) \qquad b(\mathbf{p}_\mathbf{S})^{\mathrm{IV}} = 0.2\, b(\mathbf{p}_\mathbf{S})^{\mathrm{II}}_{-1} + 0.6\, b(\bar{\mathbf{p}}_\mathbf{S})^{\mathrm{IV}} - 0.3\, b(\mathbf{S}_\mathbf{A})^{\mathrm{IV}}.$$

Evidently, not much is lost or gained when we replace $b(\mathbf{S}_\mathbf{A})$ in the intention equations by $b(\overset{*}{\mathbf{S}}_\mathbf{A})$.[1] As to the actual selling prices, it seems

[1] The Von Neumann ratios of the $b(\overset{*}{\mathbf{S}}_\mathbf{A})$-analyses 209 and 215 are 1.99 and 1.89, respectively.

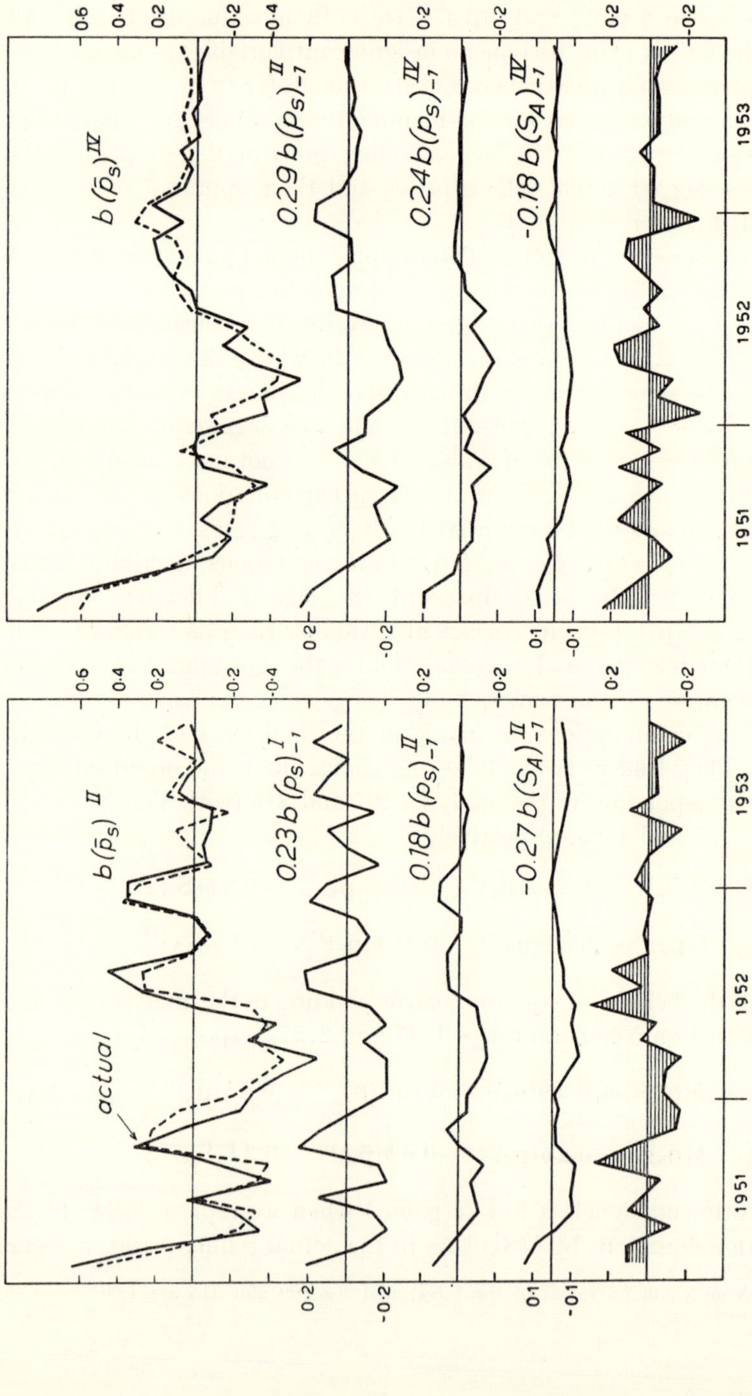

Fig. 6.8. Regressions describing the balances of the planned selling prices of the tanneries and of the shoe manufacturers: analyses 207 and 213 (German leather and shoe industry, 1951–1953)

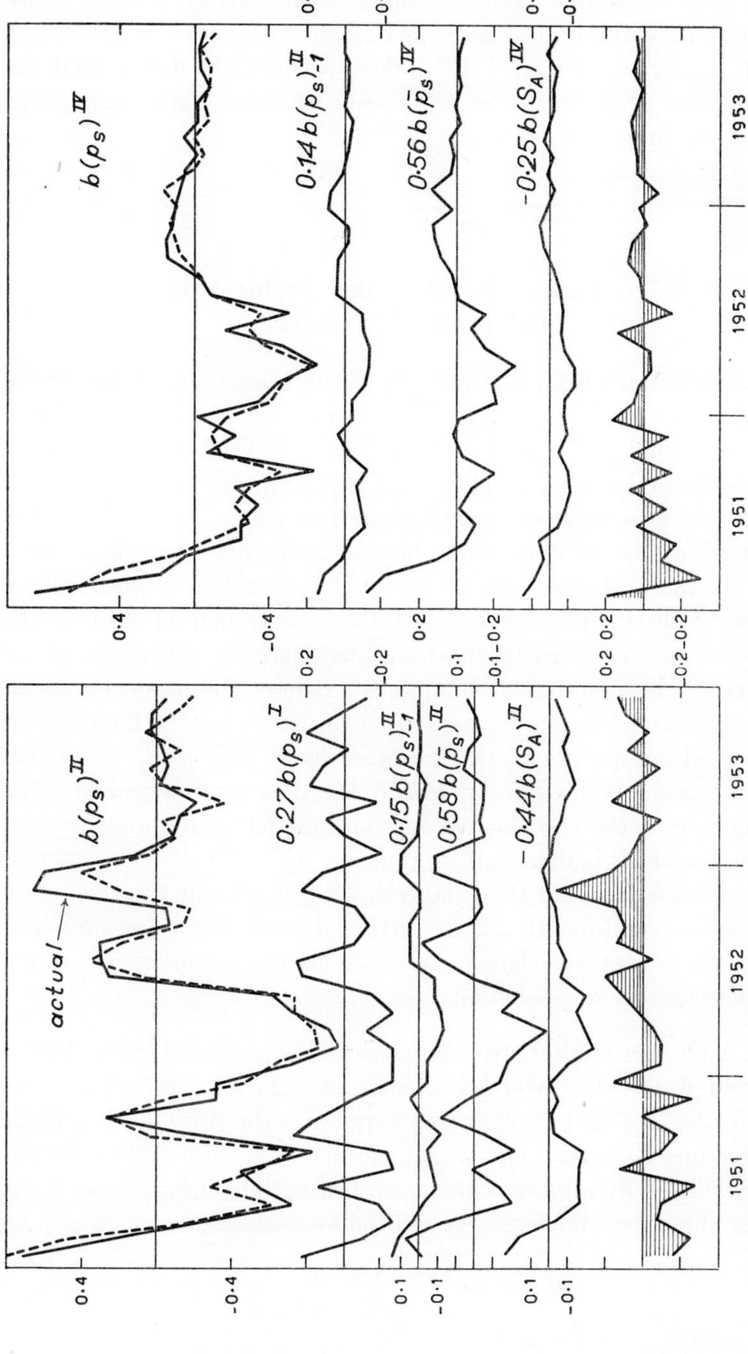

Fig. 6.9. Regressions describing the balances of the actual selling prices of the tanneries and of the shoe manufacturers: analyses 227 and 239 (German leather and shoe industry, 1951–1953)

that a lagged reaction upon suppliers' selling prices is again more pronounced for the lower stage, just as we found for the traders. A novel feature compared with the traders' pricing behaviour is that the original plans as measured by $b(\bar{\mathbf{p}}_{\mathbf{S}})$ seem to have a rather important independent influence.

The relationships (6.96)–(6.99) are sketched in the Figs. 6.8 and 6.9.

6.7. The Expected and Actual Buying Prices of the Traders in Hides

6.7.1. Finally, we must consider the factors determining the buying prices, actual as well as expected, of the traders in hides. Three analyses for the expected prices have already been presented, viz., 1, 2 and 3 in Table 6.6 of Section 6.3. They dealt with extrapolation theories and their results were bad: the correlations were small, especially for the traders whom we are considering here, $\bar{R}$ being not more than about 0.7 in all three analyses. It is conceivable that this is unavoidable because, as observed earlier in 4.1.4, the German market of hides was a very unstable one. Clearly, this may affect the possibility of describing the fluctuations in actual buying prices accurately by means of regression equations; and also, perhaps, that of describing the fluctuations in expected buying prices. On the other hand, it is also conceivable that the traders' predictions are largely based on a very simple pattern just because of the complicated mechanism that determines reality. A further analysis is therefore appropriate. This analysis is hampered, though, by the fact that the balances of the dependent variables were 1 or -1 in several months. This "hitting of the ceiling" must obviously violate the constant-variance condition on the disturbances, which underlies classical regression analysis.

6.7.2. A number of alternative regressions are presented in the Tables 6.24 and 6.25 below, which deal with expectations and realisations respectively. The first explanatory variable is the price level of hides imported into Germany. This seems reasonable because of the substantial rôle played by imported hides. No test variate information about this variable exists, however. So we need a substitute, for which we take

$$I(p_H) = \frac{p_H - (p_H)_{-1}}{(p_H)_{-1}},$$

p_H being the import price index of the traditional type; for the data used we refer to the Appendix, Section 6.F. The first-difference form $I(p_H)$ seems in reasonable accordance with the balances of our other explanatory variables. The first explanatory variables are then:

$I(p_H)$	("imported hides")
$I(p_H)_{-1}$	("imported hides, lagged")
$I(p_H)_{-2}$	("imported hides, lagged 2 months").

TABLE 6.24

SECOND SET OF ALTERNATIVE REGRESSIONS FOR THE BALANCES OF EXPECTED BUYING PRICES OF THE TRADERS IN HIDES: $b(\bar{\mathbf{p}}_{\mathbf{b}})^{\mathrm{I}}$
(GERMAN LEATHER AND SHOE INDUSTRY, 1951–1953)

$\bar{R}^2$	*Coefficients of price variables*			*Coefficients of other variables*		*Constant term*	
	imported hides, lagged	*imported hides, lagged 2 months*	*own buying, lagged*	*sales expected*	*sales, lagged*		
–0.026	1.9(1.8)	.	.	.	.	–0.06	242
0.018	3.6(2.1)	–3.2(2.0)	.	.	.	–0.07	243
0.845	.	.	.	1.33(0.10)	.	–0.05	244
0.840	.	.	.	1.34(0.11)	–0.02(0.10)	–0.05	245
0.840	–0.1(0.7)	.	.	1.34(0.10)	.	–0.05	246
0.835	–0.1(0.8)	.	.	1.34(0.11)	–0.02(0.11)	–0.05	247
0.855	.	.	0.10(0.06)	1.21(0.12)	.	–0.05	248
0.861	.	.	0.16(0.07)	1.21(0.12)	–0.17(0.11)	–0.06	249
0.857	–0.9(0.8)	.	0.14(0.07)	1.19(0.12)	.	–0.05	250

TABLE 6.25

ALTERNATIVE REGRESSIONS FOR THE BALANCES OF ACTUAL BUYING PRICES OF THE TRADERS IN HIDES: $b(\mathbf{p}_{\mathbf{b}})^{\mathrm{I}}$
(GERMAN LEATHER AND SHOE INDUSTRY, 1951–1953)

$\bar{R}^2$	*Coefficients of prices variables*				*Coefficients of other variables*		*Constant term*	
	imported hides	*imported hides, lagged*	*imported hides, lagged 2 months*	*own buying, lagged*	*sales*	*sales, lagged*		
0.155	6.5(2.3)	.	.	.	.	.	–0.03	251
0.148	7.7(2.7)	2.2(2.6)	.	.	.	.	–0.04	252
0.146	7.3(2.7)	–0.7(3.0)	–2.5(2.6)	.	.	.	–0.05	253
0.355	.	.	.	.	1.15(0.26)	.	–0.00	254
0.343	.	.	.	.	1.22(0.28)	–0.18(0.27)	–0.01	255
0.397	3.7(2.1)	.	.	.	0.98(0.27)	.	0.02	256
0.416	4.8(2.2)	.	.	.	1.09(0.27)	–0.38(0.27)	0.01	257
0.396	4.7(2.3)	.	.	0.03(0.18)	1.08(0.28)	–0.41(0.33)	0.01	258

The results are disappointing. The correction for loss of degrees of freedom makes the squared correlations in Table 6.24 for expected prices negative in one analysis (242) and positive but negligible in another (243), so that the fit is even below the level of the simple extrapolation theories (analyses 1–3). For the actual prices we do not have negative values, but $\bar{R}$ is quite small, viz., less than 0.4 (251); and the addition of lagged prices makes the correlation even smaller. Although the coefficients of $I(p_H)$ in the analyses 251–253 suggest significance, the conclusion seems reasonable that the import price level is not to be regarded as a dominant variable in the determination of the traders' buying prices. In the further analyses, therefore, this variable will play a minor rôle.

A considerably closer fit is obtained by the introduction of sales variables. For instance, if we correlate the balances of the expected buying prices of the traders in hides with their balances of expected sales, we arrive at a correlation which exceeds 0.9 (analysis 244); if we do the same with actual instead of expected variables, the correlation is about 0.6 (254). This suggests that sales expectations should be regarded as higher-order predictions which determine the expected buying prices; *vide* Section 2.3. Such an explanation seems quite reasonable, because the market of hides is a competitive one in which suppliers act as quantity adjusting rather than as price adjusting firms, so that an increased demand for hides must be expected to lead to a rise of prices. There are two objections, though. The first is that changes in demand are represented more satisfactorily by the purchases of the traders in hides than by their sales; and the correlation between the balances of their expected buying prices and those of their planned purchases is much lower, viz. 0.2, and the same is true for the corresponding actual variables (viz. 0.3). An appropriate explanation of this different outcome is perhaps that the traders' sales predictions are largely based upon general market conditions which are common to all of them, whereas their purchase plans are much more confined to their individual situation. An indication in this direction is the fact that the medians of the disconformity indices of the two sales variables are smaller than those of the corresponding purchase variables (cf. Table 4.4 in Section 4.2).

Another objection is that the correlations between prices and sales may be partly spurious. The reason is, first, that the traders' sales form a value rather than a volume variable; second, that the buying prices (the fluctuations of which they serve to "explain") have been shown to be highly correlated with the selling prices of the same month; and hence, that the buying prices are practically equivalent to the price component of sales.[1] The most satisfactory way of analysing the extent to which this is relevant is presumably the following. The spurious-correlation argument can be applied equally well to the three other sets of traders (the wholesalers and retailers in leather and in shoes). If the argument would be valid in the extreme sense that the correlation is entirely due to the price component of sales, the correlations of all four stages should be large and of comparable size. If, on the other hand, the price component does not contribute to the correlation, we should expect the correlations to decrease regularly when we approach the consumer; they should not, of course, be zero (except for sampling errors), for the propagation of the fluctuations in quantities to higher stages and that of the fluctuations in prices to lower ones must lead to a correlation between the sales of the stages III, V and VI and later values of their prices, these lags being larger for the stages close to the consumer. Hence the second hypothesis leads to the presumption of decreasing zero-lag correlations in the consumer's neighbourhood.

The actual pattern of correlations supports the second view rather than the first: the correlations between the balances of actual buying prices and those of the actual sales of the same stage are, in the order I, III, V, VI: 0.6, 0.4, 0.4, 0.0; and the analogous correlations for expected variables are: 0.9, 0.3, 0.3, 0.2. This suggests indeed that the spurious-correlation argument should not be taken too seriously. Also, we may regard this result as a further corroboration of the earlier analysis of propagation directions in Section 4.5. A graphical picture is presented in Fig. 6.10.[2] An interesting feature is that it indicates the sales of the traders in hides as a substitute for the price of a "higher" stage beyond the first.

6.7.3. Let us go back to the analyses of the Tables 6.24 and 6.25. The explanatory variables introduced in the expectation equation are [apart from $I(p_H)_{-1}$, etc.]

$$b(\overline{\mathbf{T}}) \qquad \text{("sales expected");}$$

[1] This objection can also be made to the use of sales variables in Section **6.4**; here, however, it is much more important.

[2] Stage III is omitted in Fig. **6.10**, since neither its prices nor its quantities contribute to the propagation of the actual fluctuations to an appreciable extent.

in the equation for actual buying prices:

$b(\mathbf{T})$ ("sales");

and in both equations:

$b(\mathbf{T})_{-1}$ ("sales, lagged")

$b(\mathbf{p_b})_{-1}$ ("own buying, lagged").

The last two variables are useful in the case of a lagged determination, and $b(\mathbf{p_b})_{-1}$ in particular is introduced because of its partial success in the extrapolation analyses 1–3 for expected buying prices.

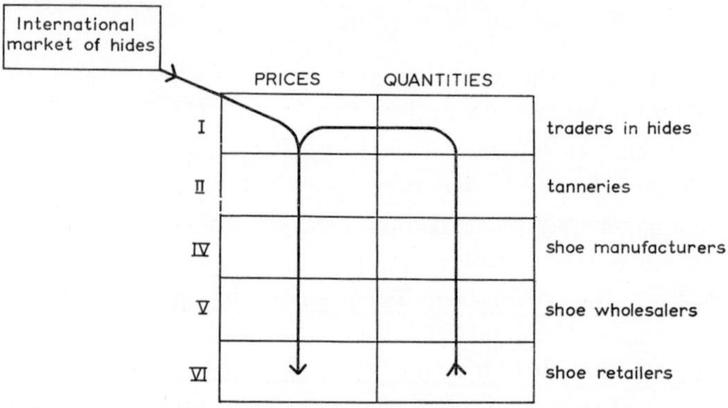

Fig. 6.10. Simplified picture of the propagation of the fluctuations in prices and quantities in the German leather and shoe industry

There is a large difference between the fit of the regressions for expected prices and that of the regressions for actual prices: the correlations of the former regressions exceed 0.9 in several analyses, whereas none of the correlations of actual buying prices exceeds 0.65. This suggests that the traders used indeed a relatively simple prediction system for a rather complicated phenomenon. Nevertheless, there is one variable, viz., the price level of imported hides, which seems significant for the actual prices but not for the expected prices (246, 247, 250, 256–258). The lagged sales are not particularly significant either (249, 257); but their equal signs in the two equations suggest that it is worth-while to accept this variable. Also, the lagged actual buying price seems to have some positive influence on the expectation for next month. Our choice is, therefore,

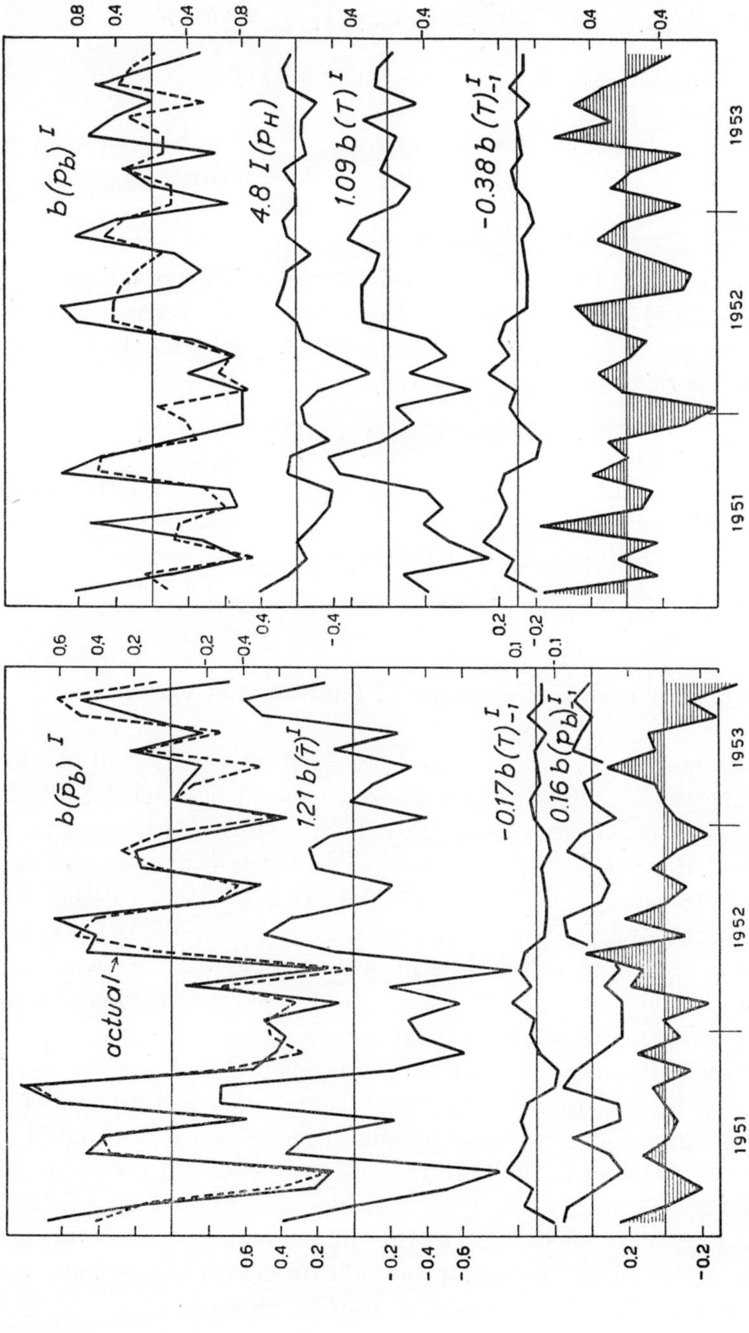

Fig. 6.11. Regressions describing the balances of expected and of actual buying prices of the traders in hides: analyses 249 and 257 (German leather and shoe industry, 1951–1953). Note the different scales of the two charts

$$(6.100) \qquad b(\bar{\mathbf{p}}_{\mathbf{b}})^{\mathrm{I}} = 0.15\, b(\mathbf{p}_{\mathbf{b}})^{\mathrm{I}}_{-1} + 1.2\, b(\overline{\mathbf{T}})^{\mathrm{I}} - 0.2\, b(\mathbf{T})^{\mathrm{I}}_{-1}$$

$$(6.101) \qquad b(\mathbf{p}_{\mathbf{b}})^{\mathrm{I}} = 5\, I(p_H) + 1.2\, b(\mathbf{T})^{\mathrm{I}} - 0.4\, b(\mathbf{T})^{\mathrm{I}}_{-1},$$

corresponding to the analyses 249 and 257 (with Von Neumann ratios 1.77 and 2.00), respectively. A picture of these analyses is presented in Fig. 6.11.

It is of some interest to note that the negative coefficients of $b(\mathbf{T})_{-1}$ can be interpreted in terms of second differences, just as we did with respect to $b(\mathbf{p}_{\mathbf{b}})_{-2}$ in the expectation equations of the buying prices of the lower stages (cf. Section 6.3). To see this, we write for the last two terms in the right-hand side of (6.100):

$$1.2\, b(\overline{\mathbf{T}})^{\mathrm{I}} - 0.2\, b(\mathbf{T})^{\mathrm{I}}_{-1} = b(\overline{\mathbf{T}})^{\mathrm{I}} + 0.2\, \{b(\overline{\mathbf{T}})^{\mathrm{I}} - b(\mathbf{T})^{\mathrm{I}}_{-1}\}.$$

So we can conclude that, given the buying prices of last month $[b(\mathbf{p}_{\mathbf{b}})_{-1}]$, these prices are expected to increase (*i*) if sales are expected to increase, and (*ii*) if sales are expected to rise more generally in the next month than they did in the present.

6.8. Conclusion; Forecasts of Facts and of Forecasts

6.8.1. By now, we have formulated preferred relations for all buying and selling prices, actual as well as expected and planned, for which test variate information is available. A brief summary of the economic features of this system follows below, after which a discussion of the statistical features is presented in 6.8.2. The relations will then be tested for the period immediately after the sample period. First, we will consider the matrix relations (in 6.8.3); after that, we will consider the relations in balances (6.8.4 and 6.8.5). The results of this testing procedure are summarised in 6.8.6.

A convenient manner of describing the system of preferred relations is provided by the use of an "arrow scheme," a tool introduced by TINBERGEN;[1] cf. Fig. 6.12. Time (in months) is measured horizontally; the various relevant variables of the successive stages of the industry are indicated vertically. Realised variables are denoted by squares, plans and expectations by circles. The circles are all placed to the left of the corresponding squares, thus indicating that predictions are

[1] Cf. J. TINBERGEN, *Econometrics* (New York, 1951), pp. 38–39.

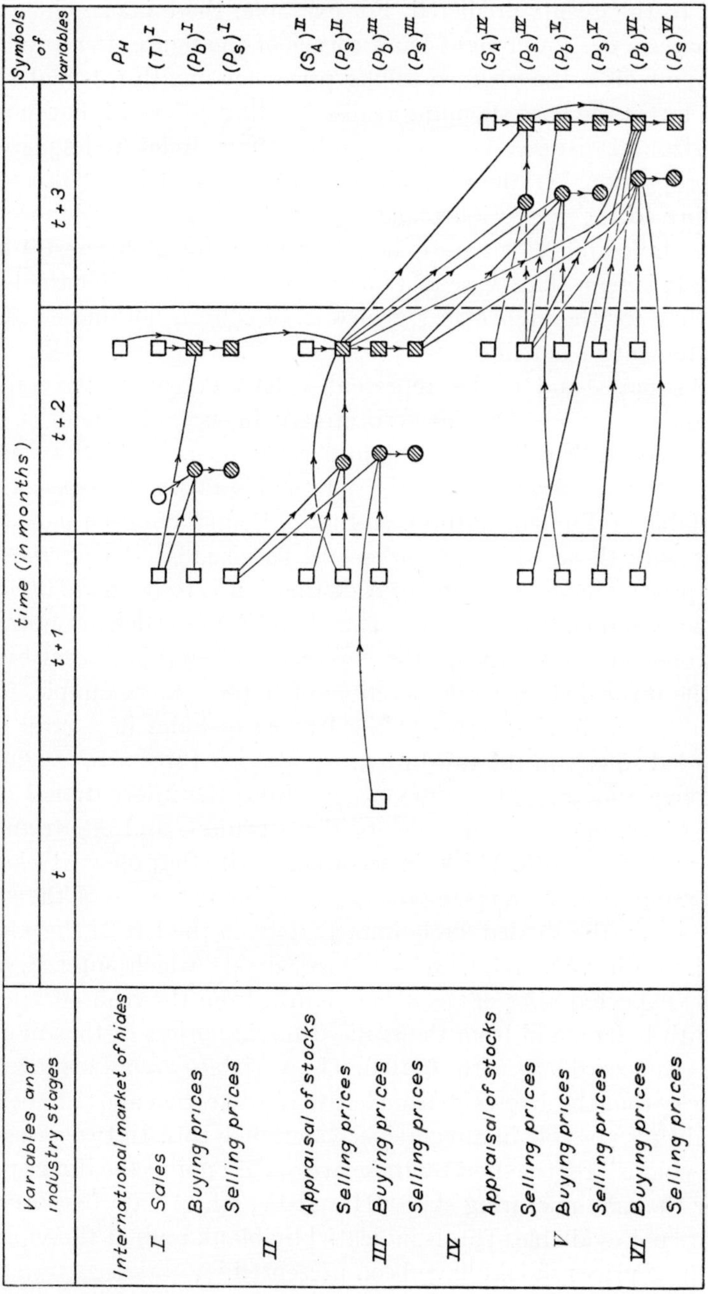

Fig. 6.12. Arrow scheme of price relationships: German leather and shoe industry, 1951–1953

"prior" to the events predicted. For example, there is one circle and one square in the lower right-hand corner of the figure, the former of which symbolises the planned selling prices for month $t + 3$ of stage VI, the latter the corresponding realised selling prices in that month. The horizontal distance between corresponding circles and squares is taken proportional to the inequality coefficient of their balance series (according to the regression plane of Fig. 4.8). A small distance between a circle and its square is hence an indicator of successful forecasting. It is seen that these distances are much smaller for the lower stages than for the higher ones, which is, of course, nothing else than a re-statement of our findings of Section 4.5.

Since squares and circles represent values taken by the various actual and predicted variables, respectively, in successive months, each intersection of a "row" and a "column" contains in principle a symbol of both categories (except of course for the appraisal of stocks, which is a variable of different nature). Not all of them have been indicated, though; only those which are necessary to visualise the price-determining process have been drawn. A distinction is to be made between the squares and circles which are shaded and those which are not. The shaded ones are "explained," the explanation being indicated by arrows; the unshaded ones are merely explanatory. For example, if we take the actual buying prices of the traders in hides in month $t + 2$ (the shaded square in the third row), we see that three arrows enter it from above and from the left, viz., one from the international price level of hides, one from the sales of these traders, and one from the sales lagged one month. This is in accordance with the preferred relation (6.101). Similarly, when taking the expected buying prices of the same set of traders (the shaded circle immediately to the left of the square in the preceding example), we see three arrows which enter it, viz., from the expected sales of the same month, from the realised sales of the month before, and from the realised buying prices of that month; which is in accordance with (6.100). The variables are all arranged in such a way that the arrows go from left to right or from above to below; this is always possible in a recursive system like this. In two cases the "causal chains" represented by these arrows are not of the direct type, viz., for the manufacturing stages II and IV, where data on purchase prices are not available. This is indicated by blank rows at those places where these prices should have been presented.[1]

[1] Relations of the Koyck type are presented in the original form; i.e., not in the derived

Several conclusions can be drawn from this summarising picture. First, there are two cases of a "separate and distinct" influence of plans on behaviour, viz., those of the manufacturers' selling prices. This is indicated by the two horizontal arrows which connect the shaded circles and squares in the months $t + 2$ and $t + 3$. In all other cases neither plans nor expectations affect "real" variables, which follows from the fact that, except for the two cases mentioned above, none of the arrows originate in circles and enter into (shaded) squares. Secondly, there are several cases of higher-order predictions. They can be divided into two groups, viz., those in which expectations affect plans, and those in which expectations affect expectations. The former group covers the determination of planned selling prices by the expected buying prices of the four sets of traders, the latter contains only one case, viz., that of the expected sales of the traders in hides affecting their expectations on purchase prices. Thirdly, there are two cases in which a judgment variable affects plans, and two other cases in which such a variable affects actual behaviour. The judgment variable is the appraisal of the size of the inventories, and the four cases belong to the two manufacturing stages. Fourthly, there are several cases of lagged determination. This follows from the numerous instances at which an arrow crosses a vertical line that separates two successive months. An interesting example is that of the dependence of the manufacturers' actual selling prices on the appraisal of their stocks in the month before, *via* their planned selling prices. If we take the preferred relations (6.98) and (6.99) for the actual selling prices, it seems that the appraisal of stocks in the present month only is effective; but if we combine them with the corresponding relations for the planned selling prices, which contain the lagged appraisal of stocks as explanatory variable, we must conclude that the appraisal of stocks in both successive months is effective, simply because the planned selling prices affect the actual ones. Finally, the arrow scheme shows that there are three different places where the quantity system influences the price system. In the simplified picture of Fig. 6.10 only one place was indicated, viz., the sales-buying price relationship of stage I. An inspection of the arrow scheme reveals that there are two others, viz., the stock appraisal—selling price relationships of the two sets of manufacturers.

form which contains the lagged dependent variable as explanatory variable. For the market relations (6.94) and (6.95) no lags beyond the first and the second order, respectively, are indicated. This differential treatment is applied because of the stronger evidence of lags for stage VI.

6.8.2. We proceed to the statistical features of the preferred relations. The discussion is simplified if we take first the matrix relations (with curvilinear amendment in some cases), the relations in balances being considered separately.

Matrix relations were employed for the description of the traders' selling prices, actual as well as planned, and for the actual buying prices of the traders in leather. It is clear from the Tables 6.13 and 6.14 that the fit of the selling price relationships is very good, which is obviously promising for prediction purposes. Further, the curvilinear amendment derived from the Figs. 6.4 and 6.5 implies that still higher correlations are obtained. As to the Von Neumann ratios of the Tables 6.13 and 6.14, a distinction should be made between those which belong to relations that are subject to the curvilinear amendment, and those which are not. There are twelve Q's which fall under the latter category, the largest of which is 2.80, the smallest 1.50, all others being concentrated in the interval (1.86, 2.57). Clearly, the hypothesis of zero autocorrelation of the disturbances need not be rejected.[1] The Q's of the other category have less validity because the specification was rejected in favour of a curvilinear one. Still, it is interesting to note that these Q's tend to be smaller: if we take the matrix relations for the fractions of increases of the stages III, V, VI, we find six Q's, the smallest being as small as 0.67, and the next four ranging from 1.30 to 1.44. This may be regarded as another indication for the appropriateness of a rejection of the rectilinear approach in these cases. The matrix relations for the actual buying prices of the leather traders are not of the same closeness of fit, and the Von Neumann ratio belonging to the fraction of increases suggests some positive autocorrelation. When viewed as a whole, however, the matrix relations do seem promising.

The eleven preferred relations in balances have multiple correlations that are decidedly lower than those of the matrix relation. An inspection of Table 6.26, in which these correlations are summarised, reveals that the lowest $\bar{R}$ is about 0.65 (for the actual buying prices of the traders in hides), the largest 0.96; the others range from 0.86 to 0.93. Although this cannot be said to be very low in comparison with many regressions based on traditional statistical data, the partial

[1] There are no constant terms in the matrix relations, but Table 6.4 can nevertheless be used for judging the adequacy of these Q's. This follows from the fact that the three explanatory variables add up to unity, so that these relations are equivalent to regressions with a constant term and two of the three original explanatory variables.

scatter diagrams of these relations, presented in the Appendix (Section 6.G), show clearly how different from the matrix relations they are in this respect. Also, several of the explanatory variables in the preferred balance relations have statistically insignificant coefficients in the analyses on which they are based. It is true, we were able to obtain more significant results by combining the analyses belonging to related processes; still, it cannot be denied that the problem of multicollinearity among explanatory variables has neither been solved nor even avoided. As to the Von Neumann ratios, when comparing these values with those of the matrix relations, we find that some positive auto-correlation among the disturbances of the balance relations is plausible. There are only two cases in which a Q exceeds or equals 2, all others being below the mean value under the null-hypothesis of independence. Still another problem is that of the constant terms, which can be regarded as trend coefficients, given the fact that balances correspond to first differences. No constant terms were introduced into the preferred relations (6.88), (6.89), ..., but they were not at all absent in the analyses on which the preferred relations are based; actually, they range from −0.06 to 0.07. No standard errors of the constant terms are available, so that it is impossible to judge their statistical significance. However, an attempt to appraise their adequacy will be made in 6.8.4 and 6.8.5, where the relations will be used for purposes of prediction.

TABLE 6.26

SUMMARY OF CORRELATIONS, VON NEUMANN RATIOS AND CONSTANT TERMS OF THE ANALYSES CORRESPONDING TO THE PREFERRED RELATIONS IN BALANCES (GERMAN LEATHER AND SHOE INDUSTRY, 1951–1953)

Preferred relation	*Dependent variable*		*Analysis*	$\bar{R}^2$	Q	*Constant term*
	balance of	*stage*				
(6.88)	$\bar{\mathbf{p}}_b$	III	15	0.737	1.98	−0.06
(6.89)	$\bar{\mathbf{p}}_b$	V	22	0.773	1.62	−0.02
			24	0.784	1.52	−0.01
(6.90)	$\bar{\mathbf{p}}_b$	VI	39	0.861	1.25	0.03
			40	0.864	1.21	0.03
(6.94)	$\mathbf{p}_b$	V	165	0.778	1.42	−0.02
(6.95)	$\mathbf{p}_b$	VI	173	0.920	1.87	0.06
(6.96)	$\bar{\mathbf{p}}_s$	II	207	0.781	1.87	0.06
(6.97)	$\bar{\mathbf{p}}_s$	IV	213	0.762	1.93	0.07
(6.98)	$\mathbf{p}_s$	II	227	0.850	1.47	−0.01
(6.99)	$\mathbf{p}_s$	IV	239	0.849	2.57	−0.05
(6.100)	$\bar{\mathbf{p}}_b$	I	249	0.861	1.77	−0.06
(6.101)	$\mathbf{p}_b$	I	257	0.416	2.00	0.01

Viewed as a whole, therefore, the relations in balances are not of the same statistical quality as the matrix relations. On the other hand, they do not compare unfavourably with traditional regressions in econometrics. This is easily seen when it is realised that balances are essentially first differences. Also, it is worth noting that the numerous turning points of the balances "to be explained" are followed rather carefully by the linear combinations of their explanatory variables. An inspection of the various diagrams of the preceding pages reveals that this is decidedly a point in their favour.

6.8.3. We proceed to consider the extent to which the preferred relations prove to be satisfactory forecasters of the data which became available after the analysis reported in the preceding sections was completed. For a survey of these data we refer to the Appendix of this chapter, Section 6.H. The predictions to be considered are all conditional forecasts, the condition being that the test variate values of the explanatory variables are as observed. They are forecasts of facts (as measured by test variates) when the dependent variable refers to behaviour or to observed exogenous variables; they are forecasts of forecasts when the dependent variable refers to plans or to expectations. In both cases, however, we shall speak of forecasts or predictions when regression predictions are discussed, and about realisations or actual values when the corresponding data to be predicted are considered, even if these data have reference to entrepreneurial plans or expectations.

Two things should be noted before we proceed to analyse the merits of these forecasts, both of which hamper the possibilities of the analysis. First, the collection of data on the traders' buying prices was discontinued in January 1955. This implies that the testing of most of the preferred relations is largely confined to the year 1954. Secondly, this testing procedure is obviously more interesting when there are sizable and varying fluctuations in the explanatory variables than in times of smaller variations. Indeed, our appraisal of the statistical quality of the preferred relations was partly based on the sharp peaks and troughs of the different variables. The year 1954 was unfortunately a rather quiet year, "no change" being very frequent, "decrease" less frequent, and "increase" very rare. Nothing can be done about this.

Fig. 6.13 gives a summarising picture of the matrix relations of the planned and actual selling prices of the four sets of traders during the

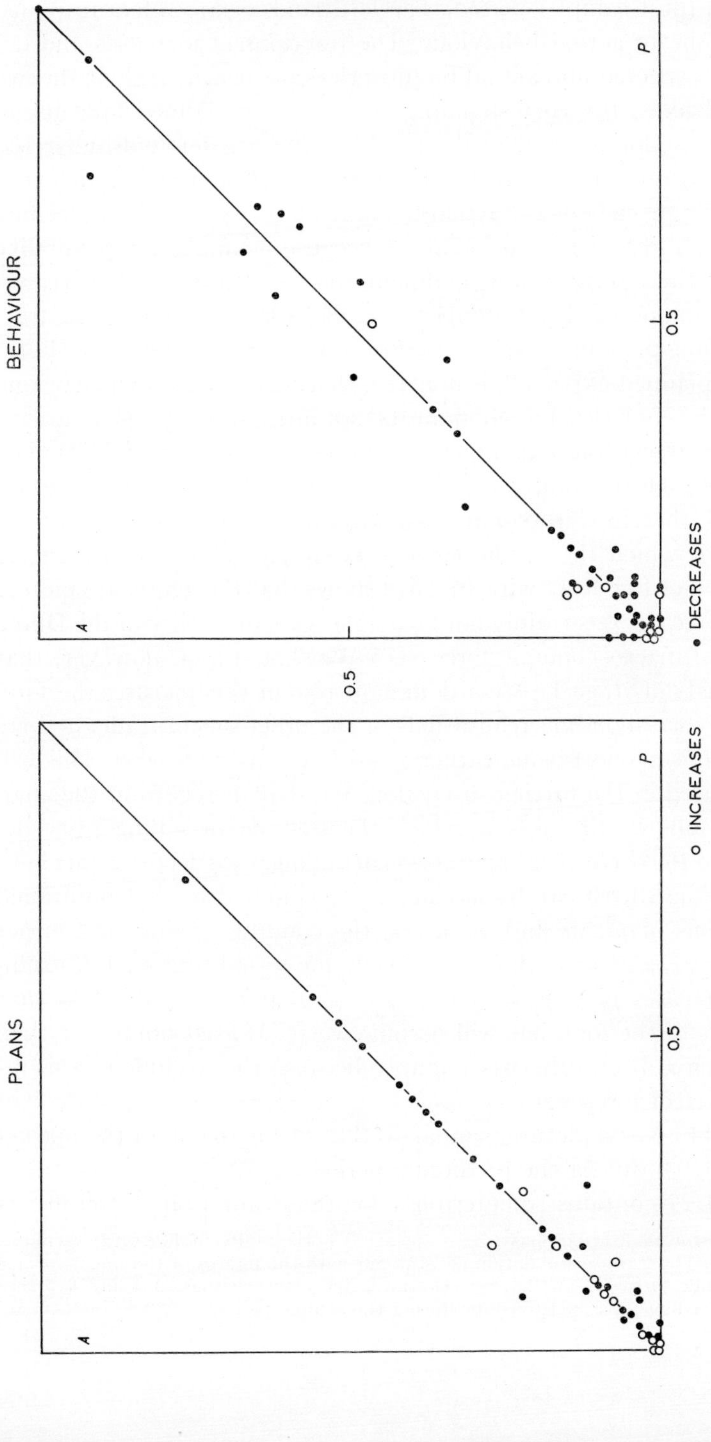

Fig. 6.13. The matrix relations of the traders' selling prices (planned and actual) during the prediction period (German leather and shoe industry, 1953–1954)

prediction (post-sample) period. The left-hand square refers to plans, the other one to actual behaviour. The fractions of increases and decreases in expected and actual buying prices are measured along the two horizontal axes, the corresponding fractions for planned and actual selling prices along the vertical axes. Increases are denoted by circles, decreases by dots. It is seen that there are very few circles, which is to be expected in view of the remarks made at the end of the preceding paragraph, and which is unfortunate because it affects the possibility of testing the curvilinear amendment for the fractions of increases. Actually, among the total number of 22 cases in which either the fraction of selling price increases, or that of buying price increases, or both, actual or planned-expected, is nonzero, there are 10 cases which belong to the traders in hides, for whom we did not introduce any curvilinearity at all. The largest fraction of increases for the three other sets of traders is 0.14, the 11 remaining fractions being smaller than 0.1. We are compelled, therefore, to confine our attention to the fractions of decreases, for which the prediction is very simple: $\overset{-3}{p}_b$ for $\overset{-3}{p}_s$, $\overset{3}{p}_b$ for $\overset{3}{p}_s$. A comparison of Fig. 6.13 with Fig. 5.2 shows that the aggregate picture of these forecasts is certainly not below the level of quality of the Dutch conditional macroeconomic forecasts.[1] We should add, however, that the forecasts of stage I play a dominant rôle in this picture, the forecasts and corresponding realisations of the other sets of traders (especially the lower ones) being rather small fractions in general. This will be elaborated in the further discussion. We shall disregard in the analysis that follows all cases in which the fraction of selling price decreases and the corresponding fraction of buying price decreases are both zero; i.e., the statistical discussion will be confined to the conditional distributions of $\overset{-3}{p}_s$, $\overset{-3}{p}_b$ and of $\overset{3}{p}_s$, $\overset{3}{p}_b$, the condition being that either $\overset{-3}{p}_s \neq 0$, or $\overset{-3}{p}_b \neq 0$, or both (and similarly for actual prices). The exclusion of the cases $\overset{-3}{p}_s = \overset{-3}{p}_b = 0$ and $\overset{3}{p}_s = \overset{3}{p}_b = 0$ implies of course that the picture of the forecasts will become worse, at least not better, than it would have been otherwise, simply because the excluded cases represent perfect forecasts.

Fig. 6.14 gives a picture, similar to that of Fig. 6.13, of the market relation (6.93) during the prediction period.

Table 6.27 contains some criteria for the evaluation of the merits

[1] Note that the realisations have been measured horizontally in Fig. 5.2, vertically in Fig. 6.13. The former convention corresponds with the figures of the unconditional macroeconomic forecasts in Chapter III, the latter with the Figs. 6.4 and 6.5 that contain the selling price relationships during the sample period.

of the forecasts. First, there is the root-mean-square prediction error,

$$s = \sqrt{\frac{1}{n}\,\Sigma(P - A)^2},$$

P being the prediction ($\bar{p}_b^3$ or p_b^3) of the corresponding realisation ($\bar{p}_s^3$, p_s^3). This root-mean-square error is compared with $\bar{s}$, the estimated standard deviation of the disturbances during the sample period. Furthermore, the table contains the number of observations n (which varies because of the varying number of cases in which the two fractions $\bar{p}_s^3$, $\bar{p}_b^3$ or p_s^3, p_b^3 are both zero), and the inequality and correlation coefficients. The results show that the root-mean-square prediction

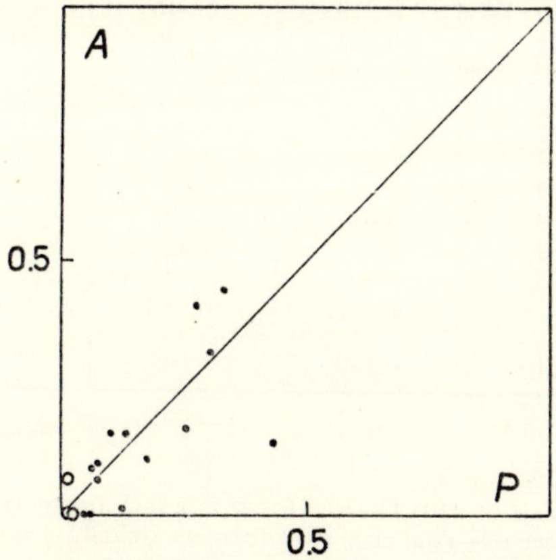

Fig. 6.14. The market relation (6.93) during the prediction period (German leather and shoe industry, 1953–1954)

errors are roughly of the same order of magnitude as the estimated standard deviations of the disturbances during the sample period [viz., about 0.05 for the selling price relationships, and two or three times larger for the market relation (6.93)]. In some cases s is decidedly smaller than $\bar{s}$. This should be ascribed, partly at least, to the fact that the fractions of the explanatory variables are mostly rather small in the prediction period, which makes the lower bounds $\bar{p}_s^3 \geq 0$, $p_s^3 \geq 0$ effective and which leads to smaller residual variance. For stage VI, for example, the fractions $\bar{p}_b^3$ range from 0 to 0.16, the fractions p_b^3 from 0 to 0.14 . As to the inequality coefficients U, furthermore, we find values that are rather small, one of them being even as small as 0.01; but for the lower stages they are larger than the corresponding values in Table 4.10 of the sample period. This, too, can be easily ascribed to the small fractions of the explanatory variables in the

TABLE 6.27

NUMBER OF OBSERVATIONS, ESTIMATED STANDARD DEVIATIONS OF THE DISTURBANCES DURING THE SAMPLE PERIOD, ROOT-MEAN-SQUARE PREDICTION ERRORS, AND INEQUALITY AND CORRELATION COEFFICIENTS FOR THE PREDICTIONS OF THE FRACTIONS OF DECREASES ACCORDING TO THE PREFERRED MATRIX RELATIONS (GERMAN LEATHER AND SHOE INDUSTRY, 1953–1954)

Industry stage	n	$\bar{s}$	s	U	r
		Planned selling prices (6.91)			
I	11	0.033	0.011	0.01	1.00
III	9	0.043	0.049	0.15	0.88
V	10	0.049	0.045	0.26	0.70
VI	14	0.044	0.020	0.13	0.88
		Actual selling prices (6.92)			
I	13	0.055	0.072	0.06	0.97
III	12	0.042	0.038	0.09	0.96
V	9	0.047	0.064	0.29	0.69
VI	13	0.047	0.028	0.28	0.66
		Market relation (6.93)			
III/II	14	0.153	0.103	0.25	0.69

TABLE 6.28

AVERAGES OF ACTUAL DATA AND PREDICTIONS, PARTIAL INEQUALITY COEFFICIENTS U_M AND BIAS PROPORTIONS U^M FOR THE PREDICTIONS OF THE FRACTIONS OF DECREASES ACCORDING TO THE PREFERRED MATRIX RELATIONS (GERMAN LEATHER AND SHOE INDUSTRY, 1953–1954)

Industry stage	$\bar{A}$	$\bar{P}$	U_M	U^M
		Planned selling prices (6.91)		
I	0.40	0.40	0.00	0.01
III	0.13	0.12	−0.04	0.05
V	0.08	0.07	−0.10	0.14
VI	0.06	0.07	0.06	0.19
		Actual selling prices (6.92)		
I	0.55	0.54	−0.01	0.03
III	0.18	0.18	0.01	0.00
V	0.09	0.07	−0.05	0.04
VI	0.04	0.05	0.10	0.12
		Market relation (6.93)		
III/II	0.16	0.17	0.04	0.02

prediction period. The correlation coefficients present a similar picture.

Table 6.28 deals with the inequality in central tendency. It contains the average values $\bar{P}$ and $\bar{A}$ during the prediction period, as well as the partial inequality coefficients U_M and the bias proportions U^M. These proportions are generally small (less than 0.1 on the average), and the partial coefficients U_M have irregular signs. This suggests that the averages $\bar{P}$ present no serious forecasting errors.

The inequality due to unequal variance and to incorrect regression slopes is considered in Table 6.29. It is seen that the partial inequality coefficient U_S is negative in all cases except two, the variance proportions being somewhat larger on the average than the bias proportions. Negativity of U_S implies, of course, that the variance of the realisations exceeds that of the predictions, which is to be expected from the hypothesis formulated in 2.5.4. Replacing U_S by U_R (which is in accordance with this hypothesis) makes the coefficient positive in all cases except three, the regression proportions being equal on the average to the variance proportions. This result is quite similar to that of Section 5.2 (cf. 5.2.3), where we analysed the conditional Dutch macroeconomic forecasts.

TABLE 6.29

STANDARD DEVIATIONS OF ACTUAL DATA AND PREDICTIONS, THE PARTIAL INEQUALITY COEFFICIENTS U_S AND U_R, AND THE VARIANCE AND REGRESSION PROPORTIONS U^S AND U^R FOR THE PREDICTIONS OF THE FRACTIONS OF DECREASES ACCORDING TO THE PREFERRED MATRIX RELATIONS

(GERMAN LEATHER AND SHOE INDUSTRY, 1953–1954)

Industry stage	s_A	s_P	U_S	U_R	U^S	U^R
			Planned selling prices (6.91)			
I	0.18	0.18	−0.01	−0.01	0.32	0.29
III	0.10	0.08	−0.05	−0.01	0.11	0.01
V	0.06	0.03	−0.15	−0.05	0.31	0.03
VI	0.03	0.04	0.03	0.05	0.05	0.18
			Actual selling prices (6.92)			
I	0.30	0.29	−0.00	0.00	0.00	0.01
III	0.13	0.13	−0.00	0.01	0.00	0.01
V	0.09	0.07	−0.08	0.04	0.09	0.02
VI	0.02	0.04	0.14	0.21	0.24	0.56
			Market relation (6.93)			
III/II	0.14	0.12	−0.04	0.06	0.03	0.06

TABLE 6.30

THE PARTIAL INEQUALITY COEFFICIENTS U_C AND U_D AND THE COVARIANCE AND DISTURBANCE PROPORTIONS U^C AND U^D FOR THE PREDICTIONS OF THE FRACTIONS OF DECREASES ACCORDING TO THE PREFERRED MATRIX RELATIONS (GERMAN LEATHER AND SHOE INDUSTRY, 1953–1954)

Industry stage	U_C	U_D	U^C	U^D
	Planned selling prices (6.91)			
I	0.01	0.01	0.68	0.70
III	0.14	0.15	0.84	0.94
V	0.19	0.24	0.55	0.83
VI	0.11	0.10	0.76	0.63
	Actual selling prices (6.92)			
I	0.06	0.06	0.97	0.96
III	0.08	0.08	1.00	0.98
V	0.27	0.28	0.88	0.95
VI	0.22	0.16	0.64	0.32
	Market relation (6.93)			
III/II	0.24	0.24	0.95	0.92

Imperfect covariation (U^C, U_C) and the regression disturbances U^D, U_D) form the subject of Table 6.30. Both the covariance proportions and the disturbance proportions are about 0.8 on the average. A summarising picture of the two sets of three proportions is presented in Fig. 6.15.

6.8.4. Our next subject is that of the predictive power of the eleven preferred relations in balances. The analysis is based on 13 observations (starting in January 1954 for plans and expectations, in December 1953 for realisations), except for the planned and actual selling prices of the two manufacturing stages, for which 30 observations are available. A picture of the development of the relevant balance series is presented in Fig. 6.16, the heavy lines of which correspond to actual development, the thin and the broken ones to alternative predictions according to the preferred relations. Three such alternative predictions have been made:

Method A. This method is straightforward: the right-hand side of the preferred relation is taken as the conditional forecast of the corresponding balance series "to be explained," with the understanding that the constant term of the preferred analysis is to be taken into consideration. Thus, for the relation (6.88) of the expected buying prices of stage III we have as conditional forecast:

$$-0.06 + 0.3\, b(\mathbf{p_b})^{\text{III}}_{-1} - 0.1\, b(\mathbf{p_b})^{\text{III}}_{-2} + 0.25\, b(\mathbf{p_s})^{\text{I}}_{-1},$$

-0.06 being the constant term of analysis 15.[1]

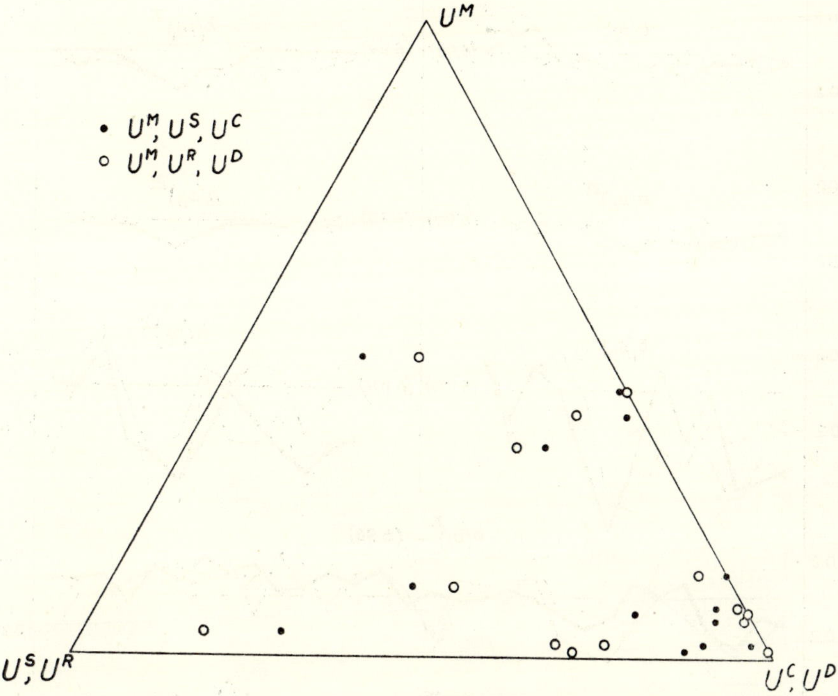

Fig. 6.15. Triangular illustration of the inequality proportions U^M, U^S, U^C and U^M, U^R, U^D for the predictions of the fractions of decreases according to the preferred matrix relations (German leather and shoe industry, 1953–1954)

Method B. Since we were not very sure about the adequacy of the constant terms (cf. the end of 6.8.2), it is useful to compare the above-mentioned method with the one in which the constant is deleted. Hence, for (6.88), we have as forecast according to Method B:

$$0.3\, b(\mathbf{p_b})^{\text{III}}_{-1} - 0.1\, b(\mathbf{p_b})^{\text{III}}_{-2} + 0.25\, b(\mathbf{p_s})^{\text{I}}_{-1}.$$

[1] In two cases [(6.89) and (6.90)] the preferred relation is based on two analyses rather than one. The average of the two constant terms has then been used; for (6.89) this average is -0.01; for (6.90), 0.03. Further, in all cases both the homogeneous linear combination of the explanatory variables and the constant term have been rounded off to the nearest multiple of 1 per cent (except when the homogeneous combination was an exact multiple of one half of 1 per cent, in which case it was not rounded off).

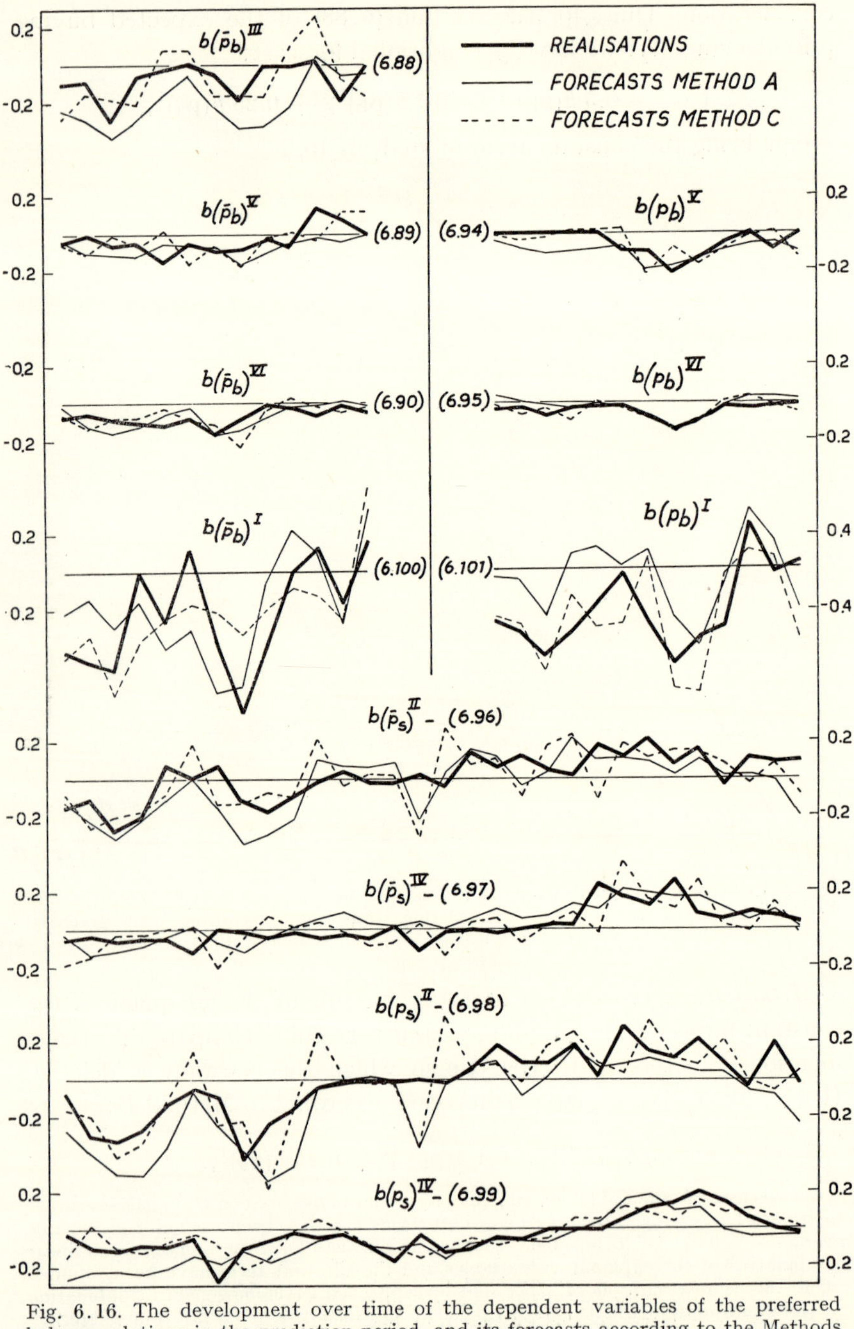

Fig. 6.16. The development over time of the dependent variables of the preferred balance relations in the prediction period, and its forecasts according to the Methods A and C (German leather and shoe industry, 1953–1956)

Method C. We were not very sure either about the absence of autocorrelation of the disturbances. Since the obvious alternative hypothesis is that of positive autocorrelation, it may be useful to predict the change in the balance rather than the balance itself. This amounts to a first-difference procedure in balances; or, given the fact that balances represent first differences themselves, to a second-difference procedure. In the case of (6.88) this predicted change is

$$0.3\, \Delta b(\mathbf{p_b})^{\mathrm{III}}_{-1} - 0.1\, \Delta b(\mathbf{p_b})^{\mathrm{III}}_{-2} + 0.25\, \Delta b(\mathbf{p_s})^{\mathrm{I}}_{-1},$$

Δ being the operator of (backward) first differences. By adding this predicted change to the lagged value of the dependent variable, $b(\bar{\mathbf{p}}_{\mathbf{b}})^{\mathrm{III}}_{-1}$, we arrive at the forecast according to Method C.[1] It will be noted that this procedure avoids the problem of constant terms.

Two of the three methods have been pictured graphically in Fig. 6.16, viz., A (the thin line) and C (the broken line). The predictions according to Method B are obtained by shifting the thin line vertically.[2] The general picture is evidently neither very bad nor very good; the forecasts are surely below the level of those of the matrix relations, which is to be expected. In particular, the figure does not show the sharp peaks and troughs that characterised the sample period. Another picture is presented by Fig. 6.17, in which the conditional forecasts are measured along the horizontal, the corresponding realisations along the vertical axes. Most of the scatters show a substantial positive—though far from perfect—correlation, especially those in the upper rows, which correspond to Method A (Method B is identical with it except for a horizontal shift);[3] but they suggest also some bias in negative direction. This will be analysed in more detail below, in 6.8.5. It is clear that the present forecasts are poorer than those of the matrix relations and also poorer than the macroeconomic forecasts of Section 5.2. We should realise, however, that this is at least partly due to the

[1] Method C for the actual buying prices of the traders in hides could have been improved by imposing the restriction that balances cannot exceed 1 or -1 (no such excesses occurred in other cases). This restriction has not been imposed.

[2] The appropriate shifts can be read from Table 6.26 above, a constant term of 0.01 corresponding with one quarter of a millimeter. For example, in the case of (6.88), where the constant term is -0.06, the B-forecasts are obtained by shifting the thin line in the upper left-hand corner of Fig. 6.16 upward by $1\frac{1}{2}$ millimeter. Only (6.101) has a different scale, implying that its B-forecasts are obtained by an upward shift of $\frac{1}{2}$ millimeter.

[3] Note that the squares of Fig. 6.17 are drawn at a larger scale than the partial scatter diagrams in the Appendix (Fig. 6.21). As to the horizontal shifts for Method B, they should be taken equal to twice the corresponding vertical shifts in Fig. 6.16.

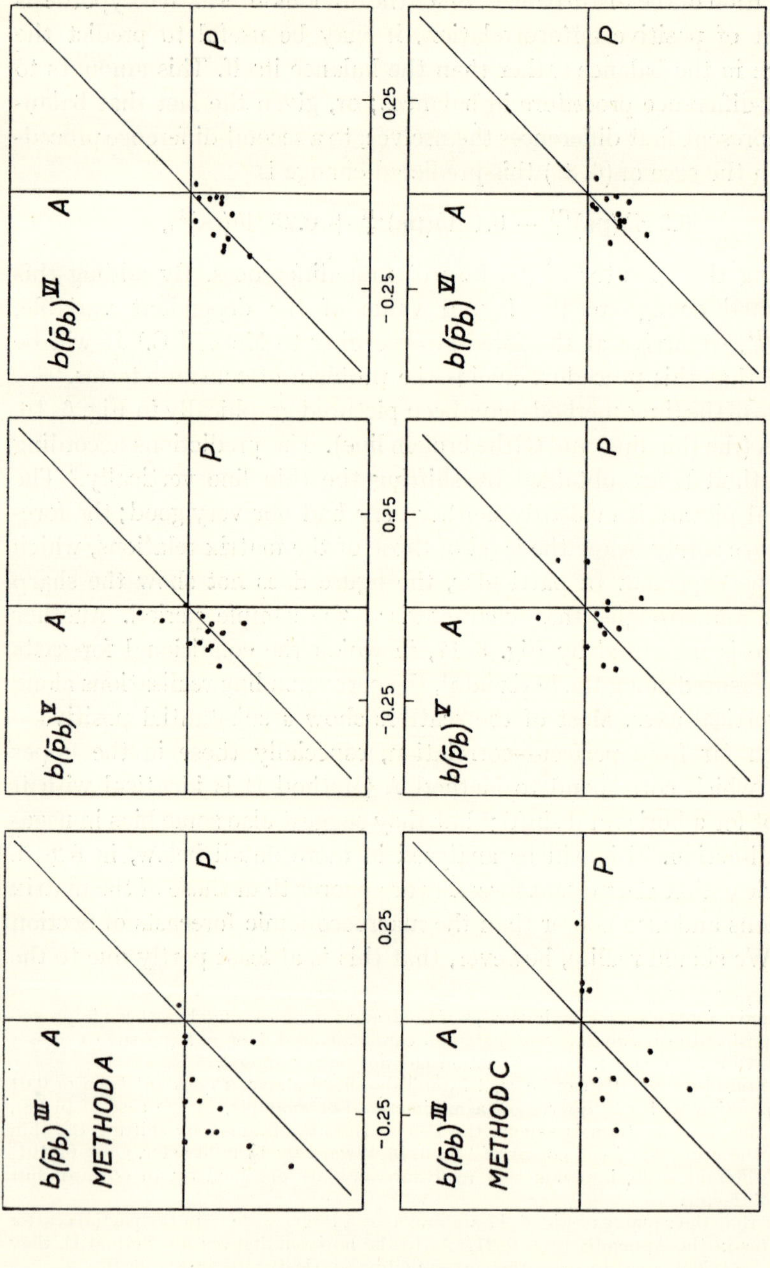

Fig. 6.17. A picture of the forecasts and realisations of the preferred balance relations. The upper row refers to Method A, the lower row to Method C. The sides of the squares are drawn at height ± 0.5, except for those which belong to the traders in hides (where ± 0.5 should be replaced by ± 1) (German leather and shoe industry, 1953–1956)

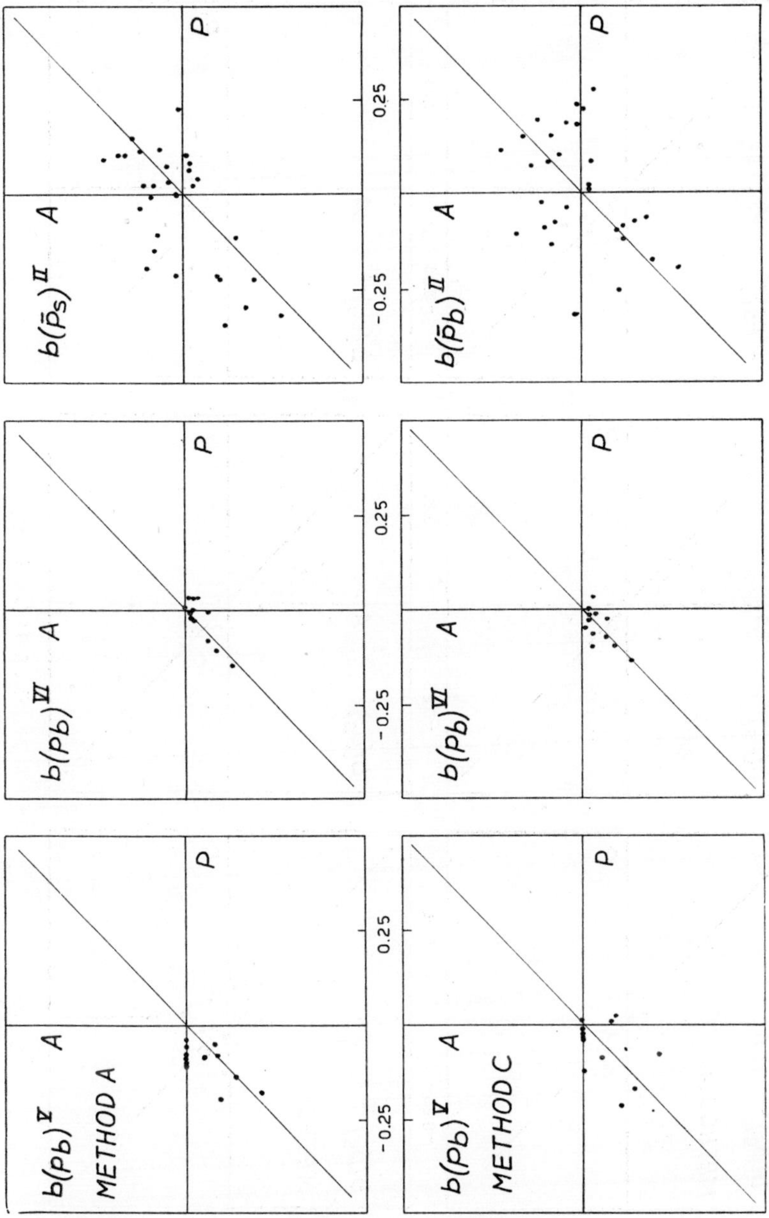

Fig. 6.17 (continued)

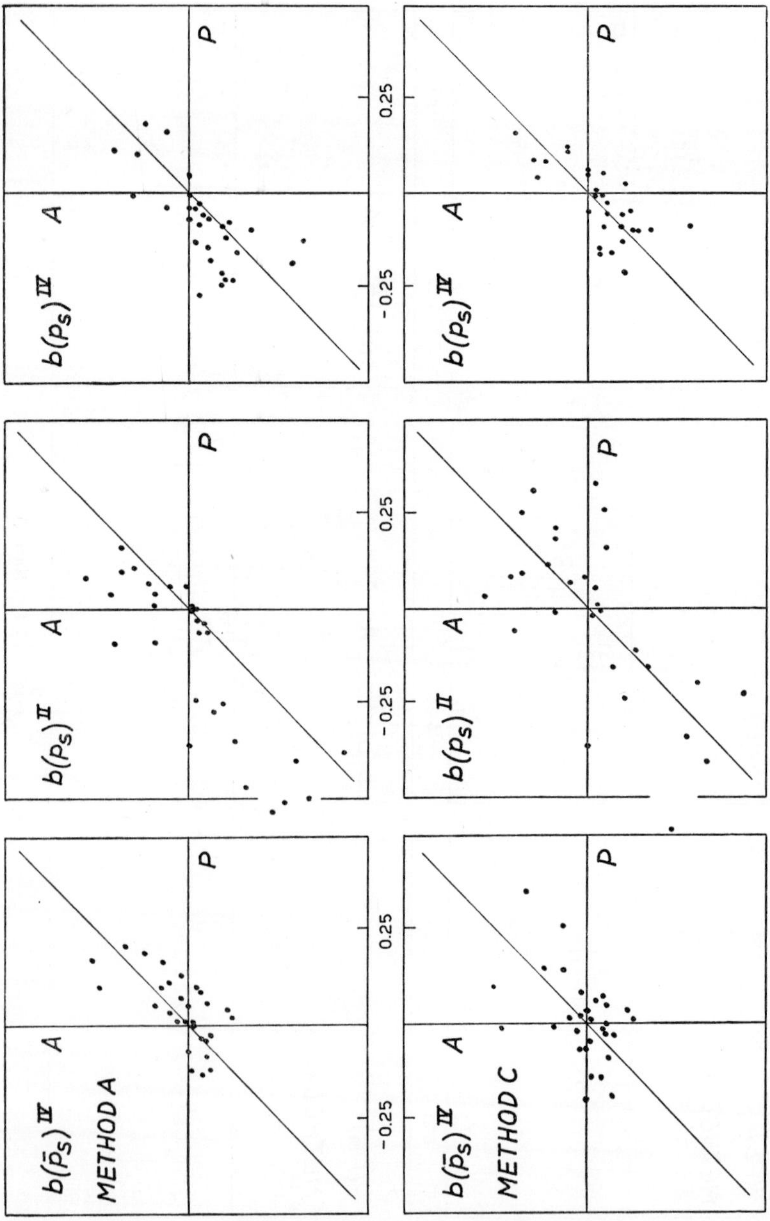

Fig. 6.17 (*continued*)

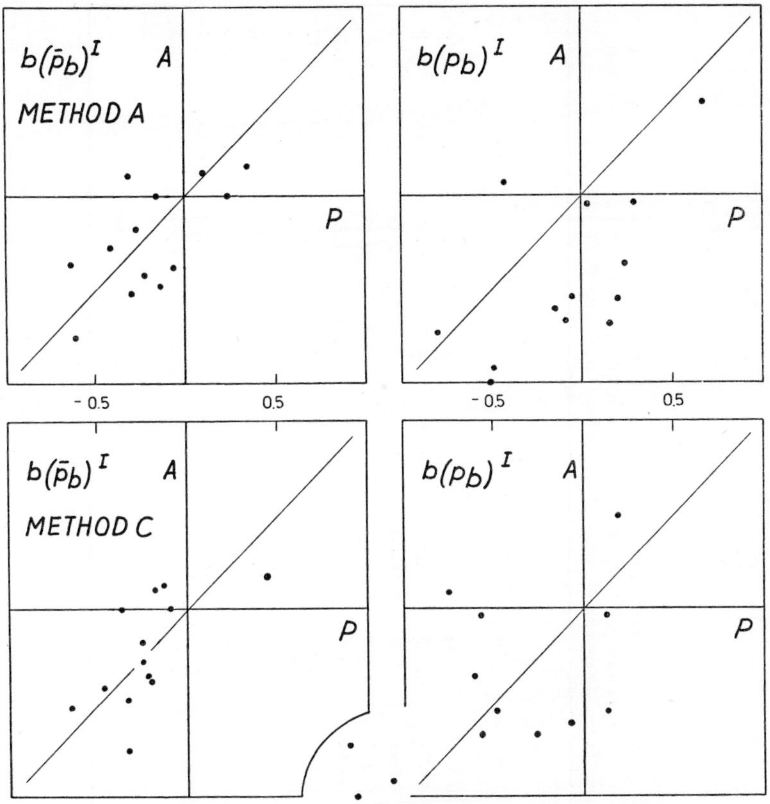

Fig. 6.17 (*concluded*)

small variations of the variables involved: if the development of the Dutch economy had been characterised by changes that are two or three times smaller than they were actually, then the conditional forecasts considered in Fig. 5.2 would have shown a much less satisfactory picture.

6.8.5. Table 6.31 contains the same information for the balance predictions as Table 6.27 for the matrix relations, but it does so for the three alternative methods A, B and C. It shows that the estimated standard deviations $\bar{s}$ of the disturbances during the sample period are about three times larger than those of the matrix relations;[1] further,

[1] For the relations (6.89) and (6.90), $\bar{s}$ has been defined as the square root of the average of the two $\bar{s}^2$'s of the underlying analyses.

TABLE 6.31

NUMBER OF OBSERVATIONS, ESTIMATED STANDARD DEVIATIONS OF THE DISTURBANCES DURING THE SAMPLE PERIOD, ROOT-MEAN-SQUARE PREDICTION ERRORS, AND INEQUALITY AND CORRELATION COEFFICIENTS FOR THREE ALTERNATIVE SETS OF PREDICTIONS ACCORDING TO THE PREFERRED RELATIONS IN BALANCES (GERMAN LEATHER AND SHOE INDUSTRY, 1953–1956)

Relation	*Dependent variable*		n	$\bar{s}$	s			U			r	
	balance of	*stage*			A	B	C	A	B	C	A, B	C
(6.88)	$\bar{\mathbf{p}}_\mathbf{b}$	III	13	0.167	0.173	0.134	0.137	0.48	0.43	0.47	0.50	0.46
(6.89)	$\bar{\mathbf{p}}_\mathbf{b}$	V	13	0.107	0.078	0.073	0.094	0.49	0.48	0.56	0.41	0.29
(6.90)	$\bar{\mathbf{p}}_\mathbf{b}$	VI	13	0.150	0.050	0.059	0.058	0.28	0.29	0.33	0.61	0.44
(6.94)	$\mathbf{p}_\mathbf{b}$	V	13	0.138	0.071	0.059	0.075	0.37	0.33	0.43	0.63	0.42
(6.95)	$\mathbf{p}_\mathbf{b}$	VI	13	0.124	0.036	0.050	0.034	0.30	0.32	0.27	0.85	0.69
(6.96)	$\bar{\mathbf{p}}_\mathbf{s}$	II	30	0.131	0.128	0.162	0.154	0.46	0.54	0.57	0.66	0.37
(6.97)	$\bar{\mathbf{p}}_\mathbf{s}$	IV	30	0.131	0.080	0.090	0.108	0.43	0.48	0.53	0.63	0.47
(6.98)	$\mathbf{p}_\mathbf{s}$	II	30	0.168	0.162	0.156	0.168	0.39	0.38	0.43	0.83	0.66
(6.99)	$\mathbf{p}_\mathbf{s}$	IV	30	0.112	0.091	0.078	0.074	0.38	0.36	0.37	0.74	0.70
(6.100)	$\bar{\mathbf{p}}_\mathbf{b}$	I	13	0.186	0.235	0.252	0.224	0.34	0.38	0.32	0.65	0.64
(6.101)	$\mathbf{p}_\mathbf{b}$	I	13	0.517	0.503	0.496	0.443	0.51	0.50	0.34	0.62	0.55
Average			.	.	.	.	.	0.40	0.41	0.42	0.65	0.52

TABLE 6.32

AVERAGES OF ACTUAL DATA AND PREDICTIONS, PARTIAL INEQUALITY COEFFICIENTS U_M AND BIAS PROPORTIONS U^M FOR THREE ALTERNATIVE SETS OF PREDICTIONS ACCORDING TO THE PREFERRED RELATIONS IN BALANCES (GERMAN LEATHER AND SHOE INDUSTRY, 1953–1956)

Relation	*Dependent variable*		$\bar{A}$	$\bar{P}$			U_M			U^M		
	balance of	*stage*		A	B	C	A	B	C	A	B	C
(6.88)	$\bar{\mathbf{p}}_\mathbf{b}$	III	−0.07	−0.20	−0.14	−0.08	−0.36	−0.22	−0.02	0.55	0.26	0.00
(6.89)	$\bar{\mathbf{p}}_\mathbf{b}$	V	−0.03	−0.07	−0.06	−0.03	−0.26	−0.20	−0.01	0.28	0.18	0.00
(6.90)	$\bar{\mathbf{p}}_\mathbf{b}$	VI	−0.07	−0.07	−0.10	−0.07	−0.01	−0.16	0.01	0.00	0.29	0.00
(6.94)	$\mathbf{p}_\mathbf{b}$	V	−0.05	−0.10	−0.08	−0.06	−0.25	−0.17	−0.03	0.48	0.25	0.01
(6.95)	$\mathbf{p}_\mathbf{b}$	VI	−0.05	−0.03	−0.09	−0.05	0.17	−0.25	−0.01	0.30	0.65	0.00
(6.96)	$\bar{\mathbf{p}}_\mathbf{s}$	II	0.01	−0.04	−0.10	0.00	−0.19	−0.37	−0.03	0.17	0.48	0.00
(6.97)	$\bar{\mathbf{p}}_\mathbf{s}$	IV	0.01	0.04	−0.03	0.01	0.12	−0.25	−0.03	0.08	0.27	0.00
(6.98)	$\mathbf{p}_\mathbf{s}$	II	−0.02	−0.13	−0.12	−0.02	−0.26	−0.24	−0.01	0.47	0.42	0.00
(6.99)	$\mathbf{p}_\mathbf{s}$	IV	−0.03	−0.08	−0.03	−0.03	−0.19	0.02	0.02	0.26	0.00	0.00
(6.100)	$\bar{\mathbf{p}}_\mathbf{b}$	I	−0.23	−0.19	−0.13	−0.23	0.05	0.15	−0.01	0.02	0.15	0.00
(6.101)	$\mathbf{p}_\mathbf{b}$	I	−0.43	−0.07	−0.08	−0.50	0.36	0.35	−0.06	0.51	0.49	0.03
Average			.	.	.	.	.	.	.	0.28	0.31	0.00

that the root-mean-square prediction errors are roughly of the same order of magnitude as the corresponding estimates $\bar{s}$. A closer inspection reveals, however, that the three root-mean-square prediction errors are uniformly smaller than their $\bar{s}$ in eight cases out of eleven. If we take all 33 root-mean-square errors and compare them with the relevant $\bar{s}$, we find that they are smaller in 27 and larger in only 6 cases. Although this aggregate outcome is obviously satisfactory from the standpoint of prediction, it should be stressed that it may be largely due to a stochastic parallelism of the following kind. Suppose that the prediction period is not only "quiet" in the sense that the explanatory variables of the regression equations show minor fluctuations, but also in the sense that the neglected variables change very little. In that case the variance of the disturbances will be reduced; an explanation which, if correct, casts some light on the applicability of the classical constant-variance assumption of regression theory.

As to the difference between the root-mean-square prediction errors according to the three competing forecasting methods, it is seen that the straightforward Method A has the lowest value ("ranks first") in 3 cases out of 11 and that it ranks last in 3 cases, that Method B ranks first in 4 cases and last in 4, and that C ranks first in 4 and last in 4 cases. A comparison of the inequality coefficients gives roughly the same picture. The differences are evidently not substantial. The correlation coefficients, however, show a clearer difference: they are uniformly smaller for C in comparison with A and B (for which they are obviously identical), the difference being slightly more than 0.1 on the average. The inequality coefficients are rather large (about 0.4 on the average for each of the three methods); this can be easily explained by pointing to the rather small variations involved. Viewed as a whole, it seems that the forecasting quality of the three competing methods is not very much different, except that C seems to be worse according to the correlation criterion. There is no evidence that C tends to be better than the other two methods for those relations that have small Von Neumann ratios.

Table 6.32 contains the averages of realisations and predictions, as well as the inequality coefficients for unequal central tendency and the bias proportions. It shows that the average of the realisations is negative in all cases except two, that Method A predicts this sign correctly in all cases except one, Method B in all cases except two, and C in all cases without exception. However, the average of the predictions tends to be more negative than the realisations justify, with the result that the partial inequality coefficient U_M is negative in about 70 per cent of all cases. Comparing the Methods A and B (which differ only by a constant), we see that the constant term employed for A brings the average $\bar{P}$ closer to $\bar{A}$ in 5 cases, and that its average $\bar{P}$ is farther from $\bar{A}$ than the $\bar{P}$ of Method B in 6 cases. Although the success of these constant terms tends to be greater for those relations which have a large constant term in the underlying analysis,[1] it is evidently impossible to say that they contribute very much to the quality of the forecasts. Still, the average level of the predictions is not without importance, for Table 6.32 shows that the bias proportions of the Methods A and B are rather substantial, their average being about 0.3. For Method C, on the other hand, the bias proportions are negligible. The results obtained so far suggest that choosing between A and B on the one hand and C on the other is largely a question of choosing between higher correlations and more accurate averages.

Table 6.33 deals with standard deviations, unequal variance and incorrect regression slopes. In most of the cases the standard deviation of the forecasts exceeds that of the realisations, so that the partial inequality coefficient U_S is positive in 8 cases out of 11 for the Methods A and B, and in 9 cases for Method C. Although the variance proportions are rather small (less than 0.1 on the average for all three methods), this effect is not without importance because of the applicability of the hypothesis of 2.5.4, which states that the standard deviations of the forecasts should be smaller. It is true, the hypothesis is not strictly applicable, since this would require knowledge of parameters rather than of point estimates. Still, it is interesting that replacing U_S by U_R leads to outcomes that are positive without exception, whereas we should have expected that they are distributed roughly symmetrically around zero. The regression proportions are larger than the variance proportions in most of the cases, their average being about 0.2 for the Methods A and B and about 0.4 for C. The larger value in the latter case is primarily due to the lower correlations of Method C, which makes the excess of s_P over rs_A larger than it would have been otherwise.

Table 6.34, finally, contains the partial inequality coefficients U_C,

[1] For the five analyses with constant terms exceeding 0.05 in absolute value, four show better predictions according to Method A. For the other six with smaller constant terms this number is only one This is, of course, hardly significant at the usual significance levels.

TABLE 6.33

STANDARD DEVIATIONS OF ACTUAL DATA AND PREDICTIONS, THE PARTIAL INEQUALITY COEFFICIENTS U_S AND U_R, AND THE VARIANCE AND REGRESSION PROPORTIONS U^S AND U^R FOR THREE ALTERNATIVE SETS OF PREDICTIONS ACCORDING TO THE PREFERRED RELATIONS IN BALANCES (GERMAN LEATHER AND SHOE INDUSTRY, 1953–1956)

Relation	Dependent variable		s_A	s_P		U_S			U_R			U^S			U^R		
	balance of	*stage*		A,B	C	A	B	C	A	B	C	A	B	C	A	B	C
(6.88)	$\bar{\mathbf{p}}_\mathbf{b}$	III	0.09	0.13	0.15	0.10	0.12	0.21	0.23	0.27	0.38	0.04	0.07	0.19	0.23	0.38	0.64
(6.89)	$\bar{\mathbf{p}}_\mathbf{b}$	V	0.07	0.04	0.09	–0.17	–0.18	0.09	0.09	0.09	0.38	0.12	0.14	0.02	0.03	0.04	0.47
(6.90)	$\bar{\mathbf{p}}_\mathbf{b}$	VI	0.04	0.06	0.06	0.13	0.11	0.13	0.21	0.19	0.26	0.21	0.15	0.16	0.59	0.42	0.62
(6.94)	$\mathbf{p}_\mathbf{b}$	V	0.07	0.05	0.07	–0.10	–0.11	0.04	0.02	0.02	0.26	0.08	0.11	0.01	0.00	0.01	0.37
(6.95)	$\mathbf{p}_\mathbf{b}$	VI	0.04	0.05	0.05	0.15	0.11	0.09	0.20	0.14	0.18	0.24	0.12	0.10	0.41	0.21	0.42
(6.96)	$\bar{\mathbf{p}}_\mathbf{s}$	II	0.12	0.15	0.15	0.13	0.12	0.13	0.28	0.26	0.40	0.08	0.05	0.05	0.36	0.23	0.50
(6.97)	$\bar{\mathbf{p}}_\mathbf{s}$	IV	0.09	0.09	0.12	0.01	0.01	0.13	0.18	0.19	0.36	0.00	0.00	0.06	0.19	0.15	0.48
(6.98)	$\mathbf{p}_\mathbf{s}$	II	0.17	0.21	0.22	0.11	0.11	0.13	0.17	0.18	0.28	0.08	0.08	0.09	0.20	0.22	0.42
(6.99)	$\mathbf{p}_\mathbf{s}$	IV	0.10	0.11	0.09	0.07	0.07	–0.02	0.17	0.19	0.12	0.03	0.04	0.00	0.21	0.28	0.11
(6.100)	$\bar{\mathbf{p}}_\mathbf{b}$	I	0.28	0.28	0.24	0.00	0.00	–0.05	0.14	0.15	0.09	0.00	0.00	0.03	0.18	0.15	0.08
(6.101)	$\mathbf{p}_\mathbf{b}$	I	0.42	0.39	0.50	–0.03	–0.03	0.06	0.13	0.13	0.20	0.00	0.00	0.03	0.07	0.07	0.36
Average			.	.	.	.	.	.	.	.	.	0.08	0.07	0.07	0.22	0.20	0.41

TABLE 6.34

THE PARTIAL INEQUALITY COEFFICIENTS U_C AND U_D AND THE COVARIANCE AND DISTURBANCE PROPORTIONS U^C AND U^D FOR THREE ALTERNATIVE SETS OF PREDICTIONS ACCORDING TO THE PREFERRED RELATIONS IN BALANCES (GERMAN LEATHER AND SHOE INDUSTRY, 1953–1956)

Relation	*Dependent variable*		U_C			U_D			U^C			U^D		
	balance of	*stage*	A	B	C	A	B	C	A	B	C	A	B	C
(6.88)	$\bar{\mathbf{p}}_\mathbf{b}$	III	0.31	0.35	0.42	0.22	0.26	0.28	0.40	0.67	0.80	0.22	0.36	0.36
(6.89)	$\bar{\mathbf{p}}_\mathbf{b}$	V	0.38	0.40	0.55	0.40	0.43	0.40	0.60	0.68	0.98	0.69	0.78	0.52
(6.90)	$\bar{\mathbf{p}}_\mathbf{b}$	VI	0.25	0.22	0.30	0.18	0.16	0.20	0.79	0.56	0.84	0.41	0.29	0.38
(6.94)	$\mathbf{p}_\mathbf{b}$	V	0.24	0.27	0.42	0.26	0.29	0.34	0.44	0.64	0.98	0.52	0.75	0.62
(6.95)	$\mathbf{p}_\mathbf{b}$	VI	0.20	0.15	0.26	0.16	0.12	0.21	0.45	0.23	0.89	0.28	0.14	0.58
(6.96)	$\bar{\mathbf{p}}_\mathbf{s}$	II	0.40	0.37	0.55	0.32	0.29	0.40	0.75	0.47	0.94	0.47	0.29	0.50
(6.97)	$\bar{\mathbf{p}}_\mathbf{s}$	IV	0.41	0.41	0.51	0.36	0.37	0.38	0.92	0.73	0.93	0.73	0.58	0.52
(6.98)	$\mathbf{p}_\mathbf{s}$	II	0.26	0.27	0.41	0.22	0.23	0.33	0.46	0.50	0.91	0.33	0.36	0.57
(6.99)	$\mathbf{p}_\mathbf{s}$	IV	0.32	0.35	0.37	0.28	0.30	0.35	0.71	0.96	0.99	0.53	0.71	0.89
(6.100)	$\bar{\mathbf{p}}_\mathbf{b}$	I	0.33	0.35	0.32	0.30	0.32	0.31	0.98	0.85	0.97	0.80	0.70	0.92
(6.101)	$\mathbf{p}_\mathbf{b}$	I	0.35	0.35	0.33	0.33	0.33	0.27	0.49	0.50	0.94	0.43	0.44	0.62
Average			.	.	.	.	.	.	0.64	0.62	0.92	0.49	0.49	0.59

U_D and their proportions U^C, U^D. Imperfect covariation is the major type of inequality, its proportion being about 0.6 on the average for the Methods A and B, and about 0.9 for C. The larger proportions U^R in comparison with U^S reduce the disturbance proportions U^D in comparison with U^C, so that the U^D's are about 0.5 on the average. Fig. 6.18 gives a picture of these proportions; a comparison with Fig. 6.15 suggests that there are some differences with the matrix predictions in favour of the latter, their proportions representing "systematic" errors being in general smaller.

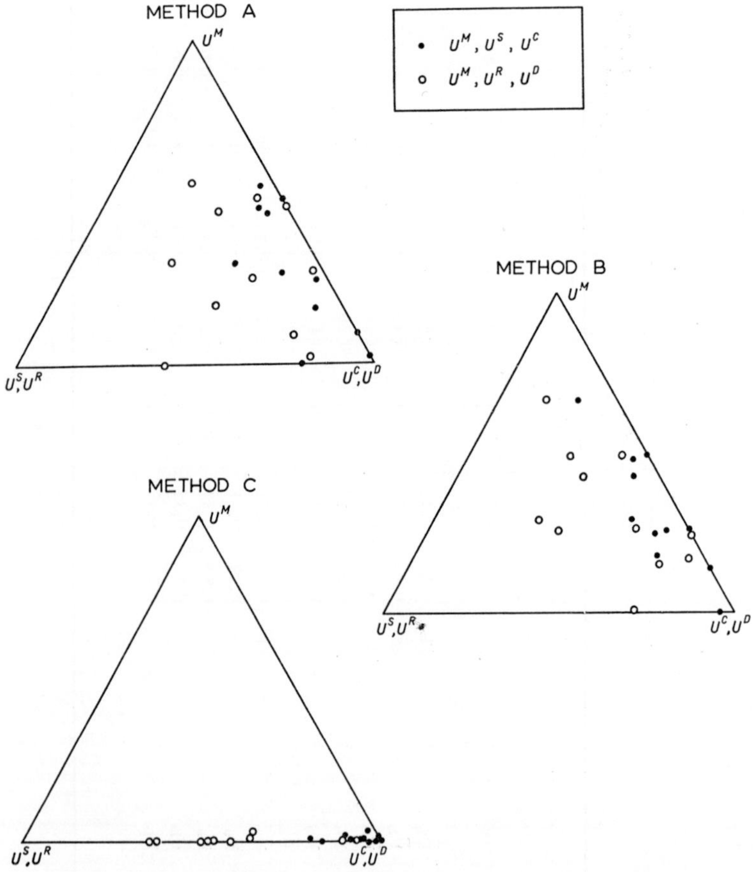

Fig. 6.18. Triangular illustration of the inequality proportions U^M, U^S, U^C and U^M, U^R, U^D for three alternative sets of predictions according to the preferred relations in balances (German leather and shoe industry, 1953–1956)

6.8.6. Looking backward, we see that the analysis has taken us from problems of methodology, *via* the estimation of relationships among plans, expectations and behaviour, to the testing of these relations in a later period. The subject of methodology will be considered again in the next two chapters, the statistics of regression and of simultaneous equations being one of their topics. The estimation carried out in this chapter is of a very simple type. Later on, we will find that this is not necessarily the best approach; but this will not invalidate the set-up for the particular case of the present chapter very much.

The economic and statistical characteristics of the estimated system have been summarised briefly in the beginning of this section; here, therefore, we can confine ourselves to the predictions for the period following the sample period. This period was short and not characterised by sizable fluctuations, which hampers our appraisal of the forecasts. Actually, the total number of forecasts is less than the number of figures which we used in order to appraise their quality. It is therefore unreasonable to stress these individual figures heavily; instead, our appraisal should be based on the aggregate picture of the tables and charts of this section. This aggregate picture, then, is not unsatisfactory. For the matrix relations, for example, we find mean-square prediction errors which are of about the same order of magnitude as the corresponding residual variances of the equations in the sample period; and by far the greater part of the inequality of forecasts and realisations is due to imperfect covariation, or alternatively, to the residual variation in the regression of realisations on predictions. For the relations in balances the estimated standard deviations of the disturbances are much larger than those of the matrix relations, so that we should expect larger prediction errors. Indeed, this is what happens; but most of the mean-squares of these errors are certainly not larger than the level suggested by the estimated variances of the disturbances. The correlations between predicted and realised balances are all positive (though smaller on the average than those of the matrix relations); and imperfect covariation and residual variation are the most prominent sources of the inaccuracy of the forecasts (though, again, they are not as prominent as they are for the matrix predictions).

On the other hand, the predictions of the balance relations show clearly some shortcomings. The merit of their constant terms is uncertain, the Von Neumann ratios of their analyses suggest some autocorrelation of the disturbances, and the forecasts show too much variation over time as well as averages that are not always satisfactory. A further analysis of the processes described in this chapter and of related behaviour patterns is obviously appropriate.

Appendix to Chapter VI

6.A. Further Notes on Business Test Methodology

6.A.1. In 6.1.3 we considered sufficient conditions on the response functions under which balances and first differences of indices are related exactly or approximately. It was also stated there that both functions can be formally regarded as cumulated distribution functions. Obviously, there is a third distribution involved in this problem, viz., that of the first differences of the underlying microvariables. In Fig. 6.19, which is otherwise similar to Fig. 6.1, this (cumulated) distribution is denoted by F.

Writing f for the density function corresponding to F and assuming

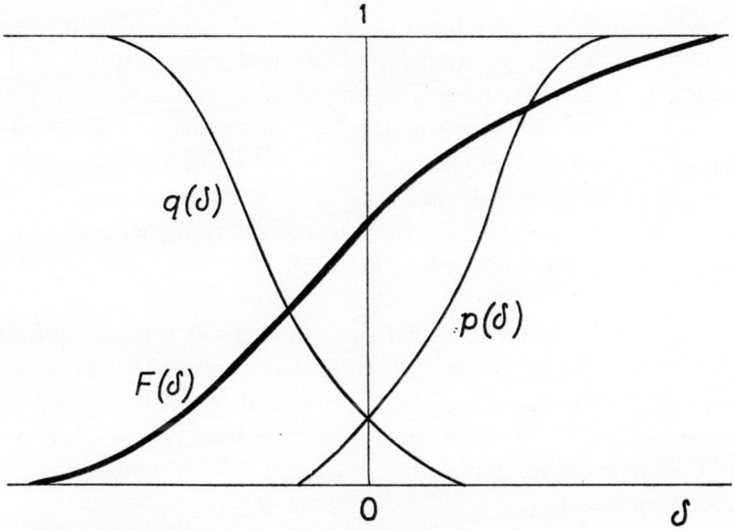

Fig. 6.19. Response functions and the cumulated frequency distribution of microchanges

continuity for p, q, f, we easily find that the fractions of increases and of decreases, respectively, are given by

$$x^1 = \int_{-\infty}^{\infty} p(\delta) f(\delta)\, d\delta; \quad x^3 = \int_{-\infty}^{\infty} q(\delta) f(\delta)\, d\delta. \tag{6.102}$$

In other words, the fraction of increases equals the mean value of "positive" response, p, the mean value being taken with respect to the distribution f; and *mutatis mutandis* for the fraction of decreases. For the balance we find

$$b(\mathbf{x}) = \int_{-\infty}^{\infty} \{p(\delta) - q(\delta)\} f(\delta)\, d\delta, \tag{6.103}$$

so that the balance is the mean value of the excess of positive over negative response. Finally, the conventional aggregate (the first difference of the index) is

$$\Delta x = \int_{-\infty}^{\infty} \delta f(\delta)\, d\delta. \tag{6.104}$$

The problem of the relation between $b(\mathbf{x})$ and Δx is then reduced to that of the relation between the two integrals of (6.103) and (6.104). As noted before, we considered in the text sufficient conditions on p and q under which this relationship is sufficiently close. It will be shown below (cf. 6.A.2) that there are also sufficient conditions on F under which this is true. Although neither set of conditions can be said to be very plausible, the mere fact that either of them is sufficient to establish this result implies that moderate deviations from these conditions do not lead in general to deviations in the relations between $b(\mathbf{x})$ and Δx which are of the same order of magnitude.

6.A.2. In order to show that there are sufficient conditions on F under which $b(\mathbf{x})$ and Δx are perfectly (and linearly) connected, we make the simplifying assumption that the variances of the two response functions are negligible; i.e., that the indifference intervals are fixed rather than stochastic.[1] This implies the existence of two nonnegative numbers a, b such that

[1] Cf. H. Theil, "On the Time Shape of Economic Microvariables and the Munich Business Test," *Review of the International Statistical Institute*, Vol. 20 (1952), pp. 105-120.

$$(6.105)\qquad \begin{aligned} p(\delta) &= 0 \text{ if } \delta < b; & q(\delta) &= 0 \text{ if } \delta > -a;\\ &= 1 \text{ if } \delta \geqq b; & &= 1 \text{ if } \delta \leqq -a. \end{aligned}$$

(Cf. Section 4.2.) Suppose then that the distribution of microchanges is rectangular, its range being constant through time. This amounts to assuming that F is represented by a straight line in Fig. 6.19, and that the F of any other pair of successive periods is found by shifting this line parallel to itself. So we may write

$$(6.106)\qquad \begin{aligned} f(\delta) &= \frac{1}{R} \text{ if } \bar{\delta} - \tfrac{1}{2}R \leqq \delta \leqq \bar{\delta} + \tfrac{1}{2}R;\\ &= 0 \text{ if } \delta < \bar{\delta} - \tfrac{1}{2}R \text{ or } > \bar{\delta} + \tfrac{1}{2}R, \end{aligned}$$

R being the range and $\bar{\delta}$ the average change:

$$(6.107)\qquad \bar{\delta} = \int_{\bar{\delta} - \frac{1}{2}R}^{\bar{\delta} + \frac{1}{2}R} \frac{\delta}{R}\, d\delta = \Delta x.$$

Applying (6.103) gives

$$(6.108)\qquad b(\mathbf{x}) = \frac{a - b + 2\bar{\delta}}{R},$$

provided that $b - \frac{1}{2}R \leqq \bar{\delta} \leqq -a + \frac{1}{2}R$, i.e., provided the range of the distribution covers the indifference interval fully. (6.108) gives a linear relation between balance and first difference of the index, which reduces to a proportionality if the indifference interval is symmetric with respect to the origin ($a = b$).

It is not difficult to proceed to more complicated cases. For example, we can assume that the response functions are polynomials in δ, which corresponds approximately with the picture of Fig. 6.19. This leads, under appropriate assumptions, to balances which are functions of the higher moments of f. However, a further analysis in this direction requires additional empirical knowledge, which is a subject that will not be pursued here.[1]

[1] For such an empirical analysis, see D. B. Jochems and H. Neudecker, "Micro-Economic Business Test Data Compared with Traditional Statistics," *Metrika*, Vol. 2 (1959), pp. 46–61.

6.A.3. To show that the matrix $\mathbf{A}$ of (6.7), when estimated according to least-squares, has the property that the sum of its rows is a row vector consisting of units, we proceed as follows. Let us write T for the number of observations, and let us define two $T \times 3$ matrices $\mathbf{X}$ and $\mathbf{Y}$ containing the observations on the $\mathbf{x}$ and $\mathbf{y}$-test vectors, respectively. (6.7) can then be written in the form $\mathbf{Y} = \mathbf{X}\mathbf{A}'$ (apart from the error term), so that the least-squares procedure gives the following estimator of the transpose of $\mathbf{A}$:

$$\mathbf{A}_e' = (\mathbf{X}'\mathbf{X})^{-1}\mathbf{X}'\mathbf{Y}; \tag{6.109}$$

and we have to show that the sum of the columns of $\mathbf{A}_e'$ is a column of unit elements. In other words, if we postmultiply $\mathbf{A}_e'$ by $\boldsymbol{\iota}$ (a column of three units), we should obtain $\boldsymbol{\iota}$:

$$\mathbf{A}_e'\boldsymbol{\iota} = (\mathbf{X}'\mathbf{X})^{-1}\mathbf{X}'\mathbf{Y}\boldsymbol{\iota} = (\mathbf{X}'\mathbf{X})^{-1}\mathbf{X}'\boldsymbol{\theta} = (\mathbf{X}'\mathbf{X})^{-1}\mathbf{X}'\mathbf{X}\boldsymbol{\iota} = \boldsymbol{\iota}.$$

The following clarifying comments can be made. First, the vector $\mathbf{Y}\boldsymbol{\iota}$ on the right of the first equation sign is equal to $\boldsymbol{\theta}$, which is a column vector consisting of T units, because each element of $\mathbf{Y}\boldsymbol{\iota}$ is the sum of all three test variates of $\mathbf{y}$ in one month and hence equal to 1. Therefore, $\mathbf{A}_e'\boldsymbol{\iota} = (\mathbf{X}'\mathbf{X})^{-1}\mathbf{X}'\boldsymbol{\theta}$. But $\boldsymbol{\theta}$ can also be written as $\mathbf{X}\boldsymbol{\iota}$ in precisely the same way as it can be written as $\mathbf{Y}\boldsymbol{\iota}$. This leads to the one-but-last expression, from which it follows immediately that $\mathbf{A}_e'\boldsymbol{\iota} = \boldsymbol{\iota}$.

6.B. Analysis of Specification Errors

6.B.1. This section contains some further results on the problems of specification analysis. First, we shall derive the expression (6.30) of 6.2.4; after that, in 6.B.2, we will consider the problem of observational errors. Third (in 6.B.3), we take the distributed-lag problems of the generalisation of KOYCK's approach. Finally, in 6.B.4, we consider the estimation under *a priori* restrictions on the parameters and the complications which arise when these restrictions happen to be incorrect.

The result (6.30) is easily derived as follows. Applying least-squares to (6.26), we find

$$\mathbf{b}_2 = (\mathbf{X}_2'\mathbf{X}_2)^{-1}\mathbf{X}_2'\mathbf{y} = (\mathbf{X}_2'\mathbf{X}_2)^{-1}\mathbf{X}_2'\mathbf{X}_1\boldsymbol{\beta} + (\mathbf{X}_2'\mathbf{X}_2)^{-1}\mathbf{X}_2'\mathbf{u}. \tag{6.110}$$

Taking mean values on both sides gives

$$\mathscr{E}\mathbf{b}_2 = \mathbf{P}\boldsymbol{\beta}_1, \tag{6.111}$$

provided $\mathbf{X}_2$ is nonstochastic; $\mathbf{P}$ has been given in (6.32). As in the text, we shall define the parameter vector $\boldsymbol{\beta}_2$ of the incorrect specification (6.26) as $\mathscr{E}\mathbf{b}_2$.

This result, though very simple, is of wide applicability in econometric analysis. One application is that of the aggregation of linear microrelations to linear macrorelations.[1] A much simpler application is the following. Suppose that (6.26) contains the same number of variables as (6.25), both being fully equivalent except for one variable; i.e., the last column of $\mathbf{X}_1$ differs from the corresponding column of $\mathbf{X}_2$. This will happen when no information concerning a relevant variable exists, so that a substitute has to be used. In such a case the two $\boldsymbol{\beta}$'s have an equal number of components and even an identical economic meaning for all components except the one corresponding to the above-mentioned variable. Still, it can be shown that in general all components are affected by the incorrect specification. For the matrix $\mathbf{P}$, which is square in this case, will now be unit matrix except for its last column; and this column will generally consist of nonzero elements. Hence

$$(\mathscr{E}\mathbf{b}_2)_\lambda = \beta_\lambda + p_{\lambda\Lambda}\beta_\Lambda \qquad (\lambda = 1, \ldots, \Lambda),$$

where $(\mathscr{E}\mathbf{b}_2)_\lambda$ and β_λ are the λ-th components of $\mathscr{E}\mathbf{b}_2$ and $\boldsymbol{\beta}_1$ respectively, and the p's are the coefficients of the auxiliary regression

$$x_\Lambda(t) = \sum_{\lambda=1}^{\Lambda-1} p_{\lambda\Lambda} x_\lambda(t) + p_{\Lambda\Lambda} x'_\Lambda(t) + \text{residual},$$

x'_Λ being the substitute for the variable x_Λ. The difference $(\mathscr{E}\mathbf{b}_2)_\lambda - \beta_\lambda = p_{\lambda\Lambda}\beta_\Lambda$ may be called the *specification bias* of the coefficient $(\mathscr{E}\mathbf{b}_2)_\lambda$. It can be easily verified that the coefficients $(\mathscr{E}\mathbf{b}_2)_1, \ldots, (\mathscr{E}\mathbf{b}_2)_{\Lambda-1}$ have no specification bias if their variables are all uncorrelated with the incorrectly specified variable x_Λ. Otherwise, however, there is such a bias in general, which is another illustration of the unfavourable consequences of multicollinearity.

[1] Cf. H. Theil, *Linear Aggregation of Economic Relations* (Amsterdam, 1954) and "Specification Errors and the Estimation of Economic Relationships," *Review of the International Statistical Institute*, Vol. 25 (1957), pp. 41–51.

6.B.2. We proceed to consider the case in which the incorrect specification is solely due to errors of observation in the explanatory variables. So we write

$$\mathbf{X}_2 = \mathbf{X}_1 + \mathbf{W}, \tag{6.112}$$

$\mathbf{W}$ being the matrix of errors. In order to simplify the analysis, we shall suppose that the errors are stochastic with zero mean, and that their simultaneous distribution is independent of the vector $\mathbf{u}_1$. In that case we may confine ourselves to conditional probability statements, the condition being that the observational errors are as they are in the sample.

Applying the general result of 6.B.1 gives then $\boldsymbol{\beta}_2 = \mathbf{P}\boldsymbol{\beta}_1$, where

$$\begin{aligned} \mathbf{P} &= (\mathbf{X}_1'\mathbf{X}_1 + \mathbf{W}'\mathbf{X}_1 + \mathbf{W}'\mathbf{W} + \mathbf{X}_1'\mathbf{W})^{-1}(\mathbf{X}_1'\mathbf{X}_1 + \mathbf{W}'\mathbf{X}_1) = \\ &= [\mathbf{I} + (\mathbf{X}_1'\mathbf{X}_1 + \mathbf{W}'\mathbf{X}_1)^{-1}(\mathbf{W}'\mathbf{W} + \mathbf{X}_1'\mathbf{W})]^{-1}, \end{aligned} \tag{6.113}$$

provided the inversion of $\mathbf{X}_1'\mathbf{X}_1 + \mathbf{W}'\mathbf{X}_1$ is not disturbed by singularity. In general, this will not be a serious problem, for we have $\mathscr{E}(\mathbf{W}'\mathbf{X}_1) = \mathbf{0}$ in the unconditional distribution where the errors are stochastic.[1] Let us then replace the matrices $\mathbf{W}'\mathbf{X}_1$ and $\mathbf{X}_1'\mathbf{W}$ by their means:

$$\mathbf{P} \approx [\mathbf{I} + (\mathbf{X}_1'\mathbf{X}_1)^{-1}\mathbf{W}'\mathbf{W}]^{-1}.$$

Expanding, we obtain an even simpler approximation:

$$\mathbf{P} \approx \mathbf{I} - (\mathbf{X}_1'\mathbf{X}_1)^{-1}\mathbf{W}'\mathbf{W}; \tag{6.114}$$

and hence, applying (6.111), we find that

$$-(\mathbf{X}_1'\mathbf{X}_1)^{-1}\mathbf{W}'\mathbf{W}\boldsymbol{\beta}_1 \ (\approx \boldsymbol{\beta}_2 - \boldsymbol{\beta}_1) \tag{6.115}$$

can be regarded as the "first-order" specification bias which results from the neglect of observational errors in least-squares estimation. The expansion (6.114) is possible only if the error moments are sufficiently small compared with the moments of the "true" explanatory variables; if this is not true, we should not have any illusions about the quality of the estimates.

Some more specific results can be obtained when it is assumed that

[1] A similar result holds if $\mathbf{X}_1$ is stochastic, the joint distribution of its elements being independent of $\mathbf{W}$. Then we should take the conditional distribution in which $\mathbf{X}_1$ is as it is in the available sample, but with $\mathbf{W}$ stochastic.

there are no current (i.e., non-lagged) correlations between the errors of different variables, in which case $\mathbf{W}'\mathbf{W}$ is a diagonal matrix.[1] If this is also true for the variables themselves, then $\mathbf{X}_1'\mathbf{X}_1$ is diagonal too; and the same holds for the matrix $-(\mathbf{X}_1'\mathbf{X}_1)^{-1}\mathbf{W}'\mathbf{W}$ by which $\boldsymbol{\beta}_1$ is premultiplied in the bias (6.115). Since the elements of the main diagonal of this matrix are between -1 and 0, it follows that the $\boldsymbol{\beta}_2$-components are biased towards zero relative to the corresponding $\boldsymbol{\beta}_1$-components. If, however, $\mathbf{X}_1'\mathbf{X}_1$ is not diagonal, then two effects occur. First, the determinant value of $(\mathbf{X}_1'\mathbf{X}_1)^{-1}\mathbf{W}'\mathbf{W}$ is increased, so that we must expect that the bias tends to be larger. Second, this matrix is no longer diagonal, which leads to relations between noncorresponding components of the parameter vectors. In the case of two explanatory variables, for example, we find, when writing all variables as deviations from their means,

$$\beta_1^* - \beta_1 \approx \frac{-1}{1 - \varrho^2}(\theta_1\beta_1 - \varrho\theta_2\beta_2) \tag{6.116}$$

$$\beta_2^* - \beta_2 \approx \frac{-1}{1 - \varrho^2}(\theta_2\beta_2 - \varrho\theta_1\beta_1), \tag{6.117}$$

where β_1 and β_2 are the components of $\boldsymbol{\beta}_1$, β_1^* and β_2^* those of $\boldsymbol{\beta}_2$, ϱ the correlation between the explanatory variables, and the θ's the ratios of error moments to the corresponding moments of the two variables; it is assumed in (6.116) and (6.117) that the latter two moments are equal, which can always be arranged by changing scales. The first effect of the nondiagonality of $\mathbf{X}_1'\mathbf{X}_1$ (that of the increased determinant value) is illustrated by the factor $1/(1 - \varrho^2)$, the other by the second term between brackets. It is not possible to specify the sign of the second effect without further assumptions concerning the signs of ϱ, β_1 and β_2.

If the errors are correlated, so that $\mathbf{W}'\mathbf{W}$ ceases to be diagonal, there is a reduction of the determinant value of $(\mathbf{X}_1'\mathbf{X}_1)^{-1}\mathbf{W}'\mathbf{W}$; but relations between noncorresponding $\boldsymbol{\beta}_1$- and $\boldsymbol{\beta}_2$-components exist even if $\mathbf{X}_1'\mathbf{X}_1$ is diagonal.

6.B.3. We turn to the problem of distributed lags that was mentioned in the last paragraph of 6.2.5. In principle, it is possible to proceed

[1] If the errors are uncorrelated in the population rather than in the sample, then $\mathbf{W}'\mathbf{W}$ is of course not diagonal; but this can be neglected, since we are only interested in first-order effects.

in the manner indicated in 6.B.1, viz., by taking (6.42) as the correct specification and (6.43) as the one which is actually used. This is, however, rather cumbersome because of the large number of moments involved. So we prefer the following related approach, which gives more specific (though less general) results.

From equation (6.40) we can derive, for an arbitrary real number ϱ,

$$(6.118) \qquad y(t) = \alpha(1-\varrho) + \beta_1 x_1(t) + \beta_2 x_2(t) + \varrho y(t-1) + \\ + (\varrho_1 - \varrho)\beta_1[x_1(t-1) + \varrho_1 x_1(t-2) + \ldots] + \\ + (\varrho_2 - \varrho)\beta_2[x_2(t-1) + \varrho_2 x_2(t-2) + \ldots] + \\ + [u(t) - \varrho u(t-1)].$$

Comparing this with (6.43), it is seen that the disturbance $u'(t)$ can be written as

$$(6.119) \qquad u'(t) = \alpha(1-\varrho) - \alpha' + (\beta_1 - \beta_1')x_1(t) + (\beta_2 - \beta_2')x_2(t) + \\ + (\varrho - \varrho')y(t-1) + (\varrho_1 - \varrho)\beta_1[x_1(t-1) + \ldots] + \\ + (\varrho_2 - \varrho)\beta_2[x_2(t-1) + \ldots] + [u(t) - \varrho u(t-1)].$$

Least-squares applied to (6.43) implies that estimation takes place in such a way that the resulting estimated disturbances of the equation have zero mean and are uncorrelated with each of the variables $x_1(t)$, $x_2(t)$, $y(t-1)$. Let us write all variables as deviations from their means; and let us denote by $C_{\lambda\lambda'}$ the product moments of $x_1(t)$, $x_2(t)$ and $y(t-1)$—indicated by the indices $\lambda, \lambda' = 1, 2, 3$, respectively—, and by $C'_{\lambda\lambda'}$ the lagged moments corresponding to any of these variables and $x_1(t-1)$ or $x_2(t-1)$ (indicated by $\lambda' = 1$ and 2). Then the least-squares implications, mentioned above, can be written in the form

$$(6.120) \qquad \begin{bmatrix} C_{11} & C_{12} & C_{13} \\ C_{21} & C_{22} & C_{23} \\ C_{31} & C_{32} & C_{33} \end{bmatrix} \begin{bmatrix} \beta_1' - \beta_1 \\ \beta_2' - \beta_2 \\ \varrho' - \varrho \end{bmatrix} \approx \beta_1(\varrho_1 - \varrho) \begin{bmatrix} C_{11}' \\ C_{21}' \\ C_{31}' \end{bmatrix} + \\ + \beta_2(\varrho_2 - \varrho) \begin{bmatrix} C_{12}' \\ C_{22}' \\ C_{32}' \end{bmatrix},$$

where lags of the second order and higher are neglected. The moments belonging to such lags are in general smaller; moreover, according to

(6.119) they are to be multiplied by powers of ϱ_1 and ϱ_2, which are numbers between 0 and 1.

Let us assume, first, that the three components of the vectors in the right-hand side of (6.120) are proportional, i.e.,

$$\begin{bmatrix} C'_{11} \\ C'_{21} \\ C'_{31} \end{bmatrix} = k \begin{bmatrix} C'_{12} \\ C'_{22} \\ C'_{32} \end{bmatrix}, \tag{6.121}$$

for some suitable scalar k. Then the right-hand side of (6.120) is a vector of zeros if we choose ϱ as

$$\varrho = \frac{k\beta_1\varrho_1 + \beta_2\varrho_2}{k\beta_1 + \beta_2}. \tag{6.122}$$

In that case we have $\beta'_1 \approx \beta_1$, $\beta'_2 \approx \beta_2$, and $\varrho' \approx \varrho$ as defined in (6.122). In general, the proportionality assumption (6.121) will be not more than a first approximation, and the same holds then for the result. If the lagged moments are close to zero, or if the difference between ϱ_1 and ϱ_2 is small, the adequacy of this assumption is not very important. If, on the other hand, there is a high degree of multicollinearity among the three variables $x_1(t)$, $x_2(t)$, $y(t-1)$, the situation is more serious because of the inversion of their matrix $[C_{\lambda\lambda'}]$; cf. (6.120).

6.B.4. We proceed to consider the possibility of using *a priori* restrictions on the parameters to be estimated.[1] Supposing that these restrictions are of the linear type, we can write them as

$$\mathbf{R}\boldsymbol{\beta} = \mathbf{r}, \tag{6.123}$$

where $\mathbf{R}$ and $\mathbf{r}$ are matrices of known numbers and $\boldsymbol{\beta}$ is the parameter vector of $\mathbf{y} = \mathbf{X}\boldsymbol{\beta} + \mathbf{u}$. We suppose that the assumptions (*i*), (*ii*), (*iii*), (*v*) of 6.2.3 and 6.2.5 are satisfied; furthermore, that the rank of $\mathbf{R}$ is equal to the number of its rows but smaller than Λ.

The obvious generalisation of least-squares is to estimate such as to minimise the second moment of the estimated disturbances, subject to the restriction (6.123) with $\boldsymbol{\beta}$ replaced by its estimator. A straightforward procedure is to eliminate part of the $\boldsymbol{\beta}$-components and to

[1] Note that the estimation procedure considered here assumes that these restrictions are exact, contrary to the case of mixed estimation considered in 6.2.8.

apply least-squares in its original form; for example, if $y = \beta_1 x_1 + \beta_2 x_2 + u$ is the equation and $\beta_2 = 2\beta_1 + 1$ the restriction, we can replace the equation by $(y - x_2) = \beta_1(x_1 + 2x_2) + u$ and take $(y - x_2)$ as the dependent and $(x_1 + 2x_2)$ as the explanatory variable. For an analysis of specification errors in the restrictions, however, it is more convenient to consider the following derivation. We introduce a vector of Lagrange multipliers, $\boldsymbol{\mu}$, and consider the extremum of

$$(\mathbf{y} - \mathbf{X}\mathbf{b})'(\mathbf{y} - \mathbf{X}\mathbf{b}) - \boldsymbol{\mu}'(\mathbf{R}\mathbf{b} - \mathbf{r}).$$

Minimisation gives

$$-2\mathbf{X}'\mathbf{y} + 2\mathbf{X}'\mathbf{X}\mathbf{b}_0 - \mathbf{R}'\boldsymbol{\mu} = \mathbf{0}, \tag{6.124}$$

$\mathbf{b}_0$ being the required estimator. When premultiplying (6.124) by $\mathbf{R}(\mathbf{X}'\mathbf{X})^{-1}$ and using $\mathbf{R}\mathbf{b}_0 = \mathbf{r}$, we obtain an expression for $\boldsymbol{\mu}$; and inserting this into (6.124), we find

$$\mathbf{b}_0 = \mathbf{b} + (\mathbf{X}'\mathbf{X})^{-1}\mathbf{R}'[\mathbf{R}(\mathbf{X}'\mathbf{X})^{-1}\mathbf{R}']^{-1}(\mathbf{r} - \mathbf{R}\mathbf{b}), \tag{6.125}$$

$\mathbf{b} = (\mathbf{X}'\mathbf{X})^{-1}\mathbf{X}'\mathbf{y}$ being the unrestricted least-squares estimator. This result implies that the difference between $\mathbf{b}_0$ and $\mathbf{b}$ is a homogeneous linear combination of the degree to which the unrestricted least-squares estimator fails to satisfy the *a priori* restrictions.

The sampling error of the restricted least-squares estimator is

$$\mathbf{b}_0 - \boldsymbol{\beta} = \{\mathbf{I} - (\mathbf{X}'\mathbf{X})^{-1}\mathbf{R}'[\mathbf{R}(\mathbf{X}'\mathbf{X})^{-1}\mathbf{R}']^{-1}\mathbf{R}\}(\mathbf{X}'\mathbf{X})^{-1}\mathbf{X}'\mathbf{u}, \tag{6.126}$$

whence it follows that the covariance matrix is

$$\begin{aligned} &\mathscr{E}[(\mathbf{b}_0 - \boldsymbol{\beta})(\mathbf{b}_0 - \boldsymbol{\beta})'] = \\ &= \sigma^2(\mathbf{X}'\mathbf{X})^{-1}\{\mathbf{I} - \mathbf{R}'[\mathbf{R}(\mathbf{X}'\mathbf{X})^{-1}\mathbf{R}']^{-1}\mathbf{R}(\mathbf{X}'\mathbf{X})^{-1}\} \\ &= \mathbf{V} - \mathbf{V}\mathbf{R}'(\mathbf{R}\mathbf{V}\mathbf{R}')^{-1}\mathbf{R}\mathbf{V}, \end{aligned} \tag{6.127}$$

$\mathbf{V} = \sigma^2(\mathbf{X}'\mathbf{X})^{-1}$ being the covariance matrix of the unrestricted least-squares estimator. It is seen that the matrix of $\mathbf{b}_0$ is obtained from $\mathbf{V}$ by deducting a positive semi-definite matrix.

Suppose, however, that some or all of the restrictions (6.123) are incorrect; i.e., that the investigator thinks that (6.123) is correct, whereas in fact

$$\mathbf{R}\boldsymbol{\beta} = \bar{\mathbf{r}},\ \bar{\mathbf{r}} \neq \mathbf{r}. \tag{6.128}$$

One might think that it is then preferable to abandon (6.123) altogether. This, however, is not correct. Whether the restricted least-squares estimator, based on (6.123), is superior or inferior depends, firstly, on the criterion chosen; secondly, on the difference $\mathbf{\Delta r} = \mathbf{r} - \bar{\mathbf{r}}$; thirdly, on some other factors, to be described below.[1] To specify the criterion, we shall consider the moment matrix of the restricted least-squares estimator around $\boldsymbol{\beta}$; this choice will be justified in Chapter VIII (Section 8.5).

The restricted estimator is then given by (6.125), as before; but it is no longer unbiased as (6.126) indicates, because its sampling error is now

$$\text{(6.129)} \qquad \mathbf{b}_0 - \boldsymbol{\beta} = (\mathbf{X'X})^{-1}\mathbf{R'}[\mathbf{R}(\mathbf{X'X})^{-1}\mathbf{R'}]^{-1}\mathbf{\Delta r} + \\ + \{\mathbf{I} - (\mathbf{X'X})^{-1}\mathbf{R'}[\mathbf{R}(\mathbf{X'X})^{-1}\mathbf{R'}]^{-1}\mathbf{R}\}(\mathbf{X'X})^{-1}\mathbf{X'u};$$

and the moment matrix is

$$\text{(6.130)} \qquad \mathscr{E}[(\mathbf{b}_0 - \boldsymbol{\beta})(\mathbf{b}_0 - \boldsymbol{\beta})'] = \sigma^2(\mathbf{X'X})^{-1} - \\ -(\mathbf{X'X})^{-1}\mathbf{R'}[\mathbf{R}(\mathbf{X'X})^{-1}\mathbf{R'}]^{-1}\{\sigma^2\mathbf{I} - \mathbf{\Delta r \Delta r'}[\mathbf{R}(\mathbf{X'X})^{-1}\mathbf{R'}]^{-1}\}\mathbf{R}(\mathbf{X'X})^{-1}.$$

The difference between the moment matrix and the least-squares covariance matrix is no longer semi-definite. Instead, we find that this difference is primarily determined by the matrix in curled brackets, viz.

$$\sigma^2\mathbf{I} - \mathbf{\Delta r \Delta r'}[\mathbf{R}(\mathbf{X'X})^{-1}\mathbf{R'}]^{-1}.$$

A little reflection suggests that a good fit of the least-squares regression (i.e., a small σ^2) pushes the elements of this matrix in negative direction, so that the unrestricted variant tends then to be preferable. Similarly, if the number of observations is large, so that $(\mathbf{X'X})^{-1}$ consists of small elements and hence $[\mathbf{R}(\mathbf{X'X})^{-1}\mathbf{R'}]^{-1}$ of large elements, the restricted variant tends to be dominated by the unrestricted variant. On the other hand, if there is a considerable degree of multicollinearity, so that $(\mathbf{X'X})^{-1}$ consists of large and $[\mathbf{R}(\mathbf{X'X})^{-1}\mathbf{R'}]^{-1}$ of small elements, the restricted variant tends to be better.

As an example, we consider the relation

$$\text{(6.131)} \qquad y(t) = \alpha + \beta_1 x_1(t) + \beta_2 x_2(t) + u(t),$$

[1] If something is known about the order of magnitude of $\mathbf{\Delta r}$, the mixed estimation procedure is preferable. Here, however, we consider the case in which (6.128) is accepted as exact (but erroneously, of course).

the restriction being $\beta_1 = r$; hence $\mathbf{R} = [1 \quad 0]$. If we standardise the three variables (zero mean, unit variance) and write ϱ for the correlation between x_1 and x_2, the moment matrix according to (6.130) becomes

$$\text{(6.132)} \qquad \frac{\sigma^2}{(1-\varrho^2)T}\begin{bmatrix} 1 & -\varrho \\ -\varrho & 1 \end{bmatrix} - \frac{\sigma^2 - (\Delta r)^2(1-\varrho^2)T}{(1-\varrho^2)T}\begin{bmatrix} 1 & -\varrho \\ -\varrho & \varrho^2 \end{bmatrix}.$$

Hence the second moment of the β_1-estimator is

$$\frac{\sigma^2}{(1-\varrho^2)T} - \frac{\sigma^2}{(1-\varrho^2)T} + (\Delta r)^2 = (\Delta r)^2,$$

which is a trivial, though not useless, result. If the specification error Δr is small, σ^2 large, ϱ^2 large and T small, the restricted estimator (= the *a priori* value $\beta_1 = r$) may be preferable in spite of the incorrectness of the restriction. For the moment of the β_2-estimator we read from (6.132):

$$\frac{\sigma^2}{(1-\varrho^2)T} - \frac{\sigma^2\varrho^2}{(1-\varrho^2)T} + (\Delta r)^2\varrho^2 = \frac{\sigma^2}{T} + (\Delta r)^2\varrho^2.$$

If $\varrho = 0$, the alternative β_2-estimators are identical and Δr does not affect the restricted estimator. When ϱ^2 increases, both the variance of unrestricted least-squares and the second moment of restricted least-squares increase. Which of these moments increases faster depends on the ratio of $(\Delta r)^2$ to σ^2/T; but for sufficiently large ϱ^2 the variance $\sigma^2/(1-\varrho^2)T$ will increase more rapidly, due to the factor $1-\varrho^2$ in the denominator.

6.C. The Estimation of Simultaneous Equations

6.C.1. This section presents a superstructure built upon the analysis of 6.2.7. The order of discussion is as follows. After a brief summarising picture of the estimation method proposed (the k-class) for a linear equation system as a whole, we pass in 6.C.2 to some alternative approaches which all lead to two-stage least-squares, as well as to a computationally simpler method for the case of just-identification. Some further extensions are presented in 6.C.3, after which simultaneous equations with autocorrelated disturbances are considered in 6.C.4. In 6.C.5 the coefficient of trace correlation is considered; it measures the extent to which the variation in all jointly dependent variables is accounted for by the set of all predetermined variables. In 6.C.6 some small-sample properties of the k-class are considered, while in 6.C.7 some alternative estimation methods are mentioned.

Consider a linear equation system,

$$\mathbf{\Gamma y}(t) + \mathbf{Bx}(t) = \mathbf{u}(t), \qquad (t = 1, \ldots, T) \tag{6.133}$$

where $\mathbf{\Gamma}$ and $\mathbf{B}$ are matrices of parameters (the former square and non-singular), and where $\mathbf{y}(t)$ is one of the T column vector of values assumed by all M jointly dependent variables, $\mathbf{x}(t)$ a column vector of values taken by all predetermined variables, and $\mathbf{u}(t)$ a disturbance vector, each component of this vector corresponding to one of the M equations. In general, of course, a great many elements of $\mathbf{\Gamma}$, $\mathbf{B}$ are *a priori* supposed to be zero.

So far, we considered only one equation of such a system; in other words, we confined the estimation to only one row of $\mathbf{\Gamma}$, $\mathbf{B}$. There are "full-information" maximum-likelihood methods for the estimation of the parameters of several or all equations simultaneously;[1] we shall come back to this subject at the end of this section. Of course, the class proposed in 6.2.7 can be used for the estimation of all equations, one by one. This can be conveniently described as follows. We denote the estimates of $\mathbf{\Gamma}$, $\mathbf{B}$ by $\mathbf{C}_e$, $\mathbf{B}_e$, the moment matrix of all predetermined variables by $\mathbf{M_{xx}}$, that of all jointly dependent variables by $\mathbf{M_{yy}}$, the "mixed" moment matrix by $\mathbf{M_{xy}}$ and the moment matrix of the least-squares residuals in the reduced form, corresponding to all jointly dependent variables, by $\mathbf{M_{vv}}$. Obviously we have, except for a factor T, $\mathbf{M_{xx}} = \mathbf{X'X}$; and similarly $\mathbf{Y'Y}$, $\mathbf{X_1'Y}$, $\mathbf{V'V}$ are submatrices of $\mathbf{M_{yy}}$, $\mathbf{M_{xy}}$, $\mathbf{M_{vv}}$, respectively. Consider then the product matrix of order $(\Lambda + M) \times M$

$$\begin{bmatrix} \mathbf{M_{yy}} - k\mathbf{M_{vv}} & \mathbf{M_{yx}} \\ \mathbf{M_{xy}} & \mathbf{M_{xx}} \end{bmatrix} \begin{bmatrix} \mathbf{C}_e' \\ \mathbf{B}_e' \end{bmatrix}. \tag{6.134}$$

Take an arbitrary column, say the μ-th, of the product (6.134), cor-

[1] Cf. T. C. Koopmans, H. Rubin and R. B. Leipnik, "Measuring the Equation Systems of Dynamic Economics," Chapter II of *Statistical Inference in Dynamic Economic Models*; and T. C. Koopmans and W. C. Hood, "The Estimation of Simultaneous Linear Economic Relationships," Chapter VI of *Studies in Econometric Method*.

responding to the μ-th row of $[\mathbf{C}_e \;\; \mathbf{B}_e]$ and hence to the μ-th equation of the system (6.133). In this row of $[\mathbf{C}_e \;\; \mathbf{B}_e]$ we put all those elements equal to zero for which the corresponding elements in $[\mathbf{\Gamma} \;\; \mathbf{B}]$ are postulated to be zero. Furthermore, we "normalise" this row by putting one of the other elements equal to -1; usually this will be the coefficient of the variable which is "explained" by the equation (say the μ'-th), for then we are sure that the element is not zero. The estimation is then confined to the remaining elements, which takes place as follows. The μ'-th row of the premultiplying matrix of (6.134), corresponding to the normalised coefficient, and the rows corresponding to the zero coefficients are deleted; thereafter, the elements are estimated by putting the μ-th column of the product matrix (6.134) equal to zero. To see this, consider the following product:[1]

$$\begin{bmatrix} \mathbf{Y}'\mathbf{y} - k\mathbf{V}'\mathbf{v} & \mathbf{Y}'\mathbf{Y} - k\mathbf{V}'\mathbf{V} & \mathbf{Y}'\mathbf{X}_1 \\ \hline \hline \mathbf{X}_1'\mathbf{y} & \mathbf{X}_1'\mathbf{Y} & \mathbf{X}_1'\mathbf{X}_1 \\ \hline \end{bmatrix} \begin{bmatrix} -1 \\ \mathbf{c} \\ \mathbf{0} \\ \mathbf{b} \\ \mathbf{0} \end{bmatrix}$$

This is the case $\mu = \mu' = 1$ and corresponds to the equation $\mathbf{y} = \mathbf{Y}\boldsymbol{\gamma} + \mathbf{X}_1\boldsymbol{\beta} + \mathbf{u}$ of 6.2.7. The variables are arranged in such a way that those which do not occur in the equation are the last ones, both in the jointly dependent and in the predetermined category. It is seen that the moments corresponding to the latter variables, as far as they are multiplied by zeros, are irrelevant for the estimation of this particular equation; this is indicated by the vertical lines in the premultiplying matrix. Similarly, the columns from the second onwards in the postmultiplying matrix, and the first, the $(m + 2)$-nd through the M-th and the last $(\Lambda - l)$ rows of the premultiplying matrix are irrelevant, the latter because they are to be deleted.

The value of k which is chosen determines the estimates numerically. In the case of limited-information maximum-likelihood it is irrelevant whether the μ'-th row of the premultiplying matrix is deleted or not; but k will then generally be different for different rows of $[\mathbf{C}_e \;\; \mathbf{B}_e]$.

6.C.2. There are several ways in which two-stage least-squares can be

[1] $\mathbf{v}$ is here the column vector of reduced-form residuals corresponding to the left-hand variable It is easily seen than $\mathbf{V}'\mathbf{v} = \mathbf{V}'\mathbf{y}$.

derived; the approach of 6.2.7 is merely one of them. KLEIN observed that it can be obtained by applying the method of instrumental variables, provided that these variables are chosen as follows: the predetermined variables of the equation considered, and the "reduced" explanatory jointly dependent variables, i.e., these variables minus their least-squares reduced-form residuals.[1] It will also be clear that the class is related to NEYMAN's B.A.N. ("best asymptotic normal") estimators.[2] Here, we shall confine ourselves to two other approaches, which have some heuristic and clarifying value.

First, it will be observed that two-stage least-squares is identical with least-squares applied to the following equation:

$$(6.135) \qquad \mathbf{y} - \mathbf{v} = (\mathbf{Y} - \mathbf{V})\boldsymbol{\gamma} + \mathbf{X}_1\boldsymbol{\beta} + [\mathbf{u} - \mathbf{v} + \mathbf{V}\boldsymbol{\gamma}],$$

$\mathbf{v}$ being the vector of estimated reduced-form disturbances corresponding to $\mathbf{y}$. This follows immediately from the fact that, in the estimation procedure, $\mathbf{v}$ enters only as $(\mathbf{Y} - \mathbf{V})'\mathbf{v}$ or $\mathbf{X}_1'\mathbf{v}$, which is zero.[3] Consider also

$$(6.136) \qquad \mathbf{y} - \bar{\mathbf{v}} = (\mathbf{Y} - \bar{\mathbf{V}})\boldsymbol{\gamma} + \mathbf{X}_1\boldsymbol{\beta} + [\mathbf{u} - \bar{\mathbf{v}} + \bar{\mathbf{V}}\boldsymbol{\gamma}],$$

$\bar{\mathbf{v}}$ and $\bar{\mathbf{V}}$ being the parent matrices corresponding to $\mathbf{v}$ and $\mathbf{V}$, respectively. It is easy to see that (6.136) is an exact, nonstochastic, equation, i.e., $\mathbf{u} - \bar{\mathbf{v}} + \bar{\mathbf{V}}\boldsymbol{\gamma} \equiv \mathbf{0}$: first, the left-hand side is a function of predetermined values and hence nonstochastic; second, the same is true for the first term in the right-hand side; and hence, the disturbance combination cannot be stochastic either, so that it must be identically equal to its mean value, viz. zero. It follows, therefore, that if we would really know the parent matrices $\bar{\mathbf{v}}$, $\bar{\mathbf{V}}$, the estimation problem would degenerate to determination rather than estimation, provided that the equation is identifiable. But we do not known them and estimate them by means of $\mathbf{v}$, $\mathbf{V}$, and this leads to a nonzero covariance matrix of the parameter estimators.

Secondly, consider the following approach. In simple terms, we may

[1] Cf. L. R. KLEIN, "On the Interpretation of Theil's Method of Estimating Economic Relationships," *Metroeconomica*, Vol. 7 (1955), pp. 147–153. Also cf. R. L. BASMANN, "A Generalized Classical Method of Linear Estimation of Coefficients in a Structural Equation," *Econometrica*, Vol. 25 (1957), pp. 77–83.

[2] J. NEYMAN, "Contribution to the Theory of the χ^2-Test," *Proceedings of the Berkeley Symposium on Mathematical Statistics and Probability* (Berkeley-Los Angeles, 1949), pp. 239–273.

[3] Cf. p. 336 n.

interpret the classical method of least-squares as the method which accepts those parameter values as estimates for which the resulting, estimated, disturbances are uncorrelated with the explanatory variables; the "reason" being that the parent disturbances are postulated to have zero parent correlations with these variables. This argument is not immediately applicable in the case of an equation which is part of a system, since no such postulate is made for the explanatory dependent variables. But we can apply it to the set of all predetermined variables of the entire system. This suggests that we might estimate according to

$$\mathbf{X}'\mathbf{y} = \mathbf{X}'\mathbf{Y}\mathbf{c} + \mathbf{X}'\mathbf{X}_1\mathbf{b}, \tag{6.137}$$

which is a system of Λ linear equations in $(m + l)$ "unknowns." If $\Lambda < m + l$, the system does not give solutions, though it does give restrictions on the estimates; it is the case of under-identification. If $\Lambda = m + l$, the system gives in general unique solutions, so that (6.137) can be used immediately to obtain point estimates; this is the case of just-identification. If $\Lambda > m + l$ (the case of over-identification), there are "too many" restrictions. However, this is not at all an uncommon situation, for we had the same thing in the classical case $\mathbf{y} = \mathbf{X}\boldsymbol{\beta} + \mathbf{u}$ with which we started; cf. 6.2.3. There, we must estimate Λ parameters, while having $T \geq \Lambda$ equations available; here, we must estimate $(m + l)$ parameters and have Λ equations available. Let us therefore consider the equation in parameters corresponding to (6.137), viz.,

$$\mathbf{X}'\mathbf{y} = \mathbf{X}'\mathbf{Y}\boldsymbol{\gamma} + \mathbf{X}'\mathbf{X}_1\boldsymbol{\beta} + \mathbf{X}'\mathbf{u}, \tag{6.138}$$

which is obtained by premultiplying (6.65) by $\mathbf{X}'$. If $\Lambda \geq m + l$, we may give Λ and $m + l$ the rôle of T and Λ, respectively, in the problem $\mathbf{y} = \mathbf{X}\boldsymbol{\beta} + \mathbf{u}$, and treat $\mathbf{X}'\mathbf{u}$ as a disturbance vector. This vector has no scalar covariance matrix in general. Actually, it can easily be shown that this covariance matrix is $\sigma^2\mathbf{X}'\mathbf{X}$, provided that $\mathbf{X}$ is nonstochastic. Also, the components of the disturbance vector $\mathbf{X}'\mathbf{u}$ are not uncorrelated with the "explanatory variables" whose values are the elements of $\mathbf{X}'\mathbf{Y}$. However, these correlations are only of the order of $1/\sqrt{T}$, so that they vanish asymptotically. The application of Aitken's generalised least-squares approach to (6.138) is therefore approximately correct. If we do so, neglecting the above-mentioned correlations and using $\sigma^2\mathbf{X}'\mathbf{X}$ for Aitken's $\boldsymbol{\Omega}$, the result is (after some re-arrangements) simply two-stage least-squares.[1] This implies automatically that, if (6.137) has a unique solution for **c**, **b** (viz., if there is just-identification), this estimate must be identical with that of two-stage least-squares.

It follows from (6.137) that the estimation in the case of just-identification is simpler than in the case of over-identification, because the matrix **X′X** need not be inverted. It can be shown that this advantage is not confined to the determination of point estimates, but that it applies to the asymptotic standard errors as well. To do so, we shall prove that the matrix

$$\begin{bmatrix} \mathbf{Y}'\mathbf{Y} - \mathbf{V}'\mathbf{V} & \mathbf{Y}'\mathbf{X}_1 \\ \mathbf{X}_1'\mathbf{Y} & \mathbf{X}_1'\mathbf{X}_1 \end{bmatrix}^{-1}$$

is identical with the product

$$(6.139)\qquad [\mathbf{X}'\mathbf{Y} \quad \mathbf{X}'\mathbf{X}_1]^{-1}\mathbf{X}'\mathbf{X}\begin{bmatrix} \mathbf{Y}'\mathbf{X} \\ \mathbf{X}_1'\mathbf{X} \end{bmatrix}^{-1}$$

in the special case $\Lambda = m + l$. Multiplication of (6.139) by the estimate of σ^2 is therefore sufficient to arrive at the asymptotic standard errors in the case of just-identification. To prove that (6.139) is identical with the square matrix mentioned above, we insert two identity matrices of the type

$$\begin{bmatrix} \mathbf{Y}'\mathbf{X}(\mathbf{X}'\mathbf{X})^{-1} \\ \mathbf{I} \;\vdots\; \mathbf{0} \end{bmatrix}^{-1} \begin{bmatrix} \mathbf{Y}'\mathbf{X}(\mathbf{X}'\mathbf{X})^{-1} \\ \mathbf{I} \;\vdots\; \mathbf{0} \end{bmatrix},$$

where **I** is the $l \times l$ unit matrix and **0** the $l \times (\Lambda - l)$ zero matrix. More precisely, we write for (6.139):

[1] In fact, this was the way in which two-stage least-squares was originally derived. Cf. H. Theil, "Repeated Least-Squares Applied to Complete Equation Systems;" and "Estimation and Simultaneous Correlation in Complete Equation Systems;" and "$R_s(k)$-Estimation of Girshick's and Haavelmo's Model of the Food Market of the United States" (mimeographed papers of the Central Planning Bureau, The Hague, 1952–1953).

$$[\mathbf{X'Y} \quad \mathbf{X'X_1}]^{-1} \begin{bmatrix} \mathbf{Y'X(X'X)^{-1}} \\ \mathbf{I} \ \vdots \ \mathbf{0} \end{bmatrix}^{-1} \begin{bmatrix} \mathbf{Y'X(X'X)^{-1}} \\ \mathbf{I} \ \vdots \ \mathbf{0} \end{bmatrix} \mathbf{X'X} \times$$

$$\times \begin{bmatrix} \mathbf{I} \\ \mathbf{(X'X)^{-1}X'Y} \ \ldots\ldots \\ \mathbf{0} \end{bmatrix} \begin{bmatrix} \mathbf{I} \\ \mathbf{(X'X)^{-1}X'Y} \ \ldots\ldots \\ \mathbf{0} \end{bmatrix}^{-1} \begin{bmatrix} \mathbf{Y'X} \\ \mathbf{X_1'X} \end{bmatrix}^{-1} =$$

$$= \begin{bmatrix} \mathbf{Y'Y-V'V} & \mathbf{Y'X_1} \\ \mathbf{X_1'Y} & \mathbf{X_1'X_1} \end{bmatrix}^{-1} \begin{bmatrix} \mathbf{Y'Y-V'V} & \mathbf{Y'X_1} \\ \mathbf{X_1'Y} & \mathbf{X_1'X_1} \end{bmatrix} \begin{bmatrix} \mathbf{Y'Y-V'V} & \mathbf{Y'X_1} \\ \mathbf{X_1'Y} & \mathbf{X_1'X_1} \end{bmatrix}^{-1} =$$

$$= \begin{bmatrix} \mathbf{Y'Y-V'V} & \mathbf{Y'X_1} \\ \mathbf{X_1'Y} & \mathbf{X_1'X_1} \end{bmatrix}^{-1}.$$

This result is due to BEGEER.[1] The assertion that the point estimate **c**, **b** of (6.137) is identical with the two-stage estimate of (6.73) is easily verified by premultiplying (6.137) by

$$\begin{bmatrix} \mathbf{Y'X(X'X)^{-1}} \\ \mathbf{I} \ \vdots \ \mathbf{0} \end{bmatrix}.$$

The following geometric picture is also illustrative (cf. also 2.5.5 and its diagram). Consider a T-dimensional Cartesian space, along the first axis of which we measure the first observation on each variable, along the second axis the second observation, etc. The values assumed by each variable are then represented by a point in this space; or alternatively, by a vector from the origin O to this point. This leads to one point Y corresponding to the left-hand dependent variable of the equation; to m points $Y_1, \ldots, Y_m$ corresponding to the right-hand dependent variables; and to Λ points $X_1, \ldots, X_l, \ldots, X_\Lambda$ corresponding to the predetermined variables. The first stage of two-stage least-squares amounts to replacing $Y_1, \ldots, Y_m$ by their "reduced" values; i.e., by those points which correspond to the right-hand y-values after the least-squares reduced-form residuals are subtracted. This gives m points $Y_1^*, \ldots, Y_m^*$ which are the projections of $Y_1, \ldots,$

[1] W. BEGEER, "Simultaneous-Equations Estimation: Two-Stage Least-Squares, Its Application, and Its Geometry." Report 5703 of the Econometric Institute of the Netherlands School of Economics (1957).

Y_m, respectively, in the Λ-dimensional plane determined by the $\Lambda + 1$ points $O, X_1, \ldots, X_\Lambda$. In Fig. 6.20 this is illustrated for the case $T = 3$, $m = 1, \Lambda = 2$. The second step is the application of least-squares with the left-hand y as dependent variable, and the reduced right-hand y's and l of the x's as independent variables. This implies that we consider the projection of Y in the $(m + l)$-dimensional plane determined by O, $Y_1^*, \ldots, Y_m^*, X_1, \ldots, X_l$, which leads to a point Y^*. After this, the decomposition of the vector OY^* in terms of the vectors $OY_1^*, \ldots,$

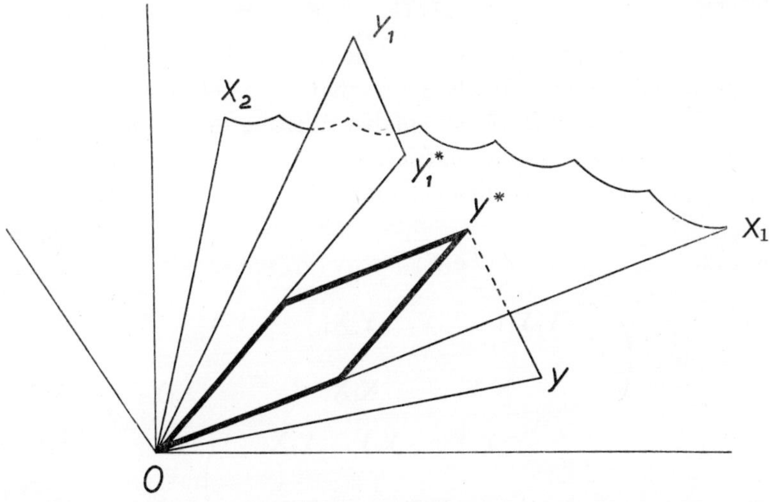

Fig. 6.20. Geometrical illustration of two-stage least-squares in the T-dimensional space, for the case $T = 3$, $m = l = 1$, $\Lambda = 2$

OX_l gives the estimated coefficients according to two-stage least-squares, as is indicated by heavy lines in Fig. 6.20 for $l = 1$. If we would have taken $l = 0$, so that the equation analysed is supposed to contain no predetermined variables, two-stage least-squares implies that we take the projection of Y on the line OY_1^* (or, more generally, in the m-dimensional plane through $O, Y_1^*, \ldots, Y_m^*$). The latter is a case of over-identification, that of Fig. 6.20—where Y_1 and Y are projected in the same plane—of just-identification. If we would take $l = 2$ in Fig. 6.20, the resulting decomposition of OY in terms of OY_1^*, OX_1 and OX_2 can be achieved in infinitely many ways. This is the case of under-identification.[1]

[1] For a more detailed geometric analysis, cf. Begeer, *loc. cit.*

6.C.3. Next, we proceed to some further extensions. The first deals with the asymptotic covariance matrix of parameter estimates of different equations. This is a problem which is of importance when the significance of a linear combination (e.g., a sum or a difference) of the coefficients of such relations has to be appraised. Suppose then that our two equations are

$$\mathbf{y}_1 = \mathbf{Y}_1\boldsymbol{\gamma}_1 + \mathbf{X}_1\boldsymbol{\beta}_1 + \mathbf{u}_1 \tag{6.140}$$

$$\mathbf{y}_2 = \mathbf{Y}_2\boldsymbol{\gamma}_2 + \mathbf{X}_2\boldsymbol{\beta}_2 + \mathbf{u}_2. \tag{6.141}$$

(Note that this and the following notation will be used in this paragraph only.) Suppose furthermore that both relations are estimated according to two-stage least-squares. Writing $\mathbf{e}_1$, $\mathbf{e}_2$ for the sampling errors and $\mathbf{V}_1$, $\mathbf{V}_2$ for the matrices of reduced-form residuals, we find in the limit when T approaches infinity:

$$\lim_{T\to\infty} \mathscr{E}(T\mathbf{e}_1\mathbf{e}_2') = \operatorname{cov}(u_1, u_2) \times \tag{6.142}$$

$$\times \operatorname*{plim}_{T\to\infty} \left(T \begin{bmatrix} \mathbf{Y}_1'\mathbf{Y}_1 - \mathbf{V}_1'\mathbf{V}_1 & \mathbf{Y}_1'\mathbf{X}_1 \\ \mathbf{X}_1'\mathbf{Y}_1 & \mathbf{X}_1'\mathbf{X}_1 \end{bmatrix}^{-1} \begin{bmatrix} \mathbf{Y}_1'\mathbf{Y}_2 - \mathbf{V}_1'\mathbf{V}_2 & \mathbf{Y}_1'\mathbf{X}_2 \\ \mathbf{X}_1'\mathbf{Y}_2 & \mathbf{X}_1'\mathbf{X}_2 \end{bmatrix} \times \right.$$

$$\left. \times \begin{bmatrix} \mathbf{Y}_2'\mathbf{Y}_2 - \mathbf{V}_2'\mathbf{V}_2 & \mathbf{Y}_2'\mathbf{X}_2 \\ \mathbf{X}_2'\mathbf{Y}_2 & \mathbf{X}_2'\mathbf{X}_2 \end{bmatrix}^{-1} \right),$$

provided the probability limit exists, and provided

$$\mathscr{E}(\mathbf{u}_1\mathbf{u}_2') = \operatorname{cov}(u_1, u_2)\,.\,\mathbf{I}, \tag{6.143}$$

which implies that there should be no lagged correlations between the disturbances of the two equations, and that their T "contemporaneous" covariances should be equal.

Second, there is the problem of general linear restrictions. Up till now, all *a priori* restrictions were assumed to be such that they exclude certain variables from the equation analysed. But it may also happen that they have the form of an equality of two parameters, of a known ratio, etc. Now general linear restrictions (with known coefficients) on the parameters of the equation considered can be easily handled along the lines sketched in the second paragraph of 6.B.4. Suppose, e.g., that it is known that $\gamma_1 = 2\gamma_2 + 1$, so that the first part of (6.64), $y = \gamma_1 y_1 +$

$+ \gamma_2 y_2$, can be written as $y - y_1 = \gamma_2(2y_1 + y_2)$. Then we should treat $y - y_1$ as left-hand dependent variable, $2y_1 + y_2$ as right-hand dependent variable, and forget all about y, y_1, y_2 until the very end when the final results are translated into the original equation. The resulting "combined" variables should be considered as jointly dependent, unless their components are all predetermined, in which case the combination is predetermined too.

Third, we should consider the problem that arises when the number of predetermined variables is large. An extreme case in this respect is the one in which this number exceeds the number of observations, $\Lambda > T$, because it implies a singular moment matrix $\mathbf{X'X}$, the inverse of which is required for $\mathbf{Y'Y} - \mathbf{V'V}$. This situation is of course irrelevant for the asymptotic theory; but we do not have infinitely large samples in practice. The standard procedure is then to disregard some of the predetermined variables, i.e., to delete some of the colums of $\mathbf{X}$.[1] The obvious objection to this method is its arbitrariness, since no clear rule about the question which variables should be retained and which deleted is available. A much better alternative seems to be the following: to determine the principal components of the series of observations on the predetermined variables, and to use these as substitutes. In practice this would imply a replacement of $\mathbf{X}$ by a matrix $\mathbf{Z}$, which contains as submatrices (*i*) the matrix $\mathbf{X}_1$ of the values assumed by the predetermined variables in the equation and (*ii*) the matrix of values assumed by the first two or three principal components of the predetermined variables outside the equation.[2] Of course, a certain degree of arbitrariness remains because of the number of principal components to be included; but it is evidently not nearly so important as it is in the usual procedure mentioned above.

Fourth, there is the problem of a linear equation which is part of a system that is otherwise nonlinear. Fifth, we should ask what happens if the values assumed by the predetermined variables are stochastic rather than fixed, as in the case of lagged endogenous variables.

The answer to the last two questions is rather simple. As long as we are willing to make suitable asymptotic assumptions—and the mere

[1] Cf. T. W. ANDERSON and H. RUBIN, "The Asymptotic Properties of Estimates of the Parameters of a Single Equation in a Complete System of Stochastic Equations," *Annals of Mathematical Statistics*, Vol. 21 (1950), pp. 570–582.

[2] This approach has been considered in some detail by T. KLOEK and L. B. M. MENNES, "Simultaneous Equations Estimation Based on Principal Components of Predetermined Variables," *Econometrica*, Vol. 28 (1960), pp. 45–61.

fact that they are asymptotic ensures that they cannot be easily refuted—, everything remains as it is in the standard case. Take e.g. the fifth problem (that of stochastic predetermined variables). As before, we find then for $T\mathbf{ee}'$ (the mean value of which leads to the covariance matrix):

$$(6.144)\qquad T\begin{bmatrix} \mathbf{Y'Y} - \mathbf{V'V} & \mathbf{Y'X}_1 \\ \mathbf{X}_1'\mathbf{Y} & \mathbf{X}_1'\mathbf{X}_1 \end{bmatrix}^{-1},$$

postmultiplied by

$$(6.145)\qquad \begin{bmatrix} \mathbf{Y}' - \mathbf{V}' \\ \mathbf{X}_1' \end{bmatrix} (1/T)\mathbf{uu}'[\mathbf{Y} - \mathbf{V} \quad \mathbf{X}_1]$$

and this in turn postmultiplied by (6.144). Assume then that (6.144) approaches, for increasing T, a finite and unique probability limit; also that (6.145) has a mean value which equals σ^2 times the inverse of this same limit, except possibly for terms that vanish with increasing T. Then, clearly, the original asymptotic covariance result (6.78) is obtained.[1]

6.C.4. A more interesting generalisation can be obtained for the case of autocorrelated disturbances. We assume:

(*ix*) *The assumptions* (vii) *and* (viii) *of* 6.2.7 *are satisfied, except for the following: first, the disturbances of* (6.65) *have a finite and non-singular covariance matrix,* $\mathscr{E}(\mathbf{uu}') = \mathbf{\Omega}$; *secondly, for each pair* t, $t'(= 1, \ldots, T)$ *and for each pair* μ, $\mu'(= 1, \ldots, m)$, *the parent reduced-form disturbances* $\bar{v}_\mu(t)$ *and* $\bar{v}_{\mu'}(t')$ *corresponding to the right-hand variables* y_μ *and* $y_{\mu'}$, *respectively, of this equation have zero mean and satisfy*

$$(6.146)\qquad \mathscr{E}[\bar{v}_\mu(t)\,\bar{v}_{\mu'}(t')] = \sigma_{\mu\mu'}\omega_{tt'},$$

where $\sigma_{\mu\mu'}$ *is independent of* t *and* t', *and* $\omega_{tt'}$ *is the* (t, t')*-th element of* $\mathbf{\Omega}$.

This condition is weaker than the one which it replaces; it bears a close resemblance to assumption (*vi*). Still, it imposes rather strong restrictions on the probability structure of the disturbances, because the covariance matrices of those in the reduced form—at least in that part of the reduced form that corresponds to the dependent explanatory variables of the equation—are supposed to be "proportional" to

[1] For a treatment of these problems in the case of limited-information maximum-likelihood, cf. Anderson and Rubin, *loc. cit.*

the covariance matrix of the disturbances in the structural equation under consideration. A sufficient condition under which this situation is reached is that the equation system be linear and that the disturbance vectors of each pair of its equations have a covariance matrix equal to $\mathbf{\Omega}$ except for a scalar. When viewed from this point, we can conclude that (*ix*), although still rather restrictive, is certainly much weaker than the assumptions which it replaces, for it allows us to take account of one important and almost common feature of disturbances in time series analysis, viz., their positive first autocorrelation.

Suppose then that the reduced form is estimated according to Aitken's method of generalised least-squares. This gives

$$\mathbf{Y} - \mathbf{V}^* = \mathbf{X}(\mathbf{X}'\mathbf{\Omega}^{-1}\mathbf{X})^{-1}\mathbf{X}'\mathbf{\Omega}^{-1}\mathbf{Y}, \tag{6.147}$$

$\mathbf{V}^*$ being the matrix of the resulting, estimated, reduced-form disturbances. Consider also the estimation equations

$$\begin{bmatrix} \mathbf{Y}' - \mathbf{V}^{*\prime} \\ \mathbf{X}_1' \end{bmatrix} \mathbf{\Omega}^{-1}\mathbf{y} = \begin{bmatrix} \mathbf{Y}' - \mathbf{V}^{*\prime} \\ \mathbf{X}_1' \end{bmatrix} \mathbf{\Omega}^{-1}[\mathbf{Y} - \mathbf{V}^* \quad \mathbf{X}_1] \begin{pmatrix} \mathbf{c} \\ \mathbf{b} \end{pmatrix}^*, \tag{6.148}$$

the last vector being an estimator of $\boldsymbol{\gamma}$, $\boldsymbol{\beta}$. Clearly, (6.148) is an immediate generalisation both of two-stage least-squares and of generalised least-squares; so we shall call this method that of "generalised two-stage least-squares." Writing $\mathbf{A}$ for the product of the first three matrices in the right-hand side of (6.148), we find

$$\begin{pmatrix} \mathbf{c} \\ \mathbf{b} \end{pmatrix}^* = \begin{pmatrix} \boldsymbol{\gamma} \\ \boldsymbol{\beta} \end{pmatrix} + \mathbf{A}^{-1} \begin{bmatrix} \mathbf{Y}' - \mathbf{V}^{*\prime} \\ \mathbf{X}_1' \end{bmatrix} \mathbf{\Omega}^{-1}\mathbf{u},$$

whence it follows that the estimator is asymptotically unbiased. Further, if $\mathbf{e}^*$ is the sampling error, we find for the asymptotic covariance matrix:

$$\begin{aligned} \lim_{T\to\infty} \mathscr{E}(T\mathbf{e}^*\mathbf{e}^{*\prime}) &= \operatorname*{plim}_{T\to\infty} (T\mathbf{A}^{-1}) \\ &= \operatorname*{plim}_{T\to\infty} T\left(\begin{bmatrix} \mathbf{Y}' - \mathbf{V}^{*\prime} \\ \mathbf{X}_1' \end{bmatrix} \mathbf{\Omega}^{-1}[\mathbf{Y} - \mathbf{V}^* \quad \mathbf{X}_1]\right)^{-1}, \end{aligned} \tag{6.149}$$

which is again an immediate generalisation.

6.C.5. Just as the coefficient of multiple correlation is the generalisation of the zero-order correlation coefficient for the case of several explanatory variables, in the same way it is possible to generalise the multiple coefficient for the case of several jointly dependent variables. Our starting point is the theory of canonical correlations.[1] Applied to our predetermined variables (whose values are arranged in a $T \times \Lambda$ matrix $\mathbf{X}$ as before) and jointly dependent variables (whose values are arranged in a $T \times M$ matrix $\mathbf{Y}_w$, the index w indicating that we are considering all dependent variables of the whole system), this theory can be briefly described as follows. Suppose that all of our $\Lambda + M$ variables are measured as deviations from their means; then there exist linear combinations of the variables $x_1, \ldots, x_\Lambda$ and $y_1, \ldots, y_M$ into other variables $\xi_1, \ldots, \xi_\Lambda$ and $\eta_1, \ldots, \eta_M$, respectively, such that

(i) All ξ and η-variables have zero mean and unit sum of squares;

(ii) Each ξ is uncorrelated with all other ξ's, and each η is uncorrelated with all other η's;

(iii) The correlation between any ξ-variable and any η-variable is zero except for Λ or M nonzero correlations (Λ if $\Lambda \leq M$, M if $\Lambda \geq M$) $r_1, r_2, \ldots$ which may be regarded as the correlations between ξ_1 and η_1, ξ_2 and η_2, etc.

The ξ's and η's thus defined are called canonical variates, the r's canonical correlations. Each pair of canonical variates, say $\boldsymbol{\xi}_i = \mathbf{X}\mathbf{h}_i$ and $\boldsymbol{\eta}_i = \mathbf{Y}_w\mathbf{k}_i$ (both written as a column vector of T observations) can be derived by imposing the constraints

$$(6.150) \qquad \boldsymbol{\xi}_i'\boldsymbol{\xi}_i = \mathbf{h}_i'\mathbf{X}'\mathbf{X}\mathbf{h}_i = 1 \quad \text{and} \quad \boldsymbol{\eta}_i'\boldsymbol{\eta}_i = \mathbf{k}_i'\mathbf{Y}_w'\mathbf{Y}_w\mathbf{k}_i = 1,$$

and by considering the condition of a stationary value of the corresponding canonical correlation:

$$(6.151) \qquad r_i = \boldsymbol{\xi}_i'\boldsymbol{\eta}_i = \mathbf{h}_i'\mathbf{X}'\mathbf{Y}_w\mathbf{k}_i.$$

The ordinary method of Lagrangean multipliers leads then to the condition

$$(6.152) \qquad [(\mathbf{Y}_w'\mathbf{Y}_w)^{-1}\mathbf{Y}_w'\mathbf{X}(\mathbf{X}'\mathbf{X})^{-1}\mathbf{X}'\mathbf{Y}_w - r_i^2\mathbf{I}]\mathbf{k}_i = \mathbf{0},$$

from which it follows that the square of any canonical correlation is a

[1] For details on canonical correlation theory, see H. Hotelling, "Relations Between Two Sets of Variates," *Biometrika*, Vol. 28 (1936), pp. 321–377; and T. W. Anderson, *Introduction to Multivariate Statistical Analysis* (New York – London, 1957), Chapter 12. The present account is largely based on J. W. Hooper's article "Simultaneous Equations and Canonical Correlation Theory," *Econometrica*, Vol. 27 (1959), pp. 245–256.

latent root of the matrix $(\mathbf{Y}_w'\mathbf{Y}_w)^{-1}\mathbf{Y}_w'\mathbf{X}(\mathbf{X}'\mathbf{X})^{-1}\mathbf{X}'\mathbf{Y}_w$. If we consider $\mathbf{X}$ and $\mathbf{Y}_w$ as sample values derived from a parent with finite moments of the second order, the corresponding parent canonical correlations are found by solving the determinantal equation

$$(6.153) \qquad |\{\mathscr{E}(\mathbf{Y}_w'\mathbf{Y}_w)\}^{-1}\mathscr{E}(\mathbf{Y}_w'\mathbf{X})\{\mathscr{E}(\mathbf{X}'\mathbf{X})\}^{-1}\mathscr{E}(\mathbf{X}'\mathbf{Y}_w) - \rho_i^2\mathbf{I}\,| = 0.$$

In the special case when $\mathbf{X}$ consists of nonstochastic elements, some of the mean values of (6.153) can be simplified.

Suppose now that $\mathbf{X}$ and $\mathbf{Y}_w$ are connected by a complete system of stochastic linear relations of which the reduced form is

$$(6.154) \qquad \mathbf{Y}_w = \mathbf{X\Pi}_w + \bar{\mathbf{V}}_w.$$

Estimating this reduced from by least-squares, we obtain

$$(6.155) \qquad \mathbf{Y}_w = \mathbf{XP}_w + \mathbf{V}_w \qquad \text{where} \qquad \mathbf{P}_w = (\mathbf{X}'\mathbf{X})^{-1}\mathbf{X}'\mathbf{Y}_w.$$

Since $\mathbf{X}'\mathbf{V}_w = \mathbf{0}$, we have

$$(6.156) \qquad \mathbf{Y}_w'\mathbf{Y}_w = \mathbf{P}_w'\mathbf{X}'\mathbf{XP}_w + \mathbf{V}_w'\mathbf{V}_w,$$

and hence, if we introduce

$$(6.157) \qquad \mathbf{D} = (\mathbf{Y}_w'\mathbf{Y}_w)^{-1}\mathbf{V}_w'\mathbf{V}_w,$$

we can conclude:

$$(6.158) \qquad \mathbf{I} - \mathbf{D} = (\mathbf{Y}_w'\mathbf{Y}_w)^{-1}\mathbf{P}_w'\mathbf{X}'\mathbf{XP}_w = (\mathbf{Y}_w'\mathbf{Y}_w)^{-1}\mathbf{Y}_w'\mathbf{X}(\mathbf{X}'\mathbf{X})^{-1}\mathbf{X}'\mathbf{Y}_w.$$

But the last matrix is the same as that of (6.152). It follows therefore that the matrix whose latent roots are considered in (6.152) is simply the inverse of the moment matrix of the jointly dependent variables postmultiplied by the moment matrix of the systematic part of the estimated reduced form, $\mathbf{XP}_w$:

$$(6.159) \qquad |\,(\mathbf{Y}_w'\mathbf{Y}_w)^{-1}\mathbf{P}_w'\mathbf{X}'\mathbf{XP}_w - r_i^2\mathbf{I}\,| = 0 \quad \text{or} \quad |\,(\mathbf{I} - \mathbf{D}) - r_i^2\mathbf{I}\,| = 0.$$

Conversely, it also follows from the above results that $1 - r_i^2$ is a latent root of the inverted moment matrix of the jointly dependent variables postmultiplied by the moment matrix of the estimated reduced-form disturbances, $\mathbf{V}_w$:

$$(6.160) \qquad |\,(\mathbf{Y}_w'\mathbf{Y}_w)^{-1}\mathbf{V}_w'\mathbf{V}_w - (1 - r_i^2)\mathbf{I}\,| = 0 \text{ or } |\,\mathbf{D} - (1 - r_i^2)\mathbf{I}\,| = 0.$$

Now the matrix $(\mathbf{Y}_w'\mathbf{Y}_w)^{-1}\mathbf{V}_w'\mathbf{V}_w = \mathbf{D}$ is a straightforward matrix generalisation of the ratio of the least-squares estimated variance of the disturbances to the estimated variance of the single dependent variable in one-equation systems. Since this ratio equals $1 - R^2$, R being the multiple correlation coefficient, it seems rather obvious to consider the $1 - r_i^2$, which are the latent roots of $\mathbf{D}$, as another generalisation. This generalisation is of a vector type, because $\mathbf{D}$ has M latent roots which can be arranged in a vector of M elements. A third generalisation of the convenient scalar type has been proposed by J. W. HOOPER, viz., the *trace correlation* $\bar{r}$ whose square is defined as

$$(6.161)\qquad \bar{r}^2 = \frac{1}{M} \operatorname{tr} (\mathbf{I} - \mathbf{D}) = \frac{1}{M} \sum_{i=1}^{M} r_i^2.$$

On comparing this with

$$(6.162)\qquad 1 - \bar{r}^2 = \frac{1}{M} \operatorname{tr} \mathbf{D} = \frac{1}{M} \sum_{i=1}^{M} (1 - r_i^2),$$

we can conclude that $\bar{r}^2$ can be naturally interpreted as that part of the total variance of the jointly dependent variables that is accounted for by the systematic part of the reduced form, and $1 - \bar{r}^2$ as the unexplained part.[1]

We can interpret the trace correlation $\bar{r}$ as an estimator of the parent trace correlation $\bar{\varrho}$ whose square is defined as the mean of the squared parent canonical correlations defined in (6.153). HOOPER showed that under the assumptions of a complete system whose disturbances are independent over time and have constant variances and contemporaneous covariances, the sample trace correlation $\bar{r}$ is a consistent estimator of $\bar{\varrho}$, and that the asymptotic sampling variance of its square is given by

$$(6.163)\qquad \lim_{T\to\infty} (T \operatorname{var} \bar{r}^2) = \frac{2}{M^2} \sum_{i=1}^{M} \varrho_i^2 (1 - \varrho_i^2)^2 (2 - \varrho_i^2),$$

provided that the elements of $\mathbf{X}$ are nonstochastic.[2] The assumption is also made that there are no multiple nonzero roots in the population. Multiple zero roots are permissible [their contribution to the sum on

[1] For a discussion of alternative scalar generalisations, such as the vector correlation and the vector alienation coefficients (proposed by HOTELLING, *loc. cit.*) and the coefficient of simultaneous correlation (proposed in the first edition of this book), reference is made to Hooper's article.

[2] Alternative conditions were considered by HOOPER in the article quoted above and in "The Sampling Variance of Correlation Coefficients under Assumptions of Fixed and Mixed Variates," *Biometrika*, Vol. 45 (1958), pp. 471–477.

the right of (6.163) is necessarily zero]; such zero roots will certainly occur if $\Lambda < M$, because the number of nonzero r's or ϱ's cannot exceed Λ.

6.C.6. Another problem of interest is whether something more can be specified about the distribution of the k-class estimators than their asymptotic covariance matrix. This problem was attacked by A. L. NAGAR,[1] who derived the bias of these estimators to the order of $1/T$ and the matrix of second-order sampling moments to the order $1/T^2$. A brief account of his results follows here.

Consider those members of the k-class for which k differs from 1 to the order $1/T$ only:

$$k = 1 + \frac{\varkappa}{T}, \tag{6.164}$$

where $\varkappa$ is a fixed number independent of T. Terms of higher order of smallness (like $1/T^2$) are not considered in (6.164), since they are irrelevant for the present purposes. It will be noted that the condition plim $\sqrt{T}(k - 1) = 0$ is satisfied for the k-class estimators falling under (6.164), so that they are asymptotically unbiased and have (6.78) as asymptotic covariance matrix. However, limited-information maximum-likelihood does not fall under (6.164), due to the fact that $\varkappa$ is taken as nonstochastic. Furthermore, it will prove useful to introduce

$$L = \Lambda - (m + l) \tag{6.165}$$

for the total number of predetermined variables in the system in excess of the number of coefficients to be estimated. It will be assumed that all random variation is normal; more precisely, it will be assumed that for each t (= 1, .., T), the M disturbances of the M structural equations form a random drawing of a stable M-dimensional normal distribution. Finally, it is also assumed that all predetermined variables take nonstochastic values.

In order to analyse the bias of the k-class estimators (6.164) to the order T^{-1}, we must introduce a matrix $\mathbf{Q}$ and a vector $\mathbf{q}$. Writing

$$\bar{\mathbf{Y}} = \mathbf{Y} - \bar{\mathbf{V}} \tag{6.166}$$

[1] "The Bias and Moment Matrix of the General k-Class Estimators of the Parameters in Simultaneous Equations," *Econometrica*, Vol. 27 (1959), pp. 575–595.

for the matrix of values taken by the explanatory dependent variables after their parent reduced-form disturbances are subtracted, we define **Q** according to its inverse

$$\mathbf{Q}^{-1} = \begin{bmatrix} \bar{\mathbf{Y}}' \\ \mathbf{X}_1' \end{bmatrix} [\bar{\mathbf{Y}} \quad \mathbf{X}_1] = \begin{bmatrix} \bar{\mathbf{Y}}'\bar{\mathbf{Y}} & \bar{\mathbf{Y}}'\mathbf{X}_1 \\ \mathbf{X}_1'\bar{\mathbf{Y}} & \mathbf{X}_1'\mathbf{X}_1 \end{bmatrix}. \tag{6.167}$$

It is seen that $\mathbf{Q}^{-1}$ is the parent analogue of the square matrix of (6.73), which itself is to be inverted for the derivation of the two-stage least-squares estimator. Next, we define $\mathbf{q}$ as the vector of the covariances of the right-hand variables of (6.65) and the disturbances of that equation:

$$\mathbf{q} = \frac{1}{T} \begin{bmatrix} \mathscr{E}(\mathbf{Y}'\mathbf{u}) \\ \mathscr{E}(\mathbf{X}_1'\mathbf{u}) \end{bmatrix} = \frac{1}{T} \begin{bmatrix} \mathscr{E}(\bar{\mathbf{V}}'\mathbf{u}) \\ \mathbf{0} \end{bmatrix}, \tag{6.168}$$

the zero vector being a column of l components. It will be noted that the fact that $\mathbf{q}$ is not zero—in other words, that there are nonzero covariances between certain explanatory variables and the disturbances of the equation—is precisely the main statistical problem of simultaneous equations.

Then it can be shown that the bias to the order T^{-1} of the k-class estimators (6.164) is

$$\mathscr{E}\mathbf{e}_k = -(\varkappa - L + 1)\mathbf{Qq}, \tag{6.169}$$

where all scalars and matrices involved are of order $T^0 = 1$ except $\mathbf{Q}$ which is a square matrix of order $(m + l)$ whose elements are of order T^{-1}. It is seen that the bias vanishes to the order T^{-1} if we take $\varkappa = L - 1$, or

$$k = 1 + \frac{L - 1}{T}. \tag{6.170}$$

Hence, if bias is our quality indicator of the estimator to be used, this result suggests that we should take $k = 1 - 1/T$ in the case of just-identification ($L = 0$), and a k-value which equals or exceeds 1 if the equation is over-identified.

But one may argue that bias is less important than variance around the "true" value; and that is our next problem. For this purpose, we must introduce some further matrices. Consider $\bar{\mathbf{V}}$; if the model is linear and if its disturbances are all normally distributed, then the elements of $\bar{\mathbf{V}}$ are also normal and moreover they can each be written as the sum of two parts, one of which is proportional to the corresponding element of the disturbance vector $\mathbf{u}$ of (6.65) and the other is independent of that vector. Hence:

$$\bar{\mathbf{V}} = \mathbf{u}\boldsymbol{\pi}' + \mathbf{W}, \tag{6.171}$$

where $\boldsymbol{\pi}$ is a column vector of m nonstochastic elements and $\mathbf{W}$ is a $T \times m$ matrix which is independent of $\mathbf{u}$ and whose rows are independent random drawings from a stable m-dimensional normal parent with zero means. Now taking second-order moments on both sides of (6.171), we obtain

$$\frac{1}{T}\mathscr{E}(\bar{\mathbf{V}}'\bar{\mathbf{V}}) = \sigma^2\boldsymbol{\pi}\boldsymbol{\pi}' + \frac{1}{T}\mathscr{E}(\mathbf{W}'\mathbf{W}); \tag{6.172}$$

or, if we enlarge each of these three matrices by zeros such that they become square of order $m + l$,

$$\mathbf{C} = \mathbf{C}_1 + \mathbf{C}_2; \tag{6.173}$$

where

$$\begin{aligned} \mathbf{C} &= \frac{1}{T}\begin{bmatrix} \mathscr{E}(\bar{\mathbf{V}}'\bar{\mathbf{V}}) & \mathbf{0} \\ \mathbf{0} & \mathbf{0} \end{bmatrix}; \quad \mathbf{C}_1 = \sigma^2 \begin{bmatrix} \boldsymbol{\pi}\boldsymbol{\pi}' & \mathbf{0} \\ \mathbf{0} & \mathbf{0} \end{bmatrix} = \frac{1}{\sigma^2}\mathbf{q}\mathbf{q}';^1 \\ \mathbf{C}_2 &= \frac{1}{T}\begin{bmatrix} \mathscr{E}(\mathbf{W}'\mathbf{W}) & \mathbf{0} \\ \mathbf{0} & \mathbf{0} \end{bmatrix}. \end{aligned} \tag{6.174}$$

It can then be shown that the matrix of second-order sampling moments to the order T^{-2} of the k-class estimator of the type (6.164) is

$$\mathscr{E}(\mathbf{e}_k\mathbf{e}_k') = \sigma^2\{(1 + \alpha_0)\mathbf{Q} + \alpha_1\mathbf{Q}\mathbf{C}_1\mathbf{Q} + \alpha_2\mathbf{Q}\mathbf{C}_2\mathbf{Q}\}, \tag{6.175}$$

where the α's are scalars, α_0 being of order T^{-1} and α_1 and α_2 of order $T^0 = 1$:

$$\begin{aligned} \alpha_0 &= (2\varkappa - 2L + 3) \operatorname{tr} \mathbf{C}_1\mathbf{Q} + \operatorname{tr} \mathbf{C}_2\mathbf{Q}; \\ \alpha_1 &= (\varkappa - L + 3)^2 + 2L - 3; \\ \alpha_2 &= 2\varkappa - L + 2. \end{aligned} \tag{6.176}$$

Evidently, the moment matrix (6.175) can be regarded as the weighted sum of three positive semi-definite matrices, viz., $\sigma^2\mathbf{Q}$, $\sigma^2\mathbf{Q}\mathbf{C}_1\mathbf{Q}$ and

[1] The relation between $\boldsymbol{\pi}$ and $\mathbf{q}$ follows directly from the definitions (6.168) and (6.171).

$\sigma^2\mathbf{QC}_2\mathbf{Q}$, where the weights are $1 + \alpha_0$, α_1 and α_2, respectively. The asymptotic moment matrix is $\sigma^2\mathbf{Q}$ in accordance with (6.78); this follows from the fact that $\alpha_0\mathbf{Q}$, $\mathbf{QC}_1\mathbf{Q}$ and $\mathbf{QC}_2\mathbf{Q}$ are all matrices of order T^{-2}. Now given the positive semi-definiteness of $\sigma^2\mathbf{Q}$, $\sigma^2\mathbf{QC}_1\mathbf{Q}$ and $\sigma^2\mathbf{QC}_2\mathbf{Q}$, the best we can do is to make their weights (and hence the α's) algebraically as small as possible. Considering (6.176), we observe that α_0 depends linearly on $\varkappa$; and given the positive sign of tr $\mathbf{C}_1\mathbf{Q}$,[1] this means that α_0 can be made arbitrarily negative by giving $\varkappa$ a sufficiently negative value. This should of course not be interpreted too literally, since a very high negative value of $\varkappa$ violates the condition that k differs from 1 to the order $1/T$ only; but it shows at least that as far as α_0 is concerned, we improve on the estimator by making $\varkappa$ negative rather than positive or zero. The situation with respect to α_2 is exactly the same, since it is also a linear increasing function of $\varkappa$. For α_1 it is different; it is quadratic in $\varkappa$ and reaches a minimum at $\varkappa = L - 3$. Hence this would be the $\varkappa$-value to be chosen on the basis of the second-moment criterion if the α_1-term were the only term of order T^{-2} in (6.175); but it is not, and given the positive dependence of α_0 and α_2 on $\varkappa$ it is obvious that the k-value to be chosen on the basis of this criterion satisfies the inequality

$$k < 1 + \frac{L-3}{T}, \tag{6.177}$$

which is certainly below the k-value (6.170) of the unbiasedness criterion. As to the question of how far below the right-hand side of (6.177) we should go, it is important to make a distinction between the case in which the elements of $\mathbf{C}_1$ dominate the corresponding elements of $\mathbf{C}_2$ and the case in which the converse is true. An inspection of (6.175) shows that in the latter case α_1 has a small effect on the moment matrix, so that the upper limit of k in (6.177) is then not very relevant. This may lead to a k-value which is substantially below 1, which in fact is not surprising given the fact that small $\mathbf{C}_1$-elements indicate that the explanatory dependent variables of the equation are largely independent of its disturbances; and in that case the objection to single-stage least-squares ($k = 0$), though still correct formally, loses much of its relevance. In the alternative case in which the $\mathbf{C}_1$-elements

[1] Proof: since $\mathbf{C}_1$ is positive semi-definite, it can be written $\mathbf{C}_1 = \mathbf{R'R}$ where $\mathbf{R}$ is a square matrix of order $m + l$, so that tr $\mathbf{C}_1 = $ tr $\mathbf{R'RQ} = $ tr $\mathbf{RQR'}$ is the trace of a positive semi-definite matrix and hence positive.

dominate those of $\mathbf{C}_2$, the size of α_2 becomes unimportant. There are then two ways in which $\varkappa$ still affects the part of the moment matrix that is of order T^{-2}, viz., linearly *via* α_0 and quadratically *via* α_1. The second effect points to the upper limit of (6.177), the first to (arbitrarily) lower values. A more precise numerical discussion of the k-choice according to the second-moment criterion requires knowledge of the matrices $\mathbf{C}_1$ and $\mathbf{C}_2$ which can at most be estimated; but it seems plausible that one will usually arrive at a k-value below 1 except when L is large,[1] and the exceptional case of large L will indeed be exceptional because T has to be larger than Λ while Λ exceeds L by $m + l$. If Λ is so large that we have to apply the principal-component procedure of the third paragraph of 6.C.3, so that we replace the matrix $\mathbf{X}$ of Λ columns by a matrix $\mathbf{Z}$ of $\Lambda' < \Lambda$ columns, then L is reduced likewise because it is replaced by $L' = \Lambda' - (m + l)$.

6.C.7. We conclude by considering some alternative estimation methods. First, we take the so-called *h-class*, which is based on the partitioned matrix

$$\mathbf{Z}_h = \left[\mathbf{Y} - (1 - h)\mathbf{V} \;\vdots\; \mathbf{X}_1 \right], \tag{6.178}$$

where h is an arbitrary real number. It is easily seen that single-stage least-squares applied to (6.65) amounts to taking the regression of $\mathbf{y}$ on $\mathbf{Z}_h$ for $h = 1$:

$$\mathbf{d}_1 = (\mathbf{Z}_1'\mathbf{Z}_1)^{-1}\mathbf{Z}_1'\mathbf{y},$$

while two-stage least-squares corresponds to $h = 0$:

$$\mathbf{d}_0 = (\mathbf{Z}_0'\mathbf{Z}_0)^{-1}\mathbf{Z}_0'\mathbf{y}.$$

[1] This result suggests that the k-value of limited-information maximum-likelihood (which is always > 1 except for the case of just-identification) is frequently too large, which may be the main reason why R. Summers found in "A Capital-Intensive Approach to the Small Sample Properties of Various Simultaneous Equation Estimators" (Cowles Foundation Discussion Paper No. 64) that two-stage least-squares gave better results in artificial sampling than limited-information maximum-likelihood. This deals with the sharpness aspects of these two methods. The simplicity effect is decidedly in favour of two-stage least-squares, as can be easily seen from H. CHERNOFF and N. DIVINSKY, "The Computation of Maximum-Likelihood Estimates of Linear Structural Equations" (Chapter X of *Studies in Econometric Method*), in particular pp. 274–277. Part of the computations on p. 274 and all on pp. 275–277 are unnecessary for two-stage least-squares.

The general h-class is defined according to

$$\mathbf{d}_h = (\mathbf{Z}_h'\mathbf{Z}_h)^{-1}\mathbf{Z}_h'\mathbf{y}, \tag{6.179}$$

and we thus see that this class is analogous to the k-class to the extent that both contain single-stage and two-stage least-squares as special cases. The classes are not identical, however. This follows from the fact that computing $\mathbf{d}_h$ amounts to solving the equations

$$\begin{bmatrix} \mathbf{Y}'\mathbf{Y} - (1-h^2)\mathbf{V}'\mathbf{V} & \mathbf{Y}'\mathbf{X}_1 \\ \mathbf{X}_1'\mathbf{Y} & \mathbf{X}_1'\mathbf{X}_1 \end{bmatrix} \mathbf{d}_h = \begin{bmatrix} \mathbf{Y}' - (1-h)\mathbf{V}' \\ \mathbf{X}_1' \end{bmatrix} \mathbf{y}. \tag{6.180}$$

On comparing (6.180) with (6.79), we can conclude that both are special cases of

$$\begin{bmatrix} \mathbf{Y}'\mathbf{Y} - k_1\mathbf{V}'\mathbf{V} & \mathbf{Y}'\mathbf{X}_1 \\ \mathbf{X}_1'\mathbf{Y} & \mathbf{X}_1'\mathbf{X}_1 \end{bmatrix} \mathbf{d}_{k_1k_2} = \begin{bmatrix} \mathbf{Y}' - k_2\mathbf{V}' \\ \mathbf{X}_1' \end{bmatrix} \mathbf{y}, \tag{6.181}$$

which is the so-called *double-k-class* introduced by Nagar,[1] who also derived its bias to the order $1/T$ and its moment matrix to the order $1/T^2$.

Other methods are the full-information methods (mentioned in the second paragraph of 6.C.1), which are based on zero constraints (and possibly other constraints) on the parameters of all structural equations simultaneously. When compared with the methods considered up till now which deal with such constraints in one equation only, these full-information estimates should be expected to be characterised by smaller sampling variability, provided at least that the additional constraints are correct. It is of some interest to add that limited-information methods can also be used iteratively to take account of constraints on parameters outside the particular equation under consideration.[2] Suppose e.g. that we start by estimating all equations, one by one, according to two-stage least-squares. We can then derive the estimated covariance matrix, $\mathbf{M}_{\mathbf{vv}}^*$ say, of the reduced-form disturbances which corresponds with the point estimates obtained. This

[1] A. L. NAGAR, "Double-k-Class Estimators of Parameters in Simultaneous Equations and Their Small-Sample Properties." Forthcoming report of the Econometric Institute of the Netherlands School of Economics.

[2] This approach was followed by A. L. NAGAR in "Simultaneous Equations Estimation: Iterative Two-Stage Least-Squares," Report 5821 of the Econometric Institute of the Netherlands School of Economics (1958).

matrix is identical with $\mathbf{M_{vv}}$ of 6.C.1 only if all equations are just-identified.[1] As soon as there is over-identification, the matrices are different; and we should expect $\mathbf{M}^*_{\mathbf{vv}}$ to be more efficient, since it is based on a larger number of restrictions. We can then repeat the second step of two-stage least-squares with $\mathbf{M}^*_{\mathbf{vv}}$ instead of $\mathbf{M_{vv}}$; this gives new point estimates, which in turn imply a third moment matrix $\mathbf{M}^{**}_{\mathbf{vv}}$, etc. This is still much simpler than full-information maximum-likelihood. We may also proceed in a less mechanical way. Suppose for example that it is known that a certain parameter is positive or zero, whereas its point estimate according to two-stage least-squares is negative. Then we may decide on a zero value and proceed with the iteration under this additional *a priori* restriction. This process can be repeated each time when unplausible point estimates (not necessarily of the wrong sign) are obtained. More experience will be necessary before a final appraisal of these iterative methods are possible; a difficulty is that there seems to be no convergence in some cases.

6.D. Implications of Multicollinearity

6.D.1. The unfavourable consequences of multicollinearity among the variables of an equation have been stressed in various places of this chapter. The best way out seems to be the method of mixed estimation, at least when there is *a priori* knowledge of some substantial quality. Since the places at which implications of the multicollinearity problem are mentioned are rather scattered, it may be worth-while to summarise them here.[2]

First, even if the classical assumptions of least-squares are all satisfied, there are large standard errors according to the formula $\sigma^2(\mathbf{X'X})^{-1}$. However, it does not follow from this approximate indeterminacy that nothing definite can be concluded from the regression analysis. On the

[1] $\mathbf{M}^*_{\mathbf{vv}}$ cannot be derived if some of the equations are not identifiable. This proviso is not very important for large systems, for we usually have over-identification there. The reason for this is that, when comparing smaller and larger systems, we find that the number of predetermined variables grows often roughly in proportion to the number of equations, whereas the number of variables in each equation is usually three or four and at most five or six. Reference is made to the article by KLOEK and MENNES quoted on p. **343**.

[2] Long ago, some of these points were stressed by FRISCH; cf. his *Statistical Confluence Analysis by Means of Complete Regression Systems*, especially the Introduction.

contrary, there are certain linear combinations of the parameters which can be determined relatively accurrately. But the economist is usually (rightly or wrongly) more interested in the parameters themselves than in these combinations.

Second, if the investigator tries to find the "true" specification by introducing additional explanatory variables, one at a time, and if he decides on the basis of statistical significance, the danger of wrong decisions tends to be greater in the case of multicollinearity. In the extreme opposite case, when the product moment matrix of the explanatory variables is diagonal, the least-squares coefficients are not affected by the question which of these variables are included. But the presence of correlations among these variables changes this radically, especially when their number is large and the multicollinearity is considerable. More generally, incorrectly specified variables affect the parameter estimates of correctly specified variables as soon as there are correlations between variables of the two groups.

Third, if the explanatory variables as such are correctly specified but observed with errors, and if they are correlated, then a similar effect results. To take an extreme example, suppose that y is a linear function of x_1 and x_2, and that x_1 and x_2 are perfectly or almost perfectly correlated. In the first case (that of perfect multicollinearity) the least-squares estimator does not exist, since the matrix $\mathbf{X'X}$ is singular. In the second case the estimator does exist, though its components have large variances. Suppose now that x_1' and x_2' have been observed, the differences $x_1' - x_1$ and $x_2' - x_2$ being observational errors. Then the least-squares estimator in the regression of y on x_1' and x_2' exists in general in both cases; but that of the first has no value at all, and that of the second very little, because the observational errors are bound to dominate the sampling distribution of such estimators.

Fourth, if the complication is that the disturbances are autocorrelated, then, whether there is multicollinearity or not, the variance expression $\sigma^2(\mathbf{X'X})^{-1}$ is no longer applicable. If there is multicollinearity, however, this expression tends to underestimate the inaccuracy of least-squares more than otherwise. It is true, this result has been derived under rather special assumptions only; but it is consistent with the general picture.

Finally, there is the problem of multicollinearity and simultaneous equations. This is really twofold. First, the mere fact that there is such a system of equations implies that the explanatory variables of each equation will in general be correlated. Second, if we decide on two-stage least-squares, then the problem is aggravated because of the subtraction of the matrix $\mathbf{V'V}$.[1]

6.D.2. Multicollinearity has only one advantage, though it is very doubtful whether we may give it this name. If there is an approximate linear relationship among the explanatory variables during the sample period, so that the coefficients found are likely to be highly disturbed; and if this approximate relationship extends to the prediction period; then the conditional prediction of the left-hand variable for this period, the condition being that the explanatory variables are as observed, is not affected by the evils of the multicollinearity. Hence the continuation of the multicollinearity in the prediction period is an "advantage." This was observed earlier in Section 5.2, and the reason is that the combination of parameters necessary for this conditional forecast belongs to those which happen to be estimated rather accurately—cf. the second paragraph of 6.D.1. However, this is not more than a qualified advantage, since its disadvantage is twofold. First, as observed in 5.2.4, it may be necessary to know other parameter combinations for policy purposes, and there is no guarantee that they belong to that favourite class. Second, the prediction result conceals the real virtues of the forecasting procedure: the forecast is "right for the wrong reasons."

6.E. Detailed Discussion of the Analyses of the Traders' Expected Buying Prices

6.E.1. It will be clear from Section 6.3 that the analyses of Table 6.6 are not to be regarded as serious attempts to ascertain the factors determining the expected buying prices. We shall therefore confine ourselves to a discussion of Table 6.7.

First, let us consider (as in the text) those analyses which contain only two explanatory variables; viz., the lagged buying price of the same set of firms of which we consider the expectations, $b(\mathbf{p_b})_{-1}$, and one lagged selling price $b(\mathbf{p_s})^{H}_{-1}$ of some higher stage H. This category

[1] This is of minor importance if $\mathbf{V}$ is small relative to $\mathbf{Y}$. In that case the difference between single-stage and two-stage least-squares (or limited-information maximum-likelihood) estimates will be small. Empirical evidence gathered in the last few years suggests that this is rather frequently the case.

is not necessarily very plausible, but it is certainly simpler than those specifications which contain a larger number of variables. Within this category, we take first the analyses the selling price of which belongs to the stage immediately above the one of the expected buying price; viz., the analyses 14, 20 and 30. It will be clear that these variants are not very plausible for the simple reason that their lagged selling prices do not supply the forecaster with much information beyond that which is contained by his own buying prices. Our lack of appreciation for them seems to be justified by the criterion of maximum correlation: the $\bar{R}^2$ is much below the highest value within the present two-variables category, the difference being about 0.2 in two of the three cases (cf. 14 vs. 13, 20 vs. 18, 30 vs. 28). There is further a negative point estimate in analysis 14; but the standard error is such that, if this specification is the right one, a positive parent value is not impossible. When viewed as a whole, however, it seems reasonable to reject the specifications corresponding to these analyses, viz.:

14, 20, 30.

The same fate seems justifiable with respect to the analyses 17 and 26. They describe the expected buying prices of the wholesalers and the retailers, respectively, in shoes, and both in terms of prices of hides. Although the coefficients of this variable are no doubt significant under classical standards if the specification is indeed the correct one, it is not plausible that this proviso is fulfilled; first, because the traders are relatively far away from the market in hides, the price movements in the leather market being a much more plausible source of information; second, because of the unfavourable evidence of the correlation criterion. So we reject:

17, 26.

6.E.2. Next, we enlarge the category under consideration by the inclusion of the lagged selling price of a second (or third) higher stage. There is evidently little justification for doing so in the case of the leather traders, since this would involve the introduction of the rather unsuccessful selling price of the tanneries (cf. analysis 14). For the same reason it is preferable to confine the experiments for the wholesalers of shoes to the selling prices of the stages II and III. This brings us, unfortunately, into a multicollinear situation, so that the result is rather inconclusive (cf. 21).

As to the retailers in shoes, there are more combinatorial possibilities because of the larger number of higher stages. For the reason mentioned above for the stages III and V, it is preferable to exclude the selling price of the next higher stage of shoe wholesalers; but it does not seem correct to exclude *a priori* the possibility that the selling price of the shoe manufacturers is relevant, even if part of their output is shipped directly to the retailers. This leads to the analyses 31 through 34, which contain two or all three selling prices of the stages II, III and IV. Again, there is little possibility to distinguish between the first two variables (which is the reason why they are not introduced both at the same time in the further regressions of Table 6.6); but the four analyses, when compared with the earlier analyses for the same set of traders, suggest that it is better not to exclude the selling price of the shoe manufacturers, nor that of at least one of the stages II and III. The value of $\bar{R}^2$ increases by about 0.05 if the selling price of IV is included (cf. 32 vs. 27, 33 vs. 28, 34 vs. 31), by more than 0.2 if the price of one of the stages II and III is included (cf. 32 and 33 vs. 29). The gain in $\bar{R}^2$ obtained by the inclusion of the selling price of IV is not impressive; on the other hand, if one of the specifications corresponding to 32, 33 or 34 is correct, these analyses suggest significance for the shoe manufacturers' prices. Also, the specification with $b(\mathbf{p_s})_{-1}^{\mathrm{IV}}$ included is rather plausible. For suppose that there has been a tendency to raise prices among the shoe manufacturers during a particular month, resulting in a positive balance; then it is not unreasonable from the retailers' point of view to expect that other manufacturers will follow suit next month for competitive reasons, thus causing a (further) rise of the retailers' buying prices by that time. These arguments lead us to reject all specifications that do not include the selling price of IV and at least one of the selling prices of II and III; viz.

27, 28, 29, 31

in addition to the specifications rejected before.

6.E.3. We enlarge the set of specifications further by considering the price variables lagged two months. First, we confine ourselves to those analyses which contain $b(\mathbf{p_b})_{-2}$, not $b(\mathbf{p_s})_{-2}^{H}$.

There is one analysis for the leather traders which falls in this category, viz. 15; and it leads to a coefficient for $b(\mathbf{p_b})_{-2}$ which is almost significant under classical standards. The same holds for one of the two alternative analyses of the shoe wholesalers (22), but not for the other one (24), nor for those of the retailers (35, 37, 39, 40);[1] the coefficients of $b(\mathbf{p_b})_{-2}$ are of the same order of magnitude as the standard errors if the selling price of II is included, and generally smaller if the latter price is replaced by that of III. This is a natural result when the number of variables increases, since the limited set of data is bound to supply decreasing additional evidence. It is tempting, therefore, to apply the simplicity criterion and to exclude $b(\mathbf{p_b})_{-2}$. On the other hand, the persistence of negative signs of the point estimates corresponding to this variable is an argument against this proposal. Also, a negative parameter value is rather plausible. As observed in the text, it means that prices are expected to rise next month if they have gathered momentum; i.e., if they rose more generally in the present month than in the month before. Since furthermore the coefficients of the other variables in the analyses containing $b(\mathbf{p_b})_{-2}$ give no reason to discredit these specifications, we may feel that it is better to include this variable. So let us reject all analyses that do not contain $b(\mathbf{p_b})_{-2}$, viz.

13, 18, 19, 21, 32, 33, 34

in addition to the earlier rejections.

Our conclusion should be less favourable with respect to the selling price $b(\mathbf{p_s})^H_{-2}$. The point estimate of its coefficient is, in all analyses 16, 23, 25, 36 and 38, of the same order of magnitude as the standard error or smaller. In addition to this, there is no persistence of sign and the $\bar{R}^2$'s are almost invariably reduced relative to the corresponding analyses without $b(\mathbf{p_s})^H_{-2}$. The plausibility argument has also less weight here, and so we reject these specifications.

As a whole, we have rejected:[2]

for III: 13, 14, 16;

for V: 17–21, 23, 25;

for VI: 26–38.

[1] In the retailers' case some experiments have been made with this variable by taking only one selling price into account; this in spite of the findings of 6.E.2. The reason is, of course, that the number of variables in the present analyses begins to accumulate. These experiments are only valuable for the purpose of making comparisons.

[2] This list includes the analyses 35 and 37, which have not yet been discussed. They were carried out for comparison purposes.

The variables which we have not rejected are:

for III: $b(\mathbf{p_b})_{-1}^{\mathrm{III}}$, $b(\mathbf{p_b})_{-2}^{\mathrm{III}}$, $b(\mathbf{p_s})_{-1}^{\mathrm{I}}$;

for V: $b(\mathbf{p_b})_{-1}^{\mathrm{V}}$, $b(\mathbf{p_b})_{-2}^{\mathrm{V}}$, $b(\mathbf{p_s})_{-1}^{\mathrm{II}}$, $b(\mathbf{p_s})_{-1}^{\mathrm{III}}$;

for VI: $b(\mathbf{p_b})_{-1}^{\mathrm{VI}}$, $b(\mathbf{p_b})_{-2}^{\mathrm{VI}}$, $b(\mathbf{p_s})_{-1}^{\mathrm{II}}$, $b(\mathbf{p_s})_{-1}^{\mathrm{III}}$, $b(\mathbf{p_s})_{-1}^{\mathrm{IV}}$.

6.E.4. The last problem is that of the correlation of the selling prices of II and III. As explained in the text, it has been "solved" by giving them equal weights; the argument being the increase of $\bar{R}^2$ when they are both introduced (especially for VI, not for V) and the approximate equality of their point estimates, to which a moderate degree of plausibility can be added. The rather plausible results obtained in Table 6.8, finally, may be regarded as an additional quality indicator for the analysis as a whole.

6.F. Some Data Used in the Analysis of the Buying Prices of the Traders in Hides

Table 6.35 below contains a price index (base: 1950 = 100) of the imported hides (*Häute und Felle*) in Germany, published in the *Statistisches Jahrbuch für die Bundesrepublik Deutschland* (Chapter XX, Section A.5). The table includes data for the sample period as well as for the prediction period.

TABLE 6.35

PRICE INDEX OF IMPORTED HIDES IN GERMANY, 1950–1954

Year	*Month*											
	J	*F*	*M*	*A*	*M*	*J*	*J*	*A*	*S*	*O*	*N*	*D*
1950	90	89	90	90	88	88	91	95	111	114	123	129
1951	139	152	155	152	152	147	137	126	123	125	116	114
1952	113	108	90	83	82	82	86	89	91	88	90	93
1953	93	93	96	94	93	92	88	90	93	94	93	93
1954	93	94	94	95	100	100	99	93	91	91	93	92

6.G. Partial Scatter Diagrams of the Preferred Relations in Balances

Fig. 6.21 contains 37 partial scatter diagrams corresponding with the preferred balance relations 15, 22, 39, 165, 173, 207, 213, 227, 239, 249, 257. In each case an explanatory variable is measured along the horizontal axis, and the corresponding dependent variable, corrected for the influence of all other explanatory variables, is measured vertically. For example, the first scatter deals with analysis 15:

$$b(\bar{\mathbf{p}}_{\mathbf{b}})^{\mathrm{III}} = -0.06 + 0.32\, b(\mathbf{p}_{\mathbf{b}})^{\mathrm{III}}_{-1} - 0.14\, b(\mathbf{p}_{\mathbf{b}})^{\mathrm{III}}_{-2} + 0.23\, b(\mathbf{p}_{\mathbf{s}})^{\mathrm{I}}_{-1};$$

the explanatory variable considered is $b(\mathbf{p}_{\mathbf{b}})^{\mathrm{III}}_{-1}$, and the corrected dependent variable

$$b(\bar{\mathbf{p}}_{\mathbf{b}})^{\mathrm{III}} + 0.06 + 0.14\, b(\mathbf{p}_{\mathbf{b}})^{\mathrm{III}}_{-2} - 0.23\, b(\mathbf{p}_{\mathbf{s}})^{\mathrm{I}}_{-1}.$$

The correction is not indicated explicitly, so that the variable which is measured vertically is simply written as $b(\bar{\mathbf{p}}_{\mathbf{b}})^{\mathrm{III}}$.

No scales are indicated in the charts; the four sides of the squares are all drawn at a distance $\pm$ 1 from the axes, the sole exception being the first scatter of analysis 257 (the vertical sides of which are drawn at a distance $\pm$ 0.1). The last two scatters are combined in one chart, the dots referring to current sales, the circles to sales lagged one month. There are some points in the scatters of analysis 257 which imply a balance outside the interval (−1, 1).

Evidently, although the correlations are far from perfect, there is little indication of curvilinearity.

6.H. Test Variate Data of the Prediction Period

Table 6.36 contains all data used for the prediction analysis of Section 6.8 (except the import price level of hides, which is summarised in Table 6.35). The organisation of this table is identical with that of Table 4.19 in the Appendix of Chapter IV.

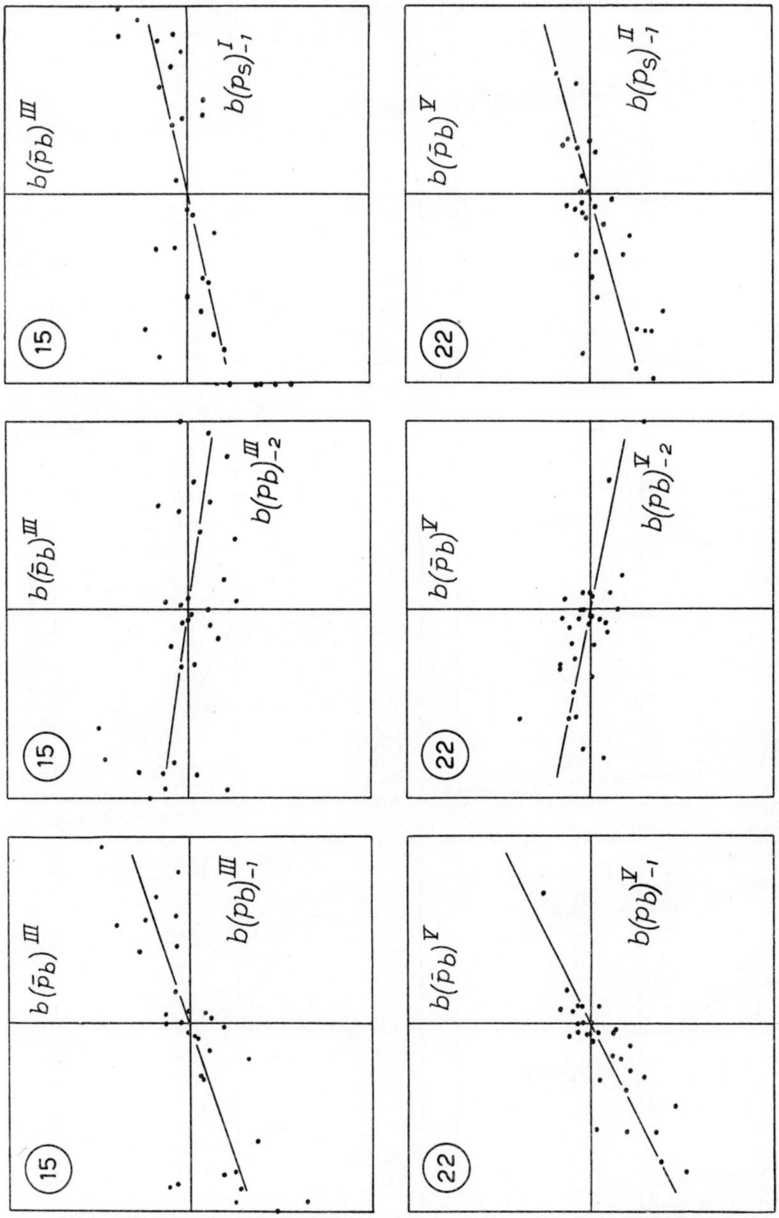

Fig. 6.21. Partial scatter diagrams of the preferred relations in balances
(German leather and shoe industry, 1951–1953)

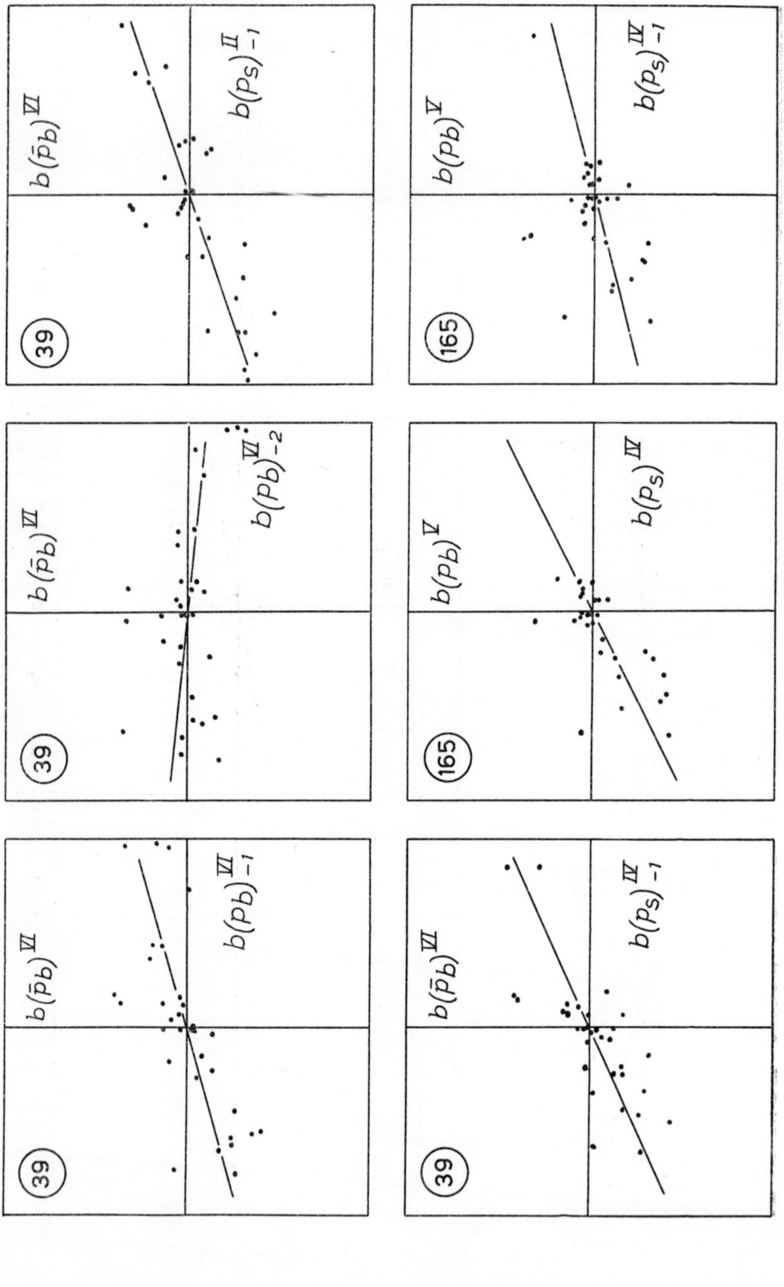

Fig. 6.21 *(continued)*

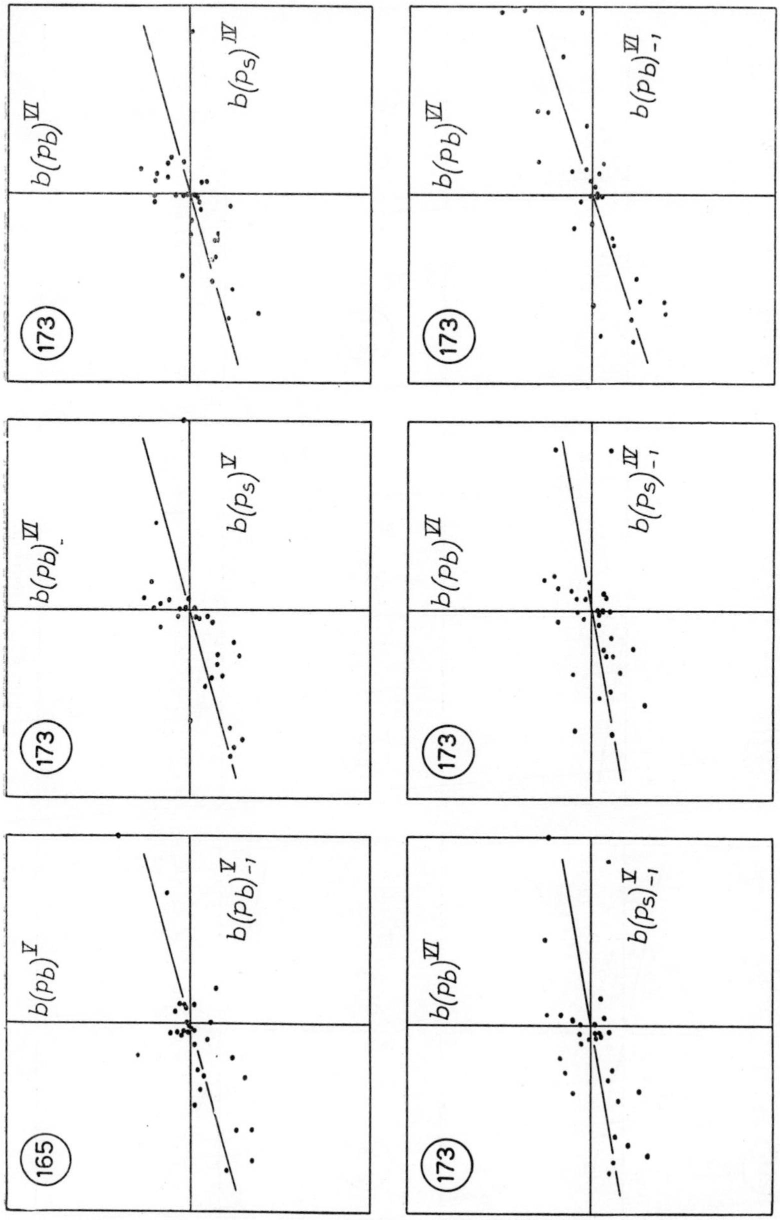

Fig. 6.21 (continued)

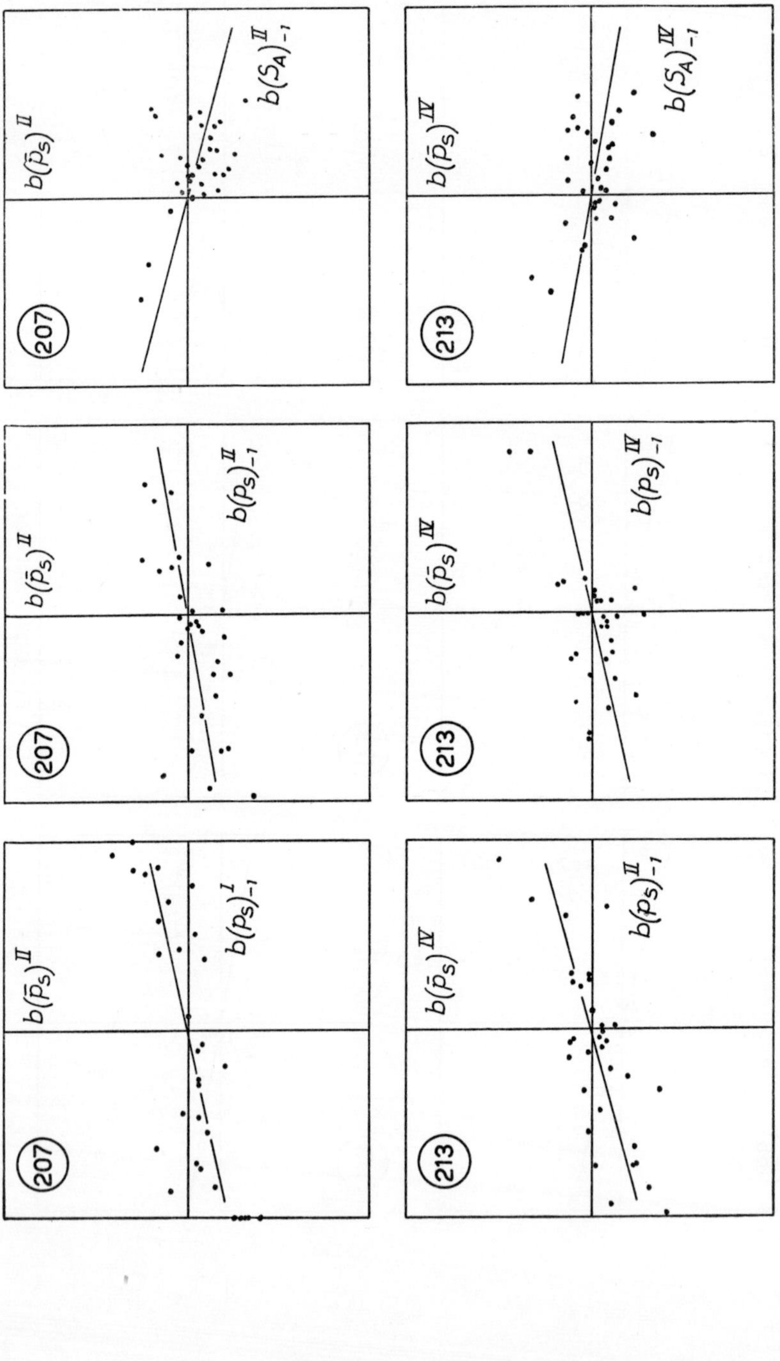

Fig. 6.21 (*continued*)

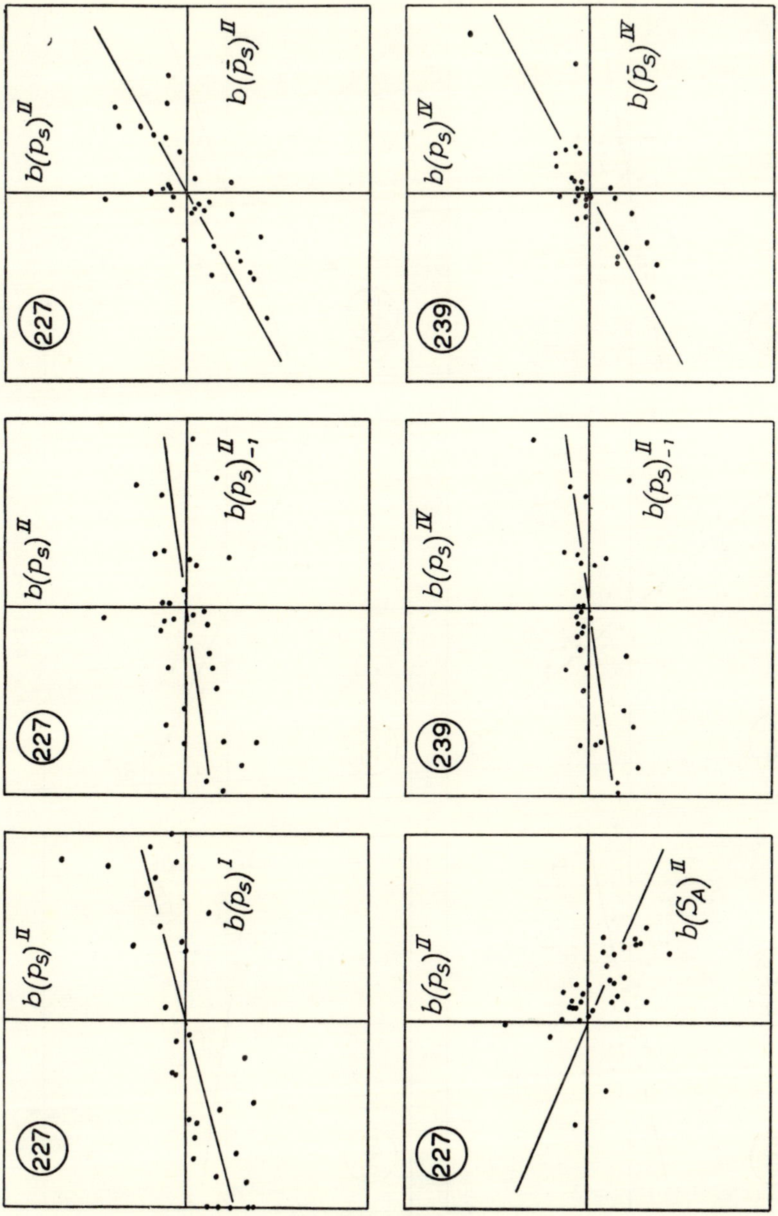

Fig. 6.21 *(continued)*

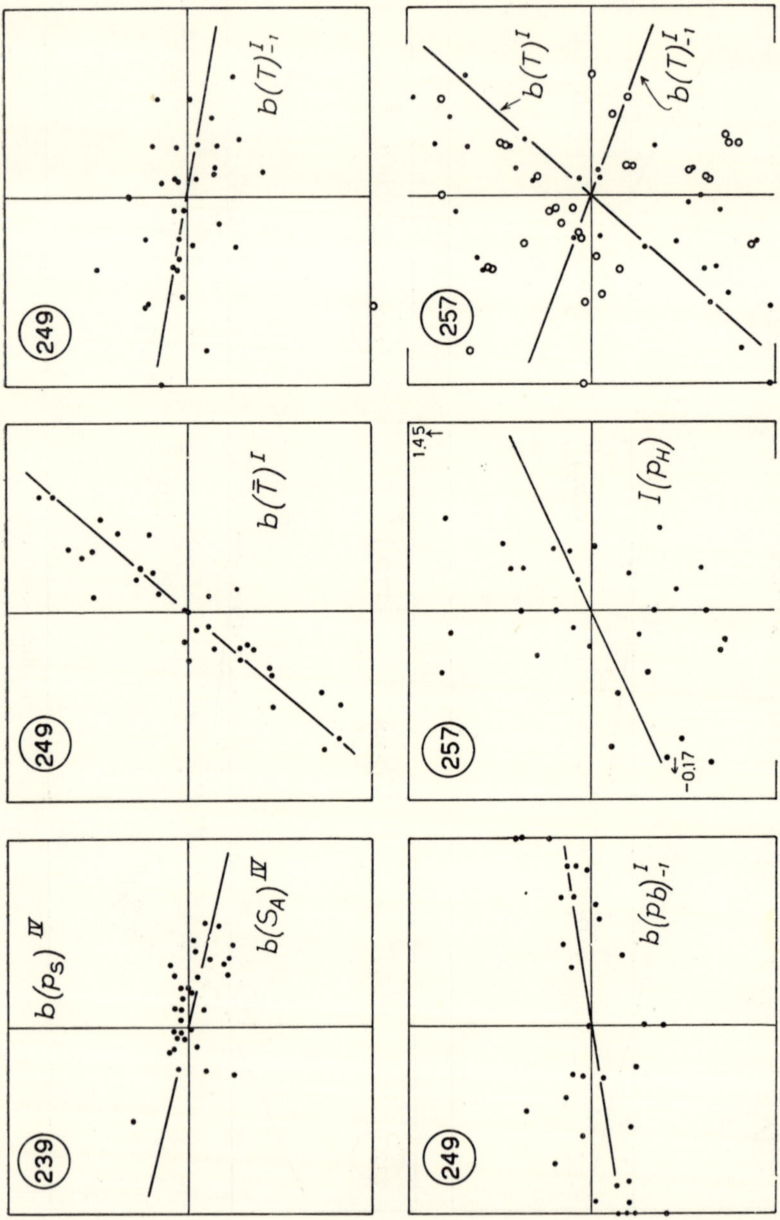

Fig. 6.21 *(concluded)*

TEST VARIATES (MULTIPLIED BY 100) OF THE GERMAN LEATHER AND SHOE INDUSTRY, 1953–1956

	Variables (and industry stages)													
	selling prices (I)		*appraisal of stocks (II)*		*selling prices (II)*		*selling prices planned (II)*		*appraisal of stocks (IV)*		*selling prices (IV)*		*selling prices planned (IV)*	
	x^1	x^3	x^1	x^3	x^1	x^3	x^1	x^3	x^1	x^3	x^1	x^3	x^1	x^3
1953, N	0	58	14	14	2	12	1	3	26	11	0	2	2	9
D	0	62	13	8	0	7	4	10	42	4	0	3	0	15
1954, J	0	61	32	6	0	30	3	18	44	2	0	10	0	6
F	0	92	34	7	0	33	2	13	35	3	0	12	0	4
M	0	65	32	8	0	27	0	27	31	2	0	9	0	6
A	0	36	28	10	0	13	0	20	25	1	0	9	0	5
M	15	11	24	3	1	6	10	3	17	4	0	5	0	5
J	0	48	32	9	0	10	4	3	25	6	0	28	0	12
J	0	100	32	6	0	43	8	0	19	1	0	10	2	2
A	0	92	31	2	2	25	3	15	17	4	0	6	0	1
S	0	67	32	4	1	17	0	18	14	10	0	2	0	4
O	46	0	26	4	3	7	0	10	15	23	1	5	0	1
N	9	13	10	19	2	4	0	1	11	29	1	4	0	5
D	13	8	16	11	4	5	6	2	20	14	0	9	0	3
1955, J	39	0	28	4	11	12	4	6	13	8	0	17	0	5
F	0	100	20	11	1	1	5	7	20	7	0	3	3	2
M	13	0	22	5	1	3	2	0	25	11	0	13	0	11
A	41	0	14	7	8	3	1	5	16	10	0	11	0	1
M	21	0	22	11	20	2	14	0	18	13	0	4	1	1
J	0	35	26	17	13	4	6	0	20	4	0	5	2	4
J	9	8	20	2	11	2	12	0	25	11	0	0	0	0
A	67	0	26	10	20	2	4	0	8	11	0	0	2	0
S	25	0	15	6	3	2	3	2	4	17	0	0	2	0
O	9	0	15	4	28	0	18	0	6	26	6	0	24	0
N	8	8	8	9	16	1	12	0	5	29	14	2	17	0
D	14	29	13	6	11	0	22	0	4	20	14	0	12	0
1956, J	13	0	13	0	21	0	8	0	9	2	22	2	26	0
F	0	0	20	0	9	0	16	0	19	5	15	0	9	2
M	28	8	27	0	7	10	7	10	22	8	7	1	5	0
A	0	6	34	2	22	2	11	0	16	2	3	3	15	6
M	0	60	35	1	0	2	9	0	26	2	3	5	9	2
J	.	.	.	.	.	.	10	0	.	.	.	.	5	2

TABLE 6.36 (*continued*)

	Variables (and industry stages)																	
	sales (I)		sales expected (I)		buying prices (I)		buying prices expected (I)		selling prices planned (I)		buying prices (III)		buying prices expected (III)		selling prices (III)		selling prices planned (III)	
	x^1	x^3	x^1	x^3	x^1	x^3	x^1	x^3	x^1	x^3	x^1	x^3	x^1	x^3	x^1	x^3	x^1	x^3
1953, N	24	40	24	19	0	65	0	43	0	43	0	1	0	12	0	1	0	19
D	12	23	8	24	0	54	0	56	0	56	0	10	0	26	0	8	0	12
1954, J	18	30	21	29	0	67	0	42	0	42	0	32	0	10	0	32	0	10
F	0	50	26	26	0	92	0	48	0	48	0	44	0	9	0	34	0	9
M	13	16	0	17	0	68	0	52	0	52	0	41	0	30	0	49	0	30
A	14	0	20	20	0	36	0	0	0	0	0	16	0	6	0	16	0	6
M	26	41	14	36	7	11	9	36	9	36	0	9	0	2	0	11	0	2
J	24	12	0	23	0	56	11	0	11	0	0	16	0	0	0	16	0	0
J	7	41	0	39	0	100	0	36	0	36	0	14	0	4	0	14	0	0
A	0	54	19	58	0	73	0	75	0	77	0	17	0	18	0	17	0	18
S	0	22	11	11	0	61	0	38	0	38	7	11	0	0	0	11	0	0
O	62	15	39	11	50	0	25	25	22	22	0	7	0	0	0	6	0	0
N	43	13	27	12	9	13	17	4	27	4	0	0	2	0	0	0	2	0
D	4	25	22	35	8	0	9	26	9	26	0	0	0	19	0	0	0	19
1955, J	57	11	29	0	.	.	17	0	17	0	.	.	0	0	.	.	0	0

TABLE 6.36 (*concluded*)

	Variables (and industry stages)															
	buying prices (V)		*buying prices expected (V)*		*selling prices (V)*		*selling prices planned (V)*		*buying prices (VI)*		*buying prices expected (VI)*		*selling prices (VI)*		*selling prices planned (VI)*	
	x^1	x^3	x^1	x^3	x^1	x^3	x^1	x^3	x^1	x^3	x^1	x^3	x^1	x^3	x^1	x^3
1953, N	0	0	0	0	0	0	0	0	0	0	0	0	0	0	0	0
D	0	0	0	5	0	6	0	5	0	4	0	4	0	7	0	4
1954, J	0	0	0	4	0	0	0	4	0	3	0	8	0	4	0	8
F	0	0	0	0	0	0	0	0	0	7	0	6	0	7	0	6
M	0	0	0	6	0	6	0	6	0	3	0	9	0	0	0	4
A	0	0	0	5	0	0	0	5	0	2	0	10	0	2	0	9
M	0	9	0	15	0	14	0	15	1	3	0	11	0	2	0	11
J	0	10	0	5	0	4	0	5	0	7	0	8	1	4	0	8
J	0	21	0	9	0	31	0	12	0	14	0	16	0	7	2	13
A	0	14	0	8	0	7	0	22	0	9	0	9	0	4	1	9
S	0	5	0	3	0	5	0	3	0	2	3	4	0	3	3	4
O	0	0	0	6	0	0	0	6	1	4	0	2	1	4	0	3
N	0	8	14	0	0	0	7	0	0	2	1	8	2	2	0	4
D	0	0	8	0	0	5	8	0	0	1	0	2	0	2	0	1
1955, J	.	.	0	0	.	.	0	0	.	.	0	5	.	.	0	6

VII. Forecasts and Policy: Problems and Tools

7.1. Predictions and Preferences

7.1.1. Up till now, numerous promises have been made to the effect that certain admittedly primitive procedures would be appraised and possibly modified in the light of the analysis of the third type of problems in the analysis of forecasts, viz., their influence on actual behaviour. This will be the topic of the present and the next chapter. An alternative way of describing this subject is "decision-making under uncertainty." Indeed, the uncertainty element is exactly the reason why forecasts are necessary; and decisions can be regarded as equivalent to behaviour. The latter statement is not correct, of course, if we want to take account of the possibility that decisions are not carried out; in that case a decision would be nothing else than a plan. We shall not follow this definition, however; i.e., taking a decision will be considered as equivalent with carrying out a decision. In the first part of the analysis, we shall go even further by excluding the possibility of plan revisions. This is the "static" approach, which is much simpler than the "dynamic" one. In the dynamic case, a policy-maker can formulate a plan in the first period, after which he decides in the second whether or not he carries it out; in other words, a distinction should then be made between a first-period decision (the plan) and a second-period decision (the behaviour). This subject, which is obviously related to the discussion of "plans having a separate influence on behaviour" [see Chapter II (cf. 2.3.5) and the empirical parts of Chapter VI], will be treated in the final section of Chapter VIII as a generalisation of the static theory.

This section gives an outline of relevant problems. Since it will appear that their solution requires certain tools some of which are, although available, scattered at different places and sometimes written in a rather technical language, the other sections of this chapter are used for a re-statement and some minor extensions of these. After this, Chapter VIII is devoted to an analysis of our third type of problem.

7.1.2. In Chapter I (cf. 1.2.1), a short description was given of the impact of forecasting on the decision-making process. A somewhat more elaborate description of man in his rôle of "decision-making animal" is the following:

(*i*) First, he should have *knowledge,* in terms of values assumed by relevant variables, *of his present state.* These variables are not necessarily of the usual quantitative type; qualitative distinctions (war or no war, Government price control or no control, etc.) are equally possible. Furthermore, it is conceivable—and even highly plausible in many cases—that the knowledge is incomplete, in which case there is an element of uncertainty even at this stage.

(*ii*) He should divide these variables into two groups: those which he controls, and those which he cannot control, but which he can at most influence indirectly and perhaps stochastically. This distinction is not in all cases a very clear-cut one; so it might seem better to speak about the degree to which a given variable can be controlled.[1] For purposes of analysis, however, we shall assume that certain variables, to be called *instruments* or *controlled variables* in contradistinction to the other, *noncontrolled variables,* exist which are fully controlled by the policy-maker. Changes in controlled variables will be called *measures* taken by the policy-maker.

(*iii*) He should make a *prediction* of the future course of the noncontrolled variables under alternative assumptions concerning his own (present and future) behaviour; i.e., he should formulate conditional expectations about the time pattern of noncontrolled variables, the conditions being alternative measures to be taken by himself in the present and in the future. It seems obvious that it is not necessary for the policy-maker to make such predictions himself, and that he may delegate this task to a staff of forecasters; but some problems are involved in this division of labour which we shall have to consider later.

(*iv*) He should *evaluate* the various outcomes of the predictions sub

[1] For example, the rate of production is usually regarded as an instrument from the standpoint of the entrepreneur. But it may be argued that no entrepreneur really controls this variable because of the possibility of earthquakes, etc.

(*iii*); i.e., he should make an appraisal of the relative merits of the results of alternative measures, this result for each set of measures consisting of (*a*) the changes in the controlled variables and (*b*) the accompanying changes in the noncontrolled variables. The second part (*b*) implies in general an element of uncertainty in addition to that mentioned sub (*i*). This appraisal is usually based on the ordering of all conceivable individual outcomes according to a preference scale; we shall come back to this later.

(*v*) Finally, he should make a *choice* among all alternatives available to him (i.e., he should choose a certain set of measures) such that the result according to the appraisal sub (*iv*) is "good" or even "best." This choice is a *decision.*

The formulation of a decision by means of the acquisition of knowledge of the present state in terms of instrument values and those of noncontrolled variables, of prediction and of evaluation—this formuation will be called the policy-maker's "policy."

7.1.3. It is clear that the above requirements are partly of a factual nature [(*i*) and (*ii*)], partly of a "behavioural" nature in the sense that a knowledge of the behaviour pattern of the policy-maker's surroundings (taken in a wide sense) is required (*iii*), and partly of a "utility" nature (*iv*). Our approach will be to use an econometric model for the "behavioural" aspect. We shall illustrate this with the following simplified example, which will be used rather frequently in the further analysis.

Suppose our policy-maker is a Minister of Finance or of Economic Affairs, who is interested in the employment level of his country and in its balance of payments. Suppose also that he knows the present values of all relevant variables; and let us write all variables, unless otherwise specified, as deviations from these present values. Suppose furthermore that the variable by means of which he can influence the above-mentioned variables is the volume of Government expenditure. Finally, suppose that the interrelationships of the relevant variables can be described by a model of the following kind:

$$P = C + I + X + G, \tag{7.1}$$

a definitional equation which describes the aggregate volume of production (P) in terms of its components: consumption (C), gross investment (I), exports (X), Government expenditure (G), all measured in constant prices;

(7.2) $$M = a_1C + a_2I + a_3X + a_4G,$$

an import equation with different "marginal propensities to import" for the separate components of P;

(7.3) $$C = \beta P,$$

a consumption function;

(7.4) $$E = \gamma P,$$

an equation describing the number of workers employed (E) as a function of aggregate production; and

(7.5) $$B = p_X X - p_M M,$$

an equation describing the balance of payments, B (in money terms, not in constant prices), as the value of exports minus the value of imports, p_X and p_M being price indices of exports and of imports, respectively. For simplicity's sake, we shall take both indices (measured with base unity in the present period, rather than as deviations from the present values) as given constants.

We may say that the model (7.1)–(7.5) is a complete one in terms of the five endogenous variables P, C, M, E, B, and three exogenous variables G, I, X (cf. 6.2.7). Under the plausible assumption $\beta \neq 1$ we can express each of the endogenous variables as functions of the exogenous ones. Two of these reduced-form relationships are relevant for our purpose, viz.:

(7.6) $$E = \frac{\gamma}{1-\beta} G + \left[\frac{\gamma}{1-\beta}(I + X)\right];$$

(7.7) $$B = -\left(\frac{a_1\beta}{1-\beta} + a_4\right) p_M G - \left[\left(\frac{a_1\beta}{1-\beta} + a_2\right) p_M I + \right.$$
$$\left. + \left\{\left(\frac{a_1\beta}{1-\beta} + a_3\right) p_M - p_X\right\} X\right].$$

The argument is then as follows. Suppose our policy-maker is interested in next year's level of employment and balance of payments. According to (7.6) and (7.7), both (unknown) quantities are determined by next year's volume of Government expenditure on the one hand, and by next year's investment and export volume on the other. Out of these, the former quantity can be controlled, whereas the latter two cannot. It is necessary, therefore, to make a (higher-order) prediction of the latter quantities such that, when this prediction is combined with knowledge (or estimates) of the parameters of the system (7.1)–(7.5), the terms in square brackets of (7.6) and (7.7) are known. They are "known," of course, only in the limited sense that a prediction is available, and this imperfect knowledge implies automatically the possibility of forecasting errors. For the moment, however, we prefer to leave this aspect aside.

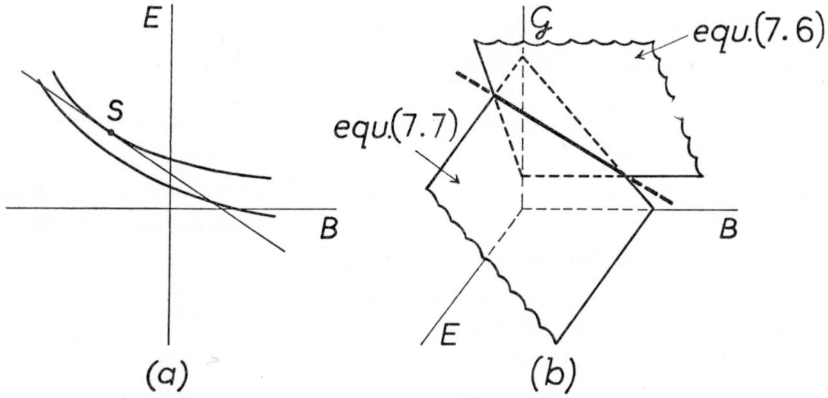

Fig. 7.1. (*a*) Constraint and indifference curves for employment (E) and balance of payments (B); (*b*) two constraints for employment, balance of payments, and Government expenditure (G)

After these operations both E and B have become linear functions of G only, the terms in square brackets being "constant terms." When eliminating G we obtain a linear relation between E and B, which is illustrated in the left-hand part of Fig. 7.1; its slope is taken as negative, which is reasonable, because the G-coefficients in (7.6) and (7.7) have opposite signs under the plausible assumptions α_1, α_4, $\gamma > 0$ and $0 < \beta < 1$. It is clear that the policy-maker can attain any point of the straight line by choosing a suitable G-value. If he can order all possible combinations of E, B-values according to increasing preference in such a way that indifference curves of the usual type exist, his "best" point on the line will be the point S where an indifference curve touches the line.

7.1.4. The above example suggests a very close formal relationship with the classical theory of consumer's demand: both there and in the example, the derivation of the "best" choice of actions is based upon a linear constraint and its point of tangency with one of the indifference curves or surfaces. Actually, we might expect certain elements of classical consumer's theory to be even more valuable for our present purposes than for consumer analysis itself, for two distinct reasons; first, because the policy-makers we have in mind, like Government officials, entrepreneurs, labour union officials, etc., are usually more "rational" than unsophisticated consumers, so that the existence of stable indifference curves seems to be a more realistic assumption for our present case; second, because consumer theory is not very realistic as to the problem of large, indivisible units of some (especially durable) commodities, whereas in the above example—and in many others—this problem does not play a significant rôle in view of the almost perfect divisibility of variables like employment and balance of payments. We shall therefore make use of this theory; and Section 7.2 will be devoted to a brief re-statement and to an extension that will prove useful in Chapter VIII, viz., in the direction of the implications of changing preferences.

There are, however, certain differences between the type of analysis we have to perform and classical consumer theory; they can be conveniently listed here. First, contrary to the sole budget restriction in consumer's theory, it is not generally true for our present problems that the number of constraints is only one. It was only one in the example of 7.1.3, but some minor modifications are sufficient to raise this to two. Suppose that our policy-maker does not consider G solely as an instrument by which he can influence E and B, but that he appraises G in its own right because of the immediate welfare implications of changes in the volume of Government expenditure (on schools, highways, salaries, etc.). In that case we should replace the indifference curves in the E, B-plane by indifference surfaces in the E, B, G-space. For our present purposes the most important consequence is that the single constraint in the E, B-plane is replaced by the two separate constraints corresponding to (7.6) and (7.7), respectively, each being represented by a two-dimensional plane; cf. the (right-hand) Fig. 7.1. The straight line which is the intersection of the planes is then the set of points out of which the policy-maker must choose. Another interesting aspect of this modification of the example in 7.1.3 is the dual nature which controlled variables may have and generally have: they serve not only as instruments in adapting noncontrolled variables, but are appraised in their own right as well. Sometimes the latter aspect is considered much more important, so that the accompanying changes in noncontrolled variables are then merely regarded as (fortunate or unfortunate) by-products.[1]

A second difference with the traditional theory of consumer demand is the fact that the constraints are usually not exact, or at least not known exactly. For the example of 7.1.3 this follows immediately from the fact that higher-order predictions had to be made of the terms in square brackets of (7.6) and (7.7), so that the intercepts of these linear functions of G are not known exactly; similarly, the multiplicative coefficients of G in both equations are usually not known exactly either. Still another cause of inexactness are the familiar random disturbances. They were not introduced in the example of 7.1.3, but there is no reason, except for that of simplicity, why they should be dropped in the behavioural equations (7.2), (7.3), (7.4). It will be observed that there is no essential difference between predicting changes in exogenous variables (like I and X in 7.1.3) and forecasting disturbances, provided the latter are interpreted as neglected variables: in both cases we have to predict changes in variables, either neglected or not.

Third, contrary to the linear budget restriction of consumer's demand theory, the constraints which we shall have to face are not necessarily linear; and even if they are linear, the multiplicative coefficients of the equations making up the constraints do not necessarily obey the simple sign rule of the consumer's budget restriction. For the coefficients of the latter restriction are simply the prices, which are never negative and usually positive. Compare this with the unequal signs of the G-coefficients in (7.6) and (7.7). Similarly, when using a utility function in order to describe the policy-maker's preferences, the marginal utilities do not necessarily obey the simple sign rule which

[1] An example is the problem of raising the compulsory minimum school-leaving age. In most cases the proposals of such measures are based on psychological, educational and social motives, yet economic effects may be quite substantial. An analysis of such effects by means of an econometric model was made by W. H. Somermeijer in "On Economic Consequences of Extending Compulsory Education," a paper read at the Hindsgavl Meeting of the International Association for Research in Income and Wealth (1955); see also W. H. Somermeijer and J. W. W. A. Wit, "Leerplichtverlenging: een poging tot kwantificering van macroeconomische gevolgen op korte termijn" (with English summary), *Statistische en Econometrische Onderzoekingen,* 1956 1st quarter, pp. 5–23.

is assumed in consumer theory. There, the marginal utilities are all positive (or zero, as in the case of saturation); but for our policy-maker the sign is not definite. An example: if employment is among a Government policy-maker's (noncontrolled) variables, an increase in this variable will usually be positively valued; hence we might speak of a positive marginal utility. But it is equally well conceivable that unemployment is one of the variables, and the resulting negative marginal utility is a proof of the indefiniteness. This example may seem almost trivial; it is nevertheless conclusive.

When applying ideas derived from consumer's theory to the policy problems as expounded in 7.1.2, it will simply be necessary to take account of these differences. But one thing has to be added here in this connection, even if it is concerned with consumers rather than with policy-makers (though our policy-maker may be a consumer, of course). It might be argued that the above-mentioned differences are not realistic, since the consumer has to face the same situation. When deciding on his expenditure during the next month (say), he does not know the prices prevailing in that period beforehand; and hence he must try to predict them. Similarly, if the consumer has no fixed income—he may earn his living as an entrepreneur—he must try to predict his income. Hence the budget restriction is not known exactly, which means that the above-mentioned second difference does not exist. Moreover, when buying larger quantities of the same commodity, the consumer can often buy at a lower price; and if the prices depend on the quantities bought, the budget constraint is no longer linear in the quantities—hence the third difference ceases to exist. It seems, therefore, that the above differences are no real ones.

The appropriate answer to this objection is that it is irrelevant. What matters for our analytical purposes is the classical theory of consumer behaviour, not the behaviour itself; and this theory, which is essentially a mathematical analysis of constrained maxima, will be amended and applied to the theory of policy-making.

7.1.5. We can now continue our discussion of 7.1.2. Suppose that the variables for which predictions must be made according to step (*iii*) are connected by a complete linear model of the type considered earlier in Section 6.2 (cf. 6.2.7):

$$(7.8)\quad \begin{array}{l} \gamma_{11}y_1 + \ldots + \gamma_{1M}y_M + \beta_{11}x_1 + \ldots + \beta_{1\Lambda}x_\Lambda = \alpha_1 + u_1 \\ \cdots\cdots\cdots\cdots\cdots\cdots\cdots\cdots\cdots \\ \gamma_{M1}y_1 + \ldots + \gamma_{MM}y_M + \beta_{M1}x_1 + \ldots + \beta_{M\Lambda}x_\Lambda = \alpha_M + u_M. \end{array}$$

Here the γ's, β's, α's are parameters, the u's random disturbances with zero mean, the y's dependent and the x's predetermined variables. This time the constant terms (the α's) are introduced explicitly—though some of them may be zero, of course. When assuming that the γ's form a nonsingular matrix, we can express each dependent variable as a linear (reduced-form) function of the x's only:

$$(7.9)\quad \begin{array}{l} y_1 = r_{11}x_1 + \ldots + r_{1\Lambda}x_\Lambda + c_1 + v_1 \\ \cdots\cdots\cdots\cdots\cdots\cdots \\ y_M = r_{M1}x_1 + \ldots + r_{M\Lambda}x_\Lambda + c_M + v_M, \end{array}$$

the r's being multiplicative reduced-form parameters, the c's constant terms and the v's reduced-form disturbances.

At this stage it is appropriate to realise that neither all y's nor all x's play the same rôle in the decision-making process. As to the y's (and reconsidering the example of 7.1.3), we observe that some do play a rôle in this process, viz., E and B in the example, whereas others (viz., P, C and M) do not. We may therefore leave out all reduced-form relations in (7.9) which belong to such "irrelevant" variables; without loss of generality we may assume that the first n equations remain. As to the x's, some of them are the policy-maker's controlled variables (G in the example of 7.1.3), but some are exogenous variables which are not at all controlled by him (I and X),[1] and some may be lagged variables. The third category creates no special problems, since the values of these lagged variables are known at the moment of decision-making. Hence their linear combinations in the right-hand side of (7.9) are known numbers, which may be combined with the constant terms (the c's). This is not true, of course, if the information concerning these values lags so much behind the events that it is not available at the moment of decision-making; nor is it true if the coefficients by which these variables are multiplied are known imperfectly. In that case it is necessary to estimate the values, which corresponds to the case of uncertainty at the level of step (i) (cf. 7.1.2). It is always

[1] It need hardly be stressed that these "noncontrolled variables" are to be carefully distinguished from the y's. In the following discussion the former category will disappear because its values are predicted beforehand, the possible forecasting errors being included in the disturbances.

necessary to predict the relevant future values of the variables of the second category (I and X in 7.1.3); similarly, it is necessary to predict the disturbances v (though it may be impossible to do more than using their mean value). Consequently, the system (7.9), as far as belonging to the "relevant" y's, can be written as

$$y_1 = r_{11}x_1 + \ldots + r_{1m}x_m + s_1 \tag{7.10}$$
$$\cdots\cdots\cdots\cdots\cdots\cdots$$
$$y_n = r_{n1}x_1 + \ldots + r_{nm}x_m + s_n$$

or in matrix form[1]

$$\mathsf{y} = \mathsf{R}\mathsf{x} + \mathsf{s}, \tag{7.11}$$

where (*a*) y is the column vector of noncontrolled variables (which the policy-maker can influence, although in general not perfectly, by means of his instruments); in the example of 7.1.3, y consists of two elements, E and B; (*b*) x is the column vector of the policy-maker's instruments or controlled variables, their number being $m \leq \Lambda$, with $m = 1$ in the example (G); (*c*) R is the matrix of coefficients belonging to x in the equations for y; in the example of 7.1.3, R is the two-elements column vector [cf. (7.6) and (7.7)]

$$\mathsf{R} = \begin{bmatrix} \dfrac{\gamma}{1-\beta} \\ -\left(\dfrac{a_1\beta}{1-\beta} + a_4\right) p_M \end{bmatrix};$$

(*d*) s, the column vector of constant terms, is a mixture: it represents the remaining part of the reduced form of the noncontrolled variables and comprises, therefore, lagged values, noncontrolled exogenous values and disturbances. In the example of 7.1.3, s is a two-elements vector, its elements being the terms in square brackets of (7.6) and (7.7); if disturbances would be introduced into the behavioural equations (7.2), (7.3), (7.4), a linear combination of them would enter into both elements. It is clear that in most cases there is considerable imperfection in the policy-maker's knowledge about both R and s, but especially about s.

Given the equations (7.11) which allow him to make conditional

[1] In order to distinguish the matrices and vectors of the present analysis from those of the statistical Section 6.2, they are printed in the sanserif type.

predictions, the policy-maker should evaluate the outcomes of alternative measures—i.e., alternative changes in $\mathbf{x}$—according to their merits. The classical way of handling this is to suppose that a utility, preference, or "welfare" function exists,

$$w = w(\mathbf{x}, \mathbf{y}), \tag{7.12}$$

which describes the ordering of alternative outcomes according to increasing preference. We applied this device in 7.1.3, where it was assumed that "welfare" depends on E and B, and hence on $\mathbf{y}$, only; but the more general situation is the one in which it depends on $\mathbf{x}$ a well, and not only so *via* $\mathbf{y}$—cf the second paragraph of 7.1.4.

The policy-maker's "best" decision is then found by maximising (7.12) subject to the constraints (7.11). Since we must assume that the policy-maker is not fully certain about the precise form of the constraints, we must conclude that his actual choice problem is that of making decisions in risk-taking situations. Therefore, we shall continue this discussion in Section 7.3, where problems of this kind will be analysed in more detail.

7.1.6. The set-up presented in 7.1.5 can be generalised in several directions; for example, the equations may be nonlinear, some of the variables may be qualitative rather than quantitative, the choice problem may be a dynamic one in the sense that present as well as future measures have to be considered simultaneously, etc. All these topics will be regarded in due course; here, we prefer to give an illustrative example which is, although still simple, somewhat less simplified than that of 7.1.3. It is based on the equation system of the Dutch economy that was described in Section 3.1, and deals with the effects of certain Government measures.

Table 7.1 gives a survey of certain consequences of four alternative measures, viz., increasing either the Government commodity purchases or the Government wage bill by 100 millions of guilders, allowing the wage rates in the private sector to be increased by 1 per cent, and allowing this and raising the wage rates of civil servants by the same percentage. Obviously, the linearity of the equation system implies that any combination of two or more measures leads to consequences that are found by combining the separate consequences accordingly; e.g., the consequences of an increase of the Government commodity purchases of 200 millions of guilders and an increase of the Government wage bill of 100 millions are obtained by adding twice the first column to the second. Hence the measures corresponding to each column may be regarded as a "unit of measure" each.

TABLE 7.1

SOME CONSEQUENCES OF FOUR MEASURES OF GOVERNMENT POLICY IN THE NETHERLANDS (changes, in millions of guilders)

Variables	*Government commodity purchases + f 100 mln.*	*Government wage bill + f 100 mln.*	*wage rate priv. ind. + 1%*	*wage rate incl. civil service + 1%*
wage-income in private sector	17	13	92	94
non-wage-income	53	42	−25	−17
total income in private sector	70	55	67	77
imports (value)	77	59	−22	−11
exports (value)	0	0	−16	−16
balance of payments	−77	−59	6	− 6

It follows from Table 7.1 that—as far as the noncontrolled variables mentioned there are concerned—an increase of the Government wage bill is about 20 per cent less effective than an increase of the commodity purchases by the same amount; that both measures are less favourable for the wage-earners as a group than for non-wage-earners (both groups having in the aggregate roughly the same income); and that the balance of payments is adversely affected. Raising the wage rate, on the other hand, is much more favourable for the wage earners, the other group being even faced with a decrease in income. A combination of additional Government expenditure and a wage rate increase is then appropriate to keep both groups in balance—provided of course the policy-maker considers this indeed as a desirable goal. As to the balance of payments, the adverse effect of additional Government expenditure is partly offset when the wage increase is confined to the private sector, but accentuated when the civil servants, too, get their share. Hence the policy-maker may feel inclined to choose the former alternative; at the same time, however, he should envisage the welfare implications of such a decision for his civil servants. And so on.

7.1.7. It is not difficult to give other examples of similar choice situations; for example, those of entrepreneurs with prices, production, etc., as instruments, and profits, assets and shares of the market as relevant noncontrolled variables. But, since the general nature of the problem of choice by means of equation systems will be clear, we proceed to a more specific problem: that of the relationship between decision-making and forecasting errors.

Let us suppose that the present values of the variables of (7.11) are known—step (*i*) of 7.1.2—, and let us measure these variables as deviations from the present values. In that case (7.11) may be regarded as a decomposition of the changes in noncontrolled variables in terms of a controlled part ($\mathbf{R}\mathbf{x}$) and a noncontrolled part ($\mathbf{s}$); $\mathbf{R}$ is considered here as a matrix of fixed coefficients. Now suppose that, at some time t, there is no noncontrolled change ($\mathbf{s} = \mathbf{0}$), but that at $t + 1$ there is such a change ($\mathbf{s} \neq \mathbf{0}$). It follows that the constraints are different in t and in $t + 1$, so that the "best" decisions—see the end of 7.1.5—will in general be different, too. Hence the policy-maker, when following these decisions, will have to take certain measures in $t + 1$. Consider then the following situation. The noncontrolled change is not known in general, but must be predicted. Suppose that the predicted change for $t + 1$ is exactly the same as in the previous case, and that it turns out afterwards that the actual change was different. In that case the "best" decision for $t + 1$, as the policy-maker saw it, is the same as before; but if his prediction had been perfect, his decision would in general have been another one. Hence the welfare level attained is lower than the welfare level that would have been obtained if the prediction had been perfect, and the resulting welfare loss is an adequate measure of the importance of the incorrect prediction. Actually, this measure is more satisfactory than the descriptive statistical devices considered in Section 2.4, and it was to this place that we referred there when stressing that counting turning point errors, etc., has primarily a heuristic value. It is necessary, of course, to specify the idea of measuring welfare losses more precisely, for, if no numerical statements are possible, our real progress beyond the usual statistical measures is very modest. It will appear in Chapter VIII that this is possible in some special cases.

Similarly, it is conceivable that some elements of $\mathbf{R}$ are incorrectly specified. Suppose e.g. that the policy-maker assumes that r_{11} is smaller than it is actually. Then he has a wrong idea as to the influence of x_1 with respect to y_1, so that we should expect a suboptimal decision leading to a loss of welfare. Still another problem arises if the policy-maker's preferences change, for one reason or another; for example, when a Government policy-maker is succeeded after an election, and his successor proceeds to evaluate the measures which his predecessor took just before leaving. Or, to take a less sophisticated example: an entrepreneur wants to minimise cost, so that his "welfare" corresponds with minus cost; if the prices of his factors of production change, his cost function and hence w change too. These and other questions will be analysed in Chapter VIII.

7.1.8. It will be clear from the above exposition that the analysis is closely related to the approaches formulated by several other authors. In a sense, the closest tie is the one with TINBERGEN's recent work on the theory of economic policy.[1] Tinbergen's approach, too, is based on the idea of using econometric models for policy purposes; but the way in which he works it out is different in several respects. First, he takes the model as it is, and pays minor regard to deviations between model and reality; and he neglects the disturbances in the equations. The second difference is related to the policy-makers' choice: Whereas in the above analysis we directed the attention to the "best" decision, based on maximising utility or welfare, Tinbergen fixes *a priori* certain desirable "target values" for the noncontrolled variables (hence his term "target variables"), and he tries to find those instrument values which are necessary in order to reach those targets.[2] His approach is as follows. He starts with a linear equation system of the type (7.8) and supposes the number of controlled and that of noncontrolled variables to be equal. In that case the matrix of β's is square and, assuming that it is nonsingular as well, it is possible to express each x in terms of all y's; this is clearly just the other way around when compared with the reduced-form relations of 7.1.5. After this, and neglecting the disturbances, we can derive for each set of target values the appropriate instrument values. When some of the x's of (7.8) are not instruments (like I and X in the example of 7.1.3), it is necessary

[1] J. TINBERGEN, *On the Theory of Economic Policy* (Amsterdam, 1952). See also his *Centralization and Decentralization in Economic Policy* (Amsterdam, 1954) and *Economic Policy: Principles and Design* (Amsterdam, 1956). For a review of the first of these three books, cf. H. S. HOUTHAKKER, "Het mechanisme der economische politiek," *De Economist*, Vol. 102 (1954), pp. 93–98, and the subsequent discussion on pp. 241–249, 455–457. Cf. also J. MARSCHAK's introductory chapter in *Studies in Econometric Method* ("Economic Measurements for Policy and Prediction"), who pays more explicit attention to the uncertainty problem than Tinbergen does.

[2] In a sense, we may say that the judgment variables of Section **2.3** and of the Munich Business Test are nothing else than series of differences between target values and corresponding actual values. For instance, if an entrepreneur reports that his stocks are too large, this means that his "target level" of stocks is below the actual level.

to predict their values for the relevant period beforehand, after which the forecasting errors are combined with the disturbances and hence neglected. If the number of instruments is larger than that of the y's, degrees of freedom arise which allow the policy-maker to take account of the immediate welfare implications of changes in his instrumental variables. If it is smaller, the targets cannot in general be reached all simultaneously, so that one or several of them must be replaced by less ambitious ones.[1]

The idea of a certain "aspiration level" with which the policy-maker is satisfied, rather than that of striving for the highest utility level that is attainable, was developed independently by H. A. SIMON.[2] There can be no doubt that it is sometimes attractive for a description of "actual" behaviour; it is even conceivable that it is appropriate for "rational" behaviour under certain circumstances. Nevertheless, it is important to make a distinction between the reduction of attainable welfare due to imperfect forecasts and the reduction of actual welfare caused by the fact that the policy-maker is satisfied with less than the attainable maximum. The further analysis will therefore be based on maximisation, not on targets or aspiration levels.

It will also be clear that our present approach has connections with certain elements of VON NEUMANN and MORGENSTERN'S *Theory of Games* and especially with statistical decision theory.[3] Our treatment is that of a general one-person game with random "moves." Of course, in the actual "game" several "persons" (competitors, pressure groups, etc.) may and will "play;" but in our approach their strategies, as our policy-maker thinks they are, are represented by the model which he uses for prediction purposes. This facilitates the treatment considerably. As to decision theory, the reader who is acquainted with it will have no difficulties in translating terms like "true state of the world," "acts," "consequences," into those which have been employed here. In particular, the loss-of-welfare concept introduced in 7.1.7 is the same as "loss" in statistical decision theory.

The policy-maker's preferences are taken as given, although we shall

[1] There may be some doubt as to the question whether the case of equal numbers of controlled and noncontrolled variables is really "normal," as Tinbergen supposes; it is not true for the example of 7.1.3.

[2] See his "A Behavioural Model of Rational Choice," *Quarterly Journal of Economics*, Vol. 69 (1955), pp. 99–118, and the references in this paper.

[3] See J. VON NEUMANN and O. MORGENSTERN, *Theory of Games and Economic Behavior* (Princeton, 2nd ed., 1947); A. WALD, *Statistical Decision Functions* (New York-London, 1950); L. J. SAVAGE, *The Foundations of Statistics* (New York-London, 1954).

investigate the impact of changes in preferences. It will be clear that we do not interpret the concept of preferences in a very narrow way, and especially that we do not confine it to bundles of commodities consumed and services rendered, as is quite usual in welfare economics. Such a limitation would restrict the applicability of the analysis. We shall not consider the problem of the relations between a Government policy-maker's preferences and those of the individuals which he is supposed to represent. This topic would lead us outside the scope of this book.[1]

7.2. Choice Subject to a Linear Constraint: A Re-Statement of Consumer's Demand Theory

7.2.1. The classical theory of consumer demand is based upon a utility function,[2]

$$u = u(q_1, \ldots\ldots, q_n), \tag{7.13}$$

which expresses the satisfaction that a consumer derives from consuming, during any given period, a batch of n commodities, as a function of each of the n quantities, $q_1, \ldots\ldots, q_n$. It is assumed that this function is twice differentiable, the second-order derivatives being continuous; moreover, that there is no saturation, so that the "marginal utilities" are positive:

$$u_i = \frac{\partial u}{\partial q_i} > 0 \qquad (i = 1, \ldots\ldots, n). \tag{7.14}$$

It follows from the continuity of the second-order derivatives that Young's theorem is true:

$$u_{ij} = \frac{\partial^2 u}{\partial q_i \partial q_j} = \frac{\partial^2 u}{\partial q_j \partial q_i} = u_{ji} \qquad (i, j = 1, \ldots\ldots, n). \tag{7.15}$$

[1] In this connection, see K. J. ARROW's contribution in *Social Choice and Individual Values* (New York-London, 1951); also L. A. GOODMAN and H. MARKOWITZ, "Social Welfare Functions Based on Individual Rankings," *American Journal of Sociology*, Vol. 58 (1952), pp. 257–262; C. HILDRETH, "Alternative Conditions for Social Orderings," *Econometrica*, Vol. 21 (1953), pp. 81–94.

[2] See e.g. the Appendix of J. R. HICKS' *Value and Capital* (Oxford, 2nd ed., 1946); or P. A. SAMUELSON's *Foundations of Economic Analysis* (Cambridge, U.S.A., 1948), Chapter V; or H. WOLD's *Demand Analysis* (New York-Stockholm, 1952); or J. R. N. STONE's *The Measurement of Consumer Expenditure and Behaviour in the United Kingdom, 1920–1938*, Vol. I (Cambridge, Engl., 1954).

The present section is based on a cardinal utility assumption; this will be weakened in Section 7.3.

The utility function is maximised subject to the constraint that the available income is exactly spent,

$$\sum_{i=1}^{n} p_i q_i = M, \tag{7.16}$$

where the p's stand for prices and M for income. It is assumed that they are all positive:

$$p_i, M > 0 \qquad (i = 1, \ldots, n); \tag{7.17}$$

furthermore, that they are data for the consumer. From (7.16) it follows immediately that the conditional maximum is not affected by proportional changes in prices and income, simply because the constraint is not affected.

7.2.2. The conditional maximisation is usually carried out by means of a Lagrange multiplier; i.e., by maximising unconditionally

$$u(q_1, \ldots, q_n) - \lambda\{\sum_{i=1}^{n} p_i q_i - M\},$$

λ being the Lagrange multiplier. This yields the conditions

$$u_i - \lambda p_i = 0 \qquad (i = 1, \ldots, n), \tag{7.18}$$

which amounts to a proportionality of marginal utilities and prices, λ being the proportionality constant. The n equations (7.18) and the budget constraint (7.16) determine, under certain general conditions, the "unknowns" $q_1, \ldots, q_n, \lambda$. We shall assume that the resulting q's are all positive; λ is of course positive as well because of (7.14), (7.17) and (7.18):

$$\lambda > 0. \tag{7.19}$$

It will prove useful to write out the $(n + 1)$ equilibrium conditions more fully:

$$\begin{aligned} u_1 \qquad\qquad & - \lambda p_1 = 0 \\ \ldots\ldots\ldots & \ldots\ldots \\ u_n \qquad\qquad & - \lambda p_n = 0 \\ p_1 q_1 + \ldots\ldots & + p_n q_n = M. \end{aligned} \tag{7.20}$$

These are the first-order maximum conditions. They are necessary and sufficient for a stationary value of u, but not more than necessary for a maximum. In order to find sufficient conditions for a maximum we introduce the determinant

$$(7.21) \qquad U = \begin{vmatrix} u_{11} \ldots\ldots u_{1n} & p_1 \\ \ldots\ldots\ldots\ldots & \ldots \\ u_{n1} \ldots\ldots u_{nn} & p_n \\ p_1 \ldots\ldots p_n & 0 \end{vmatrix},$$

which is symmetric because of (7.15). The sufficient condition is that the determinants

$$(7.22) \qquad \begin{vmatrix} u_{11} & u_{12} & p_1 \\ u_{21} & u_{22} & p_2 \\ p_1 & p_2 & 0 \end{vmatrix}, \qquad \begin{vmatrix} u_{11} & u_{12} & u_{13} & p_1 \\ u_{21} & u_{22} & u_{23} & p_2 \\ u_{31} & u_{32} & u_{33} & p_3 \\ p_1 & p_2 & p_3 & 0 \end{vmatrix}, \ldots\ldots,$$

which are the principal minors of the matrix of second derivatives in U bordered by corresponding prices, should be alternatively positive and negative.[1] This is the condition under which the second differential of u, viz.,

$$(7.23) \qquad d^2u = \sum_{i=1}^{n} \sum_{j=1}^{n} u_{ij}\, dq_i\, dq_j,$$

is negative-definite subject to (7.16). The choice of the indices 1, 2, 3, ... in (7.22) is, of course, arbitrary. The sign rules of these determinants are called the second-order maximum conditions, or stability conditions.

7.2.3. The conditions (7.20) determine the consumer's "best" decisions, given income and prices. Our next question is what happens when income and prices change. First, therefore, we consider the derivatives of the q's—interpreted as those of the "best" decision—with respect to M. This is conveniently done by partial differentiation of the $(n + 1)$ equations (7.20). Observing that the first of these equations becomes

$$u_{11} \frac{\partial q_1}{\partial M} + \ldots + u_{1n} \frac{\partial q_n}{\partial M} - p_1 \frac{\partial \lambda}{\partial M} = 0$$

and the last

[1] See e.g. Hicks, *loc. cit.*, pp. 304ff.

$$p_1 \frac{\partial q_1}{\partial M} + \ldots + p_n \frac{\partial q_n}{\partial M} = 1, \tag{7.24}$$

we can derive from Cramer's Rule that

$$\frac{\partial q_i}{\partial M} = \frac{U_{n+1,\, i}}{U} \qquad (i = 1, \ldots, n), \tag{7.25}$$

where $U_{n+1,\, i}$ is the cofactor of the $(n+1, i)$-th element in U. Nothing is known *a priori* about the sign of this ratio of determinants. Hence the derivative may be negative, which is called the case of an *inferior* commodity. If follows from (7.25) that, given the consumer's preferences, the question whether a commodity is inferior depends both on prices and on income. For example, margarine may be inferior depending on the question whether the prices of butter and margarine are close to each other; and the magnitude of the consumer's income may be important as well. Clearly, not all commodities can be inferior simultaneously, in view of (7.24) and (7.17).

In the same way, we can derive the partial derivatives with respect to prices:

$$\begin{aligned} \frac{\partial q_i}{\partial p_j} &= -q_j \frac{U_{n+1,\, i}}{U} + \lambda \frac{U_{ji}}{U} \\ &= -q_j \frac{\partial q_i}{\partial M} + \lambda \frac{U_{ji}}{U} \qquad (i, j = 1, \ldots, n), \end{aligned} \tag{7.26}$$

U_{ji} being the cofactor of the (j, i)-th element in U. This result, which is originally due to SLUTSKY, may be interpreted as follows. When the price of commodity j increases by a small amount dp_j, its immediate effect is that the consumer needs an additional income of $q_j dp_j$ in order to be able to buy the same batch as before. Now $q_j(\partial q_i/\partial M)$, which appears with a minus sign in the right-hand side of (7.26), measures exactly the influence of this hypothetical additional income on the quantity consumed of commodity i. Hence the remaining term in the right-hand side,

$$X_{ji} = \lambda \frac{U_{ji}}{U}, \tag{7.27}$$

describes the influence on q_i of an infinitesimal change in p_j, when this price change is "compensated" by a change in income in such a way that the consumer could buy exactly the same set of quantities as before if he chose to do so. We have

$$X_{ii} < 0 \qquad (i = 1, \ldots, n) \tag{7.28}$$

because of (7.19) and the alternating signs of the cofactors (7.22). Hence a compensated price increase reduces the quantity consumed of the same commodity. A non-compensated price increase, however, may increase this quantity: $\partial q_i/\partial p_i > 0$. This is the case of Giffen's paradox, which can occur only if the commodity is inferior, as is easily verified from (7.26).

7.2.4. The terms X_{ij} are called "substitution terms." Hence, according to (7.26), the price derivatives of the quantities consumed can be said to consist of two parts, one of them being concerned with income compensation (the "income effect") and the other being the substitution term (the "substitution effect"). Such terms X_{ij} may be positive, zero or negative. If $X_{ij} < 0$, then a compensated price increase of i reduces not only q_i, but also q_j. In that case i is said to be "complementary" with j. Since we have

$$X_{ij} = X_{ji} \qquad (i, j = 1, \ldots, n) \tag{7.29}$$

because of the symmetry of our determinants, j is then complementary with i as well; hence complementarity is a symmetric relation. It follows from (7.28) that each commodity is "complementary with itself;" hence complementarity is also a reflexive relation.

When $X_{ij} = X_{ji} > 0$, i and j are called "substitutes," which is likewise a symmetric relation, but not a reflexive one. There are two different reasons implying that substitution is, in a sense, a more important relation for all commodities combined than complementarity. First, we have

$$\sum_{j=1}^{n} p_j X_{ij} = 0 \qquad (i = 1, \ldots, n), \tag{7.30}$$

since the left-hand side is of the form $\lambda U^0/U$, where U^0 is a determinant in which two columns are identical. But $X_{ii} < 0$ and hence, when excluding $j = i$ in the summation and recalling that all prices are positive, the remaining sum becomes positive. It is impossible, therefore, for any commodity i to be complementary with all other commodities j simultaneously; but it is possible for each i to be substitute for each j. It follows also from (7.30) that no complementarity is possible for $n = 2$.

The second reason for the dominance of substitution relationships follows from the negative semi-definiteness of the $n \times n$ matrix $[X_{ij}]$ (its rank being $n - 1$):[1]

$$\sum_{i=1}^{m} \sum_{j=1}^{m} X_{ij} p_i p_j < 0 \qquad (1 \leq m < n). \tag{7.31}$$

Combining (7.30) and (7.31), we obtain

$$\sum_{i=1}^{m} \sum_{j=m+1}^{n} X_{ij} p_i p_j > 0 \qquad (1 \leq m < n), \tag{7.32}$$

which has the following interpretation. Suppose we divide the n commodities arbitrarily into two groups of m and $(n - m)$ commodities, respectively. Then, when taking all possible substitution terms between a commodity in the former group and one in the latter, and weighting them with corresponding prices, the sum has a positive sign—the sign of substitution rather than that of complementarity.

Other inequalities following from the negative semi-definiteness of $[X_{ij}]$ are

$$X_{11} < 0; \quad \begin{vmatrix} X_{11} & X_{12} \\ X_{21} & X_{22} \end{vmatrix} > 0; \quad \begin{vmatrix} X_{11} & X_{12} & X_{13} \\ X_{21} & X_{22} & X_{23} \\ X_{31} & X_{32} & X_{33} \end{vmatrix} < 0; \ldots . \tag{7.33}$$

The first inequality is the same as (7.28). The second may be regarded as an upper limit to the amount of substitution or complementarity:

$$X_{12}^2 < X_{11} X_{22}.$$

The $n \times n$ determinant of all X's vanishes because of the semi-definiteness.

7.2.5. The usual analysis of consumer behaviour is confined to the comparative statics of changing income and prices, given constant preferences.[2] Nevertheless, there is no reason why changes in preferences should be excluded. This will be the final topic of this section.

[1] See e.g. SAMUELSON, *loc. cit.*, pp. 113–115, 378–379.
[2] See, however, R. L. BASMANN, "A Theory of Demand with Variable Consumer Preferences," *Econometrica*, Vol. 24 (1956), pp. 47–58; and ICHIMURA's and TINTNER's contributions quoted in this article.

It will be sufficient for our purpose to consider a quadratic utility function:

$$(7.34) \qquad u = a_0 + \sum_{i=1}^{n} a_i q_i + \tfrac{1}{2} \sum_{i=1}^{n} \sum_{j=1}^{n} a_{ij} q_i q_j \qquad (a_{ij} = a_{ji})$$

This may be regarded as the simplest specification in consumer's demand theory.[1] Under this assumption the marginal utilities are linear functions of the quantities,

$$(7.35) \qquad u_i = a_i + \sum_{j=1}^{n} a_{ij} q_j \qquad (i = 1, \ldots, n),$$

and the second derivatives of u are constants: $u_{ij} = a_{ij}$. It will be immediately clear that this form has particular implications for the income derivatives (7.25). Since U and its cofactors depend no longer, *via* u_{ij} and hence the q's, on M, the income derivative is independent of income; hence the Engel curves, describing the q's as functions of M only, are straight lines, so that the question of inferiority no longer depends on the income level. But the income derivatives are still dependent on the prices: they are ratios of linear to quadratic forms in prices, and hence homogeneous of degree -1.

Changes in preferences are now analysed in the same way as those in income and prices. To do so, we replace u_i in (7.20) by the right-hand side of (7.35). Consider then an infinitesimal change in a_j; this may be regarded as a change in the marginal utility of the commodity j which is independent of the quantities consumed; cf. (7.35). Its influence on the q's is found by differentiating the $(n + 1)$ equations (7.20), which gives

$$(7.36) \qquad \frac{\partial q_i}{\partial a_j} = - \frac{U_{ji}}{U} = - \frac{X_{ji}}{\lambda} \qquad (i, j = 1, \ldots, n).$$

It follows that an increase of the marginal utility of j (which does not depend on the q's) raises the consumption of i when i and j are com-

[1] This form was also used by A. WALD in "The Approximate Determination of Indifference Surfaces by Means of Engel Curves," *Econometrica*, Vol. 8 (1940) pp. 144–175; by R. G. D. ALLEN and A. L. BOWLEY in their *Family Expenditure* (London, 1935), though in a slightly different manner; and by H. HOTELLING in "The General Welfare in Relation to Problems of Taxation and of Railway and Utility Rates," *Econometrica*, Vol. 6 (1938), pp. 242–269.

plementary and reduces i's consumption when they are substitutes. Obviously

$$\frac{\partial q_i}{\partial a_j} = \frac{\partial q_j}{\partial a_i} \quad \text{and} \quad \frac{\partial q_i}{\partial a_i} > 0. \tag{7.37}$$

Next, we consider changes in the coefficients of the quadratic part, a_{ij}, which may be regarded as measuring the sensitivity of the marginal utility of i with respect to changes in the consumption of j. When proceeding in the same way, we find for the derivative with respect to a_{jj} (i.e., the special case of equal subscripts):

$$\frac{\partial q_i}{\partial a_{jj}} = - q_j \frac{X_{ji}}{\lambda} \qquad (i, j = 1, \ldots, n). \tag{7.38}$$

Hence an increase in the sensitivity of the marginal utility of j with respect to j itself—in the sense that an increase of q_j leads to a larger (algebraic) increase in u_j than before—reduces the consumption of commodity i when i and j are substitutes and increases the consumption of i when both are complementary. Obviously

$$q_i \frac{\partial q_i}{\partial a_{jj}} = q_j \frac{\partial q_j}{\partial a_{ii}} \quad \text{and} \quad \frac{\partial q_i}{\partial a_{ii}} > 0, \tag{7.39}$$

so that an increase of the sensitivity of the marginal utility of some commodity with respect to the consumption of this commodity increases this consumption.

Finally, we take a_{jk} with $j \neq k$. When applying again the same procedure and recalling that $a_{jk} \equiv a_{kj}$, we find

$$\begin{aligned} \frac{\partial q_i}{\partial a_{jk}} &= - q_k \frac{U_{ji}}{U} - q_j \frac{U_{ki}}{U} \\ &= - \frac{1}{\lambda} (q_k X_{ji} + q_j X_{ki}) \qquad (i, j, k = 1, \ldots, n;\ j \neq k). \end{aligned} \tag{7.40}$$

It follows that an increase in the sensitivity of the marginal utility of j with respect to q_k (which is accompanied automatically by the same increase of the sensitivity of u_k with respect to q_j) leads to a change in q_i the sign of which is determined in a slightly more complicated manner. If i is complementary with both j and k, it is an increase; if it is a substitute of both, it is a decrease; and if i is a substitute of one of them but complementary with the other, the size of the substitution terms and the relative importance of j and k in the consumer's budget determine the sign of $\partial q_i/\partial a_{jk}$.

7.3. Choice in Risk-Taking Situations

7.3.1. The way in which the consumer's utility function was introduced in the preceding section suggested perhaps that utility or "satisfaction" is to be measured in just the same way as the quantity of calories or vitamins derived from consuming a certain batch of foods. This, however, is not true. It is not untrue in the sense that the possibility of making such utility measurements has to be excluded *a priori*; but rather, that such measurements need not be made in order to arrive at the results expounded in Section 7.2. This can be argued as follows.

Consider the case of two commodities ($n = 2$); larger numbers require the use of geometry in more than three dimensions, but the argument is essentially the same. Utility as a function of both quantities can then be geometrically described in a three-dimensional space, the quantities being measured along the horizontal axes and utility along the vertical axis. The resulting picture is that of a "utility mountain;" and our path on this mountain goes upward when we move away from the origin, i.e., when one or both of the quantities is increased—simply because of the positive marginal utilities. Our consumer cannot, however, climb everywhere; his movements are restricted by the budget constraint. This constraint is represented by a vertical plane in the utility-quantities space, which intersects the two horizontal axes in those points where the entire income is spent on one of the commodities; cf. Fig. 7.2, where $ABB'A'$ is the vertical plane, A' and B' its intersection points with the horizontal axes, and the curve AB represents the path along which the consumer can move: he can choose between spending his income entirely on the first commodity (then he is in A) or on the second (then he is in B) or any intermediate position. The "best" choice is the highest point of AB, which is denoted by S in Fig. 7.2.

The crucial point is that we never asked in Section 7.2 "how high" this highest point is; i.e., we were never concerned with the distance SS'. We considered only the properties of the point S', which describes fully the combination of quantities that leads to the highest attainable welfare level. Suppose then that we carry out the following operation.

We stretch or push the utility mountain in a fully arbitrary fashion by raising or lowering each of its points in vertical direction; subject, however, to the following restriction: if, for any two points Q_1 and Q_2 on the mountain, Q_1 was higher than (as high as, lower than) Q_2 before the operation, it should stand in the same relation to Q_2 afterwards. It is easy to see that, whereas the distance SS' may have been altered

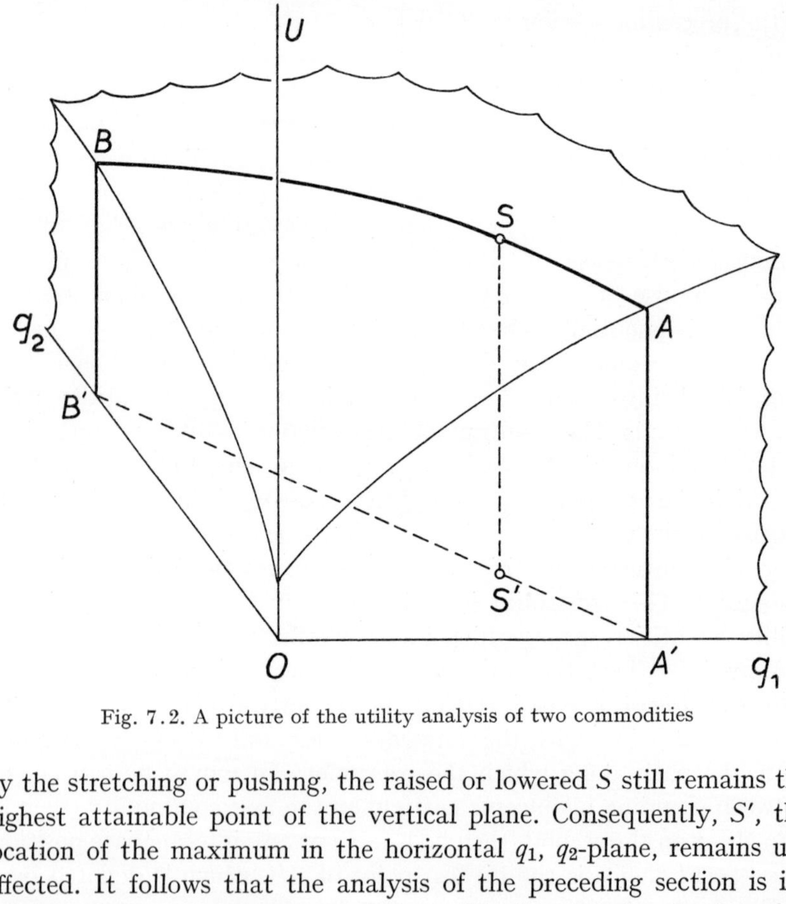

Fig. 7.2. A picture of the utility analysis of two commodities

by the stretching or pushing, the raised or lowered S still remains the highest attainable point of the vertical plane. Consequently, S', the location of the maximum in the horizontal q_1, q_2-plane, remains unaffected. It follows that the analysis of the preceding section is invariant against a replacement of the utility function by the function corresponding to the utility mountain after it has been stretched or pushed subject to the aforementioned proviso; that is, the analysis is invariant against a replacement of u by $F(u)$, where F is an arbitrary monotonically increasing function. The requirement of monotonicity follows from the fact that the replacement should not lead to a different ordering according to increasing preference. In order to preserve the possibility of differentiating the utility function, we assume that F is likewise differentiable with respect to u.

This liberty as to the choice of the utility functions has several interesting implications, some of which will be mentioned here briefly. When replacing u by $F(u)$, the marginal utility of commodity i becomes $F'u_i$ instead of u_i, F' being the derivative of F with respect to u. Hence the marginal utility is not invariant. But the first-order conditions (7.18) become

$$F'u_i - \lambda p_i = 0 \qquad (i = 1, \ldots, n),$$

and hence the proportionality of marginal utilities and prices is not affected:

$$\frac{F'u_1}{p_1} = \ldots\ldots = \frac{F'u_n}{p_n}$$

or

$$\frac{u_1}{p_1} = \ldots\ldots = \frac{u_n}{p_n},$$

F' being positive because F is monotonically increasing. Similarly, it can be shown that the second-order conditions, the symmetry of the bordered determinant (7.21), and all properties which are based on these are unaffected by replacing u by $F(u)$. Only one question has to be settled, viz., the fact that the analysis of changing preferences was based on changes in the coefficients of the marginal utilities—cf. (7.35) and ff. Since marginal utility is not invariant against the replacement of u by $F(u)$, it might be doubted whether the analysis of changes in the preference coefficients a_i, a_{ij} remains unaffected by such a replacement. However, a simple re-arrangement of the exposition shows that there is indeed such an invariance. For consider the ratio of two marginal utilities, u_i/u_j (the "marginal rate of substitution" between i and j). This ratio is not affected when $F(u)$ is substituted for u, for it becomes $F'u_i/(F'u_j) = u_i/u_j$. Consequently, the expression

$$\frac{u_i}{u_j} = \frac{a_i + \sum_k a_{ik}q_k}{a_j + \sum_k a_{jk}q_k} \tag{7.41}$$

is invariant, so that we can interpret changes in preference coefficients as certain types of changes in the marginal rates of substitution without suggesting that operations are carried out on quantities which are not invariant. It follows from (7.41) and the earlier analysis that only the ratios of the a's are relevant; furthermore, that the constant term a_0 of (7.34) is entirely irrelevant.

7.3.2. This situation, which can be briefly and roughly described by saying that an ordering according to preference of all separate alternatives is sufficient to arrive at the results of Section 7.2,[1] changes radically when we proceed to risk-taking situations. Suppose that our consumer is offered a choice between two alternatives, one of which is a batch of commodities A, and the other a 50 per cent chance of getting B and a 50 per cent chance of getting C. If A is preferred to both B and C, no problem seems to arise: by choosing A the consumer is better off independent of what the chance mechanism performs, so that his "best" choice is then A. Similarly, when both B and C are preferred to A, the "best" choice is the B, C-gamble.[2] Suppose, however, that B is preferred to A and A to C. In that case the ordering of A, B and C is not sufficient in order to conclude which is the "best" choice; and it seems then to be necessary to specify by how much B is preferred to A and A to C, and also to say something more about the consumer's attitude towards gambling. It is clear that this is precisely the situation of our policy-maker as described at the end of 7.1.5: he has to take certain measures, but he is not sure about their consequences because his forecasting technique is not perfect; he has to take a risk, therefore, and the ordering of all separate outcomes according to preference is just as insufficient as in the consumer's gambling case. It becomes necessary to order entire frequency distributions of outcomes, not only separate outcomes.

Several approaches have been developed in order to deal with this choice problem in risk-taking situations, some of which are even not probabilistic.[3] The most adequate probabilistic approach is that of VON NEUMANN and MORGENSTERN, which amounts to the following.[4]

[1] It is conceivable that an ordering cannot be represented by a numerical function, but this is a rather unplausible situation. Cf. G. DEBREU, "Representation of a Preference Ordering by a Numerical Function," Chapter XI of *Decision Processes*, edited by R. M. THRALL, C. H. COOMBS and R. L. DAVIS (New York-London, 1954).

[2] A qualification must be made: the consumer should have no moral (or other) objections against gambling, for otherwise it might be possible that A is still preferred. Similarly, in the former case the consumer should have no "love of gambling."

[3] For a survey of these approaches, see K. J. ARROW, "Alternative Approaches in the Theory of Choice in Risk-Taking Situations," *Econometrica*, Vol. 19 (1951), pp. 404–437.

[4] *Loc. cit.*, pp. 15–31, 617–632.

Under certain assumptions (to be mentioned below, in 7.3.4), it is possible to order frequency distributions of outcomes according to increasing preference, and at the same time a utility or welfare function exists with this property: the policy-maker takes his decisions as if he maximises the mean value of utility. Hence, to take the consumer's gambling case of the preceding paragraph, and assuming that u is such a utility function, there are three relevant utility levels, viz., $u(A)$, $u(B)$ and $u(C)$; and the mean value of the gambling alternative, given the 50 per cent chances of B and C each, equals $\frac{1}{2}\{u(B) + u(C)\}$. It follows that the alternative A is chosen if

$$u(A) > \tfrac{1}{2}\{u(B) + u(C)\},$$

but the B, C-gamble if the inequality sign is reversed. In the policy-maker's case as described in 7.1.5: if w is a welfare function of the above-mentioned type, he will maximise

$$\mathscr{E} w(\mathsf{x}, \mathsf{y}), \tag{7.42}$$

where y is a stochastic function of x, say $\mathsf{y} = \mathsf{Rx} + \mathsf{s}$ [cf. (7.11)] with s stochastic. In other words: he will choose that set of instrument values x for which the mean value (7.42) is a maximum.

7.3.3. Three points should be mentioned explicitly. First, not every utility function of the very general class analysed in 7.3.1 is adequate in this connection. For the analysis in Section 7.2 and in 7.3.1 it is permissible to replace u by any $F(u)$ provided only $F' > 0$; i.e., we may apply any monotonic transformation to u. But the class of utility functions which are adequate in the sense that the calculus of mean values is applicable is much more restricted. Such functions are "unique up to a linear transformation;" i.e., they are completely specified as soon as a zero and a unit of utility is fixed. In other words, measurements according to two different utility functions, to both of which the mean-value calculus is applicable, are always connected by a linear relation, just like measuring temperature according to Fahrenheit and Centigrade. The earlier utility functions are only "unique up to a monotonic transformation;" they have an "ordinal" character, contrary to the "cardinal" nature of the other group.

Second, it remains true that the "best" decision which is available to the policy-maker (though he may not know its optimality until it is too late) is the one that follows from maximising w subject to $\mathsf{y} =$

$= \mathsf{R}\mathsf{x} + \mathsf{s}$, not the one following from maximising $\mathscr{E}w$. The fact that his actual decision is found—under the assumptions of 7.3.4—by maximising $\mathscr{E}w$ does not alter this at all. Indeed, his decision is based on certain predictions; and if his forecasting technique can only specify a probability distribution of s rather than an exact s, we must expect a loss of welfare due to this imperfection. Afterwards, when information concerning s has become available, it is possible to specify what the "best" measures were; and the difference between the welfare level corresponding to these and the actual welfare level, obtained by maximising $\mathscr{E}w$ before, is a welfare loss which is as real as any other loss.

Third, it is highly important to make a distinction between maximising the mean value of utility and maximising the utility of the mean outcome; in the case of our policy-maker: between maximising $\mathscr{E}w(\mathsf{x}, \mathsf{y})$ and maximising $w(\mathsf{x}, \mathscr{E}\mathsf{y})$. It is easy to see that these procedures are highly different. Suppose we specify the three situations A, B and C of the consumer's gambling case as follows: A implies a gift of \$100,000, B one of \$1,000,000, and C a loss of \$500,000. The mean value of the B, C-gamble is a profit of \$250,000, so that maximising the utility of the mean outcome implies that this gamble is preferred to the certainty of winning \$100,000. It seems intuitively obvious, however, that most people will behave quite differently; and indeed, the process of maximising the mean value of utility does not at all imply that the gamble is chosen. Suppose e.g. that the utility of A is 0.9, that of B, 1 and that of C, -1; then the utility of the gamble is $\frac{1}{2}\cdot 1 + \frac{1}{2}(-1) = 0$, which is smaller than that of A. Such cases are sometimes called those of "risk aversion." More specifically, risk aversion means that a gamble has a smaller utility than that of the mean value of the gamble. In the example there is considerable risk aversion, for the utility of the gamble ($= 0$) is even smaller than that of the alternative A (0.9) which yields a much smaller profit than the mean outcome of the gamble. The opposite of risk aversion is called "risk preference."

7.3.4. We shall now give a brief sketch of the assumptions which lead to decisions that are based on maximising the mean value of utility. A simplified treatment of the Von Neumann-Morgenstern system has been given by MARSCHAK, and this will be followed here.[1]

[1] J. MARSCHAK, "Rational Behavior, Uncertain Prospects, and Measurable Utility," *Econometrica*, Vol. 18 (1950), pp. 111–141.

Consider first all imaginable separate outcomes of the chance mechanism. In the consumer's gambling case there were three such outcomes (A, B and C), but in general the number is of course larger. Next, consider all conceivable frequency distributions of these outcomes, anyone of which will be denoted by Z with an appropriate index. The 50–50 gamble of B and C is such a distribution, but the same is true if we replace 50–50 by any chances p and $1 - p$ such that $0 \leq p \leq 1$. Clearly, each set of measures taken by our policy-maker leads to a particular Z, viz., a set of instrument values together with a frequency distribution of values to be assumed by the noncontrolled variables; and conversely, Z specifies the measures and their consequences, as far as the policy-maker sees them (viz., in a probabilistic manner), completely. Now we suppose, first, that, for any pair of distributions Z_1 and Z_2, the policy-maker can state whether he prefers Z_1 to Z_2, or Z_2 to Z_1, or whether he is indifferent between them; furthermore that, for any triple Z_1, Z_2, Z_3, if the policy-maker prefers Z_1 to Z_2 and Z_2 to Z_3, he will prefer Z_1 to Z_3 (and similarly for indifference). Both assumptions—those of "comparability" and of "transitivity"—are also made in the classical theory of consumer's demand, but with respect to separate outcomes only, not with respect to frequency distributions. Just as in the traditional case they imply that the separate outcomes are completely ordered, in just the same way the present assumptions imply that the Z's are completely ordered according to preference.

We proceed to consider "mixtures" of different Z's. Take therefore two different Z's, Z_1 and Z_2, and an arbitrary probability p $(0 < p < 1)$. Then $pZ_1 + (1 - p)Z_2$ is another Z (Z' say), viz., the prospect of having Z_1 with chance p and Z_2 with the (remaining) chance $1 - p$. For instance, Z_1 may be the prospect of having \$2,000, Z_2 that of having \$1,000 with probability $\frac{1}{2}$ and a car with the same chance; and take $p = 0.3$. Z' is then the prospect of having \$2,000 with probability 0.3, \$1,000 with probability $0.7 \times \frac{1}{2} = 0.35$, and a car with the same chance 0.35. The following two assumptions are made. First, suppose that Z_1 is preferred to Z_2, and Z_2 to Z_3, for some triple Z_1, Z_2, Z_3; hence Z_2 is "between" Z_1 and Z_3 as far as the preference ordering is concerned. The assumption is that always some mixture of Z_1 and Z_3, $pZ_1 + (1 - p)Z_3$, exists which is indifferent to Z_2 $(0 < p < 1)$; this amounts to saying that the preference ordering is "continuous." The second assumption is the following. Consider two indifferent Z's, say Z_1 and Z_2, and an arbitrary third one, Z_3. Then any mixture of Z_1 and Z_3 should be indifferent to the same mixture of Z_2 and Z_3, i.e., $pZ_1 + (1 - p) Z_3$ is indifferent to $pZ_2 + (1 - p) Z_3$ for any p, $0 \leq p \leq 1$. An example: suppose a man is indifferent between a car (Z_1) and \$1,000 (Z_2). Then the prospect of having a house with probability 0.4 and a car with probability 0.6 is equivalent with the prospect of having a house with chance 0.4 and \$1,000 with chance 0.6; and we may replace the house by any other asset (including cars or \$1,000 bills) and do the same with the probabilities.

Under these assumptions[1] the policy-maker values the Z's according to the mean values of the utilities of their components. If we make the final assumption that the policy-maker's choice is based on maximisation of utility (and hence on maximising the mean value of utility), his actual decisions are as sketched in 7.3.2.

7.3.5. We should add here that there is an entirely different approach to this subject, which is of some relevance for our problems. Up till now, we assumed that the policy-maker takes the probabilities associated with the various alternative outcomes as given, and that there are no subjective considerations about them except in a trivial sense. However, there was a place where a more subjective or "personalistic" determination of probabilities has an element of realism, viz., in 7.1.5 when we replaced some of the x's by predictions. As long as we can assume that these variables are generated by a Markov or any other stochastic scheme, no special problem arises; but if this is not true, and if their predictions are combined with the disturbances of the reduced-form equations in a vector $\mathbf{s}$ which is assumed to have a probability distribution, then the resulting probabilities are not without subjective elements.

SAVAGE's recent contribution is valuable in this connection.[2] His approach is to formulate a simultaneous utility-probability axiomatisation; and the result is, as before, that the policy-maker takes his decisions as if he maximises the mean value of utility. The axioms are, however, not the same; Savage proves some of Marschak's axioms as theorems from his axioms. We shall not give a survey of Savage's postulates here but confine ourselves to one of them, which shows how utility and probability are connected in this approach. Suppose

[1] The proof of the following assertion involves still another assumption, which is however somewhat less interesting; cf. Marschak's three alternative Postulates III, *loc. cit.*, pp. 117–118.

[2] L. J. SAVAGE, *The Foundations of Statistics* (New York-London, 1954).

a person is offered a prize in the sense that, if an event A obtains, he receives \$100; and, if A does not obtain, he gets nothing. Suppose further that this person is offered the same prize with A replaced by another event B, and that he may choose between both alternatives. Then, if he chooses the A-gamble (and such a choice involves obviously a utility consideration), A is said to be "more probable" than B—at least not less probable—from this person's standpoint. This is a definition. One of Savage's axioms is then that on which of two events the person will choose to stake a given prize does not depend on the prize itself.[1] A further postulate is then sufficient to arrive at numerical rather than "ordinal" probabilities; i.e., to replace statements like "A is more probable than B" by quantitative probability statements.

7.3.6. This completes our preparation for the analysis which follows. We started with a general outline of the problems involved in five successive steps: knowledge of the present state, the distinction between instruments and noncontrolled variables, prediction, evaluation, and choice. We observed a parallelism between general policy-maker's problems and consumer's theory: the budget constraint corresponds to the model which is used for prediction purposes, the utility function to the policy-maker's evaluation criterion. There are differences, however. The most important of these is the fact that, in classical consumer's theory, no account is taken of the possibility that the consumer knows his budget constraint imperfectly. In our present case it is simply necessary to take account of such imperfect knowledge, since it is the corner-stone in the relation between prediction and decision-making.

[1] Cf. SAVAGE. *loc. cit.*, pp. 27–40. See also M. ALLAIS' critique in "Le comportement de l'homme rationnel devant le risque: Critique des postulats et axiomes de l'école Américaine," *Econometrica*, Vol. 21 (1953), pp. 503–546; and Savage's analysis of Allais' counter-example, *loc. cit.* pp. 101–103. Savage's work shows much similarity to DE FINETTI's and RAMSEY's theories of subjective probabilities; cf. B. DE FINETTI, "La prévision: ses lois logiques, ses sources subjectives," *Annales de l'Institut Henri Poincaré*, Vol. 7 (1937), pp. 1–68; F. P. RAMSEY, "Truth and Probability" and "Further Considerations" in *The Foundations of Mathematics and Other Logical Essays* (London, 1931), pp. 156–211.

VIII. Forecasts and Policy: Analysis and Applications

8.1. Assumptions on Constraints and Preferences

8.1.1. This preliminary section deals with the basic alternative assumptions to be made. It will be convenient to make a distinction as to whether they refer to the constraints which the policy-maker has to face, or to his preferences. The former assumptions will be indicated by a C, the latter by a P, in both cases followed by a serial number. We begin with the assumptions on the constraints.

The simplest is that of linearity,

$$y = Rx + s, \tag{8.1}$$

where R and s are matrices independent of x. This is equivalent to 7.11) in 7.1.5. Linearity may be justified either because it is an important special case, or because it is a convenient approximation when small variations in x are involved—provided of course a Taylor expansion exists and converges. The matrices R and s may be stochastic or not, but this does not interest us at the present stage.

The relations (8.1) are clearly of a reduced-form type. One might wonder whether an assumption concerning the corresponding structural equations, which are usually conceived of as underlying the reduced form (cf. Section 6.2), is perhaps more appropriate. The answer should be, first, that what really matters for the decision process is the constraint implied by the structural equations, and that this constraint is represented by any combination of these equations in precisely the same way as by the equations themselves, the reduced form being one of such combinations (and a particularly simple one); second, that the equation system is usually of an aggregated type, and that perfect aggregation is in principle attainable for the reduced form, but not in general for a complete system of macro structural equations.[1] There is, however, one objection to using the reduced form (8.1), for it is in some cases "too simple." The reason is that the y's have all coefficients unity, and that it is sometimes more convenient to give them arbitrary (positive) coefficients—just as all quantities in the consumer's budget restriction have certain coefficients (viz., the prices) none of which is fixed *a priori* at the unit level. Therefore, we replace (8.1) by

$$Qy = Rx + s, \tag{8.2}$$

where the elements of Q are positive or zero depending on whether they are on the main diagonal or not. More precisely:

ASSUMPTION C1. *The policy-maker's instruments* x *and his noncontrolled variables* y *are real-valued variables which are connected by the equation system* (8.2), *where* Q *is a diagonal matrix with positive elements in the diagonal,* R *a rectangular matrix, and* s *a column vector,* Q, R *and* s *being independent of* x.

For some purposes, however, it is not necessary to assume linearity, nor is it necessary to assume that the controlled variables are of the usual quantitative type. Let us write

$$y = f(x) + u, \tag{8.3}$$

where f is an arbitrary vector of functions $f_1, f_2, \ldots$, and u a vector of random disturbances. It will prove useful to assume that u has zero mean value independent of x—which implies no real assumption, for we can always adjust $f(x)$ such that it is true—and that its covariance matrix is independent of x. More specifically:

ASSUMPTION C2. *The policy-maker's noncontrolled variables* y *are real valued variables, and they are connected with his instruments* x *by the equation system* (8.3), *where* f *is a column vector of functions and* u *one of random disturbances, the mean value of* u *being zero for any* x, $\mathcal{E}u = \mathbf{0}$, *and its covariance matrix,* $\mathcal{E}(uu')$, *finite and independent of* x.

[1] Cf. H. THEIL, *Linear Aggregation of Economic Relations* (Amsterdam, 1954), Chapter VII. Perfect aggregation of reduced-form equations requires in general the use of different exogenous aggregates corresponding to the same microvariables in the separate macroequations. So we may have different Government expenditure aggregates by weighting separate commodity groups differently. This yields—in principle—no difficulties.

8.1.2. Next, we consider the policy-maker's preferences. The simplest assumption that we shall make corresponds to that of the consumer's utility analysis. Consider therefore the preference or welfare function

$$w = w(x, y), \tag{8.4}$$

which is the same as (7.12). We assume:

ASSUMPTION P1. *All vectors* x, y *of instruments and noncontrolled variables are real-valueda nd completely ordered according to the policy-maker's preference in such a way as to allow a representation by means of a real-valued welfare function* (8.4) *or any monotonically increasing function of this. The function is twice differentiable with respect to the elements of* x *and* y, *its second-order derivatives being continuous.*

It will be observed that this assumption implies the existence of a function corresponding to the consumer's utility function (7.13), as well as the equality of symmetric cross-derivatives corresponding to $u_{ij} = u_{ji}$ in (7.15); not, however, that the first derivatives (the marginal utilities) are positive as in (7.14). Indeed, this is, as was observed earlier in 7.1.4, one of the differences between the policy-maker's choice problem and that of the consumer. At the same time, however, it will be clear that very little is required in order to transform, for any fixed values x, y, the policy-maker's situation into that of the consumer: all we have to do is to replace a variable by minus itself when its marginal utility happens to be negative. It will prove useful to do so, and to choose for the above fixed values x, y those of maximum utility. This gives the following

SIGN CONVENTION. *All instruments and noncontrolled variables, when real-valued, are measured in such a way that in the point of maximum attainable welfare the partial derivative of welfare with respect to each of them is nonnegative, provided such a point and the derivatives exist and the point is unique.*

Three remarks should be made. First, the Sign Convention is no assumption, simply because it implies no restrictions on the quantities with which we deal. It is merely convenient in the sense that certain results can be formulated more easily and more elegantly than in the case where the Convention is not applied. Second, contrary to the consumer's utility case, we do not exclude the possibility that a marginal utility is zero; if we had done so, then indeed a restriction would be implied. Third, since the Sign Convention has reference to the point of maximum welfare, which will in general vary from case to case, we cannot exclude the possibility that some variable is introduced with a positive sign in one period, and with a negative sign in a later period. Suppose for instance that a Government policy-maker is faced in the first period with a situation in which considerable unemployment cannot be avoided, whereas in the second period employment is so close to the ceiling that inflationary pressures cannot be avoided. Then it is reasonable to assume that the marginal welfare of employment is positive in the first, and negative in the second period; hence employment is, according to the Sign Convention, the appropriate variable in the first period, and unemployment (say) in the second. Another example is that of the appraisal of stocks of the Munich Business Test—cf. Section 4.1. When stocks are considered "too small," the entrepreneur values stock increases positively; but the converse is true when stocks are considered "too large." Hence minus stocks (say) is appropriate in the latter case, and stocks in the former. This does not, of course, give rise to any essential difficulties.

8.1.3. We now proceed to quadratic welfare assumptions. Naturally, they involve only minor restrictions when the variables do not change very much, just as is true for linear model assumptions; but, since the meaning of "not very much" is not always clear in applications, especially not in this context, it seems useful to give a number of examples from which the adequacy of quadratic assumptions can be judged. We shall confine ourselves here to Government policy-makers' preferences, and leave the extension to entrepreneurs, labour union leaders, etc., to the reader. Examples of the latter kind will be considered in another connection later in this chapter.

Suppose first that the policy-maker is interested in two variables, viz., the aggregate wage bill and the total amount of profits; for the sake of convenience we assume all other variables to be constant. It is irrelevant for our present purposes whether these variables are instruments or noncontrolled variables; though in most present-day societies, of course, they are not controlled. Consider then the (left-hand) Fig. 8.1, where profits and wages are measured along the two axes. Suppose our policy-maker is a conservative man; suppose furthermore that the wage bill remains constant whereas the profits are imagined to increase from a negative value to large positive values (along the broken line). As long as the profits are excessively negative, the policy-maker will value an increase positively. Given his conservative attitude, he will presumably continue to do so even when the profits become larger and larger compared with the constant wage bill. It follows that his indifference curves have negative slopes everywhere. No doubt, after a certain point is reached he will prefer an increase in the wage bill to a further increase of profits by the same amount; however, this is not the issue, for we exclude the possibility of any increase of the wage bill. But consider now a left-wing socialist policy-maker.

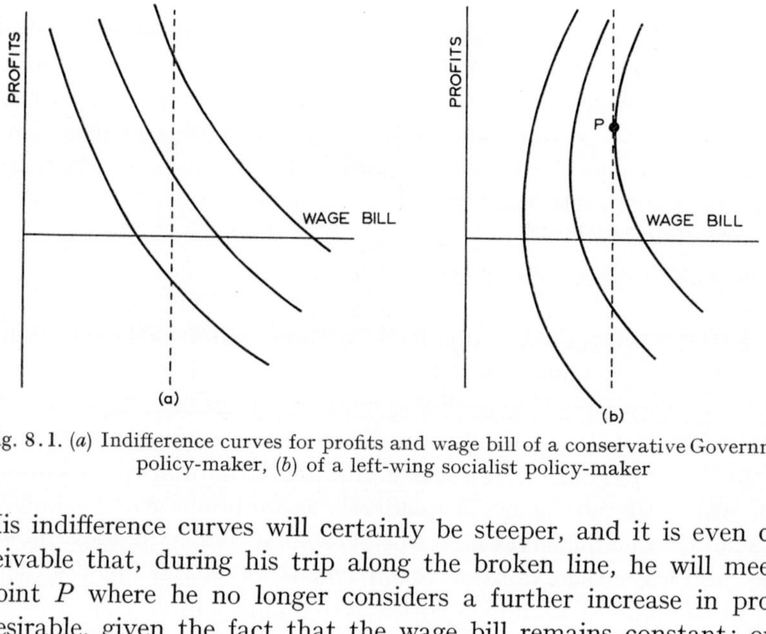

Fig. 8.1. (*a*) Indifference curves for profits and wage bill of a conservative Government policy-maker, (*b*) of a left-wing socialist policy-maker

His indifference curves will certainly be steeper, and it is even conceivable that, during his trip along the broken line, he will meet a point P where he no longer considers a further increase in profits desirable, given the fact that the wage bill remains constant; or in other words (but less precisely), beyond the point P he rejects the opportunity of having a larger national income but with still more inequality between the two groups. Clearly, the indifference curve through P has a vertical tangent in P, and above P the slopes of the indifference curves are even positive.[1]

[1] Note that the change of sign of marginal welfare does not imply that the indifference curves are, according to the Sign Convention, to be "broken" in points like P. On the contrary: if the point of maximum welfare is characterised by a positive marginal utility of profits (e.g., this points is just below P), then the picture of Fig. 8.1 (*b*) is adequate according to the Sign Convention; and if it has a negative marginal utility of profits (it is just above P, say), we should replace profits by minus profits, so that the figure is rotated around the horizontal axis. In both cases the general form of the indifference curves is the same.

Next, we consider the employment-balance of payments alternative, which was analysed earlier (though in a rather preliminary fashion) in 7.1.3; cf. Fig. 8.2. As long as there is a situation of considerable unemployment, most Government policy-makers will be prepared to accept an adverse effect on the balance of payments in order to have more employment. This willingness will of course depend on the size

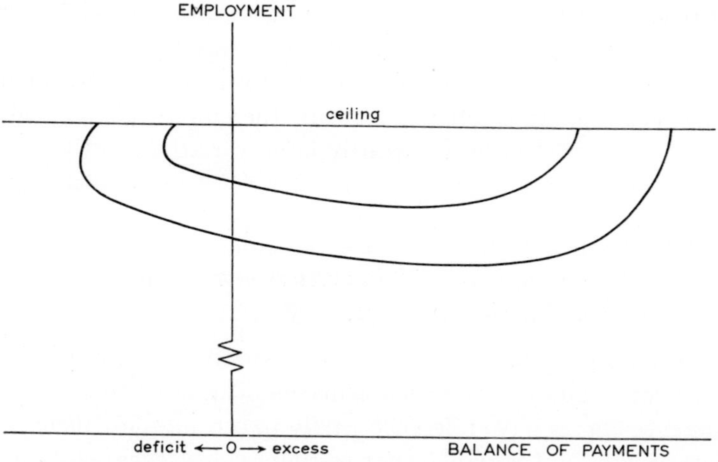

Fig. 8.2. Indifference curves for employment and balance of payments

of the balance, but it seems reasonable to say that the indifference curves will have negative slopes as long as the balance is not too far from zero and as long as employment is not very close to the full-employment ceiling. But suppose that the balance shows such a large excess that exporters are faced with difficulties because of delays in receiving their revenues, etc. Then, provided again the full-employment ceiling is not almost reached, the policy-maker will prefer to get rid of the excess, so that he values any additional excess negatively and the indifference curves have positive slopes. And suppose, finally, that employment is near the 100 per cent level. Then the attractiveness of raising employment has disappeared and it seems even reasonable to assume that it becomes negative because of the resulting inflationary pressures. Hence the indifference curves to the left of the vertical axis turn back near the full-employment line, and the same may be true to the right; cf. the figure.

8.1.4. Two conclusions are suggested by these examples. First, a quadratic welfare assumption,

$$w(x, y) = a'x + b'y + \tfrac{1}{2}(x'Ax + y'By + x'Cy + y'C'x), \tag{8.5}$$

may be quite adequate for rather large variations in the variables.[1] This is clear for the profit-wage bill indifference curves of policy-makers of different backgrounds and also for considerable parts of the employment-balance of payments indifference curves. In the neighbourhood of the ceiling one should be cautious; but this is always true when inequalities play a rôle (as e.g. in consumer's demand where quantities are nonnegative). It is not self-evident, therefore, that the following assumption is satisfied for arbitrarily large variations in the variables involved, although it will often be a rather good approximation:

ASSUMPTION P2. *Assumption* P1 *is satisfied, and* (8.4) *has the specification* (8.5), a, b, A, B *and* C *being vectors and matrices independent of* x *and* y; *and* A *and* B *are symmetric.*

A second conclusion can be drawn from the employment-balance of payments example. The arguments used in order to arrive at the indifference curves have reference partly to certain consequences of the numerical values of variables, not to these values themselves. For instance, when it is stated that increments of employment in the immediate neighbourhood of the full-employment ceiling are negatively valued because of the resulting inflationary pressures, this negativity s due to the pressures, not to the fact that the policy-maker dislikes the idea of a smaller number of unemployed workers. But suppose now that one of the variables of the model (8.2) or (8.3) happens to describe these inflationary pressures in a satisfactory manner, say a general price index. Clearly, it is then no longer necessary to take account of inflationary consequences when drawing employment-balance of payments indifference curves, since this aspect has been taken over by the price as one of the arguments of the welfare function. We may even go on and say that the price index is not a goal in itself, and that inflationary pressures as exhibited by a rise of this index are primarily important for the distribution of real income among the citizens of the society considered. All this is simply the consequence of our decision to interpret "preferences" in a wide manner, and not to go back to

[1] The constant term in (8.5) is omitted because of its irrelevance; cf. Section 7.3.

PRINTED MATTER

IMPRIMÉS

NORTH-HOLLAND PUBLISHING COMPANY

P.O. Box 103

AMSTERDAM-Netherlands

the individuals' baskets of goods consumed and services rendered (cf. the end of 7.1.8).

Therefore, we must conclude that the policy-maker is able to specify the form of his preference function only *after* all arguments of this function are specified. Perhaps this is self-evident, but the above example shows that it is worth mentioning. If the model is a small one with relatively few variables, some of these must be expected to play a rather heterogeneous and "combined" rôle; this is the case of employment when no price level is introduced explicitly. If, on the other hand, the model is specific with respect to a great many relevant variables, the heterogeneity is becoming less and less; and at the same time assumptions as those of smooth and regular preference functions will often tend to become more realistic.

8.1.5. So far, we dealt only with ordinal welfare. We now proceed to cardinal welfare in order to be able to handle the choice problem in risk-taking situations. The assumption which corresponds most closely with Assumption P2 is then:

ASSUMPTION P3. *Assumption* P2 *is satisfied, and the welfare function* (8.5) *is such that, if some of its arguments are stochastic, the policy-maker values according to the mean value of* (8.5).

Obviously, this assumption is more restrictive than Assumption P2, for it is no longer sufficient that all indifference curves are quadratic. Instead, it becomes necessary to assume that the marginal welfare of each variable is a linear function of all variables, whereas under the ordinal assumptions it is sufficient that the ratios of two marginal utilities can be written as the ratios of two linear expressions. Using the risk preference and risk aversion concepts of Section 7.3, this implication can be explained as follows. Take all x's and y's as fixed at certain arbitrary numerical levels, except y_1 which assumes the values y_1' and y_1'', with probability $\frac{1}{2}$ each. Omitting in (8.5) all terms which do not involve y_1, we find for the welfare level of this distribution[1]

$$b_1 \frac{y_1' + y_1''}{2} + \tfrac{1}{2} b_{11} \frac{y_1'^2 + y_1''^2}{2} + \sum_{j=2}^{n} b_{1j} \frac{y_1' + y_1''}{2} y_j + \sum_{h=1}^{m} c_{h1} x_h \frac{y_1' + y_1''}{2}.$$

[1] In order to stress the difference between the variables x, y which are considered here and the larger set of $\Lambda + M$ variables of the model from which they are ultimately derived (cf. 7.1.5), we shall use the indices h, k, m for x, and i, j, n for y, rather than λ, Λ, μ and M.

The corresponding welfare level of the nonstochastic outcome in which y_1' and y_1'' are replaced by their mean value, $\frac{1}{2}y_1' + \frac{1}{2}y_1''$, is given by

$$b_1 \frac{y_1' + y_1''}{2} + \tfrac{1}{2}b_{11}\left\{\frac{y_1' + y_1''}{2}\right\}^2 + \sum_{j=2}^{n} b_{1j}\frac{y_1' + y_1''}{2} y_j + \sum_{h=1}^{m} c_{h1}x_h \frac{y_1' + y_1''}{2}.$$

The difference, $\mathscr{E}w(\mathbf{x}, \mathbf{y}) - w(\mathbf{x}, \mathscr{E}\mathbf{y})$, is then

$$\tfrac{1}{8} b_{11}(y_1' - y_1'')^2,$$

the sign of which is completely determined by b_{11}. It follows that Assumption P3 allows risk preference with respect to y_1 (viz., if $b_{11} > 0$) and also risk aversion ($b_{11} < 0$), but that it excludes the possibility of risk preference for a certain range of y_1 and risk aversion for another.

For some purposes, however, the assumption is stronger than necessary, and we can replace it by that of a preference function which is quadratic in the noncontrolled variables only:

$$w(\mathbf{x}, \mathbf{y}) = A(\mathbf{x}) + \sum_{i=1}^{n} A_i(\mathbf{x}) y_i + \tfrac{1}{2} \sum_{i=1}^{n} \sum_{j=1}^{n} A_{ij} y_i y_j, \tag{8.6}$$

where $A(\mathbf{x})$ and $A_i(\mathbf{x})$ are arbitrary functions of the vector $\mathbf{x}$, which itself need not be of the usual quantitative type. The assumption, which is closely related to the earlier Assumption C2 on the constraints, is then:

ASSUMPTION P4. *All vectors* $\mathbf{x}$, $\mathbf{y}$ *of instruments and (real-valued) noncontrolled variables are completely ordered according to the policy-maker's preference in such a way as to allow a representation by means of the real-valued welfare function* (8.6), *where* $A(\mathbf{x})$ *and* $A_i(\mathbf{x})$ *are independent of* $\mathbf{y}$ *and* A_{ij} *independent of both* $\mathbf{x}$ *and* $\mathbf{y}$. *If some of the arguments of* (8.6) *are stochastic, the policy-maker values according to the mean value of* (8.6).

In this case the marginal welfare of a noncontrolled variable is a linear function of all noncontrolled variables, the multiplicative coefficients of this function being independent of the instruments. There is hence no difference between (8.5) and (8.6) with respect to the alternative: risk preference—risk aversion, as discussed above; but otherwise the marginal welfare may be an arbitrary function of the instruments:

$$\frac{\partial w}{\partial y_i} = A_i(\mathbf{x}) + \sum_{j=1}^{n} A_{ij} y_j. \tag{8.7}$$

The marginal welfare of an instrument, too, is a linear function of the noncontrolled variables, but the coefficients need not be independent of $\mathbf{x}$:

$$\frac{\partial w}{\partial x_h} = \frac{\partial A}{\partial x_h} + \sum_{i=1}^{n} \frac{\partial A_i}{\partial x_h} y_i, \tag{8.8}$$

provided the derivatives exist.

8.1.6. It may be useful to summarise the main features of the preference assumptions; those concerning the constraints are too simple to

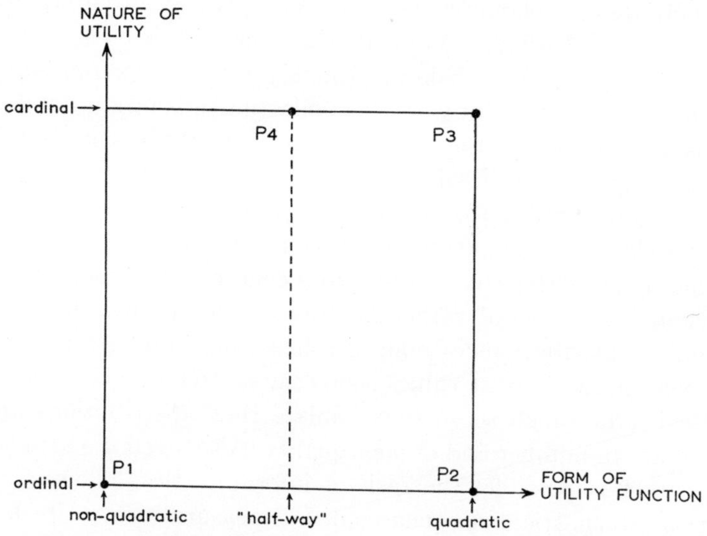

Fig. 8.3. Summary of the alternative preference assumptions made

need any re-statement. Perhaps the most adequate summary is that of a figure, where the nature of utility (ordinal or cardinal) is indicated along one axis, and the quadratic restrictions on the other; cf. Fig. 8.3. Assumption P4, which confines the quadratic restrictions to the non-controlled variables, is "half-way" in this respect. Clearly, the assumptions become more and more restrictive when we move away from the "origin," in either direction.

8.2. Certainty Equivalence and Certainty Bias

8.2.1. One of the problems in the decision-making process is the great diversity of tasks which the policy-maker has to face. He must not only make a choice (and bear the responsibility for it), but he must also be a forecaster. Naturally, the question arises whether it is possible to delegate at least the latter task to another man or to a staff, so that the "decision-making animal" is then split up into a "choice animal" and an "information animal." This is done, in the case of Government policy-making, by the establishment of a Council of Economic Advisers or of a Central Planning Bureau; in the case of firms, by establishing a secretariate or a planning staff; etc. This gives rise to a great many problems most of which are outside the scope of this book, but one of them—to be expounded below—is highly relevant for our purposes. It is, indeed, even relevant when the policy-maker's task is not divided.

It is obviously not the "information animal's" task to tell the "choice animal" how he should adjust his instruments. His task is confined to the first steps, especially step (*iii*), of the sketch of 7.1.2. Now it is clear that the prediction of the future course of noncontrolled variables under alternative assumptions concerning the policy-maker's behaviour is in general rather laborious. The specification of joint probability distributions of noncontrolled values under a great many conditions on instrument values is no easy matter, especially since the empirical data which serve to formulate these distributions are frequently few in number and of poor quality. Also, even if a satisfactory specification is possible, the task of informing the "choice animal" about the stochastic consequences of his measures can easily become inconvenient and cumbersome. To show this, let us first consider the case in which no uncertainty is present. It is then possible in principle to state uniquely what the consequences of alternative actions are: if the policy-maker takes certain (numerically specified) measures, then the noncontrolled variables will have these values; if he takes other measures, then the latter variables will have those values; etc. More formally: if $x = x^1$, then $y = y^1$; if $x = x^2$, then $y = y^2$; etc. Table 7.1 provides an example (cf. 7.1.6), and of course a very simple one, since the number of measures is only four and the number of variables is likewise limited. It is clear that the situation will become more complicated when more sets of measures are considered and when y has more elements. Nevertheless, an information of this kind is not impossible; and the "choice animal," after receiving the information, can make up his mind and choose.

But suppose now that there is no certainty. It is then no longer possible to state uniquely what the consequences are, since the factors controlling these are twofold: controlled variables (instruments) on the one hand, and disturbances on the other, the latter being determined by a chance mechanism. Confining ourselves, for the sake of convenience, to discrete distributions, we may say that the only type of information which is still possible is the following: if $x = x^1$, then $y = y^{11}$ with probability p_{11}, $y = y^{12}$ with probability p_{12}, etc.; if $x = x^2$, then $y = y^{21}$ with probability p_{21}, $y = y^{22}$ with probability p_{22}, etc. Clearly, this is a somewhat embarrassing situation, for few policy-makers will appreciate their staffs providing them with information of such an elaborate and refined nature.

8.2.2. The easiest way out is that of the neglect of uncertainty; say, by replacing stochastic consequences by their mean values. Of course, this is not a very satisfactory solution, for it is conceivable (and even plausible) that this procedure suppresses essential information. More specifically, consider the welfare function $w(x, y)$. As observed earlier, the "best" decision is the one which maximises this function subject to the actual constraints. Since the forecasting mechanism is of limited quality and provides at most stochastic statements, the policy-maker will retreat to the "next best" decision, which is the x for which

$$\mathscr{E}w(x, y) \text{ max},$$

provided w satisfies the Von Neumann-Morgenstern assumptions. On the other hand, if uncertainty is neglected by replacing y by its mean value, the policy-maker will choose the x for which

$$w(x, \mathscr{E}y) \text{ max}.$$

As stated in 7.3.3, these maximisation processes are quite different and may lead to different decisions. But under certain conditions we are in a very favourable situation: although the maximisation processes are not the same, the instrument values of the maxima are. This is shown in the following

THEOREM 1. *Suppose that the Assumptions* C2 *and* P4 *are satisfied. Then maximisation of the welfare function subject to the nonstochastic constraint* $y = f(x)$, *the disturbance vector* u *being replaced by its mean value, gives the same instrument vector (or set of instrument vectors) as maximisation of the mean value of the welfare function subject to the stochastic constraint* $\mathbf{y} = \mathbf{f}(\mathbf{x}) + \mathbf{u}$, *provided such a maximum exists.*

Let us first consider what this theorem implies. It may be that neither $\mathscr{E}w(\mathbf{x}, \mathbf{y})$ nor $w(\mathbf{x}, \mathscr{E}\mathbf{y})$ has a maximum with respect to $\mathbf{x}$; but we may discard this as an uninteresting case. Then both functions have a maximal value, which is reached for one or more instrument vectors. Theorem 1 states that the two functions have their maxima for the same vectors; in other words, that it is irrelevant whether the policy-maker maximises $\mathscr{E}w(\mathbf{x}, \mathbf{y})$ or $w(\mathbf{x}, \mathscr{E}\mathbf{y})$, since in both cases he is bound to take the same decision. In still other words, any information about the probability distribution of $\mathbf{y}$ beyond the mean value is superfluous information, simply because it does not affect the policy-maker's measures. Two conclusions follow. First, this result may be interpreted as a justification of the use of unbiased point predictions; more precisely, of the use of the mean value as the predictor of random variables. As observed in Section 2.2, point predictions have no pretention of coinciding exactly with reality; but, if they are to be "scientific," there should be a probability statement about their relationship to the actual phenomenon to which they refer. Suppose then that the conditional predictions of $\mathbf{y}$, the conditions being alternative specifications of $\mathbf{x}$, are all unbiased point predictions; Theorem 1 states that, under its assumptions, this is a sufficient basis for decision-making,[1] and that nothing is gained by making interval predictions, even if they would be extended such as to cover the entire frequency distribution of $\mathbf{y}$, given $\mathbf{x}$. The second conclusion refers to TINBERGEN's approach; cf. 7.1.8. Tinbergen, too, neglects disturbances, but his formulation involves choice of $\mathbf{y}$ (or better, $\mathscr{E}\mathbf{y}$), rather than choice of $\mathbf{x}$. Now, if it is true that $\mathbf{x}$ and $\mathbf{y}$ have an equal number of components ($m = n$), and if the choice of "target values" is such that $w(\mathbf{x}, \mathscr{E}\mathbf{y})$ is maximised

[1] Note that we deal here with unbiased point predictions which are mean values, not unbiased estimates of mean values, of random variables; Theorem 1 is concerned with such unbiased point predictions only. The example considered on p. 12 n. is illustrative in this respect: if the random variable to be predicted is y_{T+1}, then $\alpha + \beta x_{T+1}$ is the unbiased point prediction of Theorem 1, while $a + bx_{T+1}$ is also an unbiased point prediction but not the one of Theorem 1, since it is only an unbiased estimator of the mean value. The extension of the theorem for such estimates is more complicated; reference is made to J. DURBIN, "The Effect of Forecasting Errors in Dynamic Programming with a Quadratic Cost Function" (mimeographed and unpublished, 1959), and to P. J. M. VAN DEN BOGAARD, "On the Static Theory of Certainty Equivalence," Report 6010 of the Econometric Institute of the Netherlands School of Economics (1960).

by this choice, then, according to Theorem 1, the decision is not affected by the neglect of disturbances.

The proof of the theorem is as follows. Substituting (8.3) into (8.6), we find for the welfare level attained by applying the instrument values x:

$$w(x, f(x) + u) = A(x) + \sum_i A_i(x)\{f_i(x) + u_i\} + \\ + \tfrac{1}{2} \sum_i \sum_j A_{ij}\{f_i(x) + u_i\}\{f_j(x) + u_j\}.$$

Taking mean values, we find

$$(8.9) \qquad \mathscr{E}w(x, f(x) + u) = A(x) + \sum_i A_i(x) f_i(x) + \\ + \tfrac{1}{2} \sum_i \sum_j A_{ij}\{f_i(x) f_j(x) + \text{cov}\,(u_i, u_j)\}.$$

On the other hand, if the policy-maker acts under the assumption that y is equal to its mean value, $f(x)$, the relevant function is

$$(8.10) \qquad w(x, f(x)) = A(x) + \sum_i A_i(x) f_i(x) + \tfrac{1}{2} \sum_i \sum_j A_{ij} f_i(x) f_j(x).$$

Subtract (8.10) from (8.9):

$$(8.11) \qquad \mathscr{E}w(x, f(x) + u) - w(x, f(x)) = \tfrac{1}{2} \sum_i \sum_j A_{ij}\, \text{cov}\,(u_i, u_j).$$

This means that, for any instrument values x, the mean value of the welfare level attained, $\mathscr{E}w$, is derived from the welfare level corresponding to this x and to the mean values of the noncontrolled variables associated with x, $w(x, f)$, by adding a *constant*. It follows immediately that, for those x-values where one of the functions has a maximum, the other function is maximised as well. This is illustrated for the case of one instrument ($m = 1$) in the left-hand part of Fig. 8.4, where d is the constant difference (8.11).

8.2.3. This fortunate result can be briefly indicated by saying that unbiased point predictions are *certainty equivalents* in decision-making under uncertainty. Obviously, however, the validity of the result does not extend beyond that of its assumptions. If these are not satisfied, we must expect that maximisation of $\mathscr{E}w$ leads to one vector of instrument values, $\hat{x}$ say, and maximisation of $w(x, f)$ to another vector, $\bar{x}$ say. Suppose that both $\hat{x}$ and $\bar{x}$ are unique. Then we shall say that the case $\bar{x} \neq \hat{x}$ is that of *certainty bias* of the policy-maker's choice due to the use of unbiased point predictions.[1] If, furthermore, x is real-valued, we may call the difference $\bar{x} - \hat{x}$ the *size* of the certainty bias.

The remainder of this section is devoted to an analysis of this bias This will be done by removing the restrictions of Assumptions C2 and P4 one at a time, in each case supposing that all other restrictions are satisfied. First, we shall suppose (in 8.2.4) that the preference function contains cubic terms in the noncontrolled variables; in 8.2.5 we shall assume that coefficients of the quadratic terms depend on x; and in 8.2.6 we shall do the same with respect to the covariance matrix of u. A conclusion follows in 8.2.7. This one-by-one treatment may be

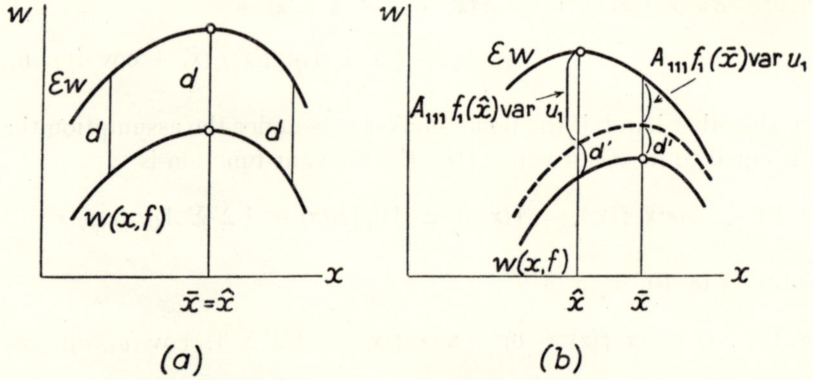

Fig. 8.4. Maximisation of the mean value of welfare, and maximisation of the welfare level associated with the mean values of the noncontrolled variables: (*a*) the case of Theorem 1, (*b*) the case of Theorem 1a, sub (*i*)

justified by pointing out that, if several restrictions are violated to a moderate degree, their combined effect is approximately found by adding the effects of the separate violations—provided, of course, a Taylor expansion is adequate.

8.2.4. Suppose the welfare function has the form

$$(8.12)\qquad w(x, y) = A(x) + \sum_i A_i(x) y_i + \frac{1}{2}\sum_i \sum_j A_{ij} y_i y_j + \frac{1}{3}\sum_i \sum_j \sum_l A_{ijl} y_i y_j y_l.$$

[1] If the vectors are not unique, so that $\mathcal{E}w$ and $w(x, f)$ are maximised for sets of x-vectors rather than single vectors, we may define certainty bias as the case when the two sets are different.

In an earlier exposition of the same subject the term "choice bias" was used. It has the advantage that it indicates clearly the nature of the quantities to which it refers; its disadvantage is that it does not indicate the cause of the bias. Cf. H. THEIL, "Econometric Models and Welfare Maximisation," *Weltwirtschaftliches Archiv*, Vol. 72 (1954), pp. 60–83, and *Linear Aggregation of Economic Relations*, pp. 178–179.

Suppose further that the constraints are given by (8.3), and that the third moments $\mathscr{E}(u_i u_j u_l)$ are finite and independent of **x**. The subtraction procedure of 8.2.2 leads then to

$$(8.13)\qquad \mathscr{E}w(\mathbf{x}, \mathbf{f}(\mathbf{x}) + \mathbf{u}) - w(\mathbf{x}, \mathbf{f}(\mathbf{x})) =$$
$$= \tfrac{1}{2} \sum_i \sum_j A_{ij} \operatorname{cov}(u_i, u_j) + \tfrac{1}{3} \sum_i \sum_j \sum_l A_{ijl}\{f_i \operatorname{cov}(u_j, u_l) +$$
$$+ f_j \operatorname{cov}(u_i, u_l) + f_l \operatorname{cov}(u_i, u_j) + \mathscr{E}(u_i u_j u_l)\}.$$

First, we take the case $A_{ijl} = 0$ for all i, j, l except A_{111}; i.e., the case of equal subscripts. This means that the rate of change of the marginal welfare of any noncontrolled variable, $\partial w/\partial y_i$, with respect to changes in any y_j (including $i = j$) is constant, as in the quadratic case; except, however, for the rate of change of $\partial w/\partial y_1$ with respect to y_1 itself, which is a linear function of y_1:

$$\frac{\partial}{\partial y_1}\left(\frac{\partial w}{\partial y_1}\right) = A_{11} + 2A_{111}y_1.$$

In terms of the risk preference—risk aversion analysis of 8.1.5, the implications are as follows. Take again all x's and y's as fixed except y_1, which assumes the two values y_1' and y_1'' with probability $\tfrac{1}{2}$ each. The excess of the welfare level of this distribution over the corresponding level with y_1 replaced by $\tfrac{1}{2}y_1' + \tfrac{1}{2}y_1''$ is then

$$\tfrac{1}{8} A_{11}(y_1' - y_1'')^2 \left[1 + \frac{A_{111}}{A_{11}}(y_1' + y_1'')\right].$$

Here, the question whether there is risk preference or risk aversion with respect to y_1 is no longer fully determined by A_{11}. If $A_{111} > 0$ the risk preference increases (or risk aversion diminishes) with increasing values of $\tfrac{1}{2}(y_1' + y_1'')$; if $A_{111} < 0$, the reverse is true. If $A_{111}(y_1' + y_1'') = -A_{11}$, there is "risk neutrality."

Under our present assumption we can re-write (8.13) as

$$(8.14)\qquad \mathscr{E}w(\mathbf{x}, \mathbf{f}(\mathbf{x}) + \mathbf{u}) = w(\mathbf{x}, \mathbf{f}(\mathbf{x})) + d' + A_{111}f_1 \operatorname{var} u_1,$$

where d' is a constant with respect to **x**:

$$d' = \tfrac{1}{2} \sum_i \sum_j A_{ij} \operatorname{cov}(u_i, u_j) + \tfrac{1}{3} A_{111}\mathscr{E}u_1^3.$$

Substituting $\mathbf{x} = \bar{\mathbf{x}}$ and $\mathbf{x} = \hat{\mathbf{x}}$ in (8.14) and subtracting, and recalling that

$$\mathscr{E}w(\hat{\mathbf{x}}, \mathbf{f}(\hat{\mathbf{x}}) + \mathbf{u}) \geqq \mathscr{E}w(\bar{\mathbf{x}}, \mathbf{f}(\bar{\mathbf{x}}) + \mathbf{u})$$
$$w(\hat{\mathbf{x}}, \mathbf{f}(\hat{\mathbf{x}})) \leqq w(\bar{\mathbf{x}}, \mathbf{f}(\bar{\mathbf{x}})),$$

we find immediately that $A_{111}\{f_1(\hat{\mathbf{x}}) - f_1(\bar{\mathbf{x}})\} \geqq 0$, so that $f_1(\hat{\mathbf{x}}) \geqq f_1(\bar{\mathbf{x}})$ if $A_{111} > 0$ and $f_1(\hat{\mathbf{x}}) \leqq f_1(\bar{\mathbf{x}})$ if $A_{111} < 0$. In words, the certainty bias is such that the mean value of the noncontrolled variable y_1 implied by the choice under neglect of uncertainty is too small if the rate of change of the marginal welfare of y_1 with respect to y_1 increases with y_1, and too large if the rate is a decreasing function of y_1. This is illustrated for the case of one instrument in the right-hand part of Fig. 8.4,[1] and stated more formally in the first part of

THEOREM 1a. *Suppose that the Assumptions* C2 *and* P4 *are satisfied, except for the addition of cubic terms in the welfare function as in* (8.12), A_{ijl} *being independent of* $\mathbf{x}$ *and* $\mathbf{y}$, *and that the third moments* $\mathscr{E}(u_i u_j u_l)$ *of the disturbance vector* $\mathbf{u}$ *of* (8.3) *are finite and independent of* $\mathbf{x}$. *Then the certainty bias, if existent, is characterised by the following rules:*

(i) If $A_{ijl} = 0$ *except for* A_{111}, *then*

$$f_1(\bar{\mathbf{x}}) - f_1(\hat{\mathbf{x}}) \begin{cases} \leqq 0 \text{ if } A_{111} > 0 \\ \geqq 0 \text{ if } A_{111} < 0. \end{cases} \tag{8.15}$$

(ii) If $A_{ijl} = 0$ *except for* A_{112}, *then*

$$\begin{aligned} 2\{f_1(\bar{\mathbf{x}}) - f_1(\hat{\mathbf{x}})\} \operatorname{cov}(u_1, u_2) &+ \\ + \{f_2(\bar{\mathbf{x}}) - f_2(\hat{\mathbf{x}})\} \operatorname{var} u_1 &\leqq 0 \text{ if } A_{112} > 0 \\ &\geqq 0 \text{ if } A_{112} < 0. \end{aligned} \tag{8.16}$$

(iii) If $A_{ijl} = 0$ *except for* A_{123}, *then*

$$\begin{aligned} \{f_1(\bar{\mathbf{x}}) - f_1(\hat{\mathbf{x}})\} \operatorname{cov}(u_2, u_3) + \{f_2(\bar{\mathbf{x}}) - f_2(\hat{\mathbf{x}})\} \operatorname{cov}(u_1, u_3) &+ \\ + \{f_3(\bar{\mathbf{x}}) - f_3(\hat{\mathbf{x}})\} \operatorname{cov}(u_1, u_2) &\leqq 0 \text{ if } A_{123} > 0 \\ &\geqq 0 \text{ if } A_{123} < 0. \end{aligned} \tag{8.17}$$

[1] Note that this deviation from the quadratic case need not necessarily lead to certainty bias. Take e.g. the situation in which the f's are stationary in $\bar{\mathbf{x}}$. Such cases are, however, not very interesting.

The second case, in which only two of the subscripts are equal, A_{112} say, is treated as follows. First, note that we may assume, without loss of generality, $A_{112} = A_{121} = A_{211}$ [cf. (8.12)]. Write (8.13) then in the form

$$\mathscr{E}w(\mathbf{x}, \mathbf{f}(\mathbf{x}) + \mathbf{u}) = w(\mathbf{x}, \mathbf{f}(\mathbf{x})) + d'' + A_{112}\{2f_1 \operatorname{cov}(u_1, u_2) + f_2 \operatorname{var} u_1\}, \tag{8.18}$$

where d'' is a function of second and third moments of $\mathbf{u}$ (and hence a constant with respect to $\mathbf{x}$). This leads immediately to (8.16). It will be seen that the sign of the correlation of u_1 and u_2 is relevant. If there is no correlation and if A_{112} is positive (negative), the difference $f_2(\bar{\mathbf{x}}) - f_2(\hat{\mathbf{x}})$ is negative (positive).

For the third case of three different subscripts, A_{123} (which we put equal to the five other A's with the same indices, like A_{132}), we find

$$\mathscr{E}w(\mathbf{x}, \mathbf{f}(\mathbf{x}) + \mathbf{u}) = w(\mathbf{x}, \mathbf{f}(\mathbf{x})) + d''' + 2A_{123}\{f_1 \operatorname{cov}(u_2, u_3) + f_2 \operatorname{cov}(u_1, u_3) + f_3 \operatorname{cov}(u_1, u_2)\}, \tag{8.19}$$

which leads to (8.17). If the disturbances u_1, u_2, u_3 are all uncorrelated, there is no certainty bias; but this is not a plausible situation for disturbances of a reduced form like (8.3).

8.2.5. Next, we turn to the case in which w is quadratic in the non-controlled variables, but where coefficients of the quadratic terms depend on the x's:

$$w(\mathbf{x}, \mathbf{y}) = A(\mathbf{x}) + \sum_i A_i(\mathbf{x})y_i + \tfrac{1}{2} \sum_i \sum_j A_{ij}(\mathbf{x})y_i y_j. \tag{8.20}$$

This implies that the rate of change of the marginal welfare of y_i with respect to y_j is a function of $\mathbf{x}$. The subtraction procedure gives then

$$\mathscr{E}w(\mathbf{x}, \mathbf{f}(\mathbf{x}) + \mathbf{u}) - w(\mathbf{x}, \mathbf{f}(\mathbf{x})) = \tfrac{1}{2} \sum_i \sum_j A_{ij}(\mathbf{x}) \operatorname{cov}(u_i, u_j). \tag{8.21}$$

First, we take A_{ij} independent of $\mathbf{x}$ except for A_{11} (the case of equal subscripts). This case may be written as

$$\mathscr{E}w(\mathbf{x}, \mathbf{f}(\mathbf{x}) + \mathbf{u}) = w(\mathbf{x}, \mathbf{f}(\mathbf{x})) + c + A_{11}(\mathbf{x}) \operatorname{var} u_1,$$

c being a constant with respect to $\mathbf{x}$. Application of the approach of 8.2.4 gives immediately $A_{11}(\bar{\mathbf{x}}) \leq A_{11}(\hat{\mathbf{x}})$; i.e., the rate of change of the marginal welfare of y_1 with respect to y_1 itself is algebraically smaller in the point of certainty maximisation.

In the second case of unequal subscripts [all A_{ij} independent of $\mathbf{x}$ except $A_{12}(\mathbf{x}) \equiv A_{21}(\mathbf{x})$, say] we can write

$$\mathscr{E}w(\mathbf{x}, \mathbf{f}(\mathbf{x}) + \mathbf{u}) = w(\mathbf{x}, \mathbf{f}(\mathbf{x})) + c' + 2A_{12}(\mathbf{x}) \operatorname{cov}(u_1, u_2),$$

so that $A_{12}(\bar{\mathbf{x}}) \leq A_{12}(\hat{\mathbf{x}})$ if u_1 and u_2 are positively correlated, and $\geq$ if there is a negative correlation. More formally:

THEOREM 1b. *Suppose that the Assumptions* C2 *and* P4 *are satisfied, except that coefficients of the quadratic terms of the welfare function, A_{ij}, are functions of $\mathbf{x}$ as in* (8.20). *Then the certainty bias, if existent, is characterised by the following rules*:

(i) If A_{ij} is independent of $\mathbf{x}$ except for A_{11}, then

$$A_{11}(\bar{\mathbf{x}}) - A_{11}(\hat{\mathbf{x}}) \leq 0. \tag{8.22}$$

(ii) If A_{ij} is independent of $\mathbf{x}$ except for A_{12}, then

$$A_{12}(\bar{\mathbf{x}}) - A_{12}(\hat{\mathbf{x}}) \begin{array}{l} \leq 0 \text{ if } \operatorname{cov}(u_1, u_2) > 0 \\ \geq 0 \text{ if } \operatorname{cov}(u_1, u_2) < 0. \end{array} \tag{8.23}$$

8.2.6. Finally, consider the case in which the covariance matrix of $\mathbf{u}$ is not independent of $\mathbf{x}$. (8.11) can then be written as

$$\mathscr{E}w(\mathbf{x}, \mathbf{f}(\mathbf{x}) + \mathbf{u}) - w(\mathbf{x}, \mathbf{f}(\mathbf{x})) = \tfrac{1}{2} \sum_i \sum_j A_{ij}\sigma_{ij}(\mathbf{x}), \tag{8.24}$$

where σ_{ij} stands for $\operatorname{cov}(u_i, u_j)$. Assuming that all σ_{ij}'s are independent of $\mathbf{x}$ except $\sigma_{11} = \operatorname{var} u_1$, we find that $\sigma_{11}(\bar{\mathbf{x}}) \leq \sigma_{11}(\hat{\mathbf{x}})$ if $A_{11} > 0$, $\geq \sigma_{11}(\hat{\mathbf{x}})$ if $A_{11} < 0$. For example, if the marginal welfare of y_1 decreases with y_1 ($A_{11} < 0$), and if y_1 is in the neighbourhood of a boundary where its variance tends to diminish, the certainty bias is such that the variance is too large; i.e., the bias is such that the mean value of y_1 in the case of maximisation under certainty, $f_1(\bar{\mathbf{x}})$, is too far from the boundary.

Next, suppose that all σ_{ij}'s are independent of $\mathbf{x}$ except the covariance $\sigma_{12} = \sigma_{21}$. In that case $A_{12}\{\sigma_{12}(\bar{\mathbf{x}}) - \sigma_{12}(\hat{\mathbf{x}})\} \leq 0$, as is stated in

THEOREM 1c. *Suppose that the Assumptions* C2 *and* P4 *are satisfied, except that elements σ_{ij} of the covariance matrix $[\sigma_{ij}] = \mathscr{E}(\mathbf{u}\mathbf{u}')$ of the* *disturbance vector* **u** *of* (8.3) *depend on* **x**. *Then the certainty bias, if existent, is characterised by the following rules*:

(*i*) *If* σ_{ij} *is independent of* **x** *except for* σ_{11}, *then*

$$\sigma_{11}(\bar{x}) - \sigma_{11}(\hat{x}) \begin{cases} \leqq 0 \text{ if } A_{11} > 0 \\ \geqq 0 \text{ if } A_{11} < 0. \end{cases} \tag{8.25}$$

(*ii*) *If* σ_{ij} *is independent of* **x** *except* σ_{12}, *then*

$$\sigma_{12}(\bar{x}) - \sigma_{12}(\hat{x}) \begin{cases} \leqq 0 \text{ if } A_{12} > 0 \\ \geqq 0 \text{ if } A_{12} < 0. \end{cases} \tag{8.26}$$

8.2.7. Our conclusions are these:

First, as observed earlier, maximisation of the mean value of welfare is different from maximising welfare after replacing the constraints by their mean values; but according to Theorem 1 there is a special case, which is not at all unplausible, under which the policy-maker's maximising decisions are the same in both cases. In other words: mean values used as unbiased point predictions form then a certainty equivalent in decision-making.

Second, if the assumptions of Theorem 1 are not fulfilled, we must expect certainty bias rather than certainty equivalence. It appears to be possible to give a specification of certain aspects of this bias; and this specification involves, in all cases analysed, quantities of at least one of the following two categories: parameters and other features of the welfare function, and similar quantities of the constraint (8.3).

Third, it is not true that there is no certainty equivalent in the cases of Theorems 1a–1c; it is only true that unbiased point predictions are then in general not certainty equivalents. There can be no doubt that, under appropriate conditions, certainty equivalents exist even if Theorem 1 is not applicable, but the point predictions of these equivalents will depend *i.a.* on the characteristics of the preference function and are hence much more complicated. In particular, it is then no longer possible for the "information animal" to supply his "choice animal" with simple point predictions without causing certainty bias, unless he has a rather detailed knowledge of the latter's preferences. Conversely, if the assumptions of Theorem 1 are satisfied, it is not only true that the "choice animal" need not know the complete distribution of **u** for taking decisions, but also that the "information animal" need not know the former's preferences in order to supply certainty-equivalent information.

This leads us at the same time to our final remark. It was observed (cf. 7.3.5) that relevant probability distributions are sometimes of the subjective type. What matters in this connection is the "choice animal's" subjective distribution, not that of his subordinate. It may be, of course, that the former is of the opinion that the latter has a much better evidential basis for determining probabilities, so that he accepts whatever the latter tells him. In that case there is effectively only one probability distribution. But if there are two different distributions and if the "information animal" supplies information based on his own convictions, this is evidently not without relevance for our present analysis. On the other hand, if the conditions of Theorem 1 are satisfied, no complications arise when the two distributions have equal means, since these form a sufficient basis for decision-making.

8.3. Optimal Decisions and Changing Constraints

8.3.1. Our next topic is the analysis of the characteristics of optimal decisions in relation to changes in the constraints which the policy-maker has to face. As before, we shall interpret the term "optimal" in an absolute sense; i.e., in the sense that optimal decisions maximise welfare subject to the actual (and generally unknown) constraints. So we leave the realm of the maximisation of welfare subject to stochastic constraints, and our next goal is such that the policy-maker, who may feel that he is in a stochastic situation (and who will in general even have wrong ideas about his distributions), will presumably never reach it, except accidentally. But still, it remains his goal. An alternative way of saying is that we shall consider welfare maximisation subject to stochastic constraints, and that all statements will refer to mean values—but this, of course, holds only if unbiased point predictions form a certainty equivalent, as in the case of Theorem 1.

Given the fact that we shall not deal with uncertainty, it will not be necessary to assume cardinal utility. So our welfare assumptions will be P1 or P2, and our results will not be affected if w is replaced by a monotonically increasing function of itself. On the other hand, we shall be more specific with respect to the constraints, for linearity will be assumed throughout:

$$Qy = Rx + s. \tag{8.2}$$

This will enable us to arrive at an immediate generalisation of the theory of consumer's demand, as summarised in Section 7.2.

In this connection, it will prove useful to give an interpretation to the elements of Q, R, s. Their meaning in terms of elementary economic concepts is in general complicated. In the employment–balance of payments example of 7.1.3, for instance, the two elements of R under the normalisation $Q = \mathbf{I}$ depend on the marginal propensity to consume (β), the reaction coefficient of the employment equation (γ), the marginal propensities to import for the consumption and the Government expenditure categories (α_1 and α_4), and next year's import price level (p_M); cf. 7.1.5. In the case of larger models, whether they are set up for a Government policy-maker or for any other decision-maker, we should expect a still more complicated dependence. Still, it is possible to give a simple interpretation to the components of Q, R, s. For it does not matter for the policy-maker that their economic meaning is complicated; what is relevant for him is that (8.2) is the set of constraints which he has to face. To grasp this more fully, suppose that the Sign Convention is applied and consider any element of R, say r_{ih}. This coefficient, which describes the influence of x_h on y_i, can be said to measure the *effectiveness* of this instrument with respect to this noncontrolled variable. It is possible, of course, that this effectiveness is negative ($r_{ih} < 0$). This means that an increase in x_h, which as such is favourable or at least not unfavourable according to the Sign Convention, has an unfavourable influence on y_i. In such a case, clearly, x_h is not a very desirable instrument with respect to y_i; but it may be desirable with respect to other y's. We shall come back to this point at the end of 8.3.2. Together with Q, the matrix R can be said to describe the *multiplicative structure* of the constraints. In this respect these matrices are fully comparable with the prices of the consumer's budget restriction, and the further analysis will illustrate this analogue. It will only be necessary to take account of the fact that R stands to the right of the equality sign in (8.2), so that a replacement of R by $-R$ is then appropriate to bring out the formal identity more fully.

The n components of s, furthermore, form the *additive structure* of the constraints. They are obviously comparable with the consumer's income; accordingly we shall refer to them as the *sources* from which the policy-maker can draw. Each source "feeds" one and only one noncontrolled variable; but the policy-maker can cause a more diversified effect of source changes by changing his instruments as well. It is easy to see that an infinitesimal increase of any of the sources leads to a higher (at least not lower) attainable welfare level. For, if s_i increases, y_i increases at the same time if no measures are taken; and this has a nonnegative effect on w. Taking no measures after the s_i-change need not be the best policy; but, since the best policy is at least as good as the no-measures policy, this proves the assertion.

As to the interpretation of Q, finally, suppose that one of its diagonal elements, say q_i (in the i-th row and the i-th column), increases; and assume further that $y_i > 0$ (which is always possible by choosing a suitable scale for y_i). Then a higher source value s_i is necessary in order to enable the policy-maker to arrive at the original level of his variables x, y. This means that we can interpret q_i as measuring the *expensiveness* of the noncontrolled variable y_i.

8.3.2. Maximisation of the welfare function $w = w(\mathsf{x}, \mathsf{y})$ subject to (8.2) is carried out, as in the case of consumer's demand, by means of Lagrange multipliers. So we consider

$$w(x_1, \ldots, x_m, y_1, \ldots, y_n) - \sum_{i=1}^{n} \lambda_i \{q_i y_i - \sum_{h=1}^{m} r_{ih} x_h - s_i\}, \tag{8.27}$$

or in matrix notation:

$$w(\mathsf{x}, \mathsf{y}) - \lambda'(\mathsf{Q}\mathsf{y} - \mathsf{R}\mathsf{x} - \mathsf{s}), \tag{8.28}$$

where λ is a column vector of Lagrange multipliers. Maximisation gives then

$$\frac{\partial w}{\partial x_h} + \sum_i \lambda_i r_{ih} = 0 \qquad (h = 1, \ldots, m) \tag{8.29}$$

$$\frac{\partial w}{\partial y_i} - \lambda_i q_i = 0 \qquad (i = 1, \ldots, n)$$

or

$$\frac{\partial w}{\partial \mathsf{x}} + \mathsf{R}'\lambda = \mathbf{0} \tag{8.30}$$

$$\frac{\partial w}{\partial \mathsf{y}} - \mathsf{Q}'\lambda = \mathbf{0}.$$

where $\partial w/\partial \mathbf{x}$ and $\partial w/\partial \mathbf{y}$ are the column vectors of the marginal welfare of instruments and of noncontrolled variables, respectively. The equations (8.30) are the generalisation of (7.18) and will hence be called the first-order (equilibrium) conditions. When combined with the constraints (8.2), they yield $(m + 2n)$ restrictions on the same number of unknowns $\mathbf{x}$, $\mathbf{y}$, $\boldsymbol{\lambda}$. It will be noted that all Lagrange multipliers are nonnegative because of the Sign Convention and of the fact that all q's are taken as positive (cf. Assumption C1):

$$\lambda_i \geq 0 \qquad (i = 1, \ldots, n). \tag{8.31}$$

It is also clear that we can eliminate $\boldsymbol{\lambda}$ by replacing (8.30) by

$$\frac{\partial w}{\partial \mathbf{x}} + \mathbf{R}'\mathbf{Q}^{-1}\frac{\partial w}{\partial \mathbf{y}} = \mathbf{0}; \tag{8.32}$$

but for our present purposes it will not prove useful to do so.

For the second-order (stability) conditions we should consider the matrix

$$\mathbf{W} = \begin{bmatrix} \mathbf{W}_{xx} & \mathbf{W}_{xy} & \mathbf{R}' \\ \mathbf{W}_{yx} & \mathbf{W}_{yy} & -\mathbf{Q}' \\ \mathbf{R} & -\mathbf{Q} & \mathbf{0} \end{bmatrix}, \tag{8.33}$$

which is obtained by bordering the matrices of second-order derivatives of the welfare function,

$$\mathbf{W}_{xx} = \left[\frac{\partial^2 w}{\partial x_h \partial x_k}\right]; \quad \mathbf{W}_{yy} = \left[\frac{\partial^2 w}{\partial y_i \partial y_j}\right]; \tag{8.34}$$

$$\mathbf{W}_{xy} = \left[\frac{\partial^2 w}{\partial x_h \partial y_i}\right]; \qquad \mathbf{W}_{yx} = \mathbf{W}'_{xy},$$

by the elements of the multiplicative structure of the constraints, with proper signs. The second-order conditions are then the following:[1] Take an arbitrary principal minor of order $(n + 1)$ in the matrix of second derivatives of w; it is irrelevant whether this minor involves derivatives with respect to instruments or noncontrolled variables. Border this minor with the corresponding elements of the

[1] See e.g. P. A. SAMUELSON, *Foundations of Economic Analysis* (Cambridge, Mass., 1948), pp. 376–378 or E. BURGER, "On Extrema with Side Conditions," *Econometrica*, Vol. 23 (1955), pp. 451–452.

multiplicative structure. The result is a principal minor of order $(2n + 1)$ of the matrix W; for example:

$$\begin{vmatrix} \frac{\partial^2 w}{\partial x_1^2} & \frac{\partial^2 w}{\partial x_1 \partial y_1} & \cdots\cdots & \frac{\partial^2 w}{\partial x_1 \partial y_n} & r_{11} & \cdots\cdots & r_{n1} \\ \frac{\partial^2 w}{\partial y_1 \partial x_1} & \frac{\partial^2 w}{\partial y_1^2} & \cdots\cdots & \frac{\partial^2 w}{\partial y_1 \partial y_n} & -q_1 & \cdots\cdots & 0 \\ \cdot & \cdot & \cdots & \cdot & \cdot & \cdots & \cdot \\ \frac{\partial^2 w}{\partial y_n \partial x_1} & \frac{\partial^2 w}{\partial y_n \partial y_1} & \cdots\cdots & \frac{\partial^2 w}{\partial y_n^2} & 0 & \cdots\cdots & -q_n \\ r_{11} & -q_1 & \cdots\cdots & 0 & 0 & \cdots\cdots & 0 \\ \cdot & \cdot & \cdots & \cdot & \cdot & \cdots & \cdot \\ r_{n1} & 0 & \cdots\cdots & -q_n & 0 & \cdots\cdots & 0 \end{vmatrix}$$

This minor should have the sign of $(-)^{n+1}$. Further, when it is bordered by another row and column of W such that a principal minor of order $(2n + 2)$ results, it should have opposite sign; and so on, up till the determinant of W itself. More precisely:

THEOREM 2. *Suppose that the Assumptions* C1 *and* P1 *are satisfied. Then, in order that values* $\mathbf{x}^0$, $\mathbf{y}^0$ *exist for which the welfare function is stationary subject to the constraints, it is necessary that* (8.30) *holds in* $\mathbf{x}^0$, $\mathbf{y}^0$. *Further, in order that this stationary value be a maximum, it is sufficient that in this point the principal minors of order* $n + 1, \ldots, n + m$ *of the matrix of second-order derivatives, bordered with the multiplicative coefficients of the constraints as in* (8.33), *have alternating signs, the first having the sign of* $(-)^{n+1}$. *Finally, if the Sign Convention is applied, all* n *Lagrange multipliers* λ_i *in* (8.30) *are nonnegative.*

It is possible to draw an interesting conclusion from the first and the third part of this theorem. Let us write (8.30) in the form

$$\begin{bmatrix} \partial w/\partial \mathbf{x} \\ \partial w/\partial \mathbf{y} \end{bmatrix} = \begin{bmatrix} -R' \\ Q' \end{bmatrix} \lambda. \tag{8.35}$$

The Sign Convention implies that all components of $\partial w/\partial \mathbf{x}$ are nonnegative; and the same is true for λ according to (8.31). A comparison with (8.35) shows that no row of R' can then consist of positive elements only. In other words, if there is a maximum and if the Sign Convention is applied, *each column of* $\mathbf{R}$ *should have at least one non-positive element*; except for the trivial case when all first-order derivatives of w vanish ("complete saturation"). Recalling that $-\mathbf{R}$ corresponds with the prices of the consumer's budget restriction, we note that the application of the Sign Convention thus removes another difference with consumer's theory, at least partly; cf. 7.1.4. It is easy to see that this result must hold. For suppose that one column of $\mathbf{R}$, corresponding to the instrument x_h (say), has only positive elements. Then a small increase of x_h — which as such affects welfare favourably, if at all — leads to increases in all y's; and this, too, affects welfare favourably. This contradicts the situation of a maximum. In the general case, when there is no saturation with respect to any of the noncontrolled variables, each column of $\mathbf{R}$ which does not consist of zeros only should have at least one negative element.[1] In other words: in equilibrium each instrument should be negatively effective with respect to some noncontrolled variable.

8.3.3. In the same way as consumer's theory describes the "best" quantities as dependent on the parameters of the budget restriction by means of demand functions, in just the same way it is possible to describe the policy-maker's optimal values $\mathbf{x}^0$, $\mathbf{y}^0$ as functions of the coefficients of his constraints. This leads to his *optimal reaction functions*

$$\begin{aligned} \mathbf{x}^0 &= \mathbf{x}(\mathbf{Q}, \mathbf{R}, \mathbf{s}) \\ \mathbf{y}^0 &= \mathbf{y}(\mathbf{Q}, \mathbf{R}, \mathbf{s}), \end{aligned} \tag{8.36}$$

the properties of which form our next subject of discussion. These functions will exist in a range of values of the elements of $\mathbf{Q}$, $\mathbf{R}$, $\mathbf{s}$ if w has a conditional maximum for any constraint $\mathbf{Qy} = \mathbf{Rx} + \mathbf{s}$ corresponding to this range; which will be assumed throughout. We shall also assume that the functions are single-valued.

Let us write all $(m + 2n)$ equations (8.30) and (8.2) below each other, as (7.20) in the theory of consumer's demand:

[1] Note that this condition is fulfilled for the employment–balance of payments example; cf. **7.1.3** and **7.1.5**.

$$
(8.37) \qquad
\begin{array}{lr}
\dfrac{\partial w}{\partial x_1} \qquad\qquad\qquad + r_{11}\lambda_1 + \ldots + r_{n1}\lambda_n & = 0 \\
\ldots\ldots\ldots\ldots\ldots\ldots\ldots\ldots\ldots\ldots & \\
\dfrac{\partial w}{\partial y_1} \qquad\qquad\qquad - q_1\lambda_1 & = 0 \\
\ldots\ldots\ldots\ldots\ldots\ldots\ldots\ldots\ldots\ldots & \\
r_{11}x_1 + \ldots + r_{1m}x_m - q_1y_1 & = -s_1 \\
\ldots\ldots\ldots\ldots\ldots\ldots\ldots\ldots\ldots\ldots & \\
r_{n1}x_1 + \ldots + r_{nm}x_m \qquad - q_ny_n & = -s_n
\end{array}
$$

Differentiation of the system (8.37) with respect to any source s_j gives

$$
(8.38) \qquad \frac{\partial x_h}{\partial s_j} = - \frac{W_{m+n+j,\, h}}{W}; \; \frac{\partial y_i}{\partial s_j} = - \frac{W_{m+n+j,\, m+i}}{W},
$$

where W is the determinant of $\mathbf{W}$ and $W_{p,\, q}$ the cofactor of the (p, q)-th element of W. Further, differentiating with respect to q_j:

$$
(8.39) \qquad \frac{\partial x_h}{\partial q_j} = y_j \frac{W_{m+n+j,\, h}}{W} + \lambda_j \frac{W_{m+j,\, h}}{W};
$$

$$
\frac{\partial y_i}{\partial q_j} = y_j \frac{W_{m+n+j,\, m+i}}{W} + \lambda_j \frac{W_{m+j,\, m+i}}{W}.
$$

And with respect to r_{jk}:

$$
(8.40) \qquad \frac{\partial x_h}{\partial r_{jk}} = - x_k \frac{W_{m+n+j,\, h}}{W} - \lambda_j \frac{W_{k,\, h}}{W};
$$

$$
\frac{\partial y_i}{\partial r_{jk}} = - x_k \frac{W_{m+n+j,\, m+i}}{W} - \lambda_j \frac{W_{k,\, m+i}}{W}.
$$

These results, as summarised in the following theorem, are so close to the corresponding equations (7.25) and (7.26) of consumer's theory as to need no further explanation.

THEOREM 2a. *Suppose that the Assumptions* C1 *and* P1 *are satisfied, and that the optimal reaction functions* (8.36) *exist and are single-*

valued. Then the first-order derivatives of these functions are given by (8.38), (8.39) *and* (8.40). *If, moreover, Assumption* P2 *is satisfied, the derivatives with respect to* s_i *are independent of* s_j, *for* $i, j = 1, \ldots, n$.

The relationship between $\mathbf{x}^0$, $\mathbf{y}^0$ and the coefficients of the additive structure of the constraints, those of the multiplicative structure being taken as constants, will prove of special importance. This relation is, for each instrument or noncontrolled variable, represented by a hyperplane in the $(n+1)$-dimensional x_h (or y_i), $s_1, \ldots, s_n$-space, and as such the obvious generalisation of the Engel curves of consumer's theory. We shall call them *Tinbergen surfaces* in honour of the man to whom the first econometric equation systems are due, and who was the first to give a clear insight into the interrelationship of such systems nd the decision process which is based on them. The second part of the theorem states that these surfaces are *flat* when the constraint are linear and the preference function quadratic.

For many years it has been the Netherlands Central Planning Bureau's practice to assume the multiplicative structure of the economy constant, and to describe the effect of outside forces and of Government measures in terms of changes in the additive structure. This is an obvious procedure, since the components of $\mathbf{s}$ are variables rather than parameters (cf. again the employment-balance of payments example), and as such more subject to fluctuations than the multiplicative structure. Alternative measures, together with their consequences in the form of unbiased point predictions as certainty equivalents, served as a piece of information to be used by the policy-maker in order to find his points on the Tinbergen surfaces; Table 7.1 (cf. 7.1.6) provides an example. The multiplicative structure of the model used was changed when additional knowledge of the structure of the economy made it advisable to do so, as happened once in every few months.

8.3.4. The further analysis will be simplified by the introduction of a more convenient notation. Let us partition the inverse of $\mathbf{W}$ according to

$$(8.41) \qquad \mathbf{W}^{-1} = \begin{bmatrix} (\mathbf{xx}) & (\mathbf{xy}) & (\mathbf{x}\cdot) \\ (\mathbf{yx}) & (\mathbf{yy}) & (\mathbf{y}\cdot) \\ (\cdot\mathbf{x}) & (\cdot\mathbf{y}) & (\cdot\cdot) \end{bmatrix}.$$

Partitioned multiplication $W^{-1}W = \mathbf{I}$ gives then the following nine matrix relations, most of which we shall have to use below:[1]

$$
\begin{aligned}
(8.42)\qquad & (xx)\,W_{xx} + (xy)\,W_{yx} + (x\cdot)R = \mathbf{I}\\
& (xx)\,W_{xy} + (xy)\,W_{yy} - (x\cdot)Q = \mathbf{0}\\
& (xx)\,R' \quad - (xy)\,Q' \qquad\qquad = \mathbf{0}\\
& (yx)\,W_{xx} + (yy)\,W_{yx} + (y\cdot)R = \mathbf{0}\\
& (yx)\,W_{xy} + (yy)\,W_{yy} - (y\cdot)Q = \mathbf{I}\\
& (yx)\,R' \quad - (yy)\,Q' \qquad\qquad = \mathbf{0}\\
& (\cdot x)\,W_{xx} + (\cdot y)\,W_{yx} + (\cdot\cdot)R = \mathbf{0}\\
& (\cdot x)\,W_{xy} + (\cdot y)\,W_{yy} - (\cdot\cdot)Q = \mathbf{0}\\
& (\cdot x)\,R' \quad - (\cdot y)\,Q' \qquad\qquad = \mathbf{I}.
\end{aligned}
$$

Obviously

$$
(x\cdot)' = (\cdot x) = \left[\frac{W_{m+n+j,\,h}}{W}\right] = -\left[\frac{\partial x_h}{\partial s_j}\right],
$$

etc. Further, we shall write $(xx)_{hk}$ for the (h, k)-th element of the submatrix (xx) of (8.41) and similarly $(xy)_{hi}$, $(x\cdot)_{hi}$, etc. The equations (8.38), (8.39) and (8.40) become then

$$
(8.43)\qquad \frac{\partial x_h}{\partial s_j} = -(\cdot x)_{jh};\quad \frac{\partial y_i}{\partial s_j} = -(\cdot y)_{ji}
$$

$$
(8.44)\qquad \frac{\partial x_h}{\partial q_j} = y_j(\cdot x)_{jh} + \lambda_j(yx)_{jh};\quad \frac{\partial y_i}{\partial q_j} = y_j(\cdot y)_{ji} + \lambda_j(yy)_{ji}
$$

$$
(8.45)\qquad \frac{\partial x_h}{\partial r_{jk}} = -x_k(\cdot x)_{jh} - \lambda_j(xx)_{kh};\quad \frac{\partial y_i}{\partial r_{jk}} = -x_k(\cdot y)_{ji} - \lambda_j(xy)_{ki}.
$$

Combining (8.43) with (8.44) and with (8.45), we find that the second terms in the right-hand side of the latter equations describe, just as in consumer's theory, the effect of combined changes. It is the effect of a change in the multiplicative structure on the optimal values of x, y, when this change is compensated by a change in the corresponding

[1] Note that the matrix (xx) is not to be regarded as a product of two vectors (which would be impossible because two column vectors cannot be multiplied); it is merely the leading submatrix of order m of the inverse of W.

component of the additive structure such that the policy-maker could remain in his original position x^0, y^0 if he chose to do so:

$$\frac{\partial x_h}{\partial q_j} + y_j \frac{\partial x_h}{\partial s_j} = \lambda_j (yx)_{jh};$$

$$\frac{\partial x_h}{\partial r_{jk}} - x_k \frac{\partial x_h}{\partial s_j} = -\lambda_j (xx)_{kh},$$

etc. In other words: a change in the multiplicative structure gives rise to a *source effect* and a *substitution effect*. Indeed, this seems a natural basis for the definition of substitution and complementarity among instruments and noncontrolled variables; and it seems also natural to define

$$U = \begin{bmatrix} (xx) & (xy) \\ (yx) & (yy) \end{bmatrix} \tag{8.46}$$

as the *substitution matrix*, on the analogy of the matrix $[X_{ij}]$ of 7.2.3. But we should be careful, since there are so many possibilities of multiplicative change. No problem arises if we take a pair of noncontrolled variables, y_i and y_j, say. There is only one coefficient attached to each such variable, and hence we may say: if q_i increases by an infinitesimal amount, and if the change is compensated by a change in s_i which is equal to the change in q_i multiplied by y_i^0; and if, finally, the policy-maker reacts to this compensated change by raising (lowering) y_j, then y_j is a substitute of (complementary with) y_i. But suppose we take two instruments x_h and x_k. Recalling that their coefficients in the constraints—the elements of R—correspond to minus the prices of the consumer's budget restriction, we should say: if r_{ih} decreases (algebraically) by a small amount, and if this is compensated by a change in s_i, and if the policy-maker reacts by raising (lowering) x_k, then x_k is a substitute of (complementary with) x_h. But this holds only for r_{ih}! It may be that, if we would take another coefficient of the same x_h — r_{jh}, say—, the policy-maker's reaction to a compensated change of this coefficient leads to the opposite conclusion. So we have defined only under what condition x_k is a substitute of (or complementary with) x_h *with respect to the i-th constraint*. The same holds if we take a pair x_h, y_i: a compensated change in r_{ih} and r_{jh} may affect y_i in opposite directions, so that the same qualification must be made. But consider

THEOREM 2b. *Suppose that the Assumptions* C1 *and* P1 *are satisfied, and that the optimal reaction functions* (8.36) *exist and are single-valued. Then:*

(*i*) *If an instrument* x_h *is a substitute of another instrument* x_k *with respect to some constraint, it is complementary with* x_k *according to none of the constraints; and mutatis mutandis for complementarity.*

(*ii*) *The same holds if* x_h *is replaced by any noncontrolled variable.*

(*iii*) *The substitution matrix* $\mathbf{U}$ *is symmetric and negative semi-definite, its rank being* m; *and it is unique except for a positive multiplicative scalar.*

(*iv*) *If, in addition, Assumption* P2 *is satisfied, then changes in the additive structure do not turn a substitution relationship into that of complementarity, nor vice versa.*

The first part is proved as follows. The influence on x_h of a compensated change in r_{jk} is given by $-\lambda_j(xx)_{kh}$; cf. (8.45). Since all λ's are nonnegative, the sign of this term is determined by $(xx)_{kh}$ and hence independent of j. Similarly, the influence of such a change on y_i is given by $-\lambda_j(xy)_{ki}$, the sign of which is independent of j, too; this settles part (*ii*). The economic meaning of this result is this: If an instrument x_k becomes more effective with respect to some noncontrolled variable, and if this change is compensated, the policy-maker's optimal reaction pattern is such that some of the x's and y's go up and others go down; but the *direction* of these movements is not affected by the question with respect to *which* noncontrolled variable the instrument x_k becomes more effective. It follows that it is possible to speak about substitution and complementarity *tout court*, without reference to a particular constraint.

That the substitution matrix is only unique except for a positive multiplicative scalar [part (*iii*)] is seen if we replace w by $\varphi(w)$ with $\varphi' > 0$. The result of this replacement is that the derivatives of w in (8.30) are multiplied by φ'; or alternatively, that the Lagrange vector $\boldsymbol{\lambda}$ is multiplied by $1/\varphi'$:

$$\frac{\partial w}{\partial \mathbf{x}} + \mathbf{R}'(1/\varphi')\boldsymbol{\lambda} = \mathbf{0}; \quad \frac{\partial w}{\partial \mathbf{y}} - \mathbf{Q}'(1/\varphi')\boldsymbol{\lambda} = \mathbf{0}.$$

The terms $\lambda_j(yx)_{jh}$, etc., of (8.44) and (8.45) are not affected by this replacement, since they are components of derivatives of the optimal reaction functions. It follows that substituting $\varphi(w)$ for w implies that all elements of the substitution matrix are multiplied by the same scalar φ'.[1]

The symmetry of this matrix follows from the symmetry of the matrix W^{-1}. This leads to a large number of relations of the Slutsky-type. Writing D_j and D_{jk} for the operator of compensated differentiation,

$$D_j = \frac{\partial}{\partial q_j} + y_j \frac{\partial}{\partial s_j}; \quad D_{jk} = \frac{\partial}{\partial r_{jk}} - x_k \frac{\partial}{\partial s_j},$$

we find

$$D_{jk}x_h = D_{jh}x_k; \quad D_j x_h = -D_{jh}y_j. \tag{8.47}$$

There are no Slutsky relations connecting two noncontrolled variables The reason is that there is no constraint which contains two such variables. But there are other relations:

$$\frac{D_j y_i}{D_i y_j} = -\frac{D_j x_h}{D_{ih} y_j} = \frac{D_{jk} x_h}{D_{ik} x_h} \quad \text{for all } h, k, \tag{8.48}$$

provided the denominators do not vanish. Furthermore, since the ratio of any principal minor of order $(m + 2n - 1)$ of W to the determinant itself is negative, we have

$$(xx)_{hh} < 0; \quad (yy)_{ii} < 0, \tag{8.49}$$

which means that complementarity is reflexive. In words: if x_h becomes less effective with respect to some noncontrolled variable and if this change is compensated, then x_h is lowered; which means a sacrifice in general, since $\partial w/\partial x_h \geq 0$ according to the Sign Convention. The same happens with y_i if this variable becomes more expensive (q_i going up). The property (8.49) is one of the features of the negative semi-definiteness of the substitution matrix.[2] Another implication is the dominance of substitution. Let us therefore postmultiply the substitution matrix by the multiplicative structure. This gives

$$U \begin{bmatrix} -R' \\ Q' \end{bmatrix} = \mathbf{0} \tag{8.50}$$

[1] Note that the substitution matrix, thus defined, differs slightly from the matrix $[X_{ij}]$ of consumer's theory. The latter matrix is invariant against monotonic transformations of the utility function. The same result can be obtained here, viz., by multiplying U by any of the n Lagrange multipliers.

[2] For a further analysis in this direction, cf. SAMUELSON, *loc. cit.*, pp. 378–379.

in view of the third and the sixth equation of (8.42). Postmultiplying (8.50) by λ gives

$$(8.51) \qquad U \begin{bmatrix} \partial w/\partial \mathbf{x} \\ \partial w/\partial \mathbf{y} \end{bmatrix} = \mathbf{0}.$$

It follows from (8.49) that each row of U has a negative element on the main diagonal. Combining this with (8.51), we obtain $(m + n)$ inequalities of the type

$$\sum_{k=2}^{m} (xx)_{1k} \frac{\partial w}{\partial x_k} + \sum_{j=1}^{n} (xy)_{1j} \frac{\partial w}{\partial y_j} \geqq 0.$$

Since the derivatives of w are all nonnegative according to the Sign Convention, at least some of the substitution terms must be nonnegative; except for the possibility of complete saturation, $\partial w/\partial \mathbf{x} = \mathbf{0}$, $\partial w/\partial \mathbf{y} = \mathbf{0}$. This result suggests that, as in the consumer's case (cf. 7.2.4), substitution among pairs of different variables is more widespread than complementarity. It is easy to see that the second reason for the dominance of substitution, formalised in equation (7.32) of consumer's demand theory, is also satisfied; we should simply replace the prices of (7.32) by the derivatives of w.

The last part of Theorem 2b follows from the fact that, if w is quadratic as in (8.5), the additive structure of the constraints does not affect W (and hence not the signs of the U-elements) *via* the second-order derivatives of the welfare function.

8.3.5. So much for the derivatives of the optimal reaction functions with respect to the coefficients of the multiplicative structure. Now we turn to the additive structure; i.e., to the $(m + n)n$ derivatives $\partial x_h/\partial s_j$, $\partial y_i/\partial s_j$, which are all slopes of Tinbergen surfaces. Just as the derivatives $\partial x_h/\partial r_{jk}$ and the substitution terms $(xx)_{kh}$, etc., these quantities will play an essential rôle in the further analysis, so that it is appropriate to pay some detailed attention to them here.

Let us take first the derivative of a noncontrolled variable y_i with respect to the source of its "own" constraint, $\partial y_i/\partial s_i$. Suppose that s_i increases, all other coefficients of the constraints remaining constant. Then, if the policy-maker decides to keep his instruments unchanged in spite of this increase, y_i will increase by $1/q_i$ times the change in

s_i. Excluding for a moment the possibility of saturation with respect to y_i, we should conclude that the changing constraint enables the policy-maker to reach a higher welfare level than before. But, as indicated at the end of 8.3.1, it does not follow that unchanging instrument values are indeed in accordance with the optimal reaction pattern. Take for instance the employment-balance of payments example of 7.1.3 (cf. also 7.1.5). If the s corresponding to the balance of payments increases such as to change the sign of this balance from negative to positive, the policy-maker will appreciate this effect. However, he may prefer a smaller positive balance, if this relative disadvantage can be compensated by raising the volume of Government expenditure in such a way that the number of unemployed workers is reduced. More generally, the policy-maker's optimal reaction pattern implies that an s_i-change leads to changes in all x's, and hence in all y's as well, except for degenerate cases. It is even conceivable that an increase in s_i leads, *via* the instrument changes, to a lower value of y_i. This effect as such leads to a lower welfare level, whereas a higher level would have been possible by keeping the instruments at their original values; it will occur only if the accompanying increases of other variables are such as to make a full compensation. In other words, the case $\partial y_i/\partial s_i < 0$ will occur if constraints and preferences are such that the policy-maker considers y_i a relatively undesirable variable.

In view of these considerations it seems natural to define inferiority of a noncontrolled variable y_i as the case $\partial y_i/\partial s_i < 0$. But, as in the case of substitution and complementarity, we should be careful. There are n sources, and it may be that $\partial y_i/\partial s_i > 0$, whereas $\partial y_i/\partial s_j < 0$. The first derivative (with equal subscripts) plays no doubt a special rôle, and the preceding paragraph was entirely concerned with derivatives of that type; so one might think that it is appropriate to define inferiority entirely on the basis of the derivative of the noncontrolled variable with respect to its "own" source. However, the problem of what to do with the other derivatives remains. There is no theorem which excludes opposite effects: $\partial y_i/\partial s_i > 0$, $\partial y_i/\partial s_j < 0$, as for substitution and complementarity; and a negative influence of "alien" sources s_j on y_i according to the optimal reaction pattern is certainly not to be disregarded as an indicator of the desirability of y_i, for y_i is then "sacrificed" in the case of a (favourable) change in s_j. Further, the above remarks are confined to the noncontrolled category; we still have the problem of inferiority of instruments.[1] The question arises whether it is appropriate to consider the effect of a simultaneous change in all sources, rather than that of one separate change. The following analysis will then prove useful.

Consider the matrix of slopes of the Tinbergen surfaces:

$$T = -[(\cdot x) \quad (\cdot y)]. \tag{8.52}$$

Postmultiply it by the multiplicative structure of the constraints:

$$T\begin{bmatrix} -R' \\ Q' \end{bmatrix} = \mathbf{I}. \tag{8.53}$$

This follows from the last equality of (8.42). Postmultiplication of (8.53) by λ gives

$$T\begin{bmatrix} \partial w/\partial x \\ \partial w/\partial y \end{bmatrix} = \lambda = Q^{-1}\,\frac{\partial w}{\partial y}. \tag{8.54}$$

In scalar form:

$$\sum_h \frac{\partial x_h}{\partial s_j}\frac{\partial w}{\partial x_h} + \sum_i \frac{\partial y_i}{\partial s_j}\frac{\partial w}{\partial y_i} = \frac{1}{q_j}\frac{\partial w}{\partial y_j} \quad \text{for } j = 1, \ldots, n, \tag{8.55}$$

or

$$\sum_h \frac{1}{\lambda_j}\frac{\partial x_h}{\partial s_j}\frac{\partial w}{\partial x_h} + \sum_i \frac{1}{\lambda_j}\frac{\partial y_i}{\partial s_j}\frac{\partial w}{\partial y_i} = 1. \tag{8.56}$$

Consider also the matrix

$$T_\lambda = \begin{bmatrix} \frac{1}{\lambda_1}\frac{\partial x_1}{\partial s_1} & \cdots & \frac{1}{\lambda_1}\frac{\partial x_m}{\partial s_1} & \frac{1}{\lambda_1}\frac{\partial y_1}{\partial s_1} & \cdots & \frac{1}{\lambda_1}\frac{\partial y_n}{\partial s_1} \\ \cdot & \cdot & \cdot & \cdot & \cdot & \cdot \\ \frac{1}{\lambda_n}\frac{\partial x_1}{\partial s_n} & \cdots & \frac{1}{\lambda_n}\frac{\partial x_m}{\partial s_n} & \frac{1}{\lambda_n}\frac{\partial y_1}{\partial s_n} & \cdots & \frac{1}{\lambda_n}\frac{\partial y_n}{\partial s_n} \end{bmatrix} \tag{8.57}$$

and its separate elements

$$t_{h,j} = \frac{1}{\lambda_j}\frac{\partial x_h}{\partial s_j}; \quad t_{m+i,j} = \frac{1}{\lambda_j}\frac{\partial y_i}{\partial s_j}. \tag{8.58}$$

[1] Note that the question of "inferiority" of instruments should be decided, not only by their immediate welfare implications as measured by their rôle in w, but also by their effectiveness with respect to the noncontrolled variables; i.e., by the multiplicative structure of the constraints. This is entirely comparable with consumer theory; whether a commodity is inferior or not depends *i.a.* on the prices.

According to (8.56) each row of T_λ has unit weighted average, provided we put the weights equal to the corresponding derivatives of w; and the same set of weights applies to all rows of T_λ. Further, the factors $1/\lambda_j$ applied to each row of this matrix are such that the derivatives of $\mathbf{x}, \mathbf{y}$ with respect to different components of $\mathbf{s}$ are "normalised" relative to each other, in the following manner. Suppose s_j increases by ds_j. If the policy-maker would decide to keep his instruments unchanged, y_j would increase by $(1/q_j)ds_j$ and hence w by

$$\frac{1}{q_j}\frac{\partial w}{\partial y_j}\,ds_j = \lambda_j ds_j.$$

So the division by λ_j in the j-th row of T_λ implies that we are considering the effect on the optimal values of $\mathbf{x}, \mathbf{y}$ of infinitesimal changes in the components of $\mathbf{s}$ which are each such that, if the policy-maker would decide not to change his instruments, they have identical effects on the welfare level. This division is of course only possible if $\partial w/\partial y_j \neq 0$ which is assumed here.

These results suggest that we should not base the inferiority definition on the effect of a change in only one component of $\mathbf{s}$; but, instead, on the effect of a combined change in all components, each of them eading to the same w-change under the assumption of unchanged $\mathbf{x}$. In other words, we should analyse the signs of rates of change in all variables along well-defined (and common) directions along the Tinbergen surfaces. So we shall say that an instrument x_h or a noncontrolled variable y_i is *overall-inferior* if

(8.59) $$t_h = \sum_j t_{h,\,j}; \quad t_{m+i} = \sum_j t_{m+i,\,j},$$

respectively, is negative. Further we shall say that x_h (y_i) is *specifically inferior* with respect to the j-th constraint if $t_{h,\,j}$ $(t_{m+i,\,j})$ is negative. Consider then:

THEOREM 2c. *Suppose that the Assumptions* C1 *and* P1 *are satisfied, that the optimal reaction functions* (8.36) *exist and are single-valued, and that there is no saturation with respect to any of the noncontrolled variables* ($\partial w/\partial y_i \neq 0$ *for each* i). *Then:*

(*i*) *The matrix* $\mathbf{T}_\lambda$ *is unique except for a positive multiplicative scalar.*

(*ii*) *Postmultiplying* $\mathbf{T}_\lambda$ *by the column vector of first-order derivatives of the welfare function,* $\partial w/\partial \mathbf{x}$, $\partial w/\partial \mathbf{y}$, *gives a column vector of units.*

(iii) At least one instrument or noncontrolled variable is not overall-inferior; and the same is true for specific inferiority with respect to the i-th constraint, for each $i = 1, \ldots, n$.

(iv) If, in addition, Assumption P2 *is satisfied, changes in the additive structure of the constraints do not affect any specific inferiority; but the same is not true with respect to overall-inferiority, unless the variable considered is specifically inferior with respect to none or to all of the constraints.*

Part *(i)* is proved in the same way as the corresponding part of Theorem 2b. Part *(ii)* follows from (8.56). The proof of part *(iii)* is trivial. It may be interpreted in the sense that non-inferiority is a dominant property for separate instruments and noncontrolled vari ables, just as substitution is a dominant property for pairs of such variables.

The first assertion of *(iv)* follows from the fact that the sign of $t_{h,j}$ and $t_{m+1,j}$ is determined by that of $(x\cdot)_{hj}$ and $(y\cdot)_{ij}$, respectively, which is independent of $\mathbf{s}$ if w is quadratic as in (8.5). For the second assertion it is useful to note that the vector of Lagrange multipliers is given by

$$\lambda = T\begin{pmatrix} a \\ b \end{pmatrix} - (\cdot\cdot)\,s, \tag{8.60}$$

where a, b is the vector of coefficients of the linear part of (8.5). This follows immediately from the system (8.37) when we replace its first equation by

$$\begin{aligned} a_{11}x_1 + \ldots + a_{1m}x_m + c_{11}y_1 + \ldots + c_{1n}y_n + \\ + r_{11}\lambda_1 + \ldots + r_{n1}\lambda_n = -a_1, \end{aligned} \tag{8.61}$$

and so on. Furthermore, when writing the seventh and the eighth equation of (8.42) in the form

$$-T\begin{bmatrix} A & C \\ C' & B \end{bmatrix} + (\cdot\cdot)\,[R \quad -Q] = \mathbf{0},$$

postmultiplying by T', and using the last equation $[R \quad -Q]\,T' = -\mathbf{I}$ of (8.42), we find

$$(\cdot\cdot) = -T\begin{bmatrix} A & C \\ C' & B \end{bmatrix} T'. \tag{8.62}$$

Combining (8.60) and (8.62), we observe that the Lagrange multipliers are general linear functions of all sources and, of course, unique except for a common positive multiplicative scalar. So the sign of

$$\sum_j \frac{1}{\lambda_j} \frac{\partial x_h}{\partial s_j} \quad \text{and} \quad \sum_j \frac{1}{\lambda_j} \frac{\partial y_i}{\partial s_j}$$

is *not* independent of **s**; unless the derivatives $\partial x_h/\partial s_j$ $(\partial y_i/\partial s_j)$ have the same sign for each j, in which case the positive λ's have no effect on the sign of the sum. This result differs from that of quadratic consumer's analysis, where inferiority is independent of the (scalar) income variable.

8.3.6. Finally, we turn to the effect of changing preferences on the policy-maker's best decisions. This implies that we give a wider interpretation to the optimal reaction functions. Supposing that Assumption P2 is satisfied, we should write them now as

$$\begin{aligned} x^0 &= x(a,\ b,\ A,\ B,\ C;\ Q,\ R,\ s) \\ y^0 &= y(a,\ b,\ A,\ B,\ C;\ Q,\ R,\ s). \end{aligned} \tag{8.63}$$

As in 7.2.5 for the consumer's case, we shall investigate here the derivatives with respect to the preference coefficients.

Again, consider the system (8.37) and replace the first $(m + n)$ equations by those of the type (8.61). Differentiation with respect to a_k and b_j gives

$$\begin{aligned} \frac{\partial x_h}{\partial a_k} &= -(xx)_{kh}; \quad \frac{\partial y_i}{\partial a_k} = -(xy)_{ki} \\ \frac{\partial x_h}{\partial b_j} &= -(yx)_{jh}; \quad \frac{\partial y_i}{\partial b_j} = -(yy)_{ji}, \end{aligned} \tag{8.64}$$

so that

$$\frac{\partial x_h}{\partial a_k} = \frac{\partial x_k}{\partial a_h} = \frac{1}{\lambda_j}\left(\frac{\partial x_h}{\partial r_{jk}} - x_k \frac{\partial x_h}{\partial s_j}\right) = \frac{1}{\lambda_j}\left(\frac{\partial x_k}{\partial r_{jh}} - x_h \frac{\partial x_k}{\partial s_j}\right) \text{ for any } j,$$

etc.[1] We may summarise the relations (8.64) briefly as

$$\frac{\partial(x',\ y')}{\partial(a,\ b)} = -U, \tag{8.65}$$

[1] Note the division by λ_j, which we also met in 8.3.5.

where the left-hand side stands for the square matrix of order $(m + n)$ of the derivatives of **x**, **y** with respect to the linear preference coefficients.

The same procedure applied to the quadratic preference coefficients gives

$$(8.66)\qquad \begin{aligned}
\frac{\partial x_h}{\partial a_{kg}} &= -x_g(xx)_{kh} - x_k(xx)_{gh} && \text{if } k \neq g \\
&= -x_k(xx)_{kh} && \text{if } k = g; \\
\frac{\partial y_i}{\partial a_{kg}} &= -x_g(xy)_{ki} - x_k(xy)_{gi} && \text{if } k \neq g \\
&= -x_k(xy)_{ki} && \text{if } k = g; \\
\frac{\partial x_h}{\partial b_{jl}} &= -y_l(yx)_{jh} - y_j(yx)_{lh} && \text{if } j \neq l \\
&= -y_j(yx)_{jh} && \text{if } j = l; \\
\frac{\partial y_i}{\partial b_{jl}} &= -y_l(yy)_{ji} - y_j(yy)_{li} && \text{if } j \neq l \\
&= -y_j(yy)_{ji} && \text{if } j = l; \\
\frac{\partial x_h}{\partial c_{kj}} &= -x_k(yx)_{jh} - y_j(xx)_{kh}; \\
\frac{\partial y_i}{\partial c_{kj}} &= -x_k(yy)_{ji} - y_j(xy)_{ki}.
\end{aligned}$$

These results are so closely related to those of consumer analysis that we may refer to 7.2.5 for their interpretation.

THEOREM 2d. *Suppose that the Assumptions* C1 *and* P2 *are satisfied and that the optimal reaction functions* (8.63) *exist. Then the first-order derivatives of these functions with respect to the elements of* **a**, **b**, **A**, **B**, **C** *are given by* (8.64) *and* (8.66).

8.3.7. When concluding, we may say that the celebrated distinction between income and substitution effect is equally well applicable in the policy-maker's case. We may even add that it is of wider importance here because of the fact that the substitution effects of changes in corresponding coefficients of different equations appear to be proportional. In the same way, there are other similarities with consumer theory. Indeed, we must say that the analysis of the present section has pushed the policy-maker so far in the consumer's direction that the term "noncontrolled variable" has almost lost its meaning. There is no uncertainty in the determination of these variables, and so it is irrelevant which m of the total of $(m + n)$ variables are chosen by the policy-maker, the remaining n being determined by the nonstochastic equation system $Qy = Rx + s$.[1] This is comparable with the consumer's situation: it is sufficient that he decides upon all quantities but one, and the last follows then from the budget restriction. There is only one element of asymmetry between x and y left in the policy-maker's case: each constraint contains only one noncontrolled variable, whereas it contains in general all instruments. The further analysis of this chapter will, however, restore the noncontrolled variables in their original position.

A few remarks on the equation system from which the reduced form $Qy = Rx + s$ has been derived may be appropriate. The analysis of this section gives no answer to the question: What is the influence of a change in a coefficient of the system of structural equations on instruments and noncontrolled variables? At least, it gives no direct answer. This question has been considered already in 8.1.1 and 8.3.1, and it is not difficult to see why an analysis in terms of structural equations rather than in terms of the reduced form is less promising. Disregarding any aggregation complications, we may say that the coefficients of the former equations have a simpler economic meaning if we look at the equations as such, but that they are much less transparent if we look at the coefficients as measuring the constraints which the policy-maker has to face; and this second aspect is relevant here. In particular, it is not possible to interpret the coefficients of x in the structural equations as indicating the effectiveness with respect to some noncontrolled variable. Also, if we maximise w subject to the structural equations rather than to the reduced form, the resulting values of the Lagrange multipliers are no longer necessarily nonnegative, even if the Sign Convention is applied. Furthermore, the definition of substitution and complementarity can be easily and naturally based on reduced-form coefficients; the same is not true for structural coefficients.

If we want to analyse the implications for the optimal values of x, y of a change in a structural coefficient, this can be carried out most

[1] Strictly speaking, this statement pre-supposes that none of the determinants of order n in the matrix $[Q \ -R]$ vanishes.

conveniently *via* the reduced form. Take for instance the employment-balance of payments example of 7.1.3 and suppose that β (the marginal propensity to consume) increases, for one reason or another. Writing $d\beta$ for the increase, we find for the increase of r_{11}:

$$\frac{\gamma}{1-(\beta+d\beta)} - \frac{\gamma}{1-\beta} \approx \frac{\gamma\, d\beta}{(1-\beta)^2}$$

(cf. 7.1.5); for the increase of r_{21}:

$$-\left[\frac{\alpha_1(\beta+d\beta)}{1-(\beta+d\beta)} + \alpha_4\right] p_M + \left[\frac{\alpha_1\beta}{1-\beta} + \alpha_4\right] p_M \approx -\frac{\alpha_1 d\beta}{(1-\beta)^2} p_M;$$

and the changes in $\mathbf{s}$ can be obtained similarly. The effect of the change $d\beta$ on Government expenditure, employment and balance of payments according to the optimal reaction functions is then found by adding the separate effects of the implied changes in $\mathbf{R}$ and $\mathbf{s}$. Since the latter effects can each be described in terms of source and substitution effects, the same holds for the effects of the change $d\beta$.

It is also appropriate to stress the advantages of the Sign Convention. It is due to this Convention that all Lagrange multipliers are nonnegative; and this in turn enabled us to define substitution and complementarity without reference to a particular constraint. Again, it is not true that the Sign Convention plays any crucial rôle in this definition; it is merely convenient. For, if it is not applied, we should make the definition of substitution and complementarity dependent on the signs of the first-order derivatives of the preference function in the point of maximum welfare. The main virtue of the Sign Convention is simply that it specifies these signs in a convenient manner.

In principle, it is possible to verify empirically the restrictions laid down in the theorems of this sections. If we specify the policy-maker as an ordinary consumer, so that $\mathbf{Qy} = \mathbf{Rx} + \mathbf{s}$ reduces to the familiar budget restriction, we arrive at a classical field of empirical research. The same is true, though to a lesser degree, if we replace consumers by entrepreneurs. But the empirical determination of the behaviour pattern of Government policy-makers is an almost untouched field. It is not our intention, however, to go in that direction. The main use of the preceding analysis is its application in the next section, where it will be combined with the results of Section 8.2.

8.4. The Loss of Welfare due to Imperfect Predictions (1)

8.4.1. We shall now recognise the fact that the policy-maker does not know his constraints, but that he must predict them. This will be done under the strongest assumptions which we have introduced, viz., C1 and P3. The "true" constraints are supposed to be

$$y = Rx + s, \tag{8.1}$$

which is in accordance with the constraints of Assumption C1 under the normalisation $Q = \mathbf{I}$; nothing will be gained in the analysis of this and the next section by adopting another normalisation, and this one is chosen because of its simplicity. The policy-maker does not know R, s; but we suppose that he makes his decisions on the basis of an estimate of these matrices, possibly a mere guess. So the constraints are, in his eyes,

$$y = R_e x + s_e, \tag{8.67}$$

R_e and s_e being estimates of R and s, respectively. The policy-maker may well think that he is justified in doing so. He may argue that $R_e = R$, or at least approximately so; and that s is random with mean value equal to his estimate, $\mathscr{E}s = s_e$, and variance-covariance matrix $\mathscr{E}[(s - s_e)(s - s_e)']$ independent of x. In so far as this is true, and given the quadratic preference assumption P3,

$$w(x, y) = a'x + b'y + \tfrac{1}{2}(x'Ax + y'By + x'Cy + y'C'x), \tag{8.5}$$

we must admit that Theorem 1 provides indeed a justification for this procedure. But it will be realised, of course, that the measures based on it will not be in accordance with the optimal reaction functions (simply because a probabilistic knowledge of s is not sufficient to achieve this), so that even then there is a "loss of welfare" due to an imperfect prediction.

Before specifying any special forecasting procedure and its errors, it will be possible to arrive at a general result for the loss of welfare which is due to a decision that differs from the best one, irrespective of the question how this decision is arrived at. This is shown in 8.4.2. The remainder of this section is mainly devoted to the analysis of the case $R_e = R$, $s_e \neq s$; i.e., to the case in which the multiplicative structure of the constraints is known. The special attention given to this situation may be justified to some extent by recalling the results of Section 5.2: it appeared there that we cannot reject the hypothesis that the Dutch macromodel has a multiplicative structure which is at least approximately adequate. Also, a comparison of the results of that section with those of Chapter III showed that erroneous estimates of exogenous changes were by far the most important sources of the errors of the unconditional forecasts; and such changes, as far as they refer to noncontrolled exogenous variables, are components of s, not of R. After this, finally, the more general case $R_e \neq R$, $s_e \neq s$ is discussed in Section 8.5.

8.4.2. Let us write w_x for the welfare level that is attained when the instrument vector x is applied. Combining (8.5) and (8.1), we find for w_x:

$$w_x = w(x, Rx + s) = k_0 + k'x + \tfrac{1}{2}x'Kx, \tag{8.68}$$

in which k_0 is a scalar, k a column vector and K a square and symmetric matrix:

$$\begin{aligned} k_0 &= b's + \tfrac{1}{2}s'Bs; \\ k &= a + R'b + (C + R'B)s = [\mathrm{I} \quad R'] \begin{bmatrix} a & C \\ b & B \end{bmatrix} \begin{bmatrix} 1 \\ s \end{bmatrix}; \\ K &= A + R'BR + CR + R'C' = [\mathrm{I} \quad R'] \begin{bmatrix} A & C \\ C' & B \end{bmatrix} \begin{bmatrix} \mathrm{I} \\ R \end{bmatrix}. \end{aligned} \tag{8.69}$$

Maximisation of (8.68) with respect to x gives

$$x^0 = -K^{-1}k, \tag{8.70}$$

and it will be clear that this is identical with the optimal reaction functions of the instruments. Substituting for K and k in (8.70) the corresponding expressions of (8.69) gives immediately the functions (8.63) under the specification $Q = \mathrm{I}$.

Furthermore, substituting (8.70) into (8.68), we find for the maximal welfare level attainable

$$\begin{aligned} \hat{w} = w_{x^0} &= k_0 - \tfrac{1}{2}k'K^{-1}k \\ &= k_0 - \tfrac{1}{2}x^{0\prime}Kx^0. \end{aligned} \tag{8.71}$$

Suppose now that another instrument vector x, leading to a welfare level w_x, is applied. Then we define the difference $\hat{w} - w_x$ as the *loss of welfare* which is due to the application of $\mathbf{x}$. This concept is the subject of[1]

THEOREM 3. *Suppose that the Assumptions* C1 *and* P3 *are satisfied and that the optimal reaction functions* (8.63) *exist. Then the application of any vector of instrument values* $\mathbf{x}$ *leads to a loss of welfare equal to*

$$(8.72) \qquad \hat{w} - w_{\mathbf{x}} = -\tfrac{1}{2}(\mathbf{x} - \mathbf{x}^0)'(\mathbf{xx})^{-1}(\mathbf{x} - \mathbf{x}^0),$$

where $(\mathbf{xx})$ *is that negative-definite submatrix of the substitution matrix* $\mathbf{U}$ *that corresponds to the instruments. The loss is unique except for the choice of a welfare unit.*

It is useful to interpret this result before proceeding to the proof First, the fact that the right-hand side of (8.72) is a homogeneous quadratic expression in the "decision error" $\mathbf{x} - \mathbf{x}^0$ implies that an error which is of the first order of smallness leads to a loss of welfare which is small of the second order. This is of course hardly surprising, since we are maximising a quadratic function subject to a linear constraint; but lack of surprise does not mean lack of usefulness, especially since no policy-maker can hope to avoid errors at every occasion. Second, the loss (8.72) can be interpreted, in geometric terms, as the square of a distance. To see this, take first the simple case in which $(\mathbf{xx})$ equals minus the unit matrix of order m. Then (8.72) states that the loss of welfare equals one half times the sum of squares of the decision errors. Consider also the m-dimensional Cartesian space, each of its axes corresponding to one of the instruments. The best decision $\mathbf{x}^0$ is then represented by a point X^0 in this space, the other ($\mathbf{x}$) by a point X; and the square of the distance XX^0 corresponds then to twice the loss of welfare. In the more general case $(\mathbf{xx}) \neq -\mathbf{I}$ we have the same picture, except that the m-space is no longer Cartesian; the axes are in general not orthogonal, nor are their units of measurement the same. The general picture is not affected, however, as is illustrated in Fig. 8.5 for $m = 3$.

Third, it appears from (8.72) that the question of substitution and complementarity among instruments plays an important rôle. Consider the case $m = 2$; in scalar form (8.72) can then be written as

[1] In all Theorems 3, 3a, etc., Assumption C1 is to be interpreted in the sense of (8.1); i.e., the normalisation is $\mathbf{Q} = \mathbf{I}$.

$$\hat{w} - w_x = \frac{1}{2} \frac{-(xx)_{22}(x_1 - \overset{0}{x}_1)^2 - (xx)_{11}(x_2 - \overset{0}{x}_2)^2 + 2(xx)_{12}(x_1 - \overset{0}{x}_1)(x_2 - \overset{0}{x}_2)}{(xx)_{11}(xx)_{22} - \{(xx)_{12}\}^2}.$$

Suppose that x_1 and x_2 are substitutes, so that $(xx)_{12} > 0$. If the errors are in opposite direction (i.e., $x_1 > \overset{0}{x}_1$, $x_2 < \overset{0}{x}_2$ or *vice versa*), we should expect that this reduces the loss of welfare in that case. Indeed, this is what happens, for the third term in the numerator is then negative. The converse holds in the case of errors in the same direction; and similar results hold for complementarity, *mutatis mutandis*. As to the

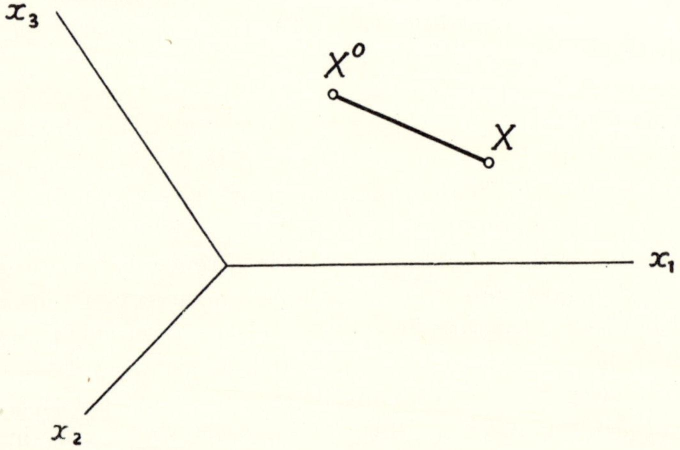

Fig. 8.5. Illustration of the loss of welfare in the space of instruments

quadratic terms, we can grasp these most easily if we disregard the substitution term $(xx)_{12}$. The loss becomes then

$$\hat{w} - w_x = \frac{(x_1 - \overset{0}{x}_1)^2}{-2(xx)_{11}} + \frac{(x_2 - \overset{0}{x}_2)^2}{-2(xx)_{22}},$$

a result which implies that a given decision error in x_h tends to be very serious if $(xx)_{hh}$ is close to zero; i.e., if preferences and constraints are such that, according to the optimal reaction pattern, the change in x_h in response to a (compensated) change of its effectiveness is small. This, too, seems rather natural.

The proof of Theorem 3 is as follows. From (8.70) we have $k = -Kx^0$. Combining this with (8.68) gives

$$w_x = k_0 - x^{0\prime}Kx + \tfrac{1}{2}x'Kx$$

so that, using (8.71),

$$(8.73) \qquad \hat{w} - w_x = -\tfrac{1}{2}[x^{0\prime}Kx^0 - 2x^{0\prime}Kx + x'Kx] = -\tfrac{1}{2}(x - x^0)'K(x - x^0).$$

Hence we must prove

$$(8.74) \qquad K = (xx)^{-1},$$

or, using (8.69),

$$(xx)\,[\mathbf{I} \quad R'] \begin{bmatrix} A & C \\ C' & B \end{bmatrix} \begin{bmatrix} \mathbf{I} \\ R \end{bmatrix} = \mathbf{I}.$$

This is verified by straightforward partitioned multiplication and applying the first three equations of (8.42) under the normalisation $Q = \mathbf{I}$.

8.4.3. Two additional remarks are in order. First, combining (8.70) with (8.69), we find

$$x^0 = -K^{-1}k = -K^{-1}(a + R'b) - K^{-1}(C + R'B)s.$$

Since K does not depend on s, it follows that $-K^{-1}(C + R'B)$ must be the matrix of slopes of the Tinbergen surfaces that correspond to the instruments; i.e.,

$$(8.75) \qquad (x\cdot) = K^{-1}(C + R'B) = (xx)\,(C + R'B).$$

This can also be verified directly by applying the second and the third equation of (8.42). It is of some interest to consider the economic interpretation of the matrix

$$(8.76) \qquad D = C + R'B,$$

the typical (h, i)-th element of which is

$$d_{hi} = c_{hi} + \sum_j r_{jh}b_{ji} = \left(\frac{\partial}{\partial x_h} + \sum_j r_{jh}\frac{\partial}{\partial y_j}\right)\frac{\partial w}{\partial y_i}.$$

Evidently, D is a matrix of second-order cross-derivatives of the preference function, in the following way: each element is the derivative of the marginal welfare of some noncontrolled variable y_i with respect to some instrument x_h, provided we take account of the fact that an infinitesimal change in x_h involves, *via* the constraints, certain changes in all noncontrolled variables. In other words: whereas $\mathbf{C}$ gives the derivatives of the marginal welfare of noncontrolled variables with respect to instruments under the specification that all other variables remain constant, $\mathbf{D}$ does so under the specification that all noncontrolled variables vary with the instrument considered as the constraints specify. Combining (8.75) and (8.76), finally, we find

$$(\mathbf{x}\cdot) = (\mathbf{xx})\mathbf{D} \tag{8.77}$$

or in scalar form

$$\frac{\partial x_h}{\partial s_i} = -\sum_k d_{ki}(xx)_{hk}.$$

This means that the slope in the s_i-direction of the Tinbergen surface of the instrument x_h is equal to a linear combination of all of its substitution terms with other instruments x_k; and that the weights of this combination are (apart from sign) the derivatives in the $\mathbf{D}$-sense of the marginal welfare of the noncontrolled variable corresponding to the source s_i with respect to the latter instruments x_k.

Furthermore, it was stressed in 8.4.2 that the loss of welfare due to small decision errors is small of a higher order; but it should also be stressed that, if this error is caused by an erroneous prediction, the difference between the predicted welfare level and the actual level attained is not small of a higher order. Returning to (8.71) and 8.4.1, we may say that the predicted welfare level based on maximisation subject to the predicted constraint $\mathbf{y} = \mathbf{R}_e\mathbf{x} + \mathbf{s}_e$ equals

$$w_e = (k_0)_e - \tfrac{1}{2}\mathbf{k}_e'\mathbf{K}_e^{-1}\mathbf{k}_e,$$

where $(k_0)_e$, $\mathbf{k}_e$ and $\mathbf{K}_e$ are the same functions of $\mathbf{R}_e$ and $\mathbf{s}_e$ as k_0, $\mathbf{k}$, $\mathbf{K}$ are of $\mathbf{R}$ and $\mathbf{s}$; cf. (8.69). The excess of w_e over the actual welfare level attained is then

$$w_e - w_{\mathbf{x}} = (k_0)_e - \tfrac{1}{2}\mathbf{k}_e'\mathbf{K}_e^{-1}\mathbf{k}_e - k_0 + \mathbf{k}'\mathbf{K}_e^{-1}\mathbf{k}_e - \tfrac{1}{2}\mathbf{k}_e'\mathbf{K}_e^{-1}\mathbf{K}\mathbf{K}_e^{-1}\mathbf{k}_e,$$

the subscript $\mathbf{x}$ of $w_{\mathbf{x}}$ being given by $\mathbf{x} = -\mathbf{K}_e^{-1}\mathbf{k}_e$. The right-hand expression can be written as the sum of two components, the first of which involves only k_0 and $(k_0)_e$ and does not affect the policy-maker's decisions [cf. (8.70)]:

$$(k_0)_e - k_0 = \mathbf{b}'(\mathbf{s}_e - \mathbf{s}) + \tfrac{1}{2}(\mathbf{s}_e'\mathbf{B}\mathbf{s}_e - \mathbf{s}'\mathbf{B}\mathbf{s}).$$

This part is evidently independent of the errors in the estimated multiplicative structure and may be of either sign; it is not small of a higher order in errors of the additive structure. The second part can be written as

$$-(x - x^0)'Kx - \tfrac{1}{2}x'(K_e - K)x,$$

x being again given by $x = -K_e^{-1}k_e$. This is not of the second order either. It follows immediately that the same is true with respect to the difference between the predicted welfare level and the attainable maximum, $w_e - \hat{w}$.

8.4.4. In the remainder of this section we shall assume that the policy-maker knows the multiplicative structure of his constraints: $R_e = R$. This implies that he is in a position to make perfect conditional forecasts of changes in his noncontrolled variables, given specified changes of his instruments. We may also say that he then knows his Tinbergen surfaces, but does not know the numerical values of his sources; a situation which is entirely comparable with that of a consumer who must decide on how to spend his income and who knows the prices of the relevant period, but not his income. Such a consumer knows his Engel curves of the different commodities, but he cannot be sure that he chooses the best point on each curve.

Our first problem is the underestimation of changes. In our present terminology, this phenomenon can be said to amount to the following. The additive structure of the constraints of the next period (which is to be predicted) is given by s; it is predicted as s_e; and in the period before it was s_{-1}. Then there is a general underestimation of changes if each component of s_e lies between the corresponding components of s_{-1} and s. In a looser sense, there is a tendency towards underestimation of changes if the majority of the s_e-components lies in these intervals. The justification of this definition is, of course, that the change in the corresponding noncontrolled variable, $y_i - (y_i)_{-1}$, is then underestimated in the conditional forecast for unchanged instrument values, $x = x_{-1}$, provided the multiplicative structure of the prediction period is the same as that of the period before (R_{-1}, say). If this proviso is not fulfilled, so that $R_{-1} \neq R$, the change in the noncontrolled vector becomes

$$y - y_{-1} = (R - R_{-1})x_{-1} + s - s_{-1},$$

in which case conclusions about under or overestimation of y-changes would be more complicated.[1]

Our question is: will this underestimation lead to too small measures? In other words: will maximisation of w subject to $\mathbf{y} = \mathbf{R}\mathbf{x} + \mathbf{s}_e$ (with the $\mathbf{s}_e$-components between those of $\mathbf{s}_{-1}$ and $\mathbf{s}$) lead to instrument values that are all closer to their level of the preceding period than those of $\mathbf{x}^0$ are? This point was raised in Section 5.1 and will be considered here in more detail.

First, take $n = 1$. In that case $\mathbf{s}$ is a scalar, s say, just as income in the consumer's constraint; and each component of $\mathbf{x}$ will go up or down with s according to the policy-maker's optimal reaction functions,

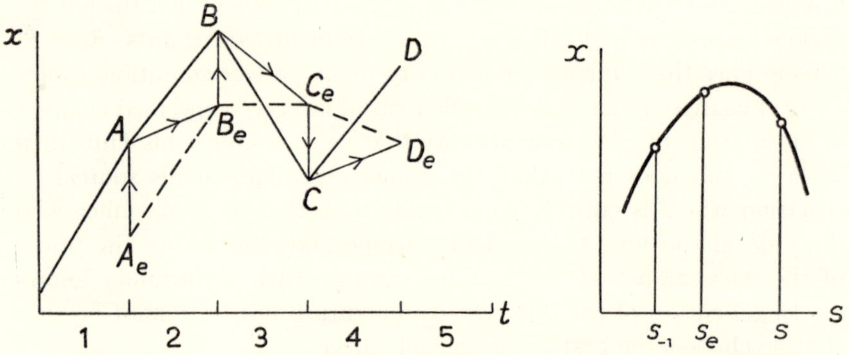

Fig. 8.6. Underestimation of changes and its effects on decision-making: (*a*) period analysis in the case of one constraint, (*b*) a case of nonlinearity

depending on the question whether this component is inferior or not. Also, specific and overall-inferiority are identical concepts in this case; and these properties are, for each instrument, independent of s. Now let us single out one instrument which is not inferior, and suppose that the multiplicative structure of the constraints, $\mathbf{R}$, remains constant during a set of successive periods $t = 1, 2, \ldots$ Consider also the left-hand Fig. 8.6, but disregard in this and the next paragraph the lines with arrows. At the end of the period $t = 1$ a forecast is made of the s-value during $t = 2$. If this prediction had been perfect, the policy-

[1] It should further be noted that it is not irrelevant which quantity is underestimated; a point stressed earlier in Section 5.4. Take e.g. the employment-balance of payments example of 7.1.3 and consider in particular investment, which is one of the variables that are part of $\mathbf{s}$. Suppose that next year's investment level is estimated by means of the outcomes of an investment survey. Since it is known that such a survey tends to underestimate the level of investment rather than its change, this is a factor which affects $\mathbf{s}_e$ rather than $\mathbf{s}_e - \mathbf{s}_{-1}$.

maker would have decided to put his x equal to the level indicated by A, so that his measure would correspond to the upward sloping straight line from the vertical axis till A. But in fact, he underestimates the s-change; hence his actual decision is A_e. At the end of the second period he predicts another increase. By this time he realises that the s-value of the period now completed was larger than predicted, and his forecast is that it will increase further in $t = 3$, though not very much. Accordingly, he decides on B_e; and the measure which he actually takes is indicated by the broken line A_eB_e. However, his prediction turns out to be an underestimation, so that the best point was B, not B_e. The best measure, therefore, was the transition from A_e to B. Since the straight line connecting these two points (which has not been drawn in the figure) has a larger slope than A_eB_e has, we may indeed say that the measure taken is too small. The same conclusion does obviously not hold if we say that the best measure is from A to B; the slope of AB being smaller than that of A_eB_e. But this statement involves another definition of the concept of measure: the instrument change AB is not measured as deviation from the original level, but as deviation from the preceding optimum. So we may disregard this variant, at least for the moment.

In the fourth period a decrease of s takes place, so that the optimal reaction function implies that the policy-maker should reduce x to the level of C; but again, he predicts a smaller decrease at the end of the third period and does not change his instrument at all, B_eC_e being a horizontal line. This is the extreme case of measures which are too small. In the fifth period, finally, there is an increase in s which leads to the best point D. There is also an increase predicted and the decision is D_e. But, since his decision for the fourth period, C_e, was much too "high," the measure taken is a decrease, C_eD_e being a line with negative slope. The best measure, on the other hand, viz. C_eD, is an increase. Hence the policy-maker's actual decision, C_eD_e, involves a turning point error; and this means that it is *not* true that underestimation of changes in s implies necessarily a measure which is too small. The consequence may also be a measure of the wrong sign.

This is a rather negative result; but it can be avoided by a simple re-interpretation. It was observed above that we obtain different results when we do not take the instrument changes as deviations from their preceding actual levels, but as deviations from their optimal levels of the preceding period. Let us do so here, but in the following manner:

we say that the actual measure taken at the end of the first period, A_eB_e, consists of two parts, the first of which serves to correct the decision error of the period just completed (A_eA), the second to adjust the instruments to the expected constraints during the future period (AB_e). This is indicated by the lines with arrows in the figure. It is not difficult to justify this decomposition, since the first part is a heritage of the preceding period and has nothing to do with forecasting errors for the period under consideration. Now, when accepting this point of view, it is easy to see that the second part (a measure according to the modified definition) is always too small if the change in s is underestimated, and always of the correct sign.

Let us then take $n \geq 2$, and accept the modified definition of measures. Suppose first that there is a proportionate underestimation of the changes in the **s**-components; i.e., there exists a scalar θ such that

$$\mathbf{s}_e = \theta \mathbf{s}_{-1} + (1 - \theta)\mathbf{s} \qquad (0 < \theta < 1). \tag{8.78}$$

Since the optimal $\mathbf{x}$ is a linear combination of the elements of $\mathbf{s}$, the instrument values chosen under assumption (8.78) must be equal to θ times the values which are appropriate under $\mathbf{s}_{-1}$ plus $(1 - \theta)$ times the values that are adequate under the true $\mathbf{s}$. Clearly, all instrument changes, as measured from their optima in the preceding period, are then too small. The same is not true, however, if we abandon the assumption of proportionate underestimation. Take e.g. the case in which the optimal reaction function for some instrument, given $\mathbf{R}$, is

$$\overset{0}{x}_h = 2s_1 - 3s_2;$$

and suppose $(s_1)_{-1} = (s_2)_{-1} = 0$; $s_1 = 10$, $s_2 = 5$. Then the optimal value of the preceding period, $(\overset{0}{x}_h)_{-1}$, equals 0, and that of the prediction period is $\overset{0}{x}_h = 5$. Suppose further $(s_1)_e = 5$, $(s_2)_e = 4$. Then the x_h chosen is -2, which amounts to a turning point error. Alternatively, suppose $(s_1)_e = 9$, $(s_2)_e = 1$. Then the x_h chosen is 15, and the measure taken is too large.

In summary, we should say that the question whether underestimation of the **s**-change leads to smaller measures than the optimal ones can be answered affirmatively to a large extent, but with several qualifications. First, measures should be interpreted as instrument changes from the optimum of the preceding period, not as changes from the preceding actual level. The question can then be answered affirmatively for the case of one constraint, at least under the assumptions made. These assumptions imply *inter alia* that the optimal reaction functions are linear in s. If this is not true (because the welfare function is not quadratic, say), we may have a situation of the type which is illustrated in Fig. 8.6, sub (*b*). The dependence of x on s according to the optimal reaction function is curvilinear there; hence the x-coordinate corresponding to s_e may be larger than both that of s_{-1} and that of s, even if s_e lies between s_{-1} and s. This will occur only if the instrument shifts from inferiority to non-inferiority in the interval (s_{-1}, s), or *vice versa*. Furthermore, as to the case of several constraints, the assertion concerning actual measures smaller than the optimal ones is correct if the change in $\mathbf{s}$ is underestimated proportionally; but it need not be correct otherwise. For the Dutch macroeconomic forecasts of Chapter III this proportionality is not more than an approximation, and the same is then true for the assertion itself. Finally, it should be stressed again that the entire analysis is based on the assumption of an unchanging multiplicative structure of the constraints, $\mathbf{R} = \mathbf{R}_{-1}$.

8.4.5. We leave here the subject of the instrument consequences of $\mathbf{s}$-errors and proceed to their welfare implications. In 8.4.2, we defined the loss of welfare due to applying the instrument values $\mathbf{x}$ as the difference $\hat{w} - w_{\mathbf{x}}$, $\hat{w}$ being the attainable maximum. In the same way, we shall define the *loss of welfare due to an incorrect prediction* (or estimate) $\mathbf{R}_e$, $\mathbf{s}_e$ as the difference between $\hat{w}$ and the welfare level $w_{\mathbf{x}}$ that is obtained if the policy-maker decides on that $\mathbf{x}$ that would maximise w if the constraints were $\mathbf{y} = \mathbf{R}_e\mathbf{x} + \mathbf{s}_e$ (whereas in fact, of course, the constraints are $\mathbf{y} = \mathbf{R}\mathbf{x} + \mathbf{s}$). Writing $w[\mathbf{R}_e, \mathbf{s}_e]$ for the latter level, the loss of welfare due to the prediction $\mathbf{R}_e$, $\mathbf{s}_e$ becomes

$$\hat{w} - w[\mathbf{R}_e, \mathbf{s}_e] = w[\mathbf{R}, \mathbf{s}] - w[\mathbf{R}_e, \mathbf{s}_e].$$

In our present case, where it is assumed that the policy-maker knows the multiplicative structure of the constraints, this can be specialised to

$$\hat{w} - w[\mathbf{R}, \mathbf{s}_e] = w[\mathbf{R}, \mathbf{s}] - w[\mathbf{R}, \mathbf{s}_e].$$

Furthermore, it will be observed that the loss-of-welfare concept, whether applied to decisions or to forecasts, determines utility measurements except for the choice of a unit. Indeed, the Von Neumann-

Morgenstern utility concept is fully numerical except for the choice of a zero and a unit; and the zero has been chosen, viz., as the loss of welfare which corresponds with the perfect decision (or prediction). It will prove useful in the discussion which follows to choose a unit as well and to take for this the difference between $\hat{w}$ and that welfare level that is obtained when the policy-maker decides on the $\mathbf{x}$ which would maximise w if the constraints were $\mathbf{y} = \mathbf{R}\mathbf{x} + \mathbf{s}_{-1}$. This leads to what will be called the *failure* of the prediction $\mathbf{s}_e$:

$$\text{(8.79)} \qquad \text{fail } \mathbf{s}_e = \frac{w[\mathbf{R}, \mathbf{s}] - w[\mathbf{R}, \mathbf{s}_e]}{w[\mathbf{R}, \mathbf{s}] - w[\mathbf{R}, \mathbf{s}_{-1}]}.$$

The failure of $\mathbf{s}_e$ is zero if the prediction is perfect: $\mathbf{s}_e = \mathbf{s}$. It is 1 if the forecast gives the same welfare result as the no-change extrapolation $\mathbf{s} = \mathbf{s}_{-1}$; and it has no finite upper limit under our present welfare assumptions, as will become clear below. The use of this particular utility scale (or better, disutility scale) can be justified by pointing out that the policy-maker is always in a position to keep it between zero and one, provided his information service is of sufficient quality. The reason for this is that he can derive $\mathbf{s}_{-1}$ as the difference between the recent values $\mathbf{y}_{-1}$ and $\mathbf{R}_{-1}\mathbf{x}_{-1}$, at least when data on these lagged values are sufficiently rapidly available. The matrix $\mathbf{R}_{-1}$ presents no problem if we assume that it is equal to $\mathbf{R}$, or at least that it is known; which seems reasonable, given our earlier assumption that $\mathbf{R}$ is known. Hence, by making no $\mathbf{s}$-forecast at all and using simply $\mathbf{s}_{-1}$, the policy-maker arrives at a failure equal to 1. It will also be observed that the choice of the denominator of (8.79) is closely related to the modified definition of measures in 8.4.4: there, we took the optimal instrument values of the preceding period as our starting point; here, we do so with the welfare level $w[\mathbf{R}, \mathbf{s}_{-1}]$ resulting from the lagged additive structure of the constraints, $\mathbf{s}_{-1}$.

We shall also make use of the *success* of a forecast $\mathbf{s}_e$. This, too, is a numerical utility concept, measured in the same unit $w[\mathbf{R}, \mathbf{s}] - w[\mathbf{R}, \mathbf{s}_{-1}]$; but it gives the excess of the welfare level attained, $w[\mathbf{R}, \mathbf{s}_e]$, over $w[\mathbf{R}, \mathbf{s}_{-1}]$:

$$\text{(8.80)} \qquad \text{suc } \mathbf{s}_e = \frac{w[\mathbf{R}, \mathbf{s}_e] - w[\mathbf{R}, \mathbf{s}_{-1}]}{w[\mathbf{R}, \mathbf{s}] - w[\mathbf{R}, \mathbf{s}_{-1}]}.$$

We have

(8.81) $$\text{suc}\ s_e + \text{fail}\ s_e \equiv 1;\ -\infty \leq \text{suc}\ s_e \leq 1;$$
$$0 \leq \text{fail}\ s_e \leq \infty.$$

In the same way as the policy-maker can reduce the failure to 1, he can enforce the success to be nonnegative.

Let us then apply the failure concept to our present analysis. The numerator of (8.79) can be written, according to Theorem 3, as

$$-\tfrac{1}{2}(x - x^0)'(xx)^{-1}(x - x^0),$$

where x^0 is the set of instrument values that maximises w, and x stands for that set that would maximise w if the constraints were $y = Rx + s_e$. But it follows from the analysis of Section 8.3 that the decision error $x - x^0$ is then given by

$$x - x^0 = -(x\cdot)(s_e - s),$$

because this error is by definition identical with the instrument change according to the optimal reaction functions that would take place if the additive structure would change from s to s_e. Hence the numerator of (8.79) becomes

$$-\tfrac{1}{2}(s_e - s)'(\cdot x)\,(xx)^{-1}(x\cdot)\,(s_e - s).$$

Similarly, we find for the denominator:

$$-\tfrac{1}{2}(s - s_{-1})'(\cdot x)\,(xx)^{-1}(x\cdot)\,(s - s_{-1}).$$

If we agree to measure s and s_e as deviations from s_{-1} — which will facilitate slightly the further analysis — we obtain the following

THEOREM 3a. *Suppose that the Assumptions* C1 *and* P3 *are satisfied, that the optimal reaction functions* (8.63) *exist, and that the policy-maker chooses those instrument values which would maximise welfare if the constraints were given by* (8.67), R_e *being equal to* R. *Then the failure of the forecast* s_e *is given by*

(8.82) $$\text{fail}\ s_e = \frac{(s_e - s)'F(s_e - s)}{s'Fs}$$

(s_e *and* s *being measured as deviations from* s_{-1}), *provided that the denominator does not vanish.* F *is the negative-definite or negative semi-definite matrix*

(8.83) $$F = (\cdot x)(xx)^{-1}(x\cdot) = D'(xx)D = (\cdot x)D.$$

The interpretation is very close to that of Theorem 3. The numerator of the failure is a quadratic function of the forecasting error $s_e - s$, just as the loss of welfare (8.72) of Theorem 3 is a quadratic function of the decision error $x - x^0$. Taking account of the denominator, we must conclude that a forecasting error $s_e - s$, the components of which are small relative to the corresponding components of the change $s - s_{-1}$, implies a failure which is small of the second order. The geo-

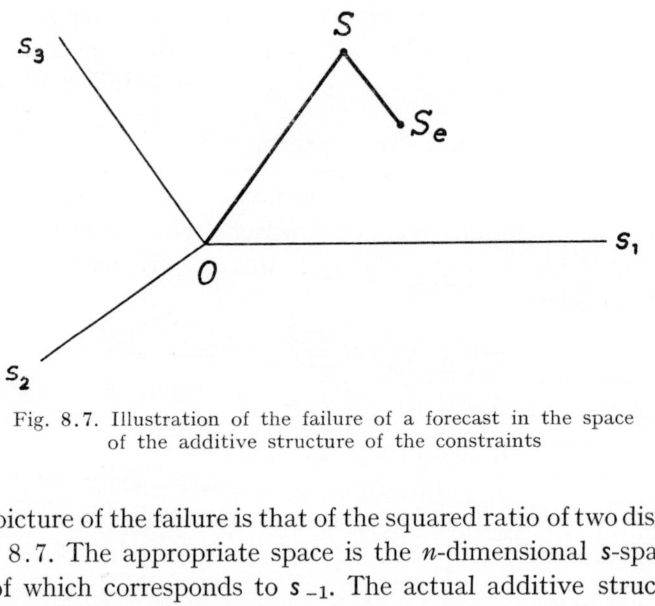

Fig. 8.7. Illustration of the failure of a forecast in the space of the additive structure of the constraints

metric picture of the failure is that of the squared ratio of two distances; cf. Fig. 8.7. The appropriate space is the n-dimensional s-space, the origin of which corresponds to s_{-1}. The actual additive structure of the prediction period and its prediction are represented by two points, S and S_e respectively. The distance SS_e, measured as a fraction of OS and squared, gives the failure of s_e.

It is tempting to compare this failure measure with the inequality coefficient of Section 2.5. Both coefficients are essentially ratios of two quadratic expressions. Also, the numerators of the coefficients are both quadratic functions of the forecasting errors. When multiplying numerator and denominator of (8.82) by -1, we can even say that the squared numerator of the generalised inequality coefficient U^* of (2.29) is identical with the numerator of the failure of s_e, provided we interpret $\mathbf{p}$ as s_e, $\mathbf{a}$ as s and take $\mathbf{Q}$ equal to the positive-definite (or semi-definite) matrix $-\mathsf{F}$.[1] There are two differences. First, the denominators are not the same. The denominator of fail s_e is such that this measure may vary from zero to infinity, whereas U^* is confined to the interval (0, 1); but this is mainly a question of normalisation.[2] Secondly, most of the applications of measures like U, especially those of Chapter IV, have reference to series of predictions and actual changes over time. The series to which the failure refers are the components of s_e and s, and they belong to one period. To take again the employment-balance of payments example, the failure is obtained by squaring the s-error of employment and multiplying by an appropriate constant, doing the same with the s-error of the balance of payments, taking their product and multiplying this by an appropriate constant, adding the results, and dividing by a certain denominator; not, however, by taking a quadratic expression of such errors belonging to a set of successive periods.

Another interesting point is the following. It was observed at the end of Chapter III that the accuracy analysis presented there made no distinction between the different quantities to be predicted on the basis of their relative importance. Now, if we specify these quantities as the components of s, Theorem 3a shows how this should be done, under its assumptions at least. We should take a quadratic form in the s-error and take F (to be called the *failure matrix*) as the matrix of this form. Since

$$\mathsf{F} = (\cdot \mathsf{x})\,(\mathsf{xx})^{-1}(\mathsf{x}\cdot),$$

this implies that we should premultiply the forecasting error $\mathsf{s}_e - \mathsf{s}$ by $(\mathsf{x}\cdot)$, which gives the decision error $\mathsf{x} - \mathsf{x}^0$, after which the latter

[1] Note that F is semi-definite as soon as $m < n$, i.e., as soon as there are fewer instruments than noncontrolled variables. In that case nonzero errors may lead to a zero loss and hence a zero failure, as can be easily verified.

[2] The inequality measure which is normalised in the same manner as the failure is $\sqrt{\Sigma(P-A)^2}/\sqrt{\Sigma A^2}$. This coefficient was used in H. THEIL, "Who Forecasts Best?," *International Economic Papers*, No. 5 (1955), pp. 194–199. It has the disadvantage of a less convenient range, but the advantage that the denominator is independent of the forecasts. To see that this is an advantage, consider the case of two alternative forecast series P_i, P_i' such that $|P_i - A_i| = |P_i' - A_i|$ and $|P_i| \geqq |P_i'|$; i.e., such that corresponding prediction errors are equal apart from sign, one of the prediction series being always larger in absolute value than the corresponding forecast of the other series (an example: $A_i = 2$, $P_i = 5$, $P_i' = -1$). Then the numerator of U is the same for both series, but the denominator is larger for the P-series. Hence the P-series has a smaller inequality coefficient than the P'-series in spite of the fact that the second moments of their prediction errors are equal, whereas the alternative coefficient is the same for both. Cf. also p. 166 n.

error is to be handled in the manner described in 8.4.2. In other words, we should "weight" the forecasting errors according to their influence on decision errors,[1] and the decision errors should be weighted, in turn, according to the inverse of the substitution matrix $(\mathbf{xx})$, as Theorem 3 prescribes. This is the most direct interpretation. For an alternative interpretation we start from [cf. (8.83)]

$$\mathbf{F} = \mathbf{D}'(\mathbf{xx})\mathbf{D},$$

which gives for the diagonal elements

$$f_{ii} = \sum_h \sum_k (xx)_{hk} d_{hi} d_{ki}.$$

If there is no substitution or complementarity among pairs of instruments, so that $(xx)_{hk} = 0$ if $h \neq k$, these diagonal elements are equal to a weighted sum of squares d_{hi}^2, the set of weights $(xx)_{11}, \ldots, (xx)_{mm}$ being the same for all. In that case those components of the forecasting error $\mathbf{s}_e - \mathbf{s}$ are most serious which belong to a constraint the non-controlled variable of which has a marginal welfare that is highly responsive with respect to instrument changes. This can be easily understood. For suppose that it is not true that y_i has a welfare derivative, $\partial w/\partial y_i$, which is highly responsive in the $\mathbf{D}$-sense with respect to instrument changes; and suppose that s_i is considerably over or underestimated, thus leading to an important forecasting error in y_i. In that case a more correct prediction of s_i will not affect the decisions made very much, since changes in them will not influence the position of y_i appreciably. Conversely, if the d_{hi}'s for this i are substantial, a correct prediction of s_i does affect the decisions to a large extent. In the absence of substitution or complementarity this gives rise to a large failure. If there is substitution or complementarity, the situation becomes more complicated, since the weights $(xx)_{hk}$ in f_{ii} do not have all the same sign. Still, if we compare two sources s_i and s_j such that $d_{hi} = pd_{hj}$ with $p > 1$ for all h, so that $\partial w/\partial y_i$ is uniformly more responsive to instrument changes than $\partial w/\partial y_j$, then the seriousness of s_i-errors exceeds that of numerically equal s_j-errors; at least, as far as the quadratic terms s_i^2 in fail $\mathbf{s}_e$ are concerned.

8.4.6. We proceed to consider more specifically the welfare implications of underestimation of $\mathbf{s}$-changes. First, we take the case of propor-

[1] Note that this influence is zero in the special case mentioned on p. 459, n. 1.

tionate underestimation. This corresponds to (8.78); or, recalling that we agreed to measure s and s_e as deviations from s_{-1}, to

$$s_e = (1 - \theta)s. \tag{8.84}$$

Substituting (8.84) into (8.82) gives immediately

$$\text{fail } s_e = \theta^2. \tag{8.85}$$

This result is independent both of the parameters of the constraints (R, s) and of those of the preference function (a, b, A, B, C). If we apply it to the Dutch macroeconomic forecasts of Chapter III and take for θ the average underestimation found there (30 per cent), the outcome is a failure of 0.09 and hence a success of 0.91. This is clearly very favourable. That it is so favourable is due to the fact that small forecasting errors lead to a failure which is small of the second order; but the actual success is not really so overwhelming, as will become clear below.

If the underestimation is not of the proportionate type, this derivation cannot be applied; but it is always possible to find an average (in some sense) which describes this phenomenon. It will prove instructive to do so, and to take for this a regression of s_e on s and one of s on s_e, the separate components of these two vectors being considered as the "values" assumed by two "variables." The introduction of these two alternative ("first" and "second") regressions will be useful for a comparison with the underestimation analysis of Section 5.1. Also, it will be convenient to use, not the ordinary least-squares regressions, but regressions leading to multiplicative coefficients of the following type:

$$b_1 = \frac{s'Fs_e}{s'Fs}; \quad b_2 = \frac{s'Fs_e}{s_e'Fs_e}. \tag{8.86}$$

Going back to 6.2.6, we see that b_1 and b_2 are regression coefficients of the Aitken-type; i.e., coefficients of the generalised least-squares regressions (without constant term) of s_e on s and s on s_e, respectively, where the rôle of $\mathbf{\Omega}^{-1}$ is taken over by the positive-definite or positive semi-definite matrix $-F$. We shall call them *failure regressions*; or briefly "regressions," since the failure type is the only type that we shall meet in this section. For the same reason, we shall not attach asterisks to the b's and further similar symbols, as we did for $\mathbf{\Omega}$-type in 6.2.6. One of these further concepts will be useful even at this stage, viz., the *failure correlation* between $\mathbf{s}$ and $\mathbf{s}_e$:

$$(8.87) \qquad r = \frac{-\mathbf{s}'\mathbf{F}\mathbf{s}_e}{\sqrt{\mathbf{s}'\mathbf{F}\mathbf{s}.\mathbf{s}_e'\mathbf{F}\mathbf{s}_e}}.$$

It will be hardly necessary to stress that these statistical concepts are not more than auxiliary in the present analysis. In particular, it is not correct to consider $-\mathbf{F}^{-1}$ (if existent), on the analogy of $\mathbf{\Omega}$ in 6.2.6, as the covariance matrix of the disturbances in a parent regression of $\mathbf{s}_e$ on $\mathbf{s}$ (or $\mathbf{s}$ on $\mathbf{s}_e$). This follows simply from the fact that none of the quantities with which we deal has been defined as stochastic. We use the terminology of a branch of statistics, but do not apply the meaning of its concepts. The justification of this procedure is its convenience; and the cause of this convenience is twofold. First, the terminology has heuristic value; second, both the present analysis and this branch of statistics, being an analysis of quadratic forms, are quite similar from a mathematical point of view.

It is very simple to apply these concepts to the failure of $\mathbf{s}_e$, as given in Theorem 3a:

$$\text{fail } \mathbf{s}_e = 1 - 2\,\frac{\mathbf{s}'\mathbf{F}\mathbf{s}_e}{\mathbf{s}'\mathbf{F}\mathbf{s}} + \frac{\mathbf{s}_e'\mathbf{F}\mathbf{s}_e}{\mathbf{s}'\mathbf{F}\mathbf{s}} =$$

$$= 1 - 2b_1 + (b_1/r)^2 = 1 - 2r^2/b_2 + (r/b_2)^2.$$

Replacing failure by success—which gives slightly more convenient expressions—, we find

COROLLARY to Theorem 3a. *Suppose that the assumptions of Theorem* 3a *are satisfied. Then the success of the forecast* $\mathbf{s}_e$ *is given by*

$$(8.88) \qquad \text{suc } \mathbf{s}_e = 2b_1 - (b_1/r)^2 = r^2(2/b_2 - 1/b_2^2),$$

where b_1 *is the coefficient of the failure regression of* $\mathbf{s}_e$ *on* $\mathbf{s}$, b_2 *that of the failure regression of* $\mathbf{s}$ *on* $\mathbf{s}_e$, *and* r *the failure correlation between* $\mathbf{s}$ *and* $\mathbf{s}_e$, *as defined in* (8.86) *and* (8.87).

It is possible to draw a few interesting conclusions. First, the earlier suggestion that the success of the Dutch forecasts was as high as 0.91 is too optimistic. The validity of this figure implies $r = 1$; and there is certainly no perfect correlation, neither in the failure sense, nor in any other product-moment sense. It is clearly difficult to determine the actual figure, since this requires knowledge of the failure matrix $\mathbf{F}$. Rather than making guesses, it is preferable to illustrate the dependence of the success on r, b_1 and b_2 graphically. This is done in the Figs. 8.8 and 8.9, the first of which describes the success as a function of b_1 for various levels of r^2, the second as a function of b_2. These graphs show several other interesting features. First, Fig. 8.9 suggests that success is always maximal, given r, if $b_2 = 1$. This can be easily verified from (8.88). It means that, for whatever correlation r, the success of the forecast $\mathbf{s}_e$ is maximised if the regression of $\mathbf{s}$ on $\mathbf{s}_e$ gives a unit coefficient. Clearly, this is of some relevance for the analysis of Chapter III. At the end of Section 3.3 we tried to eliminate the bias towards underestimation of changes of the Dutch and Scandinavian forecasts by multiplying them all by $1\frac{1}{2}$ and 2, respectively. The result was a considerable increase in variance, which raised some doubts about the adequacy of such a bias elimination. Here, we find the answer to this question: we should not raise the predicted changes in such a way that their regression on the actual changes has a unit coefficient (i.e., such that $b_1 = 1$), but we should raise or lower them until the failure regression of the actual changes on the predicted changes, thus modified, has a unit coefficient, $b_2 = 1$.[1] This result makes the problem of underestimation of changes somewhat less important than it seemed in earlier chapters (cf. Section 5.1). Still, in the Dutch and the Scandinavian case there is underestimation of changes in this sense (cf. 3.3.4); but raising the actual predictions made by 2 or $1\frac{1}{2}$ is evidently too much. We should add, of course, that the analysis of Chapter III and Section 5.1 was concerned with values assumed by certain variables, which are at most components of our $\mathbf{s}$; also, that we did not use failure regressions there. Nevertheless, this result does help to make the situation clearer.

Confining ourselves to the range of positive and finite b_2, Fig. 8.9 shows further that the success of $\mathbf{s}_e$ is zero if, and only if, $b_2 = \frac{1}{2}$; which is again independent of r. This case obviously corresponds with overestimation of changes in the sense of the regression of $\mathbf{s}$ on $\mathbf{s}_e$; but it is not necessarily overestimation in the other sense. Take e.g. $r^2 = 0.4$; then $b_2 = 0.5$ gives $b_1 = 0.8$ according to $b_1 b_2 = r^2$, and $b_1 < 1$ means underestimation of changes in the b_1-sense.

So we find that the b_2-diagram gives a clear insight into two distinct

[1] Note that such a uniform change leaves r unchanged.

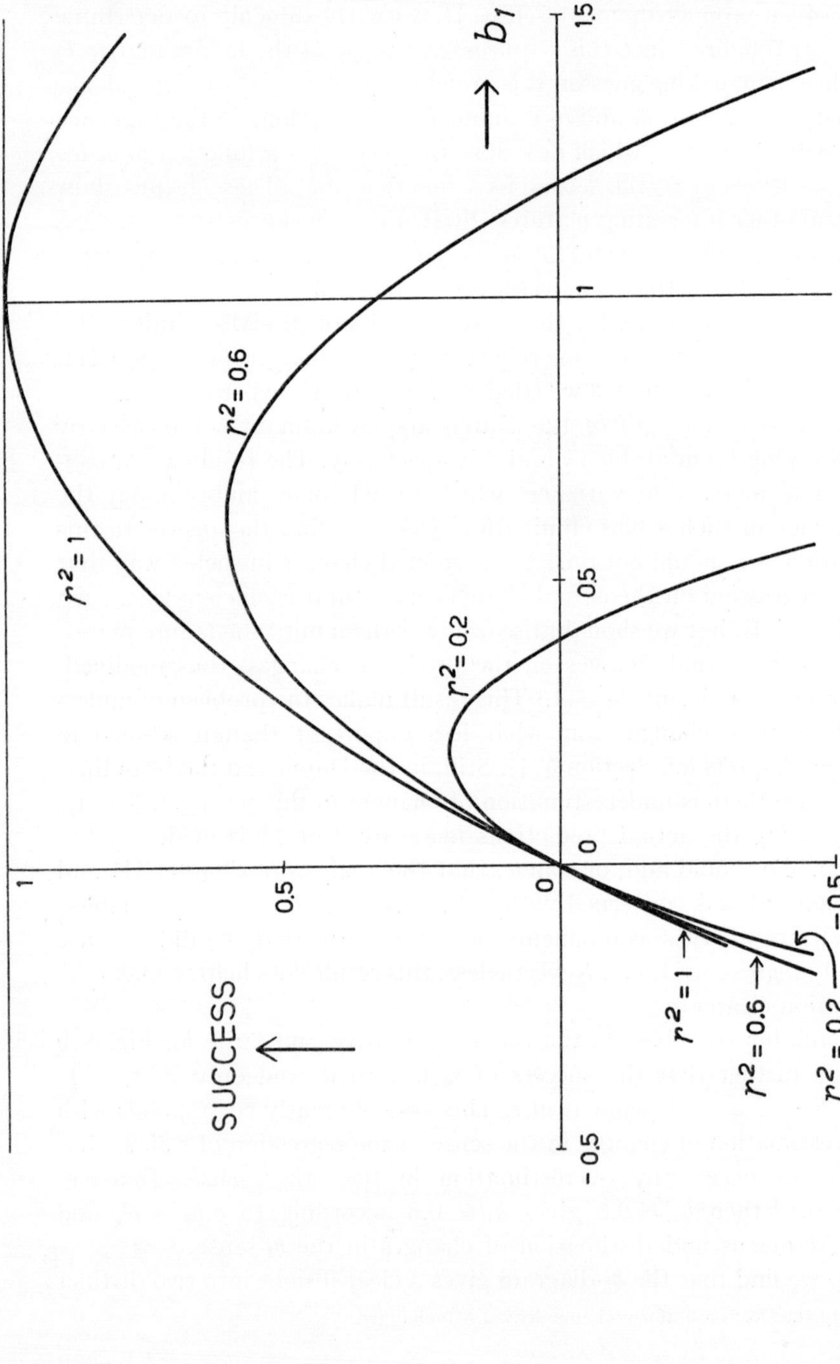

Fig. 8.8. The success of forecasts according to the Corollary to Theorem 3a: illustration based on the failure regression of s_e on s

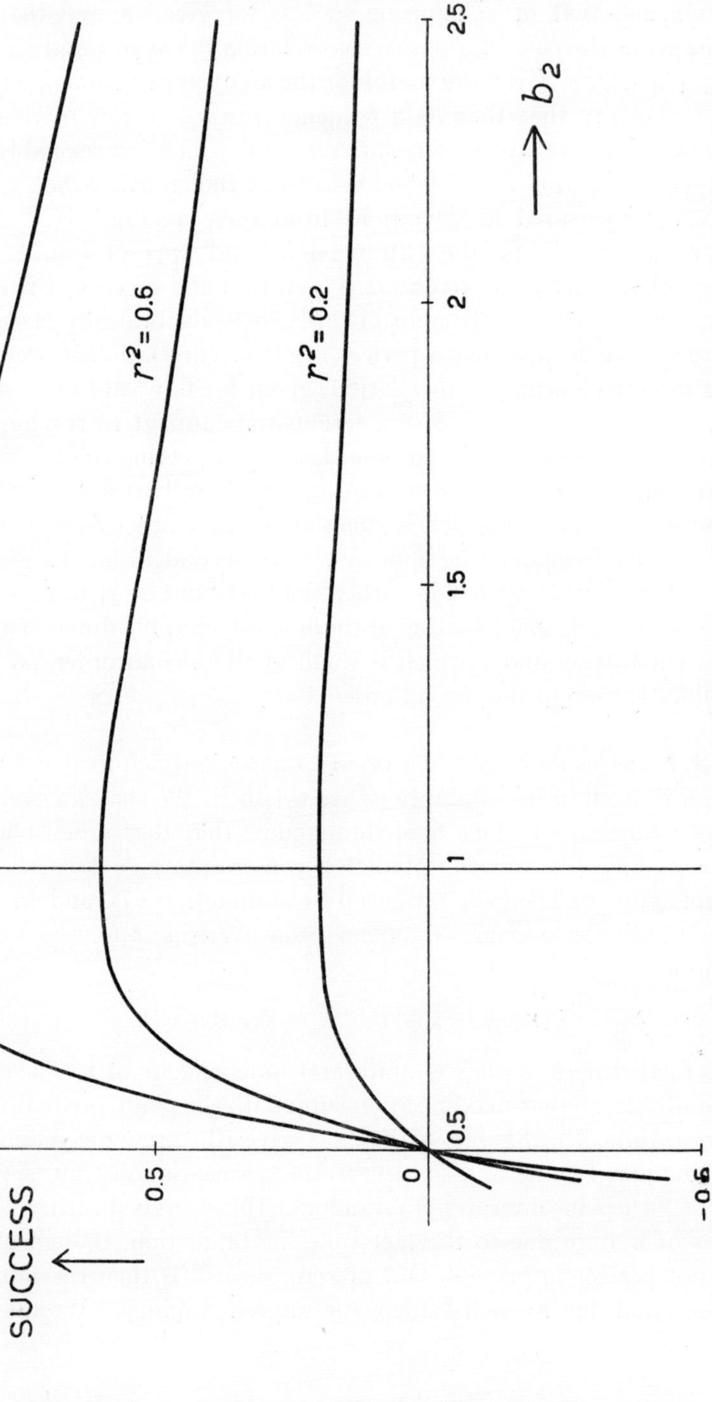

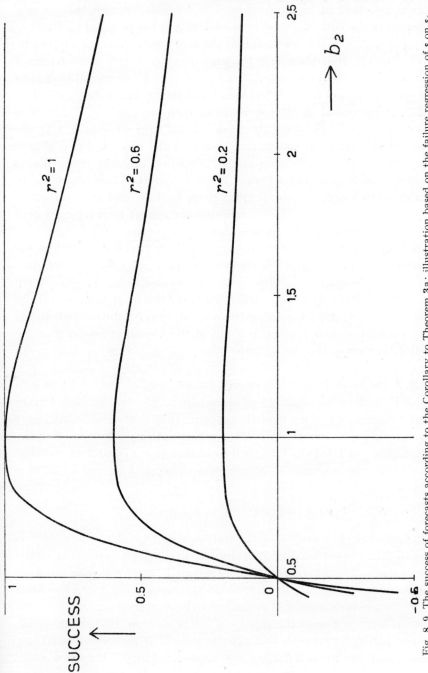

Fig. 8.9. The success of forecasts according to the Corollary to Theorem 3a: illustration based on the failure regression of s on s_e

problems: that of maximising success for given r, and that of zero success in the case of a positive correlation between $\mathbf{s}$ and $\mathbf{s}_e$. Its companion, Fig. 8.8, is more useful for the analysis of turning point errors We may say that there is a tendency towards errors of that kind if $\mathbf{s}$ and $\mathbf{s}_e$ are negatively correlated, $r < 0$; which is reasonable in view of the convention $\mathbf{s}_{-1} = \mathbf{0}$ and because of the fact that the "variables" are not measured as deviations from their average. If $r < 0$, then $b_1 < 0$ as well. So the extreme left-hand area of Fig. 8.8 is the area of turning point errors. It is seen that the success of $\mathbf{s}_e$ is always negative there; but that, for given b_1, it is algebraically larger if r^2 is larger. This means that a perfect negative correlation is preferable to an imperfect negative correlation, given b_1. Low and even moderate correlations are in any case a serious impediment to reaching a considerable success, as will become clear by inspecting the two figures.

Finally, (8.88) as well as the figures show that a reduction of the correlation below 1 which is small of the first order leads to a failure of $\mathbf{s}_e$ which is small of the same, not of the second, order. This may seem in contradiction with our earlier findings; but it is not. As can be easily verified, small $\mathbf{s}$-errors of the first order imply a difference between the correlation and 1 which is small of the second order, so that the failure is then of the second order, too.

8.4.7. Let us go back to Theorem 1 on certainty equivalence and suppose that all of its assumptions are satisfied. We shall go even farther and assume, as is done here throughout, that the "true" constraints are $\mathbf{y} = \mathbf{R}\mathbf{x} + \mathbf{s}$ and the predicted constraints $\mathbf{y} = \mathbf{R}\mathbf{x} + \mathbf{s}_e$. For the application of Theorem 1 we need to assume that $\mathbf{s}$ is random and that the prediction $\mathbf{s}_e$ equals its mean value. Writing $\bar{\mathbf{s}}$ for the mean, this implies

$$(8.89) \qquad \mathbf{s} = \bar{\mathbf{s}} + \mathbf{u}; \quad \mathbf{s}_e = \bar{\mathbf{s}}; \quad \mathscr{E}\mathbf{u} = \mathbf{0}.$$

If, furthermore, $\mathscr{E}(\mathbf{u}\mathbf{u}')$ is finite and independent of $\mathbf{x}$, Theorem 1 is applicable, so that maximisation subject to the point prediction of the constraints, $\mathbf{y} = \mathbf{R}\mathbf{x} + \mathbf{s}_e$ with $\mathbf{s}_e = \bar{\mathbf{s}}$, gives the same $\mathbf{x}$ as maximisation of the mean value of w subject to the stochastic constraints, $\mathbf{y} = \mathbf{R}\mathbf{x} + \bar{\mathbf{s}} + \mathbf{u}$, $\mathbf{u}$ being interpreted as random. Still, as argued earlier, there is a loss of welfare due to the fact that the prediction, though unbiased, is not perfect in general. Our present subject is then the failure of a prediction due to such "stochastic unpredictability." We must make a distinction here between success and failure in a particular sample and the same concepts in the population. The former quantities are relevant if we are interested in a specified case in which the probability mechanism has produced a certain numerical vector $\mathbf{u}$. The latter quantities are more interesting from a broader point of view; they are obtained by replacing sample moments of random elements by corresponding parent moments and will be noted by Suc and Fail, respectively. It is then easy to see that the parent success of $\mathbf{s}_e$ under assumption (8.89) is given by

$$\text{(8.90)} \qquad \text{Suc } \mathbf{s}_e = \varrho^2 \qquad (\text{if } \mathbf{s}_e = \bar{\mathbf{s}}),$$

where ϱ is the parent failure correlation between $\mathbf{s}$ and $\bar{\mathbf{s}}$:

$$\text{(8.91)} \qquad \varrho = \frac{-\mathscr{E}(\mathbf{s}'\mathbf{F}\bar{\mathbf{s}})}{\sqrt{\mathscr{E}(\mathbf{s}'\mathbf{F}\mathbf{s})\cdot \bar{\mathbf{s}}'\mathbf{F}\bar{\mathbf{s}}}}.$$

The result (8.90) follows immediately from (8.88), since the parent regression of $\mathbf{s}$ on $\mathbf{s}_e$ has a unit coefficient under assumption (8.89).

A few interesting conclusions can be drawn from this result. First, combining it with the Corollary to Theorem 3a, we find that Suc $\bar{\mathbf{s}}$ is the highest value that success can attain for alternative values of the parent coefficient in the regression of $\mathbf{s}$ on $\mathbf{s}_e$, given the correlation. Second, this value is always positive, at least nonnegative; though it is small or moderate if the correlation is not high. Third, equation (8.90) throws some light on the second decomposition of the inequality coefficient; cf. 2.5.4. The first decomposition of U in terms of U_M, U_S, U_C treats forecasts and corresponding actual data symmetrically by distinguishing between the two means, the two standard deviations and the covariance. The second (in terms of U_M, U_R, U_D) is not symmetrical, which was justified by the theory which states that predictions are equal to the mean values of the future actual values to be predicted. We now find that this basis—if true—has an optimal property according to the first conclusion of this paragraph.

We proceed to weaken assumption (8.89) by taking account of the possibility that the policy-maker may not succeed in predicting $\mathbf{s}$ according to its mean value: $\mathbf{s}_e \neq \bar{\mathbf{s}}$. Further, we shall assume that he makes an effort to predict the disturbances $\mathbf{u}$. Frequently, this will be in vain; but this is not necessarily true. Suppose for example that the constraints are the reduced form of an econometric model which is used for prediction purposes, and that one of the dependent variables of this model is also predicted by means of a survey; then it is conceivable that the survey forecast is used to predict the disturbance which is associated with this dependent variable in the model. Let us then summarise these assumptions as follows:

$$s = \bar{s} + u, \quad \mathscr{E}u = \mathbf{0} \tag{8.92}$$

and

$$s_e = \beta_s \bar{s} + \beta_u u + v, \tag{8.93}$$

where

$$\beta_s = \frac{\mathscr{E}(\bar{s}'Fs_e)}{\bar{s}'F\bar{s}}, \quad \beta_u = \frac{\mathscr{E}(u'Fs_e)}{\mathscr{E}(u'Fu)}. \tag{8.94}$$

Equation (8.93) is nothing else than a regression which defines the vector of "forecast disturbances" v, given the fact that the parameters β_s and β_u have been defined in (8.94). The latter definition is such that the β's are parent coefficients in the multiple failure regression of s_e on $\bar{s}$ and u. Also, $\bar{s}$ and u are uncorrelated in the failure sense, simply because $\bar{s}$ is taken as nonstochastic; this feature is implicit in the definition (8.94). It will further be convenient to introduce the multiple failure correlation, R, corresponding to the parent regression (8.93). It is determined by

$$\frac{1 - R^2}{R^2} = \frac{\mathscr{E}(v'Fv)}{\beta_s^2 \bar{s}'F\bar{s} + \beta_u^2 \mathscr{E}(u'Fu)}. \tag{8.95}$$

Comparing these definitions with the earlier case (8.89), we easily find that this corresponds with $\beta_s = R = 1$, $\beta_u = 0$.

If we substitute (8.92) and (8.93) into the numerator of the parent failure of s_e, we find for this numerator

$$(1 - \beta_s)^2 \bar{s}'F\bar{s} + (1 - \beta_u)^2 \mathscr{E}(u'Fu) + \mathscr{E}(v'Fv).$$

Writing

$$\mathscr{E}(u'Fu) = (\varrho^{-2} - 1)\bar{s}'F\bar{s},$$

ϱ being the parent failure correlation between s and $\bar{s}$; and, using this and (8.95),

$$\mathscr{E}(v'Fv) = (R^{-2} - 1)[\beta_s^2 + (\varrho^{-2} - 1)\beta_u^2]\bar{s}'F\bar{s},$$

we find for the numerator of Fail $\mathbf{s}_e$:

$$[(1-\beta_s)^2 + (\varrho^{-2}-1)(1-\beta_u)^2 + (R^{-2}-1)\{\beta_s^2 + (\varrho^{-2}-1)\beta_u^2\}]\bar{\mathbf{s}}'\mathbf{F}\bar{\mathbf{s}}.$$

The denominator equals $\varrho^{-2}\,\bar{\mathbf{s}}'\mathbf{F}\bar{\mathbf{s}}$; and so we obtain, after some further rearrangements,

THEOREM 3b. *Suppose that the assumptions of Theorem* 3a *are satisfied; furthermore, that* $\mathbf{s}$ *is stochastic with mean value* $\bar{\mathbf{s}}$ *and finite covariance matrix. Then the parent success of the forecast* $\mathbf{s}_e$ *is given by*

$$\text{(8.96)}\qquad \text{Suc } \mathbf{s}_e = \varrho^2[2\beta_s - (\beta_s/R)^2] + (1-\varrho^2)[2\beta_u - (\beta_u/R)^2],$$

where ϱ *is the correlation between* $\mathbf{s}$ *and* $\bar{\mathbf{s}}$, β_s *and* β_u *the coefficients in the regression of* $\mathbf{s}_e$ *on* $\bar{\mathbf{s}}$ *and* $\mathbf{u} = \mathbf{s} - \bar{\mathbf{s}}$, *respectively, and R the multiple correlation coefficient of this regression, all of them being taken in the parent failure sense in accordance with* (8.91), (8.94) *and* (8.95).

The result (8.96) implies that Suc $\mathbf{s}_e$ is the sum of two expressions, each of which is mainly concerned with one of the two independent variables in the regression (8.93). Alternatively, we may say that the success is a weighted average of the policy-maker's "forecasting achievements" with respect to the systematic ($\bar{\mathbf{s}}$) and the unsystematic ($\mathbf{u}$) components, respectively, of the true additive structure $\mathbf{s}$,

$$2\beta_s - (\beta_s/R)^2 \text{ and } 2\beta_u - (\beta_u/R)^2;$$

the weights being nonnegative with sum unity. It does not make much sense to derive the optimal values of β_s and β_u for given ϱ and R, simply because R is not independent of β_s and β_u according to (8.95). But it is clear that, given β_s and β_u, a high multiple correlation is always preferable to a lower one; also, that the forecasting achievements with respect to $\mathbf{u}$ are of importance if ϱ is not very large. In most cases these achievements will be somewhat meagre, thus leading to a small β_u. If ϱ is sufficiently close to unity, this is not important; otherwise, however, it is evidently desirable to pay more attention to the prediction of $\mathbf{u}$ than is usually done. In the extreme case $\beta_u = 0$, (8.96) reduces to

$$\text{(8.97)}\qquad \text{Suc } \mathbf{s}_e = \varrho^2[2\beta_s - (\beta_s/R)^2],$$

where R is now the zero-order failure correlation of $\bar{s}$ and s_e. This result implies that the success is then equal to the success that would have been realised if s_e had been equal to $\bar{s}$ [in accordance with Theorem 1 under the further assumption that $\mathscr{E}(uu')$ is independent of x], multiplied by the success that would have been realised if the true s had been equal to its mean value $\bar{s}$, s_e being as it is (cf. the Corollary to Theorem 3a).

8.4.8. Again, we go back to Chapter III. It was observed there that the variance of the forecasting errors, when corrected for the systematic error of underestimation, tends to increase when the changes to be predicted are larger. More specifically, this variance could be approximately described as a linear function of the square of either the actual or the predicted change. We shall make use of this property in order to derive a more specific result. It will not be necessary to assume in the analysis which follows that this holds for all forecasts individually; it will be sufficient to suppose that this holds for a particular combination. The results can be further generalised by taking account of the possibility that the policy-maker tries to predict the u-component of s. This leads us back to the parent regression (8.93). If we assume that v has the above-mentioned hyperbolic properties, we are indeed in a situation corresponding to that of Chapter III; which is easily seen if it is realised that the parameter β_s serves to correct the forecasting errors for under or overestimation of changes. The most convenient form of our assumption is

$$\mathscr{E}(v'Fv) = h_u\,\mathscr{E}(u'Fu) + h_s\bar{s}'F\bar{s}, \tag{8.98}$$

h_u and h_s being fixed positive scalars. This relation describes the mean value of a quadratic form in v as a linear function of the same quadratic form in $\bar{s}$. The "constant term" of this linear relation is $h_u\mathscr{E}(u'Fu)$. This is a constant only if it is independent of the policy-maker's instruments, which is true if the covariance matrix $\mathscr{E}(uu')$ is independent of x; we shall assume that this is the case.

The relevance of the form (8.98) for our present subject is immediately seen of we apply a linear transformation to v, u and $\bar{s}$. Let us define $v^* = Pv$, $u^* = Pu$, $\bar{s}^* = P\bar{s}$ such that $P'P = -F$; the negative definiteness (or semi-definiteness) of F ensures that such a matrix P exists. Then (8.98) implies that there are positive numbers h_u and h_s such that

$$\sum_i \mathscr{E}v_i^{*2} = h_u \sum_i \mathscr{E}u_i^{*2} + h_s \sum_i \bar{s}_i^{*2}.$$

It follows that it is not necessary that each of the v_i^* satisfies the above-mentioned variance assumption; it is sufficient that this is true for the sum (or the average) of their variances.

Combining (8.98) with (8.95), we find

$$(8.99) \qquad 1/R^2 = \frac{(\beta_s^2 + h_s)\bar{\mathbf{s}}'\mathbf{F}\bar{\mathbf{s}} + (\beta_u^2 + h_u)\mathscr{E}(\mathbf{u}'\mathbf{F}\mathbf{u})}{\beta_s^2\bar{\mathbf{s}}'\mathbf{F}\bar{\mathbf{s}} + \beta_u^2\mathscr{E}(\mathbf{u}'\mathbf{F}\mathbf{u})}.$$

If we substitute this into (8.96), we find, after some rearrangements:

THEOREM 3c. *Suppose that the assumptions of Theorem 3b are satisfied; furthermore, that the disturbances* $\mathbf{v}$ *of (8.93) satisfy (8.98) with fixed positive scalars* h_u *and* h_s*, and that the covariance matrix* $\mathscr{E}(\mathbf{u}\mathbf{u}')$ *is independent of the instruments. Then the parent success of the forecast* $\mathbf{s}_e$ *is given by*

$$(8.100) \qquad \text{Suc } \mathbf{s}_e = p(2\beta_s - \beta_s^2 - h_s) + q(2\beta_u - \beta_u^2 - h_u),$$

where

$$(8.101) \qquad p = \frac{\bar{\mathbf{s}}'\mathbf{F}\bar{\mathbf{s}}}{\bar{\mathbf{s}}'\mathbf{F}\bar{\mathbf{s}}+\mathscr{E}(\mathbf{u}'\mathbf{F}\mathbf{u})} \; (= \varrho^2); \quad q = 1 - p.$$

As in the case of Theorem 3b, we find here that the success of the forecast $\mathbf{s}_e$ is a weighted average of two expressions, each of which deals with one of the two components $\bar{\mathbf{s}}$ and $\mathbf{u}$, respectively, of $\mathbf{s}$. The weights are positive and have sum unity; and they are numerically determined, given the failure matrix, by the size of the systematic change $\bar{\mathbf{s}}$ relative to the stochastic variation of $\mathbf{u}$. If $\bar{\mathbf{s}}$ is a vector of sufficiently large elements, (8.100) gives

$$(8.102) \qquad \text{Suc } \mathbf{s}_e \approx 2\beta_s - \beta_s^2 - h_s,$$

which implies that the forecasting achievements with respect to $\mathbf{u}$ are then irrelevant. The maximum value of (8.102), given h_s, is reached at $\beta_s = 1$; and the maximum equals $1 - h_s$. This can be safely regarded as positive for the Dutch and Scandinavian forecasts of Chapter III.[1] If,

[1] The scedastic curves of Chapter III have a coefficient 0.1 if the actual changes are taken as right-hand variables; 0.3 if we take the predicted changes instead; cf. 3.3.2 and 3.3.4. Although neither variant is fully satisfactory for our present purposes for several reasons, it seems unlikely that $h_s > 1$.

on the other hand, $\bar{s}$ is a vector of very small elements, (8.100) gives

$$\text{Suc } s_e \approx 2\beta_u - \beta_u^2 - h_u. \tag{8.103}$$

In that case everything depends on the policy-maker's forecasts of the random component u. If he is unable to achieve anything in this direction, i.e., if $\beta_u = 0$, then (8.103) gives a *negative success*. In such a situation he should not use his forecast s_e at all. He should act under the assumption of zero change, $s = \mathbf{0}$ $(= s_{-1})$, in which case his success is zero. In other words, he should go from A_e to A in Fig. 8.6, and stay there; his further trip from A to B_e is bound to lead to a welfare reduction—not necessarily in one particular sample case, but surely in the parent population of all such cases.

It is not difficult to see to what cause this is due: First, if $\bar{s}$ is a vector of small elements, its prediction is characterised by large relative errors. This follows from (8.98), which states that the random variation of v does not decrease indefinitely with decreasing components of $\bar{s}$; indeed, upon comparing (8.100) and (8.103), we find that this forecast has practically no value. Secondly, we assume that the forecaster achieves nothing with respect to the random component of s; i.e., we assume $\beta_u = 0$. So the best thing which the policy-maker can do is to neglect the forecast by extrapolating according to the no-change rule, for then he ensures at least $v = \mathbf{0}$, thus avoiding the negative value $-h_u$.

8.4.9. This completes the first part of our analysis of welfare losses due to imperfect decisions and imperfect forecasts. We started with the general problem of the welfare implications of decision errors, after which we specialised it to that of forecasting errors in the additive structure of the constraints. We analysed the consequences of underestimation of changes in the additive structure and found that this error will often, but not always, lead to decisions which are closer to the optimum of the preceding period than the actual constraints to be predicted justify. In that sense (and with appropriate qualifications) we may say that underestimation of changes in the sphere of expectations leads to measures which are too small. Further, we tried to measure welfare losses due to such imperfect forecasts; and we found that they may be substantial, even when they are compared with the modest achievement of zero-change extrapolation. But this is not all: the analysis was based on the drastic assumption $R_e = R$, which implies that the policy-maker is in a position to make perfect conditional forecasts of changes in his noncontrolled variables, given specified instrument changes. Clearly, if this assumption is realistic, this as such implies a rather favourable situation. It will be removed in the next section, at the end of which a more complete survey of the subject can be presented.

Before proceeding to this generalisation, we shall discuss one final application. It deals with the experience of the Netherlands Central Planning Committee (a Government Committee advising on matters of the Central Planning Bureau); and it will be considered here in general, rather than in numerical, terms. In all cases in which members of this Committee advised the Bureau to revise its preliminary forecasts, this amounted to an advice to predict a smaller change. This was not as bad as it may seem, for the advice as such was correct in about one half of the cases. The question arises whether it is appropriate to revise the forecasts in the manner indicated. There is an argument which suggests that such proposals should be rejected. For suppose that the reduction proposed by the Committee is of the proportionate type; i.e., there exists a positive scalar $k < 1$ such that the Committee's $\mathbf{s}_e$ equals k times the Bureau's $\mathbf{s}_e$. Then the failure correlation is the same for both, but the Committee's b_2 (the coefficient in the regression of $\mathbf{s}$ on $\mathbf{s}_e$) is larger than that of the Bureau. Since the Bureau's b_2 is already > 1 and hence too large (cf. 8.4.6), we must conclude that its own forecasts will have a higher success value.

However, the assumption of a proportional reduction proposed by the Committee is not very plausible. Most of the Bureau's forecasts underestimated the actual changes, and hence, if the Committee's advice to predict a smaller change was correct in 50 per cent of the cases, it seems rather obvious that these proposals were concentrated at those forecasts which were relatively sizable. It can then be argued that accepting these proposals would increase the failure correlation, since this would change the forecasts in such a way that the ratios of predicted to actual changes have a smaller range. It is then no longer obvious that the Bureau's original forecasts have a higher success, for the advantage of a better regression slope may be compensated by the disadvantage of a lower failure correlation. Also, it should be admitted that, so far, we considered only two alternatives; viz., accepting either all, or none, of the proposals. It may seem self-evident that the best procedure is to accept all those proposals which would lead to a smaller numerical difference between prediction and actual change. But this remains to be seen. Let us therefore consider the numerator of the failure of $\mathbf{s}_e$,

$$(\mathbf{s}_e - \mathbf{s})'\mathbf{F}(\mathbf{s}_e - \mathbf{s}).$$

If the failure matrix is diagonal, this numerator is a weighted sum of squares of the components of the forecasting error in the additive structure, the weights having all the same sign. In that case a numerical reduction of any component of $\mathbf{s}_e - \mathbf{s}$ is desirable, irrespective of the question whether the error component obtains a different sign. For the alternative case, in which the failure matrix is not diagonal, it is sufficient to consider an example; say, $n = 2$ and

$$-\mathbf{F} = \begin{bmatrix} 1 & -0.9 \\ -0.9 & 1 \end{bmatrix}.$$

Take further for the forecasting error $\mathbf{s}_e - \mathbf{s} = \{1 \quad 1\}$. The numerator of the failure of $\mathbf{s}_e$ is then equal to 0.2, apart from sign. Suppose also that it is suggested to change the forecast of the second component of $\mathbf{s}$ from 1 to a. The numerator of the failure becomes then (apart from sign)

$$1 - 1.8\,a + a^2,$$

the minimum of which is 0.19, which is reached at $a = 0.9$; and it exceeds the level 0.2 mentioned above whenever a is outside the interval (0.8, 1). Clearly, the non-diagonality of $\mathbf{F}$ implies that the elimination of the second component of the prediction error is far from desirable; replacing $\mathbf{s}_e - \mathbf{s} = \{1 \quad 1\}$ by $\{1 \quad 0\}$ increases the failure five-fold! This holds more generally: If the failure matrix is not of the diagonal type (and there is no reason why it should be), then a reduction of one particular component of the prediction error $\mathbf{s}_e - \mathbf{s}$, the other components remaining the same, does not necessarily lead to a failure reduction. It may be that it is better to raise the component than to reduce it. To take again the above example, if the original error $\mathbf{s}_e - \mathbf{s}$ equals $\{1 \quad \tfrac{1}{2}\}$, then the failure is reduced, not by lowering the second component, but by raising it up till the level 0.9; given, of course, the value 1 of the first component. This effect is simply due to the fact that, if $\mathbf{F}$ is not diagonal, the components of the error $\mathbf{s}_e - \mathbf{s}$ may compensate each other *via* their influence on the decision error; cf. 8.4.5.

This result has not only implications for the question whether the suggestions of the Central Planning Committee should be adopted or not, but also for the analysis of the revisions of the Dutch preliminary forecasts in Section 3.2. There, we considered all revisions separately; here, we find that it is preferable to consider them combined in the light of the relevant failure matrix.

8.5. The Loss of Welfare due to Imperfect Predictions (2)

8.5.1. Not knowing the multiplicative structure of the constraints is obviously the more general case, especially when the equality $R_e = R$ is interpreted in an exact, not approximate, manner. There is little need to give numerous examples of under or overestimation of multiplicative coefficients, since they occur in abundance. World reformers are frequently sure of the great effectiveness of one particular instrument with respect to some important noncontrolled variable, while being equally sure that other instruments are practically without influence. This amounts to an R_e which consists of many zeros and one or two very large elements. Another example is that of the insufficient "weight" attached by the traders of Chapter VI to the inertia of recent changes in their buying prices, together with the excessive weight attached to observed recent changes in prices of higher markets. The corresponding coefficients are not, of course, elements of R for these traders, since they belong to variables which are not controlled by them. Nevertheless, they may be coefficients in an equation system the reduced form of which is $y = Rx + s$; and in that case they may give rise to an $R_e \neq R$.

If the policy-maker does not know the multiplicative structure of his constraints, then he does not know his Tinbergen surfaces either. Also, it is no longer reasonable to assume that he knows the additive structure belonging to the preceding period, s_{-1}; for its derivation from lagged values, $s_{-1} = y_{-1} - R_{-1}x_{-1}$, requires knowledge of R_{-1}, which is in practice not very much different from knowledge of R. Clearly, this affects the usefulness of the concepts of success and failure, since it is no longer permissible to say that the policy-maker is able to reach a zero success (or unit failure) by acting under the no-change assumption $s = s_{-1}$. We can, however, still use the concept of loss of welfare,

$$\hat{w} - w[R_e, s_e],$$

for this quantity is independent of s_{-1}.

The approach is then a straightforward application of Theorem 3, which states that the loss is a quadratic expression in the decision error $x - x^0$. Let us write for the errors of forecasting

$$dR = R_e - R; \quad ds = s_e - s, \tag{8.104}$$

and for their elements: dr_{jk}, ds_j. Just as we did in 8.4.5, we can say that the decision error $x - x^0$ is, under the assumption that x maximises w if the constraints were $y = R_e x + s_e$, identical with the instrument change according to the optimal reaction functions if the constraints would really change from $y = Rx + s$ to $y = R_e x + s_e$. But there is a difference with the situation described in 8.4.5. There, we had

$$x - x^0 = -(x\cdot)(s_e - s) = -(x\cdot)\, ds;$$

i.e., we had a linear relation between decision and forecasting errors, which is exact. Here, we have no exact linear relation between $x - x^0$ and the prediction errors dR, ds, because the optimal reaction functions are not linear in R. If the forecasting errors are not too large, however, we can approximate by means of a linear function and write

$$x_h - \overset{0}{x}_h \approx \sum_j \sum_k \frac{\partial x_h}{\partial r_{jk}} dr_{jk} + \sum_j \frac{\partial x_h}{\partial s_j} ds_j;$$

or, using Theorem 2a,

$$x_h - \overset{0}{x}_h \approx -\sum_j (\cdot x)_{jh} \{\sum_k \overset{0}{x}_k dr_{jk} + ds_j\} - \sum_k (xx)_{kh} \sum_j \overset{0}{\lambda}_j dr_{jk},$$

where $\overset{0}{\lambda}_j$ is the j-th Lagrange multiplier (= the marginal welfare of y_j) in the point of the maximum. In matrix notation:

$$x - x^0 \approx -(x\cdot)[dRx^0 + ds] - (xx)\, dR'\lambda^0. \tag{8.105}$$

Substituting this into (8.72), we find immediately

THEOREM 3d. *Suppose that the Assumptions* C1 *and* P3 *are satisfied and that the optimal reaction functions* (8.63) *exist. Then, neglecting terms of the third and higher degree in the errors of forecasting, the loss of welfare due to the prediction* R_e, s_e *of the constraint parameters* R, s *is the sum of three components*:

$$\hat{w} - w[\mathsf{R}_e, \mathsf{s}_e] \approx L_o + L_u + L_m, \tag{8.106}$$

viz., the source component:

$$L_o = -\tfrac{1}{2}(d\mathsf{R}\mathsf{x}^0 + d\mathsf{s})'\mathsf{F}(d\mathsf{R}\mathsf{x}^0 + d\mathsf{s}), \tag{8.107}$$

the substitution component:

$$L_u = -\tfrac{1}{2}\lambda^{0\prime}d\mathsf{R}(\mathsf{xx})\,d\mathsf{R}'\lambda^0, \tag{8.108}$$

and the mixed component:

$$L_m = -(d\mathsf{R}\mathsf{x}^0 + d\mathsf{s})'(\cdot\mathsf{x})\,d\mathsf{R}'\lambda^0, \tag{8.109}$$

where $d\mathsf{R}$, $d\mathsf{s}$ *are the forecasting errors* $\mathsf{R}_e - \mathsf{R}$ *and* $\mathsf{s}_e - \mathsf{s}$, *respectively, and* λ^0 *that marginal welfare vector of the noncontrolled variables which is attained if* $\mathsf{x} = \mathsf{x}^0$. *The source and substitution components are both nonnegative*:

$$L_o \geqq 0; \quad L_u \geqq 0, \tag{8.110}$$

and the mixed component satisfies the inequality

$$L_m^2 \leqq 4\,L_o L_u. \tag{8.111}$$

There is only little to be added to this result. If we would prefer to have a less approximate result than (8.106), it would be necessary to analyse higher-order derivatives of the optimal reaction functions; but we refrain from doing so here. The interpretation of the three components is rather obvious. The decision error $\mathsf{x} - \mathsf{x}^0$ consists of a source effect,

$$-(\mathsf{x}\cdot)\,[d\mathsf{R}\mathsf{x}^0 + d\mathsf{s}],$$

and a substitution effect,

$$-(\mathsf{xx})\,d\mathsf{R}'\lambda^0;$$

and hence the loss of welfare, being a quadratic form in the decision error, must be a quadratic form in the source effect plus a quadratic form in the substitution effect plus a bilinear form in the two effects. As is to be expected, the matrix of the source component is $-\frac{1}{2}$ times the failure matrix. That of the substitution component is $-\frac{1}{2}(\mathsf{xx})$, whereas the inverse $(\mathsf{xx})^{-1}$ appeared to be relevant for the decision errors of Theorem 3. To understand this difference, take the simple case of one constraint ($n = 1$); then L_u is, apart from a constant ($\frac{1}{2}\lambda_1^2$), equal to

$$-\sum_h \sum_k (xx)_{hk} dr_{1h} dr_{1k}.$$

Suppose further that x_1 and x_2 are substitutes, so that $(xx)_{12} > 0$. Then the contribution to L_u of the two terms for which $(h, k) = (1, 2)$ and $(2, 1)$ is negative if the errors dr_{11} and dr_{12} have equal signs, positive if the errors have opposite sign; and *mutatis mutandis* for complementarity. This is indeed intuitively plausible, because the substitution effect of dr's with equal signs implies that the decision error caused by this double error will be relatively small if there is substitution rather than complementarity. As to the contribution to L_u of the terms with equal subscripts, $-(xx)_{hh} dr_{1h}^2$, this is clearly always positive. Given the error dr_{1h}, the contribution is larger if the policy-maker's response according to the optimal reaction function for x_h is larger; which is obvious, too.

8.5.2. It is clear that the substitution and the source components, being both positive (at least nonnegative), reinforce each other; but the mixed component may work either way. This third component, too, is a quadratic form in prediction errors; it is not a definite one, however, for its matrix is the rectangular matrix of slopes of the Tinbergen surfaces of instruments. Naturally, we should not have much hope that it can easily reduce the loss of welfare to zero (except for terms of the third order), for its algebraic minimum is $-2\sqrt{L_o L_u}$; and this makes $\hat{w} - w[\mathsf{R}_e, \mathsf{s}_e] \approx 0$ only if $L_o = L_u$.

Consider then the following situation. Suppose that the multiplicative structure of the constraints of the prediction period and that of the period before are the same, $\mathsf{R} = \mathsf{R}_{-1}$, so that these constraints are

$$(8.112) \qquad \mathsf{y} = \mathsf{R}\mathsf{x} + \mathsf{s}; \quad \mathsf{y}_{-1} = \mathsf{R}\mathsf{x}_{-1} + \mathsf{s}_{-1},$$

respectively. We shall interpret x and y as variable, but x_{-1}, y_{-1} as those vectors of fixed numbers that have been actually realised. Suppose then that the policy-maker stands just at the beginning of the prediction period, that the predicted constraint for this period is $\mathsf{y} = \mathsf{R}_e\mathsf{x} + \mathsf{s}_e$, and that the constraint of the past period, as he sees it now, has the same multiplicative structure. In other words, these two constraints as imagined by the policy-maker at this particular moment are

$$y = R_e x + s_e; \quad y_{-1} = R_e x_{-1} + (s_{-1})_e, \tag{8.113}$$

respectively. Needless to say, the estimated additive structure $(s_{-1})_e$ is not necessarily the same as the prediction of s_{-1} which the policy-maker had to make when deciding on x_{-1}; in other words, $(s_{-1})_e \neq \neq (s_e)_{-1}$ in general. The difference between both is that, in the case of $(s_{-1})_e$, he can make use of the information that became available during the recent period. In fact, when comparing (8.113) with (8.112) and recalling that x_{-1}, y_{-1} are vectors of fixed numbers, we find

$$(s_{-1})_e = s_{-1} + (R - R_e) x_{-1}. \tag{8.114}$$

Suppose further that the effectiveness of all instruments with respect to all noncontrolled variables is proportionally under or overestimated:

$$R_e = \zeta_R R, \tag{8.115}$$

ζ_R being a positive scalar. For $\zeta_R < 1$ this would mean that, in the policy-maker's eyes, all coefficients are proportionately reduced in the direction of zero, relative to their true values. Combining (8.114) and (8.115), we find

$$(s_{-1})_e = s_{-1} + (1 - \zeta_R) R x_{-1}. \tag{8.116}$$

We suppose also that there is a proportionate under or overestimation with respect to the change in the additive structure:

$$s_e - (s_{-1})_e = \zeta_s (s - s_{-1}), \tag{8.117}$$

ζ_s being a positive scalar.This assumption is obviously a generalisation of the corresponding assumption (8.78) of 8.4.4. Finally, we suppose that the instruments are "purely instrumental" in the sense that they are not arguments of the welfare function. This implies

$$a = \mathbf{0}; \quad A = \mathbf{0}; \quad C = \mathbf{0} \tag{8.118}$$

for the coefficient vectors and matrices of the function (8.5).

Following (8.69) and (8.70), we find for the optimal instrument values of the prediction period:

(8.119) $$x^0 = -(R'BR)^{-1}R'(b + Bs).$$[1]

The decision taken under the assumption that the constraints are given by (8.113) rather than by (8.112) is

(8.120) $$x = -(R_e'BR_e)^{-1}R_e'(b + Bs_e) = \frac{-1}{\zeta_R}(R'BR)^{-1}R'(b + Bs_e),$$

where use has been made of (8.115). As to s_e, it follows from (8.117) and (8.116) that this prediction equals

$$s_e = \zeta_s s + (1 - \zeta_s)s_{-1} + (1 - \zeta_R)Rx_{-1}.$$

Combining this with (8.119) and (8.120), we find

(8.121) $$x = \frac{1}{\zeta_R}[\zeta_s x^0 + (1 - \zeta_s)x_{-1}^0 - (1 - \zeta_R)x_{-1}],$$

where x_{-1}^0 is given by the right-hand side of (8.119) with s replaced by s_{-1}. Since $R = R_{-1}$[cf. (8.112)], x_{-1}^0 is simply the optimal vector of instrument values of the preceding period, as its notation indicates. The result (8.121) implies that the decision taken, x, is a weighted average of the present and the preceding optimal decisions and of the preceding actual instrument values. The weights,

$$\zeta_s/\zeta_R, \qquad (1 - \zeta_s)/\zeta_R, \qquad -(1 - \zeta_R)/\zeta_R,$$

have sum unity; but they are not necessarily nonnegative. The geometric picture of Fig. 8.10 is instructive in this connection. The three vectors x^0, x_{-1}^0 and x_{-1} can be represented by three points in an m-dimensional instrument space, viz. X^0, X_{-1}^0 and X_{-1}, respectively. Since the actual decision, x, is a weighted average with sum of weights equal to 1, its point (X) must lie in the two-dimensional plane determined by these three points. This plane is sketched in Fig. 8.10. If it is true that all three weights are positive, X lies inside the triangle $X_{-1}X_{-1}^0X^0$. It is rather plausible that the weights of x^0 and x_{-1}^0 are positive, for this corresponds with underestimation of the changes in the additive structure: $0 < \zeta_s < 1$. It is not so self-evident, however, that the weight of x_{-1} is positive, since this would imply $\zeta_R > 1$ and

[1] Note that the existence of the inverse $(R'BR)^{-1}$ requires $m \leq n$; i.e., there should be as many noncontrolled variables as instruments, or more. This condition is rather easy to understand: if there are more instruments than noncontrolled variables, and if the instruments are excluded from the set of arguments of the preference function, then the level of maximum welfare is reached for more than one set of instrument values.

hence exclude the possibility of an underestimation of the effectiveness of the instruments. In fact, when re-writing (8.121) in the form

$$\zeta_R \mathrm{x} + (1 - \zeta_R)\mathrm{x}_{-1} = \zeta_S \mathrm{x}^0 + (1 - \zeta_S)\mathrm{x}^0_{-1}, \tag{8.122}$$

we see that the case $\zeta_R < 1$ has even a certain merit: it implies that a weighted average of the successive actual decisions is identical with a weighted average of the successive optimal decisions, all four weights being positive. In geometric terms, this corresponds with the point $\bar{X}$ of Fig. 8.10. This result suggests the actual decisions may be acceptable "on the average" when there is an underestimation of both types;

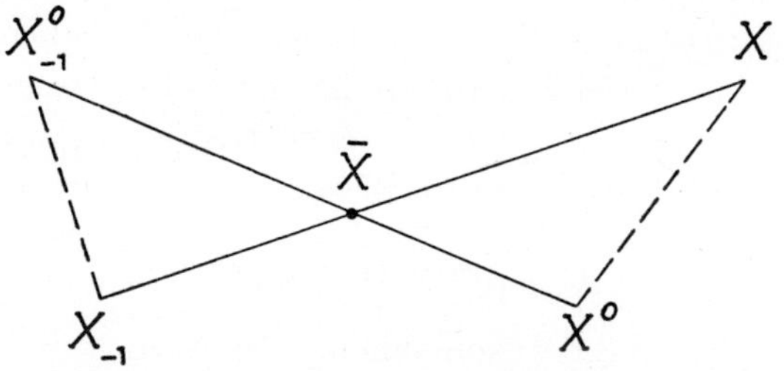

Fig. 8.10. Decision errors in two successive periods under assumptions of proportionality and of "pureness" of instruments

especially so if $\zeta_R = \zeta_S$, for the two pairs of weights are then identical. But we should be careful, since "on the average" is not sufficient; there may be a problem of variance. This we will now consider.

8.5.3. Consider the following specific question. Take ζ_S fixed and suppose $0 < \zeta_S < 1$; is it then possible to indicate the size of the appropriate compensating error (if any) in the multiplicative structure such that the loss of welfare is reduced to zero (except for higher-order terms)? In such a case, clearly, the mixed component must be negative (cf. the first paragraph of 8.5.2), for the presence of errors in both the additive and the multiplicative structure implies in general positive source and substitution components.

Within the present framework, it is hardly possible to give an affirmative answer, since only one parameter (ζ_R) can be adjusted. Suppose, however, that there is only one instrument ($m = 1$). Then, as can be easily verified, (8.121) gives $x = x^0$ (in scalar form) if and only if

$$1 - \zeta_R = (1 - \zeta_S)\frac{x^0 - x^0_{-1}}{x^0 - x_{-1}}. \tag{8.123}$$

This means that, if the change in the additive structure is underestimated, there exists a number ζ_R such that the consequences of this error are reduced to zero if the policy-maker takes $R_e = \zeta_R R$ instead of R for the multiplicative structure (provided the present optimum differs from the preceding actual instrument value, $x^0 \neq x_{-1}$). More specifically, this "compensating" error amounts to an underestimation of the effectiveness of the instrument, $\zeta_R < 1$, if the optimal instrument change as measured from the preceding actual value $(x^0 - x_{-1})$ is about equal to the same change but measured from the preceding optimum $(x^0 - x^0_{-1})$. The relationship of these two alternative differences with the concepts considered in 8.4.4 will be obvious.

This possibility of a complete reduction of the consequences of $\zeta_s < 1$ does not exist in general when there are several instruments; but the following special cases are at least instructive. First, assume $\zeta_R = 1$. This takes us back to the analysis of Section 8.4 and we obtain

$$(8.124) \qquad \mathbf{x} = \zeta_s \mathbf{x}^0 + (1 - \zeta_s)\mathbf{x}^0_{-1},$$

which implies that the decision taken is between the two successive optima; this amounts to the case $X = \bar{X}$ in Fig. 8.10. The policy-maker is then always "behind the events." Second, take $\zeta_R = \zeta_s$. Then

$$(8.125) \qquad \mathbf{x} - \mathbf{x}^0 = -\frac{1 - \zeta_s}{\zeta_s}(\mathbf{x} - \mathbf{x}^0)_{-1},$$

which describes the decision error as negatively proportional to the decision error of the preceding period. For whatever ζ_s in the interval (0, 1), successive decision errors have then alternating signs; but there is an important difference between the alternatives $0 < \zeta_s < \frac{1}{2}$ and $\frac{1}{2} < \zeta_s < 1$. In the former case – that of "gross underestimation" —the oscillatory movements of the errors have an increasing amplitude, so that $\zeta_R = \zeta_s$ is then a very poor forecasting method. In geometric terms, this means that the distance between X and X^0 is always larger than that between X_{-1} and X^0_{-1}; cf. the broken lines of Fig. 8.10. In the second case the oscillations are damped with zero as limit, which is surely an acceptable situation.

Needless to say, this result is determined by the idealised assumptions which we have made. If ζ_R is not equal to ζ_s, we should write

$$(8.126) \qquad \mathbf{x} - \mathbf{x}^0 = -\frac{1 - \zeta_R}{\zeta_R}(\mathbf{x} - \mathbf{x}^0)_{-1} + \frac{\zeta_s - \zeta_R}{\zeta_R}\Delta\mathbf{x}^0,$$

where Δx^0 is the difference between successive optimal decisions, $x^0 - x^0_{-1}$. To make further progress, it is necessary to make certain assumptions about the time pattern of this first difference. The simplest assumption is the following: the successive vectors $\ldots, \Delta x^0_{-1}, \Delta x^0, \ldots$ are stochastic and distributed independently with zero mean and the same finite covariance matrix $E = [e_{hk}]$. The second term in the right-hand side of (8.126) can then be regarded as a disturbance vector with zero mean and covariance matrix

$$\left(\frac{\zeta_s - \zeta_R}{\zeta_R}\right)^2 E;$$

and the decision errors, which now satisfy a multidimensional first-order Markov scheme, have also zero mean and the following covariance matrix:

$$\mathscr{E}[(x - x^0)(x - x^0)'] = \tag{8.127}$$

$$= \frac{1}{1 - \left(\frac{1 - \zeta_R}{\zeta_R}\right)^2} \left(\frac{\zeta_s - \zeta_R}{\zeta_R}\right)^2 E = \frac{(\zeta_s - \zeta_R)^2}{2\zeta_R - 1} E,$$

provided $\zeta_R > \frac{1}{2}$. If $\zeta_R \leq \frac{1}{2}$, the process (8.126) is not stationary, so that the decision errors would have an indefinitely increasing variance; this will be excluded. Also, it is assumed in (8.127) that initial conditions can be disregarded. They vanish in the course of time if $\zeta_R > \frac{1}{2}$.

The covariance matrix (8.127) enables us to derive the parent loss of welfare by means of Theorem 3:

$$\mathscr{E}(\hat{w} - w_x) = -\tfrac{1}{2}\mathscr{E}[(x - x^0)'(xx)^{-1}(x - x^0)] = \tag{8.128}$$

$$= -\frac{1}{2}\frac{(\zeta_s - \zeta_R)^2}{2\zeta_R - 1} \sum_h \sum_k (xx)^{hk} e_{hk},$$

where $(xx)^{hk}$ is an element of the inverse matrix $(xx)^{-1}$. Since the double sum is negative and constant with respect to ζ_R, the parent loss is minimised if the ratio before the summation signs is minimised; i.e., if

$$\begin{aligned} \zeta_R &= \zeta_s && \text{if } \zeta_s > \tfrac{1}{2} \\ &= 1 - \zeta_s && \text{if } \zeta_s < \tfrac{1}{2}. \end{aligned} \tag{8.129}$$

This remarkable result, which is independent of preferences and constraints, implies that the consequences of underestimation of the changes in the additive structure of the constraints, $0 < \zeta_s < 1$, can be reduced if the effectiveness of instruments is likewise underestimated, but in a particular manner. As long as the former underestimation is not too large ($\zeta_s > \frac{1}{2}$), the latter should be numerically equal; however, if the former becomes larger and larger ($\zeta_s < \frac{1}{2}$), the appropriate underestimation of the instrumental effectiveness is correspondingly reduced. It is not difficult to make this result intuitively plausible. Consider again the autoregressive scheme (8.126). A reduction of ζ_R from the unit level in the direction of ζ_s is favourable in so far as it reduces the covariance matrix of the vector $(\zeta_s/\zeta_R - 1)\Delta \mathbf{x}^0$, but unfavourable in so far as it raises the multiplicative parameter $-(1/\zeta_R - 1)$ numerically. The first effect is dominant up till $\zeta_R = \zeta_s$ as long as $\zeta_s > \frac{1}{2}$, for $\zeta_R = \zeta_s$ implies zero disturbances while keeping the multiplicative parameter below unity in absolute sense. When ζ_s becomes smaller and smaller, however, the effect of changing values of ζ_R on the disturbance vector becomes smaller too; in the extreme case $\zeta_s = 0$ this vector is $-\Delta \mathbf{x}^0$, which is independent of ζ_R. Obviously, the unfavourable influence of a reduction of ζ_R on the multiplicative parameter becomes then more important, thus leading to a higher optimal ζ_R.

If $\zeta_s > \frac{1}{2}$ and $\zeta_R = \zeta_s$, then the parent loss (8.128) is exactly zero. This is, of course, a consequence of our simplifying assumptions. We can obtain some further insight by assuming that (8.126) does not hold exactly, but that—due to the lack of validity of some of our assumptions—an additional disturbance vector $\mathbf{e}^*$ is necessary:

$$(8.130) \qquad \mathbf{x} - \mathbf{x}^0 = -\frac{1 - \zeta_R}{\zeta_R}(\mathbf{x} - \mathbf{x}^0)_{-1} + \left[\frac{\zeta_s - \zeta_R}{\zeta_R}\Delta \mathbf{x}^0 + \mathbf{e}^*\right].$$

Suppose then that the successive vectors..., $\mathbf{e}^*_{-1}, \mathbf{e}^*, \ldots$ are stochastic and distributed independently with zero mean and the same finite covariance matrix $\mathbf{E}^*$; further, that they are independent of all vectors ..., $\Delta \mathbf{x}^0_{-1}, \Delta \mathbf{x}^0, \ldots$; finally, that $\mathbf{E}^* = k\mathbf{E}$ for some positive scalar k. The last assumption in particular may seem quite drastic, but it is not entirely unrealistic. As far as the diagonal elements (the variances) are concerned, it means that the degree to which (8.126) is inaccurate for the separate components of the decision error tends to increase with the magnitude of the corresponding first difference of the optimal decision. These assumptions then, together with the earlier one on $\Delta \mathbf{x}^0$, imply that the covariance matrix of the term in square brackets of (8.130) is

$$\left[\left(\frac{\zeta_s - \zeta_R}{\zeta_R}\right)^2 + k\right] \mathsf{E},$$

so that the parent loss (8.128) is to be replaced by

$$(8.131) \qquad \mathscr{E}(\hat{w} - w_{\mathsf{x}}) = -\tfrac{1}{2}\frac{(1+k)\,\zeta_R^2 - 2\zeta_s\zeta_R + \zeta_s^2}{2\zeta_R - 1}\sum_h\sum_k (xx)^{hk}\, e_{hk}.$$

Writing $\zeta_R^{(k)}$ for the minimising ζ_R, we find

$$(8.132) \qquad (1+k)\zeta_R^{(k)}(1-\zeta_R^{(k)}) = \zeta_s(1-\zeta_s) = \zeta_R^{(0)}(1-\zeta_R^{(0)}),$$

$\zeta_R^{(0)}$ being given by (8.129). Since $k > 0$ and $\zeta_R^{(k)} > \frac{1}{2}$, it follows that $\zeta_R^{(0)} < \zeta_R^{(k)} < 1$. In other words, there should still be underestimation of the effectiveness of instruments, but its optimal size is less than in the case where (8.126) holds exactly, without $\mathbf{e}^*$.

In summary, we can say that the welfare consequences of change underestimation in the additive structure of the constraints can be reduced by acting on the assumption that the instruments are less effective than they are actually. This conclusion is supported in an intuitive manner by the following argument: Underestimation of additive changes induces the policy-maker to take measures which are too small; underestimation of the effectiveness of instruments induces the policy-maker to take measures which are too large; hence the two errors tend to compensate each other. Still, there are several qualifications. One of them deals with the proportionality assumptions (8.115) and (8.117); the analysis of Section 8.4 showed that the case of approximate rather than exact proportionality is not without consequences. Another is that of the purely instrumental character of the instruments. It is not difficult to understand why this assumption is necessary, for the above heuristic argument pre-supposes that the policy-maker is indifferent with respect to his instruments except in so far as they affect noncontrolled variables.[1]

[1] Note that the absence of instruments from the set of arguments of the welfare function can always be enforced in a trivial manner; viz., by introducing "noncontrolled" variables $y_{n+1}, y_{n+2}, \ldots$ each of which is identical with an instrument that is not purely instrumental. We can then replace the latter x's by the corresponding y's as arguments of the welfare function and enlarge the constraints $\mathbf{y} = \mathbf{R}\mathbf{x} + \mathbf{s}$ by including these identities. There is no formal objection against this procedure; but the coefficients of these additional identities are of course of a particular nature. They are $\pm$ 1 or 0, and the assumption of under or overestimation of the effectiveness of instruments with respect to these "noncontrolled" variables is unrealistic.

8.5.4. The twofold feature of underestimation of changes in $\mathbf{s}$ and underestimation of the effectiveness of instruments is of special relevance in connection with statistical *estimation* problems; which is our next subject.

First, we observe that the assumption of given matrices of fixed coefficients $\mathbf{R}_e$, $\mathbf{s}_e$, although highly relevant from the "choice animal's" point of view, is by no means the sole reasonable assumption from the "information animal's" standpoint. It is indeed relevant for the former in so far as $\mathbf{R}_e \approx \mathbf{R}$, $\mathbf{s}_e \approx \mathscr{E}\mathbf{s}$ is an adequate approximation (cf. Theorem 1); and the decision-maker may consider the information which he obtains in this way the best he can get, and act accordingly. The "information animal," however, will realise that the coefficients of the constraints which he uses for prediction purposes are obtained by means of some statistical procedure. So he may ask whether it is possible to derive results on the *parent loss of welfare* in the population of all possible estimated coefficients obtained by the same procedure; and he may hope that in this way he can arrive at certain statements which enable him to make a discrimination between various statistical methods according to their quality for decision purposes. This can be regarded as the decision-theoretical treatment of the sharpness criterion for point estimates; cf. 6.2.2. We shall approach this problem by confining ourselves first to the substitution component; which amounts to saying that the errors in $\mathbf{R}$ are supposed to be compensated in the Slutsky-sense, $d\mathbf{R}\mathbf{x}^0 + d\mathbf{s} \equiv \mathbf{0}$. The parent loss of welfare is then equal, apart from third-order terms, to the parent value of the substitution component, Λ_u say; and this is given by

$$(8.133) \qquad \Lambda_u = -\tfrac{1}{2} \sum_h \sum_k (xx)_{hk} \sum_i \sum_j \lambda_i^0 \lambda_j^0 \mathscr{E}(dr_{ih} dr_{jk}),$$

where dr_{ih} is to be regarded here as the sampling error of the coefficient r_{ih}. Let us then write

$$(8.134) \qquad r_h^0 = \sum_i \lambda_i^0 r_{ih}.$$

This is nothing else than the effect of an infinitesimal change in x_h on w *via* all noncontrolled variables in the point of the maximum. So we may call r_h^0 the *aggregate effectiveness* of x_h in this point.[1] Combining (8.134) with (8.133) gives

[1] Note that this is an "overall-concept" comparable with the overall-inferiority of 8.3.5. Here, we consider the welfare effect of an instrumental change *via* all non-

$$(8.135) \qquad \Lambda_u = -\tfrac{1}{2} \Sigma \Sigma (xx)_{hk}\, \mathscr{E}(dr_h^0 dr_k^0),$$

which is the mean value of a positive-definite quadratic expression in the errors of the aggregate effectiveness of the various instruments. Obviously, the best statistical method is the one which minimises this mean—given, of course, the quadratic preference and linear constraint assumptions and the further assumption that the sampling errors $\mathbf{dR}$ are compensated in the Slutsky-sense. The latter assumption will be removed in 8.5.5.

Several interesting things can be noted about the quadratic form (8.135). First, its matrix is not independent of the policy-maker's preferences, nor of his constraints. It is easily seen that a given second moment $\mathscr{E}(dr_h^0)^2$ is less serious if the corresponding substitution term $(xx)_{hh}$ is less negative, i.e., if constraints and preferences are such that the policy-maker does not react sharply to a compensated change in the effectiveness of x_h; similarly, a positive cross-moment of the errors dr_h^0 and dr_k^0 is favourable if x_h and x_k are substitutes, unfavourable if they are complementary. Secondly, the vector of the quadratic form (8.135), viz., that of the error in the aggregate effectiveness of the various instruments, is not the same at different occasions even when all underlying sampling errors dr_{ih} are the same. This follows from the fact that these errors are to be multiplied by λ's, which assume different values when the point of the maximum shifts.

The question arises whether we can say anything about familiar statistical methods in relation to the requirement of minimising Λ_u. Let us consider then in particular the method of least-squares, which has been considered earlier in Section 6.2. It can be shown (for the proof we refer to the Appendix of this chapter, Section 8.A) that this method is "best linear unbiased," which means the following. Suppose that the assumptions (*i*), (*ii*), (*iii*) and (*v*) of Section 6.2 are satisfied;[1] and consider the class of all linear unbiased estimation methods, i.e., the class of all estimators of the vector of multiplicative parameters ($\boldsymbol{\beta}$ in the notation of 6.2.3) which are unbiased and linear in the dependent variable. Then the mean value of any quadratic form in the least-squares sampling errors, for whatever positive-definite matrix of

controlled variables; there, we considered the effect of a combined change of all sources on an instrument or noncontrolled variable. In both cases the Lagrange multipliers play a determining rôle.

[1] Cf. also p. 208, n. 2. If assumption (*ii*) must be replaced by the more general assumption (*vi*), the same argument can be applied with least-squares replaced by generalised least-squares.

this form, is smaller than the same form in the sampling errors of any other linear unbiased estimator. Let us disregard for a moment the adjectives "linear" and "unbiased;" these criteria will be discussed in 8.5.5. So "best" remains, and it means that least-squares minimises the mean value of every positive-definite quadratic form in the sampling errors. Comparing this with (8.135), we can conclude that the method of least-squares has indeed the required optimal property for any policy-maker whose preferences are quadratic and who faces linear constraints; at least, provided we confine ourselves to the substitution component and to linear unbiased estimation methods.[1]

This result is also relevant for the estimation of simultaneous equations, although not in the sense that single-stage least-squares has optimal properties for decision purposes. We have written the policy-maker's constraints in a reduced form, and so we should ask whether least-squares applied to the reduced form is optimal and, if this is true, what this implies for the estimation of structural equations. When realising that the explanatory variables of reduced-form equations are all predetermined, it is easily seen that the first question can be answered affirmatively, provided the system is not characterised by over-identification. If this proviso is fulfilled, there is an exact correspondence between the least-squares estimates of the reduced form and the two-stage least-squares estimates of the structural equations, provided the latter estimates exist (which means in the present case that there should be just-identification throughout). As soon as one of the equations is overidentified, we have the complication that least-squares applied to the reduced form does not take account of all available *a priori* restrictions. Hence, in that case least-squares estimation does not lead to minimal Λ_u. Two-stage least-squares, however, when applied to such an overidentified equation, does take account of

[1] It is highly interesting that this justification of the method of least-squares was anticipated in an intuitive manner by Gauss in 1839. Originally, Gauss had advocated this method on the basis of what we would call now the maximum-likelihood principle, but then he changed his mind: "I must consider it of less importance to derive that value of an unknown quantity of which the probability is maximal (for this probability is infinitely small anyhow); instead, I consider it more appropriate to choose that value which is such that, if one sticks to it, one has the smallest disadvantage in the long run." He then proceeds to consider a quadratic loss function and continues: "To choose a quadratic function is purely arbitrary, and this arbitrariness is inherent to the problem. The quadratic has, as is well-known, extraordinarily great advantages; but otherwise one can choose functions corresponding to other conditions, and this is indeed done in very special cases." See *Briefwechsel zwischen Gauss und Bessel* (Leipzig, 1880), pp. 523–524, and also E. T. Whittaker and G. Robinson, *The Calculus of Observations* (London-Glasgow, fourth ed., 1944), p. 224.

the overidentifying restrictions.[1] It is true, the way in which this is done is not exactly the same as that of other estimation methods, like limited-information maximum-likelihood, which have the same asymptotic covariance matrix. Nevertheless, it will be clear that these results, together with those of Sections 6.2 and 6.C, imply that—except possibly for the deviations just mentioned—two-stage least-squares applied to structural equations is an optimal estimation method with respect to the reduced form. It is not necessarily optimal with respect to the structural equation which is the immediate object of estimation; this has been argued before (cf. the end of Section 6.2). But the present analysis suggests that, for decision purposes, the reduced form is more important.

8.5.5. The analysis of 8.5.4 is subject to several qualifications. First, we confined ourselves to the substitution component, Λ_u. Second, we neglected the adjectives "linear" and "unbiased" when considering least-squares. Third, the assumptions underlying least-squares are rather restrictive, and so it is useful to take account of deviations from these assumptions.

Let us start with the restriction to linearity. It seems clear from the form (8.135) that there is no cogent reason for such a restriction; nevertheless, the following arguments suggest that it has some merits. First, linearity is simple, both computationally and conceptually. Second, if the estimator is not linear in the dependent variable, then it is not linear in the disturbances either. This means that the second-order sampling moments of the estimator will in general depend on moments of the disturbances of higher order than the second. This, in turn, has two effects: it reduces the computational simplicity of the moment matrix of the estimator; and, given the fact that the expression to be minimised, (8.135), depends on this moment matrix, the question of the superiority of such an alternative estimator depends on the higher moments of the disturbances. In the case of least-squares it is not necessary to make assumptions on moments beyond those of the second order. It follows, therefore, that the restriction to linearity can be

[1] This method does not take account of the restrictions on other equations than the one under consideration. So we should expect full-information methods (cf. 6.C.1 and 6.C.7) to lead to still smaller Λ_u. This aspect is neglected here. Another complication which is neglected is that of the aggregation implications when the structural equations are macroequations; and, more generally, that of specification errors. If the additional restrictions which a full-information method uses are the result of an incorrect specification, then it is of course not necessarily true that the Λ_u of such a method is smaller.

regarded as a gain in simplicity and validity; and that the price is a loss of sharpness as measured by the difference between the Λ_u of least-squares and the Λ_u of the sharpest method which is not characterised by the linearity restriction.

Our next problem is that of unbiasedness. This criterion was in rather high esteem until recently. At present, however, it is realised that it is not of great importance.[1] It is easy to see that this is a correct appraisal in the present context. For one thing, unbiasedness as such has nothing to do with either simplicity or validity; for another, it has little to do with sharpness. To see this, let us reconsider (8.135) and take for simplicity $m = n = 1$. Minimisation of Λ_u amounts then to minimisation of $\mathscr{E}(dr_{11}^2)$, not within the class of unbiased estimators, $\mathscr{E}dr_{11} = 0$, but without such a restriction. This means that a biased estimator is preferable to an unbiased estimator, whenever the variance of the latter exceeds the variance (about its mean) of the former by more than the square of the bias. More generally, with m, n possibly $\neq 1$, any biased estimator is preferable to least-squares if its Λ_u is smaller than the least-squares value, irrespective of the size of the bias. It will be noted, of course, that the bias must not be too large, for its contribution to Λ_u is necessarily positive.

An obvious question is then: If we confine ourselves, in accordance with the preceding remarks, to linear estimators, what is then the estimator which is optimal in the sense of the last paragraph? This question is considered in detail in the Appendix to this chapter (Section 8.B); here, we shall take the simplest case of an equation

$$y(t) = \beta x(t) + u(t), \tag{8.136}$$

where $x(t)$ for $t = 1, \ldots, T$ is a nonstochastic value taken by the single predetermined variable x, $y(t)$ a value taken by the dependent variable and $u(t)$ a disturbance. We shall assume, as in the classical case, that the disturbances have zero mean, $\mathscr{E}u(t) = 0$, that they have all the same variance, $\mathscr{E}u(t)^2 = \sigma^2$, and that the covariances vanish, $\mathscr{E}[u(t)u(t')] = 0$ for $t \neq t'$. Applying the general result of the Appendix, we find for the minimum-second-moment estimator of β:

$$b^0 = \frac{\Sigma xy}{\dfrac{\sigma^2}{\beta^2} + \Sigma x^2}, \tag{8.137}$$

[1] See e.g. L. J. Savage, *The Foundations of Statistics* (New York-London, 1954), pp. 244–245 and H. S. Houthakker, "The Specification Problem in Regression Analysis," *Econometrica*, Vol. 21 (1953), pp. 488–489 (abstract).

where the summation takes place over the T observations. The sampling moment of the second order of b^0 around β is

$$(8.138)\qquad S(b^0) = \frac{\sigma^2}{\dfrac{\sigma^2}{\beta^2} + \Sigma x^2}.$$

Comparing this with the corresponding moment of the least-squares squares estimator ($b = \Sigma xy/\Sigma x^2$),

$$(8.139)\qquad S(b) = \frac{\sigma^2}{\Sigma x^2},$$

we find for the "second-moment efficiency" of least-squares relative to b^0:

$$(8.140)\qquad \frac{S(b^0)}{S(b)} = \frac{\Sigma x^2}{\dfrac{\sigma^2}{\beta^2} + \Sigma x^2} \leq 1.$$

It follows that b^0 is "sharper" than the classical least-squares estimator. The question arises what is the price to be paid. Again, this is a double price. First, b^0 is less simple than b, not only because of the more complicated denominator, but also and especially because the additional term in the denominator is unknown. The ratio σ^2/β^2 can at most be estimated (e.g., by means of least-squares). This leads us immediately to the second disadvantage: if σ^2/β^2 is replaced by an estimate, this affects the validity of (8.138) as the sampling moment of the resulting estimator. So the rival of least-squares, (8.137), is inferior in two respects; it is superior in sharpness. This superiority should not be overestimated, though. Writing ϱ for the correlation between x and y (based on moments around zero, not about the means),

$$(8.141)\qquad \frac{T\sigma^2}{\beta^2 \Sigma x^2} = \frac{1 - \varrho^2}{\varrho^2},$$

we find

$$(8.142)\qquad \frac{S(b^0)}{S(b)} = \frac{\varrho^2}{\varrho^2 + \dfrac{1 - \varrho^2}{T}}.$$

This ratio will be close to 1, unless ϱ^2 and T are both very small.

It seems then natural to ask whether it is at least possible to formulate an estimator which is linear in the dependent variable, not necessarily unbiased, but the computation of which does not require knowledge of β. Obviously, such estimators exist; and they may be superior to least-squares. An example corresponding to (8.136) is $b' = \Sigma xy/(1 + \Sigma x^2)$. Since the ratio σ^2/β^2 may be equal to 1, either exactly or approximately, the second moment of b' around β may be smaller than the least-squares variance. But it is clear that this question of superiority depends on the unknown parameters. If we make alternative assumptions about these parameters, it appears that there are values for which the second moment of b' is larger than the variance of the least-squares b; it is shown in the Appendix (Section 8.B) that this holds more generally.

So the conclusion is that neither the restriction to linearity nor that to unbiasedness reduces the value of least-squares estimation very much. The final problem is then the restriction to the substitution component and the restrictiveness of the classical least-squares assumptions. There is a certain amount of arbitrariness as to the question which assumptions are to be generalised; but, given the fact that it is not necessary to generalise in Aitken's sense, [1] the most obvious assumption to be removed is that of the absence of errors of observation in predetermined variables. This, as will be argued below, leads us back to the remark made in the beginning of 8.5.4, viz., that the twofold feature of underestimation of changes in the additive structure of the constraints and underestimation of the effectiveness of instruments is important for problems of statistical estimation.

Obviously, the forecasting errors in the additive structure, $\mathbf{ds}$, are usually not such that the errors $\mathbf{dR}$ are compensated in the Slutsky-sense. It is impossible to give rules for the errors $\mathbf{ds}$ which are valid under all circumstances; but the empirical evidence gathered in the preceding chapters suggests that underestimation of changes is a dominant feature of $\mathbf{ds}$. Now we found in 8.5.2 and 8.5.3 that the welfare consequences of this error tend to be reduced if the effectiveness of the instruments is likewise underestimated. In statistical estimation, however, errors of measurement in predetermined variables achieve exactly this: they cause a bias of the least-squares estimator in the direction of zero—cf. 6.2.4. Needless to say, such a bias does not imply that the elements of $\mathbf{R}_e$ are all reduced proportionately relative to $\mathbf{R}$, as we assumed in 8.5.2; and besides the bias in the direction of zero, there are other effects of observational errors—cf. 6.2.4. Similarly,

[1] Cf. p. 487 n.

the underestimation of changes in the additive structure is in general not proportionate either. Still, the compensating effect of the tendency towards underestimating the effectiveness of instruments, resulting from a neglect of observational errors in least-squares estimation, may be of considerable importance; although it cannot be maintained, of course, that the occurrence of errors of compensating sign but of unknown size constitutes a final solution for all estimation problems.

The main conclusion from this analysis is not that least-squares estimation is perfect; but rather that it is difficult to defeat this method. The same conclusion holds with respect to two-stage least-squares estimation, provided we use this method to find the reduced form; though not necessarily if we are interested in the separate structural equations—cf. the end of Section 6.2.

8.5.6. So much for statistical estimation. For the decision-maker himself (the "choice animal"), the immediate problems have a somewhat different nature: he has to make decisions and should do so on the basis of the knowledge which is available at the moment. There is then the problem of the optimal organisation of this available knowledge. In this connection, we shall consider the following situation, which is closely connected with the subject of 8.4.8.

Suppose that the decision-maker argues that R_e is the best estimate of the multiplicative structure which he has and that he acts accordingly, though he recognises the possibility of nonzero errors dR. There is then still the problem of the additive structure of the constraints. The forecast is s_e; so the obvious decision is the one which maximises w subject to the predicted constraint $y = R_e x + s_e$. However, it was observed in 8.4.8 that, if $R_e = R$, the use of the forecast s_e is sometimes inferior to that of the no-change extrapolation $s = s_{-1}$. The policy-maker may therefore ask whether it is perhaps better, under similar circumstances, to work under the same assumption. It is true, the present situation differs from that of 8.4.8 in several respects. First, $R_e \neq R$; second, the policy-maker does not know s_{-1}. He knows $(s_{-1})_e$, which is in general different from s_{-1}. Still, it is conceivable that maximisation of w subject to $y = R_e x + (s_{-1})_e$ gives a better result than maximisation subject to $y = R_e x + s_e$; and this is our problem.

Clearly, the answer depends on the sign of

$$w[R_e, s_e] - w[R_e, (s_{-1})_e],$$

which can be written as the difference between two welfare losses:

$$\{\hat{w} - w[R_e, (s_{-1})_e]\} - \{\hat{w} - w[R_e, s_e]\}.$$

Applying Theorem 3d, we find that this difference is equal to

$$(8.143) \qquad [s_e - (s_{-1})_e]'[FdRx^0 + (\cdot x)\, dR'\lambda^0] + \tfrac{1}{2}(s_e - s)'F(s_e - s) - \\ - \tfrac{1}{2}[(s_{-1})_e - s]'F[(s_{-1})_e - s].$$

Further assumptions are necessary to make some progress. We shall do so by making the following combination of assumptions of 8.4.8 and of 8.5.2. First, we write

$$(8.144) \qquad s = \bar{s} + u; \ \mathscr{E}u = \mathbf{0}; \ s_{-1} = \mathbf{0}.$$

Secondly, we assume that the predicted change in the additive structure, $s_e - (s_{-1})_e$, is determined by

$$(8.145) \qquad s_e - (s_{-1})_e = \beta_s \bar{s} + \beta_u u + v,$$

where the β's are defined as

$$(8.146) \qquad \beta_s = \frac{\mathscr{E}\{\bar{s}'F[s_e - (s_{-1})_e]\}}{\bar{s}'F\bar{s}}; \ \beta_u = \frac{\mathscr{E}\{u'F[s_e - (s_{-1})_e]\}}{\mathscr{E}(u'Fu)},$$

and v satisfies

$$(8.147) \qquad \mathscr{E}(v'Fv) = h_u \mathscr{E}(u'Fu) + h_s \bar{s}'F\bar{s}$$

for some positive h_u, h_s. Comparing these assumptions with the earlier ones in 8.4.8 and 8.5.2, we easily see that the present ones form a generalisation of the analysis of 8.4.8 in the same way as the proportionality condition (8.117) is a generalisation of (8.78).

After some rearrangements we find that the welfare difference (8.143)—which should be positive in order that s_e be preferable to $(s_{-1})_e$—is equal to

$$(\beta_s \bar{s} + \beta_u u + v)'[FdR(x^0 - x_{-1}) + (\cdot x)\, dR'\lambda^0] - \\ - \tfrac{1}{2}(2\beta_s - \beta_s^2)\, \bar{s}'F\bar{s} - \tfrac{1}{2}(2\beta_u - \beta_u^2)\, u'Fu + \tfrac{1}{2}v'Fv - \\ - (\beta_s + \beta_u - \beta_s\beta_u)\, \bar{s}'Fu - (1 - \beta_s)\, \bar{s}'Fv - (1 - \beta_u)\, u'Fv,$$

where use is made of the property $(s_{-1})_e = -dRx_{-1}$, which follows from (8.114).[1] Taking mean values and using (8.147), we find that

[1] It is assumed throughout that neither the multiplicative structure itself, nor its estimate, change in the two successive periods under consideration.

$$\begin{aligned}(8.148)\qquad &\mathscr{E}\{[\beta_s\bar{s} + \beta_u u + v]'[F dR(x^0 - x_{-1}) + (\cdot x)\, dR'\lambda^0]\} - \\ &- \tfrac{1}{2}(2\beta_s - \beta_s^2 - h_s)\,\bar{s}'F\bar{s} - \tfrac{1}{2}(2\beta_u - \beta_u^2 - h_u)\,\mathscr{E}(u'Fu)\end{aligned}$$

is the mean value of the welfare excess of the forecast s_e over the no-change extrapolation $(s_{-1})_e$.

Let us first confine ourselves to the second and the third term of (8.148). It is then easy to see that, if $\bar{s}'F\bar{s}$ is sufficiently small in absolute sense relative to $\mathscr{E}(u'Fu)$, the second term is small. In that case the forecasting achievements with respect to $\bar{s}$ are irrelevant; and, just as in the case $R_e = R$ of 8.4.8, a negative value $\frac{1}{2}\, h_u\mathscr{E}(u'Fu)$ for the last two terms of (8.148) is obtained if the forecaster's achievements with respect to u are such that $\beta_u = 0$. So the conclusion is independent of the equality $R_e = R$ as long as we confine ourselves to the last two terms of (8.148). As to the first, suppose (in accordance with the remarks made above) that the s-elements and β_u are sufficiently close to zero; then this term becomes

$$\mathscr{E}\{v'FdR(x^0 - x_{-1})\} + \mathscr{E}\{v'(\cdot x)dR'\lambda^0\}.$$

Now x^0 is a linear function of s according to the optimal reaction functions with slope matrix $-(x\cdot)$; see 8.4.3. But $s \approx u$ according to (8.144) if $\bar{s} \approx \mathbf{0}$; hence:

$$x^0 = K^{-1}k = -(xx)\,(a + R'b) - (x\cdot)\,u.$$

Similarly, λ^0 is the vector $\partial w/\partial y$ evaluated in x^0, y^0 and therefore a linear function of these two vectors:

$$\lambda^0 = b + C'x^0 + By^0 = b + (C + R'B)'x^0 + Bs.$$

After applying the x^0-expression and replacing s by u, we find that λ^0 too is linear in u. Gathering our results, we see that the first term of (8.148) is of the form

$$\mathscr{E}(v'FdR)m_1 + \mathscr{E}(v'FdR\,M_2u) + \mathscr{E}\{v'(\cdot x)dR'\}m_3 + \mathscr{E}\{v'(\cdot x)dR'\,M_4u\},$$

m_1, M_2, m_3, M_4 being matrices which are fixed at the beginning of the period considered. Now if we assume that the error matrix dR is distributed independently of forecast disturbances v and the unsystematic part of the additive structure u (the latter vectors having zero means), then our first term in (8.148) vanishes. Hence

$$(8.149)\qquad \mathscr{E}\{w[R_e,\ s_e] - w[R_e,\ (s_{-1})_e]\} \approx \tfrac{1}{2}h_u\mathscr{E}(u'Fu),$$

which means that no-change extrapolation is preferable to small-change prediction even if the multiplicative structure used is subject to sampling errors, provided these errors are independent of u and v.

8.5.7. Our last topic in this section is that of the loss of welfare due to the application of both imperfect forecasts and "irrelevant" preferences. As observed earlier, this is a subject which is of some importance when a policy-maker is succeeded or changes his mind for objective or subjective reasons, after which a re-appraisal of measures taken earlier takes place. So we assume, as before, that the true constraint is $y = Rx + s$ and that maximisation takes place subject to $y = R_e x + s_e$; further, that the function which is maximised is not (8.5), but

$$w_e(x, y) = a_e'x + b_e'y + \tfrac{1}{2}(x'A_e x + y'B_e y + x'C_e y + y'C_e'x), \tag{8.150}$$

A_e and B_e being symmetric. Let us write $dA = A_e - A$, etc.; then we can apply Theorem 2d in order to find the differential dx which is associated with maximisation of (8.150) instead of (8.5). The result is

$$dx = -(xx)[da + dAx^0 + dCy^0] - (xy)[db + dBy^0 + dC'x^0] = -(xx)\,dw,$$

where

$$dw = [da + dAx^0 + dCy^0] + (xx)^{-1}(xy)[db + dBy^0 + dC'x^0]. \tag{8.151}$$

If, in addition to this, there are errors in the constraints, the difference $x - x^0$ is found by adding the two effects:

$$x - x^0 \approx -(x\cdot)[dRx^0 + ds] - (xx)[dR'\lambda^0 + dw], \tag{8.152}$$

higher-order differentials being neglected. This leads to the following generalisation of Theorem 3d:

THEOREM 3e. *Suppose that the Assumptions* C1 *and* P3 *are satisfied and that the optimal reaction functions* (8.63) *exist. Then the loss of welfare due to the prediction* R_e, s_e *of the constraint parameters* R, s *and to the fact that the irrelevant welfare function* (8.150) *is maximised rather than* (8.5), *is equal to the sum of three components,*

$$L_o + L_u^* + L_m^*, \tag{8.153}$$

except for terms of the third and higher degree in the forecasting errors $dR = R_e - R$, $ds = s_e - s$ *and in the differences*

$$da = a_e - a;\ db = b_e - b;\ dA = A_e - A;$$
$$dB = B_e - B;\ dC = C_e - C$$

between the parameters of (8.150) *and those of* (8.5).

The three components are: the source component (8.107); *the enlarged substitution component*

(8.154) $$L_u^* = -\tfrac{1}{2}(dR'\lambda^0 + dw)'(xx)(dR'\lambda^0 + dw);$$

and the enlarged mixed component

(8.155) $$L_m^* = -(dRx^0 + ds)'(\cdot x)(dR'\lambda^0 + dw),$$

dw *being given by* (8.151). *The enlarged substitution component is non-negative*:

(8.156) $$L_u^* \geqq 0,$$

and the enlarged mixed component satisfies the inequality

(8.157) $$L_m^{*2} \leqq 4\, L_o L_u^*.$$

Our comments can be brief. There is no enlargement of the source component when irrelevant preferences are introduced, simply because a change in preference coefficients has no source effect. Further, we see that here for the first time another submatrix of the substitution matrix U plays a rôle than (xx) alone; viz., (xy) *via* dw in (8.151).

8.5.8. When reviewing the results of this and the preceding section, the following can be concluded.

Under the assumptions of quadratic preferences and linear constraints it is possible to derive the loss of welfare due to suboptimal actions. This loss, which is equal to a quadratic form in the decision errors (the deviations between suboptimal instrument values and the optimal ones), is the principal basis of the further results. Part of these results is directly concerned with the characteristics of the quadratic form. It appears that substitution and complementarity play a dominant rôle in this form; also, that errors of the first order of smallness give rise to a loss of welfare which is small of the second order. Other results are obtained with respect to the empirically observed tendency towards underestimation of changes. We found that this will frequently lead to measures which are too small, but that this is certainly not necessarily true. Further results are derived on the impact of prediction errors on the welfare level attained. If we assume that the policy-maker knows the multiplicative structure of his constraints, but that his knowledge of the additive structure is imperfect, then we arrive at the loss of welfare due to actions based on such imperfect forecasts; or simply, the loss of welfare due to the imperfect forecast of the additive structure. This loss is a quadratic form in the errors of prediction; and hence, if these errors are of the first order of smallness, the resulting loss is small of the second order. If there is a proportionate under or overestimation with respect to all components of the additive structure, the loss can be calculated in a straightforward way; and it is then independent of the numerical characteristics of constraints and preferences. These calculations can be carried out conveniently by means of a utility scale, the zero of which corresponds to the welfare level attained when the policy-maker acts under the assumption that the additive structure of the constraints is the same as that of the preceding period, and the unit to the highest welfare attainable. If the under or overestimation of the additive structure is not of the proportionate type, the use of certain statistical concepts becomes convenient. It can then be shown that the loss of welfare is minimised if a particular product-moment regression of the actual changes in the additive structure on the predicted changes has unit coefficient. This situation corresponds with the absence of under and overestimation in the third sense of Section 5.1. As observed there, the occurrence of this third-degree underestimation is not so dominant as that of the other two types, so that the seriousness of this error appears to be less than it seemed in earlier chapters. Nevertheless, in the Dutch and Scandinavian case (cf. Chapter III) even this type exists, and so it is certainly not reasonable either to discard the phenomenon of underestimation of changes as unimportant.

There are other interesting applications of the analysis reported so far. One of them deals with the seriousness of the various forecasting errors. We asked a question about this problem at the end of Chapter III, but we had to postpone the answer. Given the assumptions made (which includes perfect knowledge of the multiplicative structure of the constraints), the answer appears to be the following: Since prediction errors in the additive structure lead to a loss of welfare which is a quadratic form in the errors, their seriousness is measured by their coefficients of this form; and these coefficients are determined (*i*) by substitution and complementarity relationships between the various instruments, and (*ii*) by the slopes of their Tinbergen surfaces, in a manner that has been analysed in detail. Another application is that of the inequality coefficients discussed in Chapter II. The inequality coefficient U was defined as a ratio, the numerator of which is a quadratic form in the prediction errors. Clearly, this is closely related to the loss-of-welfare concept; but there is a difference: the quadratic form of U is applied to forecasting errors in one variable for a series of successive periods (at least, this is the way in which we applied it in the Chapters III and IV), whereas the quadratic form of the loss of welfare refers to the components of the additive structure of the constraints in one particular period. In the next section, where a dynamic generalisation is presented, the loss concept considered there will exhibit dynamic features; but it will still refer to all components of the additive structures in the various periods. In this connection, it is also interesting to note that the alternative decompositions of the inequality coefficients (U^M, U^S, U^C *versus* U^M, U^R, U^D) have some relevance. The second composition (U^M, U^R, U^D) was justified in Section 2.5 by means of the hypothesis which states the phenomenon to be predicted consists of a systematic and a stochastic part, and that the forecaster predicts the former part perfectly but the latter as zero (= its mean value). It can be proved that, if the phenomenon predicted is the additive structure of the constraints, and if the first part of this hypothesis is true, prediction according to the second part is optimal in the sense that it minimises the loss of welfare in the population. Actually, the policy based on such a prediction is nothing else than decision-making according to Theorem 1 on certainty equivalence.

The preceding paragraphs, as far as they deal with the loss of welfare due to imperfect forecasts, are confined to the case in which the multiplicative structure of the constraints is known. If this is not true, the loss of welfare consists of three components: a source component (which is the only one if the multiplicative structure of the constraints is known), a substitution, and a mixed component. The first two are nonnegative; the third is a bilinear form (its matrix being that of the slopes of Tinbergen surfaces), so that its sign is not definite. Indeed, the mixed component can be negative and even such that the loss of welfare is reduced considerably below the level suggested by the other two components. An interesting case where this occurs is the one in which there is (*i*) a proportionate underestimation of the changes in the components of the additive structure and (*ii*) a proportionate underestimation of the effectiveness of all instruments with respect to all noncontrolled variables. If these two conditions are satisfied, the loss of welfare can be reduced, possibly even to zero. It can be shown that, given a certain degree of underestimation of the change in the additive structure, the "optimal" degree of underestimation of instrumental effectiveness is an increasing function of the former degree, up to a certain point; thereafter, it is a decreasing function, though the optimal adjustment of instrumental effectiveness remains an underestimation throughout. This feature is of some interest for problems of statistical estimation. For we found in Section 6.2 that, if there are errors of observation in exogenous variables, this frequently implies a bias of the least-squares estimator in the direction of zero. Hence the effectiveness of instruments is then underestimated if the coefficients are derived by least-squares—at least, there is a tendency in this direction; and so the neglect of observational errors in least-squares estimation may be regarded as an approximate compensation for the underestimation of changes in the additive structure. A further analysis leads to a similar conclusion with respect to two-stage least-squares estimation of structural equations: If the statistician is interested in the reduced form rather than in the separate structural equations, two-stage least-squares estimation is a method which, though not perfect, is difficult to surpass appreciably. So our final appraisal of simultaneous-equations estimation is indeed somewhat more favourable than the preliminary appraisal formulated at the end of Section 6.2 could be. There is no contradiction; the present appraisal is concerned with the reduced form, the earlier one with the separate structural equations.

There was one result which reduced our forecasting enthusiasm: If the predicted changes in the additive structure of the constraints are small, then it is in general better for the policy-maker to correct his prediction errors of last period's additive structure by adjusting his instruments accordingly, rather than to act on the basis of the new forecasts. This holds independently of the question whether the multiplicative structure of the constraints is known or not, at least to a large extent; and this result is based on the pattern of the forecasting errors of the Dutch and the Scandinavian predictions analysed in Chapter III, which show an increasing variance around their central tendency when the corresponding actual change increases. Indeed, our picture of the quality of these forecasts deteriorated gradually. In the beginning, we thought in terms of a success of 91 per cent (cf. 8.4.6); later, we found that the actual success must be lower, because this figure is based on the assumption of a perfect correlation between the components of the predicted additive structure and those of the actual structure to be predicted; at the end, we found that the policy-maker must expect a larger loss of welfare when he acts on small-change predictions than by acting on the basis of no-change extrapolations.

8.6. A Dynamic Generalisation

8.6.1. So far, the analysis has been essentially static. It is true, several places can be mentioned where dynamic elements entered into the picture. The definition of failure and success, for instance, involves the lagged additive structure of the constraints, $\mathbf{s}_{-1}$. Another example is the stochastic-process analysis of decision errors. Still, the analysis was not dynamic in the sense that explicit account is taken of the possibility that present as well as future instrument values affect the same future noncontrolled values; and in particular that the policy-maker's present actions can (and should, if he wants to be rational) be based on a recognition of the fact that, later, he may revise his position, given the information which he will have by that time. This subject can be approached most conveniently by means of the following example.[1]

Suppose our policy-maker is a rich speculator who has the choice between investing his money in an industry that may be declared illegal by the legislature and using the money for a less dubious venture. The former alternative will be denoted by A, the latter by B. The choice must be made now; and after a year, the speculator will know whether the industry has been outlawed. At the beginning of the second year he can then change his investment from the one industry to the other; but he has to pay a conversion penalty for doing so, in whichever direction he makes the switch. So we must make a distinction between first-period and second-period decisions. The alternative decisions for the first period are "investing in A" and "investing in B;" those of the second period, "keeping A" and "switching to B" if he had chosen

[1] This example was considered by Professor H. A. SIMON and the author during a conversation and worked out by the former in "Surrogates for Uncertain Decision Problems" (mimeographed and unpublished, 1956). The author is indebted to Professor Simon for his permission to quote the example in its final form.

the first alternative in the first year, "keeping B" and "switching to A" if he had chosen the second. We shall further assume that the speculator wants to maximise the mean value of monetary gain.[1] So our w is simply identical with this gain, which is specified as follows. If A is chosen in the first year and if the law is passed and if the speculator keeps A (in symbols: AlA), the gain is minus \$5 millions. If A is chosen and retained and if the law is not passed (in symbols: AnA), the gain is plus \$5 millions. If B is chosen and kept, then, whether the law is passed or not (BlB and BnB), the gain is \$2 millions; and the conversion penalty is \$1 million, both for switching from A to B and for switching from B to A. As a whole, there are then eight possibilities; and the corresponding gains are, under the assumption that the receipts from the alternative investments belong entirely to the second year and later, the following amounts in millions of dollars:

$$\begin{array}{llll} AlA: & -5 & AnA: & 5 \\ AlB: & 1 & AnB: & 1 \\ BlA: & -6 & BnA: & 4 \\ BlB: & 2 & BnB: & 2. \end{array}$$

Suppose further that the speculator takes the chance that the law will be passed equal to p. The following argument seems then reasonable. There are four possibilities: select A for both periods (in symbols: AA), select B for both periods (BB), select A for the first and B for the second (AB), and select B for the first and A for the second (BA). The mean values of the gains of these four alternatives are:

$$\begin{array}{ll} AA: & -5p + 5(1-p) = 5 - 10p \\ AB: & p + (1-p) = 1 \\ BA: & -6p + 4(1-p) = 4 - 10p \\ BB: & 2p + 2(1-p) = 2. \end{array}$$

It follows immediately that AB is always inferior to BB, and BA to AA. So the only serious rivals are AA and BB. A comparison of their

[1] This assumption is justified to some extent by MARKOWITZ' findings, who argued that the utility function of wealth has an inflexional point in the point of present wealth. In that case a linear approximation of w as a function of monetary gain (which amounts to the same thing as an identity of w and this gain, given a suitable choice of zero and unit) is an adequate approximation, provided however the speculator is sufficiently wealthy. Cf. H. MARKOWITZ, "The Utility of Wealth," *Journal of Political Economy*, Vol. 60 (1952), pp. 151–158.

average gains shows that the former is preferable if $p < 0.3$, the latter if $p > 0.3$; in other words, the two relevant intervals are

$$(8.158) \qquad 0 \leqq p < 0.3; \qquad 0.3 < p \leqq 1,$$

respectively. In particular, if $p = 0.4$, the speculator will choose BB and invest his money in B in the first year. He will realise, of course, that the law may not be passed (the chance of which is even greater than that it will be passed), in which case it is preferable to switch to A in the second year. His actual decision is then BA, whereas BB was the original one. However, this is irrelevant, since he has to act on the basis of the available information. Also, whether he chooses AA or BB, the only interesting thing is what he selects for the first year; the decision for the second year is a matter of later concern, which is to be based on the information available at that time.

The argument of the preceding paragraph is not satisfactory. Take for instance AA. This policy implies that the speculator selects A for the first period and keeps it in the second, irrespective of whether the law is passed or not. He can also consider the following *chain of decisions*: to select A for the first period; and to switch to B in the second if the law is passed (which he knows by that time), but to keep A if the law is not passed. In symbols: $A(lB; nA)$. It may seem that this is an irrelevant refinement, because such a selection process does not involve any knowledge beyond that considered earlier for the four alternatives AA, AB, BA, BB. Hence we might think that this extension, though possibly of some importance for a formulation of clearer ideas about the second period, does not imply any innovation for the first; and in particular that the intervals (8.158) continue to determine whether A or B is to be selected for the first period. But this remains to be seen. There are three other decision chains of the type $A(lB; nA)$, viz.: to select A for the first period, to keep it if the law is passed and to switch otherwise, $A(lA; nB)$; select B first, keep it if the law is passed and switch otherwise, $B(lB; nA)$; and select B first, keep it if the law is not passed and switch in the opposite case, $B(lA; nB)$. These are the only four, since decision chains of the type $A(lB; nB)$, in which the second-period decision is not made contingent on the event, belong to the category considered in the preceding paragraph (viz., AB in this case). The mean values of the gains of these four are then

$$\begin{aligned}
A(lA; nB)&: \quad -5p + (1-p) = 1 - 6p \\
A(lB; nA)&: \quad p + 5(1-p) = 5 - 4p \\
B(lA; nB)&: \quad -6p + 2(1-p) = 2 - 8p \\
B(lB; nA)&: \quad 2p + 4(1-p) = 4 - 2p.
\end{aligned}$$

As is to be expected, the first and third alternatives are inferior. The second, however, is uniformly better than AA (except for a "tie" in the case $p = 0$); and the fourth is always better than BB (except for $p = 1$). So the only alternatives which can be worthwhile are $A(lB; nA)$ and $B(lB; nA)$; no longer $AA = A(lA; nA)$ and $BB = B(lB; nB)$. A comparison of average gains shows that the former is preferable if $p < 0.5$, the latter if $p > 0.5$. Hence the two relevant intervals are *not* those of (8.158), but

(8.159) $\qquad 0 \leq p < 0.5; \qquad 0.5 < p \leq 1.$

In particular, if $p = 0.4$, then the best decision is $A(lB; nA)$, so that the first-period selection is then A, not B. It is not difficult to understand intuitively why the results are different. If the policy-maker confines his attention to alternative actions the second-period selection of which is not made contingent on the law, the only decisions which involve a first-period selection of A are AA and AB. The latter can be ruled out, since it is always inferior to BB, the difference in gain being the conversion penalty. So AA remains. But this variant gives a picture of the profitability of A which is too unfavourable; it distinghuishes between only two alternative outcomes, viz., a large gain and a large loss; and it fails to point out that there is a possibility to avoid the loss, viz., switching to B. This feature is recognised by the variant $A(lB; nA)$, which leads to a larger p-interval for the selection of A in the first period.

The idea of considering not only chains of decisions of the type AA, AB, etc., but also chains in which later decisions are made contingent on the information which the policy-maker will have at the moment when he has to take them, is largely due to VON NEUMANN.[1] Such a

[1] Cf. J. VON NEUMANN, "Zur Theorie der Gesellschaftsspiele," *Mathematische Annalen*, Vol. 100 (1928), pp. 295–320; J. VON NEUMANN and O. MORGENSTERN, *Theory of Games and Economic Behavior*, Chapter II. Von Neumann was anticipated to some extent by BOREL and ZERMELO. Cf. E. BOREL, "La théorie du jeu et les équations intégrales à noyau symétrique gauche," *Comptes Rendues de l'Académie des Sciences*, Vol. 173 (1921), pp. 1304–1308, and some further papers by Borel, translated and commented in *Econometrica*, Vol. 21 (1953), pp. 95–127; E. ZERMELO, "Über eine Anwendung der Mengenlehre auf die Theorie des Schachspiels," *Proceedings of the Fifth International Congress of Mathematicians*, Vol. II (Cambridge, Engl., 1913), pp. 501–504. I am indebted to Professor H. A. Simon for his reference to Zermelo's article.

chain is called a *strategy*. It should be stressed that the adoption of a strategy does not imply any restriction on the policy-maker's future actions. On the contrary, the strategy specifies only conditional plans for future periods under all conceivable conditions (in the above example: if the law is passed or not passed); and hence, it does not specify any specific unconditional plan at all.

8.6.2. Let us go back to the beginning of Section 8.2. It was observed there that maximising the mean value of welfare is rather inconvenient and that maximising the welfare level of the average outcome is preferable in this respect. Here, the situation is even more extreme. To take again the example of 8.6.1, if the policy-maker would choose among the four alternatives AA, AB, BA, BB the one with the highest average gain, he surely maximises the mean value of his welfare; but he does so only within a subset of the set of strategies available to him. At present, there are at least three levels at which maximisation can take place: that of choosing the maximising strategy (which is of course the best policy, given the probability information); that of choosing the best of those chains of actions for which no future action is made contingent on information that becomes available later on; and that of choosing the best chain under the assumption that all random elements are equal to their mean values. In general, all three policies lead to different decisions, even for the first period; and hence, the last two policies are inferior to the first. This can be further illustrated with the following example, which is due to H. A. SIMON.[1]

Suppose that an entrepreneur tries to minimise the mean value of cost over time. The period considered is divided into subperiods, $t = 1, 2, \ldots, T$. We assume that the total cost during the period as a whole can be written as the sum of cost allocations belonging to each subperiod; further, that each such allocation is the sum of three components,

$$C = \sum_{t=1}^{T} \sum_{i=1}^{3} C_{it}, \tag{8.160}$$

viz., the cost of production (C_{1t}), the cost of changing the rate of production (C_{2t}) and the cost of holding inventories (C_{3t}). We suppose further that these components are each quadratic functions of the relevant determining variables:

[1] H. A. SIMON, "Dynamic Programming Under Uncertainty With a Quadratic Criterion Function," *Econometrica* Vol. 24 (1956), pp. 74–81.

$$(8.161)\qquad \begin{aligned} C_{1t} &= a_1 + b_1 P_t + c_1 P_t^2 \\ C_{2t} &= a_2 + b_2 \Delta P_t + c_2 (\Delta P_t)^2 \\ C_{3t} &= a_3 + b_3 S_t + c_3 S_t^2, \end{aligned}$$

where P_t is the production in t and ΔP_t its rate of change:

$$(8.162)\qquad \Delta P_t = P_t - P_{t-1},$$

and S_t the stock at the end of t,

$$(8.163)\qquad S_t = S_{t-1} + P_t - T_t,$$

T_t being the quantity sold in t.

Production is the entrepreneur's instrument; its rate of change and the size of the stocks are his noncontrolled variables (though the former variable is so in a degenerate sense, since it is determined by a definitional equation involving instrument values only). All these variables for $t = 1, \ldots, T$ enter, after substitution, into the quadratic cost function (8.160). The random element is represented by the sales of the various subperiods.

If the entrepreneur would minimise cost by acting under the assumption that T_t equals its mean value, $\mathscr{E}T_t$ say, the procedure is as follows; after replacing T_t by $\mathscr{E}T_t$ in (8.163), this equation and (8.162) are substituted into (8.161), and this in turn into (8.160). Minimisation of the last form with respect to $P_1, P_2, \ldots$ gives—under certain conditions—the following numerical values:

$$\bar{P}_1, \bar{P}_2, \ldots, \bar{P}_T.$$

The decision taken for the first period is then $\bar{P}_1$. The decisions for the later periods, $\bar{P}_2, \bar{P}_3, \ldots$, are irrelevant. At the end of the first period, the entrepreneur applies the same procedure. The conditional mean values of future sales, given the information obtained in the first period, will generally be different from the original means. So he arrives at the following values:

$$\bar{\bar{P}}_2, \ldots, \bar{\bar{P}}_T,$$

where, in general, $\bar{\bar{P}}_2 \neq \bar{P}_2$. He then decides according to $\bar{\bar{P}}_2$; and so on.

If he would minimise the mean value of cost without considering the strategies defined at the end of 8.6.1, he acts in the following manner. He substitutes (8.161)—(8.163) into (8.160) and leaves T_t as it is.

Then he takes the mean value of (8.160) and minimises it with respect to $P_1, P_2, \ldots$. This gives

$$\hat{P}_1,\ \hat{P}_2,\ \ldots,\ \hat{P}_T.$$

He then decides on $\hat{P}_1$, and leaves $\hat{P}_2, \ldots, \hat{P}_T$ out of consideration. As before, the decision for the second period is found by applying the same procedure at the end of the first, which gives

$$\hat{\hat{P}}_2,\ \ldots,\ \hat{\hat{P}}_T,$$

where, again, $\hat{\hat{P}}_2 \neq \hat{P}_2$ in general.

The choice of the best strategy can be explained as follows. The entrepreneur does not try to specify numerically his future decisions, but he specifies only a *rule* by which such decisions are to be derived, given the information which he will have by the time when he has to take the decision. In this example, the information consists of previous sales. So these rules can be written as the following functions:

$$\begin{aligned} P_1 &= P_1 \\ P_2 &= P_2(T_1) \\ &\cdots\cdots \\ P_T &= P_T(T_1, \ldots, T_{T-1}). \end{aligned} \tag{8.164}$$

The information available at the time when the decision for P_t must be made consists not only of previous sales, $T_{t-1}, \ldots$, but also of previous production and inventory levels, $P_{t-1}, S_{t-1}, \ldots$. However, the latter values can be eliminated iteratively, so that the arguments of the functions (8.164) can be said to comprise all relevant information. The sales before the period $t = 1$ (T_0, $T_{-1}, \ldots$) are not introduced explicitly; they are given numbers and assumed to be known; the same holds for P_t, S_t with $t < 1$. In particular, P_1 depends only on such earlier values, which results in a degeneration of the corresponding function. The further procedure is then the following: after replacing the P's by the functions (8.164) and substituting (8.161)-(8.163) into (8.160), the mean value of the latter expression is taken; and this mean is minimised, not by varying the P's numerically, but by varying the functions (8.164) in the domain of all possible functions of the same arguments. This leads, under certain conditions, to a unique best strategy:

$$
\begin{aligned}
(8.165)\qquad P_1 &= \tilde{P}_1 \\
P_2 &= \tilde{P}_2(T_1) \\
&\cdots\cdots \\
P_T &= \tilde{P}_T(T_1, \ldots, T_{T-1}).
\end{aligned}
$$

Clearly, we must expect in general $\bar{P}_1 \neq \tilde{P}_1$; $\bar{P}_1 \neq \hat{P}_1$; $\tilde{P}_1 \neq \hat{P}_1$. As to later periods, we should have no illusions at all, simply because functions of the type $\tilde{P}_2(T_1)$ are not identical with point predictions $\bar{P}_2$, except accidentally; but this is not very important. What really matters is the first-period decision, for this is the entrepreneur's immediate concern. If $\bar{P}_1 \neq \tilde{P}_1$, then this decision, if taken under the assumption that future sales are equal to their mean values, is different from the corresponding first-period decision of the best strategy. We may say that such an inequality corresponds to *first-period certainty bias* in dynamic policy-making; conversely, that $\bar{P}_1 = \tilde{P}_1$ corresponds to *first-period certainty equivalence* of unbiased point predictions $T_t = \mathscr{E}T_t$. The latter alternative is of still more practical importance than the static analogue $\bar{x} = \hat{x}$ of Section 8.2 for the simple reason that the strategy approach may be extremely cumbersome. In the example of 8.6.1, the speculator had to consider eight strategies, which is the minimum possible; here, there is an infinity of high order, viz., T functions of a number of arguments that varies from zero till $T - 1$; in the more general case (to be considered in 8.6.3), both the number of functions and that of arguments may be much larger.

Simon's analysis was concerned with first-period certainty equivalence for the case of cost minimisation; in 8.6.3, it will be expounded in generalised form.

8.6.3. Suppose again that our policy-maker has m instruments, $x_1, \ldots, x_m$, but now with values $x_h(t)$ in the subperiod t, for $t = 1, \ldots, T$. These values are taken as variable, not as fixed. He is also interested in n noncontrolled variables $y_1, \ldots, y_n$ with values $y_i(t)$ in t. Further, the function which he wishes to maximise (the welfare function) is quadratic in all mT x's and all nT y's of the period $t = 1, \ldots, T$. This can be expressed most easily as follows. We write the x's and the y's in the form of long column vectors and group them, within each of these two vectors, according to subperiods. The result is, in partitioned form,

$$(8.166)\qquad \mathbf{x} = \begin{bmatrix} \mathsf{x}_1 \\ \cdot \\ \cdot \\ \mathsf{x}_T \end{bmatrix}; \ \mathsf{x}_t = \begin{bmatrix} x_1(t) \\ \cdot \\ \cdot \\ x_m(t) \end{bmatrix}; \ \mathbf{y} = \begin{bmatrix} \mathsf{y}_1 \\ \cdot \\ \cdot \\ \mathsf{y}_T \end{bmatrix}; \ \mathsf{y}_t = \begin{bmatrix} y_1(t) \\ \cdot \\ \cdot \\ y_n(t) \end{bmatrix}.$$

To distinguish the present vectors and matrices from those of the static case, the use of the sanserif type will be confined to those vectors and matrices which refer either to one, or to two subperiods. The quadratic preference assumption can then be written in the form

$$(8.167)\qquad w(\mathbf{x}, \mathbf{y}) = \mathbf{a}'\mathbf{x} + \mathbf{b}'\mathbf{y} + \tfrac{1}{2}(\mathbf{x}'\mathbf{A}\mathbf{x} + \mathbf{y}'\mathbf{B}\mathbf{y} + \mathbf{x}'\mathbf{C}\mathbf{y} + \mathbf{y}'\mathbf{C}'\mathbf{x}),$$

the coefficient vectors and matrices of which can be likewise partitioned; for instance

$$\mathbf{A} = \begin{bmatrix} \mathsf{A}_{11} & \mathsf{A}_{12} & \cdots & \mathsf{A}_{1T} \\ \mathsf{A}_{21} & \mathsf{A}_{22} & \cdots & \mathsf{A}_{2T} \\ \cdot & \cdot & \cdots & \cdot \\ \mathsf{A}_{T1} & \mathsf{A}_{T2} & \cdots & \mathsf{A}_{TT} \end{bmatrix}.$$

$\mathbf{A}$ and $\mathbf{B}$ are taken as symmetric; hence $\mathsf{A}_{tt'} = \mathsf{A}'_{t't}$, etc. It should be stressed that it is not necessary to assume, as we did in the cost case (8.161), that the x's and y's for different subperiods enter symmetrically into the preference function. So $\mathsf{A}_{11} \neq \mathsf{A}_{22}$, etc., is permissible.

We assume further that the y's are connected with the x's according to

$$(8.168)\qquad \mathbf{y} = \mathbf{R}\mathbf{x} + \mathbf{s},$$

where $\mathbf{R}$ is a matrix of fixed and known coefficients and $\mathbf{s}$ a vector of random elements which can be partitioned as follows:

$$(8.169)\qquad \mathbf{R} = \begin{bmatrix} \mathsf{R}_{11} & \mathbf{0} & \cdots & \mathbf{0} \\ \mathsf{R}_{21} & \mathsf{R}_{22} & \cdots & \mathbf{0} \\ \cdot & \cdot & \cdots & \cdot \\ \mathsf{R}_{T1} & \mathsf{R}_{T2} & \cdots & \mathsf{R}_{TT} \end{bmatrix}; \qquad \mathbf{s} = \begin{bmatrix} \mathsf{s}_1 \\ \mathsf{s}_2 \\ \cdot\cdot \\ \mathsf{s}_T \end{bmatrix}.$$

The vector $\mathbf{s}$ is supposed to have mean value $\bar{\mathbf{s}}$ and a finite covariance matrix; its distribution is supposed to be independent of $\mathbf{x}$. The partitioning of $\mathbf{R}$, which is such that zeros occur everywhere above and to the right of the diagonal blocks, implies that no subvector y_t depends on later instrument values:

$$(8.170) \qquad y_t = \sum_{t'=1}^{t} R_{tt'}x_{t'} + s_t.$$

This condition is satisfied by the simple constraints (8.162) and (8.163) of 8.6.2; and it is evidently a reasonable condition. It has the important implication that, given our assumption that $\mathbf{R}$ is known, at the beginning of t (when the decision for x_t must be made) the subvectors $s_1, \ldots, s_{t-1}$ are known and no longer stochastic. These subvectors correspond, of course, to the sales $T_1, \ldots, T_{t-1}$ of the example of 8.6.2.

Suppose that an optimal strategy maximising $\mathscr{E}w$ exists; it can be written as

$$(8.171) \qquad \tilde{\mathbf{x}} = \begin{bmatrix} \tilde{x}_1 \\ \tilde{x}_2(s_1) \\ \cdots\cdots \\ \tilde{x}_T(s_1, \ldots, s_{T-1}) \end{bmatrix}.$$

Consider then:

THEOREM 1′. *Suppose that the following assumptions are satisfied:*

(*i*) *The policy-maker's preference function is given by* (8.167), *where* $\mathbf{x}$ *and* $\mathbf{y}$ *are vectors of real-valued instruments and noncontrolled variables, respectively, during the periods* $t = 1, \ldots, T$, *in accordance with* (8.166); *and where* $\mathbf{a}$, $\mathbf{b}$, $\mathbf{A}$, $\mathbf{B}$, $\mathbf{C}$ *are vectors and matrices of coefficients which are independent of* $\mathbf{x}$ *and* $\mathbf{y}$, $\mathbf{A}$ *and* $\mathbf{B}$ *being symmetric. If some of the arguments of* w *are stochastic, the policy-maker values according to the mean value of* w.

(*ii*) *The policy-maker's vector of noncontrolled variables,* $\mathbf{y}$, *is connected with his instruments* $\mathbf{x}$ *by the constraints* (8.168), *where* $\mathbf{R}$ *is a matrix of known coefficients (independent of* $\mathbf{x}$*) which can be partitioned according to* (8.169)*; and where* $\mathbf{s}$ *is a vector of random elements with mean value* $\bar{\mathbf{s}}$ *and a finite covariance matrix, its distribution being the same for whatever* $\mathbf{x}$.

Then the strategy $\tilde{\mathbf{x}}$ *which maximises the mean value of* w *subject to the constraint* (8.168), *if existent, implies the same first-period decision* $\tilde{\mathbf{x}}_1$ *as the vector* $\bar{\mathbf{x}}$ *which maximises* w *subject to the constraint* (8.168) *with* $\mathbf{s}$ *replaced by* $\bar{\mathbf{s}}$.

The interpretation of this theorem is analogous to that of Theorem 1 for the static case: the policy-maker need not consider strategies and can decide for the first period by replacing $\mathbf{s}$ by its mean value $\bar{\mathbf{s}}$ as unbiased point prediction. At the end of the first period, the same situation arises; he should apply the same procedure with the subvectors and submatrices x_1, y_1, R_{t1}, etc., deleted, and replace s_2, s_3, ... by their conditional means, given the information available at the end of $t = 1$. The present result is stronger than Theorem 1 in one respect, weaker in another. It is stronger in so far as we have here a dynamic strategy generalisation. It is weaker in so far as we did not have to make the assumption that x is real-valued in the earlier case. This, in turn, has two consequences: first, the preference condition is stronger here, since Assumption P4 requires quadraticity in y only; second, the assumption on the constraints is stronger because it implies linearity, contrary to Assumption C2. It is not difficult to understand intuitively why these additional restrictions are required in the dynamic case. The reason is that future instrument values are stochastic within the framework of a strategy; and in that respect they are not different from the noncontrolled variables, for which quadraticity, etc., must be assumed anyhow.

The proof of the theorem is as follows. The welfare level attained by applying any vector of instrument values $\mathbf{x}$ equals

$$w_{\mathbf{x}} = w(\mathbf{x}, \mathbf{Rx} + \mathbf{s}) = k_0 + \mathbf{k}'\mathbf{x} + \tfrac{1}{2}\mathbf{x}'\mathbf{Kx}, \tag{8.172}$$

where

$$\begin{aligned} k_0 &= \mathbf{b}'\mathbf{s} + \tfrac{1}{2}\mathbf{s}'\mathbf{Bs} \\ \mathbf{k} &= \mathbf{a} + \mathbf{R}'\mathbf{b} + (\mathbf{C} + \mathbf{R}'\mathbf{B})\mathbf{s} \\ \mathbf{K} &= \mathbf{A} + \mathbf{R}'\mathbf{BR} + \mathbf{CR} + \mathbf{R}'\mathbf{C}'. \end{aligned} \tag{8.173}$$

This is similar to (8.69). It will be noted that $\mathbf{K}$ is square, symmetric and nonstochastic.

Any strategy $\mathbf{x}$, whether equal to $\tilde{\mathbf{x}}$ or not, can always be written in the form[1]

$$\mathbf{x} = \tilde{\mathbf{x}} + \varepsilon\boldsymbol{\xi}, \tag{8.174}$$

where ε is a scalar and $\boldsymbol{\xi}$ a vector of the type

[1] See e.g. R. COURANT, *Differential and Integral Calculus*, Vol. II (London-Glasgow, 1936), pp. 495–497.

(8.175)
$$\boldsymbol{\xi} = \begin{bmatrix} \xi_1 \\ \xi_2(s_1) \\ \cdots\cdots \\ \xi_T(s_1, \ldots, s_{T-1}) \end{bmatrix}.$$

Substituting (8.174) into (8.172) and taking mean values gives

(8.176)
$$\mathscr{E} w_{\tilde{\mathbf{x}}+\varepsilon\boldsymbol{\xi}} = \mathscr{E} k_0 + \mathscr{E}(\mathbf{k}'\tilde{\mathbf{x}}) + \tfrac{1}{2}\mathscr{E}(\tilde{\mathbf{x}}'\mathbf{K}\tilde{\mathbf{x}}) + \\ + \varepsilon[\mathscr{E}(\mathbf{k}'\boldsymbol{\xi}) + \mathscr{E}(\tilde{\mathbf{x}}'\mathbf{K}\boldsymbol{\xi})] + \tfrac{1}{2}\varepsilon^2\mathscr{E}(\boldsymbol{\xi}'\mathbf{K}\boldsymbol{\xi}).$$

The first three terms in the right-hand side are independent of ε and $\boldsymbol{\xi}$ (and hence of $\mathbf{x}$), which follows from the fact that they are mean values of expressions involving $\mathbf{s}$ only, and that $\mathbf{s}$ is independent of the strategy chosen.[1] A stationarity value of $\mathscr{E} w$ in $\tilde{\mathbf{x}}$ implies then that the linear term in ε vanishes identically in $\boldsymbol{\xi}$:

(8.177)
$$\mathscr{E}(\mathbf{k}'\boldsymbol{\xi}) + \mathscr{E}(\tilde{\mathbf{x}}'\mathbf{K}\boldsymbol{\xi}) = 0 \qquad \text{for any } \boldsymbol{\xi};$$

and a sufficient condition for this stationary value to be a maximum is that the quadratic term in ε be negative-definite. This implies that $\mathbf{K}$ should be negative-definite, which is a sufficient condition under which a maximising strategy exists.

Consider then (8.177) and specify $\boldsymbol{\xi}$ in the following mT alternative ways. First, choose $\boldsymbol{\xi}$ such that its first element equals 1 and all others zero; second, such that its second element equals 1 and all others zero; and so on. After writing this out, we obtain a system of mT equations, viz., $\mathscr{E}\mathbf{k} + \mathscr{E}(\mathbf{K}'\tilde{\mathbf{x}}) = \mathbf{0}$; or, making use of the fact that $\mathbf{K}$ is non-stochastic and symmetric, $\mathbf{K}\mathscr{E}\tilde{\mathbf{x}} = -\mathscr{E}\mathbf{k}$. So we find for the mean value of the optimal strategy:

(8.178)
$$\mathscr{E}\tilde{\mathbf{x}} = -\mathbf{K}^{-1}\mathscr{E}\mathbf{k}.$$

Next, we take the certainty case, in which it is assumed that $\mathbf{s}$ equals its mean value, $\bar{\mathbf{s}}$. Then (8.172) and (8.173) remain valid, provided we replace $\mathbf{s}$ by $\bar{\mathbf{s}}$ throughout. This implies, first, that k_0 is changed in a manner which is irrelevant for our purposes (since the result is a constant with respect to $\mathbf{x}$); second, that $\mathbf{k}$ is replaced

[1] Note, however, that the optimal strategy $\tilde{\mathbf{x}}$ is *not* independent of $\mathbf{s}$; cf. (8.171). $\mathbf{s}$ is independent of the strategy in the sense that its distribution is the same for whatever $\mathbf{x}$; cf. assumption (*ii*) of Theorem 1′. In particular, it is required that the covariance matrix of $\mathbf{s}$ be independent of $\mathbf{x}$.

by its mean value, $\mathscr{E}\mathbf{k}$; third, that $\mathbf{K}$ remains unchanged. It follows that the $\mathbf{x}$ which maximises w in the certainty case is

$$\bar{\mathbf{x}} = -\mathbf{K}^{-1}\mathscr{E}\mathbf{k}, \tag{8.179}$$

which is the same as (8.178). But the first subvector of $\tilde{\mathbf{x}}$, $\tilde{x}_1$, is non-stochastic; cf. (8.171). Hence it is equal to its mean value, $\mathscr{E}\tilde{x}_1$, and also, according to (8.179), to the first subvector of $\bar{\mathbf{x}}$. This establishes the first-period certainty equivalence of unbiased point predictions.

8.6.4. If the assumptions of Theorem 1′ are not fulfilled, then we have in general first-period certainty bias rather than certainty equivalence for unbiased point predictions. However, we shall stick to these assumptions here, because they are so closely related to the linear constraint and the quadratic preference conditions of the analysis of optimal reaction functions and welfare losses in the static case. The treatment of these subjects for the dynamic case will be our next concern. Here, we shall consider the generalisation of Section 8.3; welfare losses will be the subject of 8.6.5 and 8.6.6.

The dynamic generalisation of Section 8.3 is almost trivial, because it excludes the problem of uncertainty. If we replace (8.168) by

$$\mathbf{Q}\mathbf{y} = \mathbf{R}\mathbf{x} + \mathbf{s}, \tag{8.180}$$

$\mathbf{Q}$ being an arbitrary diagonal matrix of order nT with positive elements in the diagonal, then we are in exactly the same position as we were in the beginning of Section 8.3. In particular, each component of the vectors $\mathbf{x}$, $\mathbf{y}$ has its optimal reaction function; it is irrelevant that the optimal reaction patterns for the subvectors x_t with $t > 1$ are not the policy-maker's immediate concern. There is a substitution matrix,

$$\mathbf{U} = \begin{bmatrix} (\mathbf{xx}) & (\mathbf{xy}) \\ (\mathbf{yx}) & (\mathbf{yy}) \end{bmatrix}, \tag{8.181}$$

the leading submatrix of which is the inverse of the matrix $\mathbf{K}$ defined in (8.173),

$$(\mathbf{xx}) = \mathbf{K}^{-1}, \tag{8.182}$$

provided that we put $\mathbf{Q} = \mathbf{I}$; and this matrix can be further partitioned according to

$$(8.183) \qquad (\mathbf{xx}) = \begin{bmatrix} (xx)_{11} & \dots & (xx)_{1T} \\ \cdot & \cdot & \cdot \\ (xx)_{T1} & \dots & (xx)_{TT} \end{bmatrix},$$

$(xx)_{tt'}$ containing the substitution terms which correspond to any instrument in the subperiod t and any instrument in t'. Just as in the static case, we have the rule: if $x_h(t)$ is complementary with $x_k(t')$ according to one of the nT constraints, it is a substitute of $x_k(t')$ according to none of the constraints. However, the question of substitution or complementarity between instruments (or noncontrolled variables) may be answered differently for different subperiods; i.e., $x_h(1)$ may be a substitute of $x_k(2)$, but complementary with $x_k(3)$.

Similarly, there is a matrix of slopes of Tinbergen surfaces, which is here of the order $nT \times (m + n)T$. It will be observed that we may have a situation in which there is inferiority with respect to $x_h(1)$ but not with respect to $x_h(2)$; also, that the dynamic Sign Convention,

$$\frac{\partial w}{\partial x_h(t)}, \frac{\partial w}{\partial y_i(t)} \geq 0 \text{ for all pairs } (h, t) \text{ and } (i, t) \text{ in equilibrium,}$$

may lead to a situation in which employment (say) is introduced for $t = 1$, but unemployment for $t = 2$. Again, this is inessential, just as in the static case.

8.6.5. The dynamic generalisation of Theorem 3 on suboptimal decisions is twofold in character. In the first place, we have the loss of welfare that is due to an $\mathbf{x}$ which is specified for the whole period $t = 1, \dots, T$. It is easily seen that this loss is given by

$$(8.184) \qquad \begin{aligned} \hat{w} - w_{\mathbf{x}} &= -\tfrac{1}{2}(\mathbf{x} - \mathbf{x}^0)'(\mathbf{xx})^{-1}(\mathbf{x} - \mathbf{x}^0) \\ &= -\tfrac{1}{2}\sum_t \sum_{t'} (x_t - x_t^0)'(xx)^{tt'}(x_t - x_t^0), \end{aligned}$$

where $\mathbf{x}^0$ is the vector $(x_1^0, x_2^0, \dots, x_T^0)$ according to the optimal reaction pattern and $(xx)^{tt'}$ a square submatrix of order m of the inverse matrix $(\mathbf{xx})^{-1}$. It follows from (8.184) that the extent to which an error $x_t - x_t^0$ affects welfare is independent of the deviation $x_{t'} - x_{t'}^0$ of another subperiod ($t \neq t'$), if the instruments of all different subperiods are "independent;" i.e., if there is neither substitution nor complementarity between any instrument in one period and any in another period. In general, however, there will be some substitution or complementarity among subperiods, in which case products $\{x_h(t) - \overset{0}{x}_h(t)\}\{x_k(t') - \overset{0}{x}_k(t')\}$ with nonzero coefficients will occur in (8.184).

The second approach is that of the *first-period loss of welfare*. Since the first-period decision is more important than that of the other periods because it is the policy-maker's immediate concern, it is appropriate to ask what is the loss of welfare due to a suboptimal decision in the first period. Let us define this first-period loss as the difference between the maximum welfare which was attainable before the error was made (viz. $\hat{w}$) and the maximum which is still attainable at the end of $t = 1$, given the error. The latter, conditional, maximum can be evaluated as follows. We denote the first-period decision by x_1^*, so that the error is $\mathsf{x}_1^* - \mathsf{x}_1^0$. The conditional maximisation is carried out by means of a vector of Lagrange multipliers, $\boldsymbol{\mu}$:

$$k_0 + \mathbf{k}'\mathbf{x} + \tfrac{1}{2}\mathbf{x}'\mathbf{K}\mathbf{x} - \boldsymbol{\mu}'(\mathsf{x}_1 - \mathsf{x}_1^*),$$

which gives

$$\mathbf{k} + \mathbf{K}\mathbf{x}^1 - \begin{bmatrix}\boldsymbol{\mu}\\ \mathbf{0}\end{bmatrix} = \mathbf{0},$$

where $\mathbf{x}^1$ is the instrument vector of the conditional maximum. Hence

$$\mathbf{x}^1 = -\mathbf{K}^{-1}\mathbf{k} + \mathbf{K}^{-1}\begin{bmatrix}\boldsymbol{\mu}\\ \mathbf{0}\end{bmatrix} = \mathbf{x}^0 + (\mathbf{xx})\begin{bmatrix}\boldsymbol{\mu}\\ \mathbf{0}\end{bmatrix} =$$

$$= \mathbf{x}^0 + \begin{bmatrix}(\mathsf{xx})_{11}\\ \cdot\\ \cdot\\ \cdot\\ (\mathsf{xx})_{T1}\end{bmatrix}\boldsymbol{\mu}.$$

For the first subperiod this means $\mathsf{x}_1^1 = \mathsf{x}_1^0 + (\mathsf{xx})_{11}\boldsymbol{\mu}$. But it is given that $\mathsf{x}_1^1 = \mathsf{x}_1^*$. Hence $\boldsymbol{\mu} = (\mathsf{xx})_{11}^{-1}\ (\mathsf{x}_1^* - \mathsf{x}_1^0)$, so that

$$\text{(8.185)} \qquad \mathbf{x}^1 - \mathbf{x}^0 = \begin{bmatrix}(\mathsf{xx})_{11}\\ \cdot\\ \cdot\\ \cdot\\ (\mathsf{xx})_{T1}\end{bmatrix}(\mathsf{xx})_{11}^{-1}(\mathsf{x}_1^* - \mathsf{x}_1^0),$$

the last $m(T - 1)$ components of which give the *optimal revisions* of the decisions for the later periods $t = 2, \ldots, T$, given the first-period error. Applying (8.184), finally, we find for the first-period loss:

(8.186)

$$-\tfrac{1}{2}(\mathsf{x}_1^* - \mathsf{x}_1^0)'(\mathsf{xx})_{11}^{-1}[(\mathsf{xx})_{11} \ldots (\mathsf{xx})_{1T}](\mathbf{XX})^{-1}\begin{bmatrix}(\mathsf{xx})_{11}\\ \cdot\\ \cdot\\ \cdot\\ (\mathsf{xx})_{T1}\end{bmatrix}(\mathsf{xx})_{11}^{-1}(\mathsf{x}_1^* - \mathsf{x}_1^0)$$

$$= -\tfrac{1}{2}(\mathsf{x}_1^* - \mathsf{x}_1^0)'(\mathsf{xx})_{11}^{-1}(\mathsf{x}_1^* - \mathsf{x}_1^0).$$

To interpret these results, let us go back to (8.184). We noted there that the way in which a first-period decision error affects w is in general not independent of the deviations between later x's and the corresponding components of the optimal vector $\mathbf{x}^0$. However, a first-period error affects the optimality of x_t^0 for $t > 1$ according to (8.185). This equation defines optimal revisions for these later x's, and it is characterised by the following interesting properties. First, for each instrument and for each of the subperiods $t = 2, \ldots, T$, the optimal revision is a homogeneous linear combination of the first-period error components. Second, if some $x_h(t)$ with $t > 1$ is neither a substitute of nor complementary with any of the instruments in the first period [$x_k(1)$ for all $k = 1, \ldots, m$], then the optimal revision of this $x_h(t)$ is zero, for whatever first-period error. Third, in the scalar case $m = 1$, the revision is such that a positive error in the first period, $x_1^* > x_1^0$, is followed by a negative revision if there is substitution between the instrument in $t > 1$ and that in 1, by a positive one if there is complementarity. In the nonscalar case $m > 1$ the situation is more complicated, but qualitatively of the same type because of the negative-definiteness of the matrix $(\mathsf{xx})_{11}^{-1}$.

All these points are, qualitatively and intuitively at least, rather easy to understand. Their relevance for the problem of a "separate and distinct influence of plans on behaviour" will also be clear. Let us consider again the tanners and shoe manufacturers of Chapter VI, for whose pricing behaviour we concluded the existence of such influence. In our present terminology, this effect can be explained as follows. Suppose that the pricing behaviour takes place in two successive steps ($T = 2$). In the first stage ($t = 1$) the manufacturer plans to change the selling price in the next month, he informs his salesmen, and he reports his plan in the Business Test questionnaire. In the second stage ($t = 2$) the decision is carried out and the customers (as well as the Business Test) are informed. Suppose further that the first-period decision is carried out in the way which Theorem 1′ justifies; viz., by maximisation (of profit, say), after unknown future quantities like buying prices, etc., are replaced by their mean values. This decision is measured by the vector $\mathbf{x}_1^*$, the first component of which specifies the price change planned, the second the number of salesmen informed, etc. In general, $\mathbf{x}_1^*$ will not be identical with the optimal $\mathbf{x}_1^0$, because the replacement by mean values implies certain prediction errors. So let us assume $\mathbf{x}_1^* \neq \mathbf{x}_1^0$. Then (8.185) states that, except for the special case $(\mathbf{xx})_{21} = \mathbf{0}$, this affects the optimality of the pricing behaviour planned in the sense that the suboptimal first-period decision reduces the second-period decision (the "behaviour") that would have been optimal if the first-period decision had not been suboptimal to suboptimality. Actually, "plans having a separate influence on behaviour" can always (at least under our present assumptions) be regarded as first-period decisions which stand in a substitution or complementarity relationship to instrument values of a later period. If this influence is such that plans which are numerically too high or too low are always followed by a revision of the same sign (which corresponds to a positive influence of plans on behaviour), then, in the scalar case $m = 1$, this relationship is that of complementarity. On the other hand, if there is neither substitution nor complementarity, then the revision (8.185) is zero; and this seemed to be the case for the traders of the leather and shoe industry. The selling price planned (the first-period decision) is then determined by the expected buying price, say; and the actual selling price (the second-period decision) by the actual buying price. In such a case of independence there will in general be a close similarity between the forecaster's prediction achievements with respect to buying prices and those with respect to selling prices. If there is complementarity, however, this similarity will be reduced by the tendency to adjust the selling price in the direction of the plan. The selling price predictions are then better than the buying price predictions.[1] Of

[1] For the manufacturers of the leather and shoe industry it is unfortunately impossible to test this proposition, because data on buying prices are not available. In the case of investment surveys, however, it is possible to be more specific. It is well-known that large firms tend to be more successful forecasters of their future investments than small firms; see e.g. I. Friend and J. Bronfenbrenner, "Plant and Equipment Programs and their Realization," *Short-Term Economic Forecasting*, pp. 70ff., and O. J. Firestone, "Investment Forecasting in Canada," *ibidem*, pp. 200ff. It is very plausible that this is due, not only to the superior forecasting techniques employed by large

course, this is not due to better forecasting; it is due to the fact that the forecaster adjusts his controlled variable in such a way that his prediction error is reduced.

It is interesting to note that, whereas substitution and complementarity relationships between x's in $t = 1$ and x's in $t = 2, 3, \ldots$ play a rôle in the loss (8.184), this is not true for the first-period loss (8.186). Indeed, the optimal revisions are determined by such substitution relationships; and the first-period loss, defined as the loss of welfare for the whole period $t = 1, 2, \ldots, T$ resulting from a replacement of $\mathbf{x}^0$ by the x's of the optimal revisions, loses its dependence on $(\mathbf{xx})_{1t}$ for $t > 1$ precisely because of the way in which the revisions are determined by these substitution terms. In later periods, other substitution terms become of importance for the welfare losses. To grasp this, let us consider the first two subperiods combined. Suppose that their instruments have been fixed at the levels $\mathbf{x}_1^*$ and $\mathbf{x}_2^*$, respectively. The welfare maximum which is still attainable, given $\mathbf{x}_1^*$ and $\mathbf{x}_2^*$, can be evaluated along familar lines; and the corresponding loss is then

$$(8.187) \qquad -\tfrac{1}{2}\begin{bmatrix}\mathbf{x}_1^* - \overset{0}{\mathbf{x}_1}\\ \mathbf{x}_2^* - \overset{0}{\mathbf{x}_2}\end{bmatrix}' \begin{bmatrix}(\mathbf{xx})_{11} & (\mathbf{xx})_{12}\\ (\mathbf{xx})_{21} & (\mathbf{xx})_{22}\end{bmatrix}^{-1} \begin{bmatrix}\mathbf{x}_1^* - \overset{0}{\mathbf{x}_1}\\ \mathbf{x}_2^* - \overset{0}{\mathbf{x}_2}\end{bmatrix},$$

which is to be ascribed to the first two subperiods jointly. By subtracting (8.186) from (8.187) we find what may be called the second-period loss, which can be written in the form

$$(8.188) \qquad -\tfrac{1}{2}(\mathbf{x}_2^* - \overset{1}{\mathbf{x}_2})'\,(\mathbf{xx})_*^{22}(\mathbf{x}_2^* - \overset{1}{\mathbf{x}_2}),$$

where $\overset{1}{\mathbf{x}_2}$ is the optimal second-period vector, given the first-period error, and $(\mathbf{xx})_*^{22}$ the lower right-hand submatrix of the inverse matrix

$$\begin{bmatrix}(\mathbf{xx})_{11} & (\mathbf{xx})_{12}\\ (\mathbf{xx})_{21} & (\mathbf{xx})_{22}\end{bmatrix}^{-1}$$

[which is, except for the case $T = 2$, not the same as $(\mathbf{xx})^{22}$!]. So it appears that the second-period loss, though independent of substitution and complementarity with later periods, is not independent of such relationships with the earlier period $t = 1$. Similar results can be easily derived for $t = 3, 4, \ldots, T$.

firms, but also and in particular by the greater inertia which characterises the decision processes of large organisations. The investment realisations are then adjusted in the direction of the investment plans, just as is argued for the selling price policy considered in the text.

8.6.6. Our final problem is that of the welfare losses due to imperfect forecasts rather than imperfect decisions. It will be clear that the generalisation of Theorem 3e is straightforward. One has to realise, of course, that suboptimal first-period decisions may be due, not only to wrong assumptions regarding the effectiveness of first-period instruments with respect to first-period values of noncontrolled variables, but also to such prediction errors with respect to later noncontrolled values, and even to erroneous assumptions on the effectiveness of later instruments with respect to still later noncontrolled values. Similarly, there is a loss if the additive structure of the constraints of the various subperiods is specified incorrectly, or if the policy-maker shifts to another preference function before $t = T$.

Somewhat less obvious is the generalisation of the failure concept of Section 8.4. Let us consider again the case in which the effectiveness of all instruments with respect to all noncontrolled variables of all periods is known, and suppose that at the beginning of $t = 1$ a forecast $\mathbf{s}_e$ of $\mathbf{s}$ (the vector of all successive additive structures) is made.[1] The first-period decision error as a function of the prediction error is then

$$x_1 - x_1^0 = -[(x\cdot)_{11} \dots (x\cdot)_{1T}](\mathbf{s}_e - \mathbf{s}), \tag{8.189}$$

the $(x\cdot)_{1t}$ being matrices of slopes of Tinbergen surfaces, apart from sign. Applying (8.186), we find for the first-period loss

$$-\tfrac{1}{2}(\mathbf{s}_e - \mathbf{s})'\mathbf{F}_1(\mathbf{s}_e - \mathbf{s}), \tag{8.190}$$

where

$$\mathbf{F}_1 = \begin{bmatrix} (\cdot x)_{11} \\ \cdot \\ \cdot \\ \cdot \\ (\cdot x)_{T1} \end{bmatrix} (xx)_{11}^{-1}[(x\cdot)_{11} \dots (x\cdot)_{1T}]. \tag{8.191}$$

The *first-period failure* can then be defined as

$$\text{fail}_1\, \mathbf{s}_e = \frac{(\mathbf{s}_e - \mathbf{s})'\mathbf{F}_1(\mathbf{s}_e - \mathbf{s})}{\mathbf{s}'\mathbf{F}_1\mathbf{s}}, \tag{8.192}$$

[1] Note that $\mathbf{s}_e$ is the forecast made at the beginning of the first subperiod. In general, its subvectors $(s_2)_e \dots$ will differ from the corresponding subvectors of forecasts made in later periods.

where it is to be understood that the additive structure of the constraints during the subperiod immediately before $t = 1$ (which will be indicated by the index 0) is measured as zero: $\mathbf{s}_0 = \mathbf{0}$. This definition implies, as in the static case, a zero failure for perfect forecasts, $\mathbf{s}_e = \mathbf{s}$; and a unit failure in the case of no-change extrapolation, "no change" being interpreted in such a way that it applies to all subperiods: $\mathbf{s}_1 = \ldots = \mathbf{s}_T = \mathbf{s}_0\ (= \mathbf{0})$.

Further results, similar to those of Section 8.4, can be easily derived. Here, we shall confine ourselves to some specific dynamic features. First, the analysis of Chapter V suggests that the underestimation of changes tends to become more and more conspicuous when the horizon moves away. Let us take account of this by introducing the simplifying assumption

$$(\mathbf{s}_t)_e = \theta^t\, \mathbf{s}_t \qquad (0 \leq \theta \leq 1), \tag{8.193}$$

θ being a scalar and $(\mathbf{s}_t)_e$ the t-th subvector of $\mathbf{s}_e$. Secondly, it seems rather plausible that changes in the additive structure of future constraints have less effect on the optimal values of present instruments than the same changes belonging to a less distant future. So let us make the drastic assumption

$$(\mathbf{x}\cdot)_{1t} = \eta^{t-1}(\mathbf{x}\cdot)_{11} \qquad (0 < \eta < 1), \tag{8.194}$$

η being a scalar. Combining (8.194) and (8.191), we find

$$\mathbf{F}_1 = \begin{bmatrix} \mathbf{I} \\ \eta\mathbf{I} \\ \cdot \\ \cdot \\ \cdot \\ \eta^{T-1}\mathbf{I} \end{bmatrix} F_{11}[\mathbf{I} \quad \eta\mathbf{I} \ \ldots \ \eta^{T-1}\mathbf{I}], \tag{8.195}$$

where

$$F_{11} = (\cdot\mathbf{x})_{11}(\mathbf{xx})_{11}^{-1}(\mathbf{x}\cdot)_{11}. \tag{8.196}$$

Further, it follows from (8.193) that

$$\mathbf{s}_e - \mathbf{s} = -\begin{bmatrix} (1-\theta)\,\mathbf{s}_1 \\ (1-\theta^2)\,\mathbf{s}_2 \\ \cdot \\ \cdot \\ \cdot \\ (1-\theta^T)\,\mathbf{s}_T \end{bmatrix}. \tag{8.197}$$

Finally, combining (8.197), (8.195) and (8.192), we arrive at the following result:

$$(8.198)\qquad \text{fail}_1\, \mathbf{s}_e = \frac{[\sum_1^T(1-\theta^t)\,\eta^{t-1}\mathbf{s}_t]'\,F_{11}[\sum_1^T(1-\theta)^t\eta^{t-1}\mathbf{s}_t]}{\sum_1^T\eta^{t-1}\mathbf{s}_t]'\,F_{11}[\sum_1^T\eta^{t-1}\mathbf{s}_t]}.$$

As is to be expected, the first-period failure depends on the time pattern of the additive structure of the constraints. To make further progress, we shall make two alternative assumptions. The first is that of a jump at the beginning of $t = 1$ and constancy afterwards:

$$(8.199)\qquad \mathbf{s}_0 = \mathbf{0};\ \mathbf{s}_1 = \mathbf{s}_2 = \ldots = \mathbf{s}_T.$$

This gives

$$(8.200)\qquad \sqrt{(\text{fail}_1\, \mathbf{s}_e)} = 1 - \theta\,\frac{\sum_1^T(\eta\theta)^{t-1}}{\sum_1^T \eta^{t-1}} \approx \frac{1-\theta}{1-\eta\theta},$$

the approximation error of which tends to zero for large T. The alternative assumption is that of linear development over time:

$$(8.201)\qquad \mathbf{s}_t = t\mathbf{s}_1,$$

which implies $\mathbf{s}_0 = \mathbf{0}$ as before. In this case we have

$$(8.202)\qquad \sqrt{(\text{fail}_1\, \mathbf{s}_e)} = 1 - \theta\,\frac{\sum_1^T t(\eta\theta)^{t-1}}{\sum_1^T t\eta^{t-1}} \approx \frac{(1-\theta)\,(1-\eta^2\theta)}{(1-\eta\theta)^2}.$$

The following can be concluded. First, the expressions (8.200) and (8.202) are increasing functions of η as long as $0 < \eta,\ \theta < 1$. Hence in both cases the failure is larger than in the static situation $\eta = 0$. Second, when η is in the neighbourhood of 1, the failure is close to 1 irrespective of the value of θ (except when $\theta \approx 1$, the case of almost perfect forecasts). This, too, holds for both alternative assumptions (8.199) and (8.201); and neither of these results is difficult to understand. For, if η is far from zero, later constraints are not unimportant for present decisions; and such constraints are poorly predicted according to (8.193), unless θ is sufficiently close to 1. Another interesting feature is that the failure in the linear case (8.201) is always larger than in that of the jump, given η and θ. It should be noted, however, that these alternative situations are not fully comparable. Although they are characterised by the same prediction pattern relative to the actual vector $\mathbf{s}$ – cf. (8.193)—, the actual time pattern to be predicted is not the same. So, combining (8.199) and (8.193), we find that the implied forecasts of $\mathbf{s}_2, \mathbf{s}_3, \ldots$ amount to a reversal of trends immediately after $t = 1$; i.e., the predicted change from $t = 0$ till $t = 1$ is $(\mathbf{s}_1)_e - \mathbf{s}_0 = \theta\mathbf{s}_1$, and the predicted change from $t = 1$ till $t = 2$ has opposite sign: $(\mathbf{s}_2)_e - (\mathbf{s}_1)_e = -\theta(1-\theta)\,\mathbf{s}_1$. Similarly, for (8.201), we find that trends are supposed to change in direction, but not necessarily during $t = 2$; the reversal is predicted to occur around $t \approx 1/(1-\theta)$. At first sight, the prediction of a reversal may seem unplausible; but this is not at all the case. It happens rather frequently that the long-term development of the phenomenon to be predicted is supposed to be of a stationary type, in which case the prediction of trend reversals is even reasonable. This holds in particular when there are seasonal fluctuations.[1]

8.6.7. This completes Chapter VIII as well as its section on dynamics. A survey of the results of this chapter in connection with those of the earlier parts of this book will follow in Chapter IX; here, we confine ourselves to the findings of Section 8.6.

It appears then that the dynamic generalisation is straightforward in many respects. In the beginning the appearance was to the contrary, which was due to the concept of a strategy. However, the result of Theorem 1′ implies that, just as in the static case, the policy-maker can replace stochastic future quantities by their mean values and still arrive at those instrument values which maximise the mean value of welfare. It is true, some qualifications are necessary: Theorem 1′ is confined to first-period instrument values, and some of its conditions are stronger than those of its static analogue. But the first-period instrument values are the most important ones, since they are the policy-maker's immediate concern; for the second period he can proceed, at the end of the first period, in the same way by replacing those quantities which are still future by their new conditional means, given the information that became available to him during the first period. As to the stronger conditions of Theorem 1′ (linearity of constraints,

[1] See e.g. R. FERBER, *The Railroad Shippers' Forecasts* (Urbana, Ill., 1953), pp. 70–73.

quadraticity of preferences), it cannot be denied that this is a disadvantage for applications; but its importance should not be exaggerated, because the stronger conditions must also be imposed in the further analysis, both in the static and in the dynamic case.

Given the result of Theorem 1′, the further generalisations are indeed much more straightforward. Optimal reaction functions, substitution, complementarity, etc., are concepts which are entirely analogous to the similar concepts of Section 8.3. This does not mean that these generalisations are trivial. On the contrary, one of the results is a clarification of the idea of plans affecting behaviour. A further interesting feature is the distinction between the loss of welfare which is due to a series of decisions specified for the whole period, and the loss associated with a suboptimal decision for one single subperiod. Just as in the static case, finally, it is possible to use the concept of the failure of a forecast, and to arrive at numerical statements, provided the multiplicative structure of the constraints is known.

8.6.8. After the theoretical analysis of this chapter was completed in 1957, a number of applications were made; and this is a convenient place for a summary of their results.

The first (by P. J. M. van den Bogaard and the present author) is a pilot study dealing with the American economy in the four-year period 1933–36.[1] It is based on Klein's six-equation model of the United States as far as the constraints are concerned,[2] while the preference function was chosen in the light of the depression conditions prevailing at that time. Three instruments were used, viz., Government wage bill, indirect taxes, and Government expenditure on goods and services (all in real terms); and three noncontrolled variables, viz., consumption, net investment, and a distribution variable which effectively measures the ratio of profits to the private wage bill. The preference function was formulated in two stages: first, for each of the six variables and each of the four years "desired values" were chosen; second, a positive-definite quadratic form in the deviations between actual and desired values was taken and the minimisation of this form is then equivalent with the maximisation of the quadratic preference

[1] P. J. M. van den Bogaard and H. Theil, "Macrodynamic Policy-Making: An Application of Strategy and Certainty Equivalence Concepts to the Economy of the United States, 1933–1936," *Metroeconomica*, Vol. 11 (1959), pp. 149–167.

[2] See L. R. Klein, *Economic Fluctuations in the United States, 1921–1941* (New York – London, 1950), Chapter III (Model I).

function. In this first application a very simple quadratic form was chosen, viz., the one corresponding with the unit matrix. The behaviour of the strategy corresponding with Theorem 1′ was analysed in detail, together with its consequences for the noncontrolled variables; it appeared, for instance, that the 1936-value of national income according to this strategy was larger than the level that was actually realised in any interwar year except 1941 (under the assumptions underlying this strategy, of course!). Furthermore, (unbiased) point predictions were obtained for future behaviour according to the strategy; i.e., if we calculate the vector (8.179) whose first m components supply the appropriate first-year decision, we can use the other $m(T-1)$ components as forecasts for the decisions of later years. Furthermore, by substituting the vector (8.179) into the constraint (8.168), we obtain unbiased forecasts of the values to be taken by the noncontrolled variables. Finally, these forecasts can be revised every year; i.e., at the beginning of 1934 when the original four-year horizon is reduced to three years, the procedure can be applied again (now on the basis of a three-year strategy) and this leads to new forecasts. These predictions are unbiased too, but now conditional on the information available at the beginning of 1934. And so on.

The forecasts just-mentioned were rather accurate, which is at least partly due to the fact that it was not necessary to take account of exogenous variables which are beyond the control of the policy-maker. When there are such variables it is necessary to predict their future values and this of course leads to additional errors. In a much more extensive study by P. J. M. VAN DEN BOGAARD and A. P. BARTEN,[1] dealing with the Dutch economy in the three-year period 1957–59, this feature was an important aspect. Its constraints are based on an econometric model consisting of 41 equations (out of which 12 are behavioural) in 59 endogenous and exogenous variables. Five instruments were used, viz., the general wage rate, indirect taxes, direct taxes on wage income, direct taxes on nonwage income, and government expenditure on commodities; and four noncontrolled variables, viz., private employment, the price level of consumption, the share of wages in national income, and the surplus on the balance

[1] P. J. M. VAN DEN BOGAARD and A. P. BARTEN, "Optimal Macroeconomic Decision Rules for the Netherlands, 1957–1959." Report 5915 of the Econometric Institute of the Netherlands School of Economics. (The publications mentioned in the footnotes of the next three pages all refer to the Report Series of the Econometric Institute and the International Center for Management Science, except when stated otherwise.)

of payments. Three alternative preference functions were introduced, one of which represents an employee's point of view, the second that of an employer, and the third a viewpoint which is "neutral" with respect to the employer-employee distinction. These preference functions are all quadratic as in the case of the preceding paragraph, but they are more refined in several respects. First, no equal weights are given to discrepancies between actual and desired values of different variables, so that the matrix of the quadratic form to be minimised does not have equal elements in the diagonal. Second, this matrix contains a number of nonzero diagonal elements. This is *i.a.* due to the fact that a penalty was put on violent instrument changes in terms of a smoothing amendment, which amounts to the addition of a weighted sum of squares of successive differences of instrument values to the linear combination of squared discrepancies between actual and desired values. The result of this analysis is a set of three 3-year strategies corresponding with each of the three preference functions, together with a number of forecasts of the type discussed at the end of the preceding paragraph.

A third application has to do with the minimisation of a quadratic cost function depending on production, production changes, and inventory levels. This subject was considered earlier by C. C. HOLT, F. MODIGLIANI, H. A. SIMON and J. F. MUTH,[1] who derived an optimal strategy for production and work force; and it was taken up again by C. VAN DE PANNE and G. J. AEYELTS AVERINK[2] who analysed the additional cost (which is the interpretation of the loss of welfare in this case) due to suboptimal production and work force decisions and to imperfect sales forecasts. A related management-science application was made by E. KAPTEIN and the present author,[3] who also considered the loss-of-welfare consequences of the disturbances of Klein's equation system in the context of the first application mentioned

[1] C. C. HOLT, F. MODIGLIANI and J. F. MUTH, "Derivation of a Linear Decision Rule for Production and Employment Scheduling." *Management Science*, Vol. 2 (1956), pp. 159–177. C. C. HOLT, F. MODIGLIANI and H. A. SIMON, "A Linear Decision Rule for Production and Employment Scheduling." *Management Science*, Vol. 2 (1955), pp. 1–30.

[2] C. VAN DE PANNE and G. J. AEYELTS AVERINK, "Imperfect Management Decisions and Predictions and Their Financial Implications in Dynamic Quadratic Cost Minimization." Report 6020.

[3] H. THEIL and E. KAPTEIN, "The Effect of Forecasting Errors on Optimal Programming of Production-Inventory and Anti-Depression Policies." Report 5906; an abbreviated version of this report will be published in the Proceedings of the Sixth Annual International Meeting of The Institute of Management Sciences.

above; it appeared *i.a.* that the disturbed character of the consumption function of this model is more serious than that of the investment function in spite of the fact that the ratio of the variance of the disturbances of the former function to the variance of consumption is much smaller than the ratio of the variance of the disturbances of the latter function to that of investment.

Another application (by T. KLOEK and the present author) has to do with the uncertainty of the coefficients of the constraints.[1] In all other studies mentioned above it was assumed that the estimated coefficients of the equation system that underlies the constraints coincide with the "true" parameters, but this is in general of course not the case although it is difficult to conceive of an alternative procedure. It is possible, however, to measure the loss of welfare which is associated with the use of erroneous coefficients; and also, by taking mean values, to compute the average loss associated with the variances and covariances of their sampling errors. This was analysed for a number of alternative horizons (1, 2, 3 and 4 years) in the context of Klein's Model I. It appears that as far as the variances are concerned, the contribution of the sampling error of the marginal propensity to consume of the wage-earners to the mean loss of welfare exceeds that of the sampling errors of all other coefficients of the consumption function (in spite of the small standard error of this propensity), and that the large covariance of the current and lagged capitalists' marginal propensities to consume has a negative (and hence favourable) influence on the mean loss. This holds for all alternative horizons considered. A further detailed analysis of the consequences of alternative horizons, both for this macroeconomic application and for the production–inventory case, was made by VAN DEN BOGAARD, A. MONREAL LUQUE and C. VAN DE PANNE.[2]

Finally, there is the problem of socially optimal decisions in the case when the society has conflicting preference functions. This is ARROW's famous problem,[3] and it was reconsidered by VAN DEN

[1] H. THEIL and T. KLOEK, "The Operational Implications of Imperfect Models," Chapter 8 of *Mathematical Methods in the Social Sciences, 1959* (edited by K. J. ARROW, S. KARLIN and P. SUPPES), Stanford, 1960.
[2] P. J. M. VAN DEN BOGAARD, A. MONREAL LUQUE et C. VAN DE PANNE, "Etude sur les implications des horizons alternatifs dans la programmation quadratique dynamique." Report 6019.
[3] See the end of 7.1.8.

BOGAARD and VERSLUIS[1] in the context of the Dutch macroeconomic application which deals with three alternative preference functions. Their approach is to combine these functions linearly, and to choose the weights of this combination in such a way that the loss which i inflicts upon j if he succeeds in imposing his own optimal decision equals the loss which j inflicts upon i (where i and j stand for the authors of the competing preference functions). This symmetry condition, which amounts to an effort to impose "fairness" on inter-individual utility comparisons, cannot be met under all conditions; it is then weakened such that symmetry is approximated as well as possible in some well-defined sense. In a later paper, VAN DEN BOGAARD and G. ARNAIZ[2] considered the sensitivity of decision and welfare level attained with respect to changes in the weights of the individual preference functions.

[1] P. J. M. VAN DEN BOGAARD and J. VERSLUIS, "The Design of Socially Optimal Decisions." Report 6004; an abbreviated version of this report will be published in the Proceedings of the Second International Conference on Operational Research.

[2] See P. J. M. VAN DEN BOGAARD and G. ARNAIZ, "On the Sensitivity of Committee Decisions under Alternative Quadratic Criteria." Report 6107.

Appendix to Chapter VIII

8.A. The Minimisation of the Parent Substitution Component by Generalised Least-Squares

8.A.1. We shall show that AITKEN's method of generalised least-squares, as expounded in 6.2.6, is best linear unbiased in the sense that it minimises every positive-definite quadratic form in the sampling errors within the class of linear unbiased estimators.[1] We shall make the same assumptions as those of 6.2.6, viz., that the relationship between a dependent and certain predetermined variables is given by the matrix equation $\mathbf{y} = \mathbf{X}\boldsymbol{\beta} + \mathbf{u}$, where $\mathbf{y}$ is the T-elements column vector of values taken by the dependent variable, $\mathbf{X}$ the nonstochastic $T \times \Lambda$ matrix of values taken by the predetermined variables (its rank being Λ), $\boldsymbol{\beta}$ the column vector of parameters to be estimated, and $\mathbf{u}$ the disturbance vector with zero mean and positive-definite covariance matrix, $\mathscr{E}(\mathbf{uu}') = \boldsymbol{\Omega}$.

Any estimator of $\boldsymbol{\beta}$ which is linear in $\mathbf{y}$ can be written in the form

$$\mathbf{b} = \mathbf{Ay}, \tag{8.203}$$

where $\mathbf{A}$ is some nonstochastic matrix of order $\Lambda \times T$. Combining (8.203) with $\mathbf{y} = \mathbf{X}\boldsymbol{\beta} + \mathbf{u}$ and $\mathscr{E}\mathbf{u} = \mathbf{0}$, we find that we have unbiasedness identically in $\boldsymbol{\beta}$ if and only if

$$\mathbf{AX} = \mathbf{I}, \tag{8.204}$$

$\mathbf{I}$ being the unit matrix of order Λ. Our purpose is to show that, if $\mathbf{A}$ is chosen according to the rule

$$\mathbf{A} = (\mathbf{X}'\boldsymbol{\Omega}^{-1}\mathbf{X})^{-1}\mathbf{X}'\boldsymbol{\Omega}^{-1}, \tag{8.205}$$

[1] The "best linear unbiased" character of least-squares is stated more frequently in two alternative forms; viz., that the difference between the covariance matrix of least-squares and that of another linear unbiased estimation method is a definite matrix; and that least-squares minimises the variance of every linear combination of regression coefficients. These alternative forms are, of course, not independent of the one considered here.

this choice minimises the mean value of any quadratic form in the sampling errors,

$$(8.206) \qquad \mathscr{E}[(\mathbf{b}-\boldsymbol{\beta})'\mathbf{Q}(\mathbf{b}-\boldsymbol{\beta})],$$

for whatever positive-definite $\mathbf{Q}$, subject to (8.204) and to the condition that $\mathbf{A}$ be nonstochastic. In particular, $\mathbf{Q}$ may be the matrix of the substitution component of some policy-maker.

8.A.2. The proof is carried out by straightforward minimisation. We have

$$(8.207) \qquad \mathscr{E}[(\mathbf{b}-\boldsymbol{\beta})'\mathbf{Q}(\mathbf{b}-\boldsymbol{\beta})] = \mathscr{E}(\mathbf{u}'\mathbf{A}'\mathbf{Q}\mathbf{A}\mathbf{u}) = \text{tr } \mathbf{A}'\mathbf{Q}\mathbf{A}\boldsymbol{\Omega}.$$

This trace has to be minimised subject to (8.204). So we introduce a matrix of Lagrange multipliers, $\mathbf{M} = [\mu_{\lambda\lambda'}]$, and consider the derivatives of

$$(8.208) \qquad \text{tr } \mathbf{A}'\mathbf{Q}\mathbf{A}\boldsymbol{\Omega} - \text{tr } \mathbf{M}'(\mathbf{A}\mathbf{X}-\mathbf{I}) =$$

$$= \sum_{\lambda,\lambda'} q_{\lambda\lambda'} \sum_{t,t'} a_{\lambda t}\omega_{tt'}a_{\lambda' t'} - \sum_{\lambda,\lambda'} \mu_{\lambda\lambda'}\{\sum_{t} a_{\lambda t}x_{\lambda'}(t) - \delta_{\lambda\lambda'}\},$$

where $\delta_{\lambda\lambda'}$ is the Kronecker delta (0 if $\lambda \neq \lambda'$, 1 if $\lambda = \lambda'$), and $q_{\lambda\lambda'}$ and $a_{\lambda t}$ are elements of $\mathbf{Q}$ and $\mathbf{A}$, respectively. Putting the derivatives equal to zero gives

$$(8.209) \qquad 2\mathbf{Q}\mathbf{A}\boldsymbol{\Omega} - \mathbf{M}\mathbf{X}' = \mathbf{0}.$$

Postmultiplying this by $\boldsymbol{\Omega}^{-1}\mathbf{X}$ and using (8.204) gives $\mathbf{M} = 2\mathbf{Q}(\mathbf{X}'\boldsymbol{\Omega}^{-1}\mathbf{X})^{-1}$, from which (8.205) follows.

In order to be sure that the extremum is a minimum, we consider an arbitrary estimator in the neighbourhood of generalised least-squares, say $\mathbf{b} = \mathbf{A}\mathbf{y}$ with

$$(8.210) \qquad \mathbf{A} = (\mathbf{X}'\boldsymbol{\Omega}^{-1}\mathbf{X})^{-1}\mathbf{X}'\boldsymbol{\Omega}^{-1} + \varepsilon\mathbf{R},$$

where ε is a scalar and $\mathbf{R}$ a $\Lambda \times T$ matrix, both nonstochastic. The requirement of unbiasedness implies

$$(8.211) \qquad \mathbf{R}\mathbf{X} = \mathbf{0}.$$

Applying (8.207), we find for the mean value of this quadratic form:

$$(8.212) \qquad \mathscr{E}[(\mathbf{b}-\boldsymbol{\beta})'\mathbf{Q}(\mathbf{b}-\boldsymbol{\beta})] = G_0 + \varepsilon G_1 + \varepsilon^2 G_2,$$

where G_0 is the quadratic form of generalised least-squares, and

$$G_1 = \text{tr } \mathbf{R}'\mathbf{Q}(\mathbf{X}'\mathbf{\Omega}^{-1}\mathbf{X})^{-1}\mathbf{X}' + \text{tr } \mathbf{\Omega}^{-1}\mathbf{X}(\mathbf{X}'\mathbf{\Omega}^{-1}\mathbf{X})^{-1}\mathbf{QR\Omega}$$
$$G_2 = \text{tr } \mathbf{R}'\mathbf{QR\Omega} = \mathscr{E}(\mathbf{u}'\mathbf{R}'\mathbf{QRu}).$$

But the two traces of G_1 vanish:

$$\text{tr } \mathbf{R}'\mathbf{Q}(\mathbf{X}'\mathbf{\Omega}^{-1}\mathbf{X})^{-1}\mathbf{X}' = \text{tr } \mathbf{X}'\mathbf{R}'\mathbf{Q}(\mathbf{X}'\mathbf{\Omega}^{-1}\mathbf{X})^{-1} = 0$$

because of (8.211); and similarly for the other trace. Hence

$$\mathscr{E}[(\mathbf{b} - \boldsymbol{\beta})'\mathbf{Q}(\mathbf{b} - \boldsymbol{\beta})] = G_0 + \varepsilon^2\mathscr{E}(\mathbf{u}'\mathbf{R}'\mathbf{QRu}), \tag{8.213}$$

from which it follows that the quadratic form (8.206) is always larger than G_0, provided $\mathbf{Q}$ is indeed a positive-definite matrix.

8.B. Best Linear Estimation in Regression Analysis

8.B.1. We make the same assumptions as those mentioned in 8.A.1, but consider now the following problem. We want an estimator of $\boldsymbol{\beta}$ which is linear in $\mathbf{y}$, but not necessarily unbiased, and which minimises the mean value of a quadratic form in the sampling errors, (8.206), within the class of all estimators of $\boldsymbol{\beta}$ that are also linear in $\mathbf{y}$. It will be shown in 8.B.2 that this estimator is $\mathbf{b}^0 = \mathbf{A}^0\mathbf{y}$ with

$$\mathbf{A}^0 = \boldsymbol{\beta}\boldsymbol{\beta}'\mathbf{X}'(\mathbf{X}\boldsymbol{\beta}\boldsymbol{\beta}'\mathbf{X}' + \mathbf{\Omega})^{-1}, \tag{8.214}$$

and that it minimises (8.206) for whatever positive-definite $\mathbf{Q}$. For the special case $\Lambda = 1$, $\mathbf{\Omega} = \sigma^2\mathbf{I}$, this leads to (8.137). Furthermore, the moment matrix of this estimator,

$$\mathbf{S}(\mathbf{b}^0) = \mathscr{E}[(\mathbf{b}^0 - \boldsymbol{\beta})(\mathbf{b}^0 - \boldsymbol{\beta})'],$$

will be shown to be equal to

$$\mathbf{S}(\mathbf{b}^0) = [1 - \boldsymbol{\beta}'\mathbf{X}'(\mathbf{X}\boldsymbol{\beta}\boldsymbol{\beta}'\mathbf{X}' + \mathbf{\Omega})^{-1}\mathbf{X}\boldsymbol{\beta}]\boldsymbol{\beta}\boldsymbol{\beta}'. \tag{8.215}$$

All principal minors of this matrix of the second order and higher vanish, which means that the estimation is of the scalar rather than of the vector type. This is easily seen if we write the estimator in the form

$$\mathbf{b}^0 = \boldsymbol{\beta}\mathscr{E}\mathbf{y}'\{\mathscr{E}(\mathbf{yy}')\}^{-1}\mathbf{y}, \tag{8.216}$$

so that $\mathbf{b}^0$ is nothing else than the vector to be estimated, $\boldsymbol{\beta}$, multiplied by the scalar $\mathscr{E}\mathbf{y}'\{\mathscr{E}(\mathbf{yy}')\}^{-1}\mathbf{y}$. Clearly, this makes the generalisation of not more than limited interest.

As argued in the text, such estimation methods have not only the disadvantage that the estimator depends on the unknown parameters, but also that the quadratic form (8.206), viz.

$$\boldsymbol{\beta}'(\mathbf{AX}-\mathbf{I})'\mathbf{Q}(\mathbf{AX}-\mathbf{I})\boldsymbol{\beta} + \operatorname{tr}\mathbf{A}'\mathbf{QA}\boldsymbol{\Omega} \tag{8.217}$$

(cf. below), is dependent on this parameter vector. If we would confine ourselves to estimators of the type $\mathbf{b} = \mathbf{Ay}$ where $\mathbf{A}$ is independent of the unknown $\boldsymbol{\beta}$, then the expression (8.217) will sometimes be larger than the form (8.206) for generalised least-squares, and sometimes smaller, depending on $\boldsymbol{\beta}$. It is easily seen that, for any fixed $\mathbf{A}$, there is always a $\boldsymbol{\beta}$ such that (8.217) exceeds the form (8.206) for generalised least-squares.

8.B.2. The proof is as follows. If the estimator $\mathbf{b}$ is not necessarily unbiased, the sampling error of $\mathbf{b}$ must be written as

$$\mathbf{b} - \boldsymbol{\beta} = (\mathbf{AX}-\mathbf{I})\boldsymbol{\beta} + \mathbf{Au},$$

so that the quadratic form (8.206) becomes

$$\mathscr{E}[(\mathbf{b}-\boldsymbol{\beta})'\mathbf{Q}(\mathbf{b}-\boldsymbol{\beta})] = \\ = \boldsymbol{\beta}'(\mathbf{AX}-\mathbf{I})'\mathbf{Q}(\mathbf{AX}-\mathbf{I})\boldsymbol{\beta} + \operatorname{tr}\mathbf{A}'\mathbf{QA}\boldsymbol{\Omega}, \tag{8.218}$$

which is the same as (8.217). This form has to be minimised unconditionally by varying the elements of $\mathbf{A}$. Differentiation gives

$$2\mathbf{Q}(\mathbf{AX}-\mathbf{I})\boldsymbol{\beta\beta}'\mathbf{X}' + 2\mathbf{QA}\boldsymbol{\Omega} = \mathbf{0}$$

and hence

$$\mathbf{A}^0 = \boldsymbol{\beta\beta}'\mathbf{X}'(\mathbf{X}\boldsymbol{\beta\beta}'\mathbf{X}' + \boldsymbol{\Omega})^{-1}, \tag{8.214}$$

which is the result to be proved. The moment matrix (8.215) can then be derived in a straightforward manner.

In order to verify that the extremum is a minimum, we write $\mathbf{A} = \mathbf{A}^0 + \varepsilon\mathbf{R}$ in (8.218), just as we did in 8.A.2. The resulting quadratic form is then the sum of three expressions, viz., one which is independent of ε, one which is linear, and one which is quadratic in ε.

The first is the quadratic form that corresponds to the estimation method (8.214); the second vanishes; and the third is

$$\varepsilon^2(\boldsymbol{\beta}'\mathbf{X}'\mathbf{R}'\mathbf{Q}\mathbf{R}\mathbf{X}\boldsymbol{\beta} + \operatorname{tr} \mathbf{R}'\mathbf{Q}\mathbf{R}\boldsymbol{\Omega}),$$

which has always the required sign.

8.C. Best Quadratic Estimation of the Residual Variance in Regression Analysis

8.C.1. It is of some interest to add a similar result for the variance σ^2 of the disturbances in a regression equation. For this purpose we shall assume that the covariance matrix of the disturbances is of the scalar type, so that we can replace $\boldsymbol{\Omega}$ by $\sigma^2\mathbf{I}$, while moreover it will prove useful to assume that the disturbances are all normally distributed.

It is well-known that under these conditions the maximum-likelihood estimator of σ^2 is found by adding the squares of the least-squares estimated disturbances and dividing this sum of squares by T, the number of observations. To arrive at an optimal estimator of the type discussed in the preceding pages, we shall confine ourselves to the class of estimators which are quadratic in $\mathbf{y}$ (linear estimators do not carry us very far with respect to σ^2), so that the estimator is of the form $\mathbf{y}'\mathbf{H}\mathbf{y}$, where $\mathbf{H}$ is a nonstochastic matrix which can be assumed symmetric without loss of generality. Combining this with $\mathbf{y} = \mathbf{X}\boldsymbol{\beta} + \mathbf{u}$, we obtain

$$\mathbf{y}'\mathbf{H}\mathbf{y} = \boldsymbol{\beta}'\mathbf{X}'\mathbf{H}\mathbf{X}\boldsymbol{\beta} + \boldsymbol{\beta}'\mathbf{X}'\mathbf{H}\mathbf{u} + \mathbf{u}'\mathbf{H}\mathbf{X}\boldsymbol{\beta} + \mathbf{u}'\mathbf{H}\mathbf{u}, \tag{8.219}$$

the mean value of which is

$$\mathscr{E}(\mathbf{y}'\mathbf{H}\mathbf{y}) = \boldsymbol{\beta}'\mathbf{X}'\mathbf{H}\mathbf{X}\boldsymbol{\beta} + \mathscr{E}(\mathbf{u}'\mathbf{H}\mathbf{u}). \tag{8.220}$$

If we impose the condition that the distribution of the estimator be independent of the unknown parameter $\boldsymbol{\beta}$, this implies the restriction

$$\mathbf{H}\mathbf{X} = \mathbf{0}, \tag{8.221}$$

in which case the estimator itself is simplified to

$$\mathbf{y}'\mathbf{H}\mathbf{y} = \mathbf{u}'\mathbf{H}\mathbf{u} \tag{8.222}$$

and its mean value to

$$\mathscr{E}(\mathbf{y}'\mathbf{H}\mathbf{y}) = \mathscr{E}(\mathbf{u}'\mathbf{H}\mathbf{u}) = \sigma^2 \operatorname{tr} \mathbf{H}. \tag{8.223}$$

Now it has been shown by Hsu that if we impose the restriction of unbiasedness, which in view of (8.223) amounts to tr $\mathbf{H} = 1$, the estimator $\mathbf{y'Hy}$ which has minimum variance is the estimator for which $\mathbf{H}$ is

$$\frac{1}{T - \Lambda}[\mathbf{I} - \mathbf{X}(\mathbf{X'X})^{-1}\mathbf{X'}];$$

i.e., the estimator is the sum of squares of the least-squares estimated disturbances divided by the number of observations less the number of $\boldsymbol{\beta}$-components.[1] This is "best quadratic unbiased." It has been shown by A. L. M. Schweitzer and the present author that if we do not impose the unbiasedness restriction, the estimator $\mathbf{y'Hy}$ which has a minimum second moment around the parameter σ^2 is the estimator for which $\mathbf{H}$ is

$$\frac{1}{T - \Lambda + 2}[\mathbf{I} - \mathbf{X}(\mathbf{X'X})^{-1}\mathbf{X'}];$$

i.e., the sum of squares of the least-squares estimated disturbances is now divided by a larger number ($T - \Lambda + 2$ instead of $T - \Lambda$).[2] This will be shown in 8.C.2, which also contains Hsu's result for the case of normality. As will also be shown, the bias of this "best quadratic" estimator is $-2\sigma^2/(T - \Lambda + 2)$ and its second-order sampling moment $2\sigma^4/(T - \Lambda + 2)$.

8.C.2. The second-order moment of the estimator $\mathbf{y'Hy} = \mathbf{u'Hu}$ around σ^2 is given by

$$\begin{aligned}(8.224)\qquad \mathscr{E}(\mathbf{u'Hu} - \sigma^2)^2 &= \mathscr{E}(\mathbf{u'Hu})^2 - 2\sigma^2\mathscr{E}(\mathbf{u'Hu}) + \sigma^4 = \\ &= \mathscr{E}(\mathbf{u'Hu})^2 - 2\sigma^4 \operatorname{tr} \mathbf{H} + \sigma^4.\end{aligned}$$

In scalar terms, the first mean value can be written as

$$(8.225)\qquad \mathscr{E}(\mathbf{u'Hu})^2 = \sum_{s,s'} h_{ss'} \sum_{t,t'} h_{tt'}\mathscr{E}\{u(s)u(s')u(t)u(t')\},$$

where the s's and t's are summed from 1 to T and where the h's stand for elements of $\mathbf{H}$. Now the mean value on the right of (8.225), for each s, s', t, t'-combination, is nonzero only if the s's and t's are pair-

[1] See P. L. Hsu, "On the Best Unbiassed Quadratic Estimate of the Variance." *Statistical Research Memoirs*, Vol. 2 (1938), pp. 91–104. See also the end of 6.2.3.
[2] See H. Theil and A. L. M. Schweitzer, "The Best Quadratic Estimator of the Residual Variance in Regression Analysis." Report 5802 of the Econometric Institute of the Netherlands School of Economics; to be published in *Statistica Neerlandica*.

wise equal (including the case in which all four are equal). It is therefore useful to distinguish between four possibilities, one of which is the case in which all s's and t's are equal (because this leads to fourth moments of disturbances, which under normality conditions are equal to three times the square of the variance). For example, in the case $s = s'$, $t = t'$, $s \neq t$ we have for the right-hand side of (8.225):

$$\sum_{s \neq t} \sum h_{ss} h_{tt} \mathscr{E}\{u(s)^2 u(t)^2\} = \sigma^4\{\sum_s h_{ss} \sum_t h_{tt} - \sum_s h_{ss}^2\} = \\ = \sigma^4\{(\text{tr } \mathbf{H})^2 - \sum_s h_{ss}^2\}.$$

The four possibilities and thei- contributions to the right-hand side of (8.225) are then:

Case	*Contribution to* (8.225)
$s = s'$, $t = t'$, $s \neq t$	$\sigma^4\{(\text{tr } \mathbf{H})^2 - \Sigma h_{ss}^2\}$
$s = t$, $s' = t'$, $s \neq s'$	$\sigma^4\{\text{tr } \mathbf{H}^2 - \Sigma h_{ss}^2\}$
$s = t'$, $s' = t$, $s \neq s'$	$\sigma^4\{\text{tr } \mathbf{H}^2 - \Sigma h_{ss}^2\}$
$s = s' = t = t'$	$3\sigma^4 \Sigma h_{ss}^2$.

Adding these four components, we obtain for the mean value of $(\mathbf{u}'\mathbf{H}\mathbf{u})^2$:

(8.226) $$\mathscr{E}(\mathbf{u}'\mathbf{H}\mathbf{u})^2 = \sigma^4\{(\text{tr } \mathbf{H})^2 + 2 \text{ tr } \mathbf{H}^2\};$$

and combining this with (8.224), we find for the second moment of the estimator around σ^2:

(8.227) $$\mathscr{E}(\mathbf{u}'\mathbf{H}\mathbf{u} - \sigma^2)^2 = \sigma^4\{1 - 2 \text{ tr } \mathbf{H} + (\text{tr } \mathbf{H})^2 + 2 \text{ tr } \mathbf{H}^2\} = \\ = \sigma^4\{(1 - \text{tr } \mathbf{H})^2 + 2 \text{ tr } \mathbf{H}^2\},$$

which is to be minimised subject to (8.221). We therefore consider the extremum of

(8.228) $$(1 - \text{tr } \mathbf{H})^2 + 2 \text{ tr } \mathbf{H}^2 - \text{tr } \mathbf{N}'\mathbf{H}\mathbf{X},$$

where $\mathbf{N}$ is a $T \times \Lambda$ matrix of Lagrangean multipliers. Differentiating (8.228) with respect to the elements of $\mathbf{H}$ and putting the result equal to a zero matrix gives

(8.229) $$-2(1 - \text{tr } \mathbf{H})\mathbf{I} + 4\mathbf{H} - \mathbf{N}\mathbf{X}' = \mathbf{0}.$$

Postmultiplying by $\mathbf{X}$ and applying (8.221) gives

$$\mathbf{N} = -2(1 - \text{tr } \mathbf{H})\mathbf{X}(\mathbf{X}'\mathbf{X})^{-1},$$

which, when combined with (8.229), gives

(8.230) $$4\mathbf{H} - 2(1 - \operatorname{tr}\mathbf{H})[\mathbf{I} - \mathbf{X}(\mathbf{X}'\mathbf{X})^{-1}\mathbf{X}'] = \mathbf{0}.$$

Taking the trace, we find

(8.231) $$\operatorname{tr}\mathbf{H} = \frac{T - \Lambda}{T - \Lambda + 2},$$

which in combination with (8.230) gives

(8.232) $$\mathbf{H} = \frac{1}{T - \Lambda + 2}[\mathbf{I} - \mathbf{X}(\mathbf{X}'\mathbf{X})^{-1}\mathbf{X}'],$$

which is to be proved. The bias of the estimator follows directly from (8.223) and (8.231). For the second moment we apply (8.227) and (8.232):

(8.233) $$\mathscr{E}(\mathbf{u}'\mathbf{H}\mathbf{u} - \sigma^2)^2 = \sigma^4\left\{\left(1 - \frac{T - \Lambda}{T - \Lambda + 2}\right)^2 + \right. \\ \left. + 2\frac{T - \Lambda}{(T - \Lambda + 2)^2}\right\} = \frac{2\sigma^4}{T - \Lambda + 2}.$$

To ensure that the extremum is really a minimum, we introduce another estimator $\mathbf{y}'\mathbf{H}_1\mathbf{y} = \mathbf{u}'\mathbf{H}_1\mathbf{u}$ whose $\mathbf{H}_1$ is written as

(8.234) $$\mathbf{H}_1 = \mathbf{H} + \varepsilon\mathbf{H}_2$$

where $\mathbf{H}$ is specified in (8.232) and ε is a scalar; also, we impose symmetry on $\mathbf{H}_2$ and put

(8.235) $$\mathbf{H}_2\mathbf{X} = \mathbf{0}$$

in view of (8.221). The second moment of this estimator is $\mathscr{E}[\mathbf{u}'(\mathbf{H} + \varepsilon\mathbf{H}_2)\mathbf{u} - \sigma^2]^2$, which can be written as the sum of three terms, one of which is constant with respect to ε:

$$\mathscr{E}(\mathbf{u}'\mathbf{H}\mathbf{u} - \sigma^2)^2 = 2\sigma^4/(T - \Lambda + 2);$$

a second which is linear in ε:

$$2\varepsilon\mathscr{E}[(\mathbf{u}'\mathbf{H}\mathbf{u} - \sigma^2)\mathbf{u}'\mathbf{H}_2\mathbf{u}] = 2\varepsilon[\mathscr{E}(\mathbf{u}'\mathbf{H}\mathbf{u}.\mathbf{u}'\mathbf{H}_2\mathbf{u}) - \sigma^4 \operatorname{tr}\mathbf{H}_2] = \\ = 2\varepsilon\sigma^4[2\operatorname{tr}\mathbf{H}\mathbf{H}_2 - (1 - \operatorname{tr}\mathbf{H})\operatorname{tr}\mathbf{H}_2] = \\ = 4\varepsilon\sigma^4\left[\operatorname{tr}\mathbf{H}\mathbf{H}_2 - \frac{1}{T - \Lambda + 2}\operatorname{tr}\mathbf{H}_2\right] = \\ = \frac{4\varepsilon\sigma^4}{T - \Lambda + 2}\operatorname{tr}[\mathbf{I} - \mathbf{X}(\mathbf{X}'\mathbf{X})^{-1}\mathbf{X}' - \mathbf{I}]\mathbf{H}_2 = 0;$$

and a third which is quadratic in ε and always positive, viz., $\varepsilon^2\mathscr{E}(\mathbf{u}'\mathbf{H}_2\mathbf{u})^2$.

If we impose the condition of unbiasedness (as HSU did), we should replace the Lagrangean expression (8.228) by

$$2 \operatorname{tr} \mathbf{H}^2 - \operatorname{tr} \mathbf{N}'\mathbf{H}\mathbf{X} - \mu(1 - \operatorname{tr} \mathbf{H}), \tag{8.236}$$

where μ is the scalar Lagrangean multiplier corresponding with the unbiasedness constraint $\operatorname{tr} \mathbf{H} = 1$; see (8.223). After differentiation we obtain

$$4\mathbf{H} - \mathbf{N}\mathbf{X}' + \mu\mathbf{I} = \mathbf{0}.$$

Postmultiplying by $\mathbf{X}$ and applying (8.221) gives $\mathbf{N} = \mu\mathbf{X}(\mathbf{X}'\mathbf{X})^{-1}$; hence:

$$4\mathbf{H} + \mu[\mathbf{I} - \mathbf{X}(\mathbf{X}'\mathbf{X})^{-1}\mathbf{X}'] = \mathbf{0}.$$

Taking the trace, we obtain $4 \operatorname{tr} \mathbf{H} + \mu(T - \Lambda) = 0$; and since $\operatorname{tr} \mathbf{H} = 1$, we find $\mu = -4/(T - \Lambda)$, so that

$$\mathbf{H} = \frac{1}{T - \Lambda}[\mathbf{I} - \mathbf{X}(\mathbf{X}'\mathbf{X})^{-1}\mathbf{X}']. \tag{8.237}$$

The variance of this estimator is $2\sigma^4 \operatorname{tr} \mathbf{H}^2$; see (8.227). Hence it is $2\sigma^4/(T - \Lambda)$, which exceeds the second moment (8.233) of the best quadratic estimator. The second-order condition of the best quadratic unbiased estimator can be analysed in a way which is similar to that of the preceding paragraph.

8.D. Best Linear Unbiased Regression Estimation under Linear A Priori Restrictions

8.D.1. We conclude by presenting a generalisation of the best-linear-unbiased result of Section 8.A in the direction of (exact) *a priori* restrictions on the coefficient vector $\boldsymbol{\beta}$.[1] Thus, we suppose that certain given linear combinations of $\boldsymbol{\beta}$, to be written $\mathbf{R}\boldsymbol{\beta}$, are known:

$$\mathbf{r} = \mathbf{R}\boldsymbol{\beta}, \tag{8.238}$$

where $\mathbf{R}$ is a matrix whose rank is equal to the number of its rows

[1] This generalisation was carried out by Professor Robert Dorfman of Harvard University and the author.

but smaller than Λ. We shall be interested in the class of estimators of $\boldsymbol{\beta}$ which are unbiased and linear; but now linear not only in the values taken by the dependent variable but also in the constant-term vector of the constraints (8.238). Hence, when applying $\mathbf{y} = \mathbf{X}\boldsymbol{\beta} + \mathbf{u}$, we can write such estimators as

$$\mathbf{b} = \mathbf{A}\mathbf{y} + \mathbf{B}\mathbf{r} = (\mathbf{A}\mathbf{X} + \mathbf{B}\mathbf{R})\boldsymbol{\beta} + \mathbf{A}\mathbf{u}. \tag{8.239}$$

Applying $\mathscr{E}\mathbf{u} = \mathbf{0}$, we can conclude that the estimator is unbiased identically in $\boldsymbol{\beta}$ if and only if

$$\mathbf{A}\mathbf{X} + \mathbf{B}\mathbf{R} = \mathbf{I}, \tag{8.240}$$

in which case the sampling error of $\mathbf{b}$ is simply $\mathbf{A}\mathbf{u}$.

In 6.B.4 we considered the constrained least-squares approach; i.e., we chose the estimator $\mathbf{b}$ which minimises the sum of squares of the estimated disturbances subject to (8.238), $\boldsymbol{\beta}$ being replaced by $\mathbf{b}$. As we saw, this leads to a well-defined estimator; but such a derivation says nothing as to its optimal character. Here, we shall show that this constrained least-squares estimator is that member of the class introduced in the preceding paragraph that minimises the mean value of any positive-definite quadratic form in the sampling errors. This will be shown in 8.D.2 for the generalised case $\mathscr{E}(\mathbf{u}\mathbf{u}') = \boldsymbol{\Omega}$. The estimator is

$$\begin{aligned}\mathbf{b} = {} & (\mathbf{X}'\boldsymbol{\Omega}^{-1}\mathbf{X})^{-1}\mathbf{X}'\boldsymbol{\Omega}^{-1}\mathbf{y} + \\ & + (\mathbf{X}'\boldsymbol{\Omega}^{-1}\mathbf{X})^{-1}\mathbf{R}'[\mathbf{R}(\mathbf{X}'\boldsymbol{\Omega}^{-1}\mathbf{X})^{-1}\mathbf{R}']^{-1}[\mathbf{r} - \mathbf{R}(\mathbf{X}'\boldsymbol{\Omega}^{-1}\mathbf{X})^{-1}\mathbf{X}'\boldsymbol{\Omega}^{-1}\mathbf{y}],\end{aligned} \tag{8.241}$$

which reduces to (6.125) if $\boldsymbol{\Omega} = \sigma^2\mathbf{I}$. In plain terms, this estimator differs from the generalised least-squares estimator by a vector which is a homogeneous linear combination of the degree to which the generalised least-squares estimator fails to satisfy (8.238). The covariance matrix is given by (6.127) except that $\mathbf{V}$ should now be interpreted as $(\mathbf{X}'\boldsymbol{\Omega}^{-1}\mathbf{X})^{-1}$.

8.D.2. The positive-definite quadratic form to be minimised is the same as (8.207), but the Lagrangean expression is now

$$\operatorname{tr} \mathbf{A}'\mathbf{Q}\mathbf{A}\boldsymbol{\Omega} - \operatorname{tr} \mathbf{M}'(\mathbf{A}\mathbf{X} + \mathbf{B}\mathbf{R} - \mathbf{I}). \tag{8.242}$$

Putting the derivatives with respect to the elements of $\mathbf{A}$ and $\mathbf{B}$ equal to zero gives

(8.243) $$2\mathbf{QA\Omega} - \mathbf{MX}' = \mathbf{0}$$

(8.244) $$\mathbf{MR}' = \mathbf{0}.$$

If we postmultiply (8.243) by $\mathbf{\Omega}^{-1}\mathbf{X}$ we find

(8.245) $$\mathbf{M} = 2\mathbf{QAX}(\mathbf{X}'\mathbf{\Omega}^{-1}\mathbf{X})^{-1} = 2\mathbf{Q}(\mathbf{I} - \mathbf{BR})(\mathbf{X}'\mathbf{\Omega}^{-1}\mathbf{X})^{-1}$$

in view of (8.240). Combining (8.244) and (8.245), we find

$$2\mathbf{Q}(\mathbf{I} - \mathbf{BR})(\mathbf{X}'\mathbf{\Omega}^{-1}\mathbf{X})^{-1}\mathbf{R}' = \mathbf{0},$$

and since $\mathbf{Q}$ is nonsingular this implies

(8.246) $$\mathbf{B} = (\mathbf{X}'\mathbf{\Omega}^{-1}\mathbf{X})^{-1}\mathbf{R}'[\mathbf{R}(\mathbf{X}'\mathbf{\Omega}^{-1}\mathbf{X})^{-1}\mathbf{R}']^{-1}.$$

Furthermore, by combining (8.243), (8.245) and (8.246), we obtain:

$$2\mathbf{QA\Omega} - 2\mathbf{Q}(\mathbf{X}'\mathbf{\Omega}^{-1}\mathbf{X})^{-1}\mathbf{X}' + \\ + 2\mathbf{Q}(\mathbf{X}'\mathbf{\Omega}^{-1}\mathbf{X})^{-1}\mathbf{R}'[\mathbf{R}(\mathbf{X}'\mathbf{\Omega}^{-1}\mathbf{X})^{-1}\mathbf{R}']^{-1}\mathbf{R}(\mathbf{X}'\mathbf{\Omega}^{-1}\mathbf{X})^{-1}\mathbf{X}' = \mathbf{0},$$

so that

(8.247) $$\mathbf{A} = (\mathbf{X}'\mathbf{\Omega}^{-1}\mathbf{X})^{-1}\mathbf{X}'\mathbf{\Omega}^{-1} - \\ - (\mathbf{X}'\mathbf{\Omega}^{-1}\mathbf{X})^{-1}\mathbf{R}'[\mathbf{R}(\mathbf{X}'\mathbf{\Omega}^{-1}\mathbf{X})^{-1}\mathbf{R}']^{-1}\mathbf{R}(\mathbf{X}'\mathbf{\Omega}^{-1}\mathbf{X})^{-1}\mathbf{X}'\mathbf{\Omega}^{-1}.$$

The result (8.241) follows then from (8.246) and (8.247). The covariance matrix is the mean value of $\mathbf{Auu}'\mathbf{A}'$ and hence $\mathbf{A\Omega A}'$; combining this with (8.247) we find

$$(\mathbf{X}'\mathbf{\Omega}^{-1}\mathbf{X})^{-1} - (\mathbf{X}'\mathbf{\Omega}^{-1}\mathbf{X})^{-1}\mathbf{R}'[\mathbf{R}(\mathbf{X}'\mathbf{\Omega}^{-1}\mathbf{X})^{-1}\mathbf{R}']^{-1}\mathbf{R}(\mathbf{X}'\mathbf{\Omega}^{-1}\mathbf{X})^{-1},$$

which is the generalisation of the covariance matrix (6.127) of the scalar case $\mathbf{\Omega} = \sigma^2\mathbf{I}$.

The second-order minimum conditions can be proved along the conventional lines.

IX. Conclusion

9.1. Retrospect

9.1.1. We have reached the summit of our hill. Sometimes, especially during the beginning of the exploration, the reader may have obtained the impression that what he saw was rather heterogeneous. Later on, his impression will have become different, and it is not difficult to see the reason. There are two unifying forces throughout the analysis. The first is that of the subject matter, which can be briefly indicated as the problem of decision-making under uncertainty. The second is that of the mathematical treatment. Essentially, much of the analysis can be described as the maximisation of a quadratic function subject to linear constraints. It is true, part of the analysis is more general; but the adjectives "linear" for the constraints and "quadratic" for the preference function occurred indeed rather frequently.

In Chapter II, we divided the analysis of economic forecasts into three parts: verification and accuracy analysis, the generation of predictions, and the use of forecasts for policy purposes. These subjects have been discussed in the Chapters III–V, VI, and VII–VIII, respectively. At several occasions we had to refer to other places; and hence, it will have become increasingly clear that the subject matter as a whole is closely interwoven. It may therefore be considered appropriate to show other paths through the analysis carried out in this book in order to stress these interdependencies. This will be attempted in the present section.

9.1.2. Let us start with the following simple case. A variable y is linearly dependent on two other variables x and x'. For example, y is the employment level of some country, x the volume of Government expenditure, and x' the aggregate real income of other countries.

If we write the three variables as deviations from their present values, the constant term of the equation vanishes, so that it can be written in the form

$$y = \beta x + \beta' x', \tag{9.1}$$

β and β' being parameters (constants).

We make the problem more concrete by assuming that x is some variable controlled by a policy-maker, whereas x' is not. In the above example we can take a Minister of Finance for this purpose, who will be supposed to control the volume of Government expenditure but who does not control the real income of other countries. Clearly, since x' is not controlled, y (employment) is not controlled either; cf. (9.1). Suppose further, more specifically, that the policy-maker is interested in next period's values of x and y, though not in that of x'. The future value of x presents no problem in this connection, since it is controlled; but that of y is unknown, at least not known with certainty, even when the future x and the parameters β and β' are specified. As to the parameters, their specification is in general a problem of statistical estimation, to which we shall return below. So let us assume that β, β' and x are specified; then y is still determined by the unknown x', so that a forecast of the latter value (next period's real income abroad) is in general necessary to obtain an idea of y (next period's employment level).

If the policy-maker is interested in next period's values of x and y, he should consider all possible values of x and, *via* (9.1), the corresponding expectations about y; thereafter, he should make a choice for x. Under certain conditions this can be formalised in the following way: the policy-maker's preferences are represented by a utility or preference function of which the instrument x and the noncontrolled variable y are the arguments:

$$w = w(x, y), \tag{9.2}$$

and the best decision is then that value of x for which this function is maximised subject to the constraint (9.1). However, this constraint is not known perfectly, because the knowledge of x' is limited to the availability of a forecast. Hence, the policy-maker's choice problem is a problem of decision-making under uncertainty.

The following result is then of considerable interest. Suppose that the uncertainty of the future y is of the probabilistic type; i.e., although it is impossible to specify the future y with certainty, it is possible to specify its probability distribution, given alternative values of x. This is the case when β and β' are known, and when x' has a distribution which is known. It can then be shown that, under certain conditions, the policy-maker arrives at an optimal decision for x when he disregards the uncertainty of y by replacing its unknown future value by its mean value; where "optimal" should be understood in the sense that the resulting decision is the same as the one which follows from maximisation of the mean value of utility subject to the constraint (9.1), the latter being interpreted stochastically. The conditions underlying this result involve, among other things, that the Von Neumann-Morgenstern axioms which make the utility calculus of mean values applicable are satisfied; furthermore, that the preference function is quadratic in y.

This result has several implications. The most important is no doubt the drastic simplification resulting from the replacement of probability distributions by mean values. This, in turn, may be regarded as a justification of the requirement of probabilistic statements for scientific predictions (cf. Section 2.2): for a forecast of y to be a "certainty equivalent" in decision-making, it is necessary according to the above-mentioned theorem that it is an unbiased prediction; more specifically, that it is equal to the mean value of the y to be predicted. Another implication can be described in the following terms. Sometimes economic theorists, when dealing with expectations, realise that most individuals have no "sure" expectations in the sense that they have a particular numerical value in mind, but rather a range of possible values. Such "uncertain" expectations are rather difficult to handle for analytical purposes; and the solution is then that they are replaced by a sure expectation in such a way that, if the individual would have this expectation, he would take the same action as in the case of the uncertain expectations. The objection is, first, that it is not clear whether such a sure expectation exists; second, that it is not clear whether the sure expectation, if existent, will show the same general movement over time as the vaguely defined uncertain expectations, so that the familiar concepts of optimism and pessimism can be carried over to a similar movement of the corresponding sure expectation. However, if the conditions underlying the theorem of the preceding paragraph are satisfied, both questions can be answered affirmatively: there is such a sure expectation, and it is equal to the mean value of the uncertain expectations.

9.1.3. The constraint (9.1) is extremely simple. In general, there are several noncontrolled variables of the type of y, several equations (one for each noncontrolled variable), and several instruments. The policy-maker's choice problem involves then the maximisation of a preference function subject to several constraints. It can be shown that this does not lead to any essential changes in the results reported in 9.1.2. An example of a system of relations, which can be brought in the form of such a system of constraints by means of a reduced-form transformation, has been given in Section 3.1; it deals with the interrelationships of the Dutch economy in the postwar period. It is of some interest to note that the maximisation of a preference function subject to several constraints is nothing else than a straightforward generalisation of the maximisation of a consumer's utility function subject to a budget restriction. In particular, it is possible to distinguish between substitution and complementarity relations between two instruments or between two noncontrolled variables or between an instrument and a noncontrolled variable. We shall come back to these concepts later on.

It will be clear that, in practical applications, the quality of the actions based on this maximisation is highly dependent on the quality of the forecasts. Thus, going back to (9.1), we obtain an optimal decision result if the mean value of y, given x (or, what amounts to the same thing, the mean value of x') is correctly specified. This is surely simpler than the specification of a whole probability distribution, but it is nevertheless not self-evident that a forecaster is perfect in the art of unbiased prediction. Actually, the empirical evidence of this book suggests that forecasters are far from perfect in this respect, and that the most prominent forecasting error is the underestimation of changes. When applied to x' of (9.1), this means that the predicted value is generally closer to last period's value than the actual outcome justifies; or, given our agreement to write x' as deviation from the earlier level, that the predicted x' is generally closer to zero than the actual x'.

A large body of empirical material supports this thesis. We analysed some 200 macroeconomic forecasts which have recently been prepared by Government Agencies of the Netherlands and of the Scandinavian countries; and we found that, in a majority of the cases, the predicted changes were of the correct sign but too small numerically. When preliminary forecasts were revised, the result became somewhat better on the average; still, the picture did not change essentially. We analysed many more survey data of the German leather and shoe industry, corresponding to twenty-four variables of the different stages of the industry. We obtained the same result: for almost all of the variables, "no change" was predicted more frequently than reported afterwards. The same is true for the German textile industry: we found that the number of cases in which no change is incorrectly predicted exceeds the number of cases in which it is incorrectly not predicted. The same effect, finally, could be observed for sales forecasts according to some recent American surveys.

The causes of this phenomenon have been analysed extensively in Section 5.1. We shall not go deep into this matter here, but confine ourselves to the following aspects: first, there is the random or unsystematic component of reality, which is rather difficult to predict accurately; secondly, predictions are generally based on a theory which states that certain determining factors remain constant, whereas in fact these factors change over time. Actually, the latter feature can be extended in this sense that predicted changes are frequently closer to the observed changes during a shorter period than to the actual changes which are supposedly the object of prediction; and clearly, the hypothesis of a partial stability of determining factors is usually more realistic for shorter periods. Thus, we found that predictions over two-month periods were very frequently of the no-change type if the first month was characterised by no change and the second either by an increase or by a decrease, and that this was true to a much lesser extent when the actual development was in reverse order (increase or decrease in the first, no change in the second month).

Two further remarks are in order. First, the underestimation of changes, though generally persistent, is not equally dominant for all predictions. We found that the effect was considerable in the unconditional prediction of exogenous variables; not, however, when we analysed conditional forecasts of endogenous variables derived by means of an equation system, the condition being that the values of the exogenous variables are as observed. Similarly, in the analysis of survey forecasts, we found that the underestimation of changes does not apply to prices to be paid by firms which are close to the final consumer, like retailers. More generally, the underestimation of changes seems to be important quantitatively unless the forecaster has at his disposal a method of prediction which enables him to foresee at least the direction of change rather accurately.

Finally, it is to be noted that the idea of underestimation of changes is only unique with respect to a well-defined variable. In all cases, therefore, it is necessary to specify what variable is indeed the object of prediction. Thus, it was argued that, in the case of investment surveys among entrepreneurs, we should take the size of the firm rather than investment itself; and similarly, in the case of variables which are subject to seasonal fluctuations, that changes measured from the level of the corresponding period in the previous year may be relevant.

9.1.4. The underestimation of changes is not more than one component of the general imperfection of forecasts. So we proceed to other features of forecasts and their errors. The picture becomes then more heterogenous, and our findings are of less general validity. Nevertheless, all components of the forecasting errors are of importance and deserve our attention. To go back to the constraint (9.1): Whether, in a series of successive periods, the x'-predictions are such that changes are regularly underestimated, or whether the forecasts are imperfect in any other manner, in all cases they lead to imperfect knowledge of the constraints and hence to suboptimal behaviour.

When viewed as a whole, the forecasts analysed are neither thoroughly bad, nor unsurpassable. The Dutch and the Scandinavian annual macroeconomic forecasts are on the average considerably better than simple extrapolations of recent trends; and they follow the ups and downs of actual development in a tolerable fashion. It is true, in the Dutch case a qualification must be made, because the forecasts were published rather late in the year of prediction; but, as far as the evidence goes, the unpublished preliminary forecasts which were prepared around the beginning of the year are not very much worse. There are few turning point errors (predicted increases of actual decreases and *vice versa*), but this may be largely due to the strong upward trends which characterised the postwar period. The most important systematic error is the underestimation of changes, so that the regression of predicted on actual changes has a slope below unity. This regression is not of the classical homoskedastic type: the variance of the individual points around the regression line tends to increase when we move away from the origin. Thus, in the Dutch case, an actual increase in some variable of 10 per cent is on the average predicted as 7 per cent; and this ratio is roughly constant, so that an increase of 30 per cent is on the average predicted as about 21 per cent. But in the former case, the standard deviation of the individual forecasts around the average (7) is about $4\frac{1}{2}$, whereas it is 10 in the latter case (with average 21). These numerical results apply to the rather heterogeneous aggregate of all variables combined. There are important differences between some individual variables. The price level of imported goods, for example, is predicted rather accurately. On the other hand, the level of Government expenditure is badly predicted; and this in spite of the fact that the forecaster is a Government Agency!

The German survey data are not of the conventional numerical type. The participating entrepreneurs are asked to give their plans, expectations and reports about facts in three alternative forms, viz., increase, no change or decrease; and the data used in the analysis are in the form of percentages of firms planning (or expecting or reporting) either an increase, or no change, or a decrease in some variable in some month. Various combinations of these data have been made in Chapter IV; here, however, we confine ourselves to the following. There is a rather close relation between the quality of the survey forecasts and the distance of the forecasters from the ultimate consumer. Retailers and wholesalers in shoes, for example, are generally more successful in forecasting than wholesalers in hides. This holds, in the aggregate, for all predicted variables (buying and selling prices, purchases, sales, and inventories); but it seems plausible that the reasons are not the same for all variables. It is rather obvious that prices can be predicted more easily by retailers in shoes than by wholesalers in hides, because the former can observe the fluctuations in leather prices, whereas the latter have no comparable source of information at their disposal. For sales, however, this argument cannot be applied; and it is conceivable that the superior forecasting achievements of firms close to the consumer with respect to this variable are due to more pronounced seasonal movements, so that the effect is then partly spurious. As to the forecasting differences between separate variables, prices have generally been better predicted than sales and purchases, and the latter better than inventories. The forecasts of changes in stocks were usually not satisfactory; those of changes in buying and selling prices, especially the prices of the traders in shoes, much more satisfactory. It is also interesting to note that there is little difference between the forecasting quality of instruments and that of the exogenous variables which are the main numerical determinants of these instruments, i.e., between the predictions of selling and buying prices, and of purchases and sales.

9.1.5. The relationship between corresponding plans and expectations, mentioned at the end of 9.1.4, is of considerable interest for the analysis of 9.1.2. This can be shown as follows. Suppose now that our policy-maker is a trader, that y is his profit, x his selling price and x' his buying price. Suppose further that his preference function is identical with profit, y (so that in this special case x is not an argument of the preference function). If there is a change in the buying price, then, of course, the optimality of the present selling price is affected. Indeed, we should expect the former change to be followed by a change of x in the same direction. But suppose now that the entrepreneur tries to predict the change in his buying price in order to formulate his selling-price policy, and that he does so imperfectly; suppose, for instance, that he underestimates the change in the buying price. Then it seems plausible that the selling price change on which he decides is smaller than the change that corresponds to a perfect forecast. Actually, it can be shown that, under certain conditions, expected changes that are too small lead usually to a similar effect for instrument variables. This feature is no doubt related to the phenomenon mentioned at the end of 9.1.4.

More generally, if there is an element of uncertainty and hence of forecasting in a decision-making process (and there usually is), and if the forecasts are not perfect, than the result is an action which deviates from the best action; and of course, such an action leads to a utility level which is below the attainable maximum. The difference between these two utility levels (the loss of welfare) is a natural measure for the seriousness of the forecasting error. Actually, there is a loss even in the case when the policy-maker acts according to the theorem mentioned in 9.1.2. For, if a man replaces uncertain future values by mean values (which, according to the theorem, leads to the same action as the one implied by maximising the mean value of utility subject to the stochastic constraint), this is certainly not perfect forecasting, simply because stochastic quantities are not identical with their means except in the trivial zero-variance case. Such an action is "optimal" only in the limited sense that it is "best," given the available probability information. But to say that there is not more than probability information is nothing else than admitting in a sophisticated manner that one's forecasting power is limited; and hence, acting according to the theorem just mentioned leads to a loss of welfare compared with the case of perfect forecasting, just as in any other situation of imperfect predictions.

More specific results can be obtained if it is assumed that the policy-maker's preference function is quadratic and his constraints linear. It is useful, furthermore, to make a distinction between the case in which the multiplicative structure of the constraints is known, and the case in which it is not. In the example of 9.1.2, the former case amounts to knowledge of β and β'. The forecaster is then able to make a perfect prediction of the change in y caused by a change in x; but the level of y is also determined by x', and hence errors in predicting x' still play a rôle. It can be shown that the loss of welfare which is due to such forecasting errors is a quadratic form in these errors; furthermore, that the matrix of this form is determined by the substitution terms which are obtained when we consider the present analysis as a generalisation of consumer's demand theory, in accordance with the remarks made in the first paragraph of 9.1.3. One of the implications of this result is that small forecasting errors lead to a loss of welfare that is small of the second order; which is a fortunate, though not surprising, result. Another implication is that acting according to the theorem mentioned in 9.1.2 gives a better result than no-change extrapolation [i.e., by predicting that x' remains unchanged ($= 0$) in the example of 9.1.2]; the difference between the two losses, when expressed in a suitable unit, being equal to the square of a product-moment correlation. A third implication can be explained as follows. It has been stated in 9.1.4 that the regression of the Dutch predicted changes on the corresponding observed changes has a slope of about 0.7. If there were no variance around this regression line, the determination of the line would be unique. This is not true, of course, and the result is an indeterminacy in the sense that we could equally well consider another regression line; for instance, the regression of the actual on the predicted changes. Underestimation of changes according to this regression occurs if it has a slope exceeding unity; and there are cases in which there is underestimation of changes in the sense of the former regression and not in that of the latter, but not *vice versa*. Hence underestimation in the second sense is stronger. The following result is then interesting in this connection. Suppose we multiply all predicted changes by a positive number. By choosing this number adequately, it is always possible to remove the underestimation in the second sense; and similarly, by choosing a still larger number, it is possible to remove the underestimation of changes in the first sense. But it is also possible to select this number such as to minimise the loss of welfare. It can then be shown that this minimising number is the same as the one for which the underestimation in the second sense (the regression of actual on predicted changes) is exactly removed. In other words, underestimation of changes in the first sense is not necessarily undesirable; but both under and overestimation in the second sense are undesirable, and overestimation in the second sense is not incompatible with underestimation in the first sense. It is of some interest to add that, in the Dutch and the Scandinavian case, there is underestimation of changes in the first as well as the second sense, so that raising all predicted changes by a common percentage would have reduced the loss of welfare.

The above deals with the case in which the multiplicative structure of the constraints is known. This is usually not the case, of course, since parameters like β and β' of (9.1) have to be estimated in general. So, in general, the multiplicative structure is not correctly specified. This, too, leads to suboptimal actions and hence to a loss of welfare, which can be described as follows. If the policy-maker bases his actions on an estimate $b \neq \beta$ of β, the actions which he takes are, by definition, precisely those actions that would maximise utility if the structure of his constraints would change in such a way that β is replaced by b. Now the rôle played by β in the constraint (9.1) is entirely comparable with that of a price in a consumer's budget restriction, simply because both β and such a price act as multiplicative coefficients in the linear constraint subject to which maximisation takes place. When there is a price change, then, as is well-known from classical consumption theory, the result is an income effect and a substitution effect for each of the quantities bought. Similarly, when there is a change from β to b, there is such a double effect for the values of the policy-maker's instruments; and hence, if maximisation takes place with b in the constraint, whereas it should be β, the deviations between the actual and the maximising instrument values can also be described in terms of this double effect. In the general case, there are errors both in the multiplicative structure and in the additive structure of the constraints; the preceding paragraph was confined to the latter type. The two types of forecasting errors combined lead, under certain conditions, to a suboptimal decision which deviates from the maximising instrument values in a manner that can also be described in this way. Since the loss of welfare is a quadratic form in these deviations, it is also a quadratic form in the two effects; and hence, it is the sum of two quadratic forms, viz., in each of the two separate effects, plus a bilinear form in the two effects jointly. We shall come back to this feature when dealing with problems of statistical estimation.

9.1.6. In the empirical analysis of Chapter VI we found some examples of an incorrectly specified multiplicative structure. The traders of the leather and shoe industry, for instance, when forecasting the change in their buying prices during the next month, seemed to do so on the basis of observed price changes in markets farther from the consumer and of recent actual changes of the buying prices to be predicted. This forecasting procedure as such seems more or less tenable; however, too much weight appears to be attached by the traders to the former price changes, and too little to the latter. This is only one result of the empirical analysis; we went through the entire field of the determination of prices, expected, planned, as well as actual, and arrived at several other interesting conclusions. One of them deals with a curvilinear relationship between buying and selling prices, both actual and predicted; and we concluded that this feature can be related to the theory of the kinked oligopoly demand curve. A further result was obtained for the actual and the expected buying prices of the wholesalers in hides. The market of hides was a rather unstable one in the period investigated; so it appeared impossible to obtain a high correlation in the regression describing the fluctuations of actual buying prices. But it was possible to describe the fluctuations in the expected buying prices with a high correlation in a satisfactory manner. This suggests that the traders, confronted with a very complicated mechanism by which their buying prices are actually determined, do not attempt to go into detail in order to predict the changes in these prices; but instead, they use a rather simple theory for the formulation of their forecasts. This effect seems to have more general validity. For the Dutch macroeconomic forecasts, for instance, we found that predicted changes show a higher degree of interdependence than the actual changes justify. This is presumably due to the fact that reality is not so much impressed by simple economic theories as the forecasters are. A third result pointing in the same direction is the greater unanimity of forecasts in the German surveys, compared with the corresponding reports on actual development.

There is, finally, one result of the analysis of Chapter VI which deserves more detailed attention; viz., the influence of plans on the corresponding actual behaviour. In general, of course, there is such an influence in the trivial sense that plans are at least sometimes carried out, so that the plan is then identical with the corresponding action. However, there is a more interesting and subtle relationship, which occurs if the policy-maker feels committed (partly at least) to the fulfilment of his plan, even if circumstances appear to be different from those which he expected at the time when he decided on the plan. We found such an effect for the manufacturers of the German leather and shoe industry: their selling prices appeared to be dependent, not only on buying prices and the appraisal of the size of their inventories, but also on the selling price changes which they had planned before. This behaviour seems reasonable if the entrepreneur feels that his plan may have leaked out; and it can be formalised as follows.

The analysis sketched in 9.1.2, where we considered the maximisation of a preference function subject to one or several constraints, is essentially static; it is confined to one period. But in the example of the preceding paragraph, we need a two-period analysis: in the first period there is the plan, in the second the action. Let us simplify this by distinguishing between two possibilities only, viz., raising and not raising the selling price. They will be indicated by A and B, respectively, in the case of plans, by A' and B' for behaviour. So, if the manufacturer plans to raise the price but decides later on to keep it at the old level, his chain of decisions is indicated by AB'. At first sight it may then seem sufficient for the manufacturer to compare the profitability of the four alternatives AA', AB', BA', BB'; and to choose A for the first period (i.e., to plan a raise) if either AA' or AB' is the best chain, but B (to plan no raise) if BA' or BB' is the best. This is not true, however; it can be shown that such a first-period choice may be suboptimal. This is because chains like AA', AB', etc., imply that the second-period choice is not made dependent on the information which the manufacturer will receive before he has to make the choice (viz., during the first period). Chains of decisions in which later-period decisions are made contingent on the information which the policy-maker will have at the time when he has to take them are called "strategies;" and it can be shown that such strategies are superior to chains of the type AA', etc., even when we confine our attention to the first-period choice.

More generally, if the decision problem is dynamic in the sense that present as well as further values of instruments and noncontrolled variables enter both into the preference function and into the constraints, then the use of strategies is appropriate. However, if the preference function is quadratic and if the constraints are linear, then a simplification is possible which is entirely comparable with that of the theorem mentioned in 9.1.2: if the policy-maker replaces all unknown future quantities (like changes in buying prices in the manufacturer's example) by their mean values, and thus disregards all aspects of uncertainty, then he arrives at the same first-period decision as in the case when he would maximise the mean value of utility by considering all possible strategies. Hence the laborious strategy approach is unnecessary in that case, at least for the first period. But the first-period decision is the really important one; for the decision of the second period he can proceed in the same certainty-equivalent manner at the end of the first period.

The further dynamic generalisation is straightforward. Just as in the static case, it is possible to define substitution and complementarity relationships for pairs of instruments and noncontrolled variables; but in the dynamic case we should specify this temporally by taking an instrument in a certain period and, similarly, another instrument or a noncontrolled variable in a certain period. Thus, an instrument x_1 in period 1 may be complementary with another instrument x_2 in the same period 1, but a substitute of the x_2 of the next period 2; and so on. It is of some interest in this connection that the phenomenon of plans which have a separate (positive) influence on behaviour is, under appropriate conditions, nothing else than the result of a complementarity relation between a first-period and a second-period instrument value.

9.1.7. We mentioned the problem of statistical estimation when discussing the parameters β and β' of (9.1). This subject can be brought easily into the range of subjects considered here. Indeed, the relationship between statistics and decision-making is not new; it is known as "statistical decision theory."

At the end of 9.1.5, we considered the possibility that an estimate b is used instead of β. Two alternative views are possible in such a case: either we take the numerical value of b as it is and we consider the loss of welfare resulting from the error $b - \beta$, or we regard b as the result of a particular estimation method and consider the parent loss of welfare in the population of all b's resulting from this same estimation procedure. In the first case b is interpreted as an estimate, in the second as an estimator. Our position in 9.1.5 corresponds to the former interpretation; for the appraisal of alternative estimation methods, however, the latter is appropriate.

A second result mentioned in 9.1.5 is also of interest in the present connection. In the general case, there are not only errors in the multiplicative structure of the constraints ($b \neq \beta$), but also in the additive structure; and, as stated in 9.1.5, the result is then a loss of welfare which consists of three components (two quadratic forms and a bilinear form). The discussion will be simplified if we confine ourselves, first, to "purely" multiplicative errors; i.e., to erroneous estimates of the effectiveness of instruments with respect to noncontrolled variables which are "compensated" by an error in the additive structure in the same way as compensated price changes are considered in the theory of consumer demand. Thus, in the example of 9.1.2, there is an error in the multiplicative structure if the parameter β, which measures the effectiveness of x with respect to y, is replaced by $b \neq \beta$; and the compensation by means of an error in the additive structure implies an appropriate forecasting error in x'. If there is such a compensation, two of the three components of the loss of welfare vanish, the remaining one being the "substitution component." This component is a (positive-definite) quadratic form in the multiplicative errors; in the example, it is the square of the error $b - \beta$, multiplied by a positive constant. Clearly, then, the best statistical method is that method which minimises the mean value of this quadratic form.

At this stage, it is appropriate to pay special attention to the method of least-squares. Under certain conditions, this method is "best linear unbiased;" i.e., among all estimation procedures which are linear in the dependent variable and which yield an unbiased estimator, least-squares is best in the following sense: it minimises the mean value of every positive-definite quadratic form in the sampling errors of the regression coefficients. This implies that, as long as we confine ourselves to linear and unbiased methods (and also, in accordance with the preceding paragraph, to the substitution component), least-squares is the best method, at least for those policy-makers whose preferences are quadratic and whose constraints are linear. Some qualifications should be made, however, since there is no reason why we should confine ourselves to linear and unbiased methods. In particular, if there is a statistical procedure which yields a biased estimator of β in (9.1) but with such a small variance that the second moment of the estimator around β is smaller than that of the least-squares estimator, then the former method is preferable. It is of some interest to compare the present appraisal of unbiased estimation of parameters with that of unbiased predictions in the case of the certainty-equivalence theorem of 9.1.2; here, we find no justification for this criterion; there, unbiasedness appeared to be a necessary condition in order that decisions based on such predictions be the same as those which follow from maximisation of the mean value of utility subject to the stochastic constraint. Nevertheless, even if there is no special reason for imposing the criteria of linearity and unbiasedness in statistical estimation, it appears that dropping these criteria is associated with considerable difficulties; and so the method of least-squares, although perhaps not "best," does not seem to be very far from "best."

Least-squares, under its classical assumptions, deals with the estimation of equations which contain one "dependent" variable and one or several "predetermined" variables. Equation (9.1) provides an example: y is dependent, x and x' predetermined. However, when there are several dependent variables (usually called "jointly dependent") and hence several constraints, the equation system underlying such a system of constraints is frequently "simultaneous" in the sense that some of the constituent equations contain two or more jointly dependent variables. Least-squares is in general not consistent when applied to such equations. There are consistent methods, like limited-information maximum-likelihood; and we formulated a class of methods (the k-class), which contains least-squares, limited-information and a third method, two-stage least-squares, as special cases. The third method is asymptotically equivalent with limited-information, but it is considerably simpler. The serious rivals are, therefore, straightforward least-squares ("single-stage least-squares") and two-stage least-squares. The former method, contrary to the latter, gives inconsistent estimates of the parameters of simultaneous equations; however, there are good reasons to believe that its variances are generally smaller. So it is conceivable that single-stage least-squares, applied to simultaneous equations, is preferable, in spite of its lack of consistency. However, the situation changes if we are not interested in the separate simultaneous equations as such, but in the system of constraints which is implied by these equations; more precisely, if we are interested in the reduced-form relations of the system, which describe each of the jointly dependent variables separately in terms of predetermined variables only. It can be shown that the application of two-stage least-squares to the separate equations of the simultaneous system, followed by a transformation of the estimates obtained to the reduced form, is characterised by similar optimal properties with respect to the reduced form as least-squares has with respect to equations which contain only one dependent variable. But the results reported in the preceding pages all deal with reduced forms, rather than with the underlying systems; and hence, these optimal properties are of considerable relevance when an appraisal of two-stage least-squares must be made. It is highly interesting to compare this result with the analysis of the Dutch and Scandinavian macro-economic forecasts. There, we found that the predicted changes are on the average smaller than the corresponding observed changes; further, that this "bias" could be eliminated by increasing all predicted changes by a suitable percentage; finally, that this elimination was accompanied by such a large increase of the variance of the forecasting errors that we had some doubts about the desirability of this bias elimination. Later, we concluded that increasing the predicted changes is desirable only up to the point where the regression of actual on predicted changes has unit slope; in the Dutch and the Scandinavian case, the appropriate percentage increase is then rather small. This situation is indeed comparable with that of the choice between single-stage and two-stage least-squares estimation, at least to a large extent. Single-stage least-squares has the disadvantage of bias, but the advantage of smaller variance; so this statistical method can be compared with the Dutch and Scandinavian forecasts which have been actually made, and two-stage least-squares with the predictions after their bias is eliminated. The conclusion is also comparable as long as we confine ourselves to the constituent equations of the simultaneous system: single-stage least-squares may be preferable. However, the conclusion is reversed if we take the reduced form instead; here, single-stage least-squares applied to the simultaneous equations loses its optimal characteristics.

Some final qualifications must be made. The following are the most important: least-squares (and two-stage least-squares) disregard observational errors in predetermined variables; and we confined the attention to only one of the three components of the loss of welfare, viz., the substitution component. It can be shown that the former feature leads to least-squares estimates which are in general biased towards zero, which implies an underestimation of the effectiveness of instruments. As to the latter feature, we have to take account, in the general case, of both multiplicative and additive errors in the constraints; and, given the empirical evidence reported in the preceding pages, it seems worth-while to pay special attention to the possibility of an underestimation of changes in the additive structure. As stated in 9.1.5, if there are no errors in the multiplicative structure, then the underestimation of changes leads in general to instrument changes which are too small. But if there is also an underestimation of the effectiveness of instruments, then the instrument changes have a tendency to become too large; hence the two errors tend to compensate each other. However, we mentioned above that least-squares estimation under disregard of observational errors leads, in general, to such underestimation of the effectiveness of instruments. The combination of these two errors, viz., the underestimation of changes in the additive structure and the neglect of observational errors in least-squares estimation, is hence not necessarily undesirable. Of course, it is much better to make no errors at all, and the only thing we can really say in most cases is that two errors of opposite sign but of unknown size are added. Nevertheless, it will be clear that least-squares is an estimation method which, though not perfect, cannot be easily surpassed; and the same is then true for two-stage least-squares in the estimation of simultaneous equations.

9.1.8. Our final topic is a result which seemed, in a sense, surprising; viz., that the forecast which seems "best" is sometimes inferior to a simple no-change extrapolation.

Let us go back to the Dutch macroeconomic forecasts. It was mentioned in 9.1.4 that their characteristics in relation to the corresponding observed changes can be described in the following statistical terms: the slope of their regression implies an underestimation of changes; and the variance of the individual points around the regression line has a minimum when the actual (or the predicted) change is about zero, and it increases for larger changes. Let us specify this further in order to bring this situation within our theoretical framework. Suppose then that the change in the additive structure of the constraints consists of two parts, viz., a systematic and a nonsystematic part, the latter being stochastic and the former nonstochastic. Suppose further that the predicted change consists of three parts; viz., the systematic part mentioned above, multiplied by a positive constant; the nonsystematic part, multiplied by a nonnegative constant; and a residual part. If the former constant is smaller than one, the systematic part of the change in the additive structure is underestimated. If the latter constant is zero, this implies that the forecaster's achievements with respect to the unsystematic part are likewise zero.

By specifying the first constant in a suitable manner, we can take account of the underestimation of changes. By specifying a suitable statistical structure of the residual part, we can take account of the behaviour of the variance of the individual pairs of forecasts and observations around the regression which formalises the underestimation. By specifying, finally, alternative constants by which the unsystematic part of the change in the additive structure is multiplied, we can take account of the various levels of the forecaster's achievements with respect to this part. The results can then be described in the following terms. If the systematic part of the change in the additive structure is sufficiently large compared with the stochastic variability of the unsystematic part, the forecasting achievements with respect to the latter part are irrelevant in the sense that they do not affect the loss of welfare materially. The opposite is true when the systematic part is small. When this is the case to a sufficiently large extent, the loss of welfare is no longer influenced by the forecasting achievements with respect to the systematic part; instead, it is fully determined by the unsystematic part and its prediction. If the forecaster is unable to achieve anything in this direction, i.e., if the constant by which the unsystematic part is multiplied in the prediction vanishes, then the loss of welfare is larger than it would have been if the policy-maker had acted on the assumption of no change in the additive structure. In other words, even if the policy-maker is convinced that his forecast is the best one (and, in particular, better than a no-change extrapolation), and even if he is right in the extreme sense that the forecast is perfect as far as the systematic part of the change in the additive structure is concerned, even then it is not necessarily true that the forecast is preferable to no-change extrapolation. For this systematic part may be small, and the forecaster's prediction power with respect to the unsystematic part may also be small, in which case no-change extrapolation may lead to a smaller loss of welfare. The reason is this: if the systematic part is very small, and if the coefficient by which the unsystematic part is multiplied in the prediction is also small or even zero, then the forecast is effectively equal to the residual part. Although the residual part has minimum variance for small changes, this minimum is not zero (cf. the preceding paragraph). This residual part does not contribute anything to the quality of the forecast; instead, it is a nuisance. So it is better to avoid it; and this is what effectively happens when no change in the additive structure is predicted.

9.2. Prospect

9.2.1. Having looked backward, it is now our task to look forward, in the direction of the unexplored areas that have become visible. Naturally, this task involves many unknowns and much speculation; which is the main reason why the present section will be shorter than its predecessor.

In the first place, there is the obvious necessity to extend our knowledge, both in the empirical and in the theoretical area. Much computational work will have to be done before our understanding of plans and expectations is really satisfactory; also, further theoretical progress has to be made. The introduction of relevant inequalities among instruments and noncontrolled variables provides an example.

Secondly, as to decision-making in practice, much will be gained if policy-makers act in a more conscious manner by realising explicitly what are their goals, what are the things over which they have direct command, what are their unknowns; and especially, what are the interrelationships among all these variables. TINBERGEN'S *On the Theory of Economic Policy* did much to clarify these issues. The present analysis is related to his, but it attaches more weight to the unknowns of the decision problem by focusing on forecasts. The conclusion that forecasts should become better than they are now is obvious and even trivial; more significant conclusions are possible, however. In particular, it will be necessary to make more efforts in forecasting those components of reality which are commonly called unsystematic; a point the relevance of which is clear from the last paragraphs of the preceding section. Frequently this will be a difficult task; but it is not impossible, sometimes at least. Suppose for example that one of a Government policy-maker's noncontrolled variables is net investment. Predictions can be made by means of an econometric equation system; but, in general, there will be rather considerable disturbances. An investment survey can then be used to reduce the margin of errors. Naturally, the results of such a survey should not be used in an uncritical way.

We know that investment surveys tend to underestimate the future level of investments; so we found that raising the Dutch predicted investment changes by some suitable percentage raises their forecasting quality. More generally, additional factual and theoretical information, whenever useful, should be used for forecasting and hence for decision-making.

9.2.2. The greater part of economic theory (including the present analysis) is based on the maximisation of some preference function. This procedure has obvious analytical advantages. It has the further advantage that it gives a rather accurate description of the utility level which is actually attained, for this level is never higher than the attainable maximum and, if it is lower, the distance is of the second order in general. This is not true, however, for the instrument values leading to this utility level. In most cases, the penalty associated with moderate deviations of the actual instrument values from the maximising ones is small. Clearly, this is not without relevance for the usual price theories which pretend (at least implicitly) that actual selling prices are those prices which maximise profit.

However, if it is true that moderate deviations of instrument values from the maximising ones are not very serious, then a more fortunate conclusion is possible in the normative sphere; viz., that approximations are much more acceptable here than in the analytical sphere. It is conceivable that, in many cases, this fact can be fruitfully used in order to arrive at a certain degree of "automation," in the following sense. Suppose that the policy-maker takes the multiplicative structure of his constraints as constant over time, whereas the additive structure is supposed to change. Then, whenever a change in the additive structure is predicted, the instruments are changed accordingly and automatically. This implies, of course, that the appropriate rate of change of the instruments is specified (which amounts to knowledge of the slopes of the Tinbergen surfaces). Also, it is appropriate to formulate certain minimum changes in the additive structure below which the instruments are kept constant, for otherwise the results of 9.1.8 are neglected. It is hence necessary to solve certain problems; but otherwise the procedure has several advantages. First, the policy-maker can delegate part of his authority to subordinates; his actions are confined to deviations from the automatic adjustment, so that they will be less frequent. Secondly, such a procedure removes part of the uncertainty. For, if it is known how one policy-maker will react to certain environmental changes, this contributes to the knowledge which other policy-makers have about their constraints. Thirdly, the procedure removes the following "irrational" behaviour. There is a widespread tendency among policy-makers "to do something" (i.e., to revise instrument values) when things become worse, but "to do nothing" (i.e., to keep instrument values constant) when things become better. Naturally, when a policy-maker's constraints change such that the attainable utility level increases or decreases, then, in both cases, the optimal instrument values will change in general. If there is an automatic adjustment of instrument values, this should apply to either case. There is also a chance that the introduction of such a procedure contributes to a more "rational" appraisal of a policy-maker's behaviour pattern by those to whom he is finally responsible. For the problem is no longer whether, in each special case, a certain action should be taken; instead, the problems become of a much more general nature, which facilitates objective attitudes. In particular, such an increase of "rationality" can contribute to a clearer distinction between a reduction of the utility level attained which is due to changing constraints, and a reduction below the maximum attainable. The latter reduction is to be ascribed to the policy-maker's imperfections, but the former is not; and such a distinction is often not adequately made in practice.

There are examples of automatic adjustments, like sliding scales in wage rate determination. Needless to say, there are also disadvantages associated with the introduction of procedures of this kind. Some of them deal with the complicated field of human relations and are hence outside the scope of the analysis just completed; one of them, however, is closer to our topic. When instruments are adjusted automatically, they may cease to be predetermined variables in the statistical sence. Since statistical estimation of stochastic equations is largely based on zero-correlation conditions on predetermined variables and disturbances, a reduction of the number of these variables reduces the possibility of estimation. But such features are simply the result of scientific progress, which consists of solving problems by posing other problems.

INDEX

Figures in italics refer to pages on which the term is explained in detail